The Heritage of Bay County, Florida

TABLE OF CONTENTS

The Heritage of Bay County, Florida has been organized in two sections. The first section of the book is the Topical. General subject headings are listed in the Table of Contents, and the stories are in alphabetical format under each subject heading. As an example, one can go to the page where the topic Schools begins and find individual schools in alphabetical order. Many place names are not listed in the index because they are easily located under the proper headings. Many also appear on almost every page of the book. The reader should follow the alphabetical design under the subject headings to locate most place names. The second section of the book consists of Family stories in alphabetical order.

The index is primarily a surname index. This is necessary due to the voluminous number of names included in the book. Every surname has been listed and is accompanied with the number of page on which the name occurs. Stories contained in the Family Section of the book are also in alphabetical order. However, all surnames in the family headings, stories and Topical section are indexed.

Published by:
Heritage Publishing Consultants, Inc.
P.O. Box 67
Clanton, AL 35046
1-800-568-1611

© 2005

Heritage Publishing Consultants, Inc.,
and
The Bay County Heritage Book Committee

LOC 20-03110112
ISBN 1-891647-76-8

Limited First Edition

THE HERITAGE BOOK COMMITTEE

OFFICERS
Linda Pazics Kleback — Chair
Ann Johnson Robbins — Family Coordinator
Rebecca Brown Saunders — Topical Coordinator
Janie Ruth Ammons — Treasurer

PARTICIPANTS
Neta Cauley
Sara T. Cross
Theresa Hill-Rickard
Rose Hughes
Gail Layton
Mona Anita Lucas
Georgia T. Henry-Pearson
Mildred Penton Richbourg
Ellen J. Rumph
Nelda Shores

Introduction

Bay County was formed in 1913 from land that had been part of Washington and Calhoun counties. From the beginning we were an interesting mix of people from many places, and this continues today. While the rest of the country recognizes us as a vacation and Spring Break destination, we who live here year round know we are much more than that. Our history is a rich one, populated by people with a deep love for our land, our waters, our history, and each other. We are proud to share our stories.

All of these stories were published as written. Each author drew upon the sources of their choice, their memories, and their family legends. For further information, please contact the individual authors listed at the end of each story.

The Committee would like to thank all the staff of the Bay County Public Library and George W. Vickery, Library Director, for their enthusiastic support of this project. We would also like to thank the Panama City *News Herald* and Tony Simmons for their help in publicizing the book. The *Seniors for Seniors* television program, currently produced by Florida State University, helped us spread the word as well. We also appreciate all the civic groups that welcomed us to their meetings to share our excitement about our book.

We especially want to thank all the current and former Bay County residents and their descendants who shared their wonderful stories with us. Without your words, this book would not exist. We have loved reading what you've so generously shared with us and are proud to know that this book will be an enduring record of your memories. We are honored to have helped create this collection of Bay County's heritage.

Linda Pazics Kleback, Committee Chairman

Disclaimer

While attempting to publish an accurate and actual account of the people and history of Bay County, there may be misplaced dates, misspelled names, and other similar errors. We apologize for any such problems and have done our best to avoid them. The content of this book was based on material submitted and certain judgments by the committee. Should you have any questions concerning the content of any family or topical story, please contact the author submitting the story, who alone is responsible for its content. Family stories containing more than 500 words were either submitted by an author having a pioneer ancestor in the county, or the author purchased additional space.

Communities and Towns

Around the Beach
"Panama City Beach"

St. Andrews State Park, now St. Andrews State Recreation Area, attracted the crowds as it does today. In the 1970's, a $10 annual fee allowed fishermen and bathers unlimited access to the park for one year.

Several sections of "open beach" existed along Thomas Drive for swimmers and sun bathers in the 1970's. The first was located near where Thomas Drive veers west along the Gulf. Schooners now occupies the site. Condominiums, motels and restaurants were gradually built on most of the other undeveloped spaces, with everyone wanting a piece of that "all precious waterfront."

The biggest problem beachgoers faced was making certain their cars were parked on hard-surfaced areas. Otherwise, they experienced a troublesome dig out from the sand. Near the foot of Joan Avenue and Thomas Drive, one of the last towering sand dunes remained, an example of what the beach had once been like when many of these "sand mountains," averaging 50 to 100 feet in height, guarded against storm surges along the coast. They also served as lookouts for those searching for fishing boats at sea.

At the intersection of Front Beach and Middle Beach roads, Sir Loin, a huge plaster giant, greeted tourists arriving on Panama City Beach. Across the road, Petticoat Junction Amusement Park attracted the crowds. A huge, one-eyed pirate marked its front entrance.

Farther west, hundreds of red brick homes, constructed near the end of World War II, were slowly being demolished at Edgewater. Front Beach Road, in this section, was then moved to accommodate the construction of towering condos, townhouses and a golf course in the new Edgewater complex.

Miracle Strip Amusement Park at the corner of Alf Coleman and Front Beach Road drew both families and teens, many of whom sought their first employment at this popular fun spot along the Gulf.

Just west of Miracle Strip, the county pier served as another popular destination of tourists and locals alike. Men could fish from the pier while their families swam in the water. Parking was free and spots were usually available. No fee was charged for the use of the wooden pier.

The City Pier, just east of Highway 79 at Wayside Park, charged a nominal fee. Fishermen seemed to flock more to this pier because it extended farther out into the Gulf. In the late 1970's, the Wayside Park area became the site of the annual Seafood Festival.

Down the road, the abandoned, half-finished Peppertree Condo, a victim of the recession, bore graffiti and flapping pieces of insulation that blew in the breeze on the upper floors.

At the western end of the beaches, Pinnacle Port Condos towered near Lake Powell. A few other townhouse-condos and motels extended east from this location. But long stretches of open beaches remained thanks to farsighted early promoters, who dedicated this waterfront property as permanent beachfront.

Hurricane Eloise struck in 1975, forcing massive clean ups and reconstruction in this section of the beach and farther west.

Written by: Marlene Womack.

Auburn

Auburn, near today's drone launch on Tyndall AFB, was established by Charles Jackson Raffield of Georgia. After leaving that state, Raffield and his family lived first at Wetappo before settling on East Bay in 1900.

They lived off the land by hunting and fishing and either sailed by boat to Cromanton, St. Andrews or Panama City to pick up other food and supplies or made the long wagon trip to Blountstown. Raffield's wife knitted him his first fishing net, which he quickly put to use gathering mullet and other fish to salt and sell.

South Auburn was a small addition to Auburn. It was located south of what's now U.S. 98 on the sound and bay. The Auburn post office was established in 1911, but consolidation of the smaller post offices forced the 32 families to begin using the Farmdale post office in 1929.

The Raffields had a large family. Most of the men built their own boats and engaged in the lucrative fishing industry. They too were forced to leave their decades old homes to make way for Tyndall AFB.

Submitted by: Marlene Womack, 2101 Norwood Place, Panama City, FL 32405.

Bay County Growth

North of Panama City, off Highway 20, magnificent, deep, clear springs bubbled up from the ground near Econfina Creek. Both the springs and creek drew local crowds on steamy summer days. Lake Merial also attracted swimmers to its sparkling, spring-fed water. The water was so clear bathers could stand neck-deep and still see their feet. Here again, the only difficulty visitors and picnickers might encounter was getting stuck in the deep sand beds in the roads leading in and out of the lake.

During different times of the year, scouting troops came to the lake and nearby woods to camp for a weekend. Jesse Womack was on such a trip at Lake Merial when a Bay Line train derailed in Youngstown, causing massive ecological problems.

White Western, Crystal and Court Martial Lakes were more locations popular with area residents. On the west side of Highway 77, insulators and poles still marked the old Birmingham, Columbus and St. Andrews Railroad, which earlier in the century ran from Chipley to Southport.

In the 1970's scallops covered the bay floor at places such as Spanish Shanty Cove, Redfish Point, Wild Goose Lagoon and along the northwest end of Shell Island. They were there - thousands of them - free for the taking with no licenses or diving flags required, only masks and snorkels, to dredge these juicy bivalves from the sandy bottom. Kings, Spanish mackerel, ling and redfish were also plentiful during this period in the bay and Gulf .

Submitted by: Marlene Womack, 2101 Norwood Place, Panama City, FL 32405.

Bellisle

Bellisle still remains on some area maps, near the entrance to Alligator Bayou and Strange Bayou on the southern shore of East Bay. M.E. Rogerson established a turpentine still here on the East Peninsula in 1910. A small community grew up around the still in 1910. It became the largest turpentine operation on the peninsula. A post office opened the following year.

The William Strange family made its home near Bellisle, where bears, deer and panthers could be found in the early 1900s. The post office closed in 1921 and delivery was changed to Auburn. The site of the old community is now in a restricted military training area.

Submitted by: Marlene Womack, 2101 Norwood Place, Panama City, FL 32405.

Early Days of Callaway

In May of 1855 the United States government gave a land patent to E. Langston. Mr. Langston died and later in 1855 Pit M. Callaway, a Baptist minister, became the assignee of this property for the heirs of Elbridge Langston. Mr. Callaway died before his claim was granted but his family was able to establish his claim. Mr. Callaway's daughter, Ella and her husband M.N. Carlisle were among the first settlers of the area. Their son, Pit M. Carlisle platted out the property in 1908.

In 1936 in order to build a new school the community decided to incorporate and hold elections. For $20.00 the fees were paid and a lawyer, Mr. Sellers, was hired and ballots printed. The first mayor was Albert R. Patterson. He held this position until 1956 and a new election was held. The first Town Marshall was Frank F. Fox. A.R. Patterson was also one of Five School Trustees. The city, after the school was built, decided to become inactive. When the city of Parker tried to annex part of Callaway in 1956, the men's club reactivated the city and Mayor Patterson called for new elections. Albert Patterson served as mayor from 1936 to 1956 when the new elections were held. The election inspectors for the second election were Ethel Elmore, Miss Ranew, and Ethel Hoover. The new mayor was Charlie Allan. The Charter for the city was approved in 1964 and the Mayor was E. Singleton, police chief, R. Preston, City Clerk, Clyde Patterson.

The Patterson Park is named after Albert Patterson, one of the early Callaway residents. Other early families were the Foxs', Creamers', Scott, Burkett, Baxter and Pippin. The first post mistress was Mrs. Joyner and the early occupations were turpentine, fishing, farming and lumber. A saw mill was located where the Callaway Community building is now and it was later planned for use as a train depot The saw mill was burned out by Yankees two years after the civil war ended and the train never actually came to that part of Callaway. It later became the men's club and now is J.B. Gore Park. The original school has been moved to the park as a museum.

Some of the early stores were owned by Fisher and Carlisle. One of the things that the new city charter insisted on was no new taxation unless property owners could vote on them. This brief history on Callaway was related to me by Lillian Patterson daughter-in-law to Albert Patterson and wife of Clyde Patterson.
Submitted by: Nancy Patterson, 1405 Hubert Rd., Bonifay, FL 32425, nacp@wfeca.net.

Early St. Andrew
To get to the Gulf Beach from St. Andrew, we would drive over the new Hathaway Bridge. The bridge was two lanes with a drawbridge span to let the boats pass. We could leave Highway 98 shortly and take a single lane dirt track, which is now Thomas Drive, and go to Brown's Beach. Over a wooden bridge at Grand Lagoon, you arrived a short distance from the Gulf. There was a parking area paved with shells and there were very few people. There were sand dunes as far as you could see and the beautiful Gulf Waters. Or you could continue on Highway 98 for about five miles to Long Beach Casino which had a bathhouse. A few cottages back from the beach were the only rental cottages west of Hathaway Bridge. As more tourists arrived, motels were built in St. Andrew along Highway 98. The Log Cabins were one of the first motels to be built.

The only paved street was Beck Avenue. The Baptist and Presbyterian Churches were close by and the new Grammar School was within walking distance. In the village we had Davis Grocery and the Dykes' Serve-U-Well Grocery; also there was Brown's Drug Store, Mr. Aaron's Filling Station and the Weller Fish House. There was a Library where Mrs. Zelina Brown was always glad to help you find a book. The Railroad Station stood abandoned.

Everyone received their mail at the village Post Office as there was no home delivery. Most people walked to get their mail and the boardwalk was useful for mail and shopping. The Boardwalk was eventually destroyed by a hurricane.

The City Pier was at the foot of Eleventh Street where you would see the fleet of fishing smacks. These fishermen had migrated from New England states bringing their boats with sail power. I am told fish were plentiful and they could catch thousands of pounds from the Gulf. Red Snapper was in abundance.
Submitted by: Gene Howell Sapp, 1409 Deer Avenue, Panama City, FL 32401.

Farmdale
Civil War veteran W.W. Woodford settled on a 160-acre homestead near the head of East Bay across the water from Sandy Creek in the late 1880s. He intended to develop his property and other acreage into a large town on the Intracoastal Canal, proposed since the 1830s. Woodford opened the Farmdale post office in 1889.

He also built a hotel on the bay and even paid for an expensive survey of the entire East Peninsula intending to bring a railroad to this section. Others operated turpentine stills and fishing businesses. Woodford became ill and did not see the canal was completed in 1915. The town grew slowly, and those living here were dependent upon wagons and boats for travel.

Along with other towns on the East Peninsula, Farmdale disappeared when Tyndall took over the land in 1941.
Submitted by: Marlene Womack, 2101 Norwood Place, Panama City, FL 32405.

Fountain and Betts
My parents and I moved to the Tom Cane Farm between Fountain and Betts, Bay County Florida in 1934. It was one of the last Satsuma orchards in the area. The farm was about three miles north of the Fountain Post Office and about a mile south of Betts. Fountain is about thirty miles north of Panama City on Highway 231. In 1937, my parents bought and moved to the Slick Gay place just south of the Tom Cane Farm.

I began attending the Fountain school in 1935. My brother James and I, along with cousins David, Claudia and Charles walked three miles to the school. We walked the old road that paralleled the railroad tracks to Fountain and took a trail that led from the railroad section houses through the woods to the school. Later we rode with Mrs. Messer on her Model-A Ford to school.

The school was two-room white wood building sitting on blocks

with a small front porch. There were two outhouses behind the school. There were about twenty students in the first through eighth grades. The yard was sandy and had sand spurs, rusty nails and broken glass, as if previous buildings had been located there. There

Fountain School, 1936-37. Front row, L-R: Benny Messer, Unknown, Melborn Freeman, Unknown, ____ Rayborn, ____ Murray, David Jr. Cooley, James Cooley, Charles Cooley and John Cooley. Back row, L-R: Mrs. Williams, Unknown, ____ Savage, Iris Murray, Nell Bryant, T.D. McQuagge, Myrsteel Freeman, Floyd Freeman, Vasti Savage, ____ Rayborn, Claudia Cooley and Mrs. Murray.

were no trees in the schoolyard, but pine trees and a swampy area surrounded the schoolyard. Our source of water for drinking and washing hands was from a hand pump in the northwest corner of the yard.

The boys would often gather in a patch of gallberry bushes to play and eat lunch. There was no stock law at that time so hogs and cows ran loose. Occasionally a hog would get one of our lunches. Our entertainment consisted of climbing pine saplings and bending them to the ground and riding up and down on them. Also, we would build a flying jenny on a stump by putting a bolt through a board into the stump and with someone on each end of the board another person would spin it round and round. We also played baseball using sponge balls.

The Fountain Cemetery was located east of the school and the two-trail road to the cemetery ran along the north edge of the schoolyard.

The school was closed and moved to Youngstown about 1938. A year or so later a tornado destroyed the Fountain school building while a family was living in it.
Submitted by: John W. Cooley, 309 Dublin Circle, Madison, Alabama 35758.

Goethe
In 1925 when Wid Rodgers and Mamie Adams moved their family to Crystal Lake, the nearest school was in Greenhead. Mamie took a job as bus driver for Washington County using her four-door Buick automobile. Every morning she transported her six and picked up other kids along the way. The route to Greenhead was not direct because many of her riders lived off the main road. Every child had another in his lap and several kids rode the running boards and fenders regardless of the weather. Although no one was ever hurt, Jimmy Rodgers recalled losing his grip once and tumbling off the fender.

At the end of the school term the community usually had a fish fry. This was held on the north side of Big Blue Pond from 1926 until 1931 because there were no fish in Crystal Lake. To make room for planting, the horticultural enterprise Seminole Farms had cleared the large pines, hauled them to the lakes on ox carts, and dumped them into the water. Unexpectedly, the logs changed the acidity of the lakes and the fish disappeared. After about 5 years, the lake chemistry stabilized, fish were transferred from other lakes, and soon they began to see large trout again, or bass as they are called today.

When the depression put Seminole Farms out of business, its abandoned commissary at Crystal Lake became the schoolhouse about 1931. The series of teachers included Bev Gainer, Arthur Rogers, Marvin Johns, Kate McMillan and a young Mrs. Owens from Chipley. Raymond Powell, who played a number of musical instruments, lived near the schoolhouse and was easily persuaded to perform for the kids.

In 1938, the State paved Highway 77. Deward Lisenby was guard for the gang of convicts who placed the sand clay base for the highway. The convicts shoveled clay by hand from around Tank Pond onto trucks for transporting to the construction site.

The clay base was covered with a couple inches of asphalt which was Topped with steel mill slag and left for traffic to compact. The slag was rough on bare feet and would have helped the shoe industry a lot if more people had the money. Even with shoes, the loose slag made obtaining traction too difficult to walk. Jimmy Rodgers returned from a junior CCC camp near Jacksonville by train the week the highway was completed. He arrived at Chipley and started walking home around 9 PM. Unable to get traction on the loose slag, he walked the railroad bed to Crystal Lake. He reached his folk's yard at 6 AM, just as the mail car passed; the only vehicle he saw the entire night.

In 1946, the Rodgers moved to St. Andrews which provided more dependable schooling for the younger children.
Submitted by: BeeBee Russell Deal, 15116 Highway 77, Southport, FL 32409.

Growing Up in Millville

Remember the ice trucks delivering blocks of ice to homes in Panama City. Remember running behind the truck to grab slivers of ice for a special treat in the hot summer time. The block of ice would be placed in the icebox to keep food cold. No hot water but we did have a shower. In the winter, the old wash tub would be placed in the bathroom for baths. The water heated on the stove.

Trading comic books was a serious business with children in those days. We would walk to each other's house and take an hour or more wheeling and dealing our comics. My cat Tick-Tock would follow me from house to house and sit under the house until I finished my trading. I had over 100 comics under my bed at home but if my Uncle Junior Stricklen dropped by on his way to his tug boat job, my mother would give him most of my comics to read aboard the tug boat. She didn't seem to understand the importance of comic collecting.

Playing paper dolls was next to comics in importance. We would take our paper dolls (a lot of them were the current movie stars of that time), and we would make them furniture and houses from Sears and Roebuck Catalogs. We would take them to each other's house and play for hours.

There was a girl who lived near us who loved cats. She had a dozen or more cats. While she was at school one day, her father caught all her cats, put them in bags, took them to the woods and turned them loose. When she came home and found out what he had done she got so upset that he went back to the woods and caught every single cat and brought them home again.
Submitted by: Ann Robbins, 435 South Palo Alto Ave., Panama City, Florida 32401.

Gulf Beach

In the 1930s the "Gulf Beach" was mostly stunted magnolias and sand dunes with very few homes and buildings beyond Long Beach. One of the few houses was an old deserted place with out windows or doors. It had a leaky roof and was located a couple of blocks from the gulf. This house stood alone in this area and had been abandoned by the owners, from the looks of it, for a number of years. On occasions locals would camp in it for two or three days at a time. Somewhere between 1934 and 1936 my parents decided we would spend a few days at the gulf and we camped in the old house. I remember it rained one night while we were there and everything got wet. While this was a real treat for us kids I feel certain my parents did not have such a good time.

Joe Rubash, my dad, built boats and snapper fished the local waters until World War II. With the outbreak of the war the government asked anyone who had been in the merchant marines to reenlist. He went to New London, CT to reenlist but his hearing

was not good enough so they wouldn't take him. He then went to Camp Blanding to work on the buildings coming home only on weekends. When they started the buildings at Tyndall A.F.B. he worked there until all the buildings were completed.

In subsequent years so many people came to Panama City to work at the "Shipyard" and "Tyndall" there was a housing shortage. The government asked any person that had an empty room to rent it to the workers. Since my parents owned a whole block of land in the 1700 block of Drake Ave., Dad decided to build another house next door to where we lived and our family moved there. He then divided our old house into two apartments and we rented it to shipyard workers.

There was bus service from St. Andrew to Panama and on to Millville every hour or half hour during the day until the war started. With so many people working at the Shipyard, though more buses were added and running more often still, there was usually standing room only.

I can remember coffee, sugar, meats, butter, shoes, tires and gas all being rationed. People were required to sign up for coupon books to buy these products. A family was allotted a certain number of coupons each month based on the size of the family. These items were all needed for the war effort. I particularly remember my dad's comments about having plenty of coffee since none of the kids were old enough to drink it.

Since Panama City was on the coast, people were required to put heavy, dark covers over their windows at night to make sure homes could not be seen. Monitors were even appointed to check the neighborhoods to insure no light was visible from any home. If any hint of light could be seen coming from a home the occupants were asked to cover their windows better. People were also required to black out the top half of their car headlights. Each evening around 6:00 pm everyone would sit around their radios and listen to news reports on how the war was going. World War II really changed the quaint little fishing village of St. Andrew to where it would never be the same again.
Submitted by: Pat Murfee, 1714 Drake Ave., Panama City, Fl. 32405.

Lake View Inn

My brother Bill, (William Daniel Cain), was born in 1925. The Phillips Inlet Hotel burned in 1926. My folks decided to replace it on our property. They named it Lake View Inn. It had six bedrooms, plus a two room cottage. It had big hallways down the middle with a big porch on the front. The porch was not covered and we had benches all around. The porch was used for dancing. The next year the porch was covered with tin top and screened.

We had dances at the Inlet. People came from all around. We were the only Inn or hotel on the north side of the Lake. There were three hotels on the south side of the Lake. Inlet Beach was where Camp Helen (Avondale Mills) located. Vickers was between Inlet Beach and the Walton County line. Boines Beach was where Pinacle Port was located.

My family bought a new Model T. Ford car. We still lived in our log house. It had a big dining room and kitchen off to the side with a boardwalk between the buildings. The yard was fenced with pickets to keep animals out. We had a small launch with a one cylinder motor (Palmer). My brothers would take the guests to the Gulf every morning and evening. The trip was all done in less than two hours so no one would get sunburned. Other part-time activities was to go fishing with hook or seine. They would dance, sing or play at night. There was no where to go but stay at home. We ate seafood, crabs, vegetables, syrup and coffee. For breakfast we had ham, bacon, sausage, eggs, cornbread, biscuits, syrup or honey and coffee. Families would come and stay a week or a month. When the rooms were all taken, families slept on pallets, wagons, porches or in the open.

My past time was bringing in wood and washing dishes. The blessing was said before each meal. Somebody read from the Bible on Sundays, we sang night and day. Everybody had big families, six to twelve children. I washed tubs full of dishes. Everybody helped with the fish crew, cut wood, helped with the cows, hogs and garden, for their room and board.

There was a ferry where Hathaway Bridge is now. The first bridge was built in 1928. Highway 98 was built with convict labor and mules, no tractors or trucks. By this time, there were lots of cars, but people still used horses, mules and wagons. At this time there was a bridge at West Bay and Lynn Haven. You could go to West Bay, Crooked Creek, Burntmill Creek, Vicksburg, Southport, Lynn Haven, St. Andrews, Panama City and Millville by car. The railroad came to South port via Chipley. There was no railroad bridge. The railroad also came from Dothan to Panama City. We could go by launch to Panama City and St. Andrews by way of the Gulf. We parked our boat at the west end of St. Andrews Bay and walked home if the Gulf was rough. When the Gulf got calm, we would go back and get the boat. Will Pate had a seine and motor boat. He would come down to St. Andrews Bay to the Gulf and on to Philips Inlet to fish from late August to December. He had to salt all the fish (no ice) and he would take a barrel of fish back home. He would put them in a barn or smoke house and the fish would keep up to one year. During fishing season you could catch boat loads of fish.

Written by: Clifford Hilliard Cain. Submitted by: Jo Ann Cain, 204 Cascade Street, Panama City, Fl 32405.

Lynn Haven

Although no one ever verified it, many believe the statue of the Yankee soldier in Lynn Haven was the only monument ever erected by Northern people in the South, east of the Mississippi River.

In 1911, promoter W.H. Lynn of New York established Lynn Haven in a warm climate for aging northern veterans of the Civil War. Lynn advertised his town in the National Tribune, a Grand Army of the Republic newspaper, subscribed and read by most veterans of the war. Fifty by 150-foot lots were first sold at a cost of $50 each by the St. Andrews Bay Development Co. and distributed through a lottery. Along with the lot purchase came 5 free acres on the outskirts of town for growing vegetables and fruits. E.P. and Mollie Truesdale (who became known as the "titi queen" because of some of the swampy property she sold) served as real estate agents for the development company.

Lynn Haven was not Lynn's first venture in Florida. He also helped promote the first veterans' colony in Florida at St. Cloud in 1909.

For the most part, the old soldiers and their families enjoyed living in Lynn Haven. The veterans received their military pensions from the government each month so they had a steady income. But lack of industry or investments forced the Lynn Haven bank to close in 1915 and the St. Andrews Bay Dev. Co. to file for bankruptcy a few years later.

Minor C. Keith, a distant relative of Lynn, bought the company's land and infused funds into the town. In 1920, veterans each donated money for the erection of a Yankee soldier always facing "north." Decades later, Lynn Haven residents changed the monument to a soldier commemorating military personnel in all services and wars.

For the most part, the old veterans enjoyed their years spent in Lynn Haven. They formed many organizations including the G.A.R., the women of the G.A.R., etc. They worked together to build churches, the G.A.R. hall, and other community buildings. The women held fundraisers to open the first school. They also held the Chautauqua each year, which brought in lecturers, soloists, singing and acting groups and even Sidney J. Catts, one of Florida's most colorful and unusual governors.

In 1926, W.C. Sherman opened his 18-hole golf course at the old community of Gay in eastern Lynn Haven that became known as the Panama Country Club. The following year, Bob Jones College held its first classes at College Point. The popular golf course remained, but the college closed in 1933, a victim of the Depression, and moved to Cleveland, TN.

Lynn Haven continued as a small town until about 1985 when real estate lots were gobbled up and resold at higher prices as more and more families chose to live in Lynn Haven. The property that once held many of the "5 free acres" quickly became part of new subdivisions in eastern Lynn Haven.

Submitted by: Marlene Womack, 2101 Norwood Place, Panama City, FL 32405.

Memories of Parker

Fishing is arguably the first industry that attracted workers to this area. G.M. West in his book, *St. Andrews* calls fishing a direct cause of drawing many to the bay. About 1529, Spanish explorers noted the abundance of fish the Indians had and commented on the oysters and fish in the bay.

A British coast survey in 1771 said Spanish fishing smacks reported $2,000.00 worth of cured fish per trip from Havana.

West wrote that there were 1500-1600 people in St. Andrews City between 1850 and 1863.

During the Civil War Federal bombardment destroyed fisheries and saltworks, and there was little fishing until after the war. By 1873 more fish and oysters were being caught than ever before.

In Parker, the families built boats and netted mullet up and down the coast. Daddy said "everyone wanted a skiff built by Robert and Dan Parker." Grandpa Pratt built his own sailboat and proceeded to out-sail anyone on the bay. We have the Free-for-all Race first-place cup he won. Arthur may have been born in Minnesota but he was a seaman. Must've been his Maine ancestors' DNA. Grandma Pratt's Parker brothers were net fishermen. Arthur was a carpenter and worked on boats and lighthouses-and farmed a little, too.

Submitted by: Ann Houpt, 1128 Loftin St., Parker, FL 32404.

Millville

Millville takes its name from the sawmill that was built by Henry Bovis, J.C. Gray and others on the eastern side of Watson Bayou in the late 1890s. Once successful, it was sold to the German American Lumber Co., a large foreign concern, which built the mill and the property it acquired into one of the largest lumber concerns in the country. Foreign ships docked in the bayou and transported lumber to many locations overseas.

Life was hard for the men and boys that worked at the mill. Many were maimed or killed in the dangerous machinery and buried in the Millville Cemetery, established by W.W. Holmes family, settlers after the Civil War. The post office opened in 1899.

Millville grew up around the mill and in 1910 became Bay County's largest town. The company's logging railroad conveyed lumber hundreds of miles to the mill from around Northwest Florida. The Bay Line transported the finished product to points north, out of the county, and ships carried lumber to ports all over the world.

The U.S. Government seized the German American Lumber Co. in 1917 under the Trading With the Enemy Act. During the war it operated as the American Lumber Co. After the armistice, W.C. Sherman, an owner of sawmills, and Minor C. Keith of the United Fruit Co. fame, purchased the mill and the Bay Line Railroad. They operated the mill as the St. Andrews Bay Lumber Co. until 1930 when all the available forests had been cut in the surrounding area.

The International Paper Co. opened its mill in nearby Bay Harbor in 1931, using scrap timber. That same year, the huge St. Andrews Bay Lumber Co. went up in a huge fire, which also claimed several residences close to the mill.

Millville became part of Panama City in 1926. Life continued in the old town but gradually ebbed away as residents moved elsewhere around the county. Third Street and Sherman Avenue were the main roads in Millville. The old mill was located near the western end of Third Street. Its property stretched along the east bank of Watson Bayou.

In recent years, people have begun renovating old homes and moving back to the historic town.

Submitted by: Marlene Womack, 2101 Norwood Place, Panama City, FL 32405.

Old St. Andrew During the Depression

The St. Andrew Bay area had known more prosperous times and there were large homes built along its shore. An especially fine home named Magnolia Manor, was built on the Bay in the West End area. Mrs. Theodore Roosevelt lived in the residence one winter. There was no longer Ware Mercantile which had attracted shoppers from all along the Bay. The Bank had been closed.

During these depression years everyone was poor. Most people had iceboxes not refrigerators. The children would line up when the iceman delivered the ice. He used a saw to cut the proper size and we would place our hands in position to collect the shavings to eat. I never got sick! The laundry was washed in iron kettles where they were boiled over a wood fire. Then dried outside on a clothesline. Later they ironed sheets and all. The iron often had to be

heated on the wood burning stove. Washing machines, clothes dryers and electric irons were scarce or did not exist. Many did not have indoor plumbing and had to pump their water from a well.
Submitted by: Gene Howell Sapp, 1409 Deer Avenue, Panama City, FL 32401.

Cities in Bay County
Panama City
When one looks at Harrison Avenue today, it's hard to imagine that all of this land was once nothing more than pines, palmettos, sand and swamp. In the mid-1800s, squatters occupied any property they wished, moving here and there wherever they thought they might find better soil that would grow something to eat.

In the late 1800s, men by the names of Samuel J. Erwin, Green B. Thompson, Clark B. Slade, C.J. Demorest and G. W. Jenks attempted to promote the communities of "Floriopolis," "Park Resort" and "Harrison" in what's now the downtown area but did not meet with much luck.

George M. West, a northern railroad man, first came to this area in 1886 during the land promotion of the St. Andrews Bay Railroad, Land and Mining Co. He built a home along what is now Beach Drive in St. Andrews, moved his family here for their health and became a frequent visitor until his retirement from the railroad in 1906.

Once settled in St. Andrews, West began to promote Harrison along with R.L. McKenzie and A.J. Gay, who already owned large sections of this land. They sold lots through the group's Gulf Coast Development Co. A.B. Steele, who built the Atlanta & St. Andrews Bay Railway (the Bay Line), changed Harrison's name to Panama City in 1906 for the Panama Canal under construction at that time.

Panama City was incorporated in 1909. This entire area belonged to Washington and Calhoun counties until July 1, 1913 when it became part of the newly created Bay County. Through a vote, Panama City became the county seat, and the new courthouse was completed in 1915.

The railroad and the steamer Tarpon brought in food, supplies and people, wishing to settle here and the town grew so that it reached a population of 1,722 in 1920.

St. Andrews and Millville remained separate towns until 1926 when they both were incorporated into Panama City. The Cove Hotel, the Dixie Sherman Hotel and Bay High were built about that time while real estate boomed all over Florida.

Until the International Paper Co. built its first mill in Florida and opened it in 1931, the towns offered little opportunities for employment except fishing and work in the sawmills and turpentine stills. IPC brought increased wages, overtime pay and benefits such as medical insurance, vacation time and holidays.

Shipments from the paper mill increased the need for a deeper channel in and out of St. Andrew Bay. The new pass opened in the autumn of 1934.

World War II brought thousands of military personnel to work at Tyndall Field and train at the Army-Air Forces gunnery school. Clark Gable attracted attention while he attended gunnery practice at Tyndall in late 1942 and early 1943. Wainwright Shipyard was constructed early in the war and produced 102 Liberty ships and six tankers between 1942 and 1945. With the men gone, women jumped into the labor fields as welders and in other fields. The shipyard employed thousands of men and women from all over Northwest Florida during the war. Across from the shipyard, the government erected the Navy base, which closed at the end of the war but was reopened a few months later.

Many of the individuals who came for training or to work in the Panama City area during the war never forgot the beauty of the bay and beaches. They returned to find jobs or to retire in Bay County.

Downtown Harrison Avenue remained the heart of the business district. But businesses slowly began moving from the center of town with the construction of shopping centers in Parker and along 11th and 15th streets in the 1950s and 1960s. When the Panama City Mall opened in 1976, shops and stores gradually made the move to that complex and 23rd Street. The downtown area became a ghost town in the 1980s. The 1990s brought about the successful Mainstreet project. Harrison Avenue once again draws shoppers, tourists and those desirous of an evening on the town.
Submitted by: Marlene Womack, 2101 Norwood Place, Panama City, FL 32405.

Panama City Beach
For centuries, the location we know of as Panama City Beach today remained a long, lonely stretch of sugary white sand and sparkling turquoise water. Travelers avoided the location. Those sailing along the coast came ashore only in cases of shipwrecks because they feared the Indians who hunted and fished along the beaches.

After most of the Indian bands had moved west and south, fishermen came to the Lakeside area to stay in their fishing shacks while netting and salting mullet in the autumn of the year. Their families sometimes joined them, and their children enjoyed romps in the beach and in the water. But fishing ceased during the Civil War, as many earned a living boiling seawater to make salt, desperately needed by the Confederacy.

In the late 1800s, small settlements grew up around Lake Powell to the west and Bear Point on St. Andrew Bay. Several people also took up homesteads around Grand Lagoon and on land now covered by the Navy Base.

Other homesteads were available all along the coast, but no one wanted the "worthless white sand" when they could have dirt to grow crops and gardens.

In the early 1920s, visionary individuals saw more than the sand at the beach. People such as M.E. McCorquodale, J.B. Laban, W. W. Sharpless, H. Brown and Gid Thomas laid claim to large sections of the waterfront. No real development took place, however, until Hathaway Bridge opened in 1929 and the Coastal Highway (now U.S. 98) was completed along the Northern Gulf Coast, giving access to the beaches.

Sharpless was killed, and J.E. Churchwell took over Sharpless' and Brown's property to develop Long Beach. Thomas built the first Panama City Beach (near the extreme western end of Thomas Drive as it curves to join Front Beach Road). McCorquodale established Sunnyside and Lahan, Laguna Beach. Several other individuals established their own separate beaches.

After World War II, places such as Long Beach, Edgewater Gulf, Panama City Beach and a few others became their own separate incorporated cities in 1953. West Panama City Beach, which extended from just east of Laguna Beach to the western edge of Edgewater Gulf Beach, was incorporated in 1959, and included several other beaches, such as the Old Dutch Beach area and Larkway Villas.

In 1970, all of these towns were incorporated into Panama City Beach. Land at the extreme eastern and western end of what we collectively call Panama City Beach still remains in the county, however.
Submitted by: Marlene Womack, 2101 Norwood Place, Panama City, FL 32405.

The Pass at Phillips Inlet
In the 1920's the Channel at Phillip's Inlet was about six feet deep and straight out. All of the shipwrecks, lumber, trees, logs, and shells washed up on the west side. Everything was shipped by boats and barges. Whiskey rum runners from Cuba going to Camp Walton (Fort Walton now) would toss coconuts in their husks and we kids thought they came from across the Gulf. We did not know about South Florida in 1926. We had two big hurricanes. There was lumber, boats, and sand all buried six or eight feet high. The Pass stayed straight out.

In the early 1930's a drawbridge was built over the Pass to get from Destin to Panama City. In 1934 they started the first bridge from Red Fish Point (east side) to Yellow Bluff (west side). There was a hotel on the west side but it had closed up. Mrs. Hicks bought them out and it is now known as Camp Helen. In 1926 a hotel on the north side known as Phillips Inlet burned down. My Dad, C.H. Cain, built one further east on his homestead known as Lake View Inn. At one time we had five hotels on Phillips Inlet.

About 1945 or 1946 I was gone from Phillips Inlet for four years. In 1942 to 1946 Patton's Third Army fought and walked through France and Germany and was in Austria until we met the Russian Army. The War was over in August 1945. I had a son I had never seen. My wife was six months pregnant with our first son, Mike, when I left to go overseas.

After Camp Helen built the pier about 200 people came through the Channel daily during the summer months. We were afraid the Channel was going to move so the County Commissioner at that time kept it straight. You could put a seine or net out for 200 feet of the pier. Still a good Channel remained. Prosperity boomed at that time.

In 1977 Pinnacle Port was being built. In 1979, Hurricane Eloise wiped everything out. The Pass moved west and was filled with sand and construction junk from the Pinnacle Port. Then the big environmentalists took over. There was not much sand there and the old timers depended on fishing for a living. Since then, no fish came in the Lake. You see the fish would go from St. Andrews to Destin each way. When they got to Phillips Inlet they came in to get away from pelicans and sharks. All fish eat other fish except mullet.

Written by: C.H. Cain. Submitted by: Jo Ann Cain, 204 Cascade Street, Panama City, FL 32405.

Raising Cash in the Sand Hills

In the late twenties investors were paying $1500 an acre for a piece of the horticultural enterprise Seminole Farms. They paid $300 down and the balance over five years and expected to profit

Howard Murfee ca 1934

through sale of concord grapes or satsumas. Wid Rodgers ran the farms around Crystal Lake for a salary of $2.50 per day. A typical farm worker was paid a dollar a day, about the same as a turpentine woodsman. Although the community was actually on River Pond, it was called Crystal Lake. Mr. Rodgers erected a 50 foot high water tank, and on the west side of the road, a large firewood platform to serve the B C and St. Andrews Line there. The railroad was the first leg of the journey to northern markets for the produce.

Several young boys worked for Seminole Farms. The kids could work under the low hanging arbors upright which served them well when they needed to escape an adult. As a five year old, Jimmy Rodgers pruned and harvested grapes and picked up roots all day, six days a week. He drew five cents a day, enough to buy a gallon of kerosene.

Seminole Farms folded in 1930 because of the depression. The Rodgers stayed on their place, raising hogs and selling any wood which might be convertible to currency. The 19th century loggers who had clear cut the trees for lumber dropped the limb wood and left the stumps in the ground. This dead pine wood had gone through the lightering process and was soaked with pitch and called light wood or tar wood. Mr. Rodgers, like many others gathered light wood (stumped) and cut pulpwood from new growth pines as a livelihood.

The B C locomotive's boiler was fired by burning some coal, but mainly light wood limbs which produced considerable smoke. Up to four cords of wood was maintained on the Crystal Lake racks. If the train happened to encounter enough empty racks along its trek, it had to stop until the crew could gather fuel. A young man from Goethe down the road named Tom Banks was a locomotive fireman awhile. The fireman Jimmy Rodgers remembers most was a black man from Chipley called Will Harmon who went completely blind from the glare of the open firebox. Local boys thought Harmon was terminated by the railway without a pension when he could no longer work. One day he bought 106 freshly caught fish from Bunyon Hammock and Jimmy. The boys sold fish to the passengers and crew while the train stopped for fuel, water, or produce. Starting at the age of five and continuing after Bunyon and his brothers came to live with him at age 12, Jimmy sold bluegill and trout for a penny each, regardless of size.

A number of men and boys cut pulpwood from young pine trees

of four to twenty inch diameter for the paper mills. Young Arthur Davis of Court Martial was killed when a tree he had cut fell into another, then fell onto him while he was cutting the support tree. When Jimmy Rodgers was a young teenager he partnered with Charlie Flowers who had a young family. They would camp in the woods for a week at a time, cutting pulp wood all day, every day with a cross cut saw. Their goal was 300 sticks (sections of trunk six feet long) a day for which they could expect a penny a stick.

By the 1920s retorts in Freeport and Pensacola were converting dead light wood into pine oils, tars, and charcoal through destructive distillation. There were millions of pine stumps left in the woods from lumbering days. The stumps had to be blown from the ground with dynamite, often using nimble footed teenagers. After digging a hole to access the tap root, a cavity long enough to hold two or three sticks of dynamite was drilled into the root. The dynamite was placed into the drilled hole. A dynamite cap with a twelve to eighteen inch long fuse was attached and the access hole closed tightly using wood chips. They usually prepared several stumps and blew them in series. Jimmy Rodgers worked at this as young as twelve years old; he would go down the line from stump to stump lighting fuses until the first one blew, which was his signal to take cover. The explosion usually split the stump into two pieces. Sand hill stumps were sent by rail to Southport, loaded upon barges, and shipped to Pensacola where they were inspected for payment from $4 to $10 per ton depending on the pitch content.

One December day in 1934 eighteen year old stumper Howard Murfee and Orin Chambers were destroying an old box of unstable dynamite caps when the box exploded, gutting Howard and blinding Orin. Orin recalled Howard helping him find his seat in the truck and repeatedly promising to get him out of the woods. Without stomach muscles Howard could only steer and direct Orin who had to operate the truck's foot petals. Howard died two or three days after reaching his father's home at Lake Merial. Orin recovered and eventually regained his vision.

There were other ways to raise cash in the sand hills. Most popular by far was gum turpentining; and some raised livestock. People grew vegetables in the poor soil and some had fruit trees. Whatever the occupation, the work was always hard and usually dangerous. On the other hand, people didn't have to worry about what their children would do.

Submitted by: Debbie Rodgers Green, 15223 Highway 77, Southport, FL 32409.

Redfish Point

Jose Massalina, a free Spanish black, came to St. Andrews in the early 1800s. He lived first on Massalina Bayou where most of his children were born. After the Civil War, Massalina settled on Redfish Point, which is directly across the water from Panama City. His son, Hawk, joined him on nearby Davis Point. The Gainers, Lees and other men and women, some of whom had been slaves in Econfina and Jackson County chose to lead free lives on Redfish Point.

Fishing was the main livelihood. Others grew vegetables and small crops. The boat trips the black families made from Redfish Point to Panama City each week became legendary. They came across the bay to sell fruits and vegetables and to pick up clothes and linens, which they washed, ironed and returned on their next trip to town.

The Redfish Point Cemetery was established in the late 1800s. It remains today near the golf course but contains only a few marked graves even though hundreds of people were buried here through the decades, including Jose Massalina and Hawk Massalina's first wife, Belle. Like Cromanton and other towns on the peninsula, the residents of Red fish Point were forced to vacate their land on July 7, 1941 to make way for the establishment of Tyndall Field.

Submitted by: Marlene Womack 2101 Norwood Place Panama City, Fl 32405.

St. Andrews

St. Andrews surprises many when they learn this old town actually saw activity as early as the 1820's, two decades before Florida became a state. Ex. Georgia Governor John Clark and William Loftin, a sheriff from Jackson County, were two of its first settlers. Plantation owners from inland towns brought their families to summer here in the 1840's and 1850's. They organized the

St. Andrews Development Co. to sell lots along Beach Drive.

Caroline Lee Hentz, a noted Southern writer from Massachusetts, made numerous visits, from Marianna and Quincy with her husband, Nicholas Marcellus Hentz, in the late 1840's and early 1850's to visit her daughter, Julia Hentz Keyes. While in St. Andrews, she also spent time writing her novels.

The Civil War changed things, however. Men and some of their families came to St. Andrew Bay to make salt, not to spend time enjoying the bay breezes. Sailors from the Eastern Gulf Coast Blockading Squadron were stationed on Hurricane Island, which once was located in the Old Pass. From aboard their ships, they attempted to impose the blockade ordered by President Abraham Lincoln. The Union forces had hundreds of small clashes with the salt-makers, who made salt from seawater for the Confederacy.

On March 20, 1863, several Union sailors were killed after they landed with others to obtain fresh water from the famous Tavern Spring in St. Andrews.

After the war ended, those who could afford it returned to spending their summers on the bay. The fishing industry grew along the coast.

In the 1880's the St. Andrews Railroad, Land and Mining Co. promoted the St. Andrews Bay area in a huge nationwide mail-order real estate scheme. Thousands invested in the land sight unseen.

St. Andrews grew slowly but was held back by the company, which experienced financial difficulties and could not build the railroad promised to investors. A.B. Steele of the lumber trade eventually brought his Atlanta & St. Andrews Bay Railway into Panama City in 1908, opening the area.

J.H. Drummond, a large landowner and St. Andrews' first mayor, had plans to make St. Andrews the county's largest town. But he lost out when the vote went to Panama City for the County Seat.

In the 1960's and 70's at the St. Andrews marina, locals and tourists gathered on late afternoons to watch the boats offload their catches. Others wandered around the Shrimp Boat Restaurant at Smith's Yacht Basin to view the fishing boats as they glided into the dock along Beck Avenue. Then some boat captains began making the move to Grand Lagoon on Panama City Beach.

Several old homes existed in St. Andrews from the boom days of 1880's. The prospect of renovating some of these homes slowly gained in popularity. But in the mid-1970's, the country experienced a recession, evidenced in many subdivisions around the county. Abandoned, half-finished homes at places like Delwood, North Shore and Venetian Village looked like weathered tombstones in a forgotten cemetery. But the economy recovered quickly.

After several ups and downs, St. Andrews has undergone revitalization and is once again one of the area's popular seaside towns with big plans for development along its waterfront. Less than a decade ago, St. Andrews became the first section of Panama City to host a Mardi Gras celebration which continues each year.

Submitted by: Marlene Womack, 2101 Norwood Place, Panama City, FL 32405.

San Blas

Three women by the names of Fredericka Payne, Evelyn Young, and Amanda Birch each took up 160-acre homesteads in the town that became San Blas, which was located near what's now the flight line on Tyndall AFB. Developer J.J. Powers promoted San Blas as the "Naples of Tropical America" in 1912. He sold lots from $4 to $12.50 and suggested buying them as Christmas gifts.

Holly boughs were cut and shipped north at Christmas, along with grapefruits, Ponderosa lemons and some oranges, which grew here in abundance until cold weather claimed the trees.

In 1912, Payne opened the San Blas post office. It closed in 1941 to make way for Tyndall Field. Payne died a short time before the families were forced to give up their land. She was the last person to be buried in Cromanton Cemetery.

Submitted by: Marlene Womack, 2101 Norwood Place, Panama City, FL 32405.

Small Towns and Communities, Some of Which No Longer Exist in Bay County

Allanton - Andrew Allan gave this place its name when he and his family settled near the head of East Bay in the early 1900s. The community had formerly been known as Baxter and was the home of L.C. Davis, John Beadnell and the Kirvin family. The Baxter post office was in operation from 1893 until 1896. Allan opened his Allanton post office in 1902. This post office closed in 1933 when it was moved to Farmdale across the bay. Early settlers engaged in the lumbering industry.

This community remains on area maps and is currently seeing an increase in development because of its location on the Intracoastal Canal and beautiful, undeveloped East Bay.

Anderson - The Stephen W. Anderson family settled here on North Bay in the 1850s, across from what is now Lynn Haven. During the Civil War, members of the Anderson family served in the Southern Army or provided fish to the Confederacy. The location became well known around Northwest Florida as a place for purchasing salt fish. The Anderson post office opened in 1893.

The huge Sale Davis Sawmill was erected in Anderson in the early 1900s. The post office was changed from Anderson to Southport in 1907. The Birmingham, Columbus & St. Andrews Bay Railroad was completed into Southport in 1912.

The mill brought a lot of new people to Southport, many of whom remained after the sawmill burnt a few years later. Southport has seen growth in recent years with the erection of a high-rise condominium and new waterfront subdivisions.

Bay Harbor - This town existed along the eastern side of Watson Bayou near the bay. It was the site of the Moore Timber Co., a large sawmill that operated in the early 1900s near the foot of what's now Everitt Ave. Numerous mill houses for workers, stores, and a hotel stood along the surrounding streets.

A post office was established in 1914, but the mill eventually burnt. When officials were trying to decide where to erect the International Paper Co.'s first paper mill in Florida, they decided on Bay Harbor, in almost the same location as the old sawmill. The paper mill opened in 1931. Some still refer to the area as Bay Harbor, but the post office closed in 1953 and delivery was changed to Panama City.

Bayhead - This community is actually the oldest in what is now Bay County. Its choice location near the mouths of Econfina, Cedar and Bear creeks in the early 1820s drew settlers who wished to take advantage of North Bay and use it as a shipping point to the Gulf.

During the Civil War, blockade-runners took advantage of the secluded creeks to load cotton and sail it down the bay. In the 1880s, Bayhead became the "gateway to St. Andrews," the town promoted by the St. Andrews Bay Railroad, Land & Mining Co.

A post office was not established until 1895. It closed in 1937 and delivery was changed to Youngstown. Bayhead, an old logging and turpentining area, is another location seeing big development in recent years.

Bayou George - This name has been on the maps since the early 1800s as either George's Bayou or Bayou George. But as to George's last name, no one is certain.

During the Civil War, Union sailors captured the blockade-runner Florida in Bayou George in 1862. Hundreds of travelers came through this area from Marianna, Chipley and other inland locations in the late 1800s and early 1900s as they made their way to the coast and St. Andrews.

Logging and turpentining were big industries during that period. The Bayou George post office was opened in 1921, then closed in 1938 when delivery was changed to Panama City. During the last 30 years, Bayou George has seen tremendous growth. Many businesses are now located in the Bayou George area.

Beacon Beach - A long road that parallels the water on Tyndall AFB still bears the Beacon Beach name. The community was located where Tyndall Yacht Club and nearby government housing stands today.

The location took its name from the beacons visible in the water used to guide vessels in and out of St. Andrew Bay through the Old Pass. The Episcopal Church ran Camp Weed, a retreat for young people, at Beacon Beach for several years. The Beacon Beach post office operated from 1920 until 1941 when the government took the land to build Tyndall Field.

Bennett - The Charles Bennett family gave this farming community its name. It remains on area maps at the intersection of Highways 388 and 2301, near Econfina Creek. Several older families by the names of Mashburn, Cox, Hobbs, Porter, McQuagge and

Brown once called this location home.

During the Civil War, Richard Mashburn joined the Confederate army; Stephen, his younger brother, the Union army. After the war, family members held a reunion, which continues today each May after more than 130 years.

The Bennett post office opened in 1905 and continued until 1946, when service was changed to Youngstown.

Betts - Betts once was a neighboring community of Fountain to the south. It existed in the vicinity of US. 231 and State Highway 167.

The Betts Naval Stores Company built a huge sawmill here in the early 1900s. A.B. Steele rushed to complete his Atlanta & St. Andrews Bay Railroad south from Dothan to meet the demands of the mill, which needed goods, supplies and a means to ship their lumber.

Hundreds of people lived and worked at the Betts mill. The post office was established in 1912, but it closed in 1919 and moved to Fountain after most of the timber was gone. A few houses remained, but Betts soon died.

Cook - The community of Cook takes its name from Cook Bayou in eastern Bay County. Old lore tells of a religious man who came through the area and gave it his name.

The location had a steam sawmill in the 1840s, run by men named Robinson and Rogers. They moved on and squatters came and went until the 1880s when homesteaders took up land. Families such as the Colloms, Swearingens, Olivers, Cushions, Fowlers and Browns made Cook Bayou their home. Huge oysters filled the bayou bottom and residents always had plenty to eat.

Emil Schmidt obtained homestead land in 1890 and built a model farm. The farm drew numerous visitors through the years. They came to view his fruit trees, crops and garden where he proved that with fertilizer anything could be grown in the sandy soil. The Cook post office existed from 1898 to 1920.

Cook is another location that has seen great development in recent years. Schmidt's old farmhouse is now a Bed & Breakfast.

Econfina - Property along Econfina Creek was taken early by settlers who first viewed the beautiful creeks and its springs when they came to Florida with Gen. Andrew Jackson's army in 1818. Members of the William Gainer, Elijah Robbins, Wiley Jones, Silas Wood and Rev. Soliden families settled here, but then some of them moved on to Texas and other locations.

Those who remained, such as the Gainers, built large plantations with the help of slaves. The Econfina post office opened in 1855 but closed soon after the war ended in 1867. Once more homesteaders moved into Econfina, the post office was reopened in 1871 and existed until 1919 when it was changed to Bennett. Econfina's magnificent springs remain at a constant temperature year round. The old community is the location of numerous cemeteries that date back to the early days.

High Point - This old community was situated on the southern edge of Bayou George and along what is now Deer Point Lake. High Point was a popular place for picnics and outings for those boating on North Bay. Stephen A. Spiva, whose son W.E. Spiva became a harbor pilot in St. Andrew Bay and the Gulf, took up a homestead here in the late 1800s.

Located as it was on the water, High Point was expected to grow into a large town but it remained a sparsely settled area. A post office was operated from 1912 until 1915 when service was changed to Bayhead. High Point did not have a passable road until 1928, which hindered development.

Like most other places beside waterways, the High Point area has seen great development over the past few decades.

Lawrence - Those traveling on the old Marianna Road to St. Andrew Bay often stopped at a place called Lawrence in the late 1800s. Lawrence took its name from an early resident. Those living here in the early days grew crops of peanuts, cotton, corn, beans, oats, velvet beans and sweet potatoes.

Thomas B. Young, a man who helped create Bay County and oversaw the building of the north-south roadway that later became U.S. 231, moved to this area. The Lawrence post office opened in 1905, but officially became the Youngstown post office named for Young in 1908. D.M. Ross operated a huge mercantile business here, beginning about 1910.

Maxwell - John W. McAllister, a Confederate war veteran, took up a 160-acre homestead near the mouth of Bear Creek in the 1880s. McAllister opened a combination store/ post office in 1889 and called his place Maxwell. But the post office lasted only a few years then it was moved to Bayhead. For many years during the 1800s several individuals operated a ferry across Bear Creek. From Bear Creek or any of the other creeks and bayous, they could sail down North Bay directly to the Gulf. The construction of Deer Point Dam in 1961 put an end to boat traffic from above the dam and changed the water level all around the bay, which became Deer Point Lake.

McCloy - McCloy was also known as Ft. McCloy. It was planned to rival Lynn Haven on North Bay in late 1911. Those visiting the location found it on the east side of Mill Bayou.

McCloy's post office existed from 1914 to 1917. Bay front lots sold from $100 to $500; interior lots began at $50. But few pieces of property were sold because lots in Lynn Haven were less expensive and not as rural as land at McCloy.

Merial - Merial had a short-lived existence along the Birmingham, Columbus & St. Andrews Bay Railroad tracks and what is now Highway 77, near Lake Merial in Northern Bay County. A post office existed from 1914 until 1918 when service was moved to Greenhead, farther north up the tracks. Those who lived around Merial farmed and raised cattle. The old community has seen great development in recent years, especially through new subdivisions and the construction of the Bozeman Learning Center, just north of the lake.

Mill Bayou - John Lindsey Grant homesteaded property here off North Bay and what's now U. S. 231 in the late 1800s. He operated a gristmill and farmed, fertilizing his corn with fish heads. Grant built the first bridge across Mill Bayou. The Mill Bayou post office opened in 1915 and closed in 1922 when it was moved to Panama City.

Murfee - James G. Murfee, a Civil War veteran, settled on Burnt Mill Creek off West Bay and gave the location his name. He opened a combination store/post office in 1904. Murfee believed this location would develop into a large town on the bay. Turpentining was the main occupation of those living at Murfee. The post office closed in 1919, and the mail was transferred to Southport. Workmen completed the Intracoastal Canal past here in 1938.

Plans for the future call for a new airport and massive development around Burnt Mill Creek and nearby Crooked Creek.

Nixon - About 1880, Robert Nixon liked the area around Bear Creek where it crosses what is now U.S. 231 and began the Nixon community. It was located south of Youngstown. Nixon earned a little money ferrying travelers across this creek. Residents came from all around to attend the community's popular Pleasant Hills Baptist Church when few other churches existed in the area.

Nixon was known for its logging and as a stopover place for those traveling from Marianna to St. Andrews. Its post office existed for 20 years from 1892 until 1912.

Pine Log - Although Pine Log dates back to the 1800s, the community did not get its post office until 1914. Indians had their camps here before they faced removal in the 1830s. Some hid out in the forest and managed to live undetected, often passing for white. Union troops attacked a Confederate outpost near Pine Log in 1864.

In the late 1800s, lumbermen moved in to take advantage of the huge forests. A steamboat delivered supplies up Pine Log Creek. In the early 1900s, Pine Log boasted a school, commissary, church and cemetery. The post office was operated from 1914 until 1927. Pine Log State Forest now covers some of this area.

Pittsburg - Noah W. Pitts established the community of Pittsburg on Long Point in 1886, near the foot of what now is the northeast end of DuPont Bridge.

Pitts built a big mercantile store and furnished food and supplies to some of those who lived up East Bay. He also shipped large quantities of turpentine and rosin for processors aboard the J.P. Williams and the Tarpon, which came to his landing.

From 1892 until he was ready to retire in 1903, Pitts operated his post office. Then service was transferred to Parker.

Porter - This community existed along the present State 2301 from Moccasin Creek to Mulberry Branch. Porter took its name from members of the Charles and Eliza Loftin Porter family, some of whom settled here in the mid-1800s to farm.

For a time, their son, William Porter, operated a ferry across Bear Creek. He also ran a store and in 1884 opened a post office, which existed until 1888 when service was transferred to Econfina.

Saunders - This community, named for the Jones-Saunders Co. of Pensacola, is unusual because it was located in two different places and at two different times. It first appeared on the maps near Cook Bayou where the firm was involved with the logging operations and running a small logging railroad. The company also engaged in the naval stores industry. A post office existed in Saunders from 1904 until 1906.

But when the company reestablished a new community, Saunders was located between Fountain and Youngstown, near the Bay Line tracks. The Saunders post office was operated in this location from 1910 until 1915.

Seminole Hills - Seminole Hills was a huge plantation spread between West Bay Creek and Pine Log Creek in western Bay County that began as early as 1905. The company sold 100-acre lots to investors throughout the country. These investors were encouraged to grow blueberries, pecans, oranges and grapes, which the company would plant, tend, then pick and sell for them for a percentage of the profits.

Those who lived on the plantation had housing, a school, church, commissary and hotel. The post office existed from 1927 until 1930. The Great Depression brought about the company's demise. Pine Log State Forest now covers some of this land.

Shinetown - This community, which was formerly called East End, took its name from a black man named Shine. It was part of Panama City and included property north of Sixth Street, along Massalina Bayou.

The section grew, and its first official school opened in 1928. A post office existed in Shinetown from 1944 until 1949 when it was transferred to Panama City.

Tompkins - Calvin Tompkins founded this community in the late 1800s on the west shore of what is now Deer Point Lake. He ran a sawmill and had plans for a town, but his mill burned in 1906 and was never rebuilt. The Tompkins post office operated from 1898 until 1907.

Vicksburg - A man named Vickers joined in partnership with R.L. McKenzie. They established a huge turpentining concern north of Southport, along the Birmingham, Columbus and St. Andrews Bay Railroad tracks and what's now Highway 77. The company's huge piece of property stretched over thousands of acres from Cedar Creek to Burnt Mill Creek. Vicksburg's post office existed from 1905 until 1907.

T.D. Sale purchased the still in 1910. Individuals living around Vicksburg continued to produce naval stores for many years.

Wainwright Park - World War II brought about the establishment of Wainwright Park in western Panama City. The government built this community which contained housing for employees of the huge Wainwright Shipyard on the other side of the Coastal Highway (now U.S. 98). The shipyard built 102 Liberty ships and 6 tankers during the war.

The yard took its name from Gen. Jonathan Wainwright, who became an early prisoner of war in the South Pacific. The first ship that the yard produced was named the E. Kirby Smith. A post office was operated at Wainwright Park from 1943 until 1946.

Wetappo - This creek that flows into East Bay attracted visitors prior to the Civil War. They came to spend time in summer at cottages built for that purpose near the creek and bay. After the Civil War, more people located here at the head of the bay. The Wetappo post office existed on the bay from 1888 until 1933.

At nearby Sandy Creek, Joseph Dyer and J.J. Kronmiller, two early settlers, produced bricks from the clay deposits found along its banks.

Submitted by: Marlene Womack, 2101 Norwood Place, Panama City, FL 32405.

Small Towns that Grew into Larger Cities

Callaway - This town had its beginning prior to the Civil War when Pitt M. Callaway, a Baptist minister, came south from Alabama and purchased the E.G. Langston sawmill on Callaway Bayou, available after Langston died.

He sold the mill and others operated it for a few years. Callaway returned decades later. He built another sawmill and intended to develop the town that bore his name. Then Callaway sold most of his property to his father-in-law, Moses Carlisle, in the early 1900s. Lillian Carlisle was one of Carlisle's children. She went on to marry George M. West, editor of the Panama City Pilot.

The Foxes were one of the early settlers in Callaway. In 1911, Hettina Wilhemina Krusinga Fox appealed to the Carlisles for land for a school, which was opened in 1911. Some of the other early settlers were the McCalls, Browns and Burketts.

Parker - About 1835, William Loftin, a former Jackson County sheriff then later a resident of St. Andrews, obtained 80 acres of land in what now is Parker. He intended to build a thriving town on the St. Andrews & Chipola Canal Co., proposed at that time. He named the location "Austerlitz" for Napoleon's victory over Austria and Russia, which made worldwide news.

Joseph M. White, Florida's first territorial delegate; and Henry Riviere, a Jackson County farmer, joined Loftin in this project. But St. Joseph, 40 miles to the east down the coast, drew the attention and became one of the territory's largest towns. As a result, little actual settlement took place in Austerlitz. Loftin operated a ferry across the bay but died in 1838.

Peter F. Parker, a German fisherman, his family and their descendants soon made Austerlitz their home. In the 1880s, three different Parker families lived in Parker, each from different roots. When asked for a name for the post office, the reply was "Parker." It was established in 1886.

Springfield - Plans for "Springfield" were drawn up in 1935 on vacant fields with a pretty spring so workers at the paper mill could live near their employment site. W.B. Gray, the owner of a large hardware business, platted the town in 1937.

Buddy McLemore became Springfield's first mayor. Springfield has its own police force, city hall, library, fire house, etc.

Cedar Grove - The town was called Cedar Grove because of its numerous cedar trees. It was incorporated in 1951. Later, a total of five commissioners and a mayor were charged with running the city government.

The Cedar Grove School opened on 15th Street in 1957. In recent years, Cedar Grove has expanded up Highway 231.

Submitted by: Marlene Womack, 2101 Norwood Place, Panama City, FL 32405.

Towns that Existed on the East Peninsula, But Were Lost with the Establishment of Tyndall Field (later Tyndall AFB)

Hundreds of the people who came to St. Andrews Bay to invest in the development company's land in the 1880s found more desirable property and homesteads available elsewhere around the bay. Several communities and towns were established as a result of this company's advertisements of this area.

Cromanton - W. C. Croman, a Methodist minister from Baltimore, took up a homestead across the bay from Parker in 1886. He sold land, built a store and a hotel. He preached in St. Andrews and at the Methodist church that he and others built in Cromanton. The post office opened in 1888. Visitors came and wintered at the hotel. But Cromanton remained a small community because people could access the town only by boat or after a long ride around the head of East Bay.

The mailboat delivered mail, freight and passengers on its sail up and down East Bay each day. The town's beautiful springs attracted visitors from Panama City, who came across the bay to drink the sulphur water, considered an excellent health remedy.

The town had few industries but did well in the beginning with its palmetto nuts, which were gathered, dried and sent to drug houses up North to be converted to different medicines. One of the men owned a big rabbit farm. Some also grew citrus trees that yielded large lemons, grapefruits and oranges.

Another promotion of Cromanton was attempted in 1912. By then the hotel had been converted to a private school. Students rode a launch back and forth each day from Panama City. But after a few years, the school closed.

After the construction of DuPont Bridge in 1929 and what's now U.S. 98, the town underwent significant growth in the 1930s. Residents were happy living here until the U.S. Government took all the property on the East Peninsula to build Tyndall Field. Final removal date was set for July 7, 1941. Families had to turn in the keys to their homes and leave never to return. Many faced difficulties obtaining housing in town. Payment for the Cromanton land was set at farmers' prices, not waterfront. Only those who could afford to sue the government received a just price for their land.

Marywood, Cromanton's cemetery, remains on the road that leads to the old town site on the bay. It was the burial place of several Civil War veterans and many others who lived in and around the old town. The markings of many of the graves have been lost to time and cemetery cleanups.
Submitted by: Marlene Womack, 2101 Norwood Place, Panama City, FL 32405.

Turpentine Side Camp and Semoal Hill Plantation

Half way between Philips Inlet and West Bay, about five miles, the Laird family had a side camp. About twenty-five families of Negroes lived in shanty houses for workers. They worked the trees for gum, resin, etc. One of the Negroes Eli Green had a place of business which was called in those days a Jook Joint. On Saturday night there would be a lot of jooking (dancing) going on. There was a commissary store which the Laird family owned. Will Morrison had the job of overseer which was what they called a woods rider. Was Bass Man was the only white man and family that lived there. Later on the Cauleys moved there.

The Semoal Hill Plantation was going strong in them days. They had a huge farm. They grew grapes, oranges, sugar cane, corn, peas, butterbeans and okra. The had miles and miles of produce. They had a school and even a high school. There was a hotel, hundreds of mules and a house for the farm workers to live in. The farm went from West Bay Creek, both sides, to Walton County and to the river, to where Highway 79 is today. It was a dirt wagon road in them days to the side of West Bay Creek to West Bay to the Side Camp Road.
Written by: Clifford Hilliard Cain. Submitted by: Jo Ann Cain.

The View From the Top

On a wall in my house is a mid-1950s photo of my future wife and her six brothers and sisters. They are in the Sunnyside neighborhood, posed in front of a house that bears the name *Suits Us*. The picture represents what the word "vacation" meant to many Alabamians back in those days - a trip to the beach. Anyplace else was usually out of the question.

Eleven years ago, after countless summer vacations, week-end get-aways and other spur-of-the-moment trips to our beautiful beaches, my wife and I retired, left Birmingham, Alabama behind and settled on the tranquil west end of the beach. During our years as Alabama tourists, however, such peace and quiet wasn't always to be had.

We had two children and like most kids they wanted to go places where there was an abundance of two things - noise and lots of other people. Year after year, our two kids never missed visiting Goofy Golf, Petticoat Junction, Miracle Strip Park, the old Volcano, go-kart tracks and various other Front Beach Road attractions. Before setting sail into the hubbub of a summer night, we often captured a last few minutes of serenity atop the old Miracle Strip Tower.

The tower sat directly on the beach, across from Miracle Strip Amusement Park. There was a gift shop at the bottom and an elevator. For a small fee, visitors could ride up to the observation deck

Jeff Webb with children Chris and Cindy. The Panama City Beach Tower is in the background, June, 1980

and stay as long as they wanted. For some reason, or perhaps just luck, we never found it crowded at the top. In fact, most of the time the four of us had the place to ourselves. The tower was reputed to be the tallest structure on the Strip, with an unobstructed view in all four directions. The "chop-chop" of tourist helicopters flying nearby was the only noise other than that made by the always-blowing wind. It was a beautiful place for picture taking. The accompanying photo, snapped in June, 1980, looks east from the tower. It's interesting to note the open space on both sides of Front Beach Road. The Edgewater development hadn't taken place yet.

There's an interesting tale about the tower's grand opening. So the story goes, an unusual individual reportedly was given the honor of cutting the ribbon. 'Tis said the job was done by Jo-Jo, a trained monkey wielding a pair of scissors.

The kids grew up and though my wife and I still visited quite often, there came a time when trips up the tower came to an end. Vacations became days spent at Saint Andrew State Park and nights that featured dinner followed by an after-the-news bedtime. After we moved to the beach, even though we drove by the tower frequently, we didn't stop.

Hurricane Opal dealt the tower a fatal blow and within months it was torn down. The view from the top is a memory now, one kept alive only by old photographs.
Submitted by: Jeff Webb, 21305 Caribbean Lane, Panama City FL 32413.

Neighborhoods

Crime in Millville

We lived right on the corner so there were large crowds of men going back and forth to the paper mill, walking during the day and night. We always kept our doors unlocked and the garage unlocked. We had a separate garage. We never had any trouble about losing our goods and wares and nobody was a burglar in those days.

We had the first telephone in Millville, Florida. The Berry family lived down the street from us and every Saturday night Mrs. Berry would come up and knock on the floor of the back porch and say, "Call the law to Ed. He's drunk and he's raising cain down here again." Many a time I stood and watch down a block away, my father and two policemen trying to get one-armed Ed Berry in the back of a police car. I don't know how many times he was arrested, but Ed finally beat his mother to death.

J. D. Blackwell and Mr. Brown were both policeman that lived in Millville. Mr. Brown lived out near Callaway. Mr. Brown's daughter married Mr. Harrison and he was the Oldsmobile dealer here.

My mother was a state's witness when Judge Hutchison was the prosecuting attorney and Judge Jones from Chipley was a circuit Judge over here when they tried Mrs. Belle Withers for murder. She and Charlie Rathel were both charged with mur-

der and Mr. J. Ed Stokes represented her. It resulted in a hung jury and she was never tried again. Her son, Dallas was tried, convicted and executed for murder in Panama City.

I remember when Chief Barrett shot and killed Solly Hutto in Millville and Barrett was Chief of police of Panama City. This was after 1926. I was just a small boy about eight years old. Chief Barrett said he did it in self defense; that Solly Hutto was advancing on him with a knife. Somebody had taken a knife out of Solly's hand so it was said and they had given it to my father for safekeeping. So my daddy brought that knife home and put it on the mantelpiece and told all of us children, "Now none of you touch that knife. Just don't touch it." It was like a dragon in the family. Every time we'd go by the mantelpiece, we'd look at that knife laying there, but nobody dared touch it A grand jury met and declared that Chief Barrett did, in fact, fire in self defense. He fired two shots, one in the ground to let Solly know he had a gun and not to advance on him any further and then he fired at Solly. I remember seeing Solly laying on the ground and he had a bullet hole in his left hand shirt pocket and they said it went through his heart. My future brother-in-law Harold Harmon, who was then a high school student, was up at Troy Gilbert's drug store when the first shot was fired and he found himself about five blocks away, getting out of there, running down Main Street of

Millville near the graveyard.
Submitted by: Fred Turner, 2694 Island View Dr., Panama City, FL 32405.

The Fight and Flight of Furniture

Adam Levi Welch's first wife Margaret Pristell died during the Yellow Fever. Adam Levi remarried Delilah Glisson and had many children who were raised in Old Town, or St. Andrews as it was later called. Bessie Montgomery, a daughter and Adam Levi and his wife Delilah lived in the backyards of each other.

One of the only possessions left of Adam Levi's first wife was a beautiful large center table. As the story goes, no one knows who actually had sole possession of the table, but Bessie and Delilah fought over the table frequently.

The table would go missing from Adam's house and Delilah would sneak into Bessie's and take it back. The next day Bessie would sneak into Delilah's house and retrieve the table. This magic appearance and covert recovery of the table from one house to the other went on for many months.

One sunny afternoon, Adam Levi heard a loud commotion in his back yard. Upon investigation he discovered both his wife Delilah and his daughter Bessie on ether side of the center table. To his amazement a tug-of-war had been waged over the table. Both women had tight holds on the table and the struggle was vicious. Both women landed in the dirt and neither one would give up their hold. Fearing that the table would be destroyed, Adam Levi recovered the table, but not before receiving some blows from both women and the table. After securing the table he stored it in a safe place and that seemed to end the disagreement. The center table survived and is now in the home of a family member who will remain anonymous for fear of another Family Feud.
Submitted by: Donna Rankin, 210-N East Baldwin Rd., Panama City, FL 32405.

Fond Memories of Sunnyside and Santa Monica Beaches

Introduction of Bay County Beaches was in the late 40's or early 50's through an invitation from a co-worker in Atlanta. My friend, her sister and brother-in-law had rented a cottage on Bid-a-Wee Beach. My experience prior to this trip was several weekend trips to Daytona Beach. I was overwhelmed at the difference; the calm Gulf and the beautiful white sand.

In the late 50's and through the 60's my friend Mary Broome, her parents (Ms Bessie and Walton Fletcher) invited me and my two very young daughters for short vacations at their home on Buena Vista (Santa Monica Beach). We three remember so well their happy home and kindness.

Friends at the Beach, L-R: Loretta Moore, gentleman not known, and Shirley who is wearing Sol Tepper's boots which are his trademark

Mary and I would have a wonderful time on the beach with the girls. In the evening, the little ones tucked in bed, well, supervised by Ms Bessie "Granny and Pa" Broome, Mary and I would head out to the few places on the beach for a little night life. The Paradise Lounge, 'Little B. Ham, and the Holiday Restaurant and Lounge at the Bridge. They were so different we mood picked. We met a lot of nice people and had a good time at these gatherings. In the 70's when looking for a place to purchase my happy times on Santa Monica was foremost in my mind. I called a real estate sales lady, Nell Blanchard and requested something on Sunnyside, (not knowing Buena Vista all this time was Santa Monica). They are side-by-side and have similar covenants (property owners owning the beach front).

The cottage she showed me was just what I was looking for, price wise and Beach wise. An earlier trip to Destin, anything I could afford was so far from the beach it defeated my purpose. This was a true Beach cottage. Having been brought in and placed on concrete supports, on a quiet deadend street, only a block and a half from the unobstructed beach that was my view from the cottage's screened-in front porch. The Cottage on the back end of the lot was similar to mine and there was an easement for them to enter.

This was to be my second home and my wants were few.

However, some years later my cottage burned and the owners of the back cottage sold me theirs. In the 90's this cottage was renovated. I was there when I had to leave because of "Opal". The last big hurricane in our area struck our beach. My cat (C.B.) and I headed for Atlanta for safety. Since that time my permanent home has been built on Sunnyside where the first cottage stood. The builders were the sons of Nell Blanchard, who sold me the property 20 years ago, Greg and Jim Blanchard of Blanchard Construction Co. on the beach. Many of my neighbors inherited their beach residences from their parents, the nicest form of hand-me-downs I know of. On my street the Teppers, the Wise cottage, The Watson's, Anne Black is in her Mother's Beach Home and Mr. Harris, even Ms. Mary Emma McCorqadale Munser resides on Sunnyside whose Mother and Father developed and fought for the Beaches so long ago that we enjoy their efforts today.

We are really "Old" and "New" families. A wonderful place to live! I'm selfish for my family, trusting this beautiful spot God created and the McCorqadale's and former owners fought so hard to retain it's natural beauty, will remain very much as it is for my children's children, to enjoy what is here today. The fear of over-growth is imminent.
Submitted by: Loretta B. Moore 204 3rd Street Panama City Beach, Florida 32413.

Growing up in The Cove

Looking back, it was a somewhat idyllic time. The roads were all soft dirt. We had chickens in the back yard. One friend had a pony and another friend had a horse (all in the backyard). We rode all over the Cove.

There was no Cove Shopping Center but there was the Three Arts Playhouse located near where the shopping center sits today. Going towards town, Tarpon Dock Bridge was wood and a little scary if you looked down between the cracks.

Cove School was our school and our center. I learned to play tennis there when I was in the 3rd grade. We could roller skate on the concrete court. We had a huge halloween carnival every year and the fathers built the booths for the classes to use. We played softball there in the summer; we also boarded buses there in the summer and were taken to Magnolia Beach to learn to swim. Every year, my dad came to the school and lined up each class and took the class picture-we did not have individual photos at that time.

There was a talent contest at the Ritz Theater (now Martin Theater) every Saturday morning. I actually won, once. It wasn't that I was any good at singing, it was that my dad had painted my white sweatshirt front and back with beautiful renditions of the Auburn tiger and the War Eagle, and Donnell Brookins made a big deal of it.
Submitted by: Susan Jones Moore, 310 S. Palo Alto Ave., Panama City, FL 32401.

Growing Up On Grace

After having been born at High Point on Williams Bayou and living all over the County (Washington County first, Bay County after 1913) my father chose to build the only house he ever built on Grace Avenue, at the corner of 10th Street. In the early 1930's, his new house was built with cutting-edge materials, a large screened porch, indoor plumbing, a huge living room fireplace and two large bedrooms. The refrigerator was on the back porch, but it *was* a Norge Electric. Getting a drink of milk at bedtime meant going outside!

When I came along in 1937, another bedroom was added complete with a fuel oil heater to allow for the retirement of the fireplace.

Grace Avenue, named for the granddaughter of a pioneer settler, was the site of many grand homes of early community leaders, but it was considered "out in the country" and the pavement ended at 11th Street, which was also just a dirt road. We had a close-knit neighborhood, and I still have contact with some of our Grace Avenue friends to this day,

We had all the infrastructure of a modern city: water, sewer (which was dumped raw into the bay at the foot of Harrison

Ernest and his big sister Betty Sue in front of the house on Grace in November, 1938

Avenue), dependable electricity and telephones with consecutively-assigned numbers——-ours was number 223. My friends, the McGills, had number 598. You picked up the old, heavy black phone in the living room, heard "number please" and the operator rang your party for you.

We had a grocery store or two, schools, our church, the Gulf Station, and all the Harrison Avenue businesses——-all within walking distance. Families usually had just one car.
Submitted by: Ernest Spiva, Jr., 6141 E. Hwy 98, Panama City, FL 32404.

Panama Grammar Days

Panama Grammar School served our community in the building formerly housing the high school, which moved north on Harrison Avenue to its present location in 1926. Out in the woods, Bay High's *Alma Mater* begins with "On our city's northern border——"!!!

We walked to Panama Grammar for grades 1 through 8, after attending Mrs. Foreman's Kindergarten in the 700 block of Grace Avenue. There were no busses and only a few teachers had cars. It was very easy for teachers to send a note home to your parents at lunch to be signed and returned in the afternoon. I could hear playground noises at my house and even the single outside bell could be heard at my house.

During the war (WWII), our Grace Avenue Block Warden was our neighbor, Mr. Bill Weaver, who happened to be principal at Bay County High School. Mrs. Weaver taught at Panama Grammar. During air raid drills, a huge siren on a telephone pole nearby would signal us to pull all shades and darken the houses. Mr. Weaver would appear in his helmet and armband and check the neighborhood for any signs of light coming from the houses. Cars had their headlights partially blacked out and the street lights along the bay had their waterfront half blacked out. Pretty scary reminders of wartime for all us kids!
Submitted by: Ernest Spiva, Jr., 6141 E. Hwy 98, Panama City, FL 32404.

Jinks Junior High School

Out in the "sure 'nuff" woods on 11th Street, a new school was begun when I was in 7th Grade. It was called Jinks Junior High School, and would house grades 7, 8 and 9. As often happens, construction was not completed in time for school's opening, so the old, wartime housing complex, Annie B. Sale Project, was used for a year to house Jinks Junior High - "ad interim"-the sign. Tommy Oliver Stadium is located on the site.

My 8th Grade year was spent in an old government apartment, with the walls removed and the holes for plumbing closed up with tin nailed over them. But what a great year it was, thanks to our wonderful teacher, Miss Vivian Brady! She made our 13th year of life a happy, positive, quickly-passing one!

We moved into our new school on still-to-be-paved 11th Street for the 9th Grade, and were met with busses, a cafetorium, showers, football team and marching band! We "ran off" the yearbook in green ink all by ourselves. Why, we even had automatic bells and a school-wide PA system!

We also had something new, called an "assistant principal." But, that's a whole 'nother story. Let me just say that I could still walk home with a message in no time at all!

Our band class was taught by Bay High's director, Mr. Orin Whitley-who also lived in our neighborhood. He had a huge Great Dane named Major. Mr. Whitley came over from the high school and daily revealed to us an exciting peek at glorious things to come—our high school days at Bay County High School.
Submitted by: Ernest Spiva, Jr., 6141 E. Hwy 98, Panama City, FL 32404.

More Grace Avenue Days

"On our city's northern border—didn't quite fit Bay High when

we arrived for our first year there, our sophomore year. We *still* had to walk to school; riding bikes was *uncool*, and few 10th Graders could drive. Soooo, it was "walk yourself those two blocks, boy!" For the first time, Grace Avenue wasn't so great. Why couldn't we live in Southport or somewhere, so I could ride the bus?

High school days soon passed into the "years rolled by" as the *Alma Mater* predicted. And, when I would come home from college and later from the US Army, I would sometimes bring friends for a visit. I would drive downtown on Grace Avenue and point out where the mayor lived and the first swimming pool to be built here. I would point out my preacher's house, my doctor's house, several teachers' houses, the Judge's house, and countless houses occupied by friends and classmates, long since gone.

The once-new sidewalk where we skated with our metal skates, clamped on to our shoes by a key, is cracked and patched, now. But it ran in front of everybody's house and it hooked us all together, so I would point it out, too.

Finally, I would show my guests the First Baptist Church and tell about riding my tricycle to Sunday School, long before I was big enough to tackle riding a bicycle!

Grace Avenue is still there. A few old-timers are still there. But my memories of our "place on Grace" will never go away.
Submitted by: Ernest Spiva, Jr., 6141 E. Hwy 98, Panama City, FL 32404.

Hiland Park in the 50's

The 1950's in Hiland Park were the slow, dusty years of childhood for the five children of Charles and Pera Lee Peacock and one child of R. C. and Pauline Johnson. The children were first cousins and grew up together because their parents often visited each other. That's how this story happened.

Charles and Pera Lee and R. C. and Pauline went fishing together and left Ann (Johnson), the oldest, to "babysit" with Stony, Charlotte, Carolyn, Robert, and Pauline (Peacock). Ann's parents brought her to her younger cousins' home in Hiland Park to "babysit" while the adults took off for the day. The five younger children just adored their older cousin, Ann, and would do anything she asked of them while she stayed to care for them. She was the

Early Hiland Park School

most fun "babysitter" they could every have!

The parents would always leave a measured amount of lunch money for the kids to go to the nearby community store, Hartzog's Grocery, to buy bananas and bread for delicious banana sandwiches for lunch. One time, after the seemingly long, and positively dusty, walk to Hartzog's, the children gathered inside the store to buy their lunch supplies but spied a big watermelon that looked just wonderful to them. They loved watermelon!

They decided to use their lunch money to buy that wonderful melon. They could almost taste it right there in the store! After buying the melon, they had a problem. That was a big melon, really too big for even the oldest child, Ann, to carry by herself.

Ann tried to carry it for a while but soon got tired. Stony, the next eldest, tried to carry it for a while but soon got tired too. All the other children were too little to even think about carrying that big melon! So it was that the Hiland Park neighbors must have gotten a big kick out of seeing the troop of six young children rolling that watermelon, down the dusty road, back home.

When they got home, that was the best watermelon!
Submitted by: Charlotte Peacock Davis, 9219 Lake Forest Drive, Youngstown, FL 32466.

Living in the Cove

At the end of the third summer camp, I was met at the train station by my Aunt Ruth. She took me to Panama City, Florida to live at grandma's. Grandpa Cain had just passed away, and I guess my mother may not have been able to afford the tuition there anymore.

I entered the fourth grade at Cove Elementary School.

The teacher there was Miss Holland, and needless to say I was in love. The boys were still fighting the civil war and they took it out on me every time they could. One was Billy Creary and the other was Jerry Wiggins. There were others but I can't remember their names obviously. The two pretty girls were Virginia Dennis and Sonja Weislogel, the ones who felt sorry for me! When we played touch football during recess, which really ended up being tackle when I carried the ball, I would end up under a pile of 10 boys. I guess this made me tougher down the line.

Mike Hamlin and his mother as he fires a rifle down the beach in 1940

I lived on grits and eggs for breakfast, and syrup and biscuits for supper. We had chickens in the back yard, and grandma grew collard greens there. My job was to kill a chicken every Sunday for our dinner. Obviously I didn't enjoy that. Another staple in the diet was mustard greens.

Submitted by: Mike Hamlin 251 SE 46th Street, Cape Coral, FL 33904.

Fishing by Cove Hotel

I did a lot of fishing that year. Our house was less than a block from St. Andrews Bay, and there was a dock there on the beach in front of the Cove Hotel. This seemed to be a classy place, expensive cars pulled up and people had dinner there. I can remember hearing music coming out of the dining room, particularly Frank Sinatra with the Dorsey band singing "I'll never smile again". And "There's a Small Hotel, with a Wishing Well, etc." by Claude Thornhill's orchestra.

As soon as I got home from School (and incidentally we walked, no busses there), I would grab my cane poles and go down to the dock to catch shiners and catfish. Old Black Joe was always down there, and I would usually end up giving him my catch. One time I was going to fish with bacon so I put the bacon in the pocket of my wool swim trunks before I went to school. That afternoon, I came home, put on the trunks and went to the dock. Before you knew it, something was biting me everywhere. They were ants (you can figure this out).

Meanwhile, a huge air force base was under construction called Tyndall Field, a gunnery school. So you could see a lot of servicemen roaming the streets of Panama City (probably looking for some action).

Submitted by: Mike Hamlin, 251 SE 46th Street, Cape Coral, FL 33904.

Living in Millville

In 1928 when I started to school we had a hurricane in the fall of that year. Most of the people that lived in houses around us came to our house because our house was the strongest house in the community. Mr. and Mrs. Harrison came and Annie and Emmett. Mrs. Harrison baked cakes during the hurricane and those were the best cakes I have ever eaten in my life. Wilma Harrison could bake a cake.

My father was mayor of Millville. He was also secretary of the carpenter's union. A group of about six white carpenters came to see my father as he was sitting on the back porch. They all came up and sat down. They wanted him to fire black people who were employed with the Works Progress Administration. My father was building the Callaway School and the Millville School and he was a well-known contractor. They wanted him to fire those black people and they put up the argument that, well, you know, white folks need their jobs. My father said, "well, the black men have to look after their families too, so I'm not going to fire a one of them."

Our schools were segregated. At the St. Andrews Lumber Company, I couldn't go out on the island. My father told me not to go out there because black families lived out there and black boys were playing out there. I could see them playing. I knew what black boys looked like. They were about as big as I was and I wanted to go out there and play marbles and shoot slingshots with them. My father said no and I accepted his word. I never did go out there at the lumber yard.

I remember with great pleasure the people I knew in Millville. I was astounded by the mothers of Millville. I would go to play at Bill Harris's house because they had a city park in front and a tennis court. We young boys would go up there and play on that tennis court. If dark came, Mrs. Harris would say to me, "Freddie, have you had anything to eat?" And I'd say, "No, Ma'am." She'd say, "well, go wash your hands and come in and sit down." All the women were that way in Millville. It didn't matter whether you belonged to the family or not. They would just take you under their wing and take you in there and feed you and just treat you magnificently. I just thought Millville was a nice place to be. The people didn't use bad language, there was no cursing, but Millville was the so-called "tough district." We had several boys who played football and they had a reputation for being rough and rowdy like Brownie, Skinny Cotton, the Harmon boys and some others.

The women put up fruit in the summertime and they shared their largesse with each other. There was a sense of community and people sharing what they had with other people.

Submitted by: Fred Turner, 2694 Island View Dr., Panama City, FL 32405.

Oakland Terrace 1961

In the summer of 1961, the world of a twelve year old boy living in Oakland Terrace was quite small. Everything that counted for anything was within a J.C. Higgins bike ride. It was a time of freedom. Crime was almost non-existent; doors were left unlocked; and moms, who mostly stayed at home, did not feel compelled to know the exact location or activities of their children until suppertime. Future *baby boomers* lived at almost every house and opportunities for unsupervised play and mischief were

Fred Johnson sitting on the back step, getting ready for a day at the park and baseball

limitless. From early to late, the games were on.

The neighborhood's defining characteristic was the "park" which was the hub of all summer activities. The city operated a free recreational program out of the concrete block clubhouse. High school girls were employed at minimum wage. They provided what little supervision existed, as well as the stuff of young boys' fantasies. Tennis, ping pong, archery, horseshoes, and shuffleboard were available for one to prove his superiority over another. However, these activities were merely time fillers sandwiched between the main purpose for living - baseball.

There was a game almost every morning. If there were less than eighteen players, the more skilled would play defense

Fred Johnson in his ball uniform

for both sides and only bat for one.

There were no coaches and no umpires. Winning was of paramount importance during the game. But a victory was forgotten within an hour of the final out when everyone who had a nickel went to Blackshear's Drug Store for a large root beer in a frosted mug

Written by: Fred M. Johnson. Submitted by: Patty Sikes, 6445 Dunlieth Pl., Pensacola, FL 32504.

Remembering Millville

When I was growing up in Millville, we lived in a two-story house we bought from W. B. Gray in 1917 and that's when we came to Bay County. We paid $750 for the house and the lot on which it sat and two additional lots, one on either side of the house, one towards the Baptist Church and the other one to the south of us.

I remember when school first started because to the east of us, we lived on kind of a small hill in Millville, the ground gave way

W. Fred Turner

to a branch down below us down there about a block away and a small stream ran through there. We'd make a flutter mill which was four paddles on an axle and we would have small boats, small pieces of wood attached to a string to that flutter mill; and as the flutter mill would turn in the water, it would pull the boat upstream. It was the beginning of something that sparked in my mind about learning things. Why did the force of the water pull the boat up? Why wasn't the force equal and the boat would hang onto the string down at the end. But it didn't. The flutter mill would always pull it upstream. I didn't know anything about the laws of physics.

I remember when I was very young seeing a showman right in the middle of Springfield. He had a horse and a wagon and on the back of the wagon was his platform where he was selling all this stuff. He was selling lineament and all the things that you heard about that people were selling in those days. He had an Indian with him to impress people and people had their pictures taken with him. I remember the cameras, the little brownie camera, the little square box Kodak, we had those.

Submitted by: Fred Turner, 2694 Island View Dr., Panama City, FL 32405

The 300 Block of Linda Avenue

I moved to 309 Linda Avenue from a little house on Massalina Drive in December of 1943 with my parents, grandmother and older brother. I was only a little over a month old when we moved to 309 at Christmas time. My brother David was two

Johnnie Caldwell Walker (Mema) at 309 Linda Avenue 1964

years old. Mother later told me that you should never move at Christmas time. In 1949 my brother Richard was born.

Growing up on Linda Avenue was really great. We had many neighborhood children (more boys than girls, though). One time I decided I wanted to play football with the boys. It only took a few minutes for me to realize that I did not want to be a football player.

Since we were only half a block from Cove School we had easy access to the playground and to the summer recreation programs where we could do crafts, play games and many other activities all summer.

We were able to walk or ride bikes to homes of friends for blocks around and would often meet at the Cove Hotel dock and swim. We could also walk to town and go to the movie on Saturday. When we went to Jinks Junior High School we walked the half block to Cove School to catch the bus. We did the same thing when we got to Bay High.

The Marshall, Land, Shirley, Lawrence and Douglas families lived on Linda when we moved to 309 and were there when we all graduated from Bay High. I still consider all of the folks left from these families my friends.

Submitted by: Rebecca Brown Saunders, 2515 Frankford Avenue, Panama City, FL 32405.

The Village of Old Town in the Yesterday,
"Civil War Skirmish at Old Town"

Built on a bluff above the white sand
Where the bay's blue water meets the land
Where grows the mighty oak, the pine, and bay

A log two-story built by John Clark
On the areas history left it's mark
Porches on the front and on the side
It was his home and his pride

On March twenty-first, eighteen sixty-three
Robinson's men spied a launch in the sea
From the bark Roebuck came a launch in the bay
To search for cotton being loaded that day

Sherrel was Commander of the Roebuck bark
Roger was Commander of the launch in the bay
Hidden behind the house built by Clark
Was Robinson's twenty men on that day

Coming out fast the Feds were surprised
They were close enough to see their eyes
Firing fast and furious without delay
The Feds dropped their weapons and ran away

Snow was shot dead by the hickory tree
Thomas King died in the edge of the sea
The two on the launch worked closer in
To assist the escape of their men

The two fired back but without avail
Saw the men in the water leave a bloody trail
So they lowered their flag and asked for quarter
Fire ceased on the launch; the men in the water

Robinson gave the right to pick up the dead
Later he wished he'd stood pat instead
Moving back and forth they moved farther away
Then sailed for the gulf and out of the bay

They left behind four muskets, eight bayonets
Eight cartridge boxes, two oars was total net
They buried Snow by the old hickory tree
One wounded ran away and he was free

Sherrel said there was fifty, not twenty
Robinson said twenty, it proved to be plenty
In most cases someone wins, someone loses
The victor celebrated, loser sings the blues

A war in which you had son against dad
Had brother against brother 'twas very bad
'Twas finally over we had peace in the land
We forgave each other by the shake of a hand

Robinson's guerillas won on that day
The skirmish at Old Town on the bay
Every man wounded, the Feds had lost
Though they escaped they paid a might cost

Submitted by: Charles Franklin Peacock, 447 College Station Road, Panama City, Fl 32404.

Where in the World Is Holy Hammock?

As a child I would be very reluctant to tell anyone who asked where I lived. Holy Hammock!, They would exclaim. Where is that?

Holy Hammock was, that is past tense, because it is no more, located at the most South end of what is East Avenue now. The Hammock began approximately just South of the Millville Elementary School at Cherry Street, flanked on the East by Nelson Bayou, now Watson Bayou, circling the shore line to encompass the land to the farthest portion of the hammock touching the West shoreline back to Cherry Street as this street is known today.

A hammock is a fertile area that is usually higher than its surroundings and is characterized by hardwood vegetation and deep humus-rich soil, such was where I lived my childhood. A wonderful place for a child to grow up. We lived in a house that was built by my grandfather, Steve Scott. By the time I was born in that house it was showing its declining years and we could see the earth under the house through the flooring and had to stuff paper or old rags in the walls when the winter wind surged from the North. It was a great time to live but I personally do not wish to return to the "good old days", nor to automatic air conditioning by the weather. Summers were horrendous, and winters were tortuous, spring and fall were great. That was the weather in Holy Hammock long ago. Today winters are mild compared to when I was a child, summers were about the same as today, torrid

Most people will remember when neighbors were neighbors in every sense of the word. They helped when a need became known but otherwise left each other alone. People spoke when they met on the roads, in the stores, etc., and it was a genuine greeting. If a person asked you how you were they really wanted to know, but sometimes wished they had not asked.

Holy Hammock got its name when people began to settle into this small waterfront area of then Washington County and ministers of the gospel would hold brush arbor church meetings wherever they could find space to set up a meeting. Later as more families migrated there the preachers would pitch tents where many souls found Jesus Christ and began new lives. Some of these revival gatherings, as they were called, saw healing miracles, people delivered from alcohol and wife abusers could be found kneeling on the sawdust floors asking for forgiveness and pledging never to touch the wife in anger again. My mother was healed of leukemia in just such an environment. It was called Holy Hammock also because the singing and praising could be heard for miles around because there were no trains, cars, and planes in contest with the loud preaching and singing. Preachers prayed very loud then and women shouted very loud. Outsiders would mock these spirit filled Christians, considering them to be just a little bit demented. That's how Holy Hammock came into being.

Submitted by: Marjorie Arnold, 2304 Foxworth Drive, Panama City, FL 32405.

Families of Holy Hammock

Holy Hammock was made up of good hard working folks. Many names come to my memory like the John Spikes family who became the first owners of a radio in the community. On Saturday night folks would saunter over to the Spikes to listen to the Grand Ole Opry.

One family I remember well was the Axel Love family that lived near the water on the East side of the Hammock and I always thought of them as being the most affluent of all the people that lived there. Mrs. Dora Love and my mother became very close friends.

There was the Darbys, who lived on the waterfront in the Southeast part; The Nelsons whom a street was named from and also the bayou was called Nelson Bayou back then, it is Watson Bayou now. The Rolland, Brown, Pitts, McLeod, Darby, Yates, Nelson, Henderson, Jordan, Rice, Butler, Grice, Barlow, Maddox, Davis, Hagan, Walker, Baxley, Carr, Mauldin, Scott, Raffield, Amison, Williams, Sewell, Pittman, Andrews, Parish, Barnes, Clewis, Sanders, Loves, Danley, Lightfoot, Bridges, Spikes, Railey, Patterson, Nowell, Ganey, Faircloth and Dingler families, all have lasting memories. There were others, but

these are the ones I remember. The Dingler family had a young son who could play a guitar and would serenade my oldest sister with "Beautiful Brown Eyes" which embarrassed her to no end.

Families of Holy Hammock

The Williams family was a huge bunch of people but one lady I remember so well was Mrs. Vera who could make a cement block quicker than anyone around those parts. There was another lady named Mrs. Beatrice of the same family that had a laugh that could be heard for blocks away. She was a very short lady that was as big around as she was tall, literally, and could chew gum and crack it so loud you could hear it for the same distance, almost.

Mr. Hiram Danley was the town barber. He used those clippers that squeezed together to cut the hair and would make the back of the neck tingle with every upward stroke. He cut both male and female hair, all the same way, for a fact.

John and Winnie Williams, pioneers of Holy Hammock Community

I can't close this article without mentioning the Stanberry Scallop House were we shucked scallops for three cents a pound. We called it Blueberry Hill because that is about the time the song by that name was popular. A person could shuck scallops from sundown, when the boats came in, till dawn the next morning, when they left again to load up with this wonderful delicacy of the Bay waters. I believe that Mrs. Vera Williams and my sister Ethelene were the fastest shuckers at that time and my grandmother Lillie Scott was the most enduring.

A good place to live, a good place to remember.

Submitted by: Marjorie Arnold, 2304 Foxworth Drive, Panama City, FL 32405.

Bill Turner was a fisherman in the 1940's from the Holy Hammock Community

MILITARY

Walter Eugene (Gene) Ammons Vietnam Veteran

My husband, Walter Eugene (Gene) Ammons was born 1/18/1938, in Bainbridge Ga. We met in Panama City, Florida,

where his family was living in the 1950's. By then, Gene was already in the U.S. Navy and had come home to visit his family on Christmas leave. We were married right after my graduation from high school on June 4, 1957. We then began our life together as a military family, and that would last a total of twenty years.

It all started when Gene was 17 years of age. He joined the U.S. Naval Training Center at Great Lakes, Illinois, for basic training. He became part of Company 159, 12th Regiment, 22nd Battalion. He commenced basic training on 3/16/1955 and completed basic training on 5/17/1955. He was

Walter Eugene (Gene) Ammons

sent to Boston, Mass., in May, 1957, where he was assigned to the crew of the U.S.S. Antietam, which was an 876 foot ship. He also was stationed in Honolulu, Hawaii, between 1958 and 1960. He left the U.S. Navy in 1960 and returned to civilian life as an insurance salesman for a Nashville, Tenn., insurance company, Life and Casualty.

But civilian life wasn't what Gene really wanted. In 1961, he rejoined the military by joining the U.S. Coast Guard in Panama City, Florida. During his time in the Coast Guard, he spent two years at Subic Bay Naval Base in the Philippines, 1961-62. In 1962, he went to Mobile, Alabama, for a year. We lived in Daphne, Alabama, about a year, then we moved to Mobile, Alabama, for a year. From 1964-65, he was stationed in Pensacola, Florida, at the Naval Air Station. In 1965, Gene moved again, this time to Shreveport, Louisiana. While in Shreveport, Gene was a Coast Guard Recruiter. That assignment lasted about two years.

From 1967-68, Gene served a one-year tour of duty in Vietnam. He was serving aboard the U.S.S. Androscoggin in Miami, when it was deployed to Vietnam in November, 1967. The deployment lasted until September, 1968. Aboard ship, Gene was a BT1 Boiler Technician.

The Androscoggin, known as "Big Andy", took Gene to many foreign ports during the Vietnam deployment. He saw Pearl Harbor, Hawaii, when the ship docked there for repairs and briefings on its mission. The Androscoggin also dropped anchor at the Subic Bay Navy Base in the Philippines to load ammunition, take gunnery practice, and to have more minor repairs.

"Big Andy" finally reached Vietnam, where it docked at three different locations: Song-Ong-Doc, DaNaug, and An Thoi. The crew of the ship also got to visit Hong Kong for military briefings, communications relays, shore patrol duty and support. Gene next went to Bang Kok, Thailand, aboard the Androscoggin, as well as the U.S. Navy Ship Repair Facility in Japan. Singapore was also a final port of call on this deployment.

The ship and its crew saw plenty of action while deployed on this mission. The ship's logs show that, during this deployment, they saw 114 Viet Cong killed and 31 wounded. They also destroyed one enemy infiltration vessel and destroyed 35 enemy bunkers and damaging 24.

After returning from Vietnam, Gene was stationed in Miami, Florida, where the Androscoggin was docked at home port.

In 1970, we were stationed in Atlanta, Georgia, and lived on the Army Depot in Forest Park, Georgia, for year.

We went from Georgia to Staten Island, New York, for 3 years, where he was on the U.S. Coast Guard ship, Spence, Whec 36. His final duty station was Jacksonville, Florida. Gene

retired from there in 1975, after twenty years in the U.S. Navy and the U.S. Coast Guard. At retirement he was E 7 Chief Boiler Technician.

Submitted by: Janie Ammons, 2714 E. 7th Ct., Panama City, Florida 32401. Sources: Family Records-Military Records.

John A. Delcomyn

John Albert Delcomyn, born Nov. 23, 1924 Waynsboro, Wayne Co MS to Albert and Mazie Noble Delcomyn. He had his Basic Training in Camp Wallace, TX.

John was a Corporal in the 634th Anti Aircraft Automatic Weapons Bat. He was specialized in radio and telephone communication, trained in aircraft identification and anti-aircraft

automatic weapons. He debarked from Boston on the troop ship, *George Washington*.

He was a POW of the Germans (Battle of the Bulge) from Dec. 21, 1944 to May 23, 1945. He went from 120 to 85 pounds. After liberation, he was transported from the camp located about 40 miles south of Berlin to several other locations through Germany to France and England, sailing home on the *Liberty Excelsior* to Norfolk, VA. All along, participating in rehabilitation sessions ending at Camp Gordon Johnston near Carrabelle, FL, from where he was discharged.

Cpl. John A. Delcomyn, POW, Germany, WWII

Battles & Campaigns: D-Day Invasion, Normandy-Ardennes-Northern France, Rhineland.

Decorations & Citations: European African Middle Eastern Campaign Medal with 4 Bronze Service Stars, Purple Heart with Cluster, Good Conduct Medal, 3 Overseas bars, Sharp Shooters rifle.

Ruby Nell Penton, great-great granddaughter of John and Mary Penton and daughter of Randle A. & Hettie Warner Penton became the wife of John A. Delcomyn on April 21, 1946.

Submitted by: Families of the Patriots. Contributed by: Mildred Penton Richbourg, 3909 W. 16th Street, Panama City, FL 32401. Sources: Military Records.

Richard R. Edelen — U. S. Air Force

Richard R. Edelen enlisted in the military service at Fort Des Moines, Iowa January 1942. He was shipped to Davis Monthan Air Base, Tucson, Arizona. In May 1942 he was shipped to Officer Candidate School in Miami, Florida where he graduated in August. Clark Gable was one of his upper classmen.

In September he was shipped to Marianna Air Base, a single engine advanced flight school where he performed several administrative duties.

While at the Marianna Air Base, he met Frances Gill who was the secretary to the Air Corps Supply commander. They married in July 1944.

He was transferred to several Air Corps/Air Force assignments including the University of Chattanooga and East Tennessee State College where he supervised several hundred cadets.

In November 1944 he boarded the Queen Mary for service in the European Theater of Operations. Soon after arrival in London, he observed the departure of bandsman Glenn Miller on his fateful flight to the mainland.

Edelen was shipped to Marseilles, France where he was the Base Adjutant at this large Air Transport Command facility. Another transfer sent him to the Air Transport Command Air Base in Vienna, Austria as Base Adjutant.

After 18 months service in the European Theater of Operations, Captain Edelen returned to the States in May 1946; enrolled at the School of Business at the University of

Iowa to complete his eighth semester and earn a Bachelor of Science degree in Business. He studied for his MBA at Northwestern University in Chicago.

He and Mrs. Edelen are proud parents of two daughters, their husbands and four grandchildren. They celebrated their 59th wedding anniversary in July 2003 at their home in Panama City.

Submitted by: Richard R. Edelen, 7116 S. Lagoon Dr., Panama City Beach, FL

Robert A. "Bob" Hoxie

Bob went to work as an outside electrician in October 1952 for Electric Boat Co. in Groton, Connecticut. He worked on the old fleet type boats which were made into and for radar picket duty also new diesel as well as the new nuclear submarines. In 1955, he moved into electrical design as a marine drafts-man. Bob has a medal for working on the SSN 571 Nautilus and was at the launching. He worked on other nuclear submarines, "Seawolf," "Skate," etc. On March 6, 1956, he was called into the U.S. Navy, sworn in on the top floor of the Federal Building in New York City at 12 midnight, then travel-

Robert A. "Bob" Hoxie in Naples, Italy on a Navy Tour, 1959

ing by bus to Bainbridge, MD for Boot Camp, onto Great Lakes Training Center, North Chicago, IL for Interior Communications Electrical School, which includes gyro compasses, amplifiers, telephones, etc. In October 1956 was assigned to the MSO 473, "Vigor" in Charleston, South Carolina. In March 1958, the "Vigor" and four other minesweepers were assigned to the navy base in Panama City. In 1959, Bob and the "Vigor" went to the Mediterranean Sea on a five months cruise. The ship returned to Panama City and later in April 1960, the ship went to Charleston, South Carolina and Bob got out of the navy and returned to Groton, Connecticut to again work for Electric Boat Division of General Dynamics Corp. in electrical design, IC circuitry section.

Bob worked on the SSBN "George Washington" (598) the United States first Polaris submarine as well as other Polaris and nuclear submarines. He also had to do one year in the active U.S. Navy Reserve one weekend (Saturday and Sunday) a month. He was assigned to the U.S. Submarine Base, New London, Connecticut and worked on Submarine repair or in the gyro compass shop on base. (SAM and R Unit 3-2). He left the area and moved to warmer climate in April 1961 to Panama City, Florida and completed one year inactive Reserve and was discharged March 1962 as IC Electrician 3rd Class, which he received December, 1958.

Submitted by: Robert A. "Bob" Hoxie, 1903 Arthur Ave., Panama City, FL 32405

Sfc Truett L. Lucas, Us Army Retired
From the Cotton Fields to the White House

I was born on December 13, 1935 in Northwest Florida in a little town called Esto situated in Holmes County.

My family moved to Bay County before I started school. As a young boy I would return to Esto during the summers and pick cotton on my uncle's farm to make money for school clothes for the coming year. When I graduated from Bay County High School in 1953 I enlisted into the Regular Army. I had been in the Florida National Guard during my senior year. My basic training was taken in Ft. Sill, Oklahoma. We had Cadra from the 101st Airborne Division that was fresh back from Korea by way of the hospital to heal from their wounds. So they, thinking we would go to Korea, tried to run us ragged. But I was sent to Germany in the Field Artillery.

In 1957, I re-enlisted for the Army Security Agency, which required I be given a background investigation because I was required to have a security clearance for my work. I attended school at Ft. Gordon, Georgia in the Cryptology course where I graduated and was assigned to the 3rd USASA Field Station on the Island of Okinawa. I needed and was granted a clearance of Top Secret

Crypto with Special Handling Instructions and Top Secret Codeword. Later, I was given a clearance which included "Codeword Byman" (this is a pretty high clearance).

I stayed on Okinawa from 1957 through 1964. Then I was assigned to the USASA Training

SFC Truett L. Lucas served U.S. Army 1953-1974

Center and School, Ft. Devens, Massachusetts. I was an instructor in COMSEC (Communications Security) from 1964-1966. It was during this time that I met a young lady from home, Mona Anita Gleitsmann, through the mail. We were married just before I departed for a tour of Duty in Asmara, Ethiopia. I was assigned to the 4th USASA Field Station which is situated on a mountain plateau in northeastern Africa. I was NCOIC of the ComCenter. Anita and I were there until 1969 at which time I received my orders for Vietnam.

At the 509th Radio Research Group Station in Saigon, Vietnam, I served as Trick Chief and later was NCOIC of the Saigon Major Relay Station. While in Vietnam, I was procured for assignment to serve in the White House on the Presidential Communications Team. I was picked and sent to Washington, D.C. upon completion of my Vietnam Tour. The guys that I worked with gave me a plaque saying "From the Cotton Fields to the White House". Anita joined me in D.C.

I was assigned to the White House Communications Agency in July 1970 and served as NCOIC of the Communications Center in the White House. I was responsible for building teams to go on the road to support the President, Vice-President, First Lady and Presidential Staff when they were on travel away from the White House. I was among six personnel selected to go to computer school and then was responsible for establishing computers in the White House dedicated to full-time communications with the outside world. I was also responsible for establishing the system and writing the operating procedures for a hot line between the White House and Canada and the White House and Japan. As far as I know these procedures are still in effect. I traveled with the Presidential Team in several locations in the states and to Dublin, Ireland and Israel.

Our daughter was born in Washington, D.C. at Walter Reed Army Medical Center. I retired from the Army in July 1974 and came home to Panama City.

Submitted by: Truett L. Lucas, 3235 E. Orlando Rd., Panama City, FL

Alfred E. Penton

Cpl. Alfred Emanuel Penton, son of John and Mary Penton, born April 15, 1831 Hancock Co. MS, killed in the Siege of Vicksburg, May 25, 1863, buried in the trenches with a memorial marker in Soldiers' Rest Plot of the City Cemetery, Vicksburg, MS. "He was killed by one of our own men by mistake while he was on picket duty at night during the siege" was the information written to his wife, Amuranthe Ann Perry whom he had married on Dec. 24, 1853, Hancock Co. MS.

Alfred, and six of his brothers enlisted March 25, 1863, Gainsville, MS, Capt. D. B. Seals Hancock Co. Rebels which became Co. C, 38th MS Regt., Herberts Brigade, Price's

Cpl. Alfred E. Penton, CSA

Division, seeing action at Corinth, Tupelo, Saltello, Iuka, then to Snyder's Bluff on Yazoo River, north of the city of Vicksburg. On May 18th, on to Jackson and Graveyard Roads with the heavy assault on the center of the Confederate Siege line along a 3 mile front from Stockade Redan to Ft. Garrett. Seven days later, Cpl. Alfred E. Penton was killed.

Submitted by: Families of the Patriots. Contributed by: Mildred Penton Richbourg, 3909 W. 16th Street, Panama City, FL 32401. Sources: Military Records.

George Oliver Penton

George O. Penton, born Nov. 27, 1952, Savannah, GA, son of Joe William and Mildred Morris Penton, entered the military service January 10, 1973, Montgomery, AL. He served 3 1/2 years in the U. S. Marine Corp as a Corporal in the Military Police. He made two tours in Iwakuni, Japan. He received his honorable discharge from the Separation Center Marine Corp. Base, Camp Pemberton, CA, July 2, 1976. George received the Good Conduct Medal and the National Defense Service Medal. His home is Bay County, FL.

Cpl. George O. Penton, U.S. Marine Corp., Military Police

Submitted by: Families of the Patriots. Contributed by: Mildred Penton Richbourg, 3909 W. 16th Street, Panama City, FL 32401. Sources: Military Records.

Hewitt Hillard Penton

Hewitt Hillard Penton, great-great grandson of John and Mary Penton, born Sept. 21, 1915, Zona, LA, died April 13, 2001, Tuscaloosa, AL, buried Greenwood Cemetery, Bay County, FL. He was the son of Randle A. & Hettie Penton of Panama City, FL. He enlisted in the American Merchant Marines in Corpus Christi, TX as a radio operator, WW II. He received the U. S. Coast Guard Certificate of Service for qualification aboard American vessels of 100-tons and upward in the Deck Dept. in the rating of Radio Operator.

Hewitt H. Penton, Radio Operator, American Merchant Marines

Hewitt was awarded the Atlantic War Zone Bar, the Mediterranean Middle East War Zone Bar and the Victory Medal by the U. S. Dept. of Transportation Maritime Administration. An Honorable Discharge was presented to him by Captain, U. S. Coast Guard, Frederic J. Grady, pursuant to P. L. 95-202 for service in the 'American Merchant Marines in Oceangoing Service during the Period of Armed Conflict, Dec. 7, 1941, to Aug. 15, 1945'.

Hewitt married Jo Thelma Thomas April 11, 1937 in Bay County, FL.

Submitted by: Families of the Patriots Contributed by: Mildred Penton Richbourg, 3909 W. 16th Street, Panama City, FL 32401. Sources: Military Records.

Joe William Penton

Joe William Penton was born Aug. 1, 1917, Zona, LA, died January 27, 1992, Henderson NV, buried with Military Rites, Ft. Barancus National Cemetery, Pensacola, FL, son of Randle and Hettie Penton of Panama City, FL, and great-great grandson of John and Mary Penton. Joe's first tour was when he trained at Camp Blanding, Fl, December 23, 1942. He served as a Quarter Master Supply Tec., Hq. Co., 3rd BN, 188th P.I.R. until February 25,1946 when he was discharged from the U.S. Airborne Paratroopers, World War II. His unit was aboard one of the transport ships during the signing of the Peace Treaty with Japan.

Joe was called back into service January 2, 1951, Ft. Jackson, SC, serving in Hq. & Hq. Btry, 3444 ASU, Camp Stewart, GA before being transferred to the 301st Logistical COMD. Camp Rucker, AL as a SFC(T) Stock Supervisor. This tour of duty placed him in the Korean War Zones. He was awarded the WWII Victory Medal, WWII Occupation Medal-Japan, ATO Medal, APTO Medal, Phil. Lib. Medal, Good Conduct Medal, and the National Defense Service Medal.

Sgt. Joe William Penton, US Army

On June 12, 1941, Joe married Mildred Morris of Panama City, FL.

Submitted by: Families of the Patriots. Contributed by: Mildred Penton Richbourg, 3909 W. 16th Street, Panama City, FL 32401. Sources: Military Records.

John Penton

John Penton born 1802 GA died Nov. 14, 1883, enlisted at age 9 years on January 16, 1813 in Capt. Alex Brownlow and Capt. Pemberton's Company, in Shieldsboro, Hancock Co. MS. He was the only son of Abner and Rebecca Barnhart Penton who married in Greene Co. GA. John signed up as a musician (drummer) serving at Mobile, AL in the engagement known as the 2nd Battle at what was called Mobile Point.

John Penton, Musician, War of 1812

He was taken prisoner and carried to New Orleans LA, from then to Pass Christian, MS, where he was discharged on June 30, 1815. John married Mary Polly Dungeon, both are buried in the Penton Cemetery, Carriere, MS. Seven of their sons enlisted March 1862 in the "Hancock County Rebels, CSA" which became Co. C, 38th Mississippi Regiment.

Submitted by: Families of the Patriots. Contributed by: Mildred Penton Richbourg, 3909 W. 16th Street, Panama City, FL 32401. Sources: Military Records.

A. D. Richbourg

A. D. Richbourg, born April 21, 1923, Nocatee, FL, son of Chester L. & Mattie Dykes Richbourg of Bay County, FL did his Basic Training at Camp Blanding, FL, upon induction on Feb. 16, 1943. He was immediately shipped to Camp Hood, TX after assignment to Active Service, Feb. 23, 1943. He was being trained for the Tank Destroyers but was transferred before his outfit shipped out, to Ft. Sill, OK because he had been hospitalized with a knee injury.

A. D. was assigned to Service Battery, 241st Field Artillery BN, being trained as a Heavy Machine Gunner and Rifleman, qualifying for the Carbine 30 Cal. Expert Combat Infantry-Badge, Purple Heart (Hq. 186th), Good Conduct Medal, EAME Theater Ribbon with (3) Battle Stars, Good Conduct Medal, One (1) Overseas Bar.

Pvt. A.D. Richbourg, U.S. Army, WWII

The 241st Field Artillery Batt. left Ft. Sill on March 9, 1944 for Camp Howze, Gainsville, TX for overseas indoctrination, leaving for the final overseas movement on June 24, 1944. On July 2, 1944, their ship *Thomas H. Barry* left

Staten Island, N Y and landed in Llantarnam, Wales. August 1944 saw the battalion sailing aboard the Liberty Ship, *S S Philip A. Thomas,* for Normandy.

The war was becoming more intense requiring qualified sharpshooters to be transferred from the Service Battery and others, to the infantry for the battles in Rhineland and the Ardennes Campaigns. A. D. was wounded January 6, 1945 in Luxenbourg. At this time he was in Co. C. 104 Inf. Regt. U.S. Army and deep into the Battle of the Bulge. After being treated in hospitals in France, England, Camp Shanks N. Y, he finally reached Welch Conv. Hospital, Daytona Beach, FL. on May 4, 1945 where he remained in rehabilitation until discharged Aug. 23, 1945. When discharged, he was in Co. A, 3rd Bn Det. of Patients, Welch Conv. Hospital, Daytona Beach, FL.

On Feb. 18, 1943, Mildred Penton, great-great granddaughter of John and Mary Penton daughter of Randle A. & Hettie Penton, married A. D. Richbourg.
Submitted by: Families of the Patriots. Contributed by: Mildred Penton Richbourg, 3909 W. 16th Street, Panama City, FL 32401. Sources: Military Records.

Adrian Colter "Colt" Richbourg

Adrian Colter "Colt" Richbourg, son of A. D. & Mildred Penton Richbourg, born December 29, 1951 Bay County, FL, enlisted January 1971, Panama City, Bay Co. FL, in the U. S. Army Reserves, receiving his basic combat training at Ft. Dix, NJ. Graduation was August 27, 1971, Co. B. 1st Battalion. He served six years in the 833rd Personnel Service Co. U. S. Army Reserves in Panama City FL.
Submitted by: Families of the Patriots. Contributed by: Mildred Penton Richbourg, 3909 W. 16th Street, Panama City. FL 32401. Sources: Military Records.

Adrian Colter Richbourg, U.S. Army Reserves, Bay County

Jonas N. Whitaker

Lance Corporal Jonas Nathaniel Whitaker, served in the United States Marine Corps from August 1967 until March 1969. Jonas is the son of the late, Charley Lawson Whitaker and Veola Powell Whitaker of Lynn Haven, Florida. Jonas was born in Macon, Georgia in 1948. Jonas attended school in Bay County and graduated from Bay High School in 1966, he served his country for 13 months in DeNang, Vietnam, as a combat engineer with the 3rd Marine Division. He married Deborah Cotton a Panama City native in 1970 and together they raised two children, Joan Rene'e Whitaker and Jason Edward Whitaker.
Submitted by: Deborah Whitaker, 2002 Geralo Lane, Lynn Haven, FL 32444

Lance Corporal Jonas Nathaniel Whitaker, USMC. Served August 1967-March 1969

Florida Army National Guard

War Department muster rolls at the State Arsenal, St. Francis Barracks, St. Augustine, list the names of men living in the vicinity of St. Andrews Bay who volunteered to serve in the first militia companies organized during the Indian Wars 1835-1843 and those who volunteered during the Mexican War of 1846 and the Florida Indian War 1852-1856.

Confederate government muster rolls at St. Francis Barracks record local men who enlisted in the following area home guard companies: Company H, 4th Florida Infantry Regiment organized

at Vernon: Company A, 11th Florida "Partizan Rangers," stationed at Bayhead on Bayou George, the home guard unit which repelled Federal sailors at Old Town St. Andrews, March 20, 1863, (St. Andrews Skirmish Florida Historic Marker on Beach Drive 2003); Company C, 11th Florida organized at West Bay to protect vital government salt works located there; Company K, 6th Florida organized at Vernon; and Company C, 1st Florida Reserves. During the war these units were mustered into the Confederate States Army and suffered severe losses due to sickness and wounds. Henry Anderson of Grassy Point (Point at the north end of Bailey Bridge 2003 west of Grassy Point cemetery where he is buried), Company H, was shot through both ankles at Chickamauga. Edmund Young of Bayou George, Company K, died of wounds at Chickamauga. Peter Parker, Jr., of East Bay (Parker), Company H, died of wounds at Jonesboro. His father, Peter, born in 1817 served in the reserve company. After the surrender of the Army of Tennessee at Greensboro, North Carolina, April 26, 1865, First Lieutenant Thomas H. Gainer returned home to the Econfina community with twelve survivors of Company K, 6th Florida, all that remained of the 4 officers and 60 enlisted men who reported at Chattanooga, June 18, 1862. Richard B. Mashburn of Company K walked to his home at Econfina after release from Rock Island Prison.

The St. Andrews Bay area furnished no organized military unit during the Spanish American War; but area men enlisted in Company K, 1st Florida Infantry, 1st Florida Regiment, organized at Quincy, April 29, 1898, Captain Samuel T. Williamson, Commander. The unit was mustered into federal service May 23 in Tampa by Captain Thomas M. Wooduff, United States Army, attached to the Provisional Battalion of Brigadier General Rodgers, and moved to several camps in the Tampa-Ybor City area. August 23 the Company was transferred by train from Camp Amelia, Fernandina, Florida, to Camp Wheeler near Huntsville, Alabama, where they pitched tents the morning of August 26. By that time the war was over, and October 9 the Company left for Tallahassee for the purpose of being mustered out of service. October 15 the men of Company K were furloughed for 30 days. December 3 they were mustered out of federal service.

On the front lawn of the Bay County Courthouse (6th Street and McKenzie Avenue 2003) is located a monument listing the names of Bay County Spanish American War veterans. Several are St. Andrews Bay soldiers of Company K.

Tuesday, July 1, 1913, was the date for Bay County to become a county. For several months there was discussion of organizing a company of the State Guard at the new county. During July a petition was sent to the Adjutant General of Florida asking permission to form a company. The response of the Adjutant General was so favorable that the promoters began circulating papers for signatures of men who wanted to enlist. Among the signers was Panama City Mayor T. Calvin Stephens. The first meeting was called for Saturday, August 2, at 8:00 P.M. at the Owl's Hall (located on the city wharf). October 29 the 83 members of the unit were examined and measured by Dr. D. M. Adams, Sr.. Dr. Emmet E. Cooper was elected Captain; and Michael B. Hawkins, who had served in the Philippines, the Spanish American War and the Philippine American War of 1899, was elected First Sergeant. Company M, 1st Florida Infantry Regiment was mustered into service at Panama City January 20, 1914, by Colonel James P. Hickey, Commander of the 1st Infantry. The company numbered 3 officers and 65 enlisted men. Although 92 men were on hand to join, only 68 were accepted as that was a full company. During 1915 - 1916 Company M was commanded by Captain Ray R. Powers, and Second Lieutenant Hawkins was the Executive Officer.

Company M was disbanded November 29, 1916, during the Mexican War and became part of the 1st Separate Battalion, Florida National Guard. The Battalion served on state active duty until April 12, 1917, guarding bridges, utilities, etc. in the State of Florida.

During March of 1917 Francis M. Turner, who served in Company K during the Spanish American War, was authorized to organize a National Guard Company at Millville. After much correspondence and several trips to Tallahassee, Second Lieutenant Hawkins was authorized on May 2 to organize a 34 man platoon from Panama City and St. Andrews. The platoon would be paired with Company L at Apalachicola, Captain William J. Glaslow, Commander.

Monday night, May 14, Company M, First Regiment, National

Guard of Florida, was mustered into the service of the State by the Regiment Commander, Colonel Samuel C. Harrison, Jr. Turner was appointed Captain. About 2,000 people witnessed the muster ceremony for the 3 officers and 86 enlisted men.

During July Lieutenant Hawkins was assigned to Company C at Lake City, and the St. Andrews platoon was attached to the Millville Company. August 5 Company M, 3 officers and 129 enlisted men, was mobilized. August 6, 25 of the men were transferred to Company L. August 8, 3 officers and 104 enlisted men received their final inspection from Captain Rudisall, 2nd Georgia Cavalry.

On Friday afternoon, September 14, Captain Turner marched his company from Millville to the Bay Line Depot (Junction of Beach Drive and Sixth Street 2003) at Panama City, reaching there at 2:30 P.M. Thousands of people from all sections of the county spread out all over the station ground and onto the wharf to witness the departure and express wishes for a safe and speedy return. The men answered roll call and loaded onto three cars that had been provided by the Bay Line for the trip to Camp Wheeler, Macon, Georgia. Two days later the unit arrived at Camp Wheeler. Here the unit was disbanded and the men assigned to the 106th Engineer Regiment, 106th Field Artillery Regiment and 118th Machine Gun Battalion, 31st Division. While at Camp Wheeler the 106th Engineers constructed roads, bridges, and buildings and transported men, material and provisions. Throughout World War I they were mustered into other Federal units for service in France. Several men of Company M died of wounds and sickness.

Shown in the photograph below taken in August 1923 from Co D 114th Engs, Front Row-L-R: Sgt Thomas L. Welch, Horseshoer George D. Smith, Corp William H. Rodgers, Capt Michael B. Hawkins, CO, Wagner Arthur Danley, 1st Lt James R. Asbell, XO, Pvt. Fred P. Peach, Carpenter Christopher C. Holley, Pvt Cecil Surber, Pvt Guy Willis. 2nd Row: Pvt Jean Sowell, Pvt Henry Fox, Pvt William Oliver, Pvt Joseph Blackshear, Pvt Bert Roush, Pvt Wyat H. Seigler, Wagner Albertus J. Fox, Pvt Morris Chambliss, Pvt Charley Pitts, PFC Ernst F. Gonzalez. 3rd Row: PFC Henry S. Laird, Pvt Russell W. Danley, PFC Burma A. Pilcher, Pvt Willie A. Redmond, Pvt Mervin Rodgers, Pvt John A. Laird, Pvt Lewis B. Howell, Pvt Danley, Pvt Gilbrey D. Etheridge, Pvt Roy D. Laird. 4th Row: Pvt Danley, Pvt Terrel H. Yon, Pvt Arthur L. Kimbrough, Pvt James E. Poston, Corp Harry B. Gainer, Sgt Mitchel J. "Doc" Daffin,

Co D 114th Engrs, Florida Army National Guard, Panama City, Camp Joseph E. Johnston, AT 5-19 Aug 1923, Jacksonville, Fla.

Corp Thomas V. Becham, Sgt Irwin Wells, 1st Sgt William A. Cooper, PFC John G. Dean. Jack O. Cutchens Archives.

During the summer of 1922 Captain Michael B. Hawkins, Florida Reserves, petitioned the Adjutant General for permission to reorganize Company M. On Tuesday night, September 26, a meeting for ex-servicemen was given in the theater at Millville by the American Legion Post for reorganizing Company M. Hawkins was Commander of the Post. Monday, November 6, Hawkins was elected Captain of the Company. December 5, 1922, Company M was inspected by Florida Adjutant General Charles P. Lovell. The unit was reorganized 1st Engineer Company, the senior Engineer Company of the Florida Guard, soon after becoming Company D, 114th Engineers, 31st Division. There is a photograph of Company D taken during Annual Training August 5-19, 1923, Captain

Hawkins, Commander, at Camp Joseph E. Johnston, Jacksonville, Florida. May 28, 1924, the unit was redesignated Company D, 2nd Battalion, 106th Engineer Regiment, 31st Division. October 27, 1934, Company D was ordered to Marianna by Governor Sholtz following a week of rioting. There is a photograph of Company D taken in 1939.

Company D was redesignated Combat Engineers on May 15, 1940, and, as part of the 31st Division, mobilized for active duty November 25, 1940. At 3:00 P.M. December 17, 1940, Captain Hiram W. Sperry marched his company in parade from the armory at Sixth Street (First Baptist Church of Panama City Family Life Center, 601 Grace Avenue 2003) onto Harrison Avenue, then to Second Street, then east to the City Park (McKenzie Park 2003) where an address was made by Honorable J. M. Sapp. Leaving the park they marched on Second Street to Harrison Avenue, then south to First Street to the Bay Line Depot (Junction of Beach Drive and Sixth Street 2003).

Shortly after 4:00 P.M. the 3 officers and 69 enlisted men boarded a Bay Line train which took them to Cottondale and then east on the L & N Railroad. They arrived at Camp Blanding, Florida, Wednesday, December 18. There they joined the other units of the 31st "Dixie" Division from Alabama, Florida, Mississippi and Louisiana. While at Blanding they mapped the Post. Company D was redesignated Company A, 1st Battalion, 175th Engineers February 10, 1942, and Company A, 177th Engineers May 15,1942. Members of Company D served in Alaska, the Philippines, and the European Theatre.

During January of 1947 Colonel Hiram W. Sperry and Captain Ralph V. Sorrentino initiated efforts to reorganize a National Guard Company at Panama City. Monday, March 3, 1947, Company C, 1st Battalion, 124th Infantry, 48th Infantry Division was organized at 7:30 P.M. at the armory on Sixth Street. Initial officers were Captain Sorrentino, Commander, and Fred A. Lewellen and Lawrence B. Watson, Lieutenants. Colonel Sperry was the Post Commander at Panama City and Adjutant General of the 48th Infantry Division. Colonel Robert G. White, Assistant Adjutant General of Florida, Colonel Maxwell C. Snyder, Commander, 124th Infantry Regiment, Lieutenant Colonel Louie C. Wadsworth, 1st Battalion Commander, and Lieutenant Colonel Ralph M. Neal, Headquarters, Florida Military District, came to inspect the new company. Colonel Snyder acclaimed the unit, more than 40 strong, for "activating a unit with the largest number of personnel in the state." During 1955 the unit was redesignated Company C, 1st Armored Infantry Battalion, Captain Henry T. Sorenson, Commander, and during 1959 redesignated Company C, 1st Armored Rifle Battalion, 124th Infantry, 48th Armored Infantry "Hurricane" Division, Captain Robert F. Breedon, Commander. Panama City units weren't activated during the Korean or the Vietnam Wars, but unit members volunteered for active duty, fought and died.

February 15, 1963, the unit was reorganized, redesignated and converted to Headquarters Company, 261st Engineer Battalion (Combat) (A), Captain C. Harold McLeod, Commander. January 1, 1964, the unit was reorganized, Headquarters and Headquarters Company, 261st Engineer Battalion, Captain Harold E. Dykes, Commander. An Engineer Part Unit was authorized, First Lieutenant Donald W. Roberts, Commander.

January 20, 1968, the unit was reorganized and redesignated Headquarters and Headquarters Company, 3rd Battalion, 124th Infantry, 53rd Infantry Brigade, First Lieutenant Donald W. Roberts, Commander. January 31,1972, an Infantry Part Unit was authorized, First Lieutenant Jack O. Cutchens, Commander, Major Charles L. Boss, Sr., United States Army, inspecting officer. These units were called to state active duty during the Miami riot, Cuban boat lift, and all major hurricanes in Florida.

December 26, 2002, Headquarters and Headquarters Company was mobilized, Captain John C. Kimball, Commander, and on January 2, 2003, ordered into federal service for Operation Iraqi Freedom. January 6 at the Hiram W. Sperry Armory (3121 North Lisenby Avenue 2003) the unit left by bus and unit vehicles for Ft. Stewart, Georgia. March 29 the unit left Ft. Stewart and arrived at Kuwait, April 1-2. May 1-2 Headquarters and Headquarters Company deployed to Iraq and established combat operations in Baghdad. It was initially reported that the unit would return to

Panama City after June, later after October. During September the Secretary of Defense announced that the unit would remain in Iraq one year. The unit was tasked with the 3rd Infantry Division, the 101st Airborne Division, and the 1st Armored Division and established an outstanding combat record.

Unit members designated Infantry earned the Combat Infantry Badge and those designated Medics the Combat Medical Badge, the first award of these prestigious decorations to soldiers of a Florida Guard Battalion since World War II.

The National Guard Armory at Panama City is named in honor of Brigadier General Hiram W. Sperry.

Submitted by: MAJ Jack O. Cutchens, USA, Ret, FLARNG, 1115 Kentucky Ave., Lynn Haven, Florida. Sources: Soldiers of Florida, Panama City Pilot and State of Florida Military Publications.

Florida National Guard Unit Serves in Alaska

My husband, Wilkie Jennings, was a member of the Florida National Guard Reserves. On November 25, 1940, the National Guard was inducted into the Regular Army. After camping for several weeks in the National Guard Armory, they were sent to Camp Blanding, Florida. In October, 1941, the men who were married or over 29 years old were released.

Wilkie returned to Panama City and went back to work at the

Wilkie Jennings on the left and a friend relaxing near Anchorage, Alaska, about 1943

paper mill. He was at work on December 7, 1941 when Pearl Harbor was attacked by the Japanese. He knew that he would be reactivated and in January, 1942, he was assigned to an Army Engineering Corps unit. They returned to Camp Blanding and then were sent to Texas to train for the North African campaign.

The company was sent to Fort Dix, New Jersey, in July, 1942, to sail for North Africa. Their destination was changed, however, and from Fort Dix, they were sent by troop train to the West Coast. As the 177th Combat Engineers, they went to Anchorage, Alaska to build Elmendorf Air Force Base. After Elmendorf was built, they were sent to Attu for a time. The Florida National Guard Unit stayed in Alaska until the end of the war.

Wilkie was able to come home for a leave in December, 1944 and met his daughter for the first time. He had not been home in over two years.

The Floridians adapted well to life in Alaska and spent their off time enjoying the Alaskan countryside and outdoor activities such as fishing, snowshoeing, ice skating - some were things they certainly couldn't do at home in Florida.

When they returned to Panama City, they formed an association to keep the company together as friends. Even though many men have passed away, the remaining members of the company stay in touch with each other and socialize.

Submitted by: Frances D. Jennings, 1101 Rhode Island, Lynn Haven, FL 32444

National Guard Days

In December 1952, I was a senior in Bay County High School. I had a part-time job working after school and weekends at Christo's 5 & 10 cent Store on lower Harrison Avenue. I enlisted in the local National Guard Company on December 9 of that year. Upon graduation and after two weeks of camp with the guard, I enlisted in the Regular Army in September of 1953.

Our Guard Company was in the old Armory Building on 6th Street and Grace Avenue. We would drill up and down the street of Grace Avenue in front of what is now the First Baptist Church Day Care Center. My granddaughter attends that Day Care Center today.

My Platoon Sergeant was SFC Al Nixon, and in most recent years he was my barber at Carswell's Barber Shop on the City Marina.

We made frequent trips to Silver Lake for weapon's qualification. That was my first experience of seeing how the Army handled food. They didn't save leftovers. I saw them throw away a lot of good food.

That has stuck in my mind ever since. When on K.P. (Kitchen Police), you would wash the silverware and rinse it in very hot water, then dump it onto a wool army blanket. Two guys would grab both ends and roll it back and forth to dry and polish it. It would really shine.

We went to Fort McClellen, Alabama for two weeks of training. Jean Shepherd and Furlin Huskey just came out with the country song "Dear John Letter." It was really a hit and we would stop whatever we were doing when it started playing on the radio and just stand there and listen to the music.

We rode 2 1/2 ton trucks to and from camp. When camp was over and we were returning home we stopped at the National Guard Armory in Columbus, Georgia for the night. After we bedded down, some of us guys changed to civilian clothes, jumped the fence and went downtown to see a movie, then returning to camp, jumped the fence and went to bed on a concrete floor with only an army blanket. Up the next morning at 0500 and on the road again.

After 9 months in the guard, I enlisted in the Regular Army and was processed through Fort Jackson, South Carolina. Then on to Fort Sill, Oklahoma for basic training and A.I.T. That was 50 years ago last September 16, 2003.

Submitted by: Truett L. Lucas, 3235 E. Orlando Rd., Panama City, FL 32405

9/11/01

On the morning of September 11th, 2001, Colonel Donald N. Edmands, Jr., Director of the NORAD Systems Support Facility (NSSF), was in his office at Tyndall Air Force Base, Florida. His wife Mary called and stated, "a plane just hit the World Trade Center."

Edmands walked across the hall to the break room where a TV was located. Expecting to see heavy fog, he was surprised by the clear skies over New York. While he was watching, a second plane flew into the WTC. Edmands immediately drove down the street to the Continental NORAD Region Air Operations Center (CONR/AOC).

On arrival, he found the AOC a beehive of activity. As it turned out, the AOC was in the fifth day of a practice exercise and a full compliment of personnel were manning the stations. As Edmands stood on the upper stage, behind Maj. Gen. Larry K. Arnold, 1st Air Force commander, and staff, he watched as they fielded numerous telephone

Colonel Donald N. Edmands, Jr.

calls. Air Force fighter squadrons and navy carrier battle groups were calling offering their support to CONR. On other phones, calls were coming in reporting more hijacked aircraft and developing situations.

As Edmands watched the "chat-line," a message came across from the White House; Vice President Cheney had declared the Washington area "weapons free" ....any aircraft flying in the zone would be shot down.

Edmands' unit was responsible for the software used to operate the NORAD air defense system. That afternoon, NORAD, Petersen AFB, Colorado Springs, Colo., directed Edmands, "no changes to the system" during the current crisis. Many of the members of the NSSF were quickly assigned temporary jobs as the AOC went to a fully manned, 24-hour operation. In the ensuing hours, it was not unusual to find a major or government civilian performing guard duty as the AOC "spun-up" to full wartime manning.

Late in the afternoon, the General called a meeting of his senior staff. During the meeting, he appointed Edmands and Col. Don Hansen (1AF/IG) as co-directors of Joint Task Force for Civil Support. As this was a new tasking for 1st Air Force, they were "making it up on the run." Edmands volunteered for the night shift and started setting up the 1st Air Force civil support team in the video teleconference center.

The civil support team was designed to provide military help to civilian authorities when they were overwhelmed by casualties. As it turned out, the attack on the WTC produced a high number of fatalities, but very few injuries. The team "leaned forward," but in the end, was not called upon for help.

Edmands left work on the morning of the 12th, having worked 24 hours.

Submitted by: Colonel Donald N. Edmands, Jr., 702 CSS/CC, 164 Alabama Avenue Stop 64, Tyndall AFB FL 32403-5015

TO SEE THE WORLD

Newly arrived on the Gulf Coast, March 19, 1953 during the Korean War, I was a graduate of the Navy's Aviation Machinist Mate "A" School in Memphis. I reported to NAS Saufley Field, near Pensacola. I was assigned to the Flight Training Squadron as a plane captain on a SNJ (T6- Team).

John E. Pearson

Growing up in the Bronx on Long Island Sound, I was sea, or, water oriented. Upon arrival on the Gulf Coast I made my way to the beach. I had never seen a beach so white, water so blue, sky so vivid. A tropical paradise with Sistine Chapel sunsets and an occasional hurricane. The weekends between paydays were empty and long for young sailors. So, my buddy "Jocko" and I set out to explore our new stomping grounds. Hitchhiking on many occasions, we would head east. We discovered Panama City on the way.

Various rides would take us on two lane roads with sandy shoulders (Hwy. 98). Every thing was very bright. As we neared Panama City Beach, the road wound between white sanddunes. The side of the road was covered with palmetto, scrub oak, water myrtel - a few cottages, an infrequent store.

We had our ditty bags, all we needed. We each had a blanket, towel, bathing suit, and clean shirt. We'd catch a ride - grab a bite - take a dip - spend the night in the dunes - do some serious crabbing and shelling. When we had some money we would press on into downtown Panama City. Down Harrison, past Penny's and finally have a grilled cheese sandwich at the Walgreen Drugstore on the corner of 5th and Harrison. We lived the weekend long life of beach bums, finally sated, reluctantly returning to the regimen of Monday.

Submitted by: John E. Pearson, 7753 Shadow Bay Drive, Panama City, Florida 32404

The USCGC Cartigan, W132 (The Galloping Ghost of The Yucatan Coast)

In January 1996, I was stationed in Panama City onboard the United States Coast Guard Cutter Cartigan, a 125 foot 'Active' class

U.S. Coast Guard Cutter – Cartigan

vessel that was commissioned in 1927. I remained aboard until my discharge in August of 1968. We moored at the end of St. Andrew's marina (where the current ship's store is located now), 'starboard side to.' At the time, St. Andrew's marina was a very active place with charter boats, headboats, expensive yachts and of course, tourists. Our primary mission was search and rescue and we were assigned to the Eighth Coast Guard District out of New Orleans, LA. There were also two other Coast Guard units on the marina, an 82-foot Point class patrol cutter and a 41-foot utility boat. Whenever we were getting underway or returning to port, we drew a crowd of onlookers. When mooring, it was necessary to come in parallel to the dock, as much as possible to facilitate the process. Upon returning from a Campeche Patrol of 10 days, the Captain allowed the executive officer to "con" the ship and moor her. It was in the summer and the usual gathering of onlookers began. As a Radioman, my "special sea detail" was " a sound powered phone talker on the bridge while getting underway and returning to port. You could see that the onlookers were enjoying the sight of this ship coming in to moor.

Unfortunately, the XO brought the ship in at about a 45-degree angle and miscalculated his speed. I should mention that the *Cartigan* had a reinforced bow because she was used as an ice-breaker up north once in her career. We impacted the marina quite soundly, the bow riding up about 4-5 feet out of the water and above the edge of the marina itself. The impact onto the concrete sent chips of concrete debris flying and severing a water line that ran the length of the dock and supplied our potable water. This in itself caused quite a geyser. The look of enjoyment on the faces of the onlookers turned to shock and dismay as they broke and ran in order to get away from this "runaway" vessel and the shower of water and debris. Non-pulsed, the XO merely backed down off the marina and moored her properly the second time around. To the XO's credit, he remained quite calm and collective in the face of "adversity." He came from a 'Coast Guard Family' and was a Coast Guard Academy graduate. His father and one of his uncles were both admirals in the Coast Guard. This time, we did not have the audience that we originally had. I can only imagine the stories they told regarding our ship handling prowess. I think that everybody on the 'bridge' got a chuckle out of what happened, except for the Captain. Go figure!

Submitted by: George G. Dobos, 3116 West 20th Court, Panama City, Florida 32405; copnal89@aol.com.

HISTORICAL MARKERS AND MONUMENTS

The Gideon Versus Wainwright Case
Historic Marker

The Gideon versus Wainwright Case was recognized with the placement of an historic marker at the Bay County Courthouse on August 5, 2003.

Gideon versus Wainwright Historic Marker

This is the site of the landmark Gideon case, after which the Public Defender system was established in Florida and throughout the nation. In 1961, Clarence Earl Gideon (1910-1972) stood trial in this courthouse for the felony of burglary.

Lacking funds to hire a lawyer, Gideon requested that a lawyer be appointed to represent him at trial. Gideon's request was denied, because at that time, a person accused of a non-capital felony did not have a constitutional right to a free lawyer. Gideon represented himself at his trial and was convicted. While serving his five-year prison sentence, Gideon petitioned the United States Supreme Court to review his case. The Supreme Court issued its decision in 1963 in Gideon v. Wainwright, ruling that every poor person charged with a serious crime in this country must be provided a lawyer for his defense at public expense. Panama City attorney, W. Fred Turner (b. 1922) represented Gideon at his retrial and won an acquittal. Built in 1914, this building is one of only a few original courthouses in Florida still being used for its original purpose. A fire in 1920 gutted the building, but it was immediately rebuilt in its Classic Revival architectural style.

Sponsored by the Historical Society of Bay County and the Florida Department of State.

Submitted by: The Bay County Heritage Book Committee.

Historical Clock

The history of the clock goes back to the second bank established in Panama City, the first National Bank, located on the corner of

Harrison Avenue and Beach Drive. This was the earliest center of business in Panama City and that intersection became known as "Bankers Corner" because of the location of First National Bank as well as the Bank of Panama City on the opposite corner. This magnificent electric clock was installed around July 1926 on the corner of First National's building. With the failure of First National Bank in February 1931, Commercial Bank took over the building and the clock. Commercial Bank moved up Harrison to the corner of Seventh Street in 1957, and with it went the clock, where it resides today.

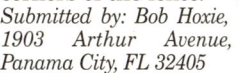

The renovated clock

Sun Trust acquired Commercial Bank in 1988. The clock had not worked properly for a number of years until a major repair and renovation was undertaken by Sun Trust in 2002, at which time both the chimes and the timekeeping mechanism were put in working order. The clock is constructed of copper and has four dials, each two feet square, which are illuminated at night. Below the face is leaded glass containing the name of the bank. The clock chimes each quarter of an hour, reminiscent of the famous Westminster chimes of London.

Interestingly, a reproduction of this clock also exists. A recent occupier of the old First National Bank building, Black Insurance, installed the reproduction about 1976 at the original location on Harrison A venue at Beach Drive. In 2002, this clock was removed by People's First Community Bank and in 2003 was reinstalled on the building at 23rd Street and Highway 77.

Years ago, T. C. Payne, cashier of First National Bank, referred to the original clock as a "gift to the citizens of Panama City." On July 16, 2003 an unveiling ceremony to commemorate renovation of the clock was held. Sponsors of this event were The Board of Directors of the Bank; Historical Society of Bay County; Chamber of Commerce and the Downtown Improvement Board.
Submitted by: Historical Society of Bay County, PO Box 1476, Panama City FL 32402

Panama City Airport Historic Marker

The Panama City Airport historic marker is located at the entrance to the airport terminal. The marker reads "Established in 1945 on Fannin Field Panama City-Bay County Airport 1964 Panama City-Bay County Airport and Industrial District 1967. Developed and

Panama City Airport Historic Marker

controlled by Representative Airport Authorities in conjunction with the Federal Aviation Agency. Control Tower erected by Federal Aviation Agency 1967."

Sponsored by Bay County-Panama City in cooperation with Florida Board of Parks and Historic Memorials
Submitted by: The Bay County Heritage Book Committee.

Panama City's Rare 4-Headed Palm Tree

Panama City's unusual 4-headed palm tree, a "Butia Capitata," commonly called "Jelly Palm" has been relocated to the The Oaks By the Bay Park in St. Andrews at the foot of Beck Avenue. It can be severely damaged with prolonged below-freezing temperatures. In the past few years, Panama City has lost many of its Palm Trees due to back-to-back cold winters. The native habitat for the "Butia

Capitata" is South America.

Bob Hoxie, V. P. of the Panama City Region of the Gulf Coast Chapter of the International Palm Tree Society, inspects the palm tree often and donated the (4) coontie located in the corners of the fence.
Submitted by: Bob Hoxie, 1903 Arthur Avenue, Panama City, FL 32405

The 4-Headed Palm that was relocated to Oaks by the Bay Park in St. Andrews

Robert Lee McKenzie Home Historic Marker

Robert Lee McKenzie's home and office on 3rd Court at Park Street is listed on the National Register of Historic Places and in addition has an Historic Marker.

The McKenzie House is a large two-story clapboard frame dwelling built in the Dutch Colonial style typical of the turn of the century houses still standing in Northern Michigan. It was built in 1909 by Belle Booth who married R. L. McKenzie in 1912; after which time the house came to be known as the McKenzie House. It stands today as it was enlarged in 1925. This house is significant because it was one of the first houses in a virtually unsettled area of Northwest Florida and because it

Robert Lee McKenzie Home Historic Marker

was the home and office of Robert Lee McKenzie. McKenzie was born in Macon County, Georgia in 1870. He moved to the Florida Panhandle in 1902 where he became joint owner of a large naval stores business. After acquiring some waterfront property here he organized the Gulf Coast Development Company. The purpose of the company was to buy more land and develop it into a town site and to secure more waterfront property for a railroad terminal. In 1906 this purpose was realized when McKenzie persuaded J. B. Steele of Atlanta to choose Gulf Coast Development Company land for his new railroad which would continue south from Dothan with connections to Atlanta. Steele said "I want this to be Atlanta's outlet to the Panama Canal;" which suggested the new city's name. In February 1909 Robert Lee McKenzie was elected Mayor of Panama City. He also served two consecutive terms as State Representative from Washington County in the Florida Legislature (1909-11, 1911-13). McKenzie was a leader in the formation of Bay County. He was instrumental in getting a highway constructed to Pensacola. His work and dedication resulted in Panama City being the location of the International Paper Company. The "Drummond Cut," completed in 1938, opened the intercoastal waterway to the west and McKenzie was a leader in this project. During the war years McKenzie was Chairman of the Bay County chapter of the Red Cross (1941-44) and a member of the Selective Services Board (1940-47). On December 4, 1964, the park across the street was renamed McKenzie Park in honor of his devoted service to the community. R. L. McKenzie's place in the development of Panama City is secure. Most of the important events of the town's development for a period of over 50 years (1902-1956) are linked with his name and efforts. For 45 years (1912-1956) the office/library of the McKenzie House was the center of his activities and as such, gives real historic importance to the house and its place in Panama City history. Sponsored by the descendants of Robert Lee McKenzie in cooperation with the Department of State.
Submitted by: The Bay County Heritage Book Committee.

Site of Loftin's Ferry Historic Marker

This site, originally known as Riviere's Landing, was named for

Site of Loftin's Ferry Historic Marker

the early settler, Henry L. Riviere, and is commemorating the founding of the City of Parker. In 1836, William M. Loftin became custom's officer and operator of a ferry from this point to Ferry point across St. Andrews Bay. This endeavor was part of the road system constructed from 1834 to 1838 under the supervision of Major J.D. Graham. The "Old Military Road" as it was known ran from Apalachicola to Marianna and beyond, and was the major land route through the bay area. Loftin's Ferry was the beginning of the community that Loftin, Riviere and U.S. Representative Joseph M. White developed and named "Austerlitz." This is significant for in 1886 the name was changed to "Parker" honoring the two separate families of Peter Parker and William Henry Parker. The City of Parker was established in September 1967, by charter and has remained a thriving, growing community ever since. Sponsored by the City of Parker. The marker is located on Pitts Avenue, where the road curves to an overlook of St. Andrew Bay.
Submitted by: The Bay County Heritage Book Committee.

The St. Andrew Bay Saltworks Historic Marker

The St. Andrew Bay Saltworks has been recognized with an historic marker. Between 1861 and 1865, the St. Andrew Bay

St. Andrew Bay Saltworks Historic Marker

Saltworks, one of the largest producers of salt in the South, contributed to the Confederate cause by providing salt, fish and cattle for southern troops and citizens. A necessary preservative in those times, salt sold for as much as $50 per bushel, and was produced in wood-fired saltworks on the perimeter of the West Bay, East Bay and North Bay and Lake Powell (a.k.a. Lake Ocala). An estimated 2,500 men, primarily from Florida, Georgia and Alabama, were exempted from combat duty in order to labor in the saltworks. The salt was transported to Eufaula, Alabama, then to Montgomery, for distribution throughout the Confederate states. Because of the importance of St. Andrew Bay Saltworks to the Confederacy, acting Master W.R. Browne, commander of the U.S. Restless, was instructed to commence a series of assaults beginning in August 1862. In December 1863, additional Union attacks occurred, which Confederate home guards could not resist. The attacks resulted in the destruction of more than 290 saltworks, valued by Master Browne at more than $3,000,000. The St. Andrew Bay Saltworks employees promptly rebuilt them, and they remained in operation through February 1865.

Sponsored by the Sons of Confederate Veterans, Camp 1319 and the Florida Department of State
Submitted by: The Bay County Heritage Book Committee.

St. Andrew Skirmish Historic Marker

St. Andrew Skirmish is recognized with an historic marker located on Business 98 between Fairland & Friendship Aves.

The U.S.S. Bark Roebuck, commanded by John Sherrill, was sent to St. Andrews Bay to prevent blockade running. On March 20, 1863, an 11-man scouting party landed in this vicinity to secure fresh drinking water. They were attacked by Confederates commanded by Captain W. J. Robinson. When ordered to surrender, the Union crew refused and two were killed and six wounded in the ensuing skirmish. The rest escaped to their ship. The Confederates

St Andrews Bay Skirmish Historic Marker

had no casualties.

Sponsored by the Florida Board of Parks and Historic Memorials
Submitted by: The Bay County Heritage Book Committee.

Union Soldiers Monument "G.A.R. Park"
Lynn Haven, Florida

My family moved from Cottondale to Lynn Haven when I was seven. I walked by the statue of the soldier each day on my way to school, but I don't remember when I learned he was a "Yankee". My ancestors for generations were Southerners, and I assumed he was a Confederate soldier. It's been very interesting to search old records for information about this unique monument. The quotes that follow are from the *Lynn Haven Tribune*, *Panama City Pilot* and *St. Andrews Bay News*.

Dr. William W. Krape, who at the age of 16 enlisted as a private in Company A, 46th Illinois Infantry, came to Lynn Haven during the month of June, 1913, and was mustered into Stanton Post No. 2, Department of Florida, Grand Army of the Republic. As Post Commander, during 1919-1920, he proposed that a memorial be built to honor those who gave their lives during the tragic war of

Stanton Post No. 2 G.A.R. Hall, ca 1921, and Union Soldiers Monument

1861-1865. By a unanimous vote the members "fully empowered Comrade Commander, William W. Krape to raise funds and erect said monument," and ordered its treasurer "to honor all bills having his okay." In order, to finance the project each member pledged to contribute a percentage of his pension check. The Lynn Haven Ladies Circle No. 7, Grand Army of the Republic, and the Charles R. Merrill Camp No. 9, Sons of Veterans contributed towards its cost from funds raised at sponsored projects. Liberal contributions were received from almost every state in the Union and from hundreds of visiting tourists.

The cornerstone was laid for the monument in 1920 by Dr. Krape. He stated, "as Mayor of Lynn Haven, Florida, I lay this memorial cornerstone as a fitting tribute to the soldiers, living and dead, whether in the infantry, cavalry, artillery, or navy, on land or sea, wherever, found, Columbia's sons have always been found at the post of greatest danger. This monument records the achievements of Washington, the father of his country, the martyrdom of Lincoln, the savior of this nation, and the nation's patriotic men and women." In less than one and a half years the monument was successfully completed and paid for through the energetic activity and personal contributions of Dr. Krape.

Erected on raised ground, surrounded by a masonry coping, the monument is ten feet square at the base and twenty six and one half feet high from the base to the crown of the bronze figure of a uniformed Federal soldier equipped, and armed. The figure was cast by the W. H. Mullins Company of Salem, Ohio, and mounted on the masonry pedestal by Comrade Francis O. Jarvis, Private, late of Company I, 106th New York Infantry and his son, David C. Jarvis, Captain of the Lynn Haven Fire Department, using the department's hook and ladder truck.

On Saturday afternoon, February 12, 1921, the one hundred and twelfth anniversary of Lincoln's birthday, the monument in honor and memory of the Union Soldiers of the War Between the States was dedicated at Lynn Haven, Florida.

Previous to the dedication ceremonies Rev. Harry Gardner Vandervoot, Private, late of Company B, 150th Illinois Infantry, of the Christian Church, delivered an exceedingly interesting address at the G. A. R. Hall, a tribute to Lincoln, to Commander Krape who had conceived and carried out this project of erecting a monument, to the surviving Comrades of the Union forces, and to those to whom...

"The muffled drum's sad roll has beat
The soldier's last tattoo;
No more on life's parade shall meet
The brave and fallen few.
On Fame's eternal camping-ground
Their silent tents are spread,
And Glory guards, with solemen round
The bivouac of the dead."

After the address every member of Stanton Post who could attend assembled on parade. A goodly number of citizens of Lynn Haven and other points, including members of the Ladies Circle and the Sons of Veterans were present. The ritual exercises of the G. A. R. were carried out perfectly by Post Officers led by Commander in Chief Krape. One commentator observed, "There it will stand silently preaching one hundred percent Americanism to those now living and to generations unborn for many years to come."

To be set at a later date were bronze tablets as tributes to their comrades and the history of the work. Three tablets were affixed to the monument pedestal and inscribed: "Monument in Memory of the Union Soldiers of the Civil War 1861-1865", the text of the "American Creed", and "Grand Army of the Republic." In an early photograph of Veterans posing in front of the monument and Stanton Hall taken before the palm trees were planted, no fourth tablet is visible on the west side. In a 1928 photograph a fourth tablet is visible and should be inscribed with "the history of the work".

The unique monument to Union Soldiers located at the southeast corn of Georgia Avenue and Eighth Street was the first of its kind erected in Florida and the Southern States. The bronze figure of an armed Federal Infantryman standing at ease atop a towering white pedestal facing North, was a living memorial to the Veterans of the Grand Army of the Republic who, in their late sixties to early eighties removed from their homes in the North to enjoy their final days among the friendly people and pleasant climate of the South. A three-inch salute gun was positioned, pointed north, on the east side of the monument's base. On December 1, 1942, Major Lorne Wilkie, Quartermaster Corps, United States Army, 4th Service Command, Atlanta, Georgia, by approval of the Commander in Chief of the G. A. R. of the state of Florida and the Lynn Haven City Commission, ordered the gun removed to Tyndall Field. It was delivered to Lt. Harvey Jernigan, Base Quartermaster, on December 9 to be sent to a U.S. Arsenal for return to active service.

Dr. Krape died in his home at Lynn Haven March 19, 1926, at the age of seventy eight. He was a soldier, a dentist, a Mayor of Lynn Haven, and the founder of the fraternal organization, Knights of the Globe. He was responsible for the monument to Union veterans located at Krape Park, Freeport, Illinois. He organized the Lynn Haven Chautauqua December 9, 1914, and left to the people of Lynn Haven the renovated James A. Gard building as a community center and lasting edifice for the Chautauqua. He was buried at his northern home, Freeport, Illinois.

Stanton Post No. 2, Department of Florida, Grand Army of the Republic, was organized by twenty five charter members in July, 1911 (probably July 4), on the second floor of the Hughey building which was completed July 5. July 22 forty veterans were recorded on the roll. The Post was named in honor of Edwin McMasters Stanton, the irascible Federal Secretary of War or in memory of Private Elias L. Stanton, late of Company I, 16th Connecticut Infantry, who was the first Federal veteran to die at Lynn Haven, June 16th, 1911. A newspaper article written in the 1930's identifies the Post as the "E.M. Stanton Post." At St. Cloud, Florida, a veterans colony was established by the developers of Lynn Haven in 1909, and a G. A. R. Post was organized there December 20 and named in honor of the first deceased veteran. The first Commander of Stanton Post was Dr. Oren Ellsworth Guiles, Private, late of Company B, 5th Michigan Cavalry. Meetings were held on the first and third Saturday of each month at 2:00 P.M. The Post's greatest enrollment occurred during 1914 when 134 were recorded.

Those identified as charter members in obituaries and newspapers were: Dr. Guiles, Stephen W. Anderson, Henry Bahl, Hammond L. Ball, Celon James Ball, John A. Barron, John D. Bodine, S. R. Burnett, James A. Gard, John M. Hughey, Jacob Laub, John G. Markham, William C. Morris, W.H. Martin, Johnson L. McLaughin, Charles R. Merrill (by mail), Henry F. Miller, Alonzo Woodruff, C.C. Palmer, Col. Ervin V. Richards, Capt. John Rogers, Alvin S. Savage, Joseph C. Sours, John Throckmorton and Emory P. Truesdell.

August 15, 1911, a chicken-pie supper at the McInnis Hotel was held to raise funds for a G.A.R. hall building. Stanton Hall was the first public building built in the "Magic City" and was partially completed during 1912. The two-story frame building faced Georgia Avenue and was situated on Lot 3 of Block 136 and owned by the Ladies Circle. The meeting hall had a seating capacity of about three hundred. Attached to the hall was a kitchen and a large dining room with three long tables seating nearly one hundred. A raised stage was centered at the east end. Curtains, green and gold, the official colors of Lynn Haven, draped the stage. Dr. Krape had the interior walls covered with paperboard. During March, 1922, cement walks were placed around the hall. A flag pole was positioned near the southwest corner of the building. Trees were planted at the site in memory of various family members. The monument was located north of the site of Stanton Hall.

Dr. Guiles was the last of the Union veterans who founded the G.A.R. colony in 1911 at Lynn Haven to die there, August 28, 1937, at the age of ninety three. Veterans Stanton and Guiles were buried at the Lynn Haven Cemetery. Stanton was buried in the northeast corner. Guiles was buried near the southwest corner.

The Lynn Haven Ladies Circle No. 7, Grand Army of the Republic, was organized in June of 1911 by sixteen charter members, Mrs. Gertrude V. Throckmorton, President.

The Charles R. Merrill Camp No. 9, Sons of Veterans, Division of Alabama and Tennessee, was organized in August of 1911, Thomas Ezra Geho, Commander.

A second Post, Abe Lincoln No. 32, was chartered during late 1912 to meet at Liberty Hall, also known as Robert's Hall and the Odd Fellows' Building.

The provision in the deed to the G.A.R. property from the St. Andrews Bay Development Company was that title to the eight lots was to pass to the City of Lynn Haven when the last veteran of the city passed away and would always bear the name of "G.A.R. Park."

Shortly after the passing of Dr. Guiles, the parcel of the property south of the monument, the site of Stanton Hall, was deeded to the Bay County School Board. During 1940 the building was used for the Lynn Haven Grade School lunch room. In the fall of 1942 a room was attached and classes held at the building. During December of 1947 the School Board sold the building for $328. The building was in very good state of preservation, erected in the days when lumber was good and especially rich in keeping qualities. It was torn down for future building material during 1948.

There are six known "official" photographs of the monument and Stanton Hall. One is most likely immediately after the monument dedication, February 12, 1921. Another was taken about the same time and pictures twenty-six veterans to include Dr. Krape and Rev. Vandervoot. These two photos are known to be made prior to 1923 as that was when the palm trees were planted. A third photo of veterans sitting on the south coping was made February 22, 1922. It was taken by Mr. Brimhall during a celebration of President George Washington's birthday organized by the Ladies Circle. A fourth photo, date unknown, is often mistaken for the dedication photo. In this photo the palm trees are pictured and the monument is weathered. A fifth photo was taken about 1928 and pictured in the Lynn Haven Chamber of Commerce brochure of 1928. A sixth photo of veterans sitting on the east coping was taken November 19, 1928, after a noon day meal for the veterans organized by the Sons of Veterans.

During 1976 the monument was refurbished by the Lynn Haven Chamber of Commerce, Lee Kinard, President. During April of 2002 the members of 1st Lt Thomas H. Gainer Camp 1319, Sons of Confederate Veterans, had the monument restored. A photo of participating Compatriots was taken May 3, 2002.

Submitted by: MAJ Jack O. Cutchens, USA, Ret, FLARNG, 1115 Kentucky Ave., Lynn Haven, Florida.

BUSINESSES

The Alcoa Theater

I remember seeing a silent movie. When I first started going to the movie theater it was silent movies and the attraction was "Tarzan and the Apes." I remember going to Mr. R F. George's store. I would take twenty cents to go to the movie. I'd get a nickel's worth of wieners and a package of saltine crackers and ten cents for admission charge. This was the old Alcoa Theater. It was first called the German-American Lumber Company Theater and then it was the American Lumber Company Theater. W. C. Sherman was the legal property custodian for the German American Lumber Company and their assets were seized in World War I, 1917. W. C. Sherman later bought those assets and he ran the mill. There was a huge fire over there, three blocks long. Our house had cedar shingles on top. All during that fire I had to get up on top of that roof and throw buckets of water on the shingles as the embers from the fire fell on the roof. My brother Wallace and I did that and our roof didn't catch on fire. If you had a fire it was usually a loss. You just suffered a loss and gritted your teeth and buried it as the old fellow said. I remember Tom Torgersen and his family lived in Millville and his house burned three times. He moved to Panama City on Harrison Ave. Dothea, his daughter, and I were in the same class together ever since Bessie Gainey's 1928 grade one. So I was sad to see Dothea move over to Panama City.
Submitted by: Fred Turner, 2694 Island View Dr., Panama City, FL 32405.

The Bay Theatre

The earliest I can remember, I guess I was about two or three years old, we lived with my Grandparents (Lucas) on a side road behind Everitt Junior High School. The street didn't have a name nor did houses have house numbers.

Everyone had a P.O. Box in the large main Post Office downtown, it is still standing today. My parents were building a house and I remember we would visit where they were working, no street name, but now it is the corner of 4th Street and Sanders Lane. We lived there until I was about age 10. During those earlier years, if we saw a movie, we had to go to the Ritz Theatre downtown on Saturday morning. First it was the "Kiddy Matinee" then the movie of the week.

Then around 1940 (don't know exactly) they built a Theatre at the corner of Hwy 22 and U.S. Hwy 98. They were called the Wewa

Howard and Truett Lucas playing in a grassy field in Springfield

Highway and The Tyndall Highway. I went to see the first movie shown at that new Bay Theatre. The movie was "The Ghost Ship".

The same movie would show on Friday and Saturday. Usually a western and some other or maybe another western or police or comedy. My family would require me and my brother to clear our yards on Friday and would let us go to the movie on Saturday. The Bay Theatre would open at 10:00 a.m. on Saturday. We would be there when it opened and stay until nearly dark, seeing the movie over and over again. The price for our age was 9 cents, we had 15 cents; show fare and enough for a 6 cent cup of chocolate ice cream that we bought in the drugstore that was part of the Theatre building.

The intersection at Hwy 22 and US 98 where the theatre

was built had four corners, one had Rowell's Service Station and the theatre; across the front of that was Champ Clark's Service Station which had a restaurant and oyster bar. Across from there was Grey Lumber Company and Hardware Store. The other corner held Clifton's Grocery Store which had been closed years before that time.
Submitted by: Truett Lucas, 3235 E. Orlando Rd., Panama City, FL 32405.

Bay Upholstery & Drapery Shop

To honor my Mother and Daddy, Alma and Frank Richardson, I would like to write down what I can remember as to how Bay Upholstery & Drapery began.

My family lived in Donalsonville, Georgia until the war started in 1941. My Dad, Frank Richardson had a large

building with a peanut sheller on one side and a grist mill to grind corn into meal on the other side and a cabinet shop in between. Upstairs there were two apartments, one in which we lived, and the other for rent. He was building houses for the government and had

Frank and Alma Richardson

about eight houses with the cement slabs down, and the plumbing roughed in. When the war started the government froze all building materials and supplies and his money as well, and he was unable to finish them.

The hotel at Wakulla Springs had just had a fire, so he and his workers went to live in Panacea, Florida to repair the fire damage at the hotel. In the summer of 1942, we moved to Lynn Haven, Florida. My Dad began working at the Wainwright Shipyard in Panama City, as many others did during the war. Shortly after, Mother began teaching Fourth grade at Lynn Haven Elementary, later helping Daddy with

his business. Before the war ended, Daddy bought a car upholstery business from a black man named, Brown, It was located in a wooden building at 520 East 6th Street. The building was owned by a Mr. Wallace. Other businesses around him were a bicycle shop run by a Mr. Morris, Hutchison Radio Shop; C. C. Walley Grocery, who also sang in a gospel quartet on Sunday mornings; Gulf Specialty Co., owned by H. H. Hathaway and wife Bonnie; Barnes Laundry; and Jimmy's Drive-In. Sixth Street or Business 98 was the main

Ann and Marshall Evans, 1983

thoroughfare to Tyndall AFB.

The upholstery shop began as a car upholstery business making seat covers, headliners, door panels and convertible tops that could most times be done early in the day and delivered back to the customer in the afternoon.

In 1953 Daddy built a two story building across the street at 523 East 6th Street with two apartments upstairs. One apartment for Mother and Daddy and one for my husband, Marshall, me and our new son, John. That next year, Daddy sold this building to a Reverend Swicord and purchased land at 527 North Cove Boulevard and built a building for his shop and one for Jack Jackson's Wheel Alignment. Mr.

Jackson's business grew so Daddy built him a larger building on the other side and rented the smaller one to Mr. Goodlake's small engine repair. Daddy had stopped doing car upholstery and was doing more furniture upholstery at this time. He operated his upholstery business for twenty-two years. In November, 1963, my Mother passed away and my Daddy died four months later in March, 1964. My husband quit working at Arizona Chemical Company and started running the upholstery shop. In the meantime, I had opened the Cloth Shop on Highway 22 in Callaway and we had started doing a few draperies along. We had both shops for a few years, but we eventually closed the Cloth Shop, rented the building and some time later sold it. I went to work at the shop downtown and we made draperies and upholstered furniture. We operated the business for twenty five more years until we retired in 1989.

We could never have operated the business without the help of our wonderful employees. I would like to name most of them. Preston McClure, W. B. Taylor, J. M. Burkett, all of whom worked for my Dad and continued on with us, Richard Burton, Mildred Floyd, Pearl Davis, Lou Whitaker, Mary Vickers, Artie Beth Davis, Marion Shehee, and Nelrea Green, who helped Daddy during Mother's illness. The designers, Ruthie Houser, Jeanne McDermott, and Rosalind Bynum Lowery were the best ever. I must not forget my customers, who were more like my friends. I could never thank them enough for the work they gave us all those years.
Submitted by: Ann Evans, 100 Cherry Street, #105, Panama City, FL 32401.

Boarding Houses

During the period from 1920's to early 1970's it was common for people with houses to rent a room to others until they could establish a place of their own. This practice led to the establishment of boarding houses such as the Pleasant Inn Boarding House and Café' owned and operated by Lauvenia Johnson Holmes Lewis in the black community on East End Avenue (Harmon Avenue).

Many of the top aspiring bands that played at the Elks Club and other local clubs would board and dine along this street. The Ink Spots, Ray Charles, Bobby Blue Bland, B.B. King and James Brown just to name a few.

The Boarding Houses, hotels and cafes provided off-base dining parties, receptions and recreation for the black military families that were incoming or outgoing of Tyndall Air Force Base, Naval Base or Ship Yard.

The numerous clergy, Bishops and Presiding Elders of the black churches would board or dine during the Northwest Conferences and other church events on East End Avenue.

Many of the black tourists in town for beach vacations always found their way to the thriving businesses along the street. The black deep-sea fishermen were known to board and have their fresh caught seafood prepared to just their style at the cafes.

On any given day there were the sounds of children playing in the street in front of their homes. Many people would sit on their front porches to watch car after car pass by with visitors and locals. There was always the distinct sound of a lone juke box playing the latest Motown sound and the dancing and laughter of the many customers.
Submitted by: Bura L. Reed, 1402 Illinois Ave, Lynn Haven, FL 32444.

Cooper's News Agency
1938-1979

Owners and Operators: Glenn Cooper (1917-1995) Mary Sue Austin Cooper (1920 - 2001)

Cooper's News Agency provided magazines and newspapers from Ft. Walton Beach to Apalachicola in the days before television. During WW II and the growth of Tyndall Air Force Base, war news and comic books were widely read for information as well as for a diversion from dreary war news. Grocery stores, drug stores, and any magazine outlet were supplied by Cooper's News Agency. The early warehouse was located in the Cove area at 224 Allen Avenue in a

garage still standing today.

Customers browsing in the Cooper's News Stand on Harrison Avenue

The Curtis Publishing Company contract was an important document because it made Cooper's the exclusive distributor of their publications in the Panama City area. Many of the early postcards picturing Panama City were paid for in advance by Cooper's News as a business decision in hopes that the images would sell to tourists. As spring approached, new magazine racks and postcard racks would be delivered to beach-area businesses for the season. Many businesses would receive stock on consignment. As Labor Day approached, collections would begin in earnest before some of the beach businesses closed up for the season without settling their accounts. Some would not open the next season and had to be found and asked to pay for the merchandise they had sold.

In addition to the wholesale operation, Cooper's News operated a retail outlet at 450 Harrison Avenue. This newsstand operated from 7:00 a.m. until 10:00 p.m. seven days a week. In addition to magazines, the newsstand sold tobacco, chocolate, and newspapers. Cooper's News was the only place to get the *New York Times, Atlanta Journal, Birmingham News, New Orleans Times Picayune, Florida Times Union* or the *St Pete Times.* Many of these papers came in by bus several times during the day, Cooper's would send a driver to the bus station to pick up recent newspaper arrivals. The Sunday *New York Times* would come in on Tuesday, and most of these newspapers were reserved a week ahead of time. Customers with reservations would come to pick up their paper during the week.

As the place to get Time Magazine, Life, Look, Good Housekeeping or any current publication, Cooper's News was a hub of local activity. Comic books, Little Golden Books, Jr. Classics Illustrated, Nancy Drew mysteries, wrestling magazines, and, after 1953, Playboy Magazine were available. The business was picketed by several religious groups over the years because of Playboy, Penthouse, and similar magazines.

Glenn Cooper attended annual magazine meetings where current authors gave signed advanced copies of their publications. Norman Mailer and Lauren Bacall were just two of the authors through the years to attend these publisher's promotional events.

As a sideline business, Coopers News operated the newspaper delivery of the *Atlanta Journal* and the *Birmingham News* along Panama City Beach from Memorial Day until Labor Day. Each night at midnight a driver would go to Opp, Alabama, or the intersection of Highway 331 and 98 to pick up the papers and begin delivery. Stops included Seagrove Beach, Phillips Inlet, and motels along Hwy. 98. About 2:00 a.m. the driver would stop at Funland for a hamburger and shake. There were over 100 stops of newspaper machines along the "route". Some racks or machines would get only 5 papers, some 25. The object was to get all the papers delivered and get off the beach before the morning traffic increased and to deliver at Cooper's News before they opened at 7:00 a.m. On Sunday night, the machines had to be "robbed" and changed from 25 cents back to 10 cents. The "take" for the week would then be counted and rolled in coin wrappers for deposit at home Monday morning. Counting and rolling several hundred dollars in dimes and quarters was quite a job. Glenn Cooper, Jr. and Ray Cooper delivered these papers for many summers to earn college money. Often times they would finish the route at 6:00 a.m. and board a fishing vessel for a day fishing or working as a deck hand before starting the whole procedure the next night at midnight. The publisher and editors of the Atlanta and Birmingham papers wanted the papers available along the beach when they came to Panama City Beach to vacation. The papers which did not sell had to be picked up and the date cut out for counting and returning to the publisher for credit. To this day, if I see someone take more than one paper out of a machine without paying for it, I'm tempted to call the police. If they only knew the LABOR involved for such small change.

Submitted by: June Cooper Lloyd, 447 Sudduth Ave., Panama City, FL 32401.

Cotton Grocery

Dorothy Eunice Cotton Stewart, born in 1936, was told she learned to walk on the counter of the wooden "mom and pop" grocery store which at that time sat in the middle of 11th Street.

Old Cotton Grocery at corner of Jenks Ave. and 11th St.

Charlie and Irma Cotton, owners of Cotton Grocery, sold everything from penny candy to fresh cut meat and were hosts to neighbors who gathered there daily to chat.

Charlie, always a good hearted man, was known to extend credit for food during the depression era, many times not collecting because he knew most folks were down and out. One example of his generosity was evident when after the death of Charlie, a box of bills was found. At the top of one bill for a woman who had passed away Charlie had penned "This debt settled by God".

Years after the transition of Irma and Charlie, a gentleman phoned Dot and said he had borrowed $100.00 from Charlie and would like to pay it back. Dot said after all this time it didn't matter, but the gentleman insisted. Dorothy said "All right, if it will make you feel better."

Around 1952 11th Street became widened and the new Cotton Grocery was built. In the early 70's Charlie retired due to ill health.

Submitted by: Dorothy Cotton Stewart, 1059 Jenks Ave, Panama City, FL 32401.

Divine Intervention

Some people believe in Divine Intervention (Guardian Angels), others don't. You be the judge of the following example.

This story involves Bose McCrary, a welder and employee at International Paper in Bay Harbor for a total of about 37 years, and is factual as related by Bose himself. Bose loved his family and was a God fearing man. He was a member of First Assembly of God Church in Millville where his family worshiped.

Welders at International Paper Company in Bay Harbor receiving a 4,000 Day Safety Award, April 1964. Bose McCrary is second from right

Bose was first employed by the mill about 1936; he left the Mill in 1942 for three years to work at the Wainwright Shipyard building liberty ships. He then returned to the Paper Mill when ship building began winding down in 1945.

In 1975, he retired from the Mill. During his employment he practiced safety and always approached his work with logic, energy and enthusiasm. He was regarded by his peers and supervisors as one of the best gas and electric welders in the Mill.

That day in June, 1965, Bose was assigned a job on the 4th floor of the pulp mill to cut a hole in a 12-inch digester blow line for removing a pulp plug from the line.

The blow line that was plugged was about 15 feet from the floor of the digester room, so Bose had to either get a ladder or find some other way to get to the blow line. Under the line was a vessel called a gas-off jug. Gasses from the digester cooking the wood chips was vented into the gas-off jug. Bose realized that the gas-off jug was just high enough for him to stand on to reach the blow line without using a ladder. He moved his acetylene and oxygen bottles to the 4th floor and unrolled enough gas hose to reach the blow line. Opening the acetylene and oxygen tank's valves, put his hoses over his shoulder and started to climb up a steel ladder attached to the side of the gas-off jug. After reaching the top of the jug, little did he know that what he stood on was an explosion door. The purpose of the explosion door was to relieve any explosive or violent pressure increase in the jug. The door can open without notice and with a violent bang to release the dangerous pressure.

Bose was standing on that explosion door and after several unsuccessful attempts at trying to light his torch, he climbed down the gas-off jug ladder to check his acetylene and oxygen bottles. When he reached the floor there was a tremendous and violent explosion that blew open the explosion door that Bose had been standing on. If Bose's cutting torch had not malfunctioned, he would have been standing on that door when it blew open and he would have been killed instantly.

Bose believes that Divine Intervention caused the torch not to light and therefore brought him down from the top of the jug to check his bottles and hoses, thus saving his life. He found that the shutoff valve of each gas bottle was closed.

Bose celebrated his 91st Birthday on October 14, 2003.

Submitted by: James L. McCrary, 12277 Brookshire Ave., Baton Rouge, LA 70815.

East End Avenue Business Life

In the 1920's to late 1960's the busy street of East End Avenue on the east side of downtown Panama City was the hub of black business activity. This street was later renamed Harmon Avenue.

There was the family owned and operated Pasco Gainer Hotel and Pasco Gainer Funeral Home. Rosa's Café' owned and operated by Rosa/Lalus Jackson, The Orange Blossom Café, Dr. Daniels Medical Office, black internal medicine doctor, and White Horse Hotel and Café was there. Cole's Café' owned and operated by Lucille Cole and family. Also East End Café owned and operated by Sye and Florence McCliren family, Wells Barber Shop, Greater Bethel A. M. E. Church, Macedonia Baptist Church and numerous residential homes were scattered in between. Many day-to-day activities and functions along with special events took place on this street. One of the most vivid memories of this period was the aroma of the special prepared foods that were cooked and served by the numerous cafes. There would be fried or smothered seafood that was in season along with chicken, porkchops, beef stew and

Seated around a table at the Pleasant Inn Café are L-R: Rufus Brown, unknown, Louise White Smith, Lauvenia J. Lewis early 1960's

28

T-bone steaks. These entrees would be accompanied by hot steaming assortment of vegetables that were in season, hot biscuits, cornbread muffins, yeast rolls, assorted beverages, iced tea, milk, coffee or sodas and an array of mouth-watering homemade pastries cakes/pies and a special treat of ice cream milk shakes and sundaes. The local workers, visiting tourist, clergy, military personnel etc. still speak fondly of the great tasting entrees that they enjoyed along the street of East End Avenue.

By the mid 1970's this glorious street was but a shell of itself. The signs of integration had taken their toll, along with the modern day shopping centers and mall. The average blacks had been drawn away from this once booming mega. There were numerous motels that had been built away from this dusty corridor. The two major churches had been built in less congested areas.

So slowly with the death of an owner, fire, lack of business, relocations, the encroachment of crime and the decline of downtown Panama City the old businesses began to close one by one.

So a ride along Harmon Avenue today is different. There are many vacant lots, many new business complexes have been built and many of the old homes still exist.

For some it is a distant memory for others it never existed but for the many who were born, lived, visited, dined, worshiped or worked on East End/Harmon Avenue just the mention of its name makes them stand a little taller and a smile will light up their face remembering the distinctness of that time and place that made us what we are today.
Submitted by: Bura L. Reed, 1402 Illinois Ave, Lynn Haven, FL 32444.

15th Street and Harrison Avenue

Fifteenth Street was home to most of the big car dealerships, then in the 1980's some moved to 23rd Street. The old abandoned, Bud Davis Drive-In Movie remained at the southeast corner of Lisenby and 15th Street. It was replaced a few years later by the Florida Triple Theater. The Gulf Drive-In Movie was located on the north side of 15th Street, west of Hamilton Avenue. The large pond, which once played host to the children's fishing contests in Spring, remains today. But most of this land is now covered by the Family Life Center.

Downtown Panama City continued as the heart of the shopping and business district as it had since the town was named "Panama City" in 1906. Sears, Penney's Woolworth's, Murphy's, Belk's, Cogburn's, Dad & Lad, Cooper's and Leitz Music drew the crowds along with numerous other businesses and stores. Motorists spent their time in search of a parking spot unless they were fortunate to find one on their first try.

Lower Harrison was the location of places such as Surplus Sales and First Federal. Talks were beginning on the updating of McKenzie Park and the restoration of the McKenzie House both one block east of Harrison.

On the downtown marina at the foot of Harrison, the Four Winds Restaurant beckoned those holding large parties and banquets. The marina was popular with teens who cruised this location on weekends, waving and beeping at one another. The nearby Bay County Public Library on Government Street was still a new building, as were the next door City Hall and Civic Auditorium on the other side of Harrison. Jane Patton served as director of the five-county library system.
Submitted by: Marlene Womack, 25 W. Government St., Panama City, FL 32401.

Fountain and Betts - Businesses

In earlier years, the Fountain and Betts area was known for its lumber, sawmills and turpentine stills, and oh yes, its moonshine stills. Location of some of the sawmills, turpentine stills and railroad beds were still visible during the 1930's and 1940's. An obvious one was about a quarter mile east of the Fountain school on Juniper Creek. Concrete pillars and a partial wood dam across the creek were still visible. Prickly pears with long

thorns covered the area. During the 1940's, I walked and rode a horse on many of the old railroad beds in the Fountain and Betts area hunting and looking after our hogs and cows. Another place where fragments of turpentine

Betts Naval Stores Company Merchandise Chip

stills, sawmills and housing were located was in the Betts area on Sweetwater Creek; about four miles north of Fountain and south of the overhead pass on Highway 231.

A Betts Naval Stores Company Merchandise Chip was found at Betts where buildings were previously located and had been torn down or rotted. The Chip dates back to the 1920's or earlier.

The Fountain Post Office was located in a combination gas and grocery store on the west side of Highway 231 about one hundred yards south of the road that went east to the Fountain School. The store was operated by Hazel Parker and later by Maude McQuagge Zingerillo. The gas pumps were hand operated by manually pumping gas up into a round glass container that was marked to show the number of gallons and it would flow by gravity through a hose to the vehicle.

In the late 1930's and early 1940's a one-car rail coach, called "The Huddler," delivered mail and hauled passengers to and from Panama City to Dothan, Alabama. The mail was picked up and delivered without stopping. A ride on "The Huddler" was quite an experience.
Submitted by: John W. Cooley, 309 Dublin Circle, Madison, Alabama 35758.

The Gallery of Art

The Gallery of Art of Panama City, 36 W. Beach Dr., Panama City's First art gallery, opened April 20, 1966 for the purpose of exhibiting and selling original paintings, pottery and sculpture of local and area artists. Mary Ola Reynolds Miller, a member of Panama Art Association, had assisted Lucille Mustin Peters in exhibiting her paintings and soon realized that many other artists had no permanent place for the public to view and purchase the fine art pieces of local talent.

First Gallery of Art Harrison Ave. & 6th St. 1966

Present Gallery of Art 36 W. Beach Drive 1999

The Gallery of Art over the years

At the corner of 6th Street and Harrison Avenue an unoccupied building was secured through the efforts of then Mayor Joe and Grodell Hutchinson, and some twenty-five area artists including Peters, Martha Van Elliott, James Chichester, Betty Tenhundfeld, Maggie Guinn, Emil Holzhauer, Mary Durgan, Ellen Bodiford, Helen Heidelberg, R.B. Aitchison, and Lillian McNulty showed their paintings on opening day. When Dan Dunn docked his boat at the Marina in July he placed his paintings in the gallery where he has continued to exhibit. Paul Brent's first exhibit of shell sculptures hung from overhead to be joined later by his early paintings, drawings and prints. Ralph Hurst, nationally known sculptor from Tallahassee, exhibited at the gallery until he closed his studio in 2003. Ana Bovard, a potter, and one of El Salvador's most famous artists, exhibited at the Gallery for thirty-five years, as well as numerous nationally renown artists. The gallery continues to be a place for young artists to exhibit their visual art and talented musicians to perform from its location since 1971.

Submitted by: Mary Ola Miller, 703 Bunkers Cove Rd., Panama City, Fl. 32401.

Glenwood Skating Arena

The deal was closed March 5, 1953 between A. D. Richbourg and wife, Mildred and A. L. Bishop and wife Cecelia Bishop of Muscogee Co, GA. A. D. and wife had purchased Lots One (1) and Two (2) Block 10 of the Glenwood Addition to Panama City, according to map on file in the office of the Clerk of the Circuit Court of Bay County, FL. [Bk. 180 p. 143].

It was time for the Richbourgs to begin their new endeavor—-building a new cinder-block, hard maple-wood floor for a skating rink for the Glenwood residents. The idea emerged as A. D. drove to work and passed young people skating on the Cove Blvd. sidewalks and road. Too, teachers needed to have a supplemental income as salaries were so low.

A. D. did most of the construction with the help of Luther J. "Luke" Newman, who lived across the street and one other fellow whose name escapes me. The rafters for the ceiling were put up by Panama Machinery & Supply Co. There was a walkway on the west side of the building with large shutters which allowed folks to watch the skaters.

Shirley B. Ramsey, Garfield Huff and Hattie L. Kent have been selected the first three contestants for a popularity contest in Panama City which will be held in the Glenwood Skating Arena

The Glenwood Skating Arena, 724 9th Court was a huge success! Music was played on a turn-table which would accommodate 45 rpm records, many we still have. The skaters would often select their favorite music. No smoking or drinking was allowed, even on the outside.

Everyone wanted to be a "skate boy" as they skated free. It was their responsibility to keep order on the floor and help beginners. Some of those remembered are Donell Campbell, Freddie James Manley, Billy Cowart, Fred Richardson, Horace Benton, and Willie Frank Pittman. Freddie, Donell and Billy went on to serve our country in the military. Fred is living up north, Willie Frank lives in Chipley and Horace is deceased.

During the time A. D. was completing his Masters Degree at FSU, Booker T. Lewis managed the rink. His primary business was Bail Bondsman located on Cove Blvd. [Now Martin Luther King Blvd]. He was shot and killed a few years ago.

In talking with ex-patrons such as Tom Bowers, James Gautier and others, all have fond memories of having a place to go "to get off the streets". Tom and James are retired Administrators of the Bay County School System. We've recently read about the goals of Mittie Gainer & Veryl McIntyre for the Glenwood Revitalization Project. Of course we can't overlook Jonathan Wilson, City Commissioner, who had the vision for the city to own this corner for the Glenwood Community Center.

At the time the Skating Arena was in its peak, other businesses and neighbors nearby were: Plato Anderson, Luther Newman, Fate Bower, Jacob Pope, Clayton Stephens, Wilson's Barber Shop, Bill's Sandwich Shop and Willis Dillard.

On occassion, white folk would come by to skate, but the Arena was reserved exclusively for the black community.

By the end of 1968 it was becoming more difficult to have time for the rink, work in education, and business began to slow down. The Richbourgs made the decision to sell the rink but didn't want something dealing in alcoholic beverages to go into the building. Luck prevailed as the Rehabilitation Services, Inc. of 628 N. Cove Blvd., negotiated a deal to purchase the building as they needed more space for their equipment and training. On February 28, 1969 the sale was closed for Lots One (1) and Two (2). [Bk. 270 p. 329].

By March 9, 1972, The Rehabilitation Service, Inc, name was changed to Easter Seal Society for Crippled Children and Adults of the Gulf Coast, Inc., 628 Cove Blvd., sold the property to Raymond Jack Jones, Lots One (1) and Two (2), signed by Ruth Houser and Tommy Cooley, officers. [Bk. 391 p.55]. Mr. Jones opened a night club, The Midnight Lounge, in the Skating Rink building, which he operated until his death in the fall of 1997.

His personal representative sold the rink property along with other property he had acquired, to the City of Panama City "—-premises described above shall be used by grantee only for public purposes, and should grantee fail to use the premises for such purposes, the property shall revert to grantor—". [Bk. 1760 p. 93].

Thus the Richbourgs' desire to have the location a place to "stand proud and be useful" now houses the Glenwood Community Center, year 2000, forty seven years after the Glenwood Skating Arena opened!

Story and pictures submitted by: A. D. Richbourg, 3909 W 16th St., Panama City, FL 3240l-1108. Sources: Land Deeds, Interviews, pictures, personal knowledge.

James Leamon Carter - Founder of Carter-Craft Boats

James Leamon Carter was born in Holmes County, Florida. As a teen, James discovered he liked wood working more than farming. He began making custom furniture. He moved to Bay County in 1942 to work at Tyndall Air Force Base. In 1948 he bought land behind the Parker Baptist Church and built a shop where he made custom furniture and counter fixtures for stores in Panama City. As his business flourished, James thought more about building boats. He modified a set of plans he was given for a fishing boat and before long his first boat was built, the *Phyllis Jean*. While continuing to make cabinets, he designed and built a larger boat for water skiing and a smaller boat for fishing.

In 1951 James officially named his business Carter-Craft Boats and only made boats. As his business grew he turned the Carter home into an office.

Carter-Craft Boats continued to grow and he acquired two business partners, Thomas J. Bingham and Raymond

James L. Carter founder of Carter-Craft Boats and one of his boats

Patrick. Tom managed the office end and Ray the sales while James managed the manufacturing side. The demand for boats for water skiing increased during the 1950s and he employed 70 men and turned out 25 to 35 boats per week. Carter-Craft boats were selling nationally with advertising in major magazines. Cypress Gardens only used Carter-Craft boats in their ski shows so the business was well represented at major ski competitions. A Carter-Craft boat was distinctive in its unique trim lines and the grooves on the bow. Tom Bingham was quoted as saying "Carter was a wood perfectionist."

In 1960 James Carter sold his interest in Carter-Craft Boats to his partners and retired. He had health problems caused from the glue and paint fumes. Carter-Craft changed from wood boats to fiberglass. The business closed in 1969.
Submitted by: Phyllis Sommers, 1826 Wales Dr., Tallahassee FL 32303.

Jessie Seale's Boarding House

My grandmother, Jessie Seale, ran a boarding house in Lynn Haven for almost 30 years. She purchased the little wooden house at 1014 Virginia Avenue from Mr. M.M. Mashburn in 1939. The house cost $700, with payments of $15 a month. Many of her boarders came from Alabama and Georgia to work at Wainwright Shipyards during WWII. For $10 a week, they got complete room and board. My Mom, June Seale Poffenberger, remembers typical meals of fried chicken, mashed potatoes and gravy with canned peaches and store-bought pound cake for dessert, served family style. My grandmother was well-known for keeping a clean house. One of her house guests was the country singer,

Jessie Seale and her Lynn Haven boarding house in 1960's

Hank Williams. He and his wife, Audrey, stayed with Jess for a week. Hank Williams would come to this area to play at square dances held above Lloyd's General Store and at Bob Jones College. Mom's cousin, Max Seale Jr. played bass guitar in Mr. Williams band.

This old house is still standing. It was a wonderful place to play when I was a kid. There were ditches full of water after a storm to wade in, and we'd draw "pretend" houses in the dirt road in front of her house, which I'm not sure Jess liked since she never wanted anything messy. I spent hours swinging in the front porch swing. That same swing is now on my porch and it always reminds me of my grandmother's house.
Submitted by: Kathy Poffenberger, 429 Georgia Avenue, Lynn Haven, FL 32444.

Lloyd Pontiac-Cadillac-GMC Truck

In 1935, Joe Hutchison operated a Standard Oil station and had the Pontiac franchise. In 1936, Rayford L. Lloyd, Sr. joined with Joe to form "Standix." The name was a cross between Standard Oil, where the dealership was located, and the Dixie Sherman Hotel, which at that time stood across the street. Lloyd soon bought out his friend and the dealership became Lloyd Motor Company. At that time, only Pontiacs were sold. Over the years, the business expanded to include Packards, Cadillacs—and even

Lloyd Motor Company at corner of 5th Street and Jenks Avenue. Dixie Sherman Hotel in the background

boats for a time after World War II and now includes GMC trucks and all types of used vehicles. The dealership was first located at Hutchison's Standard Oil station on the corner of Jenks Avenue and Fifth Street across from the downtown post office. The dealership moved in 1954 to Harrison Avenue at Tenth Street, and then again in 1980 to its present location on the corner of 23rd Street and Harrison Avenue.

Rayford L. Lloyd, Jr. took over the business upon his father's death in 1967 and ran it until 1999. In that time, the business grew from 22 employees to 120. During this time he also acquired the Nissan and Mercedes franchises and built a new dealership to house them next door to the Pontiac dealership on 23rd Street. The Lloyd dealerships then included two showrooms, a satellite used car business, a state-of-the-art body shop, and two award-winning service departments. In 1999, Lloyd sold the dealerships to Sonic Automotive, Inc., a public corporation located in Charlotte, North Carolina, and retired. The dealerships are still operating at 23rd Street under the new ownership, however Mercedes is no longer located in Panama City.
Submitted by: Lisa Lloyd Hamlin, 247 South Cove Terrace Drive, Panama City, Florida 32401.

Mr. Neeley and the Martin Theatre

The Martin Theatre was a significant part of life in Panama City for many children, teenagers and adults. It was an important part of our life because our Dad, "Mr. Neeley" was the Manager of the Martin Theatre. His Christian name was John Neeley, known as "Jack" by some but fondly called "Mr. Neeley" by most. Mr. Neeley began his "theatre" career when he was just a boy in Dalton, Georgia, sometimes playing the piano for silent movies. He worked every job at the theatre as a teenager and eventually became the manager of the Wink Theatre in Dalton, Georgia. He managed theatres in both Georgia and Alabama after returning from WW II and before moving to Panama City.

Mr. Neeley was transferred by the Martin Theatre Company of Columbus, Georgia, in 1952 as the new manager of the Martin Theatre. He brought with him his wife, Margaret Anne (Orr), and two daughters, Pat and Penny, (Patricia Anne Beach and Priscilla Elaine Daffin). The Martin was still the "Ritz Theatre" named when it was built in 1936. The Martin's owned the Theatre in partnership with Rufus Davis, Jr. of Dothan, Alabama. However, the Martin brothers bought out Davis, major remodeling occurred including the new (and current) marquee with the theatre opening on June 22, 1956 as the "Martin Theatre".

"Mr. Neeley" standing by the ticket window at the Martin Theatre

It was a great time for the movie business. It was a time when only a small percentage of people had televisions and seeing a movie was a major form of entertainment for many. There would be huge crowds at the Martin on the opening day of most new movies. Often the lines would stretch down the block of Harrison Avenue toward Walgreens Drugs on the opposite corner. There were a few live stage shows that were like vaudeville productions. Every Saturday morning there was a matinee that began at 9:45. Parents would send their younger children accompanied only by other siblings or friends and the teenagers came to socialize. The movie was often a comedy or western, all family movies. The parents knew their children were in a safe environment. Actually, the parents didn't need to worry as Mr. Neeley knew most of the kids and he did "watch them". He would say he was babysitting but he loved it.

His favorite kids were his employees. Many teenagers

earned spending money by working at the Martin Theatre. Seemingly all business, dressed smartly in suit and tie, Mr. Neeley required that employees take their job seriously but he had a talent for making his "employees" realize they were special. To this day, most of those who took tickets, sold tickets and/or sold popcorn and candy knew they were special. Most of those "former employees" of the Martin Theatre went on to be responsible citizens, many to be prominent in Panama City, the Bay County community and the State. The Martin Theatre closed in 1978. Mr. Neeley retired while managing the Florida Triple Theatre and died at age 81 in 1994.

Submitted by: Pat and Penny Neeley, 3119 Debra Blvd, Panama City, FL 32405.

The Paper Mill

On January 31, 1898, eighteen pulp and paper companies in the Northeastern United States joined to form International Paper Company. The paper industry came with International Paper Company to Bay County on April 15, 1930.

The timing was perfect for both Bay Harbor and Millville. The lumber industry had dwindled to just one large mill (in the county) at Millville. By the time operations began at the paper mill, not one sawmill was left in Bay County.

In 1930, International Paper Company, the City of Panama City and Bay County closed a deal to purchase the old Bay Harbor Sawmill property and some 190 acres adjacent to it to construct one of the largest wood pulp and kraft paper mills in the world.

Ground was broken on April 15, 1930, for the first unit. The mill was designed to have two paper machines together with their auxiliary equipment at a cost of $5,000,000 each.

The first roll of paper turned out at the new mill came off the production line on February 18, 1931. The first shipment on February 21, 1931, filled six rail cars with heavy quality paperboard, delivered to St. Louis and Kansas City. Each car carried approximately 20 tons of paper for making heavy cartons. The first shipment by water was loaded on the "Lillian" on March 5, 1931.

At the time of start-up, the paper mill employed 450 people. By the time the second paper machine went into production, the employees had increased to 1,200. The mill has modernized numerous times over the years and employed less than 600 people in 2003.

Submitted by: Charles C. Cunningham, 4731 North Star Ave, Panama City, FL 32404.

Prescott Apartment House - Bay Harbor, Florida

In 1933, Julian C. Prescott and his wife, Jennie Bell (Spencer) and their four sons Hubert, Herbert, Hobert, and Hilbert - moved from DeFuniak Springs to Bay Harbor. By 1934, they had begun to build their new home and apartment house. Just east of this location he also opened his business, "Prescott Poultry Yard".

Three of their neighbors names were: Mrs. James, Mrs. Arnold and a Dallas Miller. Of course, the streets were all unpaved but the neighborhood was clean and neat.

Prescott Apartment House

The paper mill opened about this time and there was an influx of people needing places to live within walking distance of the mill. This need made a booming business for Prescott's Apartment House.

Each apartment was furnished with a table, two chairs, bed, kerosene stove and an ice box in which a block of ice could be placed for keeping things cool. All other necessities for apartment living were furnished by the occupant.

The street in front of the apartment house ran to the entrance of the paper mill. The following stores were located on this street and made up the business district of Bay Harbor. Left side of the road was Bay Harbor Hotel and café, Ard's Grocery, Filling Station, and Johnny Warr's Barber Shop. On the right side of the road was a 5&10 Store, Drug Store, Beauty Shop, Cox's Fish Market, Drug Store, Bar and Pool Room.

It was the Bar and Pool Room across from Prescott's Apartment House where Clarence Earl Gideon committed his crime that later changed the judicial system requiring everyone to have legal representation in a court of law.

Submitted by: Joan Prescott Chance, Granddaughter of Julian C. Prescott, 851 Chance Rd., Chipley, FL 32428.

Prows Dairy

Around 1900, the Prows family saw the need for a dairy in the present Millville area. Robert Roy Prows, and his father, Simeon, introduced the dairy industry to the families which were mostly employed by the local sawmill. After opening up the small dairy, it became a fairly steady business in a short period of time due to the demand. About 1905, the production of buttermilk was added. In 1913 buttermilk was five cents a quart and sweet milk was ten cents a quart. With the building of the new ice plant in Panama City around 1909, the dairy business took on new life.

Prows Dairy

Regular horse and buggy routes were established by the elder Prows. During the first few years of operation, a sawdust covered road from Millville to Panama City was one of the best routes for the dairy. According to Alice Prows, wife of Robert Roy, customers would place jars, pitchers, and even buckets on the front porch to be filled with milk. When it was required that milk be sold in bottles, the dairy closed down for a short period of time. Several small dairies sprang up, but closed shortly after.

When the depression hit the country in 1929, the milk producers of this area formed a corporation to help keep the dairy business going. Isaac Byrd's father was one of the leaders in this movement which set up several standards not required previously. Sometimes the price guaranteed producers only 25 cents per gallon during that time.

Written by: Carolyn Prows. Submitted by: Rudolph S. Prows, 4340 College Station Rd., Panama City, FL 32404.

The Ritz Shop

In 1939, four years after my family moved to Panama City, my father opened up a newsstand next to the Ritz Theater, which is now the Martin Theater. There was a small store next to the Ritz and our shop was The Ritz Shop. I was supposed to be the manager, but Daddy was the boss. We sold magazines, newspapers, sodas, hot dogs, parched peanuts, candy and chips. The theater didn't have a snack bar, and the movie attendees would get their snacks from us.

We also distributed Alabama newspapers to the beach. My father bought a car and painted the Ritz Shop logo on the side. As soon as the papers came in, he headed for the beach with my two young brothers, Joe and Jack.

I met my husband William H. Jennings, better known as Wilkie, at the shop. Every Friday night, he would take his mother to the movies and look in the window of the shop and smile and wave. Eventually, he came in to buy the Saturday Evening Post. I told him we did not carry it, but he could buy it down the street. This went on for several weeks before he finally asked me out. We were married on March 22, 1941 - a marriage that lasted 48 years before he died in 1989.

About the time we married, the theater owners decided that no one could take food or drinks into the theater. After awhile, they opened their own snack bar. This hurt our business, so sometime in 1941 we sold the Ritz Shop.

The Ritz Shop on Harrison Avenue, 1939

Submitted by: Frances D. Jennings, 1101 Rhode Island, Lynn Haven, FL 32444.

Roads of Bay County

In the early 1970's, a section of 19th Street was also a sand-dirt road that ran east and west a short distance between Airport Road and Lisenby Avenue. Balboa and Wood Avenues from 15th Street to 19th Street had yet to be cut and were still woodlands.

East of Airport Road, a sand trail that would later connect 19th Street with Highway 231 led through one of the city's old dumping grounds to Jenks Avenue. Both State and Harrison did not extend north in the same blocks as they do today. The current traffic roundabout at State and 19th Street was a roadway tool used in other parts of the country, not in Panama City.

Bay Memorial and Lisenby were the two area hospitals at that time, while Gulf Coast existed in a few doctors' dreams.

Two-laned 23rd Street claimed some businesses, a new cemetery and a few strip malls. But it did not include Wal-Mart, Sam's, Food World, Publix, Albertson's, Peoples First, Lowe's, Home Depot or most other shopping centers and restaurants that glut the four-laned road today. Behind what is now the Wal-Mart Shopping Center, Passion Lake attracted teens as a popular, hidden swimming hole. At night the location came alive with young lovers in cars, parked around the lake. Farther west on 23rd Street past Frankford Avenue were a few ponds where cows once drank when the location was all part of Hentz's Dairy. At the northeast corner of 23rd and St. Andrews Blvd., egg hunts were held the Saturday before Easter each year on the undeveloped land.

Submitted by: Marlene Womack, 25 W. Government St., Panama City, FL 32401.

Selling Peanuts at the Shipyard

In the Spring of 1943, the Shipyard in Panama City began building the Liberty Ships that would play a vital role in the war. The " yard" ran 24 hours a day in three shifts. Each shift had 10,000 workers. I was eight years old and my father had left the paper mill in Port St Joe to work in the shipyard. Housing was extremely difficult to find because of so many new workers. We were very fortunate to rent a home on Palmetto Avenue just off St Andrew Bay near the shipyard.

There were my parents, two sisters and I. We kids thought it was a great adventure especially since we could go to the beach every day. Down the street lived Mrs. Martin. Her husband was overseas in Europe in the army. Money was very scarce in those days if you could not work and Mrs. Martin had a disability which prevented her from working away from home.

She decided to sell peanuts to the shipyard workers. She would parch peanuts in a large barrel with a crank handle, over a wood-fed fire. She could cook many pounds of peanuts at one time. Also, she would boil peanuts in a wash tub with salty water. She would place the nuts in small paper bags and distribute them to children in cardboard boxes to carry to the shipyard.

That's when I decided I wanted to be a peanut vendor. After much begging and pleading, Mother consented and I became employed for the first time. We would fill our boxes with peanuts and position ourselves at the shipyard gates. When the shift horn would blare, there would be a "tidal wave" of humanity bearing down on us from inside the yard. It was awesome. We would begin screaming over the noise, touting our peanuts. We would all sell out in minutes.

My mother had gotten a job at the shipyard and decided my six year old sister, Faye, should accompany me to sell peanuts. Mrs. Martin let her carry a small box . Of course, being a tiny golden haired girl allowed her to sell all her peanuts as soon as we arrived and caught the incoming workers. She would come crying to me that some of the other boys were stealing her peanuts. So of course, "older brother" had to get them back. This resulted in several fist fights and various scrapes and bruises. I know now this was an early manifestation of her female "wiles", which exist to this day. Anyway, Mother decided baby sister should remain at home.

I sold peanuts for two summers and made, for me, a tidy sum of money. Alas, Mother decided I should have a new suit for church and not the bicycle I planned to purchase. We moved in early 1945 as the war was winding down. I still remember the thrill when the shift siren would blast and thousands of workers would erupt through the gates.

Submitted by: Jerry Anderson, 3407 Country Club Ct., Lynn Haven, FL 32444.

Shopping Centers

For additional shopping, besides downtown Panama City, Panama Citians had the "three G's," Gibson's, Grant's and Gaylord's. Grant's was located in the Panama Plaza Shopping Center at the northeast corner of 15th Street and Lisenby Avenue. The 11th Street Shopping Center held Gibson's. Gaylord's Shopping Center just west of Jenks Ave held Gaylord's.

Submitted by: Marlene Womack, 25 W. Government St, Panama City, FL 32401.

Tarpon Dock Metal Craft

In 1942, during the depression, Charles Coonradt and Olli Peterson migrated to Panama City from Minnesota to work at the shipyard. There they worked in the metal fabricating shop where Liberty ships were being built. A few years later they opened their own sheet metal shop at the foot of the Tarpon Dock Bridge. There they built and installed gutters and began to work with stainless steel. As the city grew, they were responsible for building many of the stainless sinks and hoods for restaurants and schools.

Tarpon Dock Metal Craft building, 1945. L-R: Olli Peterson and Charles Coonradt

Mr. Peterson soon retired. With the advent of air conditioning the business was a natural because they had the means to fabricate and install metal ductwork. Therefore, they began to install central air-conditioning systems to stores and businesses. As time went on people wanted the same comforts for their homes and so began residential air-conditioning.

When Charles Coonradt retired in the late 60's, the business was bought by his son-in-law, Sam Fitzsimons and remained in the family for the next four decades. It was sold to Ben Busby and remains in operation today.

Tarpon Dock Metal Craft grew along with Bay County. As the area grew so did the size of their jobs. They were responsible for installing the first central air-conditioning units to the early buildings of Bay County including Bay High and the Auditorium.

Submitted by: Janice Fitzsimons and Charlotte Fretwell, 214 S Cove Lane, Panama City, FL 32401.

Television Comes to Panama City

I don't remember the exact date I saw my first television but I will never forget the experience. It must have been in the late 1940's. My family lived in a garage apartment in Millville near Highway 98. Someone told me that the man who owned the radio shop on Highway 98 near the Jitney Jungle Grocery Store had made a television set in his shop. I just had to see this new invention. My mom wanted me to go to the store and buy her a loaf of bread. I jumped on my bike and rode to the radio shop. It was a small, narrow shop and there on a counter was this very small television set. Playing on the black and white screen was Hopalong Cassidy the Cowboy Movie Star. He was riding across the screen after the bad guys. I was amazed. Did I mention that I had a bad habit of tearing up my empty popcorn bag while watching movies at the theater? When I could tear myself away from Hopalong, I looked down and realized that I had torn my mom's dollar bill into four pieces. There was only one thing to do. I went to the Jitney Jungle, found some scotch tape, mended my dollar and then paid for the bread and the tape. My mom never did ask me why I also bought the tape. It would be over fifty years before I would tell her my "Hopalong" story.

Not many people could afford a television set in those early days. Usually one house in the neighborhood would have a set and everyone on the street would gather at their house to watch T. V. We were lucky because our next door neighbors had one. Once a week (on wrestling night) the neighbors opened up their home for all their friends and neighbors to come over to watch T.V. We would all gather in the living room, sitting wherever we could find space (children on the floor as close to the television set as we could get), and watch the "snow" on the screen. There was only one television station here in Bay County at the time and it came on at a certain time and went off at a certain time. If you strained, you could maybe see the test pattern through all that "snow" on the screen. Sometimes, another program from somewhere else in the world of television would try to come through the snow and you would see it very faintly. That would be very exciting to see. When the test pattern for the local station came on we knew it would not be much longer until we got to see wrestling. The test pattern didn't do anything but it was there for us to see. We would watch that pattern of lines in black and white until the program came on. Afterwards, we would stay as long as we could to watch the "snow" on this wonderful, modern television set.

Living on Kraft Ave gave me another opportunity to watch television. Crazy Cooley's Television Store opened up just around the corner from my house. Mr. Cooley had a television set in the window of his store. After he closed the store at night, he would leave the television set playing. It was just like a drive-in movie. People would drive up in their cars and sit and watch television. The kids in the neighborhood would meet there and if we were lucky, someone might let us sit on the hood of their car.

Submitted by: Ann Robbins, 435 South Palo Alto Ave, Panama City, Florida 32401.

Thomas Turpentine Still

While visiting the old Callaway School House in March of 2003 with Jackie Sorensen Hogan, a 1922 photograph caption caught my eye, Thomas Turpentine Still! A group of school children are pictured with an adult. The beginning of the end of the mystery to the still's location! My Aunt Fleida Hall (daddy's oldest sister) had shown my Aunt Nona Carr the place years before so we knew the general area. Jackie knew about the still but she said Bertie Shuster could also help. Another day, my Aunt Nona, Aunt Jean Smith, Bertie, Jackie and I piled into the car and went on a guided tour in Callaway.

Winona and Beulah Streets - a few yards up from Callaway Bayou, is the intersection that led us to the "missing site." Around what is now Eleanor and Winona Street were the still and its buildings. There had been a fresh water

spring and a big dock on the bayou where boats were loaded with barrels of turpentine made from the rosin of pine trees. A cooper-shop was near where barrels were made.

A whole community of people and services included the owner's home. The Gaskins, Enfingers and

F.J. Thomas sitting on steps, Jo Thelma, Ben and Carl Thomas at car in front of a turpentine still

Britts also lived in this naval stores community. Facing the water, "shotgun houses" for the workers sat on Eleanor Street. The commissary was between Eleanor and Cherry Streets on the left under trees. The "colored" school and church were situated in this clearing. Jackie said she entered first grade in that school in 1934. She recalled white-walled and paper mill paper walls with a woodburning stove. Desks were made by the WPA and the teacher was Mrs. Pasco (Eleanor) Davis. Bertie remembered the saying about the church, "holy spirits coming through the cracks!" Fish fries and singing were regular events, On Chippiwa Street (toward Highway 22), more houses were on the right side for white children.

A gap in the F. J. Thomas history is finally filled in. More importantly, the history of Callaway. And coincidentally, my present home is on Callaway Bayou just down the road.

Submitted by: Georgia T. Henry-Pearson, 7752 Shadow Bay Drive, Panama City, Fl. 32404.

Three Arts Play House

In the 1940s Margaret and Hugh Baird operated the Three Arts Play House, located at 811 Cherry Street. The log cabin was built originally for the Cove Country Club and the location was in the Cove across from the present day Cove Shopping Center. Margaret and Hugh were dramatics teachers and taught dance, music, theater and diction.

When Ruth Martin was teaching at Cove School she scheduled a field trip to the Play House for her fourth grade students. When Margaret Baird learned the students were coming she prepared a program for the students to demonstrate what the Play House offered.

After arriving at the log cabin Miss Ruth and the students looked all around the outside of the building, even looking underneath the building. Margaret Baird could not understand why they did not come inside. So, she went out and told Miss Ruth that she had a program prepared and to come inside. Surprised to hear this Miss Ruth Martin said "Oh, I just brought my

Three Arts Play House

students by to see the best example of termites in a building I know of."
Submitted by: Eleanor Lewis, 715 Buena Vista, Panama City FL 32401.

The Villa Hotel

The Villa was built about 1885, for guests brought to St. Andrew's Bay by the Cincinnati Land and Development Company. It was multiple stories and the upstairs rooms were large, overlooking the Bay with a cool breeze. The hall bath was the custom.

In the Villa area there were homes of widows who went north for the summer that could be rented. The Oaks Hotel occupied a beautiful wooded plot on Fourteenth Street but was quite rundown. (The Lloyd family bought this property and demolished the Hotel using the building material to build modern cottages, The Oaks Cottages, which were rented to summer guests.) The Pavilion over the water no longer held dances or showed movies as in the past. It was soon to be destroyed by a hurricane.

Along the Bay front was a boardwalk from the village of St. Andrew to Isabella Avenue, West End, where there was a wharf and store. The early maps show a street beside the Bay. At this time the country was in the midst of a deep depression. Houses along the boardwalk were empty or in poor repair, My parents saw a vacant house, made inquires, and decided to buy it as their permanent home.
Submitted by: Gene Howell Sapp, 1409 Deer Avenue, Panama City, FL 32401

Working with WJHG-TV

At the time I started working with Channel 7 Television, they did not have any facilities for local news coverage. I had built an old black and white processing machine out of fishing line spools and had this set up at my house. One day there was a bad wreck near my house. I got my camera, which I had purchased earlier in Pensacola. I photographed that wreck and processed the film. I called Earl Hadaway at Channel 7 and told him I had a film of a wreck and he said he was sorry but

The News Crew of WJHG-TV

they didn't have any way of processing it. I told him I had already processed it. He asked me if I could bring it out. I said yes. I went out with the film to the beach. They were out in the old building behind where the present TV station stands now. Earl put the film on the editor and said, "Hey, I can use this." They gave me all kinds of credit for it. Unfortunately there were two girls killed in the wreck. That was the first real local film that the TV station had had. Joe Howard had a film processing machine that he filmed at football games with, but they couldn't always get in touch with Joe. A few days later they called me to come work for them. I told Mr. Shouler, the manager, I didn't know anything about news coverage. He said, "from what I've seen, you do," So I went to work for Channel 7.
Submitted by: Louie Walker, 803 Transmitter Rd., Springfield, FL 32401.

First Color Film for Television in Panama City

When Channel 7 WJHG- TV moved downtown to the old Commercial Bank building I had the film processing machine at my house. One day there was boat race going that was moved from the downtown marina to Carl Gray Park. The station, which was live at that time, couldn't get all their equipment moved that quickly so they asked us to go and get as much of it as I could. I filmed about 100 feet and came right home to process it. Earl Hadaway and Jim Tighe, the news

director, also filmed some. By alternating filming and developing between the three of us we got some of the boat activity on the news while it was still going on.

We purchased three old color processing machines at Auburn. I modified one for black and white in the boiler room of the TV station. In the meantime, I went up to the Albany TV station and helped them modify and install a machine for black and white. Perley Eppley and I also went to Eldorado, Arkansas and Monroe, Louisiana and set them up. All stations belonged to James H. Gray. The athletic director and photographer from Florida State University came over and said they would like to have the old color machine. I told them if they had some more over there I would just trade. We traded, they gave me two for the one old color. After we got the color going, we decided we should install it at the TV station. So that was the first local color film that we had because of my modifications.
Submitted by: Louie Walker, 803 Transmitter Rd., Springfield, FL 32401.

Personalities and Televisions in Panama City

When WJHG, Channel 7 was at the old TV station on the beach, Jack King, who was in the film department, also had a kid's program. Beth Lawrence and Ruth Turnipseed also worked with him. When I came in every day about 4:00 pm he wanted to use my zoom lenses on his dage black and white camera to get close ups of the kids.

During my 12 years with WJHG- TV as a news photographer I also did commercial photography like shooting slides, putting sound on film commercials for the big automobile dealers and other businesses.

I had the pleasure of meeting many personalities and movie stars like Joseph Cotton, Leif Erickson and Smiley Burnett. When WJHG- TV was downtown in the old Commercial Bank building Smiley was appearing at the Cove Shopping Center and we were having him on our noontime program. I picked him up and took him to the station. After the show he said he was hungry and did we have a place where he could get a hamburger. I said, "Well, we've got a greasy spoon around the corner. That's the Trade Winds." He said, "Oh, that would be O.K." So we had a hamburger together. He even paid for it. I took him back to the Shopping Center and never saw him again. Smiley was the side kick to Gene Autry and many more western stars. They also called him Frog Milhouse.
Submitted by: Louie Walker, 803 Transmitter Rd., Springfield, FL 32401.

Sound Cameras and Television in Panama City

During the time I was working for WJHG- TV they did not have a sound camera. So I borrowed $450.00 from Commercial Bank and went to Pensacola and bought an Aricon Sound Camera. That sound camera worked fine as long as we were using black and white film. But after they changed over to color film, the machine I made would not process the soundtrack on the color film. So we decided to go to a magnetic strip and I bought another camera from Joc Howard. It was an Aricon and I modified it. I took that camera and put a magnetic sound track amplifier in it and then we could use magnetic sound along with our color film. One day me and Buddy Wilkes went to Tallahassee to a gathering for the Governor who was going to make a speech and news conference with all the reporters. The reporters were setting up their cameras and tape recorders and I just stood my camera up with the tripod and one of the guys asked me, "where is your amplifier?" And I said, "It's in the camera." He looked at his buddy and said, "I think they are drunk." But we beat them on the air with it. We came back and processed it and put it on the air.
Submitted by: Louie Walker, 803 Transmitter Rd., Springfield, FL 32401.

James Gray Owner of WJHG TV

James Gray was the owner of WJHG- TV and he was from Albany, Georgia. I was on the beach one day photographing a political rally and I had finished and was getting in my car and there was this big black convertible with a man sitting in the passenger side and a woman driving. They backed

into the front fender of my car. It was only a little dent. I walked over to the man and said, "I hope you have some good insurance." He looked up at me and said, "you work for me don't you." I says, "well who are you?" He said, "I'm James H. Gray. I own this TV Station that you work for." I said, "I always wanted that little dent in my fender." And we left it at that. They never would let me live that one down.
Submitted by: Louie Walker, 803 Transmitter Rd., Springfield, FL 32401.

Local News and Television

A lot of times when the Panama City Music Association would have shows, Inez Jones from the Bay County High School and I would go down and go back stage where they were putting on make-up. They wouldn't allow film to be made of the actual performer but they would let us go back and film them putting their make up on and practicing around a little bit. We did that many times.

I attended many military affairs conventions, meetings, chamber of commerce banquets, Christmas parties, you name it and I had to go take pictures. Being the only news photographer around I covered just about everything that was going on. I was on call mostly 24 hours a day and during the 12 years I was with Channel 7 I only took one vacation. While I was on that vacation, they had a murder up in Brannonville and I was called back from Wewahitchka to make some pictures of that.

I also was filming football games for the local high schools. We started off with Bay High School, just me and Bibiana Neal. She worked with us a lot at the TV station and begun to help me film the football games. Between the two of us we were able to film all of Bay High's games, make copies and process the film and get it to the coaches. Then Rutherford opened up and we took on Rutherford's games. We filmed those and I had to keep getting more cameras and more help. Then Mosley High School came along and we took those on. We furnished the film and processed them. The TV station allowed me to do free-lancing work. That was one of the things that we did.
Submitted by: Louie Walker, 803 Transmitter Rd., Springfield, FL 32401.

Earl Hadaway and Donnell Brookins

Earle Hadaway and myself did a lot of documentaries. We went to Fort Pickens in Pensacola. We filmed things there like re-enactments of when the Indian Geronimo fell and we also took Linda Lou Freeland to the Marianna Caverns with us where she was to model.

I also did the photography for Donnell Brookins when he was doing Panama Profile. He set up an operation at Bay Medical Center one day for us to film. Old Dr. Morris told

me after we filmed it, (he was operating on the patient) "I could see real good with your lights, the only problem was, they barbequed my patient." I had to have those bright lights on my camera.

I was talking to the station manager Jack Shouler

Earl Hadaway with Billie and Louie Walker

and he said we need to start up a kids program. The station was located at the old Commercial Bank building at Harrison Ave and Beach Drive. I said, "Well, you got as good a man as you could possible get that is working with you." Of course he wanted to know who that was, and I said that's Donnell Brookins. I said he is working up at the transmitter that's up in Youngstown and he said I'll have a talk with him. The next thing I know Donnell was doing "The Old Professor" (Professor Fluttervein, a kid's program). Donnell

went on to do the early morning show, "Day Buster's." And during the time he was on that he decided to run for tax collector and of course there was a conflict because he was on the air and the challenger wasn't. Donnell had to get off the air to run and he won the election. He was tax collector for years.
Submitted by: Louie Walker, 803 Transmitter Rd., Springfield, FL 32401.

Wilson Funeral Home

Wilson Funeral Home is the oldest family-owned business in Bay County and one of the oldest licensed funeral homes in the state of Florida. The funeral home operates under license number thirty-eight, and of those original thirty-eight licensed funeral homes, there are only six still in existence in the state. For four generations, the Wilson family has owned and operated Wilson Funeral Home.

John Stephen Wilson moved to Panama City from Florala, Alabama, around 1910 and began to operate the Wilson Furniture, Hardware and Undertaking business. The business had been purchased from Mr. Shepherd also of Florala, Mr.

Wilson's employer. At that time, Mr. Wilson was thirty years old, married, and father of a year old son, Wilbur Preston Wilson. The founder became an active member of the community and served as mayor of the City of Panama City from 1923 to 1925.

The funeral home was relocated several times around town before Mr. Wilson built the three-story building at 413 Harrison Avenue in 1926 now occupied by the Downtown Improvement Board. The building was the first three-story building in the city and was considered "slap out of town" according to a newspaper article. The hardware store was on the ground level with the furniture on the second floor and the funeral

John Stephen Wilson, Founder of Wilson Funeral Home

home on the third floor. The telephone number for the business was "three three".

Mr. Wilson sold the hardware and furniture merchandise, and the building was leased to Rhodes Furniture. In 1940 he built the brick, colonial building at 301 McKenzie Avenue to house the funeral home. The two-story building with a basement is adjacent to the Courthouse and currently owned by the County.

During World War II metal caskets were scarce because of the demand for metal during the war. Mr. Wilson had stockpiled as many metal caskets in his basement as possible. National Casket Company in Atlanta had two seamless, copper-deposit caskets. Mr. Wilson purchased one of the caskets thinking someone of prominence might die during the war. Mr. Wilson himself was interred in the casket at the time of his death in 1956. The second casket had been purchased by a funeral home in Atlanta and was used for President Franklin Delano Roosevelt at the time of his death in Warm Springs, Georgia, on April 12, 1945.

Perhaps one of the most memorable funerals to be held in the McKenzie Avenue address was that of the 'King of the Gypsies'. He died on November I, 1948, and was interred in Meridian, Mississippi. The newspaper gave this account, "The special guard of tribesmen, stationed according to custom at Wilson's

Four Generations: Wilbur P. Wilson, Portrait of John Stephen Wilson, J. Steve Wilson, II, Steve Wilson, III

Funeral Home, yesterday permitted over 3,000 local residents to view the flower banked bier." The gypsies came from all over the country for the wake. The procession to Mississippi also saw bands of travelers at many crossroads waiting to join the procession.

At the time of Mr. Wilson's death in 1956, he was married to Grace West, grand-

Wilson Funeral Home at 301 McKenzie Avenue

daughter of George Mortimer West, one of the pioneers of the county. They are buried in Greenwood Cemetery along with his son, Wilbur Wilson, who died in 1991. The daughter-in-law, Lennie Killingsworth Wilson, still resides in Panama City.

The grandson of the founder, John Stephen Wilson, II, went to work for the funeral home in the late 1950's, He and his wife, Sandra Adams Wilson, lived upstairs in the colonial building during their first year of marriage. At that time funeral homes did emergency and non-emergency ambulance calls. Mrs. Wilson recalls the fear of being alone in the funeral home at night when her husband went on ambulance calls.

The founder's son and grandson moved the funeral home to its present location at 214 Airport Road in 1964. The founder's great-grandchildren, John Stephen Wilson, III, and Kimberly Wilson Houser carry on the family tradition of managing the funeral home.

Submitted by: Sandra Adams Wilson 2440 Pretty Bayou Boulevard, Panama City, Florida 32405.

SCHOOLS

A. D. Richbourg Gymnasium

A. D. Richbourg was honored by the P. T. O. of Hiland Park Elementary School, Faculty, Staff, Parents and Students, Friends and the Bay County School Board with the naming of the gymnasium for him.

It all began when he felt the need for the students to have a place for P. E. during bad weather. The original Hiland Park Elementary School Building was not being used for anything specific, and the dream came to him to renovate it for students' activities. This was late 1982 and early 1983. He worked unassisted on the old building, tearing out, adding load bearing studs, crawling under the building using his own jacks, etc. to level and reinforce the flooring. He worked with extension cord lighting. The school board could not afford to help, so he worked even harder to complete the task. The P. T. O. helped as much as they could. An inexpensive carpet was put down so that students could be comfortable for floor activities.

In August of 1983, A D. had a heart attack from all the stressful work He was flown to Pensacola for open-heart surgery as there was not a cardiac wing set up in Bay County at that time. Dr. Cook was the referring physician and made all the arrangements for the flight After coming home, his first stop was to ride by the school and just look at it He sat in his office chair, and it felt so good.

All the above mentioned people persuaded the Bay County School Board to allow them to name the building, the A. D. Richbourg Gymnasium. Upon his retirement in 1989, the faculty and staff honored him with a retirement reception in "his" gymnasium.

The old building is no longer on the premises, but a new building paid for by the P. T. O., Students, Parents, Faculty, Staff, School Board and SallyMae Foundation, now houses the physical education activities. It is named the A. D. Richbourg Health & Fitness Building. The dedication was in May 1997, Larry Bolinger, Superintendent of Schools. A D. is humbled by this honor and his family is very proud of his contributions to the Hiland Park Elementary School

Mildred & A. D. in front of the plaque naming the Gym

and to the children who have given him such pleasure throughout the years.

Submitted by: Mildred Penton Richbourg, wife of A D. Richbourg, 3909 W. 16th St., Panama City, Fl 32401.

Bay County High School

Graduating Class of 1931

1st Row - Seated Alma Lee Gainous, Frances Mozley, Eleanor Payne, Kathryn Yonge, Ruby Palmer, Iris Gwaltney, Marion Ingram, Carroll Weller, Rufus Allan, Shelton Gray, Jack Baxter, William Peters and James Howard.

2nd Row - Seated on Bricks - Dicie Hayes and Muriel Jones; Alma Davis, Viola Barber, Alma Turner, Pearl Murray,

My mother Alma Turner Harmon is in this picture

unknown, Gladys McBride, Doris Todd, Jewel Ellerbee, Thelma Ellerbee, June Bullard, Theodore Perkins, John Peterson, Wood Mowbray, James Look, Shellman Stevenson, Francis Marshall, and Carl Gray.

3rd Row - Standing on Bricks - Theresa Pledger and Bernice Griffin; Frances Morris, Virginia Mizell, Jack Murray, Mary Miller, Carl Long, Ruth Long, Margaret Conant, Etta Belle Fleming, Marion Roache and Johnny Hawkins.

4th Row - Ruby Gainous, Pauline McGill, James Pate, Sleepy Ogburn, Kathleen McKnight, Clarence Ware, Powell Adams, Randall Mathis, Marion Nelson and William Mozley. Not pictured - Virgil Anderson.

Picture submitted by: Shirley (Harmon) Brookins, 136 Cottonwood Cir., Lynn Haven FL 32444.

Bay High Band

When I went to Bay High, I didn't want to get into athletics. I weighed about 135 or 140 pounds and I thought I was not physically big enough to compete. So I got into the band.

In Millville over at Millville Baptist Church, now the Emmanuel Baptist Church, they had a seven shaped, seven note shaped do, re, mi, fa, sol, la, ti, do, two weeks' musical program at the church. It was Sacred Heart music and Mama sent me there for two weeks. I had a basic understanding of a bar of music and the clefs and this sort of thing. So when I went to Bay High and got into the band, I got along famously and the first thing you know I was first trombone and then I was captain of the band.

Our mothers made our first band uniforms, capes and we bought a derby hat from Kentucky which came from the Kentucky Derby. They had white tops that you could take off and wash and they cost five dollars apiece. On June 5, 1938 the band went to Cottonwood, Alabama and we serenaded an 80 year old grandmother up there. Three of the boys in the band, the Hodges boys and the Rushing boy were her grandsons. We played "Let Me Call You Sweetheart, I'm In Love With You." And she just blushed all over the place. She was Grandma Rushing. Also in the band was the Fouraker boys and Emmett Harrison. Charles Earl Hodges is now a Baptist minister retired. He was chaplain at Gulf Coast Hospital.
Submitted by: Fred Turner, 2694 Island View Dr., Panama City, FL 32405.

Bay High Band Fundraising

When I was a sophomore at Bay High School, someone formed a committee to investigate buying buses for the band and athletic departments. A fund-raising drive was instituted and my parents were active in the group. I don't remember everything they did to raise the money but eventually, three buses were purchased. The buses were painted red and white and the two departments shared those buses for several years.

As band members we were allowed to earn money towards our trips for district and state festivals with fundraisers. One time we sold light bulbs. As I remember, I sold enough to pay for my share of the trip expenses and have spending money also.

Band members also sold ads in the football programs. At that time, we had the football programs printed and gave them away free. The band sold ads to pay for the program and to raise money for the music and athletic departments. These programs contained a center section with the football players listed and the visiting team players listed, a front page with the date and the teams, a back page with a picture of the full band, the officers, the band director, and a paragraph about that night's performance. The rest of the program had pages of pictures and ads. The pictures were taken by my dad and were of the football team, the coaches, the principal, the majorettes/twirling corps, and the cheerleaders.
Submitted by: Susan Jones Moore, 310 S. Palo Alto Ave., Panama City, FL 32401, Bay High Class of 1960.

Bay High Days

After I graduated from Millville Grammar School in 1936, I started at Bay High School. The first year you go to Bay High and the first day you get off the bus, you have to run through a belt line. Here was all these Panama City boys had their belts off and would hit you across the rump with their belts. Joe Mitchell was at the end of the belt line on the right-hand side and as I passed him I left my kneecap right in his crotch. I looked back and Joe was all bent over saying, "Oh, oh, oh, let me die, let me die." He got along all right. It was just my way of getting back for that hazing that we had to take. Now, not the girls. The girls just walked off the bus and walked right into Bay High.

I went four years at Bay High. In 1937 Oren Whitley came over here as band director from Tallahassee. I was the first captain of the Bay High Band. I played trombone and my brother James played trombone before me in Sorrentino's Band. In 1923 they went to Marianna and they joined a circus band of The Mighty Hague Circus and played in a Shrine ceremonial for Morocco Temple. A lot of people were joining the Shrine. The circus band was led by a fifteen year old nephew of Mr. Hague and he was a trumpeter and his name was Harry Hague James. Harry James later became a famous trumpeter and band leader. Mr. Hague only had one arm. I remember seeing Mr. Hague several times when his circus would come to Panama City. He had a one ring circus. It was just a little bigger and better than a taffy show, but, you know,

you had performers out there, jugglers and things like that and you could buy saltwater taffy.

We also had a glee club at Bay High School. Louise Blacksheer taught glee club. I sang in 1937 at the Christmas Program for the First Baptist Church. I sang "The Holy City."
Submitted by: Fred Turner, 2694 Island View Dr., Panama City, Fl 32405.

Bay High School Band

In the early 1930's Ralph William Sorrentino started a band for Bay County High School, rehearsed that band in the evenings and never charged for his work. If a child wanted to play in the band, Ralph would see that an instrument was provided even if he had to pay for it himself. It is no wonder that the Sorrentino budget was always just sufficient to cover everything. Much was also due to Lillie, his wife, who was able to stretch household expenses to make ends meet. The Bay High Band and the Panama City Municipal Band which Ralph also began were Ralph's joy, but he also took pride in his teaching music to the young and the old and especially he took pride in his family.
Submitted by: Marie Sorrentino Waller Lee, 1002 Iowa Ave, Lynn Haven, FL 32444.

The Bay High School Class Who Had No School Annual

It was the 1942-1943 Bay High School students who were feeling the brunt of World War II. So many of the senior class boys dropped out of school to join military units, some never to return home.

Students would bring their dimes to purchase savings stamps which would be converted to bonds when the book was filled. Organizations such as the Defense Club and Victory Garden Club were ways to contribute to the war efforts.

Everything was rationed! Gas, tires, shoes and foods which curtailed the many activities young students were accustomed to. They walked, car-pooled, rode the City Transit Bus, or rode bicycles even as far as the first parking lot, past the Old Dutch Tavern on the beach.

Many of the senior girls attended the weekly USO dances which were held in the USO building at the end of Harrison Avenue.

Events such as the Junior-Senior Prom, the Halloween Carnival set up on Tommy Oliver Field (next to the school building), dances after the football games, crowning of a Halloween Queen, Mildred Penton, were continued.

Other popular places were the Glenn, the Hang Out, and dancing upstairs at the Long Beach Pavilion. Sometimes they had a band there, one being Coleman Sax! The logo was "Relax with Coleman Sax".

Sixty years later, the classmates often reminisce over what might have been in the Year Book had we had one!
Submitted by: The Bay High Alumni of 1943. Written by: Mildred Penton Richbourg, 3909 W. 16th St., Panama City, FL 32401-1108.

Bay High School Football Team 1942-1943

Top L-R: Glen Quickle, Coach Rushie, Buddy Jencks; 3rd row: Bertice Murphy, Leslie Jenks, Jim Porter, A C. Smith, L. N. Mapes, Lloyd Warren, C. G. Reeves; 2nd row: Truby Shaw, Billy Howell, Richard Davis, Harry Quickle, James Cooper, Marion Hoskins, Harrell Adams, Bill Redmond, Mitchell Johnson; 1st row. Carter Norris, Henry Pennington, Wesley Brannon, Phil Taylor, Doyl Parker, Spencer "Onion" Davis, Harold Conrad, Reggie Gainer, Charles Blackburn, E. J. Quigley, Johnny Warren.

Bay High School Football Team 1942-1943   Front   L-R:

Managers: John Albert Delcomyn, Amos Williams, _____ Bond?

Submitted by: John Albert Delcomyn, senior 1943, P. O. Box 198, Youngstown, FL 32466.

Bay High School Halloween Carnival Queen October 1942

Mildred Penton, senior, was crowned Bay High School's Halloween Queen. The crowning and grand march was in the Bay High School Gym. Alfred "Sonny" Myers was her escort.

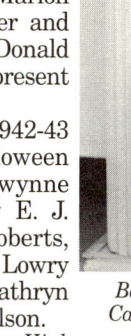

Little Miss Gretchen Nelson daughter of Mr. & Mrs. Marion Nelson, was the crownbearer and the small son of Mr. & Mrs. Donald Wasson was dressed to represent Uncle Sam.

Other candidates for the 1942-43 Bay High School Halloween Carnival Queen were: Gwynne Gainer, Junior, escorted by E. J. Quiqley; Maxine Roberts, Sophomore, escorted by J. W. Lowry and Freshman candidate, Kathryn McCabe escorted by Carl Nelson.

Bay High School Halloween Carnival Queen October 1942

Submitted by: The Bay High Graduating Class of 1943. Written by: Mildred Penton Richbourg, 3909 W. 16th St., Panama City, FL 32401-1108.

Delta Hi Social Club 1943

Bay High School Delta Hi Club members pictured in their gowns, holding their morter board, wearing bathing suits under their robes—ready for the beach!

Top L-R: Margaret "Duby" Lynch, Mildred Penton, Elizabeth "Didgie" McConnel, Gwen Newbern, Marion Gay.

Bottom L-R: Yvonne Wallace, Gene Howell, Helen Thompson, Betty Sue Spiva, Betty Jean Wilson, Ruby Williams.

Delta Hi Social Club 1943

Not pictured: Ann Coleman, Rosa Mae Lynd, Sue Hawkins, Sally Swank, Marie Everitt.

Submitted by: The Bay Hi Graduating class of 1943, 3909 W 16th St., Panama City, FL 32401-1108.

The Beginning of Cherry Street School

When my class was entering the 4th grade, the School Board decided the Cove needed another elementary school as Cove School was becoming crowded. The decision was made to take all three 4th grade classes, bus them over each morning to barracks which had been set up on the side of what is now Cherry Street School. We were bused to the barracks in the morn-

Miss Ernestine Hudson's 4th Grade Class at new Cherry Street School location in the Cove. Students were in 1960 graduating class of Bay High School

ing, bused back to Cove School for lunch, bused back to the barracks for the afternoon, and bused back to Cove after classes were over.

Now, it's only a few blocks but back then it seemed a long way.

The roads were all dirt. There was no shopping center, and few houses that far down Cherry Street.

We were told we could have the privilege of naming the new school to be built on that site. I don't know if the powers that be were actually serious; but, as I remember, Diana Fitzpatrick submitted the name Cherry Street School.

Two years later, the new school was finished and someone drew a dividing line, separating us in the 6th grade from people who had been in school with us for 5 years. In 7th grade, we all entered Jinks and a new school experience.

The photo is of our 4th grade class, Miss Ernestine Hudson, teacher.

Submitted by: Susan Jones Moore, 310 S. Palo Alto Ave., Panama City FL 32401.

Bonavista Academy, First School on St. Andrew Bay

Mr. E.W. Carswell in his book <u>Washington Florida's Twelfth County</u> observed that: "Bonavista Academy, the first center, was established on St Andrews Bay in the summer of 1827. A Mr. Wachob of Georgia was the teacher. Among those instrumental in establishing the academy were former governor John Clark of Georgia and the Rev. Peter W. Gautier, a Methodist minister who had recently come from Georgia. He had first made his home in Jackson County, where he had helped establish Webbville Academy". Bonavista Academy listed a curriculum that included these subjects: Spelling, reading, writing and arithmetic; grammar, geography, logic and natural philosophy; mathematics and the languages, according to Mr. E.W. Carswell. How long the "academy" remained operational is open to question. It might have retained the designation while being operated as a community school.

On February 8, 1838, the Florida Legislative Council approved the Charter and Incorporation of St. Andrews College to be located on St Andrews Bay. Due to the economic panic that descended on the territory the college failed to become operational.

In 1871, 30 students were enrolled at the Econfina School. By 1873, B.B. Brown was paid $18.00 per month as a Econfina teacher.

In September of 1877 schools were approved for three-month terms and the board adopted the Webster Elementary Speller for use. In the middle of 1882 the board authorized a four-month school term.

On July 2, 1883 school started at Econfina and other Washington County schools.

Allocations were made for operational expense at Bear Creek, Econfina and other schools. On December 6, 1884 Washington County levied a 4 mil tax for school purposes. Econfina School got $60.00, Sulphur Springs got $80.00, Parker School got $80.00.

On the 28th of December, 1889 Washington County School Board authorized high schools at Chipley and St. Andrews Bay, subject to approval of voters in the special tax school district. February 28,1890 brought a vote of 60 to 11 to approve the Chipley High School. On March 28, 1890 the vote for St. Andrew School carried by a 22 to 10 vote.

Submitted by: Jack Mashburn, Camp Flowers Rd., Panama City, FL.

Cove School

The gem of Panama City's historic Cove Section is the former Cove Elementary School that currently serves as Holy Nativity Episcopal School. At 205 Hamilton Avenue, the property is bounded on the east, south, west, and north respectively by Hamilton Avenue, 2nd Street, Linda Avenue, and 2nd Court. The property was originally donated for use as a school, and the original building was erected and put into use in 1937 as Cove Elementary School, with seven classrooms serving the area of Panama City roughly from 6th Street (highway 98) south to St. Andrew's

Cove Elementary School

Bay, and from Massalina Bayou on the west to Watson Bayou on the east. In the mid-1940's, responding to population growth, the Cove School building was more than doubled in size to add new classrooms and offices, with the new structure extending to the south. The old and new sections are easily distinguishable by the fact that classrooms in the original section have five windows, while the classrooms in the 1940's addition have six windows and a window for a "cloak room." Inside, the different sections are noted by the hall floor line, and especially by the use of tongue-in-groove planking in the original ceilings and hall, where the newer addition has plaster walls and ceilings. In 1950 the building was expanded further to add an auditorium and two classrooms on the northern end of the property bordering 2nd Court, and a library in the center of the main building.

Elementary grades 1 through 8 were taught there from 1937 until 1950, when Bay County opened junior high schools. At that time, Cove Elementary changed to grades 1 through 6 and so operated until 1988. In 1988 the Bay District Schools discontinued using the building as a school, boarded up the windows, and converted it to use for storage.

In 1998 the property was acquired by the Holy Nativity School Foundation. Over the next two years it underwent massive renovation to restore its original appearance and to prepare it for reopening as Holy Nativity Episcopal School. Like history repeating, the original section was renovated first and opened in August 1999 as Holy Nativity Episcopal Middle School, Grades 6-8. Renovation continued without pause, and the newer south end was opened for the fall semester 2000. Currently the building has classrooms, offices, library, auditorium, lunchroom, and maintenance facilities housing Holy Nativity Episcopal School grades 3-8.

Holy Nativity School Foundation owns the property and has leased it to the Episcopal Diocese of the Central Gulf Coast for use by Holy Nativity Episcopal School. The Foundation was established specifically to acquire and renovate Cove School for Holy Nativity Episcopal School, to ensure that this beloved, magnificent Panama City landmark is preserved, and to make the building and grounds available for public enjoyment. Foundation members and many student families in the school today have a long family history with Cove School. Some attended Cove School throughout the 1940's for their entire grades 1-8, some for grades 1-6. To all, the beautiful historic property is a source of unending pride and is the focus of much hard work and very much love.
Submitted by: Tom Weller, 2308 West Beach Drive, Panama City, Florida 32401.

Covenant Christian School

Covenant Christian School was established in the fall of 1982 to provide an educational opportunity consistent with our reformed world and life view. Additional space for the school was obtained in late 1982 when the old Callaway Elementary School building was acquired and moved across town. It was completely renovated and refurbished by the fall opening of school in 1983 when a Kindergarten and First Grade were added.

Grades two through six were added in the fall of 1984. Grades seven and eight were added in the fall of 1987 and grades nine through twelve in 1988. In the fall of 2001 three temporary modular buildings were added and the Callaway building removed to make way for the construction of a gymnasium.

Our present two story educational facility was begun in 1987. The first floor was completed and occupied by the spring of 1988. The second floor was only an empty shell in 1988 that was completed over the next five years.
Submitted by: Mona Lucas, 3235 Orlando Rd, Panama City, FL.

The Earliest Schools

The one-room log cabin school pictured here was built in 1857. My great grandfather, James Manon Mashburn donated timber and helped to build this school near Sulphur Springs on Econfina Creek. My father, Mansel D. Mashburn, the grandson of James Manon Mashburn attended this school through the fourth grade. This was during the 1870's.

Mr. E.W. Carswell in his book <u>Washington Florida's Twelfth County</u>, writing about schools in the earliest days observed that:

"As local communities developed, residents would pool their labor and other resources to build a one-room schoolhouse of round or hewn logs. A typical schoolhouse had one door and a small window closed by wooden shutters on each side.

A stick and clay chimney with a big open fireplace often stood at the end opposite the door. Such structures were often used for religious services as well as for school purposes. Pupils sat on crude four-legged benches made of split logs. Textbooks, slates and pencils were

John Daniel Cox, born February 22, 1892, standing next to the old school building

scarce, with goose quill pens and pokeberry ink often used for writing and ciphering. Emphasis in the ungraded school was placed on reading, spelling, writing and arithmetic.

There were few or no public supported schools prior to 1869 in Washington County, from which Bay County was created. It seems a strange coincidence that public school support started the year my father, Mansel D. Mashburn was born. My father loved to read and encouraged all his children to read everything, he said, "read everything, just don't believe everything you read".
Submitted by: Jack Mashburn, Camp Flowers Rd., Panama City, FL.

Econfina School House

In the early 1930's the Econfina School House had grades Primmer, as known in those days, through eight. In the period of about 1934-35 through 1942-43 is when I attended the school, walking approximately five miles. I have certificates showing I was never absent or tardy for three of those years. There was only

one teacher the majority of the time. A cast iron heater adorned the center of the one room.

The school house was used not only for school but church meetings and as an election polling place and anything else when needed. Some of the teachers that I recall were Mrs. Griggs, Mr. Archie C. Hutchison, and Mrs. Sellers.

As I was told, the school property was acquired thru a swap of property from the old Gainers, black, former slaves, for property to the northeast closer to Moccasin Creek. I knew both the old Gainers when I was a young boy as Uncle

Econfina School House

Andrew and Aunt Jenny.

In the last years of my school days, we had boys and girls outhouses. Prior to that time we simply went into the woods. I never recall seeing toilet paper; Sears Roebuck Catalogs and the like were always present. The WPA did the outhouse installation.

The pitcher pumps were not always functional/operational for water and we got water from a sweet water spring south of the school. It was likely on the Gainers' property because they did their wash, boiled their clothes and most times got their water from the spring. They also did washing for others at this source. Other family members used it as a water supply hauling the buckets on their heads for a considerable distance. There were three or four houses (more like shacks) that were owned by family members a bit south and west of the old Gainer home, most of their names were Gainer also.

There was not a black school on Econfina Creek. They were schooled in the Black Church west of this school and on the same road before crossing Econfina Creek. I would guess it is two miles away. When I was walking approximately five miles, my black friend and walking companion, Clarence Johnson, was walking seven miles or better. A tough way to get an education. There is lots of history associated with the school and it is sad that most of the individuals that had information are now deceased.

Contributed by: Jack Mashburn. Written by: William Carthell Adams, 1421 Valencia Ave., San Bernardino, CA 92404.

Goethe Schoolhouse on Banks Property

In 1929, Ed and Lucy Banks offered a one-room wooden structure for a schoolhouse on their place at Goethe, which was a whistle stop on the B C & St Andrews Line two miles south of Crystal Lake. Mrs. Banks was a RN and midwife and helped deliver many of the area's children.

Dean Delores Butler Banks and Esther Banks standing behind some children. The Goethe Schoolhouse can be seen behind the group.

Submitted by: BeeBee Russell Deal, 15116 Highway 77, Southport, FL 32409.

Grammar School Days

The St. Andrew's Grammar School was the only school from West Beach Drive to Hathaway Bridge. There was no busing and most of the students walked. We had an hour for lunch and I went to my home. A lunchroom was provided at the school and they had very good vegetable soup. I always hurried back to school to play. Jump board was my favorite. Boards were placed on top of each other and a wide board placed across the top so that two people, one on each end of the board, could jump sending the other up in the air. Mr. Merritt Brown was Principal and loved to assemble the students in the auditorium and we would sing from "The One Hundred and One Best Loved Songs" Book.

In the sixth grade we planned the Candy Club. Every Friday after school we went to a friend's home and made candy. Our agenda was to make candy and then eat it. Prom parties became popular. We made prom cards, decorating them with cut outs then numbers. We invited an equal number of girls and boys. This was held at our homes and the boy was to ask for a prom filling out the girl's card. You walked a designated route and then you proceeded with your next prom partner. Kissing was a No, No! I really never did understand the game of Post Office.

Graduation from the eighth grade was a big event. Girls wore their first formal dresses. Those with high scholastic records were recognized. Gifts were received. Many students dropped out of school at this time.

Submitted by: Gene Howell Sapp, 1409 Deer Avenue, Panama City, FL 32401.

High School Days

Going to Bay High was a great adventure! I liked riding the bus with friends. This was the only High School in the county. The school was crowded during the year 1939. Our Home Economics classes were held in the school lobby and the study hall in the auditorium was full.

There was a large wooden gym for the basketball games and band room. The football games were held at the local baseball stadium, later named Lion's Park. While in Grammar School busses took us to these football games. It was cold and you might see a bonfire on the grounds. A football field was built on Harrison Avenue adjacent to the high school with students holding a Halloween Carnival with booths and entertainment and profits for our football field. After the games there was a dance in the gym. Dates were not necessary for boys or girls. The girls sat on the bleachers and the boys formed a stag line on the gym floor and asked the girls to dance. There was not a live orchestra. The gym was not heated and during the coldest weather I covered the hood of my parent's car with blankets so the car would start later.

Prior to the football games, they would announce on the speaker system in the classroom the name of the girls who had been selected by the football players to be sponsors. It was an honor and we were excited when our name was called. This meant that you would buy a bouquet of white chrysanthemums and at the game, during half time, you presented them to selected football players. The player accepted the flowers and then gave them to his girlfriend.

Submitted by: Gene Howell Sapp, 1409 Deer Avenue, Panama City, FL 32401.

High School Days During W. W. II

My Senior year in high school the country entered World War II. Our boys were given an option of joining the service and receiving their high school diploma at mid year. Many changes took place. Tyndall Field and Wainwright Shipyard caused a great influx of people in this community. The population of Panama City increased from 15,000 to 45,000 people over night. Government housing projects were built throughout the community. Double busses with trailers were brought in to help with transportation. We all used the busses because of gasoline rationing. The new housing had ice-boxes. Ice was brought in by railroad from Wisconsin. I would see

Genevive Pouncy Rouse and Gene Howell Sapp at a 2003 Class of 1943 Reunion from Bay High School

cars in line at the St. Andrews Ice Plant to get ice for their new apartment. Milk was shipped also. Sugar and shoes were rationed.

The USO building was constructed at Harrison Avenue by the Bay as a center for the servicemen stationed at Tyndall Air Force Base. Entertainment included dances on Wednesday evenings and Saturday afternoons with the Tyndall Dance Band. This was great entertainment for the local girls and our mothers who served as chaperones also. On Thursday evenings we met at the USO and were provided transportation to the Non Commissioned Officers Club at Tyndall for the dance. You were not allowed to leave these dances with the servicemen.

My big disappointment came when I could not go to my Senior Prom; I woke up with a case of the measles.

Submitted by: Gene Howell Sapp, 1409 Deer Avenue, Panama City, FL 32401.

Hiland Park Elementary School

Hiland Park Elementary was built in 1937. The single building housed five classrooms and all other support services. In 1972, a combined media center and open classroom complex with over 9,000 additional square feet were constructed. Within this construction were five new classrooms.

In 1983, the original building was opened up on the interior to create a gymnasium for physical education classes and space for assemblies. This was done by the principal, A. D. Richbourg, and a host of volunteers.

In 1984, due to growth and deterioration of older construction, a five-room kindergarten complex was built, in addition to another 10,000 square foot building. That building now houses basic classrooms, music, art, and classes for Exceptional Education students.

In 1999, a new gymnasium was constructed with financial assistance from the Bay District School Board, the Hiland Park PTO, and Sallie Mae Serving Center. The gymnasium was named, in dedication, "the A.D. Richbourg Gymnasium".

For the next few years after that, a major renovation project refurbished most areas of the school and the original building, being used as the gym, was torn down. The old building is now, as we say, "History" and it exists only in our memories.

Today we have a comfortable and modern facility, which is both aesthetically pleasing and conducive to learning. We are, as we always have been, proud of Hiland Park Elementary School.

Submitted by: Craig Bush, Principal of Hiland Park Elementary School, 1301 Georgia Avenue, Lynn Haven, Florida 32444.

History of Southport Elementary School PTA

The first Parent Teacher Association of Southport Elementary School was organized in the school year 1936-37. Mrs. J. F. Mason was the president, Mr. E. R. Simmons was the school principal. There are no records of the PTA for the school years 1938-39 and

1939-40. In 1940-41 the PTA was again active, Mrs. Minnie Cavanaugh was president. The membership fee was 25 cents and there were 17 charter members.

For the school years 1941-42 Mrs. Maude Miller was PTA president. The minutes indicate all activities and programs for that year would center on conditions that existed in those times (WW II). The theme for 1941-42 was 'PTA and Victory'. Membership had grown to 23 people. They sponsored the lunchroom and first-aid classes for parents and staff. There are 16 former principals listed in the meeting minutes for that school year.

A few of the PTA members from the 1940's; Mrs. Frank Reeder, Mrs. Maude Miller, Mrs. Lena Richardson, Mrs. Myrtle Penny, Mrs. W.D. Gainer and Mrs. W.M. Sapp. Most of those members still have family living in Southport today. In some of these families their children, grand-children, and now, great-grandchildren have attended Southport Elementary School!

For the next few years the PTA was inactive, possibly because of the war. Today, the Parent Teacher Organization is very active at Southport Elementary! They hold fund-raisers and festivals to enrich the school in so many ways. Our parents and staff work together energetically to enable our school to be the best it can be.
Submitted by: Angela Miller, 1732 Courtland Place, Southport, Fl 32409.

Teaching School

My sister Lucille, after she graduated from Bay High, applied for a teaching certificate. If you were a graduate of a high school, you could get a teaching certificate. She got one and she taught at Southport in a one-room school house, grades one through twelve. My sister Alma, who also graduated from Bay High, would fill in for her while she and Ralph Newberry dated and went to motion picture theaters.
Submitted by: Fred Turner, 2694 Island View Dr, Panama City, FL 32405.

Memories of Hiland Park School

When starting to school, all of the children had to be carried by touring car to Panama Grammar or Cove School. It was driven by a Mr. Parker.

When I was in the seventh grade my father was told by Mr. J.C. Stewart that we might have to go to the Lynn Haven School the next year. He said a signed petition might help us to get a school in our community. Dad took a petition around for people to sign. About this time the name of the community was changed to Highland City. With the petition signed, they took it to Superintendent Hardy on July 7, 1936 and a school was organized. Cary T. Hartzog, W.R. Renfroe and J.C. Stewart began a search for teachers. H. D. Foreman donated 5 acres of land to build the school on. The people were not able to furnish enough money so Mr. A.H. Sheffield stood good for a loan at the bank and the WPA took over the construction, as they were already building the Jetties in this area. The school was finished in time for classes to start in the fall of 1937.

There were two rooms west of the hall and the east side had folding doors to make two rooms with a stage at the north end so it could be used for an auditorium when needed. Students sat in desks discarded by Panama Grammar or on benches made from planks and buckets. Water was furnished by an old hand pump and tasted of sulfur and iron. Since there was no lunchroom, we had to bring our lunches or walk home, which was for most of us too far away to walk and get back in one hour. There was no electricity and heat was provided by a wood-burning heater in each room.

Teachers in 1937-38 were Mrs. Alva M. Murray, Mrs. H.D. Foreman and Mrs. Ruby Chalker, Mr. Alva M. Murray was elected as Principal and doubled as a teacher for the higher grades. He was my teacher in the eighth grade.

Those who graduated in 1938

The first Eighth grade graduating class of Highland Park Elementary in 1938

were Sam Whithurst, Edna Hutto, Ina Coburger, Ruby Lee Hartzog, Lois Tulanne Davis and Roena Bradford. With Perfect Attendance that first year were: Frances Stuckey, Truman Hartzog, Coley Whithurst, Margaret Hartzog, Lindberg Whithurst, Iris Murray, Loette Neal, Hannah Skipper and Sam Whithurst.

Due to the impact of military personnel because of the war, the Government aided with the enlargement of the school. Three more classrooms and an office were built. Bayou George school consolidated with Highland City School.

In 1950 the seventh and eighth grades were moved to junior high schools, leaving only grades one through six in Highland City Elementary. About this time a post office substation was established in a grocery store in Highland City, forcing the name change of the city to Hiland Park, so our mail would not go to the Highland City post office in South Florida.

In the 1960's our wooden school building was moved to the back side of the property and office suites, a cafeteria and a library were built. In the 1970's five classrooms and a Learning Center were added. Then temporary buildings were added for music and SLD programs. The old wooden school became a gymnasium. In 1982 more room was needed so a new wing was added. Hiland Park School went from 4 classrooms and 3 teachers in 1937 to, at last count, 38 classroom teachers, a complete Media Center, a Cafeteria, a gymnasium, SLD, EMH Chapter one, Quest Programs, Art Classes, Guidance Counselors, a Support Staff and Administrators by 1986. It is still growing.
Submitted by: Ruby Lee "Hartzog" Strickland, 2627 Game Farm Road, Panama City, Fl. 32405.

Millville School

I remember Millville School burning in 1930. Kate Hubbard was my teacher that year. The children went to school at a flag station on the railroad, in the area where the paper mill is now. They were dynamiting for stumps across the railroad tracks. They told us not to go across the railroad tracks because we would be in danger. Those dynamite sticks would go off and our school books would jump all over the table and we'd have to hold them down. They told us to expect loud noises over there and we did. That was a kind of hiccup in my education.

I graduated from Millville Grammar School in 1936. Bill Harris was a year behind me and so was Dempsey Barron. They're the two well-known people from Millville but there were other people there such as Fred Bryant and all those girls. Judy Rigell was in the first grade with me and she was in the second grade with me and that was 1930. Her family lived where later the dock area of the paper mill was built. When the paper mill came in there, they had to move. So they moved their house over to the south side of the courthouse. Judy was my age and she and Sarah Singletary were two competitors in school on short division and long division problems. The teacher would have the problem on the board and send us to the board with a piece of chalk. It was a speed contest. Those girls would beat me like a drum. I still remember it to this day. Sarah Singletary married Megs Hallmon in 1938 and they have a son who is a dentist here, Dr. David Hallmon.
Submitted by: Fred Turner, 2694 Island View Dr, Panama City, Fl 32405.

Northside School

Our family moved into the Northside School District when Northside was the newest elementary school in the county and Joe Rogers was the well-liked principal. The woods surrounding Northside School made the location look more like "God's County" than a place inside the city limits. Northside Drive, the paved road that led south past the school from 23rd Street, changed to sand at the end of the school grounds. All this property had originally been part of the huge Moates Pond, a swamp that stretched from what is now 15th Street to Highway 231. Moates Pond was a popular place for early settlers to fish and hunt alligators.

Even at this late date, huge hawks and herons could be spied in the dead tree tops of these wetlands and whippoorwills gave their plaintive cries at night in the Spring. After a heavy rain, millions of happy frogs croaked in unison, so loud their sounds could be heard through closed windows and doors.

On rare occasions, deer, wild hogs and foxes appeared along the roads in the early morning and late evenings, reminiscent of Old

Florida. In Spring at the edge of these roads and wetlands, big, juicy wild plums dangled from the branches and huge blue dewberries swayed on their stems in the breeze. Both the plums and dewberries made excellent jellies.

Behind Northside, which was all wooded with a dirt trail running between 19th Street and the school, Fred Womack caught a beautiful bass in one of the ponds that remained from the past He yelled all the way home, letting everyone know about his prized fish.
Submitted by: Marlene Womack, 25 W. Government St., Panama City, FL 32401.

One Room School in Callaway

The One Room School in Callaway, Florida, was built in 1911 in what was then, Washington County, since Bay County was not formed until July 1913. The land was donated by Pitt Milner Carlisle who platted the area in 1911. A drive was started by Hettina Fox, (Grandma Ettie) to have a school built at what is now the south-west corner of Letohatchee and Beulah Streets. The children then had to walk to the Parker School a distance of about three miles through woods and a small creek to school. Grandma Ettie believed "Every child should have the chance to learn to read" and her persistence paid off, and the building was constructed. The first teacher was Miss Kate McMillan, from Vernon, Florida. Other teachers: were: Ruby Shutts, Mr. Baldwin, Kate Jones, Mrs. Bostick, Mr. Pollock, Thelma Jernigan, Dell Davis, Alma Davis, Miss Leah Ramey, Maida Coon, Tommie Nolan, Miss Annie Bell Phillips, (who married Mr. Rudy Gaskin while here), Beatrice Baxter, Ruth Martin, Genevieve Sorensen, Nora Burkett, among others. The first trustees were: James Burkett, Sr., Earl Bright and Leonard Coon.

Callaway School, built in 1911

The building served, not only as the school, but also was the social center for the community. There was always a community celebration at Christmas with a Live Christmas Tree that reached the ceiling, trimmed with crepe paper and real little candles clipped to the branches and lighted. Huge crepe paper bells hung in the center of the ceiling with streamers going to the corners of the room. There were bags of candy and fruit for the children and of course, Santa Claus. There were box suppers, socials, plays, parties, church, and other community activities. It was also used for voting, (national, state, and County elections) and the vote to incorporation of Callaway occurred there in 1936.

While the school was in operation, grades from "primer" through the eighth grade were taught, with several children in each grade. Sometimes as many as 30-40 were attending the school at one time. The older children helped the younger ones study, while others were at the "recitation bench" reciting, reading, spelling, arithmetic, etc. The children learned the three "R's" which formed a solid basis for their future education.

The water supply was from a well with a hand pump. There were two "Out Houses", one for the girls and one for the boys behind the school on opposite sides.

The big bell was rung about 8 A.M. for the children to come to school. About 8:30 A.M. school "took in" and school begin with roll call, The Lords Prayer, The Pledge of Allegiance and singing, There was a 30 minute recess at mid morning, an hour for lunch at noon, (some children ran home for lunch while other brought their lunch) and school was out about 3:30 in the afternoon.

The teachers boarded with families in the community, who sometimes sent the teacher a lunch by one of the children who went home for lunch. In later years, teachers drove themselves to school.

The children played hop-scotch, drop the handkerchief, tag, follow the leader, racing, etc. The older children played ball using a homemade string ball and sometimes a board for a bat.

The school was discontinued in 1936 when a larger school was built on Highway 22. The building was remodeled and used as a home until 1984. Then the land was sold with the stipulation that the building be preserved. The City of Callaway acquired the building and it was moved to its present location at 522 Beulah Avenue, at the John B. Gore Park.

The Callaway Historical Society has restored the building as nearly as possible to its original appearance. It serves as a Historical Site especially for present day school children who visit and ask questions such as "where is the lunch room", or "where are the bath rooms", or "what is recess" or "what is arithmetic".

The small Ettie Fox museum nearby contains artifacts of the area, which along, with the school reflects Callaway in its early days.

The workers for the local turpentine industry had their own school building. This was also used for their social activities and especially church. It was located between Chipewa Street and Callaway Bayou, East of Beulah Avenue.
Submitted by: Bertie Burkett Shuster, 5207 Teri Lane, Panama City, Fl. 32404.

Phillips Inlet and West Bay Schools

In the early 1920's there was a school house painted with white lime, water and color at Philips Inlet. It was later painted white with paint. The teachers were: in the early 1920's Leila Charlotte Holly Cain (my mother), 1919 to 1921 Pearl Trottman, 1920 to 1922 Jessie Hurston, 1921 to 1923 James Commander and 1922 to 1924 Dorothy Fuller.

It was a one room school but they taught primer through the twelfth grade. There were six people in the high school grades.

My first day in school a big class of two, Ray Gainous and myself. Ray stole a carton of cigarettes, first I'd ever seen. When the bell rung, we took off to the woods, hid and smoked cigarettes, Camels, at recess. We went back and played with the other kids. When the bell rung we took off to the woods. When dinnertime came, we went back to the schoolhouse. We had our lunch out of our syrup buckets (lunch pail). The teacher was a man and he told us we would have to come inside for the afternoon. When the bell rang, we run, him after us. We crawled up under the schoolhouse so he could not get us. He sent my brother Allen and Ray's brother Woodrow under the schoolhouse and drug us out. When he got through beating our butts with a paddle, we went in the schoolhouse. He made us stay for about an hour then he told us to go play for the rest of the day. He said tomorrow, we would be in the schoolhouse plus everyday after, to learn to read and write, no play. We had a spring for water but no out house. The girls used the bushes on one side and the boys on the other side, no peeping.

When I was in the second grade the school at Philips Inlet closed down. My folks got a loan of a house in West Bay. My school mates in my class that year: Grady Allen, Steve Adams, Mary Nell Pate, Johnie Sowell, Quinton McCarthy, Huts Morrison, Burdie Wovren, G. W. Corums, Clifford Marshall, Gertrude Clewis. My brothers Gene and Allen were in a higher grade that year. Billy, my younger brother, didn't go he was too young. My sisters were in St Andrews with my uncle and aunt, Will and Ada Miller. My teacher was Mozelle Rodgers Bullard. We had a two room school house with out door toilets, (out houses). One on one side for girls and one on the other side for boys. A pitcher pump for water. We went home for lunch. No electric lights no where. No plumbing. We got another house in West Bay for us to live and go to school for four months. We lived one block from the school close to the Birtchons. I was in the 3rd grade, but didn't pass. I was too short to learn much but had lots of fun being around people to play with.
Written by: Clifford Hilliard Cain. Submitted by: JoAnn Cain, 204 Cascade St., Panama City, FL 32405.

St. Andrew Grammar School
Sixth Grade Trip - 1951

The sixth graders at St. Andrew Grammar School in 1951 decided to go on an exciting adventure. It was their last year before going to Jinks Junior High, a brand new school which they would be the first class to attend for seventh, eighth, and ninth grades.

Parents, teachers and Merritt Brown, the principal, backed the plan. Money had to be raised and a trip planned. It was shortly after World War II so there was still a need for scrap metal. A lot of money was raised that way. Other things were

43

saved and sold. Entertainment earned some money. Each student earned some for personal costs.

The trip was by bus with a number of parents as chaperones. Mrs. Brock was a spearheading sixth grade teacher. The first major stop was Green Cove Springs to see large navy ships in "mothball." Then the bus headed for the Atlantic Coast and St. Augustine. The students enjoyed many "oldest" and just plain "old" places during sightseeing in contrast to the Fountain of Youth.

The group then went to Ocala and Silver Springs. The most exciting event was the Glass Bottom Boat. At that time there were hundreds of fish fighting to get close to any boat where the passengers

St. Andrew Grammar School, 6th Grade Trip, 1951 on a Jungle Cruise

fed them bread (there are fewer fish now because of the algae from fertilizer pollution in the springs). There were shops selling orange blossom perfume, beautiful palms and flowers everywhere, and a ride on the Jungle Cruise. Everyone tried to decide where the Tarzan movie had been filmed (this group grew up playing Tarzan, Cheeta, and Jane in the oak trees around Panama City).

The picture of the Jungle Cruise shows the entire group. Most of the students later graduated from the Bay High Class of 1957.
Submitted by: Sheila Scott, Panama City, FL.

St. Andrew School Glee Club

In the class of 1939-40 there was a Glee Club of St. Andrew

St. Andrew School Glee Club posing in front of the school, 1939-40

School on Beck Avenue, in St. Andrew. Mrs. Stevson was the music leader. Mr. Merritt Brown was the principal of the school. Mrs. Summers was an eighth grade teacher at the school.
Submitted by: Mrs. Beatrice F. Moates, 764 Roland Rd., Chipley, FL 32428.

The School Bus

My Dad bought a 1927 Chevrolet truck with no body. We got a man who lived in Crestview, Florida to come stay with us and build a school bus body on the truck. It had only the gas tank and windshield. My Dad had a contract to haul all the kids from Philips Inlet, Side Camp, lower form to West Bay. All the kids up to the eighth grade got off at West Bay then. All the ninth grade to twelfth was picked up and carried to Seminole Hill where there was a high school. My brother Eugene and sister Vera was the school bus drivers. We left home early and got home late. The bus had screens on the side and back. We had canvas curtains to keep rain out and wind. No heaters, one long seat down each side, got in and out from the back end and it had wood doors. The driver had doors on each side of the cab with wooden shutters between the cab and bus part.

That's where we rode every summer when school was out.
Written by: Clifford Hilliard Cain. Submitted by: JoAnn Cain, 204 Cascade St., Panama City, FL 32405.

School Photographs

Our dad donated his time over the years to take photographs for the Bay High yearbook, as well as taking photographs of the classes in elementary schools. The Bay County Library has many examples of those photographs.

This picture is of a tired annual editor and photographer sitting on his camera case in the halls of Bay High, in the 1950's. We surmise they have wrapped up the annu-

Off to the Presses! Photographer J. N. (Jimmie) Jones and Editor of the 1952 Pelican Barbara Yost

al for submission to the publisher.
Submitted by: Susan Jones Moore and J. Nelson Jones, 310 S. Palo Alto Ave., Panama City, FL 32401.

Southport Elementary School

Southport is a small unincorporated community on North Bay about 10 miles north of Panama City. There have been schools in Southport since the late 1870's -1880's. A log church was the first school, one and a half miles south of the present school. Later a two-story frame building would be used for both church services and school. A home located on Fanning Bayou close to the present school site also was used for schooling. Classes were held in other homes, often it would be the home of the teacher.

A large lumber mill was completed in 1906 and about 30 families moved into the area. They constructed a four-room, two story frame building on the present site. This building was Southport Elementary until the early 1930's when construction was started on buildings in the current school complex.

Southport Elementary School has changed quite a bit since that first building. There are now seven main buildings, with thirty classrooms, as well as administrative offices, a lunchroom, a P.E. pavilion with a lovely shaded playground, a media center and storage facilities.

The first Parent Teacher Association of Southport School was organized in the school year 1936-37. The PTO is still very strong today, and parents are always encouraged to become a part of the Southport Elementary family. Our dedicated principal is Mrs. Dianne Miller. We have a community school with involved parents and dedicated teachers.

Our Motto is "Anchored in Excellence". The school colors are Blue and White. We chose the Eagle for our School Mascot. The school Logo is an "Anchor".
Submitted by: Angela Miller, 1732 Courtland Place, Southport. Sources: Southport Elementary School, Miller Family Records.

Students of Goethe School, 1929

The Goethe School was in Bay County, the teachers were from Washington County and the children were from both counties.

Teachers were Bev Gainer of Greenhead and Hope Simmons of Vernon. The students standing in front of the schoolhouse are: 1. Etta Reeder 2. Audrey Russell (possibly) 3. Cade Rodgers 4. Esse Mae

1929 Class of Goethe School

Strickland 5. Preston Taunton 6. Pug Gainer 7. Irene Murfee 8. Annie Murfee 9. Esther Banks 10. Nellie Taylor 11. Hansel Atwell (possibly) 12. Fletcher Murfee 13. Howard Murfee 14. Etta Reeder 15. Frances Murfee 16. W A Rodgers and 17. Beulah Murfee.
Submitted by: BeeBee Russell Deal, 15116 Highway 77, Southport, FL 32409.

Students of Goethe School, 1930

In 1929, there were not many trees around which had survived the timber logging; so, each Goethe student planted a live oak tree alongside the sandy road that ran past the school. This dirt road ran from Southport to Chipley. All the trees survived to maturity. Unfortunately, the stately trees were all removed in September of 2003 so Highway 77 could be widened.

The students in the 1930 school were: 1. Bev Gainer, Teacher 2. Jimmy Rodgers 3. Steve Adams 4. Essa Mae Strickland 5. Ralph Tucker 6. Frances Murfee 7. Fletcher Murfee 8. Pug Gainer 9. Etta Reeder 10. Mitchel Limoux 11. Preston Taunton 12. Beulah Murfee 13. Nelly Taylor 14. Mamie Jewel Taunton 15. Annie Murfee 16. Cade Rodgers 17. Esther Banks 18. Alvesta Rodgers 19. W A Rodgers 20. Irene Murfee and 21. Esther Tucker.

1930 class of Goethe School

Submitted by: BeeBee Russell Deal, 15116 Highway 77, Southport, FL 32409.

CHURCHES

Calvary Missionary Baptist Church

Calvary Missionary Baptist Church is a landmark church established on May 28, 1945 at 1529 N. Mulberry Ave., Panama City led by interim pastor Bro. Fred Robbins.

On August 14, 1945, Bro. J.A. Franklin was called as its first official pastor. Charter members of this little independent "American Baptist" church were W.W. Hill, Carrie Hill, W.W. Hill, Jr., Lucille Hill, Lution Hill, J.B. Hudson, Teresa Hudson, Willie M. Lowery, Elneta Lowery, May V. Boyd, E.T. Hudson, Ellafair Hudson, Fred Robbins, Mrs. Fred Robbins, Grace King Thomason, Lucille Turner Newberry and Judith Newberry.

The pastors for the years to follow were: H.D. Donaldson, H.B. Clemmons, A.C. Goodwin, John C. Howes, David L. Morton, James Parnell, Curtis Jones, Marlin Gipson and Jim L. Hankins.

The congregation of Calvary Missionary Baptist Church taken on Easter Sunday, April 11, 1949. In the picture from L-R, 1st Row: E.T. Hudson, Walter Hamm, James Daffin, Mike Hamm, Tommy Hamm, Sue Hamm, Sue Cobb, Buddy Donalson, Patricia Donalson, Johnny Daffin, unknown, Bernadine Strickland, Mary Ellen Stanley, unknown, unknown, Annie Fay Stanley, Doris Stanley, Buddy Stanley, Ralph Newberry, Diane Newberry, Euna McNeil, Ladon McNeil, Bessie Barton, Max Barton, Sr., Glenda Barton. 2nd Row: Jimmy Thomason, Edward Douglas, Pug Hamm, Effie Daffin, Cecil Humm, Willie Lane, Mrs. Cobb, Lucille Boddye, Mrs. Harelson, Elaine Harrelson, Charlene Adams, unknown, Florence Douglas, Grace Thomason, Elizabeth Boddye Modawell, John Modawell, unknown, Carrie Hill, W.W. Hill, Pastor H.B. Clemmons. 3rd Row: Roger McNeil, Margie Smith, Judy Newberry, Nancy Sampley, Betty Smith, Bobby Smith, Betty Lane, Cathryn McLain, Elaine Newberry, Janice Newberry, Ronnie Thomason and James Stanley. Not present for this historical photo were Darrell Thomason who was at home with his younger sister Jo who had the German Measles.

Many people have shared in the accomplishments of this neighborhood church throughout the years. So many that you could not begin to call all of their names, but God in Heaven knows. To the church pioneers who had the vision to start this special ministry back in the middle of World War II in this little area of town where there were no churches, everyone who has ever been part of this loving church is grateful. And today if you are looking for a small friendly church with a tremendous love for the Lord, you are cordially invited to attend!
Submitted by: Jo Thomason Manis, 1057 Oak Avenue, Panama City, FL 32401.

Beginnings of the Central Baptist Church of Panama City, Florida

The church was organized as the Oakland Terrace Baptist Church in April of 1956 as an independent, fundamental Baptist Church. The church would be a missionary-minded Baptist church standing for the pure, undiluted gospel, attempting to reach Bay County with the message of salvation.

The first service of the church was organized in the Oakland Terrace Clubhouse. For a short time the church met in the Oakland Terrace Elementary School Auditorium, and called Rev. Bill Childs as the first pastor. A small wooden building was then moved to the corner of Fortune and 14th in Panama City where services were held until the spring of 1958.

Interior of Central Baptist Church

Rev. Hugh F. Pyle, a full-time evangelist, was called in the fall of 1957 to be the pastor, after the resignation of Brother Childs. In the spring of 1958, the church purchased the 35-acre Reaver Airport on West 11th Street and the name was changed to Central Baptist Church.

For awhile, planes and sermons started at the same time and planes frequently landed in the back yard of the new church property! After a few months, the Reaver Air Service moved to Fannin Field and the Central Baptist congregation moved into the first half of the hangar, as auditorium, and the old wooden building for Sunday school rooms. Some classes were even held under the wings of planes.

The church radio broadcast "Impact and Inspiration," was on WPCF Radio in February of 1958 and continued for almost 14 years. By means of radio, newspaper advertising and by hard work and personal visitation, Central Baptist Church became known throughout Bay County.
Submitted by: John Barton, 1104 Balboa Ave., Panama City, FL 32401.

Central Baptist Church and Panama City Christian School

In 1960 the church started a Christian day school with 32 pupils. Two rooms were built to accommodate the first two classes. As the school grew, grades (and rooms) were added year after year. By 1973 the school enrolled nearly 1000 students from childcare through high school.

In 1968 the mortgage on the 35-acres was burned and the church property debt was all cleared. Missionaries were being supported on many foreign fields, and busses were rolling through the city bringing pupils to the Christian School and to Sunday school at Central on the Lord's Day.

In 1966, plans were formulated for the construction of new facilities. Groundbreaking for the new building was in July of 1969 and members worshiped in the beautiful new auditorium for the first time on November 15, 1970, as the finishing touches were being added. On January 10, 1971, Dr. John Rice dedicated the new building. Dr. Walter Hughes, of Canada, led in the prayer of dedication.

In June of 1973, the pastor of 15 1/2 years announced that God was calling him back into the ministry of full-time evangelism and that he also needed time to devote to writing for Christian publications. Dr. Pyle was honored by the church with the title of Pastor-Emeritus. Rev. Bryant Nelson was called to the pastorate next, arriving in January of 1974. He resigned in February of 1975. Brother Milton Ker came in August of 1975 followed by Dr. Bradly Price in 1982; Dr. Richard White in 1991 and Dr. Frank Starling became pastor in 2001.

Submitted by: John Barton, 1104 Balboa Ave., Panama City, FL 32401.

Covenant Presbyterian Church

On November 18, 1973, several families from two area Presbyterian congregations met for worship in the Westside Men's Club located off 23rd Street at Posten Bayou. It was a small beginning...32 people...but from this nucleus grew our present church. The group called itself "Independent Presbyterian Fellowship." Its purpose was to form an evangelical Presbyterian church committed to subjecting every area of life to the authority and infallibility of the Scriptures, and the reformed faith, with a zeal for missions.

On January 6, 1974, Donald C. Graham supplied the pulpit (a podium borrowed each week from Wilson Funeral Home). At a meeting following the service, the group voted unanimously to request Gulf Coast Presbytery of the National Presbyterian Church to organize them as a particular church of that Presbytery and denomination. Later that year, the National Presbyterian Church changed its name to Presbyterian Church in America in deference to a local congregation in Washington, DC known as the National Presbyterian Church. We are most often simply called the PCA.

On January 20, 1974, three key events occurred. Mr. Graham was unanimously called to be the organizing pastor. The name "Covenant Presbyterian Church" was adopted, and the first offices were elected: five Elders and four Deacons.

The following Sunday, January 27, Covenant Church was officially organized by Gulf Coast Presbytery with Dr. William A. McIlwaine of Pensacola presiding. This was particularly appropriate since Dr. McIlwaine, a lifelong missionary to Japan, was one of the founding fathers of the PCA and later served as moderator of the General Assembly.

Just two weeks later on February 10, the infant congregation began to hold its Sunday services in the cafeteria of the Northside Elementary School. When the charter membership roll was closed on March 3, 1974, there were 52 communicant members including its newest, Tommy Carr, who that morning became the church's first member to join by profession of faith and baptism. (Later Tommy and his family left Covenant Church to attend Reformed Theological Seminary. Today the Carr's live in Demopolis, Alabama where Tommy pastors a PCA congregation).

The following Tuesday evening, the installation service for Mr. Graham was held in the sanctuary of the Northside Baptist Church.

The young church continued to worship in the Northside School Cafeteria for over two years. On May 12, 1974, the congregation purchased its first parcel of land, (1 & 1/4 acres) in the 2300 block of Frankford Avenue. Subsequent purchases have increased that initial parcel to eight acres.

Ground breaking for the present sanctuary was July 20, 1975. The first worship service was held in the new facility in early 1976.

Ray Lanning became the second pastor in July of 1978. He was succeeded in January of 1981, by E. Lee Trinkle, III. Our present pastor, Robert S. Hayes (one of the fifty-two charter members) followed Mr. Trinkle in November of 1984.

Covenant Church has from its start, placed great emphasis on missions. Over one-hundred missionaries (home and foreign) have visited Covenant Church over the years. Through budgeted funds and designated offerings, Covenant participates in the financial support of over seventy-five missionaries and mission projects each year. In 2001 the mission and benevolent giving of Covenant Church was nearly $90,000.

Members of Covenant Church have been key leaders in two local ministries, the Panama City Rescue Mission and the Pregnancy Center.

In January of 1999 Covenant celebrated its 25th Anniversary as over two-hundred and forty members and one-hundred Covenant children are joined by faith in Jesus Christ to make Him known as we are a "salt and light" influence in a world darkened by sin.

Currently in 2004 as we celebrate our 30th Anniversary, we are in a newly renovated and expanded sanctuary with beautiful stained glass windows. Rev. Robert S. Hayes is Pastor, Rev. Robert M. Hopper as Assistant Pastor and M. Eric Sparks is the Youth and Music Director.

Submitted by: Mona Lucas, 3235 Orlando Rd., Panama City, FL.

Early St. Andrews Methodist Church

Known by many names through the years, one of the first Methodist Churches in St. Andrews is now The Historical St. Andrews Church. During the churches early years it experienced many pastors. Thomas Welch, the son of Adam Levi Welch was a frequent preacher and often used his nephews, Lester and Chester Welch as offering collectors.

Lester and Chester would walk the isles, collect the offerings and depart to the back area to tally. After reporting the total to Thomas, if the amount was slight of what was needed, the twins were sent back down the isles to collect again. This process went on until the desired total was attained.

The question on the minds of many was if the sermon motivated the congregation to dig deeper or did they pay just to experience silence, and shorten the sermon.

Written and submitted by: Donna Welch Rankin, 210-N East Baldwin Rd., Panama City, FL 32405.

First Baptist Church of Panama City
Sixth Street and Harrison Avenue

Fourteen people with a vision met in a small frame schoolhouse, at Park Street and Luverne Avenue, on December 16, 1908 and organized The First Baptist Church of Panama City. In July, 1909 the church moved services to "Ward's Hall" located upstairs over a store near Fourth Street and Harrison Avenue. The congregation located its first building on the northeast corner of Fifth Street and Grace Avenue in the summer of 1910. The church grew, and the Gospel began to work its change in the growing area of Panama City. As the community flourished, so did the membership. A new church auditorium was erected in 1926 on the corner of Sixth Street and Harrison Avenue. Additional property was acquired and many other buildings were completed–an education building in 1951 and another in 1958. By 1969 the congregation had once again outgrown its auditorium, a cherished landmark in the heart of downtown Panama City. After much prayer, the membership voted to remain in the downtown area, demolish the building, and erect a new structure on the same site. It was completed in May, 1971. Ten years later the church purchased the old Armory Building located on Sixth Street and Grace Avenue, and renovated it for use as a Family Life Center. Extensive remodeling of the main auditorium was completed in 1998. Once again, the church has outgrown its present facilities, but the membership prayerfully chose to remain downtown. Other parcels of land have been purchased, and a new multi-level parking garage is being erected at the corner of Grace Avenue and Seventh Street. Future plans are for a still larger auditorium to be built. Church membership is now at 4200+ and continues to grow. The Sunday worship service is televised to a large portion of Northwest Florida and the tri-state region. First Baptist Church continues to be a vital, growing part of the Panama City/Bay County area. The vision of those first fourteen members has never changed–to seek, reach and teach the Gospel of the Lord Jesus Christ.

Submitted by: First Baptist Church, P. O. Box 1200, Panama City, FL 32401.

1908

First Baptist Church, Panama City through the years

1926

1910

1971

First Baptist Church Southport

In 1874 a few Baptist met in an old log schoolhouse on Grassy Point and founded the Grassy Point Baptist Church, later known as First Baptist Church of Southport.

The first pastor of record was Rev. John Stewart recorded in 1880 minutes of the West Florida Baptist Association in Washington County, Florida.

Some of the first members were Frank and Mary Jane Page, Wiley and Sarah Sullivan, Martha Ann, Lewis, Sara and Betty Anderson.

First Baptist Church of Southport

The church moved to Bradley Point in the township of Anderson because the people moved closer to Southport. Mr. T. D. Sale acquired land from Vickers & McKenzie in 1910; the Southport Lumber Co. built a large sawmill on Mill Point. With the people moving across the bay to work, Mr. Sale saw the need for the church to move, so he gave the land where the church is now located at the corner of Bridge Rd. and Market St. in Southport. The original building was started in 1912.

It was here in 1933 that the West Florida Baptist Associational meeting was held and the members decided to divide and form the Northwest Coast Baptist Association.

In 1959 a new auditorium was built and the old building was torn down. Since then there have been numerous additions to the building. There have been many pastors over the last 129 years. At the present time the church body is growing in number and Spirit under the director of Pastor, Roy M. Shortt.
Submitted by: Evelyn Mullins & Mary Lou Quick, P. O. Box 8448, 1732 Bridge St,. Southport, FL 32409.

First Presbyterian Church

Handsome red brick, stately white columns, beautiful stained glass windows and a towering colonial steeple form the structure of First Presbyterian Church located on Seventh Street just east of Harrison Avenue. Worshippers have gathered at this site for over 50 years.

First Presbyterian Church was organized in 1913 with 17 charter members. First coming together in the home of Rev. and Mrs. W.C. Wallace and then in a small building, the Masonic Hall, on First Street. The charter members included: Mrs. W.C. Wallace, Mrs. M.A. Coleman, Misses Janie and Mary Wallace, Waldo Wallace, Mr. and Mrs. Arthur Hutton, Mrs. A.A. Payne, Mrs. Daniel Gillis, Miss Joe Gillis, Mrs. C.G. Varlin, Mr. H.H. Weinass, Mrs. W.J. Lee, Mr. and Mrs. W.T. Griswold (Mr. Griswold was the superintendent of the railroad and became the first elder for he had held this position at a Presbyterian Church elsewhere.), Miss Allie Griswold and Mr. Crawford Adams.

First Presbyterian Church

Shortly afterwards, a little schoolhouse was purchased from the Gulf Coast Development Company for $500. The congregation agreed to pay $25 quarterly at 6% interest for their new place of worship. The women of the church raised much of the monies by cooked food sales, giving teas and hosting an occasional "Southern dinner."

Early in the summer of 1918, Rev. J.P. Wood was sent from Quitman, GA to serve as pastor. Rev. Wood served the church until 1926, when he was made pastor emeritus and Rev. J.C. Leckenby became pastor. In July of 1932, First Presbyterian changed its name to Wallace Memorial Presbyterian Church honoring Rev. Wallace. In 1934, the church moved in a building located at 624 Harrison Avenue, across from the Nelson Chevrolet Company. The Harrison Avenue location was remodeled several times, adding classrooms and a kitchen.

In 1943, a building fund was established to "let us build in Panama City a church, which will be a credit to God." Church minutes note the annual budget in 1945 was $7402 with a $300 pastor's salary. An organ fund for the new building was also started called, "The Penny Fund." Ground was broken on August 7, 1950 for the new sanctuary and adjoining educational building, which is the present site at 100 E. Seventh Street.

The new facility was completed in September of 1951. Rev. Richard L. Scoggins was the pastor and the church had a membership of 275 persons with an annual budget of $20,000 before Rev. Scoggins came to Wallace Memorial in May of 1950. The Harrison Avenue building was moved and became the Panama City Garden Club. Rev. Scoggins served as pastor for 25 years.

In the 1960's the former Panama Grammar School across the street was purchased. It is an educational building for Sunday School classes, Youth programs, The First Presbyterian School, in addition to church offices.

A major renovation of the sanctuary took place in 1986 and 1987. The "I am" stained-glass windows were installed and the Nelson Chapel was constructed. The church again became known as "First Presbyterian" and affiliated with The Presbyterian Church of America.

First Presbyterian Church has planted churches in other areas of Bay County, such as Bayou George, Springfield, Sunnyside Beach, Forest Park and Lynn Haven. A 1930's article in The Panama City Pilot reads, "from this church has sprung all of the churches in Panama City, as well as many of the schools." (The St. Andrews Presbyterian Church is older having been formed in the late 1800's. Travel between St. Andrews and Panama City was not easy even in the 1930's.) For more than 90 years, First Presbyterian Church has welcomed Panama Citians and visitors to follow Jesus' teaching, "I was glad when they said unto me, Let us go into the house of the Lord."
Submitted by: Elizabeth Ann Krause Percival, 322 Bunkers Cove Road, Panama City, FL.

First United Methodist Church

Panama City First United Methodist Church has served First 100 Years.

Smack in the middle of town, safely above St. Andrew Bay and Massalina Bayou, the Methodist Church was built soon after it was organized on July 28, 1907.

The lot was donated by the Gulf Coast Development Company. The Rev. S.B. Strout, was the pastor for first services, September 17, 1911.

Methodist Church, corner Fourth Street and Magnolia Avenue, Panama City Florida

The wooden structure at 4th Street and Magnolia Avenue served our new little town for about 40 years until a fire and a growing membership dictated the construction of the present church just across the bridge on 4th Street. "Old Panama" was dominated by that church steeple and the town-wide presence of its bell. It was so typical of turn-of-the-century houses of worship: wooden shutters, a great organ and palm trees out front.

Long viewed as a leader among area Methodist churches, First United Methodist became the first to televise live Sunday services under the wise guidance of the Pastor, Brother Si Mathison.

Services have been continually broadcast for 40 years, and the church has enjoyed phenomenal growth while retaining that special friendly "small church flavor" we are so proud of today.

You don't have to be in hearing range of the church bells today to feel the influence and power of this great church and its people. Many lives have been enriched by our church which sprang from such modest beginnings before Bay County existed.

Just ask anybody.

Submitted by: First United Methodist Church, 903 E. 4th Street, Panama City, FL 32401. Written by: Earnest Spiva.

Grace Baptist Church
Forty-five Years in the Making

In an old house on Harrison Avenue, (where McDonald's stands today) a group of families met on May 9, 1957 to pray for God's guidance and blessing. (The home was made available by Mrs. Waldo Wallace, Jr., or possibly a Dr. Brewer.) Sixty people attended the first regular worship service on Sunday, May 12. The congregation chose the name Grace Bible Church, and prayerfully sought a pastor.

The first pastor, Rev. Melvin Moody, served the church for seven years. During this time the church relocated to a wooded lot (the present location on Highway 77). Mrs. Blandford McKenzie loaned the church the funds to purchase the land. The congregation pitched in to clear the land and build a new sanctuary; and a home next to the church was pur-

Grace Baptist Church

chased for the pastorium. Several years later, Judge Sapp purchased five acres next to the church property and gave it to the church. The present auditorium now stands there.

After Melvin Moody, other pastors were Ralph McGilvra, Moody Roberts, Lee Larson, and Billy Baugham. In the early 70's, the name of the church was changed to Grace Baptist Church. Pastor James B. Jones served the church for twenty years, before his death from cancer in 1993.

Pastor Larry Curtis, who came in 1994, has led the church through a dramatic growth in attendance, creating the need for a larger facility. The auditorium complex was completed on May 3, 1998, coinciding with the church's forty-year anniversary.

Submitted by: Grace Baptist Church, 2745 Hwy 77, Panama City, FL 32405.

Grace Presbyterian Church, PCUSA

Grace Presbyterian Church, PCUSA was organized in December, 1984 and held its first worship service on January 6, 1985.

Following the reunification of the Presbyterian Church US and the United Presbyterian Church of the USA in late 1984, a group of 126 people met and decided to form a new church.

The group unanimously voted to call Rev. Dr. Wade H. Bell, Jr. as the organizing pastor. This call was approved by the Presbytery of Florida and on January 6, 1985, Rev. Bell preached the first sermon to the new congregation.

The name Grace Presbyterian Church was chosen and approval was granted by the Presbytery.

The Wallace Memorial Presbyterian Church voted to transfer 8.5 acres of land in the Forest Park area to the new church. Wallace Memorial had been given the land for a church site, but it had never been developed.

Grace began meeting in the Seventh Day Adventist Church on West 11th Street while the new church was being planned and built. On September 7, 1986 the first worship service was held in the new facility. In 2001, we reciprocated by sharing Grace's facilities with the Seventh Day Adventist congregation

while their new church was under construction

God has richly blessed the growth of Grace. From the original 180 Charter Members in 1985, we have grown to over 350 in 2003.

Grace has had three ministers, Rev. Bell, Rev. Ken Wilmersheer and our current minister, Rev. Tully Hunter.

Grace Presbyterian Church

Grace Presbyterian Church has an active ministry including Sunday School for all ages, traditional and contemporary worship services, men's and women's groups, Bible study groups, and outstanding programs for children and youth including Vacation Bible School and Caraway Street for K-5th graders. We have adult and children's choirs, a bell choir, and a praise band. We offer a fully accredited Pre School program and this fall we opened an After School Day Care program for K-5th grades.

We sponsor a Scottish Festival each spring and hold the Kirkin' of the Tartan to celebrate our Scottish heritage.

We pray that we will continue to serve, worship and glorify our Heavenly Father who has kept us in his loving care from our beginning through today and into the future.

Submitted by: Grace Presbyterian Church, 1415 Airport Road Panama City, Florida 32405.

Gulfview United Methodist Church

Gulfview United Methodist Church was organized in 1954 by Mattie Mae and Joe Bell, owners of Bells Cottages and Belmar Hotel where Sugar Sands now stands. A group of thirteen received permission from the Methodist Conference to build the church in Laguna Beach. In 1955, J. B. and Carolee Lahan donated the land on Rose Lane. Construction began in 1955, and was com-

Gulfview United Methodist Church

pleted in 1956. Gulfview was the first church on the beach. The Episcopal and Presbyterian Churches were established shortly thereafter. These three churches held services on successive Sundays and all would attend. Linwood Lewis was the first pastor and the church has been served by fourteen pastors since. The first worship service was conducted on February 12, 1956, the cornerstone laid in November 1956 and dedication of the church and mortgage burning was celebrated in 1962. The women blessed the event with a dinner for all. There were thirteen charter members in 1957-1958. Further building programs included a North and South Chapel to the church in 1988-89, present parsonage in 1994-95, the Mathison Educational Annex in 1997-98 in honor of Rev. Si Mathison and in loving memory of his wife Mary.

Gulfview is known for its warmth and friendliness. It is a unique church. The congregation comes from every state, Canada and visitors from countries worldwide. The snowbirds fill our pews every winter and the young "Campus Outreach" college students who arrive every summer touch our lives in a positive way, all here to worship together. Our doors are always open and we sincerely invite you to join in our ministry for the Lord.

Submitted by: Mrs. Allison Simmons, 232 Rose Lane, Panama City Beach,

Fl 32413, and Loretta Moore, 204 3rd Street, Panama City Beach, FL 32413.

Hiland Park Baptist Church in the Beginning

When I was growing up there was no church in Hiland Park. I went with my cousin to church services in a papermill paper covered tent. It had timber slab planks for seating. Then Bob Jones College boys, needing practice, came out and built a bush arbor by cutting trees from post and frame and covering it with bushes for shade. It had timber slabs for benches. This is where they preached revivals to people coming to hear them. Lanterns were used for light at night.

In 1943, Miss Juanita Woodham came from the First Baptist Church of Panama City and with the help of Brother J.C. Alexander had a Bible School in the Hiland Park School Building. They continued with Sunday afternoon Sunday School and preaching with Bro Alexander acting as Superintendent and Pastor of the services.

In December 1943, a Church was organized and Brother C.L. Wattenbarger, a missionary, came and supplied as Pastor until

Bible School group in front of the first church building of Hiland Park Baptist Church

August 1944. In September 1944 with the church still meeting at the school, Rev. A.B. Thomas accepted the call to be our Pastor. He helped to build our first auditorium and served from September 1944 to August 1945. At this time Rev. Homer Dugger accepted but could not come right away. Rev. Eugene Sloan served as Interim Pastor from December 1945 until June 1946 and was instrumental in getting benches for the church. Then Rev. Dugger came and paved the way for our first Educational Building. He left in December of 1946.

In April 1947, Rev. U.V. Rollins accepted our call and was with us until March 1950. During this time the educational building and a Pastorium was completed and used. Rev. Earl Plant accepted in April but could not be here until August so Rev. E.P. Strickland served as Interim Pastor until August.

At this time, Mrs. Fronie Hall was elected Secretary of the church and Mr. E.R. Simmons was elected as Janitor and both were put on the payroll.

Under the leadership of Rev. Earl Plant, our church started a Mission Bible School at Brannonville and it became a church. He resigned in September 1957.

In November 1957, the church called Rev. Byron Ray who was in seminary at New Orleans, Louisiana. He was obligated to help rebuild the churches in Cameron, Louisiana, which were destroyed by the hurricane. He commuted back and forth for several months. Being an architect and a great organizer many things were brought into being before he resigned in July 1959.

Rev. Robert Pender came in September 1959 and served until he answered the call to be a missionary at Rosaris, Argentina and he was here until September 1961. Dr. J.D. Allen, from Baptist Bible Institute in Graceville, Florida served as Interim until 1962 when Rev. Frank Morgan came and served until 1965. Dr. Allen helped to get the second auditorium and third educational building started. Rev. Morgan helped to finish the buildings and served until September 1965, when he resigned. Dr. Walter Draughn from Baptist Bible Institute supplied as Interim Pastor for 8 months.

In May 1966, Rev. Robert Strickland came and a song leader, Jim Cathy, was added to the payroll. In his ministry, the auditorium we are now using was completed. We also started the mission that became Temple Baptist Church in his ministry. The church is still growing and has had several pastors since Rev. Strickland left us. In the beginning the Charter Members were, to my knowledge: Mrs. Hazel Howard, Mrs. Annie Belle McNeil, Mrs. J.A. Skipper, Mrs. Alto Newsome, Mrs. Mildred Snow, Mrs.

Julian Howard, Mrs. W.C. Kelly, Mrs. Etta Porter, Mrs. J.C. Johnson, Mrs. Pallie Martin, Mrs. Aldiu Lovell, Mrs. Nora Hughes, Mrs. J.A. Newsome, Mrs. H.B. Newsome, Mr. and Mrs. H.A. Sellars, Mrs. Harvey Childs, Mrs. D.B. Hammond, Mrs. Horace Newsome, Mrs. Eva Hartzog, Miss Rubylee Hartzog, Miss Margaret Hartzog, Mr. and Mrs. A.H. Sheffield, Mrs. John Hughes, Mr. J.C. Johnson, Miss Audrey Johnson, Mrs. George Whitmire, Miss Evelyn Hammond, Miss Mavis Johnson, Mr. Howard Sheffield, Miss Jackie Carpenter, Mr. Floyd Howard, Miss Mildred Clements, Mrs. Audry Mashburn and Mr. and Mrs. Delmas Hall.

The first Deacons were: Horace Newsome, Delmas Hall, J.C. Johnson, Cary Hartzog, and A.H. Sheffield. Some early Sunday School Superintendents were Rev. J.C. Alexander, H.A. Sellers, H.B. Newsome, Linnie Kirkland, John Cooley, Cliff West and Buford Freeman.

The Training Union was organized in 1945 and some of the early Directors were: A.H. Sheffield, Amos Johnson, Amos Howard, Snow Allen, Arie Johns, Jim Cathy, L.T. Austin and Watson Shields.

Submitted by: Rubylee Hartzog Strickland, 2627 Game Farm Road, Panama City, Florida 32405. Source: The Memory and Files of Rubylee Strickland.

Historic St. Andrew Church

The Methodist circuit riders came through the Bay County area around 1821 preaching the gospel of Jesus Christ. The early settlers of St. Andrew met in homes. The first church was built in 1845, but it was destroyed during the Civil War in the federal gunboat bombardment of 1863.

The July, 1888 issue of the St. Andrew's Messenger stated that there were Methodist, Presbyterian and Baptist churches in St. Andrew. The St. Andrew Methodist Episcopal Church was organized in 1886 and the sanctuary was built on the cor-

Historical St. Andrew Church on Chestnut Avenue at 11th Street

ner of Washington Street (later charged to 11th Street) and Chestnut Avenue. Since many settlers came from the North after the Civil War, the church was organized as a Methodist Episcopal Church and not as a Methodist Episcopal Church South. The sanctuary was built in 1887. The other churches of that time have been moved or demolished and so the church sanctuary on the corner of 11th Street and Chestnut Avenue is the oldest extant church building in Bay County.

From 1887 - 1937 the sanctuary was home to the St. Andrew's Bay Methodist Episcopal Church. During this time seventeen pastors served and there were several years when there was no pastor and a temporary supply or a layman held services.

From 1938 to 1940 the Pastor to the St. Andrew Church was appointed by the presiding elder of the Alabama Conference of the Methodist Episcopal Church South.

From 1941 through 1952 the name of the church was "St. Andrews Methodist Church." During the war years of 1942 - 1945 the church was asked to share their Sunday school rooms for school use. The County School Board promised to pay for any needed improvements. There was a need for a second bathroom so the School Board paid for the plumbing and the church furnished the fixtures.

At an official board meeting in 1952, there was a discussion about whether it was appropriate to have the "s" in St.

Andrews Methodist Church. Elinor Howell said that the name was taken from a Biblical saint and that the spelling should be Saint Andrew with no 's'. So, the spelling of the name was changed.

St. Andrew Methodist Church built a new facility on 11th Street east of Frankford Avenue. The first service in their new sanctuary was on March 20, 1956, with over 600 people attending. The old sanctuary seated less than 100 comfortably. Before they moved, the St. Andrew Methodist Church gave Mr. C.M. Kelly the option to buy the property. He intended to dismantle the church and build some rental cottages. On March 23, 1954, he wrote to the Board of Trustees that "he would not exercise his option to buy."

In 1955 the sanctuary was purchased by the Panama City Christian Church for $10,000.00. They grew and built a new facility on Highway 390. When they moved in 1970, they sold their old sanctuary to a fledgling church called the First Independent Methodist Church for $10,000.00. In June, 1971,that Church called its first full-time pastor, Henry Hazard. He began his ministry in Panama City on July 9, 1971, and served until September 26, 1999.

In 1983 the name was changed to Heritage Bible Church. The congregation of Heritage Bible Church worshiped there until September 26, 1999. It had purchased land on State Avenue and on that date moved into its new facility. Nevertheless, some of its members remained at the old facility to start a new church, called the St. Andrew Bible Church. Laymen took the lead and preached each Sunday at the new church in the oldest facility in Bay County: Darin Krawczky, Jeff Lawson and Tom Seeuws.

The name of the church was changed in 2001 to the Historic St. Andrew Church. Dr. Robert Slane became pastor of the church. He retired in 2002 and since then the church has been led primarily by laymen.

Over the years the church facility at 11th Street and Chestnut Avenue, although small, has served the Lord and the people of the St. Andrew area well. Its name has changed and sometimes also its congregation, but it has continually served its purpose of being a lighthouse in the community and reaching the lost for Christ.

Submitted by: Rev. Henry Hazard, 3380 State Ave., Panama City, FL.

History of Holy Nativity Episcopal Church, Panama City, Florida

Under the direction of the Rev. Thomas D. Byrne, rector of St. Andrew's Episcopal Church on Beach Drive, ten Cove area families left that church to establish Holy Nativity Episcopal Church at 222 North Bonita Ave. in the Cove in 1955. Some of the families were headed by Abbot Browne, Wilbur James, Frank Lewis, Urban Peters and Carroll Weller. The first Holy Nativity wedding in 1957 united Tom Weller and Linda Peters from two founding families.

The first rector, the Rev. David R. Damon, held the first regular service on

Holy Nativity Episcopal Church's new sanctuary was completed in 1991

June 26, 1955, with 64 attending. What is now the parish hall was then the church. It consisted of four walls, a stage, 50 folding chairs, and several baby beds along the back wall. Minister and members added an altar, altar rail, steps, and a kitchen.

In September, 1959, the church opened a kindergarten under the direction of Mrs. Gervase Woods. In 1961 they added the first grade and thus started the Episcopal Day School.

The Rev. James Soutar served from 1970 to 1973.

The Rev. Robert D. Battin was rector from 1973 to 1995. His first service was August 19, 1973, with 27 in attendance.

Immediately Father Battin and his wife Charlotte began visiting members who had drifted away. Attendance (averaging 190 in 1995) and participation in church activities steadily increased. Choir director and organist during this time was Mrs. Kenneth (Elaine) Smith.

Under Father Battin's leadership the school and church grew in buildings, student body, and membership. He led and participated in the building of the new sanctuary in 1991and held the first service there on September 8, 1991. When Father Battin retired, the parish hall was named Battin Hall in honor of his family's contributions.

The Rev. Donald MacLeod and the Rev. Sidney Ellis served as interim priests until the Rev. Dr. John D. Richardson was called to Holy Nativity in 1996. Under his leadership the church staff increased to include youth minister Chris Mixer, priest associate the Rev. Tom Weller, followed later by the first curate the Rev. Diana Freeman, ministers of music Jeff Jordan (1999-2001) followed by Mark Pybus from England in 2003. Mrs. Richard (Karen) Duncan led the choir and attorney Jonathan Dingus played the organ in the interim.

Holy Nativity was the tenth fastest growing Episcopal church in the U.S. from 1996 to 2000. With increased programs and Sunday attendance (averaging 298 in 2001) came the need for more space. In 2001 Father Richardson led a successful building campaign to construct a Christian education building next door to the church with construction beginning in 2003. Under his leadership the school also expanded to two campuses to include a middle school in the remodeled old Cove Elementary School.

Submitted by: Joyce H. Dannecker, 933 Andrew Circle, Panama City, FL 32405.

Immanuel Baptist Church
Millville, Florida

The Immanuel Baptist Church in Millville was founded in a sawmill town, when the community was little more than a year old. The St. Andrew Lumber company was in operation in Millville and families were coming by wagons and boats from Choctawhatchee Bay and southern Alabama to find work in the saw mill or related business.

Missionary Baptist Church, Millville, Fla. and now location of Immanuel Baptist Church

The St. Andrew Baptist church, founded in April 1894, was the nearest church and before long there was a definite need for a church in the community. Several of the Millville residents were members of the St. Andrew Church but transportation was slow because boats were used more frequently than a horse and buggy. Sixteen members of the St. Andrew Church who were dedicated Millville residents asked for letters of dismissal and met at the Millville School house on August 27, 1900 to organize a church for Millville. For two years the school located at the corner of Tarpon Avenue and 3rd Street served as the church. In 1902 a building was erected on property given by Mrs. W. W. Holmes and served for 46 years as the Church house. In 1948 a new church on College Avenue was completed. The Immanuel Baptist Church has been and is a great church and is continuing to grow.

Submitted by Harold Brookins, 136 Cottonwood Cir., Lynn Haven, FL.
Source: Immanuel Baptist Church 1900-2000 To God Be The Glory.

The Lynn Haven United Methodist Church

The beginning of what is now the Lynn Haven United Methodist Church was a service held on April 30, 1911. The official meeting for organization of the Lynn Haven Methodist

Lynn Haven United Methodist Church

Episcopal Church was held on June 11, 1911, with 75 charter members.

The first building, dedicated on March 24, 1917, was on the southeast corner of 9th and Pennsylvania. Membership at this time was 57. The church was growing and active in this building for the next several decades. During this time, the name was changed to Lynn Haven Methodist Church, as various denominations united.

In 1961, the original sanctuary was completely remodeled, with the bell tower removed, the high ceilings lowered, the pulpit area relocated, and the entrance now facing Pennsylvania Avenue. Next, a block building with a gym area was constructed. Membership records from 1967 show a total of 313, with an active youth program.

On Easter Sunday, 1974, the current building was dedicated. The original building had been torn down, largely due to termite damage, and construction was to accommodate membership growth, now as a United Methodist Church.

In recent years, the church has grown substantially to a current membership of 1240. Many more group ministries and four services—two contemporary and two traditional—are now offered each week. Property has been purchased and construction begun on a much larger facility on Transmitter Road. Future plans are to grow as believers in Christ and expand ministry, as He blesses and directs.

Submitted by: Pat Garrett, 1518 Missouri Ave., Lynn Haven, FL 32444.

Millville Baptist Church

As a small boy I went to Millville Sunday School at the Baptist Church. One day it rained and we went in the auditorium for the regular church service. As they were concluding the Sunday School portion of it, they asked if anyone had anything to say and I said, "I do." I stood up and I said, "Somebody should fix the roof. It leaks over there in the Sunday School room." Ludie Bear, she lived on the corner just across from the church, said, "This is all biblical and a little child shall lead them." I felt guilty about saying anything about the leaky roof. But the roof was fixed. Later on the church burned. Ludie had the church bell. She got the bell, inverted it, turned it over and put it right at the corner and used it as a large flower pot.

Ludie's mother was Mrs. Cochran and she lived across the bay from Panama City where Thomas Drive is now. Mrs. Cochran and her husband homesteaded 140 acres over there. We would go to Mrs. Cochran's house for Sunday dinner sometimes. We had to go by boat. I remember Mrs. Cochran as being a white haired lady. I remember thinking about how they would have to bring all their groceries by boat. They had dug a well so they had water but most people didn't have hot water heaters because they were too expensive. Most people used wood to cook with in wood stoves. So they had what they called a jacket which is a metal jacket that goes in the wood compartment, the burning compartment. The metal jacket heats up. You run cold water through it and it heats the water as you cook your food. We had one of those. We had a tank and a jacket.

Submitted by: Fred Turner, 2694 Island View Dr., Panama City, FL 32405.

Palo Alto Church of Christ

The first congregation of the Church of Christ in Bay County had its beginning on November 28, 1935 when the West Hill Church of Christ in Pensacola sent the evangelist, Paul Simon, to establish a new church. A community church building located near the site of the International Paper Company in Bay Harbor was used for the first meeting. Services were held on Sunday afternoons, the only time the

Palo Alto Church of Christ

building was available. The young church moved to the Simons' home soon and then the railroad company donated land for a church building in Springfield. Charles Hannah and his pet ox did the land preparation for the building.

The church met in Springfield until 1946 when land was purchased on Hwy 98 and Palo Alto Avenue and a larger church building was built. The church grew until it was large enough to spawn several other congregations in the area. In 1959 a new building was built on the same property facing Palo Alto Avenue and the old building was torn down. Greater than half of the church's contributions were sent to missionary efforts.

By 1987 the church had outgrown the building and parking space. Over six acres was purchased from the Pettis family on Hwy 231 at Ormond Avenue for a new facility. The first service in the new 1.3 million dollar building was held May 15, 1994.

Palo Alto Church of Christ is known for its emphasis on its Childrens' Ministry. Jane Keller, head of "For the Children" at Palo Alto, received national recognition in 2003 for excellence. The church sponsors Palo Alto Daycare Center for children whose parents work outside the home. Its interest abroad continues with assistance in Thailand and the Ukraine.

The church exists to be used by God who transforms people into fully developing followers of Jesus Christ. The minister is Kenneth Grizzell, youth minister, Adam Ellis, and elders are John Johnson, Joe Keller and Jerry Harrison. All visitors are honored guests.

Submitted by: June Harrison, 336 Bunkers Cove Rd., Panama City, FL 32401.

Panama City Seventh-day Adventist Church

The church was organized in May 1931 by Seventh-Day Sabbathkeepers from the St. Andrews, Southport, and Millville areas and located at 424 N. Magnolia Avenue. There were two rooms, a front room for worship services and a back room for operating a Christian school. The land was donated by P.W. Crosby. Generous donations of time and money by members, relatives, and friends made the church a reality with 38 charter members.

In 1952 a need for more space prompted the sale of the church to a local law firm which decided to build around the church building. The pointed roof of the church can still be seen. The church / school moved to a house in the Cove area.

The first meeting in the church located at 1905 W. 11th Street was held Sabbath, January 30, 1954. The school used the Sabbath school rooms until a separate facility could be built. In 1955 a building was added behind the church for fellowship activities as well the school.

Two Churches have been spawned from this church - Maranatha in Panama City (1980) and North Bay in Southport (1995).

In mid - 2001 the 11th Street property was sold to Victory Baptist Church which graciously allowed the school to continue there until July 2002. Sabbath services were held in the Grace Presbyterian Church on Airport Road.

In September 2002 the school moved into its new building and in December 2002 regular weekly worship services and social activities began at the present location at 2700 Lisenby Avenue, Current membership is 490.

Submitted by: Pastor Scott Tyman, 2700 Lisenby Avenue, Panama City, FL 32405.

Parker United Methodist Church

Parker United Methodist Church had its beginnings in the 1800s when it met with other denominations in an old log cabin on the Parker beach front known as Riviere Landing. Later it met in another log cabin, a school just south of to day's Parker Fire Department.

Combined Methodist-Baptist services were preached by circuit riders prior to 1900. Early records show that the Rev. W.A. Prince of the Wewahitchka charge was the first pastor to serve the Parker church. First wedding recorded in the Union Church was that of Arthur Llewellyn Pratt and Gertrude Parker on Sunday, October 6, 1901. Their first son, Stuart Arthur, born Dec. 19, 1902, was baptized in 1903, according to church records.

Methodists and Baptists continued to worship together every month, alternating pastors. They met weekly for Union Sunday School. The Parker Cemetery Association deeded ground to the Methodists in 1935 and construction began on the southeast corner of the cemetery. W.G. Johns supervised construction, with the assistance of the men of the congregation. The white frame building on the corner of West Street and Pitts Avenue served Methodists and Baptists until 1939 when the Baptists began a building program to establish their own church.

In the early years the one-room building was heated by a pot-belly stove. Arthur L. Pratt donated one of his ship's bells to call the congregation to worship. It is still in use in 2003. The church remained at the cemetery location, with the parsonage across the street, until 1958, when property was acquired on the corner of Boat Race Road and U.S. Highway 98 bypass. The church building was moved to the new site during the tenure of the Rev. C.M. Tyndale. The property at Pitts and West was returned to the cemetery association.

At the new location additional Sunday school rooms were built. A fellowship hall was added in 1963. The church continued to grow and plans were made for a new sanctuary which was dedicated in June 1966.

The church in the 21st Century includes a new and expanded fellowship hall, classrooms and a youth center. The congregation, led by Pastor Paul Malson, supports a strong missions program locally, in other states and foreign countries.

Submitted by: Ann Houpt, 1128 Loftin Street, Panama City, Florida.

St. Andrew Baptist Church: A Lighthouse, a Bridge

To celebrate its 100th Anniversary in 1994, St. Andrew Baptist Church published *One Hundred Years Looking Toward the Future: A History Still in the Making.* Excerpts taken from his volume indicate that church growth paralleled that of the area, "a long, slow development...pitted against the uneven ground of Panhandle growth...[Sixteen] Baptists who had been meeting in homes gathered together and constituted the St. Andrew Baptist Church." Church records indicate these as Mary Peel Moates, Ben Moates, Gertrude Rotzein, Jessie Sowell, Elizabeth Sowell, Hawk Stephens, T.N. Knowles, Janie Sowell, Christian Sowell, Docia Singletary, Jane Stephens, Mamie Williams, Mrs. M.J. Corby, Jessy Rowell, Emma Martin and Rev. J.B. Webb. Having been first housed in a building shared by a grocery store, the church purchased its own building, Little's Hall, overlooking the bay in 1895. Continued growth in membership led to the building of the "Church on the Hill" which took its place on what is now the corner of 15th Street and Deer Avenue. The cornerstone for the sanctuary located at 3010 West 15th Street was laid in 1949 by 79 year-old Ben Moates, at 22 a charter member. Through several additions and remodeling to accommodate planned growth, the church now occupies the block at this latest address.

St. Andrew established typical foundations for itself, immediately setting up a graded Sunday School program, Baptist Young People's meetings and Wednesday night meetings "for education discussion of Baptist doctrine." St. Andrew Baptist history indicates the church soon began a mission Sunday School nearby, reflecting what was to be a continual heart of missions. The church went on to found what became Immanuel, Westview, West Bay and Ebro Baptist Churches. This emphasis has continued with contributions to state, home and foreign missions. In recent years the church has maintained its own mission programs including benevolence, the Sheltering Tree pregnancy counseling center, Women of Worth, a deaf ministry and a day care ministry. Members have undertaken mission trips to several foreign countries.

An outstanding program ministering to youth, a vital ladies ministry, the deacons and the Sunday School program have been central throughout the church's history. Members have enriched their Bible study and enjoyed current Christian literature in a well equipped media library. St. Andrew's music programs have ministered to its members and the Bay County area for many years. Today as in the beginning, St. Andrew Baptist Church has endeavored to be a spiritual lighthouse as it builds bridges to the future.

Submitted by: Carol Cowley, 2838 Longleaf Road, Panama City, FL 32405-2045.

St. Andrew/Beck Avenue/Jenks Avenue Church of Christ

The congregation first began meeting in April, 1955, with 33 members using the auditorium of the St. Andrew Elementary School. Gerald McCalister and Gilbert Wilson devoted their time in preaching for the congregation while also pursuing secular work. The St. Andrew Church of Christ met in the school until May 1956.

During this time span, the church purchased a parcel of land at the corner of 17th Street and Beck Avenue in the St. Andrew section of Panama City. Shortly after the purchase of the land, a minister's home was constructed.

On June 3, 1956, the opening services were held in the minister's home and the St. Andrew Church of Christ became the

Church of Christ, 3332 Jenks Avenue

Beck Avenue Church of Christ. Hugh Tucker, who was employed by the Bay County School System, was hired as the minister in September of the same year.

In late 1957, construction of a church building began at the same location as the minister's home. Opening services in the new facility were held on June 1, 1958.

As the congregation grew, the need for a full-time minister was evident and in June, 1959, Byron Laird was hired as the minister. Between 1959 and 1973 five different ministers served the church: Byron Laird, C.C. Arquitt, Gerald Robinson, L.E. Wright and Doyle Smith.

Then in July, 1973, the Jack Reece family moved to Panama City to take up the local work. Jack and his wife, Pam, continue to faithfully serve this congregation.

Between 1973 and 1983, the Beck Avenue Church of Christ steadily grew in membership so that two Sunday morning worship services were needed to accommodate those attending.

The congregation purchased a tract of land on Jenks Avenue in August of 1984 and a new facility was completed in July, 1993 on that property. Thus began the Jenks Avenue Church of Christ which has subsequently grown to a membership of four hundred.

A Family Activity Center was completed on the Jenks Avenue property in October, 2001, to better serve the congregation.

The Jenks Avenue Church of Christ is a non-denominational, autonomous church family with no ties to any earthly headquarters. Jesus is the head of the church, which is His body. Elders (a term used interchangeably in the scripture with

Pastor and Bishop) serve as leaders by shepherding the "flock" (spiritually feeding and protecting), giving spiritual counsel, and overseeing decisions affecting the church family. (I Peter 5:1-3)

The first two elders were Renfro Lloyd and the late Gilbert Wilson. Currently there are seven elders: Hal Burleson, Paul Calhoun, Jim Holsombake, Dale McKeand, M.C. Pippin, Hugh Tucker, and Wayne Wegner. Serving under them is the Minister, Coordinator of Youth Activities and twenty-two deacons with assigned ministries.

Submitted by: Jenks Avenue Church of Christ, Hugh Tucker, 3332 Jenks Avenue, Panama City, FL 32405.

Saint Andrew United Methodist Church

In this year of 2003 the Saint Andrew United Methodist Church at 2001 West Eleventh Street celebrates its 117th year. Its beginning dates back to 1886 when the first Methodist circuit rider rode through what is now Bay County and faced danger at every turn as he planted a seed instilling an interest in the gospel.

Sketch of the St. Andrew United Methodist Church in 1986

Following in his footsteps was a lady minister, Miss Jenny E Smith, who traveled countywide by bicycle as far as Allentown.

The first church, which is still standing today, was erected in what then was Washington County; Bay County had not yet been carved out. The little wood frame church on Eleventh Street and Chestnut Avenue in Saint Andrews had a high peaked roof with a belfry tower tipped with a cross. The tower held a huge bell, which pealed forth before every service as well as for fires and other exciting events. It is remembered how it rang with vigor when World War II was over and armistice was declared. This bell still performs the duty of call to worship in the steeple of the current church on Eleventh Street, which was built in 1955.

The women played a part in planning the inside of the new church. They visited other churches to see how the insides were furnished, One such interior was in Washington D.C at the Foundry Church. It had the divided chancel, the white marble altar and the beautiful kneeling rail of rough iron with sprays of grapes intertwined. This design was unanimously accepted and completed the beauty of the church. The devoted members volunteered their services making each area of the church function with love and appreciation. Each time one has been privileged to enter Saint Andrew United Methodist Church, they are impressed anew by the priceless preciousness of the people that still make this church so stately and strong, during the solidarity and the quiet hours worshiping our Father.

Submitted by: Janice Whitehurst, 900 De Gama Ave., Panama City, FL 32401. Written by: Nita Whitehurst, 2710 Frankford Ave., PC 32405.

St. Andrew's Episcopal Church, Panama City, Florida

Christ Church, St. Andrews, Fla.

St. Andrew's Episcopal Church had its origins in the first decade of the twentieth century as neighbors began meeting for worship in local homes. One home where such meetings took place was that of A.D. Weller at 2308 W. Beach Drive, still owned and occupied by the Weller family. Not long after 1910, property was given for the church on Beach Drive and the original wooden frame building was constructed and consecrated in 1914 as Christ Episcopal Church, St. Andrews. An early photograph around 1915 shows a large gathering of church members that included A.D. Weller and his family, with his brothers, the Rt. Rev. Reginald Heber Weller, Episcopal Bishop of Fond du Lac, Wisconsin and the Rev. Charles Knight Weller of Tennessee. As was the case with many Episcopal congregations that began as "Christ Church," the name of the local church was eventually changed to take the name of a revered New Testament saint. St. Andrew's Church has flourished over the years, serving for decades as the only Episcopal Church in Panama City and Bay County; but out of that beginning four other congregations have sprung up, from St. Thomas' Episcopal Church, Laguna Beach to Holy Nativity Episcopal Church in the Cove Section of Panama City. The original wooden church building was modified and expanded several times over the years. Finally, in the mid-1950's it was given to the local Greek Orthodox congregation and moved to their property on Baldwin Avenue. St. Andrew's Episcopal Church erected their new brick building on West Beach Drive in 1958-1959 and they are still at that historic, picturesque location looking out across St. Andrew's Bay.

Prepared by the Rev. Thomas Carroll Weller, Jr. Submitted by: Gina Weller Webb, 1025 W 19th St., 2-D, Panama City, FL 32405.

St John Missionary Baptist Church

St John Missionary Baptist Church's history dates back to the year 1923. A wood framed structure stood on the corner of Eleventh Street and Mercedes Ave. Serving as pastor from 1923 to 1929 was Rev. N. M. Hutchins, Rev. Willie Cady, Rev. G. W. McClinton and Rev. L. J. Flowers. 1929 to 1940 was Rev. William Gipson, 1940 to 1946 was Rev. W. S. Drayton, Jr., 1946 to 1952 Rev. T. J. Jones, 1952 to 1963 Rev. L. P. Davis, Sr., 1964 to 1989, Pastor Jackson E. Jones, 1989 to 1991 Rev. James B. Hamilton served as Interim Pastor, 1991 to 1992 Rev. Bernard Blount, 1992 to 2000 Dr. Rory L. Bedford and 2001 Pastor Delwynn G. Williams.

Pastor Delwynn G. Williams

Pastor Williams is a member of the National Baptist Convention of America, Progressive M. E. Baptist Convention of Florida, Progressive Baptist Association of West Florida, NAACP, SCLC (serving as Bay County chapter President), listed in Who's Who Among Business Leaders and in the 1987 edition of Outstanding Young Men Of America.

The Church has a radio ministry and is preparing for a television ministry. The Church stands proudly on the corner of Martin Luther King, Jr. Blvd and Eleventh Street. Before the old Church was demolished, three crosses appeared in the window. People came from all over to witness this mystery. St John's has just celebrated eighty blessed years. God bless St John's, Pastor Williams, his wife Susan, their children, Britni Cherell and Brandon Darnell and all the St John members.

Written and submitted by: Maureen Marshall Smith, 8009 Highway 22, Panama City, FL 32404.

Springfield Baptist Church

First meetings of the group that would become Springfield Baptist Church were held in the summer of 1943 in the Springfield Elementary School building. Assistance was given by Immanuel Baptist pastor Adolph Bedsole and several Immanuel members, including George and Mary Jane Shores.

Sunday School was begun in June, with H. D. Smith serving as the first superintendent.

Following a July revival led by C. L. Wattenbarger, superintendent of Northwest Coast Baptist Association, new converts were baptized in Parker Bayou.

Training Union was organized in October, with I. R. Culbreth serving as the first director.

Official organization with 28 charter members was December 8, 1943, at a meeting in the home of Mr. and Mrs. B. S. Outlaw. H. M. Conner was called as interim pastor.

First Service in New Building on Third Street, June 1952

Mrs. J. N. Vann was instrumental in establishing a Women's Missionary Society.

In 1944, a house on School Avenue was purchased and remodeled to serve as a church building.

In 1945, J. B. Ansley was called as first pastor, and a house on a lot adjacent to the church property was purchased for a pastorium.

With Ira Hill as finance chairman, property was purchased on Third Street in 1951, at the present site of the church. Franklin Shores prepared architectural plans for the new building that was erected, and first services at that location were held in June of 1952.

First church secretary was Betty Hughes, and first church librarian was Jim Bertha Powell.

Property was purchased on Helen Avenue for a pastorium, and the building was completed in 1964.

Members have assisted in establishing three additional Baptist churches: Midway, Howard Carlisle, and East Bay.

Current pastor is Jerry Everage.

Persons in the accompanying photograph are: First row: Larry Hicks; Ronnie Hicks; Mary June Williams; Thelma Bauler; Evon Blount; Lamar Clark; Jimmy Clark; Patricia Shores: Catherine Tharpe; Ann Johnson; Judy Tharpe; Annie Charles Tharpe. Renee Duncan; Jeff Hodges; Terry Hodges; John Tharpe; J. M. Tharpe. Second row: Mae Blount; L.T. Blount; Bobby Roughton; Billy Blount; Rev. and Mrs. C. H. Frye; Mrs. S. G. Bryan; Mrs. J. A. Hoffman; Pera Lee Peacock; Pauline Johnson; ____; Mary Jane Shores; Marie Duncan; Betty Sue Tharpe; Anita Hodges; Ira Hill; Ford Hewitt; Jerry Hicks. Third row: ____; Johnny Boyette; ____; ____; J.M. Williams; Charles Goodman; Margie Goodman; Arthur Duncan; George Shores; Jewel Clark; ____; Rubylea Futch; W. A. Futch; ____; Charles Hodges.

Fourth row: Harry Powell; Jim Bertha Powell; Gwen Boyette; Sybil Moody; Mrs. S. B. Nix; ____; ____; ____; Elvira Carroll; Mrs. J. N. Vann; W. R. Sadler; Elma Hill; Zelda Hill; _____; Editha Smith; Lorene Hughes; Effie Hughes; ____; Sherman Hicks; Jewel Hicks.

Submitted by: Springfield Baptist Church, 3615 E. 3rd St., Panama City, FL 32401

Springfield - Parkway Presbyterian Church

On January 26, 1938, a Sunday School was organized in a vacant store building at the corner of the Wewa and Coastal Highways. January 9, 1939, ground was marked for a new church building.

November 12, 1939 a petition was drawn and signed to The Presbytery of Florida for a Presbyterian church to be organized at Springfield, it was presented on November 22.

A Commission of Florida Presbytery was appointed and met on January 14, 1940 to organize the church. Rev. Thomas Watson was the organizing minister. Rev. James W. Marshall served as minister of that church longer than any other minister.

Fall of 1959, the church relocated to present location; changed its name to Parkway Presbyterian Church. The Rev. G. Davies was the first pastor there. In 1980, the church purchased the Skipper's property and the remodeled facility has been used for various community groups and youth activities. A contest was

held to name the property "Skipper's Nest". The fellowship hall was remodeled that year.

On March 3, 1985, groundbreaking services were held for a new sanctuary, choir room and administrative wing. Beautiful stained glass windows were installed. Easter worship services were held on the foundation. Dedication services were held on October 20, 1985.

In 1986, the first softball team was formed. Easter Sunrise services were held outside. We were recognized in the *Presbyterian Survey* magazine as one of the first churches to use the church seal in its stained glass design.

Stained glass window in sanctuary of Parkway Presbyterian Church

January 14, 1990, celebrated our 50th Anniversary.

In 1995: Hurricane Opal blew the steeple to the ground. That same year a pioneer member, Elder emeritus, Wilson McKinnon, disappeared and his fate was never learned.

We celebrated 60th year Anniversary in 2000.

Submitted by: Sherl Morden, Church Historian 2003-04, 505 S. Tyndall Parkway, Panama City, FL 32404.

Straightway Christian Ministries

June 2, 1991 in the home of Pastors Franklin W. (Sammy) Stewart and Sandi Stewart, The Harvestors Home Church had its first service and official start as a church body. In attendance, were nine individuals who were committed to the ministry that the Lord was raising up.

They met in Pastor Stewart's home for two weeks. The third week they were able to hold their services in their new location at 229 N. Tyndall

Straightway Christian Ministries

Parkway known as the Callaway Village Square Shopping Center. The next eleven months they experienced growth beyond their expectations. Their average attendance reached 50-60. They then secured the adjacent building next to them which was at one time a furniture store. After renovating the building, they moved in and God continued to bless them. June 12, 1994, The Harvestors Home Church was changed to Straightway Christian Ministries, Inc. and in August of 1994 they relocated to 7124 Hwy 22.

On August 30, 1995, they purchased five acres of land located at 5031 N. Star Avenue, with plans to build a new facility and relocate Straightway Ministries to its permanent home. They held a ground breaking service January 24, 1999 with a powerful attendance.

On July 18, 1999 they held their dedication service to their NEW church. Praise God! On June 8, 2003 they celebrated their twelfth anniversary and continue to look forward to what the Lord has planned ahead. Knowing that the scripture says, "He that began a good work in you will see it through to its completed state." It's exciting to know there is yet more to come and they anxiously and excitedly look forward to what lays ahead.

Submitted by: Sammy Stewart, Sr., Pastot.

Trinity Lutheran Church

Trinity Lutheran Church, Panama City, was organized in 1952 and conducted worship services at the old City Hall until the Sanctuary was built and dedicated in 1954. The Church was graced with Panama City's first stained glass window - a

Stained Glass Window in the Trinity Lutheran Church, 1001 W. 11th Street, Panama City, Florida

beautiful Crucifix above the Altar made of stained glass from Germany.

The Church built an Education Building for its most ambitious project - Bay County's first Kindergarten. Trinity educated children of all races and denominations from 1956 until 1971 when the public school system initiated a Kindergarten program.

Our pastors over the years have been: Rev. Eduard Schack, April 1952-September 1954; Rev. Henry Storm, April 1955-January 1965; Rev. Theodore Strelow, May 1965-December 1969; Rev. Alan Steinke, August 1971-June 1977; Leonard Wilhelm, February 1978-September 1979; Rev. Dr. Roland Schutz, October 1980-August 1999; Rev. Edward Meyer, August 1999- July 2001; Rev. Dr. Wesley Toncre, April 2001-Present.

Submitted by: Paul Richard Parker, 3201 W. Highway 98, Panama City, FL 32401.

Trinity United Methodist Church

In the early 1900's, Millville was a populous town on Watson Bayou. The lumber industry was booming in the South. Previously known as Watson Bayou Community, Millville derived its name from one of the largest sawmills in the nation built on the western shore of Watson Bayou in 1899.

Painting of the Trinity United Methodist Church

A group of citizens, recognizing the need for a Methodist church, organized the Millville Methodist Episcopal Church, South. The first services were at various locations until a suitable permanent site could be secured. Founding members included several prominent citizens instrumental in the formation of Panama City in 1909 and Bay County in 1913.

In the early days Miss Lillian Carlilse, and her father, would travel from Callaway in a horse-drawn buggy to teach Sunday School. Miss Carlilse wed G.M. West, founder of Panama City.

In 1902, the Board of Stewards voted to purchase the present property on Third Street from Mrs. L. V. Holmes for fifty dollars. After a payment of twenty dollars, Mrs. L. V. Holmes considered the debt paid. Plans for the church, a clapboard structure adorned with a bell, steeple and shuttered windows, were completed in 1904.

Seeing the need for a church on the east side of the bayou with no bridge at that time, the minister and other members traveled by rowboat to conduct services in the small settlement of Harrison (Panama City). In 1907, those efforts led to the organization of a church in that community. As a result, Trinity United Church is the "mother church" of First United Methodist Church. In 1948, the present sanctuary was completed and in 1949 the church changed its name to the Trinity Methodist Church. In 1968, the word "United" was added, uniting three denominations which shared a common Methodist heritage.

Trinity United Methodist Church is entering its second century, proclaiming the gospel of Jesus Christ in the Millville area.

Submitted by: Trinity United Methodist Church, 2322 E. Third Street, Panama City, Fl 32401. Written by: Wayne McLeod.

Unitarian Universalist Fellowship of Bay County

In the late 1950's, some members of the Philosophical Society extended their quest for enlightenment into a more spiritual

Unitarian Universalist Fellowship meeting place

realm by organizing a Unitarian Fellowship. Membership was open to all who wanted to engage in a free search for truth and meaning. They were also active in social causes that were considered "liberal", including racial integration and environmentalism. The Fellowship engaged in school integration activities such as the "Freedom School" that was held on Saturdays at St. John's Catholic Church to introduce white and African-American children to each other in a supportive setting.

In 1961, a national merger of Unitarian and Universalists occurred, so the local group changed its name accordingly, and they maintain membership in the Unitarian Universalist Association headquartered in Boston. The group met at the Panama City Garden Club, Oakland Terrace Recreation Center, and other rented locations until 2002 when they purchased the former Summerford home at the intersection of Airport Road and Lisenby Avenue. The house has been converted to a comfortable meeting space, and the grounds, which include a pond and historic plantings, are being managed as a National Wildlife Federation "Backyard Refuge".

The Rev. Harold Hawkins of Tallahassee has provided ministry to the Fellowship for many years on a part-time basis. Visiting ministers, lay speakers, and representatives of community groups have led the group in the thought and discussion that are a hallmark of the UU tradition.

Submitted by: Candis Harbison

West Bay Baptist Church

Church history began early in the year 1950. A group of concerned folk met on the front porch of a house that Mr. & Mrs. Angus Watford were building. Among those gathered were Mr. & Mrs. V. V. Wilson; Mrs. Lee Cauley; Mrs. Gladys Duck; Mr. & Mrs. Henry Taunton; Mrs. Alma Coram; Mrs. Myrtle Caraway and Mrs. Tiny Scott. They were having a prayer meeting seeking the direction of the Lord about some way to get a Baptist Church in the West Bay area. And thus was the humble beginning of this wonderful Church in the body of Christ.

West Bay Baptist Church

They had been meeting in different places and homes and later that year, prayers began to be answered. In June 1950 Mr. E. W. Scott and his wife Dollie donated a parcel of land to build a Church on. They also donated a parcel of ground for part of the "old" cemetery. On June 6th, 1950 Mr. & Mrs. Scott met Mr. V. V. Wilson, Mr. Angus Watford and Mr. Henry Taunton at the Bay County Court House and made the final transition on the piece of land soon to become the home of the West Bay Baptist Mission with our mother Church sponsor being the First Baptist Church of St. Andrews, now called the St. Andrews Baptist Church. Brother Bill Davis and Brother Lewin were present as witnesses.

Submitted by: Dolly Anderson, 11818 Church Road, Ebro, FL 32437.

Woodlawn United Methodist Church

The Woodlawn United Methodist Church had its beginning on October 8, 1957 in the home of Sid and Georgia Henry with approximately 12 people to plan for a new beach church. Drs. W. B. Atkinson, Sr.. District Superintendent and Carlisle Miller, First Methodist Church pastor also attended.

Earl Padgett, W o o d l a w n Subdivison developer, donated the 5 acres for the church plus a lot for the parsonage

A sketch of the original 1957 Woodlawn United Methodist Church

in addition to building the two at cost of the materials. Additional land was later provided by the Padgetts.

The first church service was held in the Padgett Construction office on Thanksgiving, November 28. 1957. A rented parsonage and Monterrey Motel served as the church until June. 1958, when the congregation celebrated their first Sunday in the new building at 202 Carolyn Blvd. The ladies lost no time before organizing work crews to landscape and raise funds for church and parsonage furniture. They made altar arrangements and asked each member for 10 cents for a building at Blue Lake Conference Grounds. But "... not to interfere with our mission pledge."

In 1981, classrooms were added and offices plus the fellowship hall were expanded. "Snowbirds" began arriving in the 1970's and an anonymous donor, in 1988, made possible an 80 seat sanctuary addition.

According to a forty year church history published in 1997, the membership for that year was 689 with a budget of $366,850 contrasted with a dozen families who initially budgeted $9,000 in 1957. The 1950's median U.S. income was $5,087.

As a result of continued growth during the decades of eleven pastors, a groundbreaking for the new church on Alf Coleman Road was led by the Rev. Ronald Ball on September 30, 2001.

Submitted by: Georgia T. Henry-Pearson, 7752 Shadow Bay Drive, Panama City, FL 32404.

LOCAL AUTHORS AND ARTISTS

Winston Chester

Winston Chester is the author of *"Full Box!": 100 years of fishing and boat building history in Bay County*. This book was the 2002 award winner of the Best Local History Monograph presented by the Florida Historical Society.

Winston is a native of Quincy, Florida and a fifth generation North Floridian. His love of the outdoors began at an early age while fishing and hunting with his dad and brothers in the woods and waters of the Florida panhandle.

Nick Wynne, Executive Director Florida Historical Society and Winston Chester, recipient of Best Local History Monograph Award 2002

After graduation from Quincy High School, he attended the University of Florida on a football scholarship and received a Bachelor of Science degree in Physical Education. He later completed a Master of Educational Administration degree from the University of West Florida and an Educational Specialist degree from Florida State University.

He has taught and coached in the Bay District School System for 30 years and currently teaches Outdoor Education and Physical Education at Mosley High School.

He and his wife, Gail, live on North Bay in Southport where they enjoy fishing for speckled trout and redfish.

Submitted by: Winston Chester, 6726 Toepfer Blvd., Southport, FL 32409

Jeannie Weller Cooper

Jeannie Weller Cooper lives in the Cove with her husband Robert, their two daughters, and an assortment of animal companions. Although her family goes back to Florida's Spanish Colonial era, Mrs. Cooper is an Atlanta native and only returned to the state in 1999. She divides her time between family, church, research and writing, and volunteer work in the community, most notably with the Historical Society of Bay County

She underscored her commitment to preserving the Cove's

unique character and history with the publication of her first book, *The Cove, Panama City's Neighborhood*, an Arcadia Publishing Images of America book in 2002.

Submitted by: Author.

Dr Samuel Homola: Panama City Author

Dr. Samuel Homola of Panama City, Florida, is one of Florida's most prolific authors. More than 200 of his articles have appeared in such magazines and journals as *Cosmopolitan*, *Scholastic Coach*, *Swimming World*, *Consumer's Digest*, *Let's Live*, *Skeptical Inquirer*, *Chiropractic Technique*, *Scientific Review of Alternative Medicine*, *Skeptic*, *Nutrition Forum*, and *Priorities for Health*. His article, "Finding a Good Chiropractor," published in the January, 1998, issue of *Archives of Family Medicine*, was the first chiropractor-authored article ever published in a journal of the American

Dr. Samuel Homola

Medical Association. *The Skeptic Encyclopedia of Pseudoscience*, a two-volume library reference published by ABC-CLIO, INC., in 2002, contains a chapter written by Dr. Homola.

Homola began writing as a hobby in 1963 when one of his articles appeared in the May issue of *Strength & Health*, a popular weightlifting and fitness magazine. His first book, *Bonesetting, Chiropractic and Cultism*, also published in 1963, was reviewed in the February 1, 1964, issue of *Library Journal* and recommended for inclusion in medical and reference libraries. His next two books, *Backache: Home Treatment and Prevention* and *Muscle Training for Athletes*, were published in 1968 by Parker Publishing Company, a division of Prentice Hall, who published 10 of his books in succession. Two of Homola's books were co-authored by Peter Lupus of "Mission Impossible" fame. Lupus opened Peter Lupus' Leisure Health World Spa on Panama City Beach in 1974, where Homola lectured regularly. In 1977, Lupus began hosting "Peter Lupus' Body Shop," a nationally syndicated television series filmed at Paramount Studios in Hollywood, California. Dr. Homola appeared as a guest on two of these shows, which led to co-authored publication of *Peter Lupus' Guide to Radiant Health and Beauty: Mission Possible for Women* in 1978 and *Peter Lupus' Celebrity Body Book: A Body Improvement Guide for Men and Women* in 1980.

Dr. Homola retired from practice as a chiropractor in 1998. His book *Inside Chiropractic* was published by Prometheus in 1999 and added to the Consumer Health Library series. His latest book, *The Chiropractor's Self-Help Back and Body Book*, published by Hunter House in 2002, is the culmination of 43 years of treating patients and writing articles on health subjects.

Submitted by: Dr. Samuel Homola, 1307 E. 2nd Ct., Panama City, FL 32401-4003

Ann Pratt Houpt

Ann Pratt Houpt, author of *Images of America Parker Florida*, is a sixth generation descendant of William Loftin, one of the early settlers of the Parker area. The first year of her life she and her parents, Stuart and Bernice Pratt, lived in the home of grandparents, A.L. and Gertrude Pratt. Gertrude was a great granddaughter of Loftin.

After attending Parker Elementary School for first through eighth grades, Ann graduated to Bay High School for grades nine through 12. She attended Florida State University with a Lewis Scholarship, planning to teach Spanish and French. She left FSU after two years to marry Roy L. Houpt, Jr., who was stationed at Tyndall Air Force Base.

They lived in Lenni, Pennsylvania for five years before moving back to Parker. She enrolled in classes at Gulf Coast Community College attending evening classes while substituting in Bay County Schools. Other employment included five years as a reporter/feature writer/state editor at the Panama City *News Herald*, and a year at the Bay County Chamber of Commerce before coming to the Bay County Public Library in December 1977 as a young adult assistant in the Youth Department.

Ann Pratt Houpt

Ann completed the picture history of Parker in May 2003. She is currently planning two similar projects, hopefully for Arcadia Publishing. The Houpts reside in Parker. They have two sons, three granddaughters and one great grandson. The family also includes Ann's mother Bernice Pratt. A Yorkie named Hamish is in charge of security.

Submitted by: Ann Pratt Houpt, 1128 Loftin St., Parker, FL.

Linda Pazics Kleback

I had always dreamed of being a writer. I'd attended writers' conferences and workshops in Pennsylvania and had some modest success publishing poetry and short stories in literary magazines. What I had never expected was to find my niche in writing about family history. When genealogy became a passion, sharing information did as well. Since I had such varied backgrounds to research in the Pazics and Kleback families, I was exposed to a wide variety of record sources. Working at the Bay County Public Library required me to become familiar with Southern records. As I discovered

Linda Pazics Kleback

resources that had not been published, I found a new calling.

Getting genealogy information in print is vital to me. I have written 150+ articles on Florida and Pennsylvania source records which were published in a variety of journals including *The Florida Genealogist*, the *Western Pennsylvania Genealogical Society Quarterly*, *West Florida Footprints*, *The County Line*, and the *Southern Genealogist's Exchange Society Quarterly*. From 1990 to 1994, I served as the editor of *The Florida Genealogist* and was able to get some wonderful information published that helped many researchers including some working on their Florida Pioneer Descendant certificates.

Since 1991 I have written "Tracing Pasts", a weekly genealogy column in the Panama City *News Herald*. This has given me the opportunity to spread the word about record sources, books, conferences, and other genealogical current events. A highlight was the chance to let readers know about the ongoing battle to save the Florida State Library and Archives in 2003.

As long as there are records out there that we genealogists need, there will be a demand for articles about them. I hope to contribute to the body of genealogical literature for many years to come.

Submitted by: Linda Pazics Kleback, 1607 Belmont Blvd., Lynn Haven, FL 32444-3343.

Barbara Mulligan

Barbara Mulligan has been painting and printing woodblocks for over thirty years in Panama City. She began painting local landmarks and created over 300 scenes in the northwest Florida area. Her best known work was of the old Cove Hotel which was

located (1926-1976) on Cherry Street in the cove section of Panama City. Senator Bob Graham owns the original of this work.

Barbara's first career was in public education where she worked as teacher and administrator for over 30 years. Upon retirement in 1992 she began working as a professional artist creating images for a national market sold by a local company. Painting and printing woodblocks using only watercolors has led to the development of three major shows. Her first show, *At A Window*, was based on the poetry of Carl Sandburg. It has twenty painting/prints chosen as a cross-section of the famous poet's work.

Barbara Laird Welch Mulligan, 1957. Photo taken the year she married George

The show was so large that it had to be edited to sixteen works. The second show, *Bay Windows*, is based on nostalgic 'stained glass' scenes from Bay County. The last show, *A Muse Looks On*, is based on poetry the artist wrote.

Barbara and her husband George are parents and grandparents of ten who all live in Panama City. They represent five generations who have lived in Bay County since 1912.

Submitted by: Studio Gallery, Barbara Mulligan Landmarks, 1016 Buena Vista Boulevard Panama City, Florida 32401.

George Mulligan

George Mulligan began a hobby of photography in his native state of New Jersey over fifty years ago. He joined the navy after college graduation from Rutgers University and trained in Pensacola. He met and married his wife Barbara in Panama City. George served as a blimp pilot at various air stations. After service he began a career in education and taught in his home state where they started their family of two sons and two daughters. The family moved back to Florida in 1970. The couple worked in public schools for the next thirty years.

Upon retirement in 1992 George embarked on a second career in videography. He built an edit studio next to his wife's studio and has created over 100 videos. His subject matter is as varied as his life experiences. Foreign travel, local events, unusual family activities and 'underground art' dominate most of his video productions. He captured scenes such as a visit with Dylan Thomas' friends in Swansee, Wales, the climbing of Mt. Krizvac in Bosnia, a tour of Israel, Easter Mass at the Vatican, the Chinese gardens in Vancouver, British Columbia, the 'Spirit Mounds' of South Dakota as well as the vanishing scenes of Bay County. He now produces DVDs with music and text using the latest technology. He also enjoys the role of father and grandfather in his adopted state of Florida.

Submitted by: George R. Mulligan, "Take A Mulligan," 1016 Buena Vista Boulevard, Panama City, FL 32401.

George Mulligan, 1957. Taken the year he married Barbara

Tommy Smith

Tommy Smith was born in Huntsville, AL in 1911. His family moved to Panama City in 1916. He attended Panama Grammar School and Bay High School. He received a Masters in Arts Degree from the University of Florida in 1934. He is a local author of several books on Bay County history; including "The History of Bay County from the Beginning."

He taught at Bay High School from 1934-1937. He was elected Superintendent of Bay County Schools in 1948 and served until 1960. In 1978, he was elected to the School Board and served until 1990. He held many state wide positions including being President of the Florida Superintendent Association in 1951. He was made a Life Member of the Florida PTA in 1960.

Local Author, Tommy Smith

His list of community organizations includes being a charter member of Panama City Elks Club, Moose Lodge and St. Andrews Bay Yacht Club. He has served as President and Lt. Governor of the Kiwanis Club and was Kiwanis Citizen of the Year in 1959 and 1995. He is a Past President of the Bay County Historical Society and an active member today. He is a Sunday School teacher and the historian of First Methodist Church where he has been a member since 1916.

Tommy Smith is a gentleman, historian and story teller who has left a rich legacy to the citizens of Bay County, Florida.

Submitted by: Tommy Smith, 801 Florida Avenue, Panama City, FL.

Marlene Womack, Local Author

Marlene Minch Womack is the author of four books on Bay County and Northwest Florida, where she has researched local history for the past 30 years. She also is a frequent speaker on historical subjects in this area.

Womack, who was born in Elizabeth, N.J., grew up in neighboring Linden. She attended Linden public schools, then graduated from Newark Prep in Newark, N.J. The writer's interest in history extends back to her youth. She lived a block away from where George Washington traveled from New York City to Philadelphia and saw many of the landmarks from those early days. Womack's paternal grandmother, uncle and father instilled a love of history in her by taking her to old cemeteries, historical homes and sites and vacant houses, supposedly

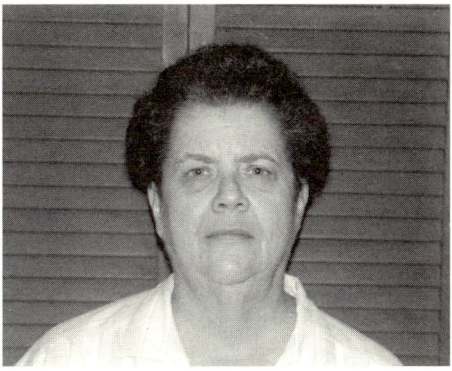
Marlene Womack

occupied by "ghosts." Her grandmother had been part of New York City's "Gibson girl" era and told her many stories about the city, Coney Island and Long Island in the late 1800s and early 1900s.

Her maternal grandmother wintered in Florida each year. She sent post cards and brought home souvenirs, which kindled Womack's interest in the state. Comedian Arthur Godfrey became one of the first to broadcast television from Miami. During freezing winters up north, viewers saw him in the evening on the beach in balmy Miami, which gave Womack an even greater interest in the semi-tropical state.

At 19, the author married Loy A. Womack of Dallas County, Arkansas, whom she met the previous year on a weekend with girlfriends in Washington, D.C. He was in the Air Force and transferred from Ft. Belvoir, VA to Sheppard AFB in Wichita Falls, TX From that base it was on to Little Rock, AFB, AR; Tin City, Alaska (an isolated tour without dependents); Eglin AFB, FL; Hickam AFB, Hawaii; and McGuire AFB, NJ. After spending his final years at Tyndall AFB, FL, he retired in this area.

In the meantime, their three sons were born: Matthew in 1964, Michael in 1967 and Fred in 1974.

When Womack arrived in Panama City with her family in 1973, she immediately began researching, locating and indexing each of the 60 or more cemeteries and grave sites in Bay County. While at McGuire AFB, Womack had read minister and writer H. Charlton Beck's books about old towns in South and North Jersey. Womack enjoyed tromping through the woods with her boys locating these old sites.

From Beck's writings and her own previous research in New Jersey she knew the importance of tombstone records to genealogists when old birth and death certificates or the family Bible were not available. Besides her cemetery research, Womack spent three years reading all the old newspapers available in preparation for a county cemetery book.

But interest in learning more about the area in which each graveyard was located took preference. In the early 1980s, she took courses in journalism and creative writing at Gulf Coast Community College and Florida State University. Her professor at FSU took time one day to take her to the assistant editor of the News-Herald, Ken Cazales, to tell him Womack needed to be published.

She began writing her weekly "Out of the Past" column in April 1982 and continues it today. "Along the Bay," her first book, and "The Pictorial History of Panama City Beach," her third book, were printed by publishers and are no longer available.

"The Bay Country" is a collection of 40 articles that have appeared over the years in her newspaper column. "War Comes to Florida's Northern Gulf Coast" tells about life at Tyndall Field; Eglin Field; the Navy Base; Apalachicola Airfield; Camp Gordon Johnston, near Carrabelle; Marianna Airfield; and Dale Mabry Field in Tallahassee during World War II. This book contains about 40 pages on the activities at Wainwright Shipyard in Panama City where 102 Liberty ships and six tankers were built during the war. This also gives glimpses of the South Pacific through a local woman's diary while she served as a World War II nurse.

Submitted by: Marlene Womack, P.O. Box 15631, Panama City, FL 32406.

HISTORICAL STORIES

Aftermath

A convoy of vehicles rolled out of Montgomery, Alabama, on the morning of October 5, 1995, headed back to Bay County after the passage of Hurricane Opal. Traffic wasn't as slow as the previous day's northward journey, when it seemed everyone in the Florida Panhandle and southern Alabama was running from the storm.

After being turned away by numerous motels my son Chris and I luckily found shelter with an ex-college buddy of his. We spent a horrible night being pounded by a Category 1 hurricane nearly 200 miles inland!

Damage at Front Beach Road and Riviera Drive done by Hurricane Opal in October of 1995

As we rolled south on U. S. 231, we didn't know what to expect down on the beach. We couldn't pick up any radio stations and didn't find anyplace with power until we got to Ozark. From there we detoured and backtracked our way into Florida and just outside of Bonifay, we finally picked up a radio station. Two guys were describing damage in Bay County. They never identified the station, but they kept repeating things like, "Remember the Treasure Ship? It's gone. Remember Pineapple Willie's? It's gone, too." On and on they went citing a litany of destruction. Chris and I looked at each other, stomachs churning. That wasn't what we wanted to hear.

The depressing duo did make us aware that no one was being allowed into Bay County. Highway 79 was blocked at the county line. We drove to DeFuniak Springs, came south on 331 and turned east on U. S. 98, hoping we could sneak in from the west. Unfortunately we found the road blocked at the east end of the Phillips Inlet bridge. The troopers had no idea when, or if, the road would be opened.

I could tell Chris was pondering over something. Finally, he told me he was going to walk in. If his truck was okay, he'd drive to the other side of the barricade and tell me. If he didn't show up, then the truck couldn't be driven and I could expect the worst. He slipped into the nearby woods and headed toward Pinnacle Port. I walked up to the barricades to wait.

About an hour later, here came Chris in his little red Toyota. He got out grinning and I knew everything was all right. The feeling of relief I had can't be described. A few shingles were blown off my house and a window was blown out. There was no damage to his house and he even had power! Both houses were only a block off Front Beach Road and about two blocks apart. The accompanying photo shows the devastation on the stretch of Front Beach Road between our houses.

Later that night they let us in and I drove to Chris' house. I stayed there several days until I got power back. Our wives hadn't returned yet, but we survived. We quickly saw the spirit of Bay County. Neighbor helped neighbor and everyone worked together to overcome Opal's effects. But it was something most folks never want to do again.
Submitted by: Jeff Webb, 21305 Caribbean Lane, Panama City, FL 32413.

Depression Times

During the Depression years food was simple but the mother's knew how to make the most from what was available. Heating was by fireplaces and oil burning stoves. It is understandable that I would think winters were cold. I do remember ice along the Bay. The unpaved streets were frozen. The summer was hot and windows stayed open to catch a breeze. These old houses did not have screens at their windows. The houses were designed by people from northern climates and often had a steep roof to shed the ice and snow. They did use cross ventilation in their plans and the high ceilings added to our comfort. We were not afraid of intruders and used screen doors.

Our main entertainment was swimming in the Bay from the Villa and Oaks piers. The school ground was a gathering place for ball games. We enjoyed paper dolls, cutting them from the Montgomery Ward or Sears Roebuck catalogs. We used wallpaper books to design our houses. This cost nothing and we became totally involved on hot summer afternoons.
Submitted by: Gene Howell Sapp, 1409 Deer Avenue, Panama City, FL 32401.

The Final Flight of Second Lieutenant Edwin L. Gorbet
"Greater love hath no man..."

People living in Panama City in the autumn of 1953 will never forget the horrendous explosion that rattled windows and broke downtown plate glass windows that fateful Monday at noontime on September 28, 1953. I personally was sitting at the table in the lunchroom at Panama Grammar School, along with students from Mrs. Wilma McFatter's sixth grade class, and it scared the students so badly that many dove under the dinner tables out of fear for their safety's sake.

Second Lieutenant Edwin Leroy Gorbet notified the Tyndall Control Tower of the emergency and they gave him permission to go ahead and abort the plane immediately. He saw the area he was in with several schools and a heavily populated residential area close by. He informed the Tyndall authorities that he would eject but would not do so until he reached St. Andrews Bay to where there would be no possible ground casualties. However, he never made it to the bay waters. While still talking to the Control Tower personnel, the F86-D sabre jet exploded into many pieces with most of the debris landing in the empty field next to the Panama City Garden Club on what was then Ninth Street, only a few blocks away from the bay, where he would have ejected to safety.

My brother, Darrell Thomason, worked at the Panama City *News Herald*, and had come home for lunch. We lived on North Mulberry Avenue and when he arrived home, my little sister, Edna, ran out to meet him. About the time he scooped her up, they heard the loud explosion and he saw the plane debris falling from the sky. He jumped back in the car, along with my little sister, and drove in the direction of the falling aircraft. Arriving at the crash site, a few people had already congregated. He stated that the pilot's helmet was laying there on the ground amidst debris. My brother, Jim, also went to the scene of the crash.

Lt. Gorbet, age 22, was from Isconido, California, and had been in the Air Force for two years. He was stationed at Ent AFB, Colorado Springs, Colorado, and was on temporary duty at Tyndall.

It was determined that the cause of the crash of the F-86-D was its fueling system.

Tommy Smith, School Superintendent, and the Bay County School Board recommended that Lt. Gorbet receive a medal of honor for his heroism for not ejecting when he had the opportunity...but rather taking a chance in order to reach the bay to prevent the possibility of the plane falling on the school grounds. Superintendent Smith stated that Lt. Gorbet was a true hero, and was to be commended for his unexcelled bravery. Members of the Garden Club later stated that they were recommending that Lt. Gorbet's name be added to a war memorial for Bay County's heroes that was being erected in the area close to where the plane crashed.

My Mother, Grace Thomason, had a very close friend, Mrs. O.O. (Marie) Turner, who wrote a letter to the family of Lt. Gorbet following the crash, expressing her sympathy, and expressing her appreciation for the sacrifice he made...and she included a Bible verse taken from St. John 15:13... "Greater love hath no man than this, that a man lay down his life for his friends." Mrs. Turner, whose husband was Mr. Ollie D. Turner, who owned the little neighborhood Turner's Drugs on 15th Street, received a letter back from Lt. Gorbet's mother stating that of all the letters and expressions of sympathy she had received that her letter had meant the most to her of all.

Actual site where the plane of 2 Lt Edwin L. Gorbet crashed

Submitted by: Jo Thomason Manis.

Gideon v. Wainwright

On July 5, 1963, I accompanied a big bosomed client to the Bay County Courthouse to get her a divorce and as I was leaving Judge Joseph Bailey's Chambers on the Second Floor, Judge McCrary was standing in the balcony entrance to the Courtroom and motioned for me to come to him, which I did, and he there told me that he had just appointed me to represent Clarence Earl Gideon. On August 5, 1963 trial was held in State of Florida vs. Clarence Earl Gideon with me as Defense Counsel and the verdict reached by the Jury was Not Guilty. Two time Pulitzer prize winner, Anthony Lewis (Author of GIDEONS TRUMPET) was present as were several other people. The case was not especially difficult to try and the only incriminating evidence was Gideon's prior criminal record and his pocket full of coins (in excess of $20.00) when arrested when the evidence tended to show several coin-operated machines had been burglarized. Factually Gideon had been in an all-night penny ante poker game and could not have gotten away with the "swag" (12 cans Budweiser; 12 cans Coca Cola and four 5th's of Wine) inasmuch as he was on foot and direct testimony was that his clothes did not bulge (as if he were hiding the "loot" under his clothing.) I was no super counsel and a law student could have won an acquittal in my estimation. Of course the U. S. Supreme Court's decision had already altered the criminal law procedure in the whole United States. We all (Gideon included) drank a toast to Gideon's victory in champagne at Mike Darley's Office (Editor of Panama City NEWS-HERALD) with Dixie cups (we couldn't find enough glasses).

Submitted by: Fred Turner, 2694 Island View Dr., Panama City, FL 32405

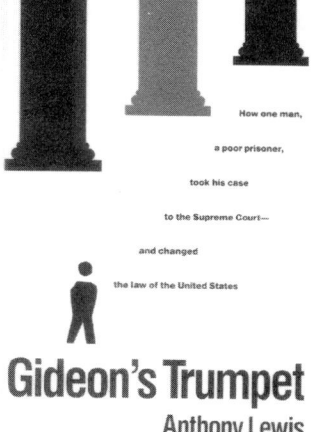

How one man,

a poor prisoner,

took his case

to the Supreme Court—

and changed

the law of the United States

Gideon's Trumpet
Anthony Lewis

Book cover of the latest edition of Gideon's Trumpet

Hathaway Bridge

Both ends of the old Hathaway Bridge, built in 1929, continued to be popular fishing spots until 1990. Then, because they represented liabilities, the city had them removed and sunk as fishing reefs in the Gulf.

But the area around the 1959 Hathaway Bridge continued to attract fishermen, especially along the western bridge abutment, where locals and tourists congregated each day to net mullet, trap crabs and catch fish.

Those crossing Hathaway Bridge from the west saw ship after ship anchored off Port Panama City, awaiting salvaging. A boat ride between these haunting hulks gave one the feeling of being sandwiched by giants.

Some of the old Wainwright Shipyard buildings remained in this location from World War II. West Florida, then Florida State University held classes in one of these two-story buildings until FSU's beautiful new branch campus opened to the

north along the bay. The school board occupied another of the Wainwright buildings before moving to its new headquarters on Balboa Avenue in the 1990's. After these structures were vacated, they were torn down to make way for the expansion of the port.

Gulf Coast College, across the highway, continued to grow, adding new buildings every few years. Married students, needing day care, could drop off their youngsters at Choo-choo College, an old converted caboose, while they attended classes.

Highways 77, 79 and 231 saw increasing traffic as large numbers of people chose to move north of town. The beaches witnessed tremendous growth with the erection of many new condos, hotels, motels, water parks, homes and golf courses. Petticoat Junction gave way to a large shopping center.

Then Hurricane Opal struck in 1995, causing extensive damage to low-lying sections and to structures along Panama City Beach. But within six months Bay County was well on its way to recovery from the storm.

Panama City and St. Andrews marinas underwent extensive renovations. About this same time, redevelopment began taking place in downtown Panama City and St. Andrews. St. Joe, the huge property owner in Northwest Florida, changed from growing timber to building subdivisions on thousands of its acres. The Lynn Haven-Southport section witnessed the construction of its first condo on North Bay.

Submitted by: Marlene Womack, 2101 Norwood Place, Panama City, FL 32401.

Survivor Describes Ordeal When Freighter "Tarpon" Sank

This is the story of the sinking of the freighter Tarpon, which went down on the morning of Sept 1, 1937, in the Gulf about eight miles off Laguna Beach. A survivor, William C. McKnight second engineer of Carrabelle retold the story of the wreck and his 33 hours in the squally Gulf waters, to a former shipmate, Stuart Pratt of Parker, who had left the ship on Sept 1 1934 to go to work at International Paper Company.

They agreed there were many occasions when the old ship, which had been built in 1887 in Wilmington, Delaware and brought to the Gulf coast in 1904 by Capt. Barrow, nearly had been lost. After throwing over a carload of freight, they could make it to the harbor.

According to McKnight, "We left Pensacola Tuesday evening, heavily loaded as usual and were soon wallowing in a heavy southeaster. At midnight I relieved First Engineer Lloyd Mattair on duty in the engine room."

As he went up, Lloyd said, "Call me if you need me, Will."

The ship was rolling and the decks were awash. The dunnage—lumber that holds freight off the deck—was loose and was white with a messy paste of flour, feed and other wet cargo. Deckhands, tossing freight out the ashport, slid around on the slippery surface.

At 2 a.m. I sent for Mattair. When he saw how it was, he went to tell the Captain.

He returned and said the Captain told him to keep working and we'd make it all right. For the rest of the night we fought the water, and Lloyd kept trying to convince the Captain the situation was hopeless.

I went up and told the Cap'n the pressure was awful low and we needed to stop engines.

First Mate Danford said not to stop-"just slow'em down. I need steerage, we're heading north now."

That meant he was going to beach her. Or at least we'd have a shorter swim. We had turned toward Phillip's Inlet.

The crew worked like fury to man the pumps. The maid was scared half out of her wits, and as she huddled in a corner I thanked God my wife, Viv, had changed her mind about coming.

Next time I saw the Cap'n he'd told Danford to pull her offshore—we were headed south-southeast again.

"We'll save all or nothing," he said.

Along about daybreak the water was up to within two or three inches under the fire (oil burners) and I knew we didn't want to be in there when the two met. So I called out to Cecil

Smith and Adley Baker, "Come on, boys, it's time to go." It wasn't my place to say, but the Cap'n hadn't told the crew to go and Lloyd couldn't get him to beach or abandon her.

We went to the hurricane deck and began cutting the girdings on the lifeboat. It was raining hard and the old ship was tossing. We had cut half the ropes, when a sea washed over us. The boat flew up and when it came down it crushed Secondmate Billy Russell against the deck. The rest of us washed over.

Deckhands were freeing the other lifeboat. They put the frightened woman in the boat and tied her so she wouldn't be thrown out. But the boat capsized and by the time they got it righted she had drowned.

I was in the water trying to keep my head and looking around for something to hang on to. Those cork life jackets would float if you kept your head underwater; if you raised it up, you sank till the water was up past your eyes.

Around 8 a.m. the Tarpon sank down at a 45-degree angle. The boiler didn't blow so the whistle still had pressure. Something fell across the rope and the whistle kept gurgling. The water had killed the fires.

I was still looking for something to grab hold of when the after mast came straight up out of the water and landed about 10 feet away. The gib hatch cover from the front of the pilot house floated by with Cap'n Barrows, First Mate Danford, Lloyd and one of the seamen on it a perfect lifeboat.

I called out to Lloyd, "Hey, is there room for me on that?"

"No, Will," he said. "It's full up now. One more would sink it."

The kitchen room had blown off and was floating upside down with the purser, Wolfe, and his son, who was the cargo checker, on it. It had hundreds of nails sticking up; it made an uneasy bed.

Well, that after-spar was looking better and better. I grabbed hold with one arm. Davis, the quartermaster, got on too. People were dying all around and that spar was a hard thing to live on. The seas were running high and the mast would go up one side and down the other.

Adley paddled by on a hunk of dunnage. Afterward he said he paddled right on until his dunnage fell apart and he had to start swimming. He swan all night and went ashore and crawled up to the highway. He was 25 hours in the water.

Meanwhile, we were hanging on to our spar and it was the middle of the night and we could see lights way in on the beach road. Davis said he had seen one shark.

Around noon the next day an airplane flew low overhead but it was too rough for it to land. Then, about 4 or 5 p.m. three boats came in sight. There was a Coast Guard boat and two seine boats. When they picked us up, there was Lloyd Mattair and Danford. The Cap'n, I learned, was dead, from exposure. We had been in the water 33 hours and he was a pretty old man. Somebody gave me a jigger full of water-I could've drunk

a gallon. And they gave me a Coast Guard uniform to put on. When we got to Pensacola, they sent all survivors to the hospital.

An insurance company paid me $150 "courtesy money" for what I'd lost with the ship.

"Is that all I get for all the work I did to stay alive out there?" I asked them. The guy said, "You weren't swimming to save the boat, buddy!"

"No," I said, "but if I'd drowned, it would've cost you $10,000!"

Melvin Beck was the first to sight the survivors. He climbed a hill this side of Destin and saw them. He went into Destin and sent two seine boats to pick them up.
Submitted by: Ann Houpt, 1128 Loftin St, Parker, FL.

The Turner House

Built in 1914 by Mr. George Stephenson at the corner of

The house at Center Avenue and 2nd Plaza, Millville, Florida

Center Avenue and 2nd Plaza in Millville this house was sold by William Benjaman (W. B.) Gray, a local realtor and uncle of broadcaster Carl Gray, to W. F. and Fronia T. Turner in September of 1917. The Turner's came to Millville from Alabama with their children, James Henry Turner, Verlie Turner Stanley, Connie Turner Beckham, Howard S. Turner, Lucille Turner Newberry, Alma Turner Harmon, Wallace N. Turner and (Judge) W. Fred Turner (who was born in this house). W. F. Turner died in 1945 and in 1950 the family sold the house, which still stands as a reminder of the past.
Submitted by: James Ray Brookins, 516 Harvard Blvd., Lynn Haven, FL 32444.

Turpentine Days

Dallas Withers was a woods rider. They were called that because what they would do is put kind of a tin or metal cup on a pine tree and let the rosin run into that cup and then they'd come out and collect that rosin for the mills that would refine it as turpentine. Mr. Withers was working up there at Southport. They moved him up there for one year but then his family moved back to Panama City. They moved down the street from us but down a block. We knew all the families, Miner and Ruth and the Girls and they used to come over and visit Alma and Lucille Turner.
Submitted by: Fred Turner, 2694 Island View Dr., Panama City, FL 32405.

CLUBS

AMVETS Post 2298 Helps Veterans Help Themselves

One of the most active community service organizations in Bay

AMVETS Post 2298 is located at 5519 W. Highway 22 in Callaway near the intersection of Highway 22 and Tyndall Parkway

County is the AMVETS (American Veterans) Carl J. Luksic Post 2298 located at 5510 East Highway 22 in Callaway. The Post is part of a nationwide organization chartered by the U.S. Congress and is the only congressionally chartered veterans organization that is open to all veterans, honorably discharged

or released, and those now serving in the military.

Post 2298 is a non-profit organization and the largest veterans organization in Bay County with its own facilities and one of the largest in Florida. It is named for Carl Luksic of Callaway, a World War II fighter ace, who shot down five enemy aircraft on one mission and later was taken as a prisoner of war.

The Post, with over 600 members, provides volunteer work, programs and services to veterans, their families and the community as a whole. During 2003, the Post and Auxiliary have logged over $50,000 in service credits to the community. It began with 100 members in March 1987, with Franklin Hawley, Jr. of Springfield, its first commander. Roger Wilkinson of Callaway, is the present post commander.

The Ladies Auxiliary was chartered in October 1987 with 83 members. Betty Caple of Panama City, was its first president. Linda Gfell of Springfield, now occupies that position.

In late 2003 the post received a charter to form a "Sons of AMVETS Squadron." The squadron has 13 charter members and Mike Fuqua of Panama City, is the squadron commander.
Submitted by Frank Gregory, Public Relations Officer, AMVETS Post 2298,

5510 E. Hwy 22, Callaway, FL 32404.

Apalachee Society C.A.R.

The Apalachee Society Children of the American Revolution was organized at Cove Elementary School on February 13, 1960 when Miss Ruth Martin was Regent of the St. Andrew Bay Chapter DAR (1958-1960). Mrs. Harold S. Butler, Jr., was Senior President.

The Charter members were: Judy Beth Anderson, Laura Robb Butler, Anne Daffin, Charles Daffin, Melinda Daffin, Linda Davis, Rebecca Leitch, Nancy Murphy, Ruth Louise White, Richard Wills, Jr. and Michael H. Wells.

Mrs. Dorothy Daffin Randall (Mrs. W.S.), current Senior President (1994-2003) also served as Regent of St. Andrew Bay Chapter DAR (1960-1962). Her daughter Anne Daffin Harris (Mrs. Carl J.) served as Senior President from 1980-1984 and from 1987-1988.

The Apalachee Society C.A.R. hosted the State C.A.R. Conference in March 1979. Mrs. Malcolm Traxler was Senior President and served from 1977-1980 and 1984-1987. Malcolm Traxler, Jr., served as State Jr. Registrar 1978-1980. Ashby Lippitt served as State Organizing Secretary 1979-1980 and State Corresponding Secretary from 1980-1981.

Miss Ruth Lucille Martin established a scholarship to recognize Apalachee C.A.R. Seniors who are graduates of Bay County High Schools and who demonstrate service, leadership, patriotism and loyalty to the C.A.R. as well as to the United States of America.

Membership in the C.A.R. is by lineal descent from a person who served the American Revolution.

Submitted by: Dorothy Daffin Randall (Mrs. W.S.), 5801 Thomas Dr., Unit 1224, Panama City, Beach, FL 32408. Courtesy of: Martha Lee Traxler (Mrs. Malcolm).

The Bay County Genealogical Society

The Genealogical Society of Bay County was organized on 2 September 1980 with nineteen charter members. Nancy Roberts was elected as the first president. The name of the group was changed to Bay County Genealogical Society in 1996.

Projects of the Society have included surveying the county's tombstones and creating a printed list which was filmed by the Latter Day Saints and made available through the church's microfilm loan program and at the Bay County Public

Working to keep the Past Alive: Bay County Genealogical Society Members, 2003

Library. Members of the Society also have an ongoing project to copy and publish information from the Bay County Marriage Records.

The Society actively supports the Genealogy Collection of the Bay County Public Library and has donated many books and microfilm to the collection. Members have also volunteered in the Genealogy Room over the years, helping library patrons and keeping the shelves in order.

The Society has sponsored many seminars featuring beginning and intermediate topics presented by local genealogists. They have also held seminars taught by major national speakers including Desmond Walls Allen, Arlene Eakle, and Michael J. Neill. Their monthly meetings have featured speakers on a wide variety of genealogical topics presented by genealogists from Canada, Georgia, Florida, and other areas.

The *County Line*, the newsletter of the society, began publication in 1982 under the leadership of Katherine Krauth. Other editors have included Linda Pazics Kleback, Cliff Loper, Sondra Taylor, Wallie W. Waltonen, and Billy Nale.

Since its formation, the Bay County Genealogical Society has worked to teach, inform, encourage, and applaud local genealogists of all levels of expertise. Many of us here owe a great debt of thanks to this organization.

Submitted by: Linda Pazics Kleback, 1607 Belmont Blvd., Lynn Haven, FL 32444-3343.

Bay County Sporting Club

My dad, John William Douglas, belonged to a hunting camp, the Bay County Sporting Club. It was out towards Eglin Air Force Base. We would go out there and a lot of Judges, Police Captains and everybody belonged to it. Mr. Cowser that owned Cowser Filling Station down on Harrison Avenue was a member. Ted Barefield who was a detective at the Police Department was a member. George McCall, John McCall, Mr. Russell, all were members of the Sporting Club. We would sometimes have our Thanksgiving at the Sporting Club. We didn't have to get dressed up. We wore dungarees. Everybody could just be themselves.

Bay County Sportsman's Club after a successful hunt. L-R: T.L. Cowser, Grady Mixon, Coy Rushing, John Newbern, Custer Russ, John McCall, Dabet Cox, George McCall

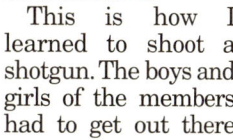
Bay County Sportsman's Club enjoying Econfina Stew at the Rocky Bayou Club House. L-R: Marvel Holley, Stump Starling, Tili Cowser, Judge Bailey, Red Catherl, John Douglas

This is how I learned to shoot a shotgun. The boys and girls of the members had to get out there with shotguns and learn how to hit glass bottles. They would put the bottles on a fence and we would shoot. We also went fishing while at the Sporting Club.

Submitted by: Frances Bunnie Douglas Powers, 925 Oak Ave.., Panama, City, Florida 32401.

The Bear Beach Club

The Bear Beach Club, a local chapter of Enesco's Cherished Teddies Club, was organized in June of 1997 under the sponsorship of Jane's Hallmark Shop. At our monthly meeting, club "membears" share news about Cherished Teddies figurines and collectibles. Members have also traveled to Cherished Teddies conventions in various cities in the Southeastern U.S. including Charlotte, North Carolina, and Birmingham, Alabama.

Members of the Bear Beach Club

We have also been involved in charity work. We have raised money for St. Jude Children's Research Hospital, the chosen charity of the Cherished Teddies Club. In 1998 we came in 6th in the country for the amount donated in the yearly fund raiser. In 2002 we raised $1300 for the charity. Locally, our group participated in Pick An Angel in 1998-2000 and have filled wish lists of Seniors through the Council of Aging since 2000. We have also helped fill Christmas gift bags for the St. Andrews Nursing Home and donated books and school supplies to Parker Elementary School and Early Childhood Services.

Submitted by: Linda Pazics Kleback, 1607 Belmont Blvd., Lynn Haven, FL 32444-3343.

Captain James Day Chapter
Colonial Dames XVII Century

A luncheon meeting to officially organize a chapter of Colonial Dames XVII Century was held October 19, 1965. The Chapter meets four times a year, originally at the Cove Hotel, and has out of town members. The name Captain James Day was selected in honor of an ancestor of the Misses Catherine and Ruth Martin. Captain Day was born in 1654 and served in the Virginia Militia.

Chapter Members placing a Colonial Dames XVII Century Marker on their founder's grave at the Parker Cemetery, 2003

By 1966 it had the 21 members required for a charter. Those signing it on April 14, 1967 were Catherine Martin, Ruth Martin, Grace Elzea, Georgia Merriam, Amelia Hollis, Fredericka Benton, Martha Coleman White, Lou Ellen Coleman, Louise Dumaree, Arabelle Grant, Evelyn Swann, Millicent Armogast, Frances Waller, Doris Anderson, Eleanor Howell, Linnie LaRue, Gene Sapp, Martha Lee Traxler, Georgia Campbell, Elizabeth Fensom, Romenia Haidt, Grace Wilson, Eleanor Drake, Louise Porter, Dorothy Daffin, Janie Bell, Nathalie Scarlett, and Linnie Dooley.

Membership is limited to those having lineal descent from an ancestor who rendered service and lived in one of the 11 British Colonies in the Continental United states prior to 1701. This ancestor must be an immigrant colonist or the descendant of one.

The objects of the patriotic society are:

To aid in the preservation of the records and of the Historical Shrines of our Country.

To foster interest in Historical Colonial research.

To aid in the education of the youth of our country.

To commemorate the noble and heroic deeds of our ancestors, the founders of our Great Republic.

To maintain zealously those high principles of virtue, courage, and patriotism which led to the independence of the Colonies and the foundation and establishment of the United States of America.

To aid in the establishment of a Library of Heraldry, working with various Genealogical Societies.

To develop a library specializing in 17th. Century American Colonial data.

Submitted by: Carlton Tompkins Price, 1937 W 27th Street, Panama City, FL 32405.

City Basketball League

The Panama City City Basketball League in the late forties had the following teams: Coca Cola, Creel & Sons, Holland Lumber, Wallys, Bay Gulf Oil, Navy and Tyndall.

Coca-Cola Basketball Team of the Forties

They played at the Bay High Gym and played for the fun of it.

In the accompanying photograph are: Kneeling left to right - Pete Holman, Winston Johnson, Alex Mathis, George Thomas. Standing left to right - Al Sabo, J. Q. Floyd, Tom Haney and ____ Sampley

Submitted by: Sarah

Haney, 3304 Robinson Bayou Court, Panama City, FL.

Emerald Coast Poets

A community group, Emerald Coast Poets (Poets) is open to anyone who is a writer, a reader or anyone who wants to write poetry. A Chapter of State and National Federation of Poetry Societies, this chapter was formed in November, 1994. Having experienced the benefits of a regular gathering of poets in the state of Georgia, a returning Bay Countian, Georgia Thomas Henry (Pearson) began talking with other writers in the community and instructors at Gulf Coast Community College (GCCC) with similar interests in poetry. The opening luncheon meeting was held December 3, 1994 at the Harbour House with a program by Lynn Wallace, Assistant Professor, GCCC. Officers elected were Georgia Henry, president; Janice Lucas (GCCC), vice-president;

Georgia Henry-Pearson and Barbara Wilkins-Roman at the First Gulf Coast Writer's Festival, 1998

Nancy Ford-Railey, secretary; Jane Hamm, treasurer and Denise Clark, hospitality. Thanks to Bill Payne and Jennifer Fenwick of Bay Arts Alliance, an ongoing poetry page was reserved for members' poems to be published in Bay Arts and Entertainment. Presentations were also made at local clubs, on TV and radio.

Barbara Wilkins (Roman) attended that meeting and became the second president. Henry moved to vice-president and Dave Shreck, secretary\treasurer. Roman was reelected in 1997 with Leo Carpenter, vice-president; Phyllis Varner, treasurer, and Henry, special projects coordinator. A noteable program that year was delivered by George and Barbara Mulligan about Dylan Thomas. A contest was sponsored and won by Floyd Regan and Nancy-Ford Railey.

Lucas, Wallace, Henry and Roman represented the Poets in planning the initial Florida Gulf Coast Writers' Festival. Also in '97 a monthly critique session was begun at Henry's home. Janice Lucas was president in 1998 when the Poets hosted the state association at the Harbour House. Norma Hubbard became an entertaining Emily Dickinson in Henry's one-act play.

Currently, Emerald Coast Poets meet monthly at the Bay County library. Following Roman's four years, presidents were Zan Miller, Floyd Regan and Pat Bastendorf.

Submitted by: Barbara Wilkins Roman, 523 Palermo Road, Panama City, Fl 32405.

GFWC Gulf Coast Woman's Club, Inc.

GFWC Gulf Coast Woman's Club formed February, 1991, with 92 charter members who desired to serve their community under the international banner of the General Federation of Woman's Clubs.

Members are actively involved in community projects providing

Charter Officers - GFWC Gulf Coast Woman's Club 1991-1992

manpower as well as donations within six departments: Arts, Conservation, Education, Home Life, International Affairs, and Public Affairs. During 2003, over 13,000 hours and $27,900 were given by our 149 members through club activities. Some of the first projects adopted 1991-92 continue today: Red Cross Blood Drive, Baldwin Road Trash Pickup and making shifts for rape victims who have to leave their clothes as evidence when examined at hospital emergency rooms.

Some other club projects involve: Very Special Arts; Music Association, Visual Arts Center; Young Writer's workshop; Teen Parenting Program; Kid Fest; Earth Day; Coastal Cleanup; Nature's Gallery; ZooBoo; local libraries; Bay Education Foundation; Junior Museum, Take Stock in Children mentoring; scholarships; Meals on Wheels; Red Ribbon Week; Canine Companions; March of Dimes; Special Olympics; Council on Aging; UNICEF; ESOL students; CARE; Rescue Mission; Operation Smile; Valentines for Veterans; Domestic Violence prevention; Bay Medical Foundation; Hacienda Girls Ranch; and Bay Town Trolley shelters.

The club twice won national recognition for Make A Difference Day projects and a Community Improvement Project award was received in 2002 from Florida Federation of Women's Club for spearheading restoration of local cemeteries. In May, 2003, Gulf Coast Woman's Club was named for the 4th consecutive year as one of the five most outstanding women's clubs in Florida.

In the accompanying photograph are the GFWC Gulf Coast Woman's Club officers of 1991-1992: L to R: Jimmie Ann Graham-Corresponding Secretary; Judith Nelson-Parliamentarian; Anita Segler-Treasurer; Carolyn Finlayson-Recording Secretary; Mona Hughes-President; Judy Houser-President Elect; Carol Crisp Garrison-Vice President.

Submitted by: Anita Segler, 2508 Pretty Bayou, Island Drive, Panama City, FL 32405.

Greater Panama City Dog Fanciers' Association, Inc.

The Greater Panama City Dog Fanciers' Association, Inc. was chartered by the American Kennel Club and incorporated in the state of Florida in 1972. The founders and charter members included Mr. Gus Tingle, Mrs. Evelyn Tingle, Mrs. Barbara Bryan, Mrs. Betty Christian, Lt. Col. James Christian and Mrs. Helen Shuh. The first President was Gus Tingle. Other past presidents include Lester Doty, Florence Doty, Mary Bratsen, Mary Ann Olson, James Christian, Biff Hunt, Polly Hunt, Judy Purvis, Kathi Edwards, Jim Vagenas, Jean Moseley and Margaret Adcock.

Greater Panama City Dog Fanciers' Association Dog Show 1987

The purpose of the club was and is to promote purebred dogs through proper care, training and careful knowledgeable breeding and to provide information and education for dog enthusiasts and the general public.

To that end, the club sponsors two American Kennel Club licensed dog shows, and two American Kennel Club sanctioned dog matches each year. Other activities include puppy handling classes, educational programs at the monthly meetings, Pet Week poster contests through the Bay County schools, Halloween Dog-a-Ween costume contests and Oktoberfest wiener dog contests. The club participates in many other local activities including, but not limited to, the Panama City Christmas parade, St. Andrew Bay Center's Spring Fling, the Scottish Festival, Junior Museum educational programs, and the Bay County Fair. The club also maintains a breeders index and a web site linked to the American Kennel Club.

The first competitive match was held in 1973 for local and surrounding area dogs, and the club was approved for regular point shows by the American Kennel Club after successfully completing 3 of these matches. The first American Kennel Club licensed regular point dog show was held in Panama City in 1975, with Mr. Lester Doty as the first Show Chairman. Dogs from 48 states and many foreign countries were entered to earn show points towards becoming an AKC champion of record.

Through the years, the club has offered scholarships to Gulf Coast Community College, financially supported improvements to the A. Z. Bessant Park in Panama City Beach, and donated to many local causes such as the Humane Society and hurricane relief.

Submitted by: Ann Robbins, 25 W. Government St, Panama City, FL 32401

History of the Panama City Lions Auxiliary

The year of 1949 the Panama City Lions Club had their annual Fish Fry at the Panama City Country Club for installation of officers. Mrs. Andy C. McNeil (Betty C.) and Mrs. T. Brannon Copeland (Imogene) enjoyed attending with the other Lions' wives. They decided to organize a Lions Club Auxiliary, with permission from the Lions Club President William H. Sapp and T. Brannon Copeland and Andy C. McNeil. The organization date was June 21, 1949.

The charter meeting was held at the Dixie Sherman Hotel on the Mezzine floor, with twelve members attending. Three of the charter members are still active with the club, Betty McNeil (Mrs. Andy C.), Louise Danzey (Mrs. Byron) and Sarah Haney (Mrs. Tom). The object of this auxiliary is to promote a friendly feeling among the ladies and assist the Lions Club in their projects and socials. The first By-Laws and year book were composed by Betty McNeil and Louise Danzey. The first president was Louise Danzey.

Mrs. Andy C. McNeil and Mrs. William Lawrence presenting a scholarship to Frank Eiseman

Our first project was conducting hearing tests with audiometer machines and vision tests with eye charts in the public schools of Bay County.

We helped the Lions Club with their auctions, and the Gopher Races held annually on the 4th of July. The environmental protection agency was against using live gopher turtles, therefore Opal and Johnny Reaver built mechanical gophers to continue the races to date.

Through the past 54 years, we have been active in supporting many Lions projects and community projects. We have made a difference in our community and we are proud of our Lions Auxiliary.

In the accompanying photograph Mrs. Andy C. McNeil and Mrs. William Lawrence are shown presenting a scholarship to Frank Eiseman for Gulf Coast Community College from the Panama City Lions Auxiliary.

Submitted by: Mrs. Andy C. McNeil (Betty C.), 137 Hombre Circle, Panama City Beach, FL. Mrs. William R. Rumph (Ellen J.), 161 Marin Drive, Panama City, FL.

Historical Society of Bay County, Inc.
About Our Logo

At the turn of the new millennium, the Bay County Historical Society experienced a resurgence of energy and activity. New bylaws were drawn up and new corporate papers were filed renaming the organization the Historical Society of Bay County, Inc. Membership and participation grew rapidly. Wanting a new logo that would be representative of Bay County's history, the Board approached local artist, Barbara Mulligan. Barbara, a third generation Bay Countian, is the granddaughter of John Henry Laird who was a prominent businessman in this area. Barbara is also a member of the Historical Society of Bay County and has been awarded signature/life membership in the Florida Water Color Society.

Barbara created a pen & ink line drawing depicting a circa 1910 Bay County scene. It features a common boat of the era, a launch, in the foreground and the Bay Fisheries Company building and schooners in the background. A launch was a multipurpose boat

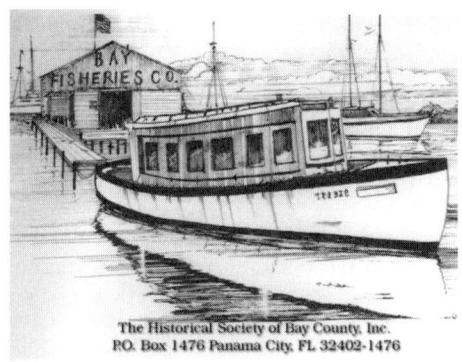

The Logo for the Historical Society of Bay County

used to transport passengers, mail and other goods and could also be used for fishing. Bay Fisheries Company was founded in 1908 and soon became Bay County's major industry. It was located on a pier in St. Andrews near the foot of present day Frankford Avenue.

Submitted by: Historical Society of Bay County, P.O. Box 1476, Panama City, FL 32402.

The Hutchison-Poplawski Chapter of the American Ex-Prisoners of War

The Hutchison-Poplawski Chapter is one of many chapters in the state Department of the American Ex-Prisoners of War. Over 1100 men in the state are members of the organization. Florida vies with Texas as having the most ex-pows.

Gerald Duval came to our community in 1994 and put a notice in the paper inviting all ex-pows to a meeting at the K-Mart on the west side of the Hathaway bridge. Names were taken and a chapter name decided on and thus began the formation of the Hutchison-Poplawski Chapter for this area. The group now meets on the first Tuesday of each month at the Mariner Restaurant, 9104 Front Beach Road at Panama City Beach. Membership is limited to ex-pows, their spouses, widows, or next-of-kin. The Chapter was named for the deceased husbands of Anne Hutchison Walker and Reba Poplawski.

March 1, 1995 the Chapter was established, officers elected, and on July 6, was recognized by a proclamation issued by the Mayor. The national organization issued a Charter on March 24, 1996. Commanders of the Chapter have been Anne Walker, Clarence Goad, Gerald Duval, John Anderson, George Hizer, and Charles Jones. Recent deaths include Donald Brown, Dan Nugent, Joseph Crea, John Galbraith, Robert Floyd, Alline Hizer, and Charles Cockrell. The Chapter will host the next state convention to be held June 18-20, 2004 at the Holiday Inn Express on Cove Boulevard.

Submitted by: John H. Anderson, P.O. Box 13753, Mexico Beach, FL 32410.

The Junior Service League

The Junior Service League of Panama City, Inc. is a not for profit service organization which was founded in 1952. The Charter members were Ann Cook, Margaret Rainey, Mary Catherine Jenks, Neil Poyner, Phoebe Fowhand, Peggy Jemison, Elizabeth Byrd, Letitia Moody, Barbara Quigley, Carolyn Fleming, Martha Jane Adams, Mary Lee Christo, Alice Coleman, Ann Gray, Carol Lark, Josephine Logue, Barbara Nelson, Sara Padgett, Ruth Sherman, and Betty Sudduth. The purpose of the organization is to foster interest in the social, economic, educational, cultural and civic conditions of the community, as well as to promote the interest of its members in volunteer service to the community.

Since its establishment, League members have donated countless hours of volunteer service to fulfill the needs of the community. The League also has started and supported many of its own projects over the years to serve the less fortunate. The largest of these projects, the Child Service Center, was begun in 1952 to provide clothing for children in our area who needed assistance. Through the now twice-yearly Child Service Center and the League's year round Happy Hanger service, the League has been able to clothe over 20,000 area children. The League has also assisted with over 70,000 hearing tests for children over the years, and been instrumental in the establishment of many other community projects, such as the Visual Arts Center, the After School Assistance Program and the preservation of McKenzie House in downtown Panama City.

The League has funded these projects through many different means. Initially, the League maintained a thrift shop, later known as the *Bargain Box*, which provided used clothing at low prices. In

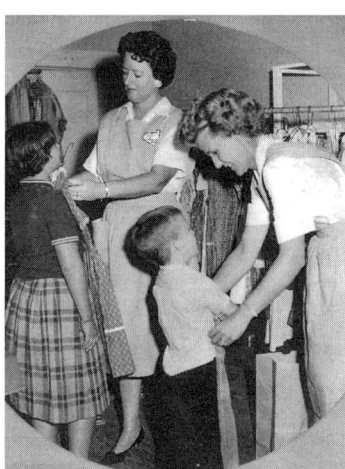

Junior Service League members working The Child Service Center

1961, the first annual Charity Ball was held and raised $2,000 in profit. This formal ball, which was at the time one of the only formal events held in the area, often was held at the Armory near the airport. The last annual Charity Ball was in 1980. Also for a time, the League sponsored a giant thrift sale, called Whale of A Sale. This project was held yearly from 1977 until it too was discontinued in 1988.

Since 1989 however, the League's largest fundraising effort by far is the annual Holly Fair. Since the first Holly Fair gift mart at the Civic Auditorium, the event has grown each year into what is now one of the most anticipated holiday shopping opportunities in our area. Through the generous donations of our Holly Fair sponsors, and the attendance of the public at the Holly Fair events, Holly Fair is able to fund entirely the Child Service Center and Happy Hanger projects. The League has also published three cookbooks and a pictorial history of Bay County. Profit from the sales of these books, which include *Bay Leaves*, *Beyond the Bay*, *Bay Fetes*, and *Along the Bay*, are also used to help fund the many good works of the Junior Service League.

Now more than one hundred members strong and no longer wearing the service uniforms of past years, the Junior Service League continues its tradition of tireless volunteerism. We are very proud of our continued efforts to improve the community in which we live.

Submitted by: Lisa Lloyd Hamlin, President-Elect, 2003-04, 247 S. Cove Terrace Dr., Panama City, FL 32401.

League of Women Voters of Bay County

Founded in 1976 by 86 Charter Members, the League was not granted full lobbying status until it published an in-depth study of county government entitled "The Bay County Handbook". Under President Pam Smoak, the first Candidate Questionnaire was published in the *News Herald* as a full page ad in 1976, which is now done as a public service by the paper. That same year the first Candidate Forum was presented, which has evolved into a bi-annual live broadcast over TV and WKGC.

The League has provided many public forums for City, County, School Board and various appointed boards to fulfill the mission as a non-partisan organization to "promote political responsibility through informed and active participation in government". The "Voter Guide" to governmental officials was first published in 1976 and is now handled by the Supervisor of Elections office. From promoting the use of an agenda and an appointed Manager for the County in 1976 to sponsoring Hurricane, CCH and Deerpoint Seminars in the 80's, then hosting Educational Town Meetings and Women in Politics Forums in the 90's the League has been actively pursuing better government. The league's goal is to hand out more "Roses" than "Brickbats" in the future as Bay County transforms from the "good ole boy" system to the 21st century!

Submitted by: LWV Historian JoAnn Cain, 204 Cascade St., Panama City, FL 32405.

Panama City Chapter of the Florida Society of the Sons of the American Revolution

The Panama City Chapter was chartered on September 27, 1973.

The objects of this Society are declared to be patriotic, historical, and educational, and shall include those intended or designed to perpetuate the memory of those who, by their services or sacrifices during the war of the American Revolution, achieved the independence of the American people; to unite and promote fellowship of the American people; to unite and promote fellowship among their descendants, to inspire them and the community at large with a more profound reverence for the principles of the government founded by our fathers; to encourage historical research in relation to the American Revolution; to acquire and preserve the records of the individual services of the patriots of the war, as well as documents, relics, and landmarks; to mark the scenes of the Revolution by appropriate memorials; to celebrate the anniversaries of the prominent events of the war and of the Revolutionary period; to foster true patriotism; to maintain and defend the institutions of American freedom, and to carry out the purposes expressed in the preamble of the Constitution of our country and the injunctions of Washington in his farewell address to the American people.

The special interest is to George Washington.

The national headquarters is in Louisville, KY.

Past Presidents have been: 1973 Tom Y. Bingham, 1974 Tom Y. Bingham, 1975 Richard Gaunt, 1976 Bobby Carswell, 1977 Henry Hinkle, 1978 Tom Y. Bingham, 1979 Bobby Carswell, 1980 Henry Hinkle, 1981 E. Terry Jack, 1982 Marvin McCain, 1983 Marvin McCain, 1984 Bobby Wing, 1985 Tom Y. Bingham, 1986 Marvin McCain, 1987 Marvin McCain, 1988 Marvin McCain, 1989 Bobby Hamilton, 1990 Bobby Hamilton, 1991 Tom Y. Bingham, 1992 Tom Y. Bingham, 1993 Marvin McCain, 1994 Russell Williamson, 1995 Russell Williamson, 1996 Russell Williamson, 1997 Russell Williamson, 1998 John H. Carter, 1999 John H. Carter, 2000 John H. Carter, 2001 John E. Cahoon, 2002 John E. Cahoon, 2003 Walter C. Sherman.

The following have been presented: Bronze ROTC medal, Law Enforcement Commendation Medal, Fire Safety Commendation Medal, Martha Washington Medal, Medal of Appreciation, and Meritorious Service Medal.

Flag certificates have been presented to those displaying the American Flag; the Eagle Scouts have been honored.

G.M. West was state Vice-President in 1922. John H. Carter was state President for the 2001/2 term.

Submitted by: Walter C. Sherman, P. O. Box 609, Panama City, FL 32402-0609.

Panama City Coastal Cruisers

The first meeting of the Panama City Coastal Cruisers was held March 1, 1997 at The Hawks Nest Restaurant. Skip Cruce (founding father) wanted to form a group that shared the joy of the water and camaraderie of boating. There were 30 members in 1997.

The first officers were Skip Cruce, Commodore; Dick Reca, Vice-Commodore; Nancy Moss, Secretary; Jim Fortier, Treasurer; and Faye Beuthin, Member-at-Large.

Our regular club meetings are currently held on the first Tuesday of the Month at the St. Andrew's

Cruisers Along the Bay

Bay Yacht Club at 7:PM. Through the efforts of Chris Moser, Manager of the Panama City Marina and Suzye Payne of the St. Andrew's Marina and members the club has grown to 58 members.

Current officers are: John Forehand, Commodore; Jim Fortier, Vice-Commodore; Jackie Nelson, Secretary; Molly Wert, Treasurer; and Member-at-large, Wayne Wert.

Skip Cruce coordinates the yearly Blessing of the Fleet in March.

Submitted by: Florence Fortier, P.O. Box 15031, Panama City, Florida 32406.

Panama City Garden Club, Inc

The Panama City Garden Club's clubhouse is located at 810 Garden Club Drive. It has taken 67 years to bring the building and its beautiful landscaped grounds to fruition. The Club was organized in 1935 with Mrs. Louise Blackshear as Chairman and Federated in 1936 with Mrs. A. M. Lewis, Sr., as the first president. The Club had 4 circles and 70 members. Due to World War

II, three of the four circles disbanded. However, the Camellia Circle continued to function. Therefore, the original Federation date still stands. In 1947, after the war, the Camellia Circle formed another circle from their membership. Other Circles were gradually added in the following years.

In 1947 patriotism was at an all-time high. The Garden Club sponsored and created the Bay Memorial Park Association. Twenty acres of undeveloped swamp land were leased from the City of Panama City to establish a War Memorial Park in honor of Bay County's war dead. Women and men rushed to join the Association. Enthusiastically, the clearing and landscaping of the park began. A nursery was established in November, 1949, with two acres under cultivation. There were three lathe houses for the propagation of plants for beautification of the park. The nursery was located on Highway 390A, one-fourth mile off Hwy. 390.

In 1952, Mr. Marion (Bubber) Nelson acquired a building and gave it to the Garden Club. This building was originally the first Panama City School. It was later moved and served as the First Presbyterian Church and after the Church built a new building it was moved to its present loction in the center of Bay Memorial Park facing what was then called 9th Street. Since that time, 9th Street between Florida Avenue and Balboa Avenue has been paved and renamed "Garden Club Drive". Renovation on the building began immediately. In 1983 the old Spanish style, flat roof was replaced with an English Manor style, changing the appearance of the building. Additions and upkeep have continued into the 2002-2003 club year.

Panama City Garden Club Building

In the 1960-61 Club year, membership reached 301. The Club has had 23 named circles. The first Flower Show Judges School was held in 1952 and the practice of holding two flower shows yearly was initiated, one in the spring and one in the fall. In the late 1960's and early 1970's, due to an aging membership and younger women joining the work force, Club membership began decreasing. Currently the Club has six active Circles with a total of 137 members.

Between 1998-99, the Bay Memorial Park Island was totally re-landscaped and a granite wall was erected bearing the names of Bay County's native-born war dead from all wars since 1940. On Memorial Day, May, 1999, an impressive ceremony was held on the Park Island, and the island was rededicated as a War Memorial Island.

Through the Club's association with Operation Cinderella, a local civic improvement organization, cooperation on beautification projects throughout the city is made possible. The Club's most popular community event is the Annual Azalea Trail which began in 1967.

Submitted by: Mrs. Opal Etheridge, member and a Former President of the Panama City Garden Club, Inc., 810 Garden Club Drive, Panama City, FL 32401.

Panama City Lions Auxiliary

The Lions Auxiliary was organized to assist the Panama City Lions Club carry out their projects and to offer our members an outlet for fellowship and service. Through the years we have supported the following sight conservation projects yearly: North Florida Eye Bank, Florida Lions Foundation, Florida Lions Conklin Center, Leader Dogs for the Blind, Southeastern Guide Dogs, Florida Lions Camp and Diabetes Research Institute. We also support local community projects including the Salvation Army, Rescue Mission, Red Cross, Family Services Agency and others. We have sponsored a scholarship to Gulf Coast Community College. The project dearest to our heart is sponsoring a vision impaired child and helping the family.

We support our projects through fund raising activities including assisting the Lions Club with their annual truck raffle. We

Many of the current members of the Panama City Lions Auxiliary

have had garage sales, card parties, recipe sales and Christmas Bazaars. We use the monies that we receive to support our various projects.

As we begin our 55th year, we are proud of our accomplishments and pleased to have maintained an organization of giving, caring ladies who enjoy fellowship with each other for good works.

Current members shown in the accompanying photograph are: From left to right: Lois Dick, Anne Johnson, Betty Heaton, Gloria Coleman, Betty McNeil, Lucille Hargrove, Barbara Hale, and Linda Lawrence. In the front row are Rose Gheesling and Jeanne Silaz. Not pictured are members: Louise Danzy, Kitty Darnell, Margaret Dozier, Shirley Fiser, Ann Garmon, Sarah Haney, Jane Highfield, Helen Hindsman, Jimmie Hutchison, Laura Landgraf, Bette Lemersal, Freda Miller, Ann Mills, Ellen Rumph and Joanne Sparks.

Submitted by: Ellen J. Rumph, 161 Marin Drive, Panama City, FL.

Panama City Lions Club

One way to gauge the depth of a community's compassion is to observe the effectiveness and generosity of its civic and service clubs. The Panama City Lions Club was organized and chartered in 1935 to provide eyesight assistance to those so deprived, and to meet the needs of those in the community who required a boost from their neighbors. After a bumpy start, the Panama City Lions Club really got rolling and by 1938 was already a positive force in the city. Early officers were Alton Boyd, W. W. Rowell, Lloyd Allen, J. G. Parker, F. E. Moon, K. M. Richards, and Carl Dennis. One of the first community projects undertaken by the club was to organize and sponsor School Safety Patrols for all area schools.

Another early project was the establishment of a Blind Operators Stand" at the Panama City Post Office. The concession was operated for many years by George Mozley, who even today (2003) is a member of the Panama City Lions Club.

A major fund raiser, the "International 600 Gopher Race", was begun in 1962 and has been run on the 4th of July every year since. Long time residents will remember how hilarious was the race commentary offered by Lions Donnell Brookins and Lowater Stafford.

The gophers race on a course that is 600 inches long, hence the designation as the International 600. The race initially involved the running of actual gopher turtles, but a few years ago that animal was placed on the endangered species list and their use was thus proscribed. To take the place of live gophers, Lion Johnny Reaver and his wife, Opal, designed and built a bionic, battery-powered version of the gopher which has been used to great effect in recent years. Since their beginning, the races have yielded some $300,000 in funds raised by the Lions Club for its sight conservation and community betterment projects.

For almost seven decades, the Panama City Lions Club has been an entity for good in the community. The current membership is committed to building on that heritage of service.

Submitted by: Johnny

Gopher Race held on Fourth of July by the Panama City Lions Club

Reaver, 1011 Buena Vista, Panama City, FL 32401, and Bill Rumph.

Panhandle Writers Guild

"On a dark and stormy night"...Martha Spiva called Barbara Mulligan about her interest in creating an organization for writers. The first meeting of the Panhandle Writers Guild met in Martha's Johnson Bayou home with twenty five members. The date was in the spring of 1975. Jane Patton, head librarian of the Bay County Public Library at the time, later invited the Guild to meet at their 'almost' new building located next to city hall on the downtown marina. This move proved to be an important step in providing an ideal location to make contacts for new members. After some evening programs the group would gather at a nearby cafe for sharing ideas.

Over time many hundreds of local citizens from the surrounding area and tourists visiting our beaches have attended workshops, seminars and monthly programs provided by the Guild. One of the first members, Marlene Womack, has become one of our most recognized local historians. Marlene has written a column about our area's history in the Sunday edition of the *News Herald* for many years.

Many changes have taken place within the Guild but it still meets at the library. The present interests of the Guild is on the topics of self-publishing and book arts. Although many of the members have been published in national level formats the new interests have served the members well. The Guild has also kept up with some modern techniques of publishing such as web sites, DVD video books and scripts for visual presentations.

Submitted by: Barbara Mulligan, 1016 Buena Vista Blvd., Panama City, FL 32401.

Ralph Sorrentino's Band

Ralph Sorrentino met a local barber who wanted to learn music. Ralph told him that he would teach him music if the barber would teach him how to barber. They shook hands on the agreement. A lot of talk was going around about a new city being built on St. Andrews Bay and Ralph missed the water. He traveled to Panama City, Florida, liked what he saw and bought one half interest in a barbershop with money he borrowed from his brother-in-law Dick Taranto In 1919 he formed the first civic band, Panama City Municipal Band. He also had a small orchestra that played for dances wherever they could make a little extra money. They rode the train to Lynn Haven to play at parties. He also found time to give free music lessons to young and old.

The old city park, now McKenzie Park, was the location of many a band concert on Sunday Afternoons and for all major holidays. He directed the municipal band until 1933.

In 1937 a fire destroyed his band hall on Magnolia at Seventh Street. He and his band members were practicing when Ralph heard the crackling sound of flames. The band hall had been constructed with money subscribed by persons who had an interest in his music endeavors. But a large portion of the expense of the construction was given by Ralph. When asked whether the loss

Ralph Sorrentino's Band on Harrison Avenue

would mean the end of his musical efforts he replied that it would not and that he loved music too well and received too much joy from the organization to allow such a matter to interfere with the future.

Submitted by: Marie Sorrentino Waller Lee, 1002 Iowa Ave., Lynn Haven, FL 32444. Sources: Panama City Pilot; Family interviews.

St. Andrew Bay Chapter National Society, Daughters of the American Revolution

The St. Andrew Bay Chapter, National Society, Daughters of the American Revolution, was organized November 12, 1948, with Mrs. M. A. Coleman as Organizing Regent, and Mrs. J. S. Wilson, Organizing Vice-Regent. Charter members were: Mrs. Aline Adams, Mrs. Olivia Byrd, Mrs. Ona Carpenter, Mrs. Lila Daniell, Mrs. Mae Freeman, Mrs. Rebecca Guidroz, Mrs. Mildred Harbison, Mrs. Louise Lewis, Mrs. Mattie Lewis, Mrs. Lady Mathis, Mrs. Georgia Merriam, Mrs. Sudie Peace, Mrs. Dorothy Randall, Mrs. Anna Sherman, Mrs. Jessie Steele, Mrs. Ida Stringer, and Mrs. Nellie Wilkerson. Two of the Organizing Members, Mrs. Dorothy Randall and Mrs. Rebecca Guidroz, are still active members in 2003. In 1948 there were 20 members; today there are 97.

The National Society was founded in Washington, D.C. on October 13, 1890, with three founding members and 18 organizing members. Miss Eugenia Washington, descendant of George Washington's brother Samuel, was given National Number 1. Mrs. Benjamin Harrison, the wife of the President of the United States, was the first President General. Their first project was the completion of the monument to Mary Washington, mother of George Washington, which had been abandoned due to a lack of money to finish it. The quickly formed chapters collected the money to finish it.

The objects of the society are "to perpetuate the memory and spirit of the men and women who achieved American independence." A service organization, the entire endeavor of the DAR is to achieve its three objectives: historic, education, patriotic.

Membership is open to any woman, 18 years of age or older, who is descended from a woman or man who served in the Revolutionary War. Today, there are hundreds of thousands of members in all 50 states and several foreign countries.

Submitted by: Lenda McCain, Regent, 1980-1982, 1988-1990, 2002-2004, 712 W. Pierson Dr., Lynn Haven, FL 32444.

St. Andrews Bay Yacht Club

Nestled under the stately oaks on beautiful St. Andrew Bay is the St. Andrews Bay Yacht Club. Residential developer H.L. Sudduth carved out the land specifically and solely for the purpose of a yacht club in the midst of his residential development. The idea began in the minds of Major Frank Wood and Phil Roll, who both loved to sail. They met with Harry Fannin—President of Commercial Bank—and H.L. Sudduth in Sudduth's office. Sudduth agreed to donate the land and Harry Fannin said if they could secure 15 prominent members of the community, he would loan the money to build the Yacht Club.

On August 9, 1933 a meeting took place at The Dixie Sherman Hotel but they had only 13 members. By the next meeting on August 16th a total of 25 men had agreed to form The St. Andrews Bay Yacht Club. Major Frank Wood became the first Commodore; Phillip Roll, Vice Commodore; Charles Bingham, Rear Commodore and Robert Mathis, Jr. was the first Secretary/Treasurer. They along with Jesse Cogburn; Burnis Coleman; J.W. Crews; M. J. "Doc" Daffin; Sidney A. Daffin, Jr.; M. H. Edwards, Jr.; Harry G. Fannin; Paul Lindsay; Will D. Muse; Malcolm Parker; Dr. W. E. Roberts; AR. Rogers; Douglas B. Sale; Thomas Sale; J. A. Smith; Ernest R. Spiva, Sr.; Capt. W. E. Spiva; H.L. Sudduth and Dell Wood comprised the charter membership.

These men had the land cleared - doing some of the work themselves-and built the original clubhouse of limestone and cypress with oak flooring. The Dixie Sherman Hotel served as the temporary location until this original building was completed in 1935. The cost to join was $50.00. Wives did the cooking

St. Andrews Bay Yacht Club

and a meal cost $1.50.

Harry Murphy and Steve Fitzpatrick were hired to run the club. On Saturdays and Sundays —sailing days — if the boats lacked crew, then Harry and Steve would fill in. In June of 1936, the first two regattas were held with four "fish-class" boats qualifying the club for the Gulf Yachting Association. During these early years many notables including Asa Chandler of Coca-Cola in Atlanta and Pete Louillard of Durham enjoyed the club as well. The beautiful silver trophies these men sponsored are still awarded today for the Chandler and Louillard-Kent regattas.

During the 1940's, the United States Coast Guard "took over" the Yacht Club in the interest of national defense. A barracks was built on the property and a better dock was also constructed. The club had to be cleared of its furniture, so many of the ladies took it into their homes until 1946 when the club was returned to the members.

Harry made the best pink lemonades, Steve was kind and respectful to all ages, and Diana was hired to cook wonderful dishes from the kitchen. From the late 1940's forward the Yacht Club has been a center of social and recreational life in Panama City hosting lavish formal dances, elegant bridal parties, Easter egg hunts and 4th of July celebrations.

In 1968, "flying scots" became the sailing vessel of choice, so "senior" sailors bid goodbye to the fish-class boats with a funeral on the front lawn. many sailing greats have called it "home," among them are Idus Darby, Floyd Davis, Allen Douglas, Julian Bennett and Jane Pope Prather. The clubhouse was reconstructed in the 1970's to its current design. For 30 years, the St. Andrews Bay Yacht Club has hosted "the Flying Scot Mid-Winters" and Greg Fisher, a 5 time National Champion, describes this event at St. Andrews Bay as "the very best!" This is quite a compliment for the race location is annually determined by The Flying Scot Association on the basis of waters, racing management, facilities and a club's warm hospitality.

The St. Andrews Bay Yacht Club is a private club located at 218 Bunkers Cove Road and a member of the Gulf Yachting Association. Its mission is to "encourage and develop activities that participate in the nature of yachting and boating in St. Andrews Bay ... and to form a close association among it's members...and members of other Yacht Clubs throughout the Gulf Coast." Members' children between the ages of 5 and 18 can enjoy the many sailing activities of the Junior Yacht Club.

Submitted by: Gay Sudduth and Elizabeth Ann Kruse Percival, 322 Bunkers Cove Rd., Panama City, FL.

The Safari Club

The Oates family had been operating a small night club, known as the Couger Lounge. It was located on Hamilton Avenue and 11th Street in Panama City. Tom and Fred Oates, were both graduates of Tuskegee University and were Commissioned Officers in the United States Air Force, they had served their Country. Tom and Fred had shared a vision for many years, of building and operating an upscale night club, to fulfill the social need, of the African-American Community. Fred and Tom Oates were knowledgeable in the field of construction. Pooling together their resources, the brothers were able to purchase the land suitable for their vision. Two years later the Safari night club stood magnificently on the corner of Hamilton Avenue and 11th Street.

The exterior of the Safari Club was most impressive, the landscape included palm trees in a criss cross manner. The spacious land surrounding the Safari Club magnified its presence. The interior of the Safari was draped in an African Motif; a wall to wall bar was located by the side entrance. The floor was covered with plush red carpet, a juke box was on the left of the front entrance. Located in the center of the Safari Club, was a dance floor surrounded by tables and chairs. Overlooking the dance floor was a balcony. The club also featured a game room with a pool table on the right side. Ladies and Gents bathrooms were on the left. The dining area on the right was very spacious. Beyond this area was an office, kitchen, and package store which also had a drive-in service window for take-out customers. The cathedral ceiling held a giant silver disco ball, which reflected diamond shadows on the dance floor, as it revolved to the rhythm of the music.

In 1974 the Oates brothers decided to sell the Safari Club to Justin Stephenson, a highly qualified club manager, who had operated clubs, throughout Europe and Southeast Asia.

Justin had met his good friend George Smith, in London, England. George was also knowledgeable in club management. George and Justin worked well together, sharing responsibility of running the club. George with his dynamic personality, operated the bar and kept the customers entertained. Exciting, high energy show bands were booked weekly to perform at the now famous Safari, it was the most popular place to be. The weekends drew tremendous crowds of people from all walks of life, employees and musicians from local clubs would frequent the Safari Club to have late night jam sessions, the music, dancing, and laughter was electrifying. Still today the memory of the hottest nightclub in Bay County lingers in the community.

The kitchen was operated at different times by the Woods Family, also Mrs. Lilly Washington and then Mrs. Katherine Steel.

Monday night football was an exciting event, Justin was from the Island of Jamaica, and was an experienced chef, able to cook many exquisite meals for the Monday night football customers.

Justin was out of town one Monday and George was the cook, everybody was anticipating the delicious food they were accustomed to. His customers were so disappointed when George presented them with plain old beef hot dogs. Many professionals patronized the Safari, enjoying the warm welcome, and the wonderful atmosphere and joyous conversations. The Safari Club was operated very professionally. Obnoxious behavior had zero tolerance. This was a family oriented club. Helen and Maureen worked with their husbands, Justin and George, the children also pitched in on the weekends cleaning up to earn their allowance.

The Safari Club had a very positive influence on Michael and Diane Stephenson the children of Justin and wife Helen, and George, Roy, Nadine and Andre the children of George and Maureen. These children attended Rutherford High School and all became highly successful people.

George Smith known by many as Smitty eventually sold his share in the Safari and pursued a career in real estate and became very successful. George is presently a Commissioner of Callaway, and doing a good job. Justin also known as Steve, continued to operate the Safari until his passing in 1999. His wife Helen who had worked by his side throughout the years, continued to manage the Safari Club, until it was sold to Bay County, and was demolished in 2002. A new juvenile justice court house has replaced the Safari Club. But oh! those great memories, the show bands, the good food, music and the laughter, and most of all the contribution of the Oates brothers who shared their vision and accomplished their goal to provide a first class entertainment spot for all people to enjoy. Thank you Fred and Tom Oates, Thank you Steve and Smitty.
Submitted by: Maureen Marshall Smith, 8009 Highway 22, Callaway, FL 32404.

Spartan Baseball Team

The Spartan baseball team was formed in the forties. It had been called the Seahawks and the Fliers at different times. They were in the Gulf Coast League. Other teams in the league were: DeFuniak Springs, Apalachicola, Wewahitchka, Port St. Joe, Blountstown and Tyndall. They played at Lion's Field which was at the corner of Nineteenth Street and Highway 231.

Members shown in the photograph of the Spartan Baseball

Spartan Baseball team

team members are as follows: L-R, Kneeling: Joe Harris, Jack Creel, Fred Lewis, Tom Haney, "Bit" Parnell and Jimmy Crump. L-R, standing: Unknown, Unknown, J.V. Snuggs, Unknown, and Paul Mainous. Not pictured are J.Q. Floyd and Ty Fleming. Photo loaned by Gladys Suggs, 1301 Lakeridge Dr, Panama City, FL 32405.
Submitted by: Sarah Haney, 3304 Robinson Bayou, Panama City, FL.

Tops #FL 56 Panama City

On December 9, 1965, four ladies met to form the first TOPS (Take Off Pounds Sensibly) in Panama City. Jean Terpstra, an Air Force wife, was the first leader and is now on the Board of Directors at TOPS HQ. Current leader is Rosemary Zickefoose. Within a year, membership had grown to sixty, and then to a hundred. Several splinter groups were formed from the original chapter.

Pictured are recent Division Winners in TOPS #FL56. Seated L-R: Norma Wallis, Rob Swearingen, Barbara Wackowski, Albert Carpenter and Ethel Lewis. Standing: Peggy Tubbs and Sara Wallace.

Peggy Tubbs joined in January, 1966, and is now treasurer. Bob Davis recently celebrated 25 consecutive years as a KOPS (Keep Off Pounds Sensibly); his wife, Mary, is active in the group. Couples at goal are Pat and Buford Nowell, Marie and Harry Revell, and Catherine and Albert Carpenter. Catherine's two sisters, Shirley Williams (KOPS) and Louise Bickford are members. Sarah and Hazel Swearingen are sisters-in-law, and Sarah's grandson is a member. Ann Swearingen and her three daughters belong, as do Ethel Lewis and nephew, Al Lazar (KOPS). Clearly, TOPS is a family affair!

State Recognition Days (SRD) are held when members statewide are recognized for their accomplishments. TOPS FL 56 has had many winners. When SRD was held in Panama City in 1992, chapter members participated in planning and in the Outer Space skit presented at the City Auditorium.

TOPS FL 56 continues to prosper. Meeting places have changed but the goal has remained the same — to Take Off Pounds Sensibly and to keep them off.
Submitted by: Ethel Lewis, 1409 Arthur Avenue, Panama City, FL 32401.

United Daughters of the Confederacy Confederate Saltworks Chapter

The Charter of the Confederate Saltworks Chapter of the United Daughters of the Confederacy was signed on February 10, 1959 with Mrs. John E. Pilcher as the organizing President and 47 Charter members.

The United Daughters of the Confederacy is the outgrowth of many local memorial, monument and Confederate home associations and auxiliaries to camps of United Confederate Veterans that were organized after the War Between the States. It is the oldest patriotic organization in our country because of its connection with two statewide organizations that came into existence as early as 1890 — the Daughters of the Confederacy (DOC) in Missouri and the Ladies' Auxiliary of the Confederate Soldiers Home in Tennessee.

The objectives of the organization are Historical, Educational, Benevolent, Memorial and Patriotic:

To collect and preserve the material necessary for a truthful history of the War Between the States and to protect, preserve, and mark the places made historic by Confederate valor.

To assist descendants of worthy Confederates in securing a proper education.

To fulfill the sacred duty of benevolence toward the survivors of the War and those dependent upon them.

Mrs. John E. Pilcher, Sr., left, and Mrs. J.M. McElvey, right, standing at the Salt Kettle on Panama City Marina, September, 1970.

To honor the memory of those who served and those who fell in the service of the Confederate States of America.

To record the part played during the War by Southern women, including their patient endurance of hardship, their patriotic devotion during the struggle, and their untiring efforts during the post-War reconstruction of the South.

To cherish the ties of friendship among the members of the Organization.

Submitted by: UDC Committee, P.O. Box 59625, Panama City, FL 32412.

The Woman's Club of Panama City, Florida, Inc.

In 1913 Bay County and the Woman's Club of Panama City were born. Since its inception, the purpose has been to serve our community.

The first meeting place for the group of thirty-two women was 101 W. Beach Drive, now the Elk's Clubhouse. That building was sold in 1935 for $4,500. In 1936 a new clubhouse was built at 350 N. Cove Boulevard.

In the years 1917-1919 the club formed the first library association, opening with 1,500 books and manned by members. In 1931 they paid the salary of the first county nurse.

Other milestones included donating $1,400 during the great depression to help pay teachers' salaries. The club received recognition in World War II for selling more than $500,000 of war bonds. In the 1960's, members raised money to open a building fund for a new library and established two annual scholarships to Gulf Coast Community College. In 1967, the club led the movement to establish the Junior Museum; in the mid-eighties, $3,485 was contributed to furnish rooms in the Anchorage Children's Home. In 2000-2001, the club was responsible for over $18,000 of donations to the Children's Advocacy Center. This past year, the 281 members gave over 60,000 hours to service projects.

Since 1947, the club has produced the famous "Red Stocking Revue." The show, to quote the local newspaper, is "nothing short of extraordinary." It is written, choreographed and directed by members and showcases local talent. The profit supports community services.

Today, the club continues to work tirelessly to make a positive difference in our community, state and nation.

Submitted by: Joan Parker, 103 Harbour Pointe Drive, Lynn Haven, FL 32444.

SERVICE ORGANIZATIONS

The Bay County Fair

"County fairs are like fishin', or huntin', or playing golf," Horace Carr allowed. "It grows on you."

Bay County and Horace Carr was honored with one of only five Heritage Awards on December 3, 2001, (which happened to be Mr. Carr's 78th birthday). The award was presented in Las Vegas by the International Association of Fairs and Expos. "It was for somebody that contributed to the state association without being a paid employee," Mr. Carr was quoted in the local News Herald. "I've been on the state fair board since, Lordy-goodness, in the 60's." Another honor came to the county and Mr. Carr in 1996 when his work with the local Fair and the Florida State Fair was presented the state's volunteer Fair Person of the Year Award. Mr. Carr, a former county agriculture agent, served as Fair manager and director for many years.

In addition to Horace Carr, many individuals and families have had a hand in the Fair's growth and success. The first Fair had its beginning in 1942 at Highway 22 and 98 in Springfield. The property was owned by Gray Lumber Company. W. C. Cooper, Sr. was one of the first volunteers. Ray C. Pilcher and D. C. Suggs were two of the early managers and directors. V. E.

Ribbon cutting for Fair Grand Opening

Banks was treasurer for many years. Mr. and Mrs. W. C. Cooper, Jr. are also active in the Fair's development and activities. Liza Jackson, Emma Benton and other Bay County Extension personnel brought variety and excellence into the exhibits. E. E. Hendley, a board member for 35 years with 10 years as director, has a film on selected years of the Fair that shows Earl Hadaway of WJHG TV interviewing various Fair workers. Joe Cooper, long

term manager, stated that the purpose of the Fair is "to set up competition within the county to further agricultural and educational development by coming together once a year."

And once a year, the county came together until 1947 when a permanent site was located at Sherman Avenue and 15th Street in Cedar Grove. Community interest has facilitated periodic changes, expansions, and renovations.

Expansion and parking are reoccurring concerns. Horace Carr relates, "We bought up all the property available around there and there's still not enough parking. We're hoping we're going to get relief if the county builds a new park off what we use to call Hog Pen Curve." A long way from his first Bay County Fair in 1955, "… a little old fair with no buildings except a tin shed 12 foot wide and 100 foot long, … with bare bulbs hanging on lines from rafters and burlap sacks lining the ceiling."

The American Legion owned and operated the Fair under the name of "Bay County Agriculture Exhibitors" for several decades. Currently, the non-profit organization is the "Central Panhandle Fair in Bay County." Rules for operation are provided by the State Department of Agriculture with an annual inspection the first day of each Fair in order to certify safety and compliance to rules.

One state requirement is the presence of livestock. In 1955, there were Hereford cows from the Jim Lowery Farm and the Bylsma Dairy, and horses from the 4-H Club. But now the livestock has dwindled. It was easier when there were 14 dairies; but there are other animals such as turkeys, chickens, ducks, and Guineas. There are plenty of cakes, canned fruits and vegetables, quilts, needlecraft, food preparation, art, horticulture, flower shows and other exhibits, but no longer any sideshows or "girlie shows."

And concession stands abound, with carnival rides lighting up the sky, announcing that the Fair is in town!

Submitted by: Georgia T. Henry-Pearson, 7752 Shadow Bay Drive, Panama City, Fl. 32404.

Bay County Health Department

The Local Health Department, also known as the Bay County Public Health Unit for brief periods, dates back to the late 1930's when a group of citizens saw a growing need for a county health unit in Panama City. On January 9, 1939 the Florida State Board of Health approved the appointment of W.H. Ball, M.D. as health officer. His staff consisted of a sanitarian, two nurses and a secretary. The main focus of the new unit was sanitary regulations and communicable disease. The unit was funded by revenue generated from the City (Race Track Funds) and County, and is currently funded by the County and State.

The Facility locations changed with growth over the 62 years. The first location was the County Court House, Third Floor. In 1940 it moved to Harrison Avenue adjacent to Lisenby Hospital; then to the west side of the Court House on McKenzie Avenue. In 1945 it moved to 624 East Coastal Highway (Bus. 98). In 1975 the Health Department moved to 605 N. MacArthur Avenue by Bay Memorial Hospital. In 1980 they opened a satellite clinic at 408 School Avenue in Springfield. The WIC (Women, Infants, Children) program had grown large enough to warrant a separate facility and was moved to 524 N. MacArthur Avenue. In 1983 WIC moved to 717 E. 7th Street. By 1987 a satellite clinic was opened at 17109 Hutchison Road in Panama City Beach. In 1988 a Primary Care Clinic was opened at 505 W. 11th Street and a Center for Women at 110 E. 5th Street. The Center for Women was consolidated to 505 W. 11th Street in 1989. An Administration Annex was opened in 1993 at 619 N. Cove Blvd. In 1995 the Springfield Clinic services at 408 School Avenue was consolidated to 505 W. 11th Street. By 1996 the services from 505 W. 11th Street and 605 N. MacArthur Avenue was consolidated to a new larger facility at 597 W. 11th Street. In 2001 the services from the Beach Branch was moved to 597 W. 11th Street.

We now have two separate divisions dedicated to sanitary regulations (Environmental Health) and communicable disease (Epidemiology). Public health services have expanded: Immunizations, HIV/AIDS, Family Planning, Child Health, Adult Health, Healthy Start, Women, Infant, and Children (WIC) Food Supplement Program, School Health, Tobacco Free Partnership, Community Services, Sexually Transmitted Disease, etc. The number of employees increased from 5 in 1939 to 135 in 2002 to meet the growth of Bay County.

The eleventh and current Director/County Health Officer is Peter P. Sylvester, M.D. who is the epitome of public health and has served our community at the Health Department for the past 14 years. The organization has also experienced tremendous change in the infrastructure of the public health system in the later years. The most significant change was the separation of health from the Health and Rehabilitative Services (HRS) system in 1996, which invoked the birth of the Department of Health. This has had a positive effect on public health by forcing legislators to address health as a separate entity. New legislation funding for intervention programs to address critical health issues facing our area has thrust public health into the 21st Century. Considering the effects of public health and the rising concerns for increased health issues we expect our growth to increase at light speed.
Submitted by: Mary Mathews, 597 W. 11th Street, Panama City, FL.

Bay County Library

The Public Library in Bay County had some shaky beginnings. It actually started in the 1930's as a "traveling library". At that time, the library had about forty books, one table and one chair and it moved from location to location over the course of several years. The library would move into a storefront that had

The Bay County Public Library Building on Jenks Avenue

been offered by a businessman and stay there until it was needed by the owner for other purposes. They would then go to the next building that was available. At times, the books and other items were simply boxed and stored until another location became available.

In about 1938 the citizens became more interested in having a permanent location for the library. Money was raised and an octagon shaped building, to house both the Chamber of Commerce and the Public Library was designed. The location was at Washington Park, a site next to the Post Office on Jenks Avenue. In September of 1941, after three long years, the building in Washington Park was dedicated.

This building was a vast improvement over the pillar to post existence; however, it was still cramped for space. For eighteen years the Library shared the building with the Chamber of Commerce and the library had only two rooms and one restroom it could call its own. During this period, the Librarian's office was simply a cubby hole hidden behind shelving.

In 1959, the Chamber of Commerce moved to a new building and the Library then had four rooms and two restrooms. In 1961, Washington County joined with the Bay County Library and the Northwest Regional Library system was formed. Bay County Library became the Headquarters Library for the system. Bookmobile service was also offered during this period.

In 1962, the Library was offered the use of a building that had housed a Public Restroom located next to the Library building. They graciously accepted this building and began painting and renovating to make it usable as a part of the Library.

The Library had been bursting at the seams since 1961 and a major campaign was started to raise money to build a new and bigger library. Library staff participated in various ways to help raise money for the new building. When Deer Point Dam was dedicated, some staff members were there selling candy for the Library fund. In 1964, the Library buildings and land at Jenks Avenue were sold to the federal government for a Post Office parking lot. The Library then moved to the Christo Five & Dime building on Harrison Avenue. The Library was supposed to be in the storefront for only one year. However, three years later the Library was still there and still growing. By this time, Gulf, Calhoun and Walton counties had joined the library system.

Finally, in 1967 the Library moved again, to the present location on the Downtown City Marina. This building has served the Library well. In 2001, there are eight locations in three counties in the Library System in addition to the Headquarters.

The library is once again bursting at the seams. Perhaps it won't be long before the Public Library gets to move again.
Submitted by: Rebecca B. Saunders, 2515 Frankford Avenue, Panama City, Florida 32405; e-mail: saunder1@ol.com; saunder@nwrls.lib.fl.us.

Bay County Public Library: Yesterday, Today, and Tomorrow

I am much nearer my last day as Director of the Bay County Public Library (BCPL) than my first, but I remember the latter with crystal clarity: the time of year, the drive to work, the library staff and trustees I met, and the ominous weather. It was a momentous occasion. It was also a dark and stormy day as Hurricane Kate was bearing down on us. The situation called for a momentous decision, so my first official act was to close the library. That was November 19, 1985.

There was also a storm brewing within the Northwest Regional Library System (NWRLS.) At that time the Bay County Public Library was the headquarters library for the NWRLS, a multi-county alliance of public libraries serving Bay, Gulf, Liberty, Calhoun, Holmes, and Washington Counties. The mission of the BCPL is to support, strengthen, and equalize library service among member libraries. The State Library of Florida strongly encouraged this regional library cooperation, but it did not provide funds for

System services. The member libraries benefitted from service functions provided by the BCPL - materials selection; cataloging and processing; administration; reference; storytelling; sharing of resources; etc. They were better able to contain costs and increase services

A computer class in the Computer Lab at the Bay County Library

and access locally than they could if operating on their own. It created an illusion of well-being on their part, and it was breaking the budget of the BCPL. In sum, Bay County Public Library was subsidizing a Systems arrangement without System funding.

Early in my tenure as Library Director, the Library Board of Directors determined to set the BCPL on a course that required member libraries to contribute to System services, and we had to weather a storm of protest from several member libraries. Ultimately, we trimmed our sails and whittled the NWRLS into a three-county library system: Bay, Gulf, and Liberty Counties. When the State Library recognized that Regional Library Systems like ours needed financial support to "work together. . . not alone," they established a Multi-County Grant Program in 1993. That put the BCPL and NWRLS on solid financial ground. The headquarters library and the member libraries benefitted significantly.

Another important turning point in Bay County Library history was the introduction of computer and telecommunications technologies. When I arrived on the scene in 1985, there was one computer in the administrative office of the BCPL and what seemed like miles of card catalog stations in the public service area. In technical services there were long rows of book carts with hundreds of books waiting to be cataloged and processed. With the help of a Library Service and Construction Act (LSCA) grant, we automated all technical operations of the library (purchasing, processing, cataloging, and circulation.) Next we automated access to the collections and established a System-wide network for sharing materials. Online Public Access Catalogs (OPACs) replaced all manual file card catalogs, much to the chagrin of many library patrons. With the shift to computer-based technical operations, online public access catalogs, and library materials in electronic form, a whole new dimension in the *means* of library service was emerging. Without the dedication of our library staff and their willing acceptance of constant technological change, redesigning library services during the 1990s would have been a nightmare.

What a time of opportunity for librarianship! Collections expanding beyond the limitations of print resources; resources and services no longer confined by the walls of library buildings; librarians extending their expertise into areas of electronic content and access. By the turn of the century, BCPL was offering a full spectrum of information resources to library users. As I write this essay in September 2003, however, the Bay County Public Library is at another crossroads in its storied history. What increasingly troubles me and my colleagues - and should concern everyone who values the library - is that our current thirty-six year old library building on the City Marina is in deteriorating condition. Especially the roofing system which lets in water by the bucket fulls. Moreover, its limited space for books, computers, and people cannot meet the demands of an ever-expanding County population. Bay County has simply outgrown its program of library service. The Library Board of Directors has lobbied the Bay County Commission to construct a new BCPL to meet the extensive demands on

our library resources and services in the future. On September 16, 2003, the County Commission in a 3 to 2 vote killed a planned 0.2 percent millage increase to build a new Bay County Public Library. Commissioners Cornel Brock and Jerry Girvin were the panels only supporters of the library tax increase. The "unkindest cut of all" came from Commissioner John Newberry who withdrew his support for the library based on a tax increase. Immediately following the approval for a static FY 2004 budget, Commissioner Newberry made a motion for the commission to find a way to fund the library project "come hell or high water." Perhaps there is a pun intended here.

So, where does library development stand as this publication goes to press? Whether a new library is to be or not to be depends on whether promises made are promises kept.

Submitted by: George Vickery, Director of the Bay County Public Library and the Northwest Regional Library System, 25 W. Government St, Panama City, FL 32401.

Changes in the Bay County Public Library

From its vantage point at various locations around Panama City, the Bay County Public Library watched the downtown section go from a small waterfront spot to a thriving metropolis over the past 90 years.

One can only wonder what library founders G.M. West, R.L. McKenzie and several others would say if they could see the way the town and organization has grown since the days when the community was known as Harrison and had only a few homes and businesses.

Harrison first saw development after West retired from the railroad in 1906 to promote the town with naval stores operators McKenzie and A. J. Gay. A. B. Steele, the builder of the Atlanta & St. Andrews Bay Railway Co. (Bay Line), renamed the town Panama City that year for the Panama Canal under construction at that time.

West built a huge wooden 1,120-foot steamer dock that extended into the bay from the foot of Harrison Ave. Since boats were the main means of transportation and travel, this pier became the center of activities in Panama City. Several businesses such as a café, the post office and the jail were all located on the dock.

In 1909, the year that Panama City was incorporated, the population was listed as 600.

Two years later in 1911, W.H. Lynn of New York founded the town of Lynn Haven for Union veterans of the Civil War. The Woman's Literary Club established the area's first library in Lynn Haven that same year. West intended to organize one for Panama City, but garnered little interest among the residents until three years later when the idea of establishing "free public libraries" swept the country.

In his Panama City Pilot, West pushed the need for a library quoting Theodore Roosevelt, who said "after the church and school, the free public library is the most effective influence for good in America."

On the blustery winter night of Jan. 5, 1914, West invited several people to his home on Beach Drive in St. Andrews. Beside a flickering fire, those in support of a library formed the "Panama City Library Association." They set membership dues at $1 per year.

Thus began the library's story as it moved from place to place with enough pages to fill a book.

The First Library

In May 1915, Panama City's first library opened in the Commercial Club House, now the Elks Club on Beach Drive, with 250 books donated by citizens. Anne Chandlee served as the first librarian and kept the room open two half days each week.

The waterfront, with long wooden pier and other docks, remained the center of activity in Panama City. Harrison Avenue extended to Sixth Street; north of that location was out of town. Huge live oaks lined the middle of the street and horses and mules drank water from troughs. Some sections of town had boardwalks which made walking easier than on the sand-filled streets. Cows and pigs wandered freely around town where an occasional Model- T appeared on the roads.

To the northeast above the trees, one could see the new courthouse with its dome and clock, which was completed in 1915. Launches carried tourists to the pavilion across the bay at Lands End, now Shell Island, where bathing apparel rental cost 25 cents.

In 1919, the Panama City Woman's Club took over the library's operation and scheduled hours Monday and Friday from 3-5 p.m. A few years later, the library offered "a cool reading room open in summer" and "a restful place in winter" by the bay.

Then in 1924, the Woman's Club was sold, and the library moved to different locations around Panama City, adding more chapters to its book. After space became tight, the library turned over many of its books and magazines to the schools.

When the Woman's Club built its new home on Fourth St. in the 1930s, the Cove stood out as one of the most beautiful sections of town with all its new homes. It was also Depression years, and the club sponsored a Works Progress Administration sewing room, which included a section for the library.

By then Harrison Avenue had been extended north to connect with the highway that became U. S. 231. Panama City Beach was beginning to attract visitors, but lower Harrison Avenue continued to be the heart of the business district. Crowds still gathered at the city pier.

Bayfront Park

In 1937, business leaders suggested improvements to the lower end of Harrison Avenue, which involved filling in a semi-circle area that extended 250 feet in each direction.

The beautiful new Bayfront Park and drive opened for traffic on Mar. 4, 1938. Included in the park were two half traffic circles, one for making a loop at the foot of Harrison Avenue, the other for pulling off along the edge of the grass. The recreational area also featured a new dock, a long wooden pier and floats for seaplanes.

Town officials soon realized that the library needed a place of its own. As a WPA project in conjunction with the Chamber of Commerce, the City of Panama City began building its own library in 1938. This structure was located on Jenks Avenue, in Washington Park next to the new post office, which opened that year. But lack of funds placed this library project on hold.

In 1939, Miss Bessie Norton, librarian at Bay High, came to the rescue and spearheaded an organization called "Friends of the Bay County Free Public Library." The group succeeded in obtaining two WPA workers by the names of Ernestine Cooley and Gina Whitehurst for this project. On May 8, these two women opened the library on Second Street with 40 books, a large number of magazines, one table and one chair. But the absence of funds forced this library to close, and the organization fell on hard times.

Then several businessmen, such as H.L. Sudduth, A.E. Rogers, A.H. Brake, allowed the library to occupy their buildings or offices. Brake's second floor had once housed a funeral parlor. By then, the organization had moved so many times, some people referred to it as "the traveling library." If patrons wanted to use the facility, they realized they better phone first to determine the library's current location, as more chapters were added to its book. Mary Brown was a librarian during this time.

The fall of 1940 found the half-finished library building on Jenks Ave. in a dilapidated condition. The need for a permanent location finally forced a few supporters to confront Mayor Harry Fannin, who forked over $750 and helped the supporters raise the $1,000 needed to complete the building.

The population of Panama City stood at 4,738; Bay County's at 20,686.

The Octagon-Shaped Library

Dedication of the new octagon-shaped building in Washington Park was held Sept. 10, 1941. It opened just in time to provide services to the thousands of military personnel, shipyard workers and the many new families that flooded into Panama City during World War II. The Chamber of Commerce occupied the front half of the building and the library, the two rooms in the rear.

Serving as librarians over the next several years were Helen McKinney, who besides working as an employee did a lot to raise funds to support the library; a Miss Sneed; a Miss Carol; and Jane Van Dike Patton.

When Patton became head librarian her primary goals and successes were extending the library services to other counties and introducing a bookmobile to bring reading material to rural areas, jails and nursing homes.

But in the Washington Park, heavy rains sometimes flooded the library, ruining books. The Chamber of Commerce relocated, which gave the library the entire building for its use.

The New Downtown Marina

As business and fishing boats began moving to St. Andrews and Panama City Beach, Panama City leaders proposed a redevelopment project through the construction of a downtown marina. Once bond money was secured in 1957, work commenced on this huge project that would replace Bayfront Park.

A section of the waterfront was purchased from the C.S. Anderson family, who for many years operated fishing and party boats from their own dock, west of Harrison Ave.

The principal development jutted 1,200 feet into the bay from the foot of Harrison Avenue. Included in this plan were the new City Hall; the marina with some 436 berths; a large auditorium, capable of seating 3,000, that became the Marina Civic Center; a big restaurant with a dancing pavilion; and concession buildings. The Panama City Marina was completed in the summer of 1959.

In 1960, the population of Bay County totaled 67,131. A few years later, the library needed more space, and plans got underway for a new building. The post office purchased the old property, and the library was forced to make its temporary headquarters in the vacant Christo Dime Store on Harrison Ave.

The new library finally opened at the city marina in May 1967 and began its next chapter. The collection included 50,000 books. In addition to the books, it offered a theater for children, a room for the blind, and a section for business and young adults. The library also featured a "quiet room" where the public could relax, enjoy a book or magazine and gaze at the beautiful bay through the large windows. The second floor was used for storage. But by 1974 when space was needed, employees and patrons began using sections of the second floor.

Through the years, books, magazines and newspapers were added, along with interlibrary loans, microforms, audio books, video cassettes, online information databases, classes in computer usage, and a small meeting room for organizations. The public now has access to the Internet on the library's 16 computers, along with many other services.

In recent years, the marina was modernized with more up-to-date boat slips, a roundabout, a ships' store and a fuel dock. The Civic Center and City Hall have also undergone extensive renovations.

Today, the library serves between 1,000-1,700 patrons per day. In 2000, Bay County's population was listed at 148,217, or double the population in 1960. The book total at the library is 116,333, again double the 1967 figure. On both the main floor and the second floor, every nook and cranny is filled with library items and equipment.

The library cannot go up because its foundation was built on wooden pilings that would not support additional weight. It cannot extend out because of a similar problem and the loss of parking spaces. During periods of heavy rain, the old building leaks in so many places 30 big plastic containers or more must be used to catch the dripping water while huge sheets of plastic protect the stacks.

Over the years, the building has had a new roof and other roof repairs, plus numerous patch jobs. Structural engineers say nothing more can be done to improve the 36-year-old building. The library needs more space.

Great progress has come to this area and surrounding towns and communities in recent years. Neighboring counties realize the importance of new, modern libraries and have built them in their communities. The Bay County Public Library awaits its next chapter.

Submitted by: Marlene Womack, P.O. Box 15631, Panama City, FL 32406.

Head Start - A Community Coming Together

The first Head Start in 1967, a federal eight-weeks summer program for preschool children in Bay County, was a start to remember. The prior year, the grant from the Bay County School Board (Board) was refused by the Office of Economic Opportunity (OEO). The Board would not agree to integrate teachers and aides or to combine centers serving these families with incomes below $3000. Also eligible were a small number of handicapped children and those above the poverty line.

In 1967, the Head Start (HS) grant was again submitted by Bob Bowden, Bay County Federal Projects Director. Georgia Henry worked with Bowden on the grant for 500 children which contained the requested changes of the year before. The program included education medical and dental, parent involvement, social services and nutrition. Teachers spent a required week at Florida State University, the state's HS training site.

However, Thomas Todd, Bay County School Superintendent, received word in May that unless additional changes were made, the proposal would be rejected! Todd's charge to OEO is that HS is being used to dictate administration and operation of the school system, and that the welfare of children is not considered. He advised OEO that Bay County was not so dependent on the federal government that school officials will agree to unreasonable demands. OEO officials accuse Bay officials with gerrymandering the boundary lines of the centers (schools) to produce segregation.

The May 11, 1967 Panama City News Herald reporter, Dorothy Beanland, followed with: "A county sponsored preschool program was approved by the Board if the federally sponsored HS project is rejected. Todd blasted the changes called for by OEO, stating the Bay proposal was in compliance with integration polices set forth by the federal court, and the OEO were overstepping their authority. He advised OEO that the project had been planned to meet the needs of children and refused to make the changes.

Two elementary principals, Curtis Jackson and James Commander, were named to work with Todd on enlisting parental and civic-club aid for the program. . . Members of the preschool planning group include Todd, Jackson, Commander, Marvin McCain, Robert Cain Fletcher Jones and Mrs. Georgia Henry."

Beanland's June 2, 1967 article reads: "OEO Rejects Bay's HS Program, Hearing Set Thursday. OEO says the federal program has been rejected because it fosters racial prejudice. . . Todd said that enrollment of students and assignment of faculty members were to follow to a "T" the guidelines given for school integration by Federal Judge Harrold Carswell. As OEO had requested, the number of centers were cut in half, and principals advised to hire staff."

Again from Beanland: "Bay Head Start Hearing Slated. Today, June 8, a hearing is scheduled in the county courthouse. It is the second hearing of its sort in the United States. Federal Projects Director, Bob Bowden and HS Director, Mrs. Georgia Henry, who planned most of the proposed program are anticipated to testify at the hearing."

The night before, my husband, school principal Sid Henry and I invited the OEO attorneys to our home. We wanted them to understand the comprehensive, quality HS program planned and the effort made to eliminate segregation as shown in bus routes to schools, with the exception of the United Cerebral Palsy Center which has specialized equipment.

The final in a series of Beanland's articles appeared June 9, 1967: "Bay Head Start Program Receives OEO Blessing, Compromise Reached. Following rejection of defense items offered by School Board Attorney Julian Bennett by Hearing Examiner Ralph Daughtry, a recess was called, and attorneys huddled in private conference with school and OEO officials throughout the day. Officials from both sides wandered in and out of the conference room shuffling papers, talking privately to each other in the hallway, and examining maps as another 20 people waited restlessly in the courtroom.

Around 4 p.m., members of the Board began showing up one at a time and disappearing into the private conference room. Shortly after a third member arrived, Daughtry returned to the courtroom. Within minutes, attorneys filed in and the official meeting again got underway.

Malcolm Mason, OEO attorney, then announced that in view of the fact that the children of the county were the most affected by the outcome, both sides had made every effort to work out a solution of a difficult problem and an agreement had been reached. Mason emphasized that this year's program is possible only through compromise, that future proposals would have to follow OEO guidelines without exception. The four centers will be located at Drummond Park, Patterson, Mowat and the United Cerebral Palsy Clinic. . . Buses will transport all of the children regardless of where they live. Extra funds will be provided, the OEO attorney said, to cover transportation cost, and the United Cerebral Palsy Center will be for handicapped children only.

The presence of Governor Claude Kirk's Special Assistant for Educational Affairs, Bill Maloy, was a contributing factor to the outcome. Julian Bennett, School Board Attorney, was also a convincing presence. School principals James Commander and Curtis Jackson were constant in their dedication to Early Childhood Education. Nor would HS become a reality with out the persistence of Thomas Todd. With his outstanding leadership, Head Start happened in 1967, and possibly the following years.

The eight week program began the following Monday. Tribute is due to all who participated. Special gratitude goes to Ida James, Assistant HS Director; Betty Rogers, Social Services; Lois Lawrence, Music; Marge McKleskie, Nurse; Dr. Floyd Humphries, Medical; Dr. Ullman, Bay County Health Department; Ruby Baggett, Nutrition and two valued volunteers, Phyllis Daniels and Mildred Richbourg.

Visitors from the state HS Training Office at Florida State University related that our project was the best summer HS in the state. As a compliment to the entire community. the Director, Georgia Henry, was hired as Florida's HS Training Director.

The school system sponsored summer HS until 1983. The directors were Phyllis Daniels, Marjorie Jones, Lois Lawrence (9 years), and Betty Rogers.

In 1983, the Board rejected the offer to convert summer HS into a full-year program. Early Childhood Services, Inc. accepted the grant and has it to this date. Approximately 355 children are served annually in 7 school-based programs. Early HS was added in 1997 serving approximately 83 children and families in 4 of the 7 centers. There are also 2 HS/Child Care Partnerships plus a Home Based Program. HS services for the 2000-01 program year included 175,500 USDA-approved meals and snacks, 379 child health screenings, 372 dental screenings, 435 developmental assessments, technical assistance, training for disability coordinators in 10 HD programs in 18 counties. 325 volunteers participated in the program

Submitted by: Georgia T. Henry - Pearson, 7752 Shadow Bay Drive, Panama City, Fl. 32404.

Junior Museum - The Adventure Place

Created in 1967, the Museum is situated on 12 acres of land located close to downtown Panama City and its business district.

Exhibits are designed for use by preschool through middle school aged children. Adult guidance and participation is recommended. In addition to permanent and special exhibits, the museum offers educational programs and classes.

The Junior Museum is located at 1731 Jenks Avenue, Panama City, Florida, 32405. It's mission is to inspire and educate children by providing interactive exhibits and programs focusing on science, history and culture.

Submitted by: The Junior Museum, 1731 Jenks Avenue, Panama City, FL 32405.

Local History Room
Bay County Public Library

The Local History Room at the Bay County Public Library is an important part of Bay County and its history. From the time I first started working for Jane Patton at the Library in the late 1950s collecting history was very important.

For many years newspaper articles, photographs and other items pertaining to the history of Bay County and Panama City resided in boxes with a staff member or two familiar with what was there. After moving into the building at 25 W. Government Street we dedicated an area of the library to housing these materials, complete with a desk and the capability of answering questions.

Rebecca Saunders, on right, shows Local History room to visitors

In 1974 portions of the George Mortimer West collection were gifted to the Library by a grandson, Charles West. This greatly enhanced the collection and the materials were moved to a location on the 2nd floor of the Library. Around 1987 additional changes were made to the area housing the Local History collection and the circulation desk from the building at Jenks Avenue was placed in the room. In 2001 the room was relocated to another area still on the 2nd floor. This allowed us additional space. Carpet was also added provided by the Friends of the Library.

The Library received grants from the Bay Youth Center Board and the Panama City Rotary Club in 1984. We worked with Shirley Howell and the 8th and 9th grade Quest students at Jinks Junior High School to begin organizing the photograph collection. This initial organization is the basis for the present collection of over 5,000 photographs.

The Bay County Public Library and the Bay District Schools were awarded a grant for the Bay County Digitized Photo Archive. In January of 2004 digitized photographs on the Internet at www.photos.nwrls.com number 3,410 photographs from the BCPL Local History Room collection and 1,972 from the Tommy Smith/Bay District Schools collection.

The Library continues to increase its holdings and the use of the room is remarkable. At the present time there are 1,287 monograph items (books, annuals, city directories, telephone books, magazines, newspapers and more).

Submitted by: Rebecca B. Saunders, Local History Room Specialist, Bay County Public Library.

National Society Daughters of the American Revolution

St. Andrew Bay Chapter, National Society Daughters of the American Revolution The St. Andrew Bay Chapter, NSDAR, was organized November 12, 1948, with Mrs. Lou Ellen Coleman as organizing regent and 19 charter members. Today, the chapter is nearly 100 members strong.. The chapter name was chosen because of the historical significance of St. Andrew Bay in Bay County.

The DAR 's many purposes include historic preservation, promotion of education, and patriotic endeavor, as well as honoring those who have given of themselves to create and defend our United States of America.

The St. Andrew Bay Chapter conducts workshops in lineage research for prospective members. It works with other Florida chapters to preserve Florida historical sites. It provides genealogical materials for Bay County Library.

The St. Andrew Bay Chapter conducts an annual American History Essay Contest in all Bay County 5th, 6th, 7th, and 8th grades. It also conducts the DAR Good Citizens Program promoting dependability, service, leadership, and patriotism among high school seniors and a Columbus Essay Contest for all high school students. Annual awards are given for excellence to JROTC cadets. Its members participate in promoting adult literacy and citizenship for newcomers to the USA.

The St. Andrew Bay Chapter joins with nearly 3000 other chapters worldwide to support selected rural and Native American education programs. Its participation in college scholarship programs occurs on both national and local levels. It promotes Constitution Week to emphasize, defend, and preserve the Constitution. It distributes American flags and flag codes.

The NSDAR is a member of the National VAVS Advisory Committee through which it provides service to veterans of all the uniformed services. The St. Andrew Bay Chapter annually presents gifts to VA medical centers serving Bay County. It promotes participation in events to honor past service by veterans and current service by today's military men and women.

Submitted by: Elizabeth D. du Mont, Regent, St. Andrew Bay Chapter, NSDAR, 6323 Thomas Drive #703, Panama City Beach FL 32408-5658.

Sgt. Robert A. "Bob" Hoxie

Bob's career in Police work began March 6, 1962, starting with short classroom training and on patrol with senior officers. Pay $69.00 a week, six-day week. Bob walked the downtown beat for five months then was assigned the west beat in a patrol car for two weeks. Then he was put in charge of the Panama City Jail until city courts were discontinued and prisoners were taken to the county jail. The police station was moved into its new quarters 1979-80. A short time later the detention cells and jailor position were discontinued. Bob was put in charge of animal control (July 1962) when the first animal shelter was built by Panama City. Animals were taken in from surrounding cities and counties until Bob and the Chief implemented a fee system. Bob controlled the animal strays, dogs running in packs, etc. and helped with writing needed animal ordinances, still in use today. The second animal shelter was larger and Bob had a shelter attendant, two trucks and four animal wardens when the Bay County Humane Society contracted to handle Panama City's animal control. In July 1962, Bob was also in charge of supply buying for the police department and inventoried all department equipment, furniture, etc., along with building maintenance.

On September 12, 1967, Robert A. Hoxie made Sergeant.

He was put in charge of special services in the early 1980's which included meter department and process serving. Finding that the parking meters were an added expense to the police department and city, he requested permission from the city manager to remove them. The city manager approved and the meters were removed.

As process server, Bob had one patrolman helping serve

Panama City's papers. In 1989, Sheriff Pitts appointed both men as special deputies to serve Panama City's papers in Bay County. Bob was appointed to serve on the D.U.I. School for the first eight years it was in operation with P.A.C. Bob spoke to the finance committee for detox and it was refunded for operating at the end of its first year on. Bob assisted Tyndall Air Force Base in starting their D.U.I. Program in 1964. After a couple of years, he also assisted Tyndall Security Police in how to catch and handle all kinds of animals and which kind of equipment to use.

Robert A. Hoxie

In 1967, he assisted Errol Sewell when he started the Boys Club. Bob implemented the use of orange rain coats and vests, also twelve traffic cones in supervisors cars. After serving as a patrol supervisor, Bob was placed in the property evidence section and received a certificate of commendation for up-dating and clearing old cases. He went on patrol and in January 1993 was hospitalized for a severe heart disease, leaving him only able to do a desk job. Bob became a station officer taking reports by phone and walk in. After a short time, he was needed in property evidence. He retired on May 31, 1995 unable to continue as a police officer. The doctor said no more physical activity.
Submitted by: Robert A. "Bob" Hoxie, 1903 Arthur Ave., Panama City, FL 32405.

Seniors For Seniors

A troubled voice was on the phone. "Where can I get the Seniors for Seniors tape I saw on TV today? I must have the information I just heard. My wife is very ill and I have to make some immediate decisions about her care. My questions are the same ones asked of and answered by the attorney on TV."

This is a true example of why Seniors for Seniors 30 minute television program has been on the air for nine years. It has served as a voice for the elderly in Bay County. "The whole purpose is to let seniors help themselves or find out where they can get help," said Frances Edelen, who co-hosts the show with her husband, Dick Edelen. Taped at WJHG- TV, it is shown twice a week during the month on the Gulf Coast Community College television station.

As sure as the first Monday in the month arrives, an assortment of retirees gather at WJHG TV to produce another month's

Senior for Seniors volunteers, L-R: Dick Edelen, Carl Borgersen, Vanda Borgersen, Otto Witt, Jerry Winkler, John Pearson, Frances Edelen, Georgia Pearson

show. Seniors write it. Seniors produce it. Seniors operate the cameras. And seniors host it. These volunteers have diverse backgrounds. . .a Navy pilot. . . an FBI agent. . . a high school teacher. . . a marketing/sales executive. . .and an electrical engineer. . . a housewife. . .Army and Air Force officers, and a human services consultant.

The origin of the show was in 1994. Producer John Pearson had been involved in a television program in Georgia. He thought such a program may be successful in Bay County after talking to Beach Cable about community access television. Next he contacted the Bay County Council on Aging Retired Senior Volunteer Program (RSVP). That search, plus conversation with friends, yielded Frances and Dick Edelen who would become the hosts and interviewers for the show. While they had never faced

television cameras before, they readily adapted to the task.

Television cameramen had to be found. Again in the Bay County Council on Aging talent was Carl Borgersen, Jerry Winkler, George Expling, Otto Witt and Bill Rumph. These volunteers readily grasped the necessary fundamentals to operate the complex machines.

The volunteers now are John Pearson producer; Georgia Henry Pearson, writer, co-producer; Dick and Frances Edelen, hosts; Vanda Borgersen, announcer; cameramen, Carl Borgersen, Otto Witt and Jerry Winkler.

Initially, sponsors expressed some reluctance to subsidize the show. However, after it became evident there was a growing viewership, sponsorships have become easier to obtain. And, an announcer was needed to introduce and close each show, and extend gratitude to the sponsor and to the television station for the use of its technicians and equipment. Vanda Borgersen was the perfect choice. WJHG provides a director plus staff.

The writer and associate producer, Georgia Henry-Pearson, first secures a list of questions from the guest for each show and provides it to the hosts. The questions serve as an outline of conversation with the guest and as a basis for the related opening and closing narration for the announcer to read.

The month-to-month continuity of the show is managed by the two producers who have established contacts among a wide spectrum of professionals such as heart specialists, oncologists, ophthalmologists, attorneys, Social Security executives, law enforcement officers, hospice personnel, legislative issues, visual art and creative writing.

As a result of the developing expertise of Seniors for Seniors, the show received two top media awards for service to seniors and to the community: The 2001 Aging with Dignity Television Journalism Award by the Florida Department of Elder Affairs, and The 2001 Quality Senior Living Award in Media by the Florida Council on Aging. The first award resulted from a nomination by the Area Agency on Aging to the Department of Elder Affairs. The second award resulted from a nomination by the Bay County Council on Aging to the Florida Council on Aging.

The Pearsons produced their last show in December, 2003. Florida State University, Panama City Campus, assumed production in 2004.
Submitted by: Georgia T. Henry-Pearson, 7752 Shadow Bay Dr., Panama City, Fl. 32404.

The Visual Arts Center

The Visual Arts Center of Northwest Florida credits its beginning to the Panama City Art Group, 17 artists who formed an association in 1955 for the purpose of exhibiting and promoting the visual arts in Bay County. In 1963, the name was changed to Panama City Art Association. Members lobbied for art teachers in elementary schools, taught studio art

Flag raising ceremony in front of the old city hall building

courses and installed art exhibits at the Fair Grounds, Junior Museum, Panama City Mall and the Marina Civic Center.

In 1986, Panama City Art Association and the Downtown Improvement Board received a grant to renovate the old Panama City Hall and Jail and transform it into permanent gallery space. The newly remodeled building was christened Visual Arts Center of Northwest Florida, and opened its doors in 1988 as the only museum-Quality exhibition space between Pensacola and Tallahassee. The new addition to the building houses the entrance foyer, elevator and Art Deco style stairway.

The original building was built in 1925 in Spanish Revival style. The stucco on the outside of the building has many pieces of multi-colored glass; the Visual Arts Center is thought to be the only building in Florida with this type of stucco. The building facade is a key element, with Greek columns, Corinthian capitals, a Roman arch with a false gable and a Spanish terra cotta tile roof. Inside, unfinished brick walls and barred windows testify to the building's history as a jailhouse. The floor molding in the original lobby is Georgia pink marble, the same that is used in the Capital Building in Atlanta, Ga.

Education is a priority of the Visual Arts Center. Through weekend and evening hours, the VAC offers opportunities for people of all incomes and schedules to visit and participate in our programs.
Submitted by: Visual Arts Centers of Northwest Florida, 19 East 4th Street, Panama City, Fl. 32401.

Women's Civic Club of Panama City Beach

The Women's Civic Club of Panama City Beach held its first meeting in October 1965. The Club was formed primarily by women owning and working in businesses on the Beach. While the early membership was 20-30, the present club has an average membership of 160.

During the past thirty seven years, the club has been instrumental in bringing improvements to the community. In early years (70-80), a "beauty of the beach" contest recognized young people. When the Christmas tree lighting and parade were begun (1980s), the Club was one of the first to participate. They worked to establish and furnish a community center and in recent years (2000-2002) a Senior Center. Life saving and fire fighting equipment were secured for City departments in 1980-90. Maggie Still Park was dedicated in memory of a member of the Club (1989) and is maintained by members. The Club assisted in building Under the Palms playground (2000). Each year, equipment for City Parks is provided.

The Club's mission is to promote civic improvements and aid worthwhile projects. To fulfill this mission members hold fund raising projects such as Gulf World Weekend, Seafood Festival activities, silent auctions, dances, arts and crafts show, flea markets, and bridge games and tournaments. Annually, the club provides three scholarships and makes contributions to Children's Miracle Network, Beach Care Services, schools, domestic violence, Library, Food Pantry, Beach Police and Fire Departments, Senior Center and other worthy projects such as Boys and Girls Club, Gibb Village, etc.
Submitted by Gail Oberst, 208 Oleander Circle, PCB 32413, cftpyramid@knology.net.

MEMORIES OF BAY COUNTY

Active Community Volunteers

Mother and Daddy both were always active in the school and church community with their children. After Daddy retired, he and Mother bought several coin laundries and ran them for several years. When Mother retired they both became very active volunteers in the community. After building a new home and moving to Lynn Haven in 1973 they joined the Lynn Haven Presbyterian Church. Both mother and daddy volunteered at Bay Medical Center (Daddy in the emergency room at the information desk and Mother in the Gift Shop). Mother still volunteers in the Gift Shop in 2004. Together they delivered bread and bakery goods from a local grocery store to the Rescue Mission and to the refuge house for abused spouses and delivered Meals on Wheels for the Council on Aging. Together they collated and prepared for mailing the church newsletter for many years. Mother has for many years been coordinator for the Mission Haven/Thornwell clothing drives. Mother for many years sent out cards to church members as a part of the outreach program. Both my Daddy before his death and Mother to this day have been faithful members, in service and attendance, of Lynn Haven Presbyterian Church.
Submitted by: Rebecca B. Saunders, 2515 Frankford Ave., Panama City, FL 32405.

Henry Clay and Christine Walker Brown 1993

Attending Church in Bay County

Attending church, I learned early in life who God and Jesus are. We had wonderful Christian ladies who taught Sunday School and the influence on our young lives helped form the men and women we later became. We were taught from small cards, a picture on the front and the reverse side told the story. I still have some of those cards that I consider real treasures.

Pastors were Pastors in every sense of the Biblical word. They were more personally involved with their church, as a whole, than Pastors seem to be today. I don't think size of membership has anything to do with holding this reverse attitude toward flocks today. Brother J.B. Davis, Brother

Sunday School Class at Millville Advent Christian church in the 1940's or 50s

Bedsole, Brother H.K. Shepard and others, were salt of the earth ministers who visited, prayed for, and had personal communion with their church members. Creating lasting memories of that particular minister.

When someone came to our church and wished to be baptized everyone that could attend would travel to Oliver Creek. Most all the churches used this small body of water, but some ministers would chose the bay waters to cleanse the repentant souls. It was many years before a church in Bay County had indoor baptistries. This gave the new Christian no room to back out of their new found faith by blaming the weather.

Going to church gave me a great religious and moral foundation to live by for a lifetime.
Submitted by: Marjorie Arnold, 2304 Foxworth Dr., Panama City.

The Big Snow of 1958

While attending St. Andrews Elementary School, I remember it snowing two times. The second time, on February 13, 1958, there was a lot of snow. It was very cold that day, instead of going out on the playground, we met in the school auditorium. Everyone was talking about the possibility that it might snow. Back then school started at 8:30. First, second and third grades ended the day at 2:30, while fourth, fifth and sixth grades ended at 3:15. On that cold afternoon when the bell

Sketch of Richard Holley and Eddienell Soderquist, playing in Richards's backyard as the snow started to fall on that cold afternoon of February 13, 1958

rang at 3:15, I ran home as fast as I could. Everyone was excited because the weather report was forecasting snow that night. As I ran into the warmth of the kitchen, I made a snack, turned on the television and watched the "Little Rascals." Changing into my play clothes,

Richard Holley playing in the snow

I wrapped a scarf around my neck and headed out the back door. My next door neighbor, Eddienell Soderquist and I met in the backyard, eagerly talking about the possibility of a night of snow. Both of us being born and raised in St. Andrews where the chances of snow are hardly never, it was an unimaginable thought. Our emotions were really high and fun and laughter were sounds in my backyard.

It was very breezy and the sky was a very dark gray color. We were all bundled up, wearing gloves and toboggans pulled down over our ears and eagerly looking for the snow to start. To have something to do, we would improvise whatever we could use to entertain ourselves. We used a 55 gallon drum with a long board laid across it for a see-saw, only

Florida snow scene; note palm tree and icicles with snow

ours was more fun than the see-saws at the parks. As we rocked up and down the drum rolled back and forth about five feet or more.

Well, there we were, Eddienell and I rocking up and down on the see-saw, praying for snow. Then it happened! The biggest snow flakes you could imagine, falling all around us, big white snowflakes. They were swirling around us and the wind was blowing the snow sideways. We thought it was a blizzard. Mother was taking pictures and we were jumping up and down like monkeys. Soon the snow started to accumulate on the ground and everything was becoming white. Yes indeed, Eddienell and I had prayed up a real snow storm! It snowed most of the night. The next morning we woke up to a white blanket of snow on the ground. The snow lasted about two days. Days later you could still find small patches of snow in areas where the sun had not shone. Wilson Hair and I pulled a wagon around picking up snow where it had not yet melted to make a snowman. That was a real treat for all of us living in St. Andrews. I will never forget the beautiful uncommon sight of seeing the ground blanketed with snow, so white and clean, as far as I could see.
Submitted by: Richard Holley, 1104 Carolina Avenue, Lynn Haven, FL 32444.

Biscuits

Margarete Gleitsmann worked at the Jinks School Lunchroom in the 50's and 60's. She was known for her school rolls, biscuits, cinnamon rolls and French bread. Kids and teachers alike would sneak through her "baker's alley" as it was called to try and snitch an extra roll or piece of bread.

But she didn't always have that reputation of being a good baker or cook. When she first came to America and was working in a hotel over in Valpariso in the 1930's she spoke hardly any English. She was taught to cook and bake by a

Greek chef through an interpreter who understood Greek and German. She made biscuits one morning for breakfast and the construction workers that were at the table in the dining room stuck the biscuits up on the hat rack hooks that were all around the room (the biscuits were so hard they couldn't eat them).

But, I know there are many junior high school students and teachers that remember Big Margarete's baking from Jinks.
Submitted by: Mona Anita Lucas, 3235 Orlando Rd, Panama City, FL.

Margarete Gleitsmann during her Jinks Junior High lunchroom days

The Bose McCrary Tornadoes

There is a saying that lightening doesn't strike the same place twice. This does not necessarily apply to tornadoes.

The Bose McCrary Tornadoes hit his property where he currently lives (2003) at the north eastern outer limits of Springfield. Both tornadoes traveled from south to north and jumped his house with little to no damage to the house.

The layout of his property at the times the tornadoes hit includes his house facing north, with T.V. antenna, a small barn behind the house (south side less than 100 feet from the house), and a small oak tree in the front yard less than 20 feet from the front porch. The oak tree was about 10 inches in diameter and about 15-18 feet tall when the first tornado hit. The oak tree, house and barn line up in a straight line.

When the first tornado struck circa 1958-1960, it took the roof

Bose McCrary at 82 years old

from the barn, the antenna from the house and put a cork screw twist in the small oak tree. The tornado traveled south to north depositing the barn roofing in the road in front of the house. After this the barn roof and antenna were replaced.

The second tornado struck circa 1967 and traveled the same path as the first. The second one took all the barn, jumped the house taking the antenna and wrinkling one corner of the roofing on the south side. The oak tree in the front yard disappeared. After this tornado damage the barn was rebuilt, the house roof repaired, and a new antenna installed. A pecan tree was later planted in the early 70's at the oak tree site.
Submitted by: James L. McCrary, 12277 Brookshire Ave., Baton Rouge, LA.

Chicago World's Fair

In 1893, members of the Goble family came to Bay County to turkey hunt with my father, Mansel Deshong Mashburn. After a successful hunt, they invited him to go home with them and stay a year working on their farm in Indiana. While visiting there, they treated him to a visit of the World's Fair in Chicago. He said he was amazed at the Florida exhibit, there were mountains of oranges and full grown tall pine trees. But, the one thing that was most memorable happened during a "wild-west" cattle show. One of the bulls with extremely long horns jumped the fence and was amongst the audience when a man sitting next to my father pulled a pistol and shot the bull dead. When the police came

Frank James from the famous James Brothers

to investigate, the man admitted he had shot the bull because he did not want to see anyone hurt or even killed. He had identification proving he was Frank James, Jessie James's brother. My father said when the gun went off it almost scared him to death, because he did not see the man pull the gun. My father got to visit with Frank James for the rest of the show.

Submitted by: Jack Mashburn, 6714 Camp Flowers Rd, Panama City, FL.

Cooking Sugarcane Juice into Syrup

I grew up on a 40 acre farm on Camp Flowers Road between Bayou George and Youngstown. My father always planted from 5 to 10 acres of Blue Ribbon sugarcane because it made the very best syrup.

We always made from 150 to 300 gallons of syrup each year. We had a 60 gallon cast iron kettle in which we cooked the cane juice. During the years of the Second World War, we cooked one batch of syrup down until it was just sugar and we would bleach it in the sun, that way we did not have to depend on rationing stamps to get sugar.

One of my jobs as a young boy was skimming the juice as it was cooking, to get the foam off as it boiled to the top of the kettle. This skimmed foam was put in one of several barrels next to the kettle. The "skimmings" as it set in the barrels would ferment and that is what is called "cane skimming buck", or to the inexperienced, beer. This was a powerful beer, I never knew the alcohol content, but I knew it was strong. If someone distilled the "buck" the end product was some of the best sugarcane rum.

Sugarcane Juice Mill

During my senior year in 1945 in Bay High School, two of my male friends came out to the farm to shoot doves during syrup making time. I told them where they could find the doves but I could not go show them because I had to keep cooking the cane juice. They saw me emptying the skimmings into the barrel and wanted to know what was in the barrels. I told them it was very powerful sugar cane beer, more commonly known as cane-skimming buck. They wanted to know if they could just *taste* the beer.

After about an hour of *tasting* the beer, I reminded them they had come out to shoot doves and that they had better get to it or they would not be able to see one, much less shoot it. By that time all reasoning had left them and it was like talking to the wind. So, it was finally too late to shoot dove and they had forgotten all about it anyway. They asked if they could take a "sample" home with them. I was more than a little aggravated with both of them so I decided to teach them a small lesson. I picked up a one gallon empty syrup can and filled it about two-thirds full and placed the lid on tight. I deliberately did not fill it full. I knew it was about five miles to U.S. 231 and the dirt road was like a washboard. Back then the roads were only graded once a month. As soon as they left, my father said "you should not have done that," and I said done what? He said I saw you did not

fill that can to the top and you know what's going to happen way before they get to the highway. This was on the weekend and the next Monday when I got to school, both of my friends jumped me right away. I gave them both my best "angelic" look and said: "What is your problem? I treated you with welcome hospitality at the farm." They both, talking at the same time, said: "Before we got to the highway, the lid blew off that can of beer and showered both of us and we had to buy a new headliner for the car to get the smell out of it." I bit my tongue to keep from laughing.

My favorite memory of all time is a sugarcane field when it is fully ripe. It smells like a perfume factory.

Submitted by: Jack Mashburn, Camp Flowers Rd, Youngstown, FL.

Coon Hunting in Bay County

Sometime prior to 1950 and after 1940, the News Herald wrote a story about my father's favorite coon hound. This dog was a natural coon hound, if you did not take him hunting as often as he wanted, he would go by himself, tree a coon and wait for you to find him. One dark night just after sundown when it was so dark you could not see your hand in front of your face, this dog decided he needed to go hunting. So, he started running a coon, at least my father thought it was a coon, and it jumped in Bear Creek. Well, the creek was full of hungry alligators and my father did not want his favorite coon hound to become a tasty morsel for a gator. He jumped in his boat and rowed out to find his dog. When he got next to the dog, he grabbed it by the neck and as he lifted it out of the water he noticed it did not have a long tail. Right away he knew he did not have the dog, but he didn't know what he had until it bit his hand. He started to drop it in the boat, but then thought better of it because the full grown wildcat appeared to have a very limited sense of humor. He knew he could not turn it loose and it was getting more difficult to hold, so he reached in his pocket with his left hand and got out his Barlow pocketknife. He placed it in his mouth sideways, to try to bite down on the blade and open it. He bit so hard he bit the handle off his knife. Meanwhile, he was holding the cat at arms length and the cat was a "clawing and a gnawing" his hand and arm. He finally stabbed the cat to death, but not before the cat got in some good licks on his hand and arm. He eventually found his dog. The moral of this story is: If you are going coon hunting, don't catch a wildcat.

Submitted by: Jack Mashburn, 6714 Camp Flowers, Rd., Panama City, FL.

Cove School Days

My parents bought a house at 308 Linda Ave in the Cove. It was a dirt road then and only about five houses on each side of the road. We went to Cove School. There were no sidewalks, eventually the neighbors got together and pooled

All dressed up for the Junior Banquet at Cove School, 1956. In the picture are: Bunnie Douglas, Annette ONeal, Patricia Luch, Wanda Barnes, Catherine Burkette, Lillian Pate, Janice Musgrove, Ed Yerby

their money to build the sidewalks. We would go to school and we would walk down to the Cove Hotel and that's where a lot of us learned how to swim. At the end of Cherry Street there were trees and a gang of us would gather up and play Tarzan and Jane and get ice cream at the little store on Cherry Street. We were like a close knit family, everybody knew everybody.

I went to Cove School from the first grade to sixth and then to Jinks from seventh grade to the ninth grade.

I went to Bay High School and one day I hooked school. I hooked school because I thought my dad was going out of town, He worked for the Police Department. A bunch of us walked from Bay High down to City Cut-Rate Drug Store. That's where they had the booths and we were sitting there with the straws, blowing the straw wrappers at each other. All of a sudden I felt this hand on my shoulder and he said, "Hi!" "Oh!" It was my dad. He said, "Are you girls having a good time?" And we said, "Oh, yes." It was my first time skipping school. He said, "Young lady I want to talk to you when you get home." I was grounded for a month, no TV, no telephone.

We had it good growing up here in Bay County. We had our Junior and Senior Proms and going to the Dixie Sherman for our Dinner there. We all got to wear strapless evening gowns. My dad knew some people over at the Yacht Club and they would have dances and we would have to wear evening gowns. I bought one white evening gown, a lace dress, at Schneider's Dress Shop down on Harrison Avenue. We took material and we changed it, the same dress, over and over again. It was red, green, purple, whatever the color, it was still the same dress.

I graduated from Bay High School in the Class of 1957. I married and moved up North. Someone asked if I like the North or the South best. I think it is both. I have learned a lot up North and since I came back to Panama City I have enjoyed getting to know some of my old friends again. I have cousins in DeFuniak Springs, Florida that I have learned to know all over again. The Gandy's, Ganey's and Gainers. Willie Mae Gandy Walker's mother and my father were brother and sister. Our grandfather built one or two of those houses on the lake in DeFuniak Springs.

Submitted by: Frances Bunnie Douglas Powers, 925 Oak Ave., Panama City, Florida 32401.

Doris Hunt

Doris Hunt gave much to the children of Bay County, her family, friends, and her church, The Antioch Temple Church of God in Christ. Doris served as a Teacher's Aide at St. Andrew and Lucille Moore Elementary Schools. Just out of Rosenwald High School, she began her trek mentoring students, working at the Trinity Luthern Church Kindergarten a short while before going into the Public School System. Her

Doris Hunt working with 3 Lucille Moore School Students

education began in Bay County at the Carrie B. Shaw Elementary School, Rosenwald High School, the Rosenwald Junior College, Gulf Coast Community College and many workshops and classes which were available to her, always endeavoring to become more proficient in her teaching skills. Students loved her and she worked hard at her assignments. People loved her. Her last employment was with the Bay County Council on Aging.

Doris had 6 children: Steffon, Patrice and Roderick Hunt, Bruce & Kelvin, Danny (dec' d) Martin. She was born August 12, 1941 to the union of Hillery and Overy "Lassie" Hunt. Doris died October 13, 2003, at the age of 62. A dedicated and faithful person to the community was buried in Redwood Cemetery, Bay County, FL, October 18, 2003.

Submitted by: Mildred Richbourg, retired teacher Lucille Moore Elem. School, 3909 W. 16th St., Panama City, FL 32401.

Early Years in Panama City

Henry Clay Brown was born 28 November 1915 in Birmingham, Alabama to Charles Gaston Brown and Annie Marie O'Neill. Henry was the seventh of eight children, six girls and two boys. In 1935 he came to Panama City in search of work. There was not much work to be found in Birmingham and his brother, the oldest child of Charles and Annie Brown, had already moved to Panama City and was working at the paper mill. Daddy also found work at the mill and had a room in the same rooming house where his brother and a sister were living.

On 25 May 1936, a Saturday evening, Daddy went sailing with friends Willard Blackburn, Robert Lindsey and David Tasker. They were enjoying a very successful sail, and feeling quite sure of themselves sailed out to the mouth of the new channel. There was quite a heavy sea coming in and it proved too

*The boat **RedWing** approaching dock.*

much for the eighteen foot sailboat and about 12:30 a.m. the boat listed and filled with water. The young men had foresight enough to throw over the anchor and cling to the boat until they were picked up about 5:45 on Sunday by Captain Bruce on the *Red Wing*.

Daddy stayed in the Panama City area until sometime in 1939 and served in the Florida National Guard in 1938 and 1939. In March of 1943 Daddy, Mother, David and Mema moved to Panama City for Daddy to work for a Gas Company. Housing was scarce and they first moved into a little home on Massalina Drive belonging to the owner of the Gas Company. At that time Allen and Linda Avenue were not cut all the way through to Massalina Drive. During the day Mother and Mema could hear the noise of lots of children. One day when Daddy got home from work, they asked him to drive them around so they could see where all the children's voices were coming from. They were surprised to learn that only three blocks away was Cove Elementary School. In December of 1943 we moved into the home on Linda Avenue where all three of the Brown kids grew up.

Submitted by: Rebecca B. Saunders, 2515 Frankford Avenue, Panama City, FL 32405.

The Fight in the Cabbage Garden

When the depression started Daddy and Mama had twelve children of their own, plus others from time to time depending on who needed a home. Most of our growing up occurred in a large house at Crystal Lake, one of several whistle stops for the B C & St Andrews Line. When friends, relatives or even neighbors needed a room overnight or for a month or a year, we kids would lay a pallet in the wide corridor or on the back porch and give them ours. Early in the depression when I was about thirteen I saw two of those neighbors in a terrible fight. That happened near Tank Pond at another whistle stop called Goethe, two miles south of our place.

One of the fighters was Tom Tyson,

Jimmy and Wib Rodgers ca 1928

who with an older sister Nettie MacDonald, lived a mile or so south of Tank Pond at Tyson Lake. Tom's brother Jim Tyson and the MacDonalds came here from North Carolina before 1920. Tom came later; the first time I saw him was right after we arrived in 1925. He had an ox and wagon then. In 1929, when Jim died, Tom buried him in their backyard. The Tysons had a few cows and hogs roaming the woods and Tom was cooper for J R Moody's turpentine operations at nearby Court Marshall Lake. He was educated and knew the Bible well and on occasion ate Mama's cooking. Tom manufactured his own chimney bricks. Some say he hid his gold in those bricks about '29 when Uncle Sam collected everybody's coins. The other fighter was a WWI veteran named Edenfield who often went to the veterans hospital and always stayed with us a week or so upon his return. Mr Edenfield was currently without a wife and had recently moved onto the old Russ place southwest of Tank Pond; he had a fine cabbage garden from which he permitted us to extract earthworms. He once lived near Lucas Lake on a peninsula with Belvi Dykes as wife where he raised hogs with the help of a dog who served as a very effective catcher. Mr Edenfield only had to point and say "catch 'em", and that dog would hold the unfortunate designee by the ear as long as required, paying no attention to the other pigs scattering back to the woods.

The day of the fight my brother Wib and I had walked from the house to Mr Edenfield's for worms.

Wib was catching the worms I snored from the soil when Tom Tyson arrived and started to remove his plow from his wagon so he could hitch it to his mule. In the eight years I had known him he had moved up to a mule from an ox, despite the hard times. Mr Edenfield came from the house and greeted Tom who opined that he was "hard to get along with today". Edenfield took offense that a black man should think he had any choice but to get along because the next thing I heard was the slapping of the plow chains over Tom's head. When I realized they were fighting I grabbed the fence with both hands and heard its rattling long before I realized my own trembling was causing it.

I never heard of Tyson hurting anybody but he reached in his wagon and turned around wielding an axe which I had no doubt he was ready to use. Edenfield ran to his wood pile and returned with a rotten pole which broke apart when he swung it. Running to his cabin he said that he "had something that will stop you" although Tom had pretty much stopped already.

I knew Mr Edenfield kept a rifle in the cabin and knew I was about to see a killing. I ran into the house after him, begging him to spare Tom's life and warning Mr Edenfield that he would be hung if he killed Tom. Mr Edenfield ignored me and I could not stop him; so, I tackled one of his legs, and he just dragged me out into the yard holding the gun in his hands. Suddenly regaining his senses, Mr Edenfield declared to Tom, who was still standing beside his wagon holding his axe, "It's over; go on with the plowing". He turned to the cabin and put his rifle behind the door. Tyson, who was plainly hurt, hooked up his mule and completed the task for which he had come as if nothing had happened. However, he had to shave a fine specimen of beard for his wounds to be treated.

Twenty years later I saw Tom Tyson at my service station at McKenzie Avenue and Fourth Street. He was moving back north to his apple farm. About 1960 Mr Edenfield and his wife traded their place for J H Deal's house in Panama City.
Submitted by: J M Rodgers, 321 Allen Avenue, Panama City, FL 32401.

Fishing For Chickens

The family of Silas and Lillie Mae Welch of St. Andrews consisted of five girls and twin boys. My father is one of the twins, Lester Allen Welch. The Welch family of St. Andrews has long been involved in boat construction and the fishing industry. During the years of The Depression this family survived on what commodities were being distributed and what my grandfather could catch during his daily fishing trips. Needless to say, after a while the family became weary of the same old diet.

The Welch family lived in the two story green home at the corner of Beck Ave. And 11 th. Next door to the Welch family lived an old woman who was not only unfriendly but down right stingy. She had a huge yard of chickens. Silas and his twin boys Lester and Chester approached her one day asking about the possibility of trading some seafood for a chicken. The stingy and unfriendly little old lady said "no", and continued to say "no" after many requests.

The family continued to eat their daily monotonous diet. One day Silas and the boys could take it no longer. The three set out to cut a hole right in the middle of the livingroom floor. The hole was about the size of a dinner plate. After a few days of baiting the chickens with bread crumbs to wander under the Welch home, a piece of corn was attached to a fishing hook. It was not long before they had a strike. Yes, a fresh chicken! After about four days of the Welch family enjoying fresh chicken, the grumpy lady next door began to complain about dogs in the area killing her chickens. To this date of publishing the story still remains a mystery. A story of the missing chickens and those awful dogs that no one ever seemed to sight. My grandfather said "In the Bible it says to fish...it's just not clear...for what."
Submitted by: Donna Rankin, (as told to her by her grandfather Mr. Silas Marion Welch), 210-N East Baldwin Rd, Panama City, FL 32405.

From Dirt Roads to Pavement

I remember when Millville was first paved. The pavement was in St. Andrews up to 15th Street and then it came down and went through Panama City on 6th Street, out to Millville on 6th Street, and out to the Millville Cemetery and stopped there. I remember when Harrison Avenue was an unpaved boulevard, a north dirt road and a south dirt road and oak trees in the middle. The Sherman Arcade was built there and a blind couple named Hodgeboom would sit there strumming a guitar. They had a tin cup that you could put your donations in. My father bought a 1927 Ford Coupe Model T and he and my mother took me over to town. I was five years old and they left me in the car while they shopped. When they got back, I was singing with this blind couple. I remember the song, "Show me the way to go home, I'm tired and I want to go to bed. I had a little drink about an hour ago and it went right to my head." The blind couple invited us to have dinner with them that night. So we came back to their house and we went inside and the blind couple forgot to turn on the lights, and I remember how embarrassed they were.
Submitted by: Fred Turner, 2694 Island View Dr, Panama City, FL 32405.

The Fun Down Under

The George C. Pringle house was built in 1919-20 at the corner of 11th Street and Harrison Avenue. The 4 bedroom, 2 bath house was one of the largest in Bay County and quite the show place of its era.

Cellars are not a common feature in coastal Florida houses. The Pringle house was an exception. It served as a garage for the family's Model T— and, as an impromptu swimming pool when the rains came. A wooden garage with double doors covered the inclined driveway. The parking area was surrounded by 3-foot high, double-bricked retaining walls. A narrow staircase allowed access into the main hall of the house. The retaining

The George C. Pringle Home, a showplace of the era

walls were backfilled, creating a 'crawlspace' that allowed children and most adults to walk upright under the full expanse of the house. The crawlspace was a kid-magnet, attracting three generations of Pringle progeny to play hide-an-seek in the darkened recesses. Windows in the exterior foundation walls allowed sunlight to penetrate into the rooms created by support walls. Long shadows and tales of secret passageways and ghostly hauntings left many a younger sibling running for the main house. An abandoned stove flue made the spectral wailings of a mischievous child echo throughout the cellar rooms. The 3-deep brick support walls resonated with the sounds of laughter.

The fun wasn't limited to the cellar. The vast front stairway provided seating for excited children waiting not-so-patiently to catch sight of Santa at the annual Jaycees Christmas parade. The wide front and back porches offered respite from long, hot summer afternoons. Lazy days visiting with cousins, sipping lemonade or cola while listening to adults reminisce, playing chase in the front yard - the memories of a childhood at the Pringle house.

The Pringle house was moved to Frankford Avenue in 1967 after the property was sold to Humble Oil Company. It was demolished in the 1990s.

Submitted by: Deanne Walton Coffield, 408 Palmetto Court, Lynn Haven, FL 32444.

Games

As a very little girl I played dolls and had teasets and all the accessories to playing house. Annice and I were first best friends and double-first cousins twice removed. She was born February 20 and I came along on July 30, so she was usually the leader unless cousin John Charles, who was a year younger, came out because he was a BOY.

We played paper dolls too, using the catalogs-Sears Roebuck and Montgomery Ward when the new one came out and they gave us the old one. We cut out whole families and our games with them were more complicated than a soap opera.

As we grew older, it seemed all our playmates were boys, and our outdoor activities included, besides playhouses, boy stuff like Civil War, Cowboys and Indians, and World War II. I was only six and a half when a quiet Sunday was shattered by the radio news of Pearl Harbor. I had no idea where that was or exactly what had happened but the aftermath of it shaped my childhood. Uncle Noah (Red) Anderson was in the US Navy on a destroyer in the thick of battle. Uncle Donald Pratt was in the Army on a Mine Sweeper in Massachusetts. And at school we saved our dimes for bonds and we collected scrap iron for the war effort. I earned sergeant's stripes by hauling in scrap metal. Red, white and blue stripes, sewed on my jacket. Grandma Anderson went to work at the Shipyard, helping build big grey troopships. There were gun emplacements at the jetties, we had blackout curtains on our windows and people said there were German submarines in the Gulf.

My dreams were filled with enemy soldiers hitting the beach in front of our house. Coming up the hill attacking the front door and hiding among the oaks. I always woke up right before they shot/tortured/raped us-in a cold sweat and scared to look out the window at the moss waving in the breeze.

When we played in the bay, we'd play like we were Marines, landing on an island and we'd fuss over who was best at getting shot and falling dramatically into the shallow water. Boys could always make gun sounds better than girls. I didn't know why. We'd gather up the seaweed that washed up along the shore and make forts. The little clear, round jellyfish became ammunition-the southern, summer alternative to snowballs. You haven't lived until you've been hit in the face with a jellyfish (these were the harmless ones, not like sea nettles that sting).

Submitted by: Ann Houpt, 1128 Loftin Street, Parker, FL 32404.

The Garage Apartment

Kraft Ave was a great place to grow up. We lived in a garage apartment on Kraft Ave in Millville above a three car garage. There were no doors on the garage, so when the wind blew strong, the linoleum rug would lift up off the floor. You could turn the radio on and off by stomping on the living room floor. No air

conditioner, but we had never had any so we didn't even notice. Very few people locked their doors. Neighborhoods were safe.

Sitting on the steps of the garage apartment, you could hear all the sounds from the Bay County Fair and see all the lights. It was wonderful. The Fair was located in Springfield where the Isle of View Drive-In Movie would later be built. We would sit on the steps and look at the stars and once in awhile see a shooting star. Once we even saw the Northern Lights.

Every time there was a hurricane warning we would leave home. Any apartment that a stiff breeze could blow the rug up off the floor would never be safe during a hurricane. Mr. Sewell, a neighbor, worked at the Bay County Health Department on Highway 98. We would go there to wait out the storm. It was great. Coke machines and candy machines available all night, examination tables to sleep on if you got too tired and windows large enough to watch the palm trees bend down to the ground from the wind. Listening to Donnel Brookins on the radio all night long to find out if we would survive the hurricane was so exciting. After the storm we would go back to our apartment which would still be just as we left it. The summer before I started to Bay High my mother and father bought a house on Kraft Ave and we moved out of that garage apartment. We have had several storms though all these years and that garage apartment is still standing today.

Submitted by: Ann Robbins, 435 South Palo Alto Ave., Panama City, Florida 32401.

Going to Church in Bay County

I am very grateful for my Christian foundation learned from my mother, grandmother and Sunday School teachers. My mother taught me to pray before going to sleep, a habit I have kept. She required her children to attend church unless we were sick. If we did not go to church we could not go any other place.

My first prayer was "God bless me and help me to be a good girl". My prayers have become longer and more mature but always asking my Heavenly Father to help me be strong in spirit and body.

Going to church was fun and our only social outlet except school and playing with friends. My brother, friends and I would walk about two miles. There was a well worn path from the corner of the graveyard to the sidewalk in front of First Assembly Church. They almost always were into their service by the time we reached that area and the singing and rejoicing could be heard long before we got there. The meeting was so lively and happy sounding, with women screaming and men yelling in loud voices as they experienced the presence of the Holy Spirit. This was very scary to young people who were not used to this type meeting.

Only one time can I remember someone getting that excited in one of our services and that was when grandmother, caught in the Spirit, began dancing, speaking in tongues and waving her arms around in such a manner that the ladies in her Sunday School class didn't know just what to do with her. They tried in vain to quiet her but she wouldn't be quieted. (Note: In those days it was called speaking in the unknown tongue.)

Submitted by: Marjorie Arnold, 2304 Foxworth Dr., Panama City, Florida.

Gopher Tortoise

Bay County and Northwest Florida lie within the heart of the domain of a unique reptile, the gopher tortoise. Gopher tortoises, more commonly called *gophers* or *cooters*, are the only tortoise native to North America, and live in areas with deep sandy soil, such as the sand hills of North Florida. Its habitat range from the southeastern corner of Louisiana to the southwest corner of South Carolina, and includes nearly all of the State of Florida, and the southern parts of Alabama and Georgia.

These slow moving tortoises are primarily nocturnal, however at times they can be seen moving about during the day. Gophers tend to avoid the heat of the day, foraging in the early morning or late afternoon. Using its shovel-like front legs, the gopher or cooter digs down into the sand at approximately a thirty-degree angle. A gopher's burrow also called a cooter hole is usually about twelve to twenty feet in length, but, some have been known to be much longer. The width is equal to the

Sketch of Gopher Tortoise by Heather McQuagge

gopher's length, thus allowing it to turn around anywhere in its burrow. Mature gophers average nine to eleven inches in length, and weigh approximately ten pounds.

Whereas today, the gopher is threatened and classified as a species of special concern, in times past it was killed for its meat. The gopher was a valuable source of protein for Native Americans and early settlers in Northwest Florida. When harvested, a gopher yielded between one and two pounds of meat.

A common method of retrieving the cooter out of its cooter hole was to attach a large metal hook onto the end of a strong vine or heavy gauge wire, which was pushed down into the gopher's burrow. When the gopher was hooked it was pulled out of its burrow backwards.

A more humane method of extraction was to determine the location of the gopher by pushing a vine or wire into the burrow, and then using a shovel or post-hole diggers to dig down to the gopher. The average depth of a gopher tortoise's burrow is usually around five feet.

During the Great Depression of the 1930's, my father Herbert "Hub" McQuagge, and his older brother, Levi "Coot" McQuagge, quit school at a very young age and went to work to earn money for the family. Jobs were scarce during this time and the pay very low. Another means of providing food for the family was to venture into the piney woods around Fountain, Florida in search of gophers. In many poor southern families, gophers were often referred to as *Hoover chickens*. Turpentine camps also relied on the gopher as a source of protein for their hard day's work. The gopher's meat was commonly used in soups or fried. It was widely believed that eating gopher meat improved one's longevity, and it was also thought to be a cure for impotence and other health problems.

Searching for gophers had its dangers though, Hub and Coot had to constantly be on the lookout for the eastern diamondback rattlesnake, which liked to use the burrows to seek relief from the intense Florida heat.

Gopher tortoise's burrows are also used for safety and shelter by many other animals, such as rabbits, skunks, armadillos, raccoons, and opossums, as well as many other species of snakes. The burrows are especially helpful to these animals's survival during times of wildfire.

Today, many of the descendants of early southern pioneers owe a debt of gratitude to the gopher tortoise, for without this unique Florida native, many of their ancestors might not have survived.
Submitted by: Gerry Dale McQuagge, 1608 Georgia Ave, Lynn Haven, FL 32444. Sources: The late Herbert McQuagge, Calvin Johns Sr., and Andrew Weckherlin.

A Great Place To Work

I had the good luck to have a wonderful Girl Scout leader, Eleanor Lewis, during my Junior High and High School years. She encouraged me to volunteer at the Bay County Library to get my book badge.

I did earn my badge and continued to volunteer at the Library cutting out newspaper articles and mounting them. I soon progressed to shelving books and reading shelves and by ninth grade was

Mary Lou Watts, Becky (Wallace) Saunders and Margaret Berry, 1978

working part time and actually getting paid. During the rest of my school years I worked shelving books, behind the circulation desk and on the bookmobile on Saturday and during the summers. I had some wonderful experiences and learned many good things. Jane Patton, Librarian, was a great boss and a good friend. She encouraged me to learn and grow over the years. After I married in 1962, I left Panama City for almost two years. When we returned to Panama City I worked briefly at another job and in 1965 returned to work at the Library. I'm still working at the Library in 2003 and enjoying every minute of it. The job has changed considerably over the years and as taught by Jane Patton I've continued to learn and grow.
Submitted by: Rebecca B. Saunders, 2515 Frankford Avenue, Panama City FL 32405.

Growing Up On St. Andrew's Bay

My Father was a soldier in World War I and suffered bad injuries. He had taken shrapnel which cut his jugular vein then he contracted encephalitis and got sleeping sickness in the flu epidemic. He received the Silver Star Medal for Gallantry in Action, the Service Medal with bars for the different battles in which he took part and The Purple Heart Medal. Upon his separation from the service he returned to Americus, Georgia and his Law Practice.

My mother was teaching in the High School. She met this handsome young man with a great singing voice and they fell in love. After they were married my father became sick as a result of his war injuries and became permanently disabled.

I was born in Troy, Alabama, my Mother's home. We enjoyed our vacations to Saint Andrew's Bay and staying at the Villa Hotel. Often there were friends and family there also. Escaping the heat of summer, we would drive to the coast, car windows open for air. I was so excited as we drew closer. You could almost smell the salt and the air was cooler. Arriving at the Villa, there was a strong breeze off the beautiful blue Bay. Ready to run to the water, I was told that I must take a nap or rest first before I could go in the water.

My father did not drive and was anxious for me to learn. There was no age limit in Florida at that time. I had a friend a year older and she was driving. I was driving at the age of ten on our dirt side streets. That year they passed legislation for an age limit of ten years old. It moved forward as I grew older and became the minimum age for drivers licenses when I became sixteen.
Submitted by: Gene Howell Sapp, 1409 Deer Avenue, Panama City, FL 32401.

Hathaway Bridge and the Gulf Coast Highway

My grandfather John Simon Johnson worked for the Florida State Road Department most of his life. He was a part of the work crew that built the first Hathaway Bridge in Panama City. There was a young man who worked on the crew that stayed with John Simon and Annie at their home in Altha, Florida. This young man's name has been lost through time but he will always be remembered as the man who was knocked off the bridge and killed while the Hathaway Bridge was being built. John Simon did not know how to read and write until his wife Annie taught him. He never did learn how to do math and numbers on paper. But he could take a board, smooth out the dirt on the ground, and draw a square on the dirt. From that square he could figure out how much lumber was needed to build a house and how the house would be built. One of the many houses that he built was a brick house on Beach Drive which is still there today.

John Simon was also on the work crew that built the first road bed on Panama City Beach. The Gulf Coast Highway went from Panama City Beach to Destin, Florida. Clarence Hansford was the Captain of the road crew. The state of Florida gave Clarence a house in Panama City to live in while working on the road. Hundreds of men worked on this road bed. Times were hard and jobs were few. Men would walk and swim inlets all the way from Pensacola to Panama City to ask for a job. John Simon got his son Robert a job on the work crew. Robert was 17 years old and it was his first real job.

Water was brought to the "free labor camp" by tugboat. It was so hot that you couldn't wear shoes to work in, but had to work barefoot. You had to grease your mouth to keep it from blistering. The men slept in tents. They used mules to pull slip pans to move the sand dunes. A slip pan looked like a big scoop. It was so sharp it could cut the legs off the mules if not handled correctly. The men could easily get hurt or killed too. At lunch time a bell would be rung so the men would know to stop working and eat and rest for awhile. There were two mules on the crew named Hub and John. The men admired these mules a lot. These mules knew when it was noon time. One of the mules would raise his head and bray and the other mule would lay down. Then the mule that brayed would lay down and then the noon bell would ring. The mules would not get up until lunch time was over. Their handler would sit on one of the mule's rump and fan them while they were resting. Then the mules would get up and a minute later the lunch bell would ring for work to begin again. The work crew got to watching the mules to see if they would ever miss beating the bell, but the mules always knew the time. The men at the work camp ate good but plain food. Whatever was available which was usually side meat and beans. One man asked the cook, "Cookie, how big was that hog you killed? We've been eating his sides for weeks. When are we going to get to the hams?" Sometimes the men killed sea turtles and ate them. Once there was a storm and coconuts washed up on the beaches. The men ate those coconuts. There was one man on the crew who would only swim in the gulf when the undertow was bad and it was storming. That's the way he liked it. Robert worked on the road crew for three months and decided he had had enough. He told Clarence Hansford that he wanted to quit. Clarence told him he couldn't leave. Robert told Clarence if he didn't take him back to Panama City he would kill him. He was joking (maybe) but he meant to leave one way or another. Clarence took him to Panama City. Robert said when he got to Panama City and walked on the city pavement, it felt like his brains were being jolted out of his head. The WPA supplied funds to complete the Gulf Coast Highway in 1934.
Submitted by: Dorothy Ann Johnson Robbins, 435 South Palo Alto Ave., Panama City, Florida.

Hawking Papers at the Beach

In 1939, when I was a young boy, my family opened a newsstand next to the Ritz Theater and we distributed newspapers. My brother, Joe and I would sell the Birmingham Age-Herald, Montgomery Advertiser, Atlanta Constitution, Jacksonville Times-Union and the Pensacola Journal to the tourists visiting the beach.

Dad had an old Model T with all the advertising on it. He would load the papers in the back and drive out to Panama City Beach. He let me off there and I started hawking newspapers cabin to cabin and walking toward Pensacola. Joe would be taken out to Laguna Beach and he'd start going cabin to cabin hawking newspapers and making his way back toward Panama City Beach. We'd meet at Wayside Park (the place with the awful sulfur water that Dad insisted we drink for our "health".)

Sometimes my older brother, Bob, went with us and helped sell newspapers. We had shoulder bags and believe me, when Dad loaded those things up with Sunday papers, you worked like the devil to sell them to lighten the load you were lugging while trudging in that hot sand (usually barefooted). Dad didn't pay us much, but Joe and I made out like bandits with tips from those rich tourists who felt sorry for the poor waifs.

I remember reaching Wayside before Dad or Joe got there and reading my surplus newspapers, especially the columnists like O.O. McIntyre or Westbrook Pegler. I think I was

molding a career there. Dad was so particular about his newspaper that I had to be careful to fold it just so even though it was one that didn't sell.
Submitted by: William J. (Jack) Duncan, 3663 Garden Valley Road, Roseburg, OR 97470.

Indoor Privy And Other Wonderful Inventions

My father built us an indoor privy. We had an outdoor privy when we moved to Millville and we built an indoor privy and on the back of our house he built a toilet and a shower. The girls could take hot showers back there and the room was large enough for them to take their clothes back there and dress there too. I remember that addition was welcomed by my Mama and my sisters. It was a pretty physical problem until Daddy put that shower bath in there. You couldn't find a shower head to buy so Daddy built one. It was a great big thing. It was large as a plate and it had holes. He had sat there and knocked holes in that shower head so that when you turned the water on you got a generous amount of water on you. It was marvelous, just marvelous. I haven't seen a shower head like that since.

All the things that I run into now in antique stores, the depression glass and all that, was stuff that we had on our table. We bought one of these refrigerators with the round unit sitting on top of it. I think it was General Electric. We put it in our dining room in Millville. My mama's kitchen was just full of smells that would make your mouth water. She had a large wooden bowl that she filled with flour. She would take a lump of lard and throw in the bowl of flour, mix it up and make her light, fluffy biscuits.

On Sunday we usually had a roast and either sweet potatoes or Irish potatoes, depending on the roast. If we had beef roast, we had Irish potatoes. If we had pork roast we had sweet potatoes. The food in our house was always very adequate. We had more food than we really needed. My mother was a good cook. She put a good meal on the table and you came and ate. No worries then about cholesterol and calories in those days.

In the dining room was a Singer sewing machine with a pedal. Mama made clothes for my sisters and me and Wallace. As we got older, she went to the store and got us jeans and shirts and things like that. But she still made some of the girl's clothes.

We first had a crystal radio set that you had to have earphones that you could listen. Only one person could listen at a time. So mama had that crystal radio set. Then we bought a radio set from Sears and Roebuck. It was called a super heterodyne. It was an oblong box about two feet long and it was about eight inches high, about eight inches deep, had a speaker sitting on the top of it and had a small dial in the front. My mama used to listen to WSM in Tennessee. She liked bluegrass music and country music. She danced all the time. She told me one time, "I almost didn't marry Wilburn Turner." I said, "Why would you not want to marry daddy?" She said, "He couldn't dance a step."
Submitted by: Fred Turner, 2694 Island View Dr., Panama City, FL 32405.

An Infamous Visitor

The Raffields were well known throughout the Southeast for fishing and being "movers and shakers" in the seafood industry. Raffields owned and fished trolling boats, party head boats, commercial snapper boats, shrimp boats, and seine boats.

My daddy, Charles F. Raffield, owned the Raffield Fish Market on Tarpon Dock in Panama City, FL. The fish house was the state-of-the-art "show case" of the commercial fishing industry. There were visitors and tours throughout the year to see how fish was taken care of on the boats, and the processing of fresh fish in large quantities while maintaining freshness. He had a trolling boat docked out back to take friends, visitors, legislators, senators, and business associates fishing for public relations. His commercial sales covered the Southeast, and one of his regular weekly commercial accounts was for the porpoise shows at Sea Aquarium in Miami.

In about 1945, while playing around the docks and fish house as I had been doing since early childhood and meeting "dignitaries" from various states and countries, I was introduced to a large man in a white suit and white dress hat, and his business associates. I thought this was so dumb for anyone to go trolling

in a white suit, but what does a 9 year old know about things like that anyway. Daddy wore suits sometimes or slacks with sport shirt, but always with a dress hat even if he was only going next door to get a cup of coffee at Jessie Cook's Restaurant. Anyway, the large man in the white suit went fishing, had his fish dressed out and packed in ice for travel as many do, and left. That 'strange' man never came back again. It was about 4 years later when I found out that this large quiet man lived in Miami, and had heard about the Raffields Through the Sea Aquarium, and had been sent by them. That large strange man was Al Capone, the Chicago gangster, "living out his remaining years" in Miami.
Submitted by: John C. Raffield, Rt 1 Box 358, Jacksonville TX 75766.

Jane Patton, Our Mother

I'm pretty sure that in mid-50's Panama City, ours was the only mother who regularly stood on her head in the living room.

She never tried to be a trendsetter and she certainly wasn't into yoga because it was 'cool'. She'd simply read a book which pointed out the wisdom of reversing gravity's pull every now and then, and this made sense to her—way before the Beatles made noise about it.

Mother was a pragmatist, which you might look at as being pretty boring. With mother, never.

Like when brother Jon shot a wild boar up on DeWitt Street, pre-houses. Mother said fine. You killed it. We'll eat it. And she (Mother grew up on a farm in Iowa) proceeded to butcher that thing right in the backyard. We were mortified. Beaver Cleaver's mother never went around butchering pigs right off the back porch.

Then there was the dry cleaning experiment. Mother was horrified at the cost of commercial dry cleaning. So she read a book. Gasoline, a barrel full of it, was dragged to the carport and our dry-cleanables were dipped and hung, dipped and hung, but never quite lost that whiff of Gulf Station. (Luckily none of us dared smoke around Mother or we'd all have been blown to kingdom come.)

Her entrepreneurial spirit was alive and well. That's how she came to lease two acres in Lynn Haven for planting cucumbers. The vision was pickles. Millions of pickles. Too much rain that year, so the pickles never made it.

She invented "The Cove Shopper" when the Cove Shopping Center first opened. Right there on our dining room table she'd write the stories, design the ads, type it all up, mimeograph those flyers. And Jon, with a small red wagon, got to distribute them all around the Cove. Together they made enough money to buy Jon a piano, probably the proudest purchase in our family's history.

Mother's pragmatism was put to excellent use in the early 60's during segregation. Mother could see no earthly reason why anyone, whatever color or background, should be denied access to books. When some people got in a huff because Mother was letting "coloreds" use the main library, she told them politely but firmly that these new patrons were there because they needed information and it's the business and purpose of a library to make that information available. Period, amen. I like to think that Mother's reasonable, calm, dignified way of handling that situation was an important contribution to Panama City's relatively civilized integration process.

Mother was a lady and that's probably the image most of us associate with her. But Mother was also a fighter, an

Jane Patton and business partner/driver Sandra Capps ready for the road. The J. V. Patton memorial rig is still "on the road" with Sandra driving.

inventor, a problem-solver, a pioneer, a stubborn Taurus, a loyal friend, a philosopher and a wonderful, original, honest and loving mother and grandmother.
Submitted by: Judith P. Lotas, 45 E. 89th St., Apt 20C, New York, NY 10128.

Judge W. Fred Turner

In the early 1940's I began to look around Panama City to see what there was. College was just out of my reach. We didn't have any financial institutions that would help with college tuition. Mrs. Steve Wilson, the undertaker's wife, called me and said, "Come here. I want to talk to you. I will pay you and pay for you to go to Julliard in New York. You have a marvelous voice and I want you to cultivate it. I will pay your expenses to go to New York so you can go through Julliard and get a musical education." I said, "Miss Wilson, I appreciate the offer very much, but I don't think I can do that. I'll go and talk to my parents and come back with you." And I did.

Mrs. Wilson's daughter Betty, was in the glee club with me and Mrs. Wilson had heard me sing at the Baptist Church. I sang at several places around here and when WDLP first went on the air, Nita Whitehurst was the first voice on the air from Panama City and I was the second. We had a fifteen-minute program and we played our horns and sang songs on WDLP.

I was taking just menial jobs here in town, nothing of importance and nothing with a future to it. I was working for Mr. Helton Harrison. He was paying me a dollar a day to work in his store. Some friends of mine, Paul Haberer and Francis Carter came by and said they were going to join the Air Force. This was a year before Pearl Harbor. I talked it over with my parents. My mother said, "Well, if that's what you want to do, but you've got to make up your mind about whether or not you want to be in the military." Phillip Roll who was a Colonel in the Reserves had talked to our classes at Bay High and said we had a future in the Air Force. So on October 4, 1940, me, Paul Haberer, Francis Carter, W. R. Sowell and Cecil Dean all met in Dothan, Alabama and joined the Air Force. We were sent to Barksdale Field, Louisiana to the 55th Pursuit Squadron and of the people that I got in the service with, only Francis Carter is still alive. Francis lives in Montgomery, Alabama. Cecil Dean was an ace in World War II from North Africa and flew P40's. Paul Haberer was a Master Sergeant in the Air Force. His father was treasurer of the paper mill and signed the checks over there for those people.

I was interviewed one time when I was circuit judge and they said to me, "Judge, have you ever killed people?" And I said, "Yes." They said, "What was it like?" I said, "I had no feeling one way or two. I killed some Japanese. All I had to do was remember Pearl Harbor."

Before I ran for office of Circuit Judge, I went to see my minister, Rev N. B. Langford, Pastor of the First Baptist Church. I asked him, "Is there anything in the Bible that would prohibit me from imposing the death penalty?" He said, "No." So I ran for circuit judge and nobody ran against me.
Submitted by: Fred Turner, 2694 Island View Dr., Panama City, FL 32405.

Kidding Around: Remembering When

What was the Downtown like in the 1940's and 50's? Here are some of my memories from that time as a kid growing up in a mom & pop hardware store:

Mullet fries and bands in City (McKenzie) Park - Hotels and other white and beige framed houses with forest green trim - Christmas parades - live oak trees lining the waterfront - five o' clock gatherings at City Pier to see boats laden with red snapper return to port - hot fudge sundaes, chocolate sodas, and banana splits at Walgreen's soda fountain - sitting on Santa Claus's lap at J.C. Penney's - 75 cents business men's lunches in the elegant Marie Hotel restaurant - slaw dogs and draggin' Jimmy's - walking from my father's store to the post office under the shade of mighty oaks - seeing my ill mother off at the old train depot - seeing my father for the first time at the old bus terminal on his return from the war - 14 cent Westerns and talent shows on Saturday mornings at the Ritz Theatre - pegged pants from Mount Harmon's Men's Wear - my first soft ice cream cone ever at the Sweetette - playing on the enormous vines in Doug Sales' trees - the wind knocked out of me in a fall from Granny Hurst's tree - toys and Spanish peanuts at the two ten cent stores - pecans under Granny Hurst's tree - neckin' in the balcony of the Ritz.

Sadly for me, my children and grandchildren might only get to experience one or two of these things. "Progress" has taken care of the rest.

Submitted by: Bob Hurst, 243 S. Cove Terrace Dr., Panama City, FL 32401.

King of the Half-Shell

Reuben Wilson Eddins fondly known as "Pop" was known by thousands who enjoyed his oysters on the half shell at the Eddins' Oyster Bar

also known as Pop's Oysters. During his 36 years in business he owned several oyster bars and restaurants in downtown Panama City with his last location at 25 West Beach Drive which he operated until his death in 1963.

Pop Eddins' oysters were famous across the nation

Reuben Wilson "Pop" Eddins

and helped make this area famous. Hundreds of local citizens and thousands of others from every section, as well as Tyndall Air Force Base and Navy Base personnel, including Clark Gable when he was stationed at Tyndall, had their taste of the cold delicious oysters, served in half of its home, so to speak.

At Pop's Oyster Bar there was an exclusive blend of atmosphere and Pop was the focal point watching him as he opened the cold, fresh oysters with pleasure and pride. During those years he served millions of oysters to eager eaters with some customers eating as few as six to one customer eating 230 at one setting.

Another exclusive blend was the sauce Pop served. It was his own product. The peppers were grown by him and he labeled the sauces according to the degree of heat. The names were borrowed from those of famous people and things that would suggest temper or temperature. Some of the labels were Atomic, Lightning, Gunsmoke, Voodoo, Possum Trot, John Dillinger, Blast Off, In Orbit and After Burner to name a few.

Pop's successful business spoke for itself as he and his wife Willie Mae educated three sons, Billy Mack, Jack, Charles and two daughters Christine and Christell who all grew up in Bay County. All the children still live here except Christell who resides in Orlando.

Submitted by: Charles W. Eddins, 311 Minnesota Avenue, Lynn Haven, FL 32444.

The Lake Huntington Raft

Wilson Hair, Richard Williams, James Williams and myself had talked for months about building a raft that we could fish on, camp on, sail on, jump off of and swim around. The plan was devised, it would be a big challenge, but the accomplishment would be worth it. The whole idea did not seem to be impossible, after all we had heard rumors of Pat and Mike Adams building a submarine. Now, how is that for good old St Andrews ingenuity. At least, we figured we could build a simple Huckleberry Finn-Tom Sawyer raft.

We obtained 55 gallon drums, two-by-fours and one-by-fours. Plenty of three-quarter-inch rope secured the drums

to the raft. A four-by-four ten feet long was used for our sail and some half inch rope to keep the mast and sail steady and a pup tent for shelter. We put our minds to this job. Before long the raft started to take shape.

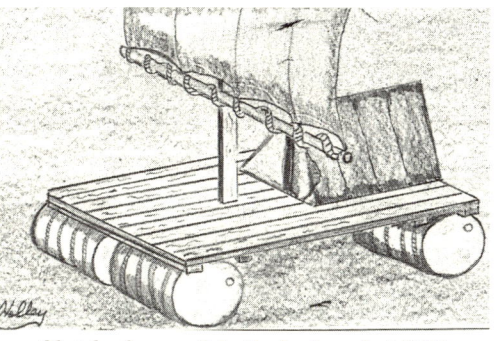

Sketch of our raft in the backyard at 1506 Wilmont Avenue, 1959

After several weeks, we finally finished. There it was; we were proud! Our next goal was to transport it to Lake Huntington. Richard and James took care of this matter. I don't know how they got it, but they pulled a trailer into the backyard and soon we were ready to start the big haul.

Now, I'm not going to tell you this was easy. There we were, Richard, James, Wilson and myself struggling just to pick up the raft and secure it to the boat trailer. After hours of work we got the raft loaded and safely secured. We would begin the move first thing next morning.

This maneuver began at the crack of dawn. Moving the raft out of the backyard was hard enough, but turning the trailer north on Drake Avenue was more of a challenge. Making it to 16th Street we began to turn west on the black asphalt. A short while later, we arrived at the stop sign approaching Highway 98. By now it was eight in the morning, and the traffic was more than we thought it would be. After waiting a long time, Wilson suggested that we start at the next break and the cars would stop for us, we started rolling with all the strength we had. We had traffic stopped both ways. We were doing pretty well until this lady jumped out of a car, started taking pictures, and hollered at us, "this was cute and she would put it in the News Herald." Wilson said, "that's all we need, Doc Daffin will put us in the Bay County jail for sure." We all started laughing. The transport was rolling so well, we just kept on going, right across Beck Avenue. Then all that remained was the parking lot of the Kwik Chek grocery store. We didn't figure so many grocery shoppers being there that early. We finally arrived at Bayview Avenue and felt good about our conquest of arriving at Lake Huntington.

The task of unloading the raft should have been another major obstacle, but our adrenaline was flowing pretty good. Picking the raft up and sliding it down the bluff into the water turned out to be a piece-of-cake. There it was, floating in the water and it looked like The *Queen Mary* to us. We all boarded our raft, jumped up and down, clapped hands and congratulated each other. First order of business was to put up the sail and make ready for the channel bridge. We could vision navigating the channel and then out into the beautiful St. Andrew Bay. But our vision was shot dead, for there was not enough wind to move our raft. By now we decided we would have to obtain long wood push poles to move the thing. The next afternoon, after church, we were ready to board our raft again. The push poles worked better than the sail and we enjoyed our first afternoon on Lake Huntington. Our adventures were short lived because we suspect that someone stole our raft, but then again it might have sank. We do have some 8mm movies, we will watch them occasionally and think Huck and Tom did not have anything on us boys growing up in St. Andrews.

Submitted by: Captain Richard Holley, 1104 Carolina Avenue, Lynn Haven, FL 32444.

Life in Panama City
A Great Place to Spend a Childhood

My first night in Panama City was spent at the Dixie-Sherman Hotel. So it was that my adventures in this new place called Florida began the next morning when my

The Dixie Sherman Hotel, Downtown Panama City

brother, Bob, took me to the rooftop of the Dixie Sherman where I could peer out over a vast, flat landscape that included St. Andrews Bay. It was an awesome sight. My former home in Moultrie, Georgia was in hilly, red clay country where the only body of water nearby was a pond or a lake. This was the first time I had seen such a large body of water. In my mind it stretched forever, but in fact the bay was a small body of captured water behind an inlet leading to the great Gulf of Mexico. St. Andrews Bay and the Gulf of Mexico would soon become an integral part of my life as I grew to manhood.

Our first house in Panama City was a old wood frame house with a screened-in front porch. There was just a spot of land in front where a struggling lawn of St. Augustine grass grew in the sand. The house was at the corner of Harrison Avenue and Fifth Street, just a block from the downtown business center. The house was built before electricity was readily available and had been wired later. Outlets were porcelain-encased receptacles with copper insets allowing electric plugs to be screwed in. Light bulbs were screwed into overhead outlets and had no shades. The naked bulbs cast eerie shadows around the room.

We lived in this house for only a short time, but I remember one time when my brother, J.T., played a trick on me. When the plug was not inserted in the outlet, the bare copper was left exposed. J.T. told me the outlet was a mouse hole and if I put my finger in it, the mouse would bite me. In all innocence, I had to try it. The electrical current "bit" me, but the trick taught me a valuable lesson. I learned to respect electricity early in my life. J.T. obviously had fallen in love with electricity because it became his lifelong work.

Submitted by: William J. (Jack) Duncan, 3663 Garden Valley Road, Roseburg, OR.

The Lost Legacy

Albert was a bottlenose dolphin. He was captured from the Gulf of Mexico in 1968 when he was about twelve to fifteen years old to be trained to perform at a new marine park that was to open on Panama City Beach. When Gulf World opened in May 1970, Albert was there - but he wasn't performing. Albert was very independent and used his intelligence to defeat his training until a highly experienced trainer came to Gulf World and worked with Albert. Once Albert decided to participate he became fully committed and rapidly learned more behaviors than any of the other dolphins. Albert adjusted well to his life in captivity. Descriptions of him included "mellow" and "laid back".

Albert with local TV personality Amy Hoyt at Gulf World Marine Park in 1998

He served as the ambassador for bottlenose dolphins year after year entertaining and educating all who visited Gulf World. Many visitors were surprised when they returned to Gulf World with their children to find Albert - the dolphin they enjoyed when *they* were youngsters - was still there. Albert grew to be a very old dolphin and at the age of about 43 he passed away. Living to this ripe old age is extraordinary in itself since dolphins only live to be about half that age. However, Albert's success story wasn't over yet.

Just before his death, it was discovered that Albert was going to be a father. After 30 years of participating in the captive-breeding program, Albert, at the ancient age of about 43 was going to be a father for the first time. When Albert died in June 1999, knowing that there was a chance to have his offspring carry on his legacy somehow eased the loss. Sadness turned to disbelief a few weeks later when two more of Albert's mates turned up pregnant. Everyone was awed by Albert's posthumous grand finale.

Four months later Allie was born. She was a beautiful, healthy baby and a very special dolphin to all who knew of her. Albert's other babies were born seven months later, in May 2000. The male was named A.J., short for Albert Junior and the female was named Jasmine. Gulf World had never been prouder, and rightfully so. Having three successful births within such a short period of time is quite rare, and the circumstances surrounding their inception was incredible.

The babies learned quickly from their mothers and soon they were stealing the show and capturing hearts. Everyone loved the youngsters, their antics and their story. What joy they brought! If only the joy had lasted. Sadly, one February morning in 2002, with no forewarning, Jasmine was found dead. A.J. died a month later, a victim of the same fast-acting viral infection. Although all precautions were taken, Albert's first-born and last surviving offspring, Allie, succumbed to the virus that October. She was three years old. Albert's legacy was over.

Albert's story is a great one and it deserves to be remembered. Certainly it lives on in the memories of all who experienced it but eventually it will only exist as this story that is entirely inadequate in expressing the emotions evoked by these wonderful beings.

Submitted by: Lisa A. Keppner, 4406 Garrison Road, Panama City, FL 32404.

A Love That Led to a Career

Everyone in my family read. It was not unusual for the five of us to be in comfortable chairs, happily enthralled in books. When I began working at Bay County Public Library, Mrs. Jane Patton took my love of reading and helped me find my life's work. She instilled in her staff the ability to use a love of books to serve people.

Current and former "Patton trained" friends and co-workers. (Left to right: Ann Robbins, Claire Calohan, Marion Papson, Anita Lucas, Rebecca Saunders and Ellen Rumph)

The patrons were very important to her and serving the needs of all people was her motto. Her legacy was the establishment of a six county regional library that, with branches and a bookmobile, took library services to the widest range of people possible.

The bookmobile carried the library to far flung areas, from fishing camps to country crossroads, it drew patrons. For areas where small schools offered limited libraries, students could get what they needed from the library on wheels. Families were supplied with materials almost at their doorways.

I left Panama City and worked in school libraries in Louisiana and Virginia. My sister, Claire, began working for Mrs. Patton after I left. She left Panama City and later returned and resumed "our" job. I worked in the Salt Lake County Library System in Utah and the Loudoun County Library System in Virginia.

I have proudly said that I was "Patton trained" and thus fully equipped to share her library philosophy of providing the best possible service to patrons. Along the way, I met many truly dedicated and wonderful people from all walks of life.

Thanks to my family for sharing their love of reading, and to Mrs. Patton for teaching me the ability to work in a job that was so rewarding.

Submitted by: Ellen J. Rumph, 161 Marin Drive, Panama City, FL 32405.

Memories - John G. Hentz

I was born and raised in Liberty County. I caught me a ride

out of those woods in September of 1931 and went to the University of Florida. It was right in the middle of the Depression. I was 20 years old at the time. I was lucky enough to get a job at 20 cents an hour on the Agricultural Experiment Station Dairy and a free room in the dairy barn. We had to run the dairy the year round so I also went to summer school. I graduated from the college of Agriculture in three and a half years with two majors, Agricultural Engineering and Animal Husbandry. I got my degree on February 4, 1935 and had already been hired as Assistant County Agricultural Agent in Walton County with headquarters in DeFuniak Springs. Bay County had not had a County Agent since 1928. I was appointed County Agent in Bay County on January 1, 1936 and sent to Panama City to re-establish the County Agent's Office. I was County Agent in Bay County for the next 14 years. A lot of good things happened during those years. On January 1, 1940, I was given a promotion and appointed County Agent in Okaloosa County with headquarters in Crestview. On October 15, 1941, I received another promotion and was appointed County Agent in Walton County with headquarters at DeFuniak Springs.

Submitted by: John G. Hentz, 2406 St. Andrews Boulevard, Panama City, FL 32405.

St. Andrews Bay Dairy

In the Fall of 1942, I received an offer from Mr. and Mrs. O.E. Miley of Panama City to buy St. Andrews Bay Dairy in St. Andrews that I simply could not refuse. It was a going business that would pay for itself and with it I got 417 acres of land, 180 acres of it in the city limits of Panama City and the other 237 adjacent to the city limits. I was in the dairy business for the next 31 years and property development. The land started at 19th Street and went north to 27th Street. It was bounded by Frankford Avenue on the east and Beck Avenue and Pretty Bayou Drive on the west. St. Andrews Bay Dairy was here 54 years. The Mileys operated it 23 years. My wife Ruth and I operated it 31 years. Meanwhile, we moved the dairy cows to Washington County in April of 1968 and developed a 910 acre dairy unit there. We developed the property in Panama City. The area where Tommy Thomas Chevrolet is, used to be in my cow pasture. We developed Pretty Bayou Heights, two large additions to St. Andrews Meadowbrook, Island View Estates and a lot of unplatted resident and business property. We dug Hentz Canal (3300 feet) and built Hentz Fish Lakes.

Submitted by: John G. Hentz, 2406 St. Andrews Boulevard, Panama City, FL 32405.

Memories of Growing Up in the Panhandle

My parents, Bernard and Margaret McCulloch, moved to Panama City in the 1940's. These are some of my memories as a child living in the Cove during that approximately 10 year span.

Saturday morning at the Ritz Theater...9 cents admission which later went up to 14 cents. Saturday included about three hours of cartoons, serials, and western movies. There were almost always candy fights, with Necco wafers flying. There were also the Saturday morning talent shows with my father as the pianist. My friend Mary Lou Waterfield and I won 1st prize once. We sang "Red Wing" and I played the ukelele. Prizes included ice cream and cowgirl outfits. Mary Lou, Susan Jones, and I were crazy over horses. We lived, breathed and drew pictures of them.

Another favorite pastime was fishing for "choffers" down

George Bernard McCulloch with Louis Weaver and his musicians

at the "Green Dock" in the bayou with our bamboo poles and bits of bacon.

The times our parents took us to the beach, it seemed as if we would never get there. After we went over Hathaway Bridge, it seemed like a long and boring ride with nothing but

George Bernard McCulloch with the Bernie Dean Band

miles of tall pines. The first beach was Panama City Beach, and then a little further was Long Beach, and then miles and miles of sugar-white sand, turquoise water and sea oats. At Long Beach there was a long slide right near the water's edge. There was also a casino with an orchestra in which my father played piano. He was the business agent for the musician's local. On occasion, if a musician came into town with nowhere to stay, my father invited him to stay at our house for the night. I often came out in the morning to find someone sleeping on our couch. My father was a very kind man, but sometimes it got him into trouble-like the time he was worried about a stray cat he found and he got badly scratched.

My mother worked part-time as dental assistant to Dr. Fields, and then later she was secretary to Walter Green, the manager of the Dixie Sherman Hotel. The hotel was completely renovated in the late 1940's. Mother and her friend, Suselee Jones, took the Dale Carnegie course offered at the hotel.

Special memories: Jimmy's Drive In had the best foot-long hot dogs, and car hops to deliver them. I loved the special relish-wow! One day, Susan's father, Jimmie Jones, took us out in St. Andrews Bay up to our knees to get scallops; and, we used to have hot dog roast out in the woods, by digging a hole in the ground. We caught tadpoles down at the creek near my house. Our roads were dirt then and one time I remember the rag man coming up the road with his mule and cart. We lavished affection on that mule because he was a live "horse." Alberta Belcher who walked all the way from her house to do housework all day for various people. I came to know and love Alberta and her dear, sweet nature. She told us how the landlord could not get electricity for them. We always drove her home at night and when we moved from Panama City, she adopted my rabbits. Alberta's mother had lived during the Civil War and one time there was an article in the newspaper with her picture.

We moved back to Massachusetts in 1953, when I was 13, and I bid goodbye to my two good friends, Susan and Mary Lou, and to my horse, Bonnie Bee, my collie dog, Laddie, and our chickens. I came back to visit in 1956 and had a reunion with Mary Lou and Susan. They both left Panama City and traveled extensively, living in various places. We kept in touch sporadically; they have both moved back to the panhandle, and we got together there in 2002. Hopefully, we will all get together again in future years.

Submitted by; Brenda McCulloch Roache, 40 Oak St., Teaticket, MA 02536.

Mrs. Silas Welch's Lye Soap
By: Donna Welch Rankin, granddaughter

My Grand Mother was a kind hearted but strict woman. She always allowed her grand children to watch her cook and was a wonderful cooking instructor. When I was about five years old, 1953, she and I were in the back yard of her home near the corner of Beck Avenue and 11th Street. I was extremely excited because she was going to teach me how to make Lye Soap (an old family recipe.) After carefully watching her and committing to memory the ingredients, I questioned her on why she would put sugar in the soap. Her reply was "cause when you grand kids say ugly words and I have to wash your mouth out I don't want it to taste too bad."

For those Grandmothers who would like to follow in her ways of discipline, here is the recipe for Granny Lillie Mae Welch's Lye Soap: Use 3 quarts of fat drippings, 1 lb. Can of Lye, 1 quart cold water, 3 tsp. Borax (Borateem), 1 tsp. salt, 1/2 cup cold water, 1/4 cup ammonia, 1/2 cup sugar. Use enamel kettle and wooden spoon for lye solution. Save fat drippings in quart jars. When you have 3 quarts, thoroughly clean it by boiling it in equal amounts of water. Place kettle in cold place to firm fat. Cut fat from kettle sides. Pour off water and waste, scrape off excess waste from bottom of lard cake. Clean kettle and replace lard cake. Melt over low heat. Dissolve lye in 1 quart water and let stand until cool. Add melted fat slowly. Stir constantly. Mix other ingredients together and add to first mixture. Stir until whole mixture is thick and honey colored. Pour into a pan lined with a clean white clothe. Mark pieces into desired sizes.
Submitted by: Donna Rankin, 210-N East Baldwin Rd, Panama City, FL 32405.

Nautical Charts and References to the Raffields

Nautical charts have been the ocean, rivers, bays, and bayou's road maps since the beginning of time. Without these nautical charts showing buoys and water depths,

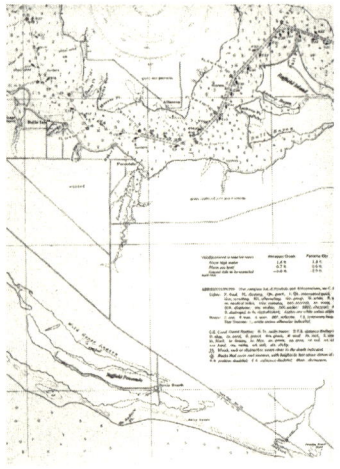

Map of Raffield Island and Raffield Peninsula

many boats and ships would be lost or run aground. These nautical charts have numerous landmarks and points of reference to steer the seaman along their plotted course.

Each coast line over the world has it's own identity. Bay County has many familiar landmarks and points of reference used by the early pioneers and settlers of Auburn, Farmdale, Allentown, Cromaton, and San Blas: examples being, Wild Goose Bayou, Davis Beach, Goose Point, Bull Bayou, Strange Point, Belle Isle, Lathrop Point, Wetappo Creek, Sandy Creek, Horseshoe Bayou, Crooked Island, Crooked Island Sound, and Deer Point to name a few.

There were two particular landmasses designated by the pioneers of those early years. One being *Raffield Island* located in the area east of Auburn, Farmdale, and Allentown. On the north side of Raffield Island was Bull Point. Bull Point was the homestead for the families of David Willis Raffield, David Charlton Raffield and Winton Earl Raffield. On the south side of the island in a tall stand of pine trees lived Charlton Raffield near Lathrop bayou. The other landmass is the *Raffield Peninsula* found directly south of Farmdale inside the Crooked Island Sound (aka St. Andrews Sound), between Wild Goose Bayou (Lagoon) and Crooked Island Sound was also called Lacy's Camp, after Lacy Jackson Raffield.
Submitted by: John C. Raffield, Rt. 1, Box 358, Jacksonville, TX 75766. Sources: Raffield Island and Raffield Peninsula can be found: U.S. Department of Commerce; National Oceanic and Atmospheric Administration; Florida Nautical Chart 11393-Intercoastal Waterway; Lake Wimico to East Bay

Need for Speed

In the mid 1940s, Bernice, Charlie, and Percy Cotton were returning from a Lake Wimico fishing trip when they noticed a boat race taking place on Watson Bayou. They immediately pulled over to the area, unloaded their gear from the 16-foot fishing boat they were pulling, and entered the last race - the free for all - which anyone could enter.

Bay County Boat races, late 1940's

They soon decided to build their own race boats. Charlie would draw out the plans on the butcher paper used at Cotton's Grocery Store and saw out parts for the boat with the store's meat saw. They would gather in Percy's backyard to build the boat. The boats were made of juniper and plywood with canvas covered bow and sides. The only wood parts were the bottom and ribs along the side. The ribs were covered with canvas and then painted. Each additional coat of paint acted as a sealant, making the canvas smoother and tighter.

The brothers built two boats. Their first boat - the *We Did It* - had a 22 h.p. Johnson motor. The second boat was named *Cotton's Grocery*. Most of the race boats were 8 ft long, 4 ft

Bay County Boat racing teams traveling to Florala, Alabama, late 1940's

wide, and weighed 75 to 100 pounds. There were only three racing motors at the time - the 10 h.p. Mercury, 22 h.p. Johnson, and 55 h.p. Evinrude. To run the boat, the driver had to kneel in the bottom of the boat and lean as far forward as possible while the motor was cranked; otherwise, he would end up with the bow straight up out of the water like a bobber, before sinking like a rock. The motors were cranked with the propellers held up out of the water because once the propellers hit the water the boat took off. There was no padding between the wood bottom of the boat beating on the water and the knees of the driver, so battered knees were a given. These boats were driven wide open and Bernice always seemed to flip the boat in the first turn.

A large group from Panama City would gather to watch the boat races at Watson Bayou or just about any place that had a large fresh water lake - traveling even to Florala, Alabama. The entourage from Panama City often was so large that the group was escorted into Florala by the

Alabama Highway Patrol. The boat races later were moved from Watson Bayou to Callaway Bayou because of the noise. Boat Race Road got its name from these boat races. Some of the Panama City people involved in the races were: Joe Hutchinson, who had a factory built boat named *Fireball* with a 22 h.p. Johnson, Bill Quigley, Charlie Philips (who was killed in a boat race at Florala), and Nick Shivers whose boat sported a 55 h.p. Evinrude.
Submitted by: Percy Scott "Scotty" Cotton, Jr. 3903 Quail Street, Panama City Beach FL. 32408.

Panama City Changes

We had the newspaper Panama City Pilot and then the Panama City News and Panama City Herald came along. Then they joined forces and combined. Stories got bigger. We finally got a Sears and Roebuck store downtown at 5th Street and Harrison Ave. Crystal Stores were big. Local people begin to emerge. We had our little "jack-of-all-trades" in Panama City. They were all competent workmen and they could get the job done. Mr. I. F. Clark was a plumber. His daughter married Charlie Powell and he ran a clothing store in the Sherman Arcade.
Submitted by: Fred Turner, 2694 Island View Dr, Panama City, FL.

Papaw's Storytelling

Tommy Welch, my husband, used to sit and tell our grandchildren stories. He would make them up as he went along and nine times out of ten, they were about wrestling alligators or something of the sort.

One day, our two grandsons by our son Jerry, were over at our house sitting on their Papaw's lap in his favorite chair. He started to tell a story and then he looked at them and said, "You know, Papaw is getting so old he can't even wrestle alligators anymore, and I don't wear my false teeth much either so I couldn't even bite the gator." Wes, our oldest grandson who was about four or five at the time, looked up at his Papaw and said, "Papaw, that's okay, you catch the gator and hold him down, and I'll bite him."
Submitted by: Jerry Welch, 1614 Molitor Ave., Panama City, FL 32401; Written by: Lillian M. Welch.

Piano/Voice Recital

Piano/Voice Recital, 1946, Mrs. Jewel Cannon, Teacher, Immanuel Baptist Church. Front Row L-R: Avis Davis, Shirley Harmon, unknown, John Henry Gill, Rita Conrad, Barbara Blue, Angeline Bedsole, Carol Smith, Elizabeth Phillips, Alice Scott, Leorita

Recital, 1946, Immanuel Baptist Church

Bryant, Marie Courtney, Barbara Pippin, Mary Elizabeth Gill, Carolyn Pitts. Back Row L-R: Unknown, Mary Elizabeth Paul, Pat Hughes, Pat Buffington, Helen Fay Walters, Marcia Campbell, Thelma Bauler, Jacqueline Stanford, Virginia Richardson, Betty Sue Thorpe, Emily Harmon, Joyce McDaniel, Polly Paul, Carolyn Price, Norma Jean Bedsole, Betty Jean McDaniel, Mrs. Jewel Cannon.
Submitted by: Shirley Harmon Brookins, 136 Cottonwood Circle, Lynn Haven, FL 32444

"Piffle," she said.

One of the most important values my mother, Jane Patton, taught me came by virtue of what I call her "Piffle" response. That's what she said when you complained about something that wasn't worthy of being complained about: "Piffle", said she. I complained a lot, too. About not being able to afford a matching sweater set. "Piffle." Or when I

whined because I had to wait till we got home to the salad and milk before I could rip open the MacDonald's hamburger wrapping. "Piffle" . When I got overly dramatic about my own self-importance, I'd get another "Piffle" response. And a big, drawn-out "PIF-FLE" when I complained at the early hour she woke me to go play golf with her at the country club.

What did the "Piffle" response teach me? To count my blessings, deal with issues, and get on with things. I'm often accused of saying "Get over it" to family, friends and co-workers when I detect an unnecessary whine. But, come to think of it, "Piffle" has a certain charm that "Get over it" lacks, don't you think?
Submitted by: Joanna Patton, 45 E. 89th St., Apt 20C, New York, NY 10128.

Plantin' Black-eyed Peas

This story is about my son-in-law's grandfather's family and it has been handed down through the years. It is a tale of how people traveled before the days of highways, motels and restaurants. It is a story from long ago, when people lived off of the land and had to rely on their instincts to survive. This tale took place in the mid 1800's, sometime before the Civil War.

Andrew Jackson had marched his troops across the Panhandle of Florida coming back from the Battle of New Orleans. Remember the old song, that said "in 1814 we took a little trip, along with Col. Jackson down the mighty Mississipp"? Well, some of those men liked what they saw in the Panhandle and came back with their families to settle here.

Once a year, these early settlers would harness the mules to an open wagon and head south to the Tampa area. They had goods of some kind to trade, but no one would admit to knowing what those goods were. The journey took several months and the food that they left with wouldn't sustain them for the whole trip. There were several forts along the way and they could camp there for a few days. They ate what they had brought, could shoot, or fish they caught. They said they "et off the land".

Along the wayside, as they went south, they planted black-eyed peas. They would come back the same way, and harvest the peas. It didn't matter if they had dried on the vines, in fact that made them easier to take with them. They planted black-eyed peas because the "bugs and critters didn't et'em". "Them beans we counted on" to eat on the way home.

There were Indians living in the area, but they had no trouble with them. When they got to Tampa, they fished and ate oysters, wild oranges and guavas. There was no meal available in the Tampa area so they had no means of making cornbread going home.

This tale of a different time, a different way of traveling, has been told and retold through the years. It is a testimony to the ingenuity and gumption of pioneer families.
Submitted by: Sally Roos as told to Ellen Rumph, 161 Marin Drive, Panama City, FL 32405.

The Porta Potty of Yesteryear

Outhouses were built by the owners of the land during the 20's to 30's with all the glory they could muster. New ones would stand tall and very old ones would be seen leaning or swaying in the wind of a storm.

In the early 1900's if a large family could only afford a one seater, it put family members in jeopardy when more than one person was in need of the facility. This was one of the first lessons a toddler learned in speed and taking turns. There were times when a short line would form on the outside of the privy and fights could break out as to whose turn was next.

The outhouse with two seats would give two needy persons a chance to use the waste station together as long as the two were of the same gender. There were man/wife and the parent/child exceptions but never unisex occupancy.

Toilet tissue was unheard of. A family fortunate enough to own a Sears Roebuck catalog waited for the expiration date and used it for cleansing. Rural folk used corncobs, leaves, fennel branches, potato sacks or paper sacks.

Then came the Great Depression when the government decided to clean up and set out to give every family a privy made with government materials at no cost. The economy allowed for only one seat buildings and the owners received a certificate of completion with their name on it. If you lived in the time of the outhouses, hopefully, you can relate to the humor intended in this article.

Submitted by: Marjorie Arnold, 2304 Foxworth Dr., Panama City, FL.

Recipe Contest

For a number of years, I have entered cooking contests. I picked up the "cooking bug" from my Mother. She was a good

Janie Ammons holding a Fruit Pizza standing next to Eliza Jackson

cook and taught me all I know and a few shortcuts. I started entering the competitions over twenty years ago.

The first recipe I entered in a contest won first place. It was called "Party Chicken Loaf." It was a cold dish made with the paper milk carton as a mold. I won $15.00 and a free cookbook. The very next year, I prepared a "fruit pizza" and went all the way to Daytona for the state level competition. In Daytona, we were paired with another contestant in a kitchen. My kitchen partner won 1st place, and her prize was a riding lawn mower. She was from Blountstown, FL.

The third year I entered the cooking competition, I prepared a Watermelon Salad, and, again, I won 1st place. My Mother entered these competitions sometimes, too. On one occasion, she entered a sweet potato cheesecake and won the local contest. She then went to Clearwater for the state level cook-off, but did not place there.

Another one of my winning entries one year was my Creamy Pecan Pie. It was almost like a cheesecake because I put pecans in the crust. Another year in Jacksonville, FL, I entered a breakfast cookie recipe and another 1st place prize, including a cookbook. The recipe included bacon, cheese, eggs and many breakfast foods. I told people if their children didn't eat breakfast, give them one of my "Cookies" for breakfast.

In more recent years, I entered the Capt. Anderson's contest and won 2nd place with my Peanut Butter Spaghetti Red Sauce Recipe.

My children have teased me over the years with comments like "Mom, when are you going to fix some 'real' food like meat and potatoes?" They would tell people that my biscuits could be used for hockey pucks and that my gravy was like target paste. It became the family joke. But, that's okay, I noticed they still ate what I cooked.

Submitted by: Janie Ammons, 2714 E. 7th Ct., Panama City, FL 32401.

Sewing Circle of Southport, Florida

Sewing Circle of Southport, Florida

Pictured left to right: Addie Nelson, daughter of Daisy & Louis Nelson, niece to Bubber Nelson; Mattie Lee Dykes md (1) Chester Lee Richbourg & md (2) T. W. Tam Campbell; Esther Corley md J. C. Stewart; Ida Wilcox md ___Gainer; Ila Corwell; Katie Smith; Annie Mae Dykes md Tom Masker; Bonnie Youngblood; Johnnie Taylor; Annie Smith. [Mattie Lee Dykes and Annie Mae Dykes were sisters, daughters of William Henry Dykes and Sarah Alice Mims. Both girls attended the St. Andrew Grammar School]. This picture made about 1912 in Southport, Florida.

Submitted by: Daisy Lee Richbourg Engelhardt and Lillian Masker Welch.

"Silver Star"

As a child I was always excited about going on trips with my Dad. He was a boat captain, and coming from a long line of mariners, running a boat was one of the things he did best.

There was something different about this trip, there was an extra twinkle in Dad's eyes, a little more excitement in his voice and my little mind just knew that we were in for something extra special.

It was not uncommon for Dad to run several boats during the year. Like most captains, it was a matter of where the work was at the time. I got to go on several different kinds of boats; I guess that is why I love the water today. I just couldn't get over how excited Dad was about this particular trip. He seemed more excited than I was and that was unusual.

When we pulled up to the dock, I saw several different boats, there was one big huge one there, glistening like new made money. I could feel the excitement rise within my little heart, as I just

Captain Winton Earl Raffield with son, Vincent Earl Raffield and friend, Calvin Bud Bradley standing in front of "Miss Clara" a homemade oyster boat

knew that was why Dad was so anxious. As we walked down to the water we passed the big boat, I tugged at Dad's shirttail, and he just kept walking. In a minute we stood in front of a tug. It looked old, battered and worn, surely this was not the boat my Dad is so excited about? My little heart sank as we got on board.

There was much to do, to get her underway, and Dad was too busy to fool with me, so I sat over in the corner as he had instructed until we were well underway. As things began to settle down and Dad could concentrate on other things, he had me come over and help him at the wheel, something that I loved to do.

Then he told me the story about when he was a boy, about my age. Dad lived at the head of East Bay as a boy, close to a place that was well known as Bull Point. His family used to live at what is now known as Tyndall, but then it was known as Farmdale, then they moved across the bay to Bull Point. He came from a large family, and in those days they actually had to cross the bay by boat or ferry just to get supplies from town. His dad, like generations before him, made a living the best way he could, which was usually fishing. The Raffield's had been well established as making some of the largest catches in the area. They came to the area in the mid to late 1800's. Some of them were farmers and others were trappers, and basically they took to fishing like it was born to them. They had little, but somehow managed on what they had, some even claimed that if you were born a Raffield, you had Saltwater in your veins, because of the love they all seemed to have for the water.

Dad was playing on the beach one day, when he saw this beautiful tug come by, he stopped playing with his sisters and brothers and just sat down and stared at it for as long as he could see it. It was beautiful to him, painted up so colorful, and massive in its strength as it pushed the barge along. For a moment at least he daydreamed he was the one pushing that barge along, and when he could no longer see the boat, he proclaimed "One day, I'll be her captain." The others laughed, and went on about their play, as Dad, still in a daze dreamed about the tug.

"Today is that day son, and I am her captain," it was my Dad's dream come true. She may have been tattered and worn, but Dad saw the Silver Star as she was years ago. His dream had come true. Dad worked on the Silver Star for a while, and took great pride in giving her a fresh coat of paint, and doing some much needed repairs. When the work was finished and his time with her was through, I could see the beauty that he saw in her, and even more I could see it through his eyes, as we pulled away from the docks to bid her farewell.

In Loving Memory of; Captain Winton Earl Raffield

By: Vince and Linda Raffield

Submitted by: Lora Nell Raffield, 3609 East Game Farm Road, Panama City, Florida 32404.

Sitting in the Middle of Thomas Drive

In 1949, Ellis and Peggy Walton lived at Long Beach Resort in a small apartment behind the juice stand. Next door was the tin-pin bowling alley, the shooting gallery, and the skating rink, which they managed. The large 2-story casino fronted the apartment area; the Hang-Out was behind. The area was noisy and the couple frequently walked along the beaches area to escape the din.

On a warm sunny day, they began walking from Long Beach down to the water, past old Panama City Beach,

Peggy Cotton Walton Malone posing on the beautiful shore of the Gulf of Mexico

under its long pier, and into the vast expanse of sugar-white sand. They walked inland toward Grand Lagoon, or so they hoped. All you could see in any direction was white, shimmering sand - no houses, no people, no cars - like a huge white desert. As the sun beamed down, with the gulf behind them and the lagoon in the distance ahead, they began to worry that they couldn't find their way back. They came upon an old weather-beaten, bent tree. Ellis was an amateur photographer. The sculptural shape of the old tree offered a picturesque backdrop for his new bride. They rested for a short while and then made the return trip home.

The site of the old tree has been replaced with asphalt roads, concrete condos, and a golf course. The couple crossed the white expanse to an area that is today near Thomas Drive and Joan Avenue. But in 1949, it was a quiet oasis offering vistas of sand dunes, beach myrtle, and sea oats.

Submitted by: Peggy Cotton Walton Malone, 2622 Michigan Avenue, Panama City FL 32405.

Summer Vacation

One summer I went to Panama City, Florida, to stay with grandma for about eight weeks. I got a job on a fishing boat making three bucks a day. I baited hooks, cut bait, and

removed people's catches and put them on ice. We were out from about 7am till 6pm. There were no fishing rods used, just hand lines, fishing at 6 fathoms about 30 miles out in the Gulf. The primary catch was red snapper and black grouper. When we would return, I would go to an oyster bar and blow the whole three bucks on oysters and beer. Back then, they served a 14 year old without batting an eyelash! I damaged my fingers something fierce handling those fish (Gill rakers). We were out there one day when on the radio they had announced the official surrender of Japan, the war was over.

On that summer I had a chance to meet the boys that used to rag on me in the fourth grade. They were very friendly, and we fished together on occasion. But they still, in a friendly way, called me a Yankee!

Submitted by: Mike Hamlin, 251 SE 46th Street, Cape Coral, FL 33904.

"Touch Of Humor" Gulfview Methodist Church

A story recalled by affiliated member Kitty Peterson of Vidalia Ga.: her Mother and Father were very active in the New Beach Church, Ms. Beulah and Alvin Martin. Ms. Beulah was the Church organist. The organ was very old and they had a saying, "They prayed while she played". A combined effort to keep the wheezing tone going, through each service. Ms. Beulah being a conscience person was always present except for one incident that made an impression on her daughter. The neighbors two doors away named Weston's had a pet monkey, that dearly loved Ms. Beulah. That 'lil fellow having traveled down the power lines to visit dropped on Ms. Beulah's head as she came out of the house ready for church. The efforts of Alvin Peterson were

Shirley, M.M. Allen, Sr., Loretta Moore

almost futile to remove him. The shock, the hat and the hair-do in shambles were too much for Ms. Beulah to face that tired 'ol organ, that morning.

The Methodist are really known for their wonderful meals. However, the cleanliness next to godliness is pretty close. Kathy Harrison, Kitty and Fred's daughter, the Martins granddaughter was a friend of Pastor Syfrett's daughter. The women of the church were having a church cleaning. The girls being tag-a-longs were invited to come in. When entering they were given a knife. Thinking they were going to make sandwiches for lunch, they joyfully hopped about until one of the ladies calmly explained to them, since they were small, their job was to crawl under the benches and scrap off all the chewing gum there. There wasn't any information about lunch that day, however the church was clean from "top to bottom."

Submitted by: Loretta B. Moore, 204 3rd Street, Panama City Beach, FL. 32413.

Rev. W. C. Wallace

The Reverend William Craig Wallace was born in Soddy, Tennessee, July 9, 1848. He graduated from King College, Bristol, Tennessee, and from Union Theological Seminary in Richmond, Virginia. He was ordained into the Presbyterian ministry in Soddy in 1871. His work as a pastor and home missionary carried him into Texas, Indian Territory, Kansas, and South Georgia.

In 1888 he met and married Viola Augusta ("Gussie") Maxwell of Cairo, Georgia. They had six children, three of whom lived to adulthood (Coe, Waldo, and Janie).

While serving in Kansas, Mr. Wallace's health failed and he was diagnosed with "tuberculosis". Because of this; he decided to give up the active ministry and move to South

Georgia where the climate was more hospitable.

In 1908 he heard about the thriving community of Panama City on St. Andrews Bay. He felt the salt air would be beneficial for his health, so he loaded his horse and wagon, and with his two sons, Coe and Waldo, set out on the two day trip to the coast.

When they reached their destination late one afternoon they pitched camp on what is now Beach Drive, near the location of the Elks Club. After a few days inspecting the area, he told the boys to take the wagon, go back to Cairo, get their mother, two sisters and their possessions, arrange for a freight car, and come back, arriving on the new Bay Line Railroad. In the meantime, he would find a place for them to live.

So far as it is known, the Reverend Mr. Wallace never left Bay County, even for a short visit, until his death December 23, 1930.

When Mr. Wallace came to Panama City there was a small congregation of Presbyterians meeting regularly. He associated with these people and assisted in their worship services, but was never the pastor of the congregation. (He was at that time a minister of the "Northern" Presbyterian Church, and this was a "Southern" Presbyterian Church.) He was however, the Sunday School Superintendent, and preached from time to time in the Panama City and St. Andrew churches.

When he was asked to preach in the St. Andrews church, he would walk the two or three miles from Panama City, preach, receive a couple of dollars, and walk home - often without being asked to have dinner.

When services were not scheduled in the Presbyterian Church Mr. Wallace was to be found in the "Amen Corner" of the First Methodist Episcopal Church, South, just down the street from his home.

About 1912 Mr. and Mrs. Wallace bought a lot in the 400 Block of Magnolia Avenue, and borrowed about $1500.00 from M. A. Coleman with which they built a home. In 2002, in order to make room for the State Attorney's Building, this house was moved to its present location on McKenzie Avenue at Massalina Bayou.

For a number of years, Mr. Wallace owned and operated a fruit and vegetable market on Harrison Avenue, near the present entrance to McKenzie Park.

Sometime after his death (which was not from "tuberculosis" but probably from prostate cancer), the Panama City Presbyterian Church was renamed Wallace Memorial Presbyterian Church in memory of W. C. Wallace. This church is now known as First Presbyterian Church.
Submitted by: Waldo Wallace, 1311 Cincinnati Ave., Panama City, FL.

Willie and Bea Findley

Summertime fun on St. Andrews Bay in the 1930's would be taking a small sailboat and sailing over to the Point to pick up scallops out of the seaweed in shallow water. On this day about 1937-1938, Lillian Welch Spinks (standing) and her two children, Roy Spinks, Jr. and Elizabeth Spinks were going with Willie and Bea Findley (standing in bathing suits in back of boat) to the Point. In the picture the Point is just beyond the trees. Chester Adam Welch who was called, "Big Bud" is the "Captain" this trip. This part of the shore line is near present day 10th Street and 11th Street. Arthur, (Sunny) (Buddie) Gill built small boats on this beach. The cottage shown in the background of the picture, were rented to summertime tourists. Willie and Bea's brother, Buddie, built this small sail boat for them.
Submitted by: Beatrice Moates, 764 Roland Rd., Chipley, FL 32428-5186.

Friends sailing onSt. Andrews Bay

Willie Eva Smith and Gospel Music

Every single day when I think of all the gifts in life, I focus on a wonderful, dedicated black woman I had the honor to share some time with, Willie Eva Smith. She was at one time a teacher at Rosenwald High School. Rosenwald played a significant part and was a major element of Bay County's history. Willie Eva would have to be compared to gospel music itself, like a giant tapestry that has been woven, intertwined and embedded in the hearts of people.

I met Willie Eva and her assistant Adeline some years ago. All my church sisters and brothers and I throughout Bay County, were part of her gospel music workshop. The workshops embraced everyone who was interested in gospel music. Once every year, she would travel from California to Panama City to make sure we received our nourishment of new gospel music. A wonderful opportunity was born of unity throughout our churches. Each one of us took back to our church a greater depth of gospel music. St. John Missionary Baptist Church under the leadership of Delwynn G. Williams, senior pastor/teacher, hosted one of the workshops. The amazing thing about Willie Eva, in spite of her declining health and her dependency on her oxygen tank, was her determination and dedication. Willie Eva would be so engulfed by the music, she would forget to reconnect her oxygen tank. What an inspiration. Willie Eva Smith passed away January 31, 2003. The wonderful memories will always be etched in our hearts. I imagine another workshop has already begun, only this time with the angels. I hope this very important gospel music workshop will continue. That someone will grasp the torch and complete this journey. Gospel music is the tapestry of life and the very essence of the soul. This great lady, Willie Eva Smith, a blessed lady, captivated it all and taught all of us to care, share, unite and feast of the essence of gospel music. What an honor!
Submitted and written by: M. M. Smith, 8009 Highway 22, Panama City, Florida 32404.

Winemaking

Ralph Sorrentino was an exceptionally good winemaker. After all he had his own grapes and friends and neighbors wore paths to his door to get a taste of his wine. Although making wine was illegal, Ralph had no problem with the Police Department or the Sheriff Department. They knew no amount of money could tempt Ralph to sell any, but if he liked you, he would give you a bottle of his wine.

Frequently ships from other countries docked near the paper mill and the sailors celebrated by going to shore and getting drunk. The law put the unruly sailors in jail and then would call Ralph to interpret for inmates and policemen so the problem could be solved. Since Ralph never lost his Italian accent, the foreigners may have felt comfortable when he talked to them.
Submitted by: Marie Sorrentino Waller Lee, 1002 Iowa Ave., Lynn Haven, FL 32444.

WE REMEMBER

Early camp grounds

Leslie Porter gazing at a captured alligator, 1919

First Hathaway Bridge, built in 1929

Building in front center was Panama City Post Office in 1907

The Bay Theatre at Third Street and Highway 98 in 1950

An early fire truck with firemen

HARRISON AVENUE/DOWNTOWN

T.M. (Woody) Smith driving an old fashioned funeral coach in a parade.

The Four Winds Restuarant

Chicken Ranch Restaurant, 1201 Harrison Avenue

Interior of Cogburn Clothing Store

Gulf Coast Development Company & Gulf View Inn at the end of Harrison Avenue, 1909

Bay County High School, built 1926

BUSINESSES OVER THE YEARS

Jimmy's Drive-In opened in 1948

The Jewel Box owned by J.A. Warren, next to the Martin Theatre, 1961

Corner of Harrison Avenue and First Street, Young's Cafe

Interior of Thompson's Appliance Company, the popular record shop in the 50's and 60's

Domestic Laundry and Cleaners, Delivery Truck, 1930's

Sears, Roebuck and company in downtown Panama City, 1960's

SCOUTING

Girl Scouts bringing canned goods for food baskets

Glenwood Cub Scouts

Cub Scout Troop visiting Tyndall Air Force Base

Girl Scout Troop marching in a parade

Girl Scout Troop on the steps of the Woman's Club building

SPORTS AND ACTIVITIES

Lynn Haven Band, 1918

Panama High School basektball team, 1937

Jack Creel and Paul Mainous at Lions Park.
Spartans Baseball team

Millville School basketball team

Skating at the Glenwood Skating Arena

PEOPLE

Roy Martin showing off the Ling he caught

Captain Barrow on the Steamer Tarpon

Young ladies all dressed up for the Azalea Trail Queen festivities

Mr. and Mrs. Maxon and Mrs. Roland

Girls Basketball Team from Rosenwald High School

PEOPLE

Panama City Police Officer with MP's from Tyndall, 1960's

Enjoying a Millville School Reunion, 1999

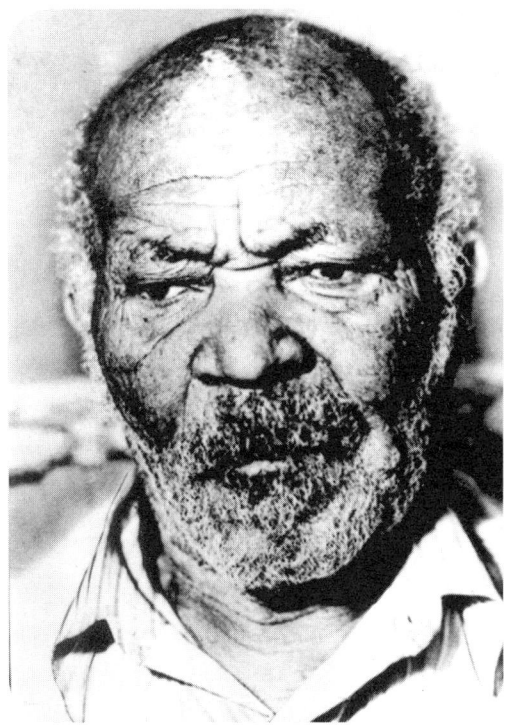

"Hawk" Massalina

*A lady and a grapegruit tree. In the early years,
fruit trees flourished in this area*

Order of the Eastern Star ladies

101

JANE PATTON, FORMER BAY COUNTY LIBRARIAN

Bay County Public Library Building at 411 Jenks Avenue

Mrs. Patton talking to school children

Mrs. Patton with her grandchildren

In memory of Jane V. Patton ("Lady Jane," as an English friend called her). She was the Head Librarian at Bay County Public Library for 22 years. A very versatile lady, she was a stern but kind director and administrator and mentor. Always an entrepreneur, she bought an 18-wheeler truck at one point. Mrs. Patton was loved and respected by all she met. She will long be remembered.

Bookmobile and patrons at a stop in Pretty Bayou in 1960's. Mrs. Patton is second from right

JANE PATTON, FORMER BAY COUNTY LIBRARIAN

Bay County Public Library at 25 W. Government Street

Jane Patton's children, Jon Patton, Joanna Patton and Judy Lotas standing with Lucy Peters and the portrait Lucy painted of Mrs. Patton

Mrs. Jane Patton, Librarian of Bay County Public Library from 1957-1979

Jane Patton at the beach with a grandchild

Climbing aboard her truck

GIDEON vs. WAINWRIGHT MARKER DEDICATION
August 5, 2003

Bay County Courthouse Built in 1915

W. Fred Turner was Attorney in The Landmark Gideon Case

Ronald Gideon, W. Fred Turner, Retired Judge, and David Gideon

Rebecca Saunders has presented Judge Turner with a plaque from the Historical Society

David and Ronald Gideon with Rebecca Saunders and Fred Turner at the Gideon marker

W. Fred Turner died at age 81 on November 23, 2003. Photography by Steve Wallace.

MILITARY

Millville National Guard Artillery Battery

The <u>John Bascom</u> being launched from the Wainwright Shipyard. Only ship built there that was sunk during WWII

GI's from Tyndall relaxing near the USO building at the Panama City Marina, 1942

Entrance to Tyndall Air Force Base, 1940's

Scuba divers from the Navy Mine Defense Laboratory in a local spring

COMMUNITIES

Fountain House Restaurant

Grand Army of the Republic Union Veteran Monument in Lynn Haven

Cedar Grove Tiny Mites

Wayne George and Jeff Morris with their trucks at St. Andrews Bay Dairy

Soda Fountain at Company Store, Millville

Class Picture at Hiland Park School, 1971-72

COMMUNITIES

Springfield Elementary School Class, 1955-56

Rural School house, Callaway, Florida

Dirego Park Assembly of God Church, 1950's

Anderson's of Southport, 1908

Tapper's Pier, Mexico Beach, Florida

Parker School Class 1920, Mrs. Baum teacher

THE BEACHES

Water view of the Miracle Strip Amusement Park and Top O' the Strip Tower

Howard Padgett, Jr., and Joyce Stevens playing in the sand at Camp Helen

Scene at St. Andrews State Park

People enjoying the Hang Out, 1960's

House at the beach that was destroyed during Hurricane Opal in 1995

TRANSPORTATION

A man driving his horse and buggy, 1900

Old St. Andrews Bay Line. Children are from St. Andrews School, 1913

Volmer Harmon and Jack Mayer on Harmon's boat "Red Wing"

Bicycling in St. Andrews, 1896

Roadster Car

Panama City Transit bus, 1950-60's

FISHING IN BAY COUNTY

Young man at old city dock with his catch

A party showing off their catches of the day, 1948

Charles and Michael Gandy pretending to ride a 432 lb. Warsaw at Treasure Island Marina

Beach Yacht Club, fishermen and women displaying their catch

Theo Strickland and Huel Claeghorn with fresh catch on Camp Helen pier, 1956

Charles Barnes and friends showing off a catch

FAMILY HISTORIES

Lowell Frederick Adams

Lowell Frederick Adams was born in Laurel Hill, Florida, on August 26, 1913, the eldest of eight children born to Ida Mae Davis Adams and Jefferson Fabian Adams. His grandfather, Fabian William Adams, was born in Barbour County, Alabama, and his grandfather's brother, John Allen Adams, was the grandfather of Drs. D. M. and Powell Adams.

The family of Lowell F. Adams moved to St. Andrews, Florida, when he was five years old, for his father to work for the German American Lumber Company in Millville. It was in St. Andrew that Lowell began his formal education, as he walked the boardwalk to school. He wrote of excursions on St. Andrews Bay, with "waters as clear as crystal...one could see the bottom very clearly and used a glass dish to see the fish swimming."

It was in Ozark, Alabama, where his father was working that Lowell met his bride, Annie Lucille Daughtry. They were married on December 22, 1932. He told that he had two dollars and fifty cents when they went to get married. The minister responded to Lowell's inquiry about how much he owed him

Lowell Frederick Adams and Annie Lucille Daughtry Adams

with, "Just give me whatever you think she is worth." He gave the minister a dollar, which was almost half of his money. Lowell and Lucille both worked at the Wainwright Shipyard during the war.

Lowell was the proverbial "Jack of all trades", because living during the depression prompted one to be innovative. He worked for Mrs. Lillian C. West for a time at the Panama City Publishing Company and also for the News and Herald newspapers. He continued to work in the printing business his entire life and worked in the printing department at Gulf Coast Community College while Dr. Richard Morley was the president. He also was the founder of Adams Printing Company.

Lowell felt God calling him into the gospel ministry and was ordained on November 14, 1948. He was able to receive his ministerial training through courses offered at the Covington County Extension Center through Howard College in Birmingham, Alabama. He, thereafter, pastored small churches in Alabama and Florida. The local churches he pastored were Midway Baptist and Howard Carlisle Baptist. He also pastored Highland View Baptist in Port St. Joe in the 1950's. He was a bi-vocational pastor, meaning that he also had to have a secular job, which was usually in the printing business.

He was passionate about preaching and printing. He wrote regularly to the 37 cent forum in the *News Herald*. He wrote a weekly column for the Port St. Joe newspaper, *The Star*, entitled "The Country Preacher", which was published up until he had a stroke in 1999, with his death following in 2001.

Lowell Adams had a way with words, and those words live on.

Submitted by: Sandra Adams Wilson, 2440 Pretty Bayou Boulevard, Panama City, Florida 32405

Alderman Family - Part I

The first of the Alderman families, Joseph (J.B.) Braswell Alderman and wife, Allene Chitty Alderman, and children, Juanita (Nita) and Joseph, Jr. (Joe), moved to Panama City from Valdosta, Georgia in 1939. Alderman had been transferred with the Martin Theatre chain to manage the Panama Theatre located on Harrison Avenue next to the Coleman Still

J.B. Alderman

Allene Chitty Alderman

store. The original theatre was on Beach Drive, but after burning, the Harrison Avenue building was constructed. The Aldermans had visited Panama City in 1931, when their first child, Juanita (Nita) was four years old. Joe, Jr. had not yet been born into the family at that time. The vacation began at the old Tarpon Dock. Alderman and a friend enjoyed an all day deep sea fishing trip. By nightfall the caught fish were cleaned and a joint fishfry was held in the dirt parking lot on the bay by the dock. A beautiful full grown oak tree spread it's foliage over everyone, and little daughter Juanita enjoyed the huge rope swing attached to the tree. As of 2003 that same oak stands tall and beautiful. During the day, Allene, Juanita and friend enjoyed swimming and sunning in the bay on West Beach Drive, near Lake Caroline. They all stayed at the old Alabama Hotel in St Andrews, at the corner of 12th Street and Cincinnati Avenue.

Allene Chitty Alderman on West Beach Drive 1931

To this day Juanita remembers the old hotel, and how the rooms were built around the courtyard where you could sit in lounge chairs and sun, and the doors built of wooden planks, and the skeleton key for the door. It was later bought by Mr. Swann, who taught at Bay High School, who tore it down and built cottages with the lumber. Moving to town in 1939 the family found it to have a slow and

Juanita (Nita) Alderman Whitehurst, age 4, on visit to Panama City-1931

easy pace, almost like a sleepy village. At the foot of Harrison Avenue, a park atmosphere, grassy knoll, benches, a long wooden dock, which housed the Coast Guard Cutter, and the Light House Restaurant adding its uniqueness to the scene.

Submitted and written by: Nita Alderman Whitehurst, 2710 Frankford Ave., Panama City, Florida 32405

The Alderman Family - Part II

The Alderman's first home was in the Cove, one block from the bay on Allen Avenue, and in view of the beautiful Cove

111

Juanita Alderman Whitehurst (age 12) and Beverly Duren (across from Byrd Bottling Plant and in front of first Radio Station, WDLP, on West Beach Drive)

Hotel. Their second move carried them to St. Andrews across from the Truesdale Park, then back to Panama City. During World War II Alderman was transferred to the newly constructed Bay Theatre in Springfield, where it was more convenient for the servicemen to attend movies than having to come all the way into town. Panama City had begun to boom. There hadn't been a radio station but when WDLP was built on West Beach Drive, Juanita, who was then twelve years old, had the honor of singing opening night and was the first voice over the airways. An unforgettable story was about the Coast Guard Cutter's mascot, a dog named "Sugarmeat", who each morning would go up and down Harrison Avenue visiting with everyone. At his death he was given a place of honor on the lawn of the "Seaside Inn", which then was used as quarters for the crews. From a sleepy village the Aldermans saw the coming of Tyndall Field, Shipyard, Project Houses, Buses with holding straps instead of seats, USO on the knoll at the foot of Harrison Avenue, Block long lines to attend movies and Ration Stamps. Many stars visited or were stationed at the bases, one very famous one, Clark Gable at Tyndall. The founding Alderman parents are gone, but the two children, along with their children still reside in Panama City. Joe, Jr. grew up to become part of the building industry, contributing his talents for art on the drawing board, and expanding the growth of the city with the construction of beautiful homes and buildings. Juanita (Nita) went on to build the first commercial Day Nursery in the city and offered her talents to community service through music, playing for Beauty Pageants, and civic affairs. The Alderman family weren't among the very early pioneers, but they take pride in saying they were part of the building and growth of such a beautiful city.

Submitted by: Joe B. Alderman, Jr., 6030 Pippen Rd., Panama City, Florida 32404; Written by: Nita Alderman Whitehurst, 2710 Frankford Avenue, Panama City, Florida 32405

Walter Dewey Ammons Family

My husband's great-grandfather, John Ammons, was born in September of 1854 in Georgia. When he was about 25 years old, he married Camilla Champion, also of Georgia. She was born in January of 1855. Together, they raised a family of seven children. Their children were: Buddie, born in May, 1877; Bryant, born in February, 1878; John, born in September, 1880; Irvin, born in October, 1882; Walter, born in December, 1885; Nettie, born in May, 1886, and Martha, born in November, 1888. John Ammons was a farmer. He died 6/26/1929, and is buried in the Welfare Church Cemetery in Covington Country, Alabama. His wife, Camilla, had died in 1926 and was also buried in the same cemetery.

One of their sons, James Bryant, was born on 2/29/1878 in Alabama. Census records indicate he was a general laborer, as an adult. He married Effie Sowell, probably around 1906. She was born in 1886 in Alabama. They had four sons together. They were: Willis, born in 1907; Walter Dewey, born in 5/25/1908; James Lester, born in 1912, and Robert, born in 1916. James Bryant Ammons died on 11/26/1950, in Covington County, Alabama. The census records of 1920 indicated he was divorced. One of Bryant and Effie Sowell Ammons' sons, Walter Dewey, became my husband's father. Walter Dewey Ammons was born on 5/25/1908 in Alabama. As an adult, "Dewey" made a living as a driver for a petroleum trucking company. He married Dollie White in Crestview, Florida, on 12/18/1927. She was born 8/10/1910, in Southport,

Left to Right Front Row: James Jimmy Ammons-Wayne Ammons-Margette Ammons-Dianne Carter- Back Row- Dolly Ammons-Dewey Ammons-Joyce Ammons-Flossie Dawsell (Doswell)

Florida. Together, they raised a family of nine children. My husband, Gene, was among them. Their children were: Inez, born 1/14/1929; Betty, born 12/19/1932; Lavern, born 4/6/1935; Walter Eugene (Gene), born 1/18/1938; Mary, born 5/13/1940; Joyce, born 12/18/1942; Margaret, born 5/7/1945; James F. (Jimmy), born 12/6/1948, and Wayne, born 4/24/1951. Walter Dewey Ammons died 9/31/1978. Dottie White Ammons died 2/7/1993 at age 88, in Bainbridge, Ga.

I met my husband's parents and siblings before I met him. After their move to Panama City, they settled in the area of town where I lived with my parents, near the paper mill. The area was called Millville, because of its close location to the mill, where my father and so many others worked. I met Gene's sister, Mary, and we became friends. We both liked to roller skate. We went skating almost every weekend at a local skating rink called Rainbow Roller Rink.

I met Walter Eugene (Gene) Ammons when he came to visit his family in Panama City on leave from the Navy in 1956, for Christmas. He was stationed in Boston, Mass., at the time. We began dating while he was home that Christmas of 1956. We kept in touch when he returned to duty after the holidays. Gene was assigned a tour of duty in Haiti in 1956, the year after we met and began dating. He purchased a set of wedding rings while in Haiti, and we became engaged. I was still in high school at this time, but I graduated on 6/3/1957, and we were married the very next day at Donaldsonville, Ga.

Submitted by: Janie Ammons, 2714 7th Ct., Panama City, FL. Sources: Family Records-Census.

George W. Anderson

George W. Anderson, (February 19, 1882-February 19, 1966) descendant of Scots who came from the Isle of Skye to Walton County by way of the Carolinas, came to Bay County from DeFuniak Springs about 1918 with his wife, Palestine (Monk) and their children, Burruss, Bernice and Grace.

He came seeking work with the Seminole Plantation, a company that produced satsumas, grapes, blueberries and other farm products. He was a foreman, and the family lived at the Lower Farm, on West Bay Creek, and at Crystal Lake.

"Papa rode a big white horse, and I thought he owned the Seminole Plantation," his daughter Margaret remembers.

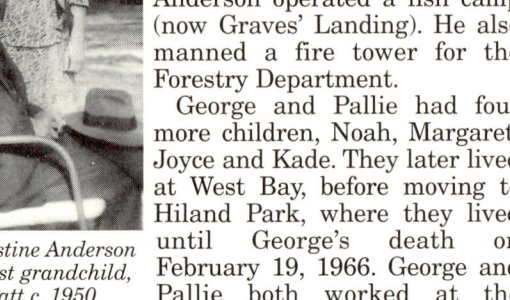

George and Palestine Anderson shown with eldest grandchild, Vera Ann Pratt c. 1950

The company produced excellent fruit, but it was difficult getting it to market. The Seminole Plantation endured freezing weather, and fruit spoilage at the railheads, but could not outlive the Great Depression. After it went out of business the family then moved to Pine Log, where Anderson operated a fish camp (now Graves' Landing). He also manned a fire tower for the Forestry Department.

George and Pallie had four more children, Noah, Margaret, Joyce and Kade. They later lived at West Bay, before moving to Hiland Park, where they lived until George's death on February 19, 1966. George and Pallie both worked at the

Shipyard during World War II. But he would have liked to be a full time freshwater fisherman. Palestine moved to Parker, where she resided near her daughter Bernice Pratt.

Palestine was a riveter's helper at the Shipyard. Later she worked for Hentz Grocery on Harrison Avenue near Sixth Street, where she made donuts. She was the first patient enrolled in the newly constructed Gulf Coast Convalescent Center, and lived there 13 years, until she died there in her 99th year. (Dec 1, 1993).

The couple had 23 grandchildren, 48 great grandchildren, and great- great grandchildren that are still being counted.
Submitted by: Bernice Anderson Pratt, 1128 Loftin Street, Parker FL 32404 and Margaret Anderson Duncan, 1609 Arthur Avenue, Panama City 32405.

Lessie Eva Anderson

Lessie Eva Anderson was born 14 October 1904 at Tinnelle Alabama and died 25 October 1994 at age 90 in Panama City, Florida. She is resting in the Evergreen Memorial Gardens, near the Open Bible in Bay County Florida.

Eva was the daughter of John Zolicoffer and Desty Lavinia "Chapman" Anderson. Her grandparents were John Wesley and Martha Ann "Olliver" Anderson and Richard Asbury and Martha Zipparahana "Baker" Chapman. Her great grandparents Henry and Rebecca "_?_" Anderson and Richard and Nancy "Goodson" Chapman and Richard and Amma "Shouter" Baker and Thomas Richard and Elizabeth "Grimmer" Chapman. Her great great grandparents were William Washington and Elizabeth "Hester" Chapman.

Eva was the oldest of 9 children in her family-Siblings listed: Youel Iverson (12 January 1907-23 August 1989) Married I.V. Campbell. Delia Inez (5 March 1908-11 July 2000) married Clarence Jordan. Mattie Mae (21 April 1910-living) married Devota Jordan. Dewey Mandolin (17 July 1911-10 April 1970) married Selma Smith. Rillie Itom (16 January 1915-Living) married Willard Woodrow Simmons. J.Z (initials only) (22 November 1917-11 June 1986) married Mary Antionette Wilkes. Audie Lee (1 November 1921-19 October 1998) married Fannie Merle McCall. John Purvis (28 October 1926-22 Feb 1993) never married. The family grew up in Coffee Springs, Alabama where their father farmed and was well known for making and selling sugar cane syrup. In the fall of the year he made syrup for many people in the community. They gave him some of their syrup as pay for his labor and he sold it.

The Anderson Family: (L to R. first Row:) Dewey Anderson, Mattie Mae Anderson, J.Z. Anderson, Delia Inez Anderson and Youel Iverson Anderson. (L to R. second row:) Lessie Eva Anderson, John Zolicoffer Anderson (father), Desty Lavinia "Chapman" Anderson (mother) and Rillie Itom Anderson. Audie Lee and John Purves Anderson were not born when this picture was taken.

He bought and drove the first school bus in Coffee Springs, Alabama, about 1930. At one time he owned two busses and had both in operation. The County paid him for his services. He was very strict on all the bus pupils but was loved and respected by all of them. When he died in 1944 the school let all the children that wanted to go to his funeral out.

Eva's mother, Desty had her gardens and grew what the family needed to eat. There was always plenty of food at grandma's house. She also pieced and quilted quilts and passed this hobby down to her daughters and some of her grandchildren.

Eva learned to sew well and made all of her children's clothes. She could look at a picture and make a dress look just like it. I always enjoyed wearing pretty clothes.

Eva saved all her scraps and made them into pretty quilts.

Eva was a hard worker and she kept her children busy too. She washed her clothes in washtubs and boiled them in the wash-pot. I always dreaded to see wash day come cause I had to rinse. In the spring of the year we had to carry everything out to sun in the yard so she could boil water in the wash-pot and scald the walls and ceilings. Then we scrubbed the floors and put everything back in place. Next our bodies had to be cleaned out by taking Calumel and following it with Epson Salts or Castor Oil. We were told that if we eat during this time it would salivate us so we were afraid to eat. Eva broke bushes from the woods and tied them together as brooms for us to sweep the yards and under the house must be as clean as any other part of the yard. She also made brooms out of broom-sage for us to sweep the floors with. Even with all of the work we had to do she always made time to play hide-and-seek with us when the work was done and dad was working late.
Submitted by: Nancy Eva Norton, 2618 Game Farm Road, Panama City, FL 32405; Written By: Ruby L. Strickland, 2627 Game Farm Road, Panama City, FL 32405. Sources: Memories, Family Bible and other family records in the files of Ruby Lee "Hartzog" Strickland

Mary Elizabeth Anderson

My Great Grandmother, Mary Elizabeth Anderson, was born July 28, 1848 and died on January 13th, 1900.

She was born in New Bern, North Carolina, the daughter of Thomas Anderson and Sarah Louise West Anderson. Sarah Louise was the daughter of Reading West and Mary Lane.

In 1855, Elizabeth moved to St. Andrews Bay and her family founded the community of Anderson, later to become known as Southport. Elizabeth's brothers were Stephen W. Anderson (born September 20, 1846 and died November 1, 1922) and William Merritt Anderson (born April 4, 1852 and died March 2, 1873).

Elizabeth's parents, Thomas and Sarah are believed to be buried at the Gay Cemetery, also known as "Dead Man's Hole" in the golf course at the Lynn Haven Country Club.

The Anderson's were fishermen and traded their salt fish for other supplies from the northern counties of Florida. As with many of the coastal families, they were trying to stay neutral during the Civil War, supplying mullett to both Confederate and Federal troops, or who ever was in need of food.

Sarah fell in love with and married a dashing young 2nd Lieutenant from the Florida 2nd Cavalry, William Jones Padgett. They were married in her father's house on May 14, 1865 at St. Andrews Bay. Depositions from her Widow's Pension Application, given by Rebecca E. Mercer, describes the wedding as a lovely candle lit ceremony with Mr. & Mrs. Mercer serving as candle bearers. She also states that the house "was filled with Blue Coated Yankees".

Following the Civil War, William and Elizabeth stayed at St. Andrews for a while, where he worked as a salt maker. They later returned to William's home in Jackson County and they farmed a large farm until his death in 1893. His death left Elizabeth a young widow with 2 minor children, Ellis Cabell Padgett and Elizabeth Matilda Padgett.

Elizabeth and William are both buried in the McQuagge Cemetery, about 6 miles south of Marianna, Florida in the community that was once the homesteads of the Padgett, McQuagge, Haynes and Gay families.
Submitted by: Gil Roberts, 2623 Highway 73, Marianna, FL 32448; E-mail: gilann@earthlink.net; Written by: Patricia Ann Roberts - Great Grandaughter, 2623 Highway 73, Marianna, FL 32448; E-mail: gilann@earthlink.net.

Palestine Monk Anderson

It must be difficult for some of the great- and great-great-grandchildren to imagine being 98 years old. It's getting easier for me.

I remember when I went to the nursing home to tell Grandma "I'm a grandma now!" It must be something, being old enough to know your granddaughter is a grandmother. And if I can be just like her, I'll be happy. As I tell you of some of our memories, I hope my grandchildren will remember me with such joy.

We remember grandma's Godliness, her strength and especially her sense of humor. She was a Lady in the fullest sense of the word: she had authority, she took care of all who depended on her, as long as she was able, and she ruled with kindness. None of us cousins (that I've talked to) can think of a time she got onto us for anything. The joy of the Lord must have been her strength, for she was always happy. (Angela says she remembers Grandma flicking the boys with her dishtowel when they got too rambunctious, however.)

Palestine Monk Anderson, September 27, 1894-December 1, 1993

Most of us remember that as Barry said once, "Grandma's a Sport." She entered into the fun — going fishing with her was about the most fun for me— and we usually caught fish. Grandma was all things to all people. Each of us grandchildren was convinced grandma loved us most of all. She told an interviewer one time that the child she loved best was the one that was sick or in need or farthest away. I know there've been times I knew she was praying for me and I know her prayers helped get me through some hard times.

We learned something about being a wife and mother from grandma. She showed me that a wife works hard, alongside her husband, to care for their family. When you kids see an old picture of "Rosie the Riveter" that was the kind of work Grandma did at the shipyard during World War II. I was really proud to say that grandma helped build Liberty Ships.

We watched her as she took care of grandpa for nine years after he had a stroke. She still never seemed to be angry or depressed. I told you, she was a strong woman. She always called grandpa Mr. George.

Grandma kept her sense of humor even in the nursing home. When she could no longer speak, she could and did always laugh.

Whatever one of us remembers about grandma, you can just about multiply by 23: Cathy said she always felt safe and secure and happy in grandma's house, and she loved to hear the rain on the tin roof. And as she was telling me, I could hear the rain too.

Nancy recalls that Grandma always said "I love you a bushel and a peck and a hug around the neck" and in the nursing home she'd always laugh when you said it to her.

Michael said tell about the biscuit hoecake— and every one of us remembers Grandma's biscuit hoecake! Breakfast with Grandma was special. "Melissa and I halved a whole hoecake one morning." Michael said. Somebody needs to learn to make a biscuit hoecake like she did. It must have been the love she put in – nobody can make 'em like she did.

Some of Tommy's best memories are of chauffeuring Grandma around. I guess the first thing Tommy did after getting his first driver's license was to call Grandma and ask "Can I take you anywhere, Grandma?"

Buddy recalls one time his dad told him to pick up Grandma in West Bay and take her home in his truck. "I forgot about it being a 4-wheel drive, and I just leaned over, opened the door and said 'let's go, Grandma', 'Buddy says. "Grandma looked up at me and said 'You'll have to get a ladder to get me into that truck."

Buddy also remembers Grandma's donuts. "I could always get a donut at her house," he said.

When she worked at Hentz' Grocery making donuts, you could always expect a baker's dozen in your box. Barry's memories are of stopping by after summer band class every day and grandma'd give him a donut. One little girl (not family) came in one day and grandma wasn't behind the counter... she knew grandma's name was from the Bible but couldn't think what it was "Where's . . miss.. miss Jerusalem?" she asked.

Miss Pally's not here now. But today we know where she is. She's probably watching us and smiling and remembering... and hoping that someday we'll be together over there. . . Won't it be something to have grandma show us around heaven? I feel like she's saying as she did on so many Sunday mornings, "Wash your face and get on your best clothes and don't be late to church! And get yourself ready to come up here." God bless you, Grandma. See you some morning.

P.S. That ends the eulogy we gave at the funeral. But it started me thinking. . . we should write about grandma and put it all together so we could all have a copy of all our memories. I know there's one set of grandchildren that can remember when Grandma and Grandpa lived in West Bay, catty-corner across the highway from Aunt Edith's house. I spent a week out there one summer when I was about five or six years old. I remember her warming water in a washtub on or near the road for me to play in/get a bath. Then when I was a big girl I remember the house in Hiland Park– and Soxie can remember visiting there after Grandpa was disabled by stroke. Then she moved to the house in Parker and another whole set of grandchildren remember that house.

Of the 23 grandchildren, George is with her now, and of the great-grandchildren, Melissa and Perry. I love to think about all the reunions in Heaven- - they were there to show her around last week, and they'll be there for us.

Submitted by: Ann Pratt Houpt

Thomas Anderson

Thomas Anderson was born in North Carolina on April 7,1817. He died February 27, 1876 in Anderson, (now named Southport) Washington County, Florida. He married Sarah L. West c.1844 and they had three children, Stephen, Elizabeth, and William Merritt, all born in North Carolina.

During 1854/55, Thomas and Sarah left New Bern, North Carolina and came to St. Andrews Bay, settling with their young family on Fannin Bayou. They homesteaded 300 acres and started the town of Anderson (later changed to Southport). With his love of the sea, Thomas was a natural fisherman and supported his family in this manner. There was no ice available, so to preserve their catch, they would salt down the fish and store them in barrels, to be either sold or bartered for other goods. Farmers would come from Jackson County, to the north, and as far away as Alabama and Georgia, in their horse drawn wagons loaded with vegetables, beef, cotton, pine lumber and any goods that could be traded for the fish.

Thomas was the original Captain Anderson, and his son and grandsons would continue the family business over the years, building the reputation as having the best seafood in Bay County. Their fishing business evolved into a restaurant, and was sold, in 1967, to the current owners of the now "world famous", fabulous Captain Anderson's Restaurant.

Thomas' daughter, Elizabeth, married 2nd Lieutenant William J. Padgett on May 4, 1865 in a candlelit ceremony in her father's home on beautiful Fannin Bayou, where she had lived during her childhood. This young couple would remain there until the late 1870's when they moved to Jackson County to raise their family.

Thomas and Sarah are believed to be buried in the Anderson family plot in Southport Community Cemetery. They are my G-G-Grandparents, and have left a wonderful family legacy to all of their descendants.

Submitted by: Patricia A. Roberts, 2623 Highway 73, Marianna, FL 32448 gilann@earthlink.net. Sources: "Full Box" by Winston Chester; Family History.

Henry C. Bailey

Henry C. Bailey was a man who made a difference. He was born in Henry County, Alabama. Realizing the importance of a good education, he attended the Tuskegee institute, earning an Alabama Teaching Certificate. Mr. Bailey dedicated many years in the public school system in Geneva, Alabama and Henry County. Over a period of time, Mr. Bailey accumulated many talents and certainly put his talents to good use. Eventually, Mr. Bailey and his family settled in Panama City, Florida. In 1941, immediately building a nice house, Mr. Bailey became one of Panama City's leading Black activists. He also became the president of the Negro Improvement Association.

Mr. Bailey earned a great deal of respect and strived for better living conditions for his people such as, sewage, street lights and pavements. Mr. Bailey attended St. John Missionary Baptist Church. He became a deacon and superintendent of the Sunday School. When the Sunday School children received a certificate recently, one could not help but to focus on the absence of Deacon Bailey. Pastor Williams and many members expressed how very much we missed Deacon Bailey, a man of substance, striving for excellence constantly. Every man's task is his life preserver. Deacon Bailey had a voice that was barely a whisper, which echoed to the right ears and truly made a difference.

Deacon Henry C. Bailey died July 8th 2003. He was 96 years old, leaving behind a tremendous legacy for all mankind.
Submitted by: Maureen Marshall Smith, 8009 Highway 22, Panama City, Florida 32404.

Tom Baker

Tom Baker was born in 1864. He was living in Campbellton, Florida with his grandmother, Mariah Powell. They moved to the St. Andrew Bay area when Tom was a child, so Mariah could find work among the families who had summer homes along the bay. Tom worked with the early fishermen who shipped salted fish to towns west of St. Andrews Bay. Tom met and married Amanda Gainer in the 1880s.

Penny (seated) Jincy at Cabin built on Hog Island

He brought her back to the bay along with her mother, Penny and her sister, Jincy.

Tom homesteaded 160 acres of land on Hog Island in what is now part of Tyndall Air Force Base. He built a log house and lived off the wild hogs, deer and fishing from the Bay. There he and Amanda raised 10 children, one of which was Alonzo.

Alonzo Baker was born on September 25, 1893, Stephen's Hammock, Hog Island. "Lonnie" worked with his father in a sawmill when he was a child. He also fished and turpentined in the wooded areas of Hog Island. During the early 1900s the family moved to Red Fish Point. Alonzo married Susie McKinney of Campbellton. Alonzo was in the army when his oldest child was born November 15, 1918.

Lola Mae Baker was one month old when her father returned from the army and took Susie and Lola Mae to Red Fish Point to live. "Lonnie" and Susie raised 8 children on the Point. Alonzo continued to work at various jobs and Susie did laundry for people in Panama

Susie Baker

City. During the week Alonzo would row across the Bay to the City dock with laundry for Susie's customers. If the weather would not permit his rowing across the bay, families would drive on Highway 98, cross the newly constructed DuPont Bridge, (1929), drive

Alonzo Baker

down dirt and shell roads to Red Fish Point to pick up clean laundry and drop off the dirty.

Lola Mae recalls once she and one of her brothers, Lorenzo, heard their father calling to them from the woods, "Bring me my rifle and two shells!" When the children returned with the rifle and shells, Alonzo said for them to get away from him. Alonzo fired once and missed his target. With the second shot he killed the biggest rattlesnake Lola had ever seen. Alonzo had stepped over the snake and narrowly missed being bitten.

Susie Baker died January 26, 1949 and is buried in Campbellton. Alonzo died March 27, 1987 and is buried in the Garden of Memories in Panama City.

Alonzo's father, Tom, his brother, Tommy, his maternal grandmother, Penny, and his Aunt Jincy are all buried in the cemetery on Davis Point. Lola Mae lives in the same house on Eighth Street her parents built in 1941-42 when they moved

Lola Mae Barker with Ray Hatton

across the bay after Tyndall Air Force Base was being built.

Lola Mae has helped raise many nieces and nephews. She has worked for numerous families in Panama City. Lola is one of the best cooks in the area. She has become a beloved friend to many.

There are articles that have been written about the Baker family in the News Herald. One of these articles is dated September 8, 1986 and another shortly before Alonzo passed away.
Submitted by: Lola Mae Baker, 529 E. 8th St., Panama City, FL 32401.

The Judson Barber/Mollie Halley Barber Family

Judson Barber was born in Blountstown in 1872. His wife, Mollie Halley Barber, was born in Blountstown in 1878. They were married in 1892, when Judson was 20 and Mollie was fourteen. At first, they had nowhere to live except in the woods under a lean-to made from branches. They hung their laundry on bushes to dry.

Within a few years, Judson and Mollie moved to Bay County, where Judson worked as a blacksmith. It is believed that Judson and a brother both left the Blountstown area about the same time because of an Indian uprising, but Judson never

Mollie Halley Barber and Hilton A. Barber

returned to the place of his birth. He died in Bay County in 1921.

Judson and Mollie had two children, Stellar Ann, born in 1894, and Hilton Allen, born in 1908. Stellar married George Perkins, who became a railroad engineer, and remained in Bay County. After military service, Hilton relocated permanently to the Atlanta area.

Stellar and George had three daughters, Myrtle Perkins Presley, Mildred Perkins Scott, and Madrid Perkins Skipper/Enders. Of the three, Mildred remained in Bay County.

Mollie lived out the rest of her life in Bay County. Both Judson and Mollie were buried in the Millville Cemetery.
Submitted by: Myrtle Perkins Presley (Granddaughter of Mollie Halley Barber), 9960 Atrium Way, Box 220, Jacksonville, FL 32225; Written by: Merle Presley Parker.

Oscar and Arvie Barnes Family - Part I

Oscar and Arvie Barnes were married April 24, 1927 in Jackson County, Florida. They

moved to Bay County in 1935 or 1936. Oscar was born February 29, 1908, Mary Arvie was born October 2, 1908, both in Jackson County, Florida. Oscar passed away October 25, 1983 and Arvie on September 17, 1982.

Their first child was still born January 31, 1929 followed by six more children.

Oscar Lamar was born April 1, 1931, he married Bertie Mae O'Neal in 1949. They adopted one child, Gregory Scott. Greg had two sons, Gregory Allan and Scott Thomas. Lamar passed away February 27, 1993 and Bertie Mae, March 23, 2000.

Oscar and Arvie Barnes 50th Anniversary April 23, 1977

Roy Gene was born July 14, 1933, he married Myrtle Hood in 1952. They adopted two children, Debra Genine and Stephen Lee. Debra married Thomas Statham, they have one child, Jordyn Ellen.

Herman Billie was born May 15, 1937, he married Mary Nell Hood in 1957. They have no children. Yes, Mary Nell and Myrtle are sisters.

Wanda Virginia was born August 14, 1939, she married Wayne Godwin in 1957, they divorced 1961. They had one child, Beverly Lynne. Lynne married Gary Certalich, they had three children, Shawn Michael, Rebecca Elizabeth and Kayla Nicole. In 1968, Wanda married Jerry C. Segers, he passed away December 26, 1991. They had two children, Bradley Cecil and Virginia (Ginger) Dawn. Brad never married. Ginger married Ronald Thomas, they divorced. They adopted one child, Elaina Denise.

Helen Lyvonne was born June 5, 1941, she married Edward Long, Jr. in 1961. They had three children, Teresa Marie which was still born, Edward III and Karen Michelle. Eddie married Bethel Dobson and they had two children, Jeremy Allen and Ryan Edward. Karen married Jeff W. Lewis and they have one child, William Jeffery. Jeff had two children by a previous marriage, Jessica and James. They are raising Jessica.

Robert Glenn was born April 26, 1944, he married Virginia French Foster in 1992. They never had any children but are raising a relative of hers, Brandon, who is now six years old. Virginia had three grown children when they married, Mary, Becky and Sharon. Mary has one child, Bryan.

All of the Barnes children have stayed in Bay County except Helen and she lives in Biloxi, MS. The Barnes family was a poor family but we didn't know the difference, we were a happy family and we all still enjoy life and are a very close knit family.
Submitted by: Wanda Barnes Segers, 621 Baywood Drive, Lynn Haven, Florida 32444.

Oscar and Arvie Barnes Family - Part II

In the sixties, Daddy served two terms as commissioner and one term as mayor for the City of Springfield. Mama stayed home all her married life and raised the kids to the

best of her ability and I think she did a pretty good job of it. Mama and Daddy raised us in the church, we all joined the Springfield Presbyterian Church at some point of our lives. Mama was one of the organizing members of the church in 1940. The

Arvie, Lynne, Greg, Debra, Oscar, Buddy, Eddie, Karen, Brad, Ginger April 23, 1977

church moved to Callaway in 1959 and is now the Parkway Presbyterian Church. Mama, Daddy and Lamar remained members of Parkway until their deaths. Wanda is still a member, is an elder and very active in Presbyterian Women.

When Lamar was a little boy, we lived in Martin Town, which was across the Highway 98 from the paper mill, there was a little dog that was always bothering him, Mama told him to pick up a stick and hit the dog. He came home one day feeling very proud, he had hit the dog and killed him.

When Lamar was about twelve years old, he would ride the bus to town to go to the movies at the Ritz Theatre. One day when he got off the bus in Springfield he ran into the path of a Danley Furniture truck. He was not seriously hurt but when he got to Bay High School and taking American History under Mrs. Anderson, he would tell her he couldn't learn because he was run over by a truck when he was younger. Eight years later, Wanda had Mrs. Anderson for American History, she asked Wanda about the accident, Wanda told her yes he was hit but not seriously, he just used that for an excuse.

One cold winter day our kerosene heater caught fire. Daddy told me to go outside and hand him the water hose through the window. I picked up the hose, ran to the window, Daddy reached for it and it was only about 1 foot long. It was frozen and broke when I picked it up. All of us kids thought that was funny. Then Billie got a boiler from the kitchen, got water from the bathroom and ran to daddy with it to throw on the fire. With all the commotion going on at our house, our neighbor Mrs. Musgrove came over to see what was going on, she walked in the front door and by that time our living room was full of water and she slipped down. To us kids that was so funny, we were lucky she was not hurt.

We all love to get together and we love the Lord.
Submitted by: Roy Gene Barnes, 1212 Florida Avenue, Lynn Haven, Florida 32444.

Oscar and Arvie Barnes Family - Part III

Daddy worked at the paper mill for 36 years, he retired after a stroke. While at the paper mill, we only had one car so Mama would take him to work and go get him. One day, Mama and Helen went to get him and he had to work overtime, one of the men came to the car and told her he was stuck (an expression they sometimes used for working over), Helen was young and that really upset her, she started crying, thinking her Daddy was stuck and couldn't come out. After Daddy retired, he took up fishing and loved it.

When I was a baby, Wanda wanted to hold me, Mama gave me to her, she decided she wanted to sit on the syrup bucket, so she tried, she turned the bucket over and ended up on the floor, she thought she had hurt me but I never touched the floor, it just scared Wanda.

We still get together on Thanksgiving and Christmas Eve at Wanda's house. We have kept up the tradition of having raw oysters on Christmas Eve. Virginia and I live in the house I was raised in on Central Avenue in Springfield. Our family still likes to get together and reminisce of growing up in Springfield.

Submitted by: Robert Glenn Barnes, 207 Central Avenue, Panama City, Florida 32401.

Gene, Lamar, Billie, Wanda, Helen, Glenn, Arvie and Oscar 1980

Barnes/Calloway Family - Part 1

My maternal grandmother and grandfather, John Stuart and Minnie Leonard Barnes moved their family from Falco, Alabama to Panama City in January of 1918 before Evelyn Barnes Calloway was three in April. Evelyn was the oldest daughter of Stuart and Minnie Barnes. The family settled in the sawmill town of Bay Harbor (Old Mooretown) where the Smurfit-Stone Mill now stands.

Stuart Barnes was a locomotive engineer on the log train during the sawmill days from 1918 until it closed several years later due to the fact that all the timber had been used up and no replanting process was in force at this time. The sawmill company owned several train engines along with two sawmills, one in Bay Harbor and one in Millville. Every evening when the train passed near the family's house, returning from the timber fields, Stuart would signal his return with a few blows from the train whistle. The family eagerly awaited this signal each day since they knew "daddy" would soon be home.

Stuart Barnes with hand on log train

Evelyn remembers a hurricane that hit the community when she was a small child. That was a frightening day listening to the howling, roaring wind and the rattling roof. Large oak trees that nestled the house blew down all around but fortunately none fell directly on the house. The children had their picture made standing on one of these huge trees after the storm was over. I remember visiting "Danny", the nickname we grandchildren had given our grandmother, in that big house. It had many large rooms that made off of a long wide hallway through the middle of the house. The sawmill houses were later moved to another location to make way for the paper mill.

Evelyn attended M i l l v i l l e Elementary School, then called Millville Grammar School, which housed grades one through

Evelyn (far right) after the storm

eight. She graduated from Bay High School in 1933. Her love was for books and reading. She loved also to write and she dreamed of attending college and becoming a journalist but that dream became the impossible dream because of the Great Depression. The next morning after the national announcement that the stock market had crashed, Stuart went to the bank to withdraw the college funds, but the bank was closed and he never got his money.

Submitted by: Evelyn Barnes Calloway, 2600 E. 26th St., Lynn Haven, FL 32444. Written by: Barbara Calloway Gaddie

Barnes/Calloway Family - Part 2

In January of 1936, Evelyn married my father, Eugene Millard Calloway. My paternal grandparents, Thomas Henry and Bessie Lindsey Calloway, moved to Panama City in 1930 when Eugene was in the tenth grade. They lived in a house on 4th St. and Harrison near the old First Methodist Church. He attended Bay High for a short while, then the family moved to Apalachicola where he graduated from high school. He loved sports, especially baseball and softball and received a sports scholarship to attend college, but because of the depression he immediately had to go to work to help support the family since he was the oldest son. When the family was living in Caryville in 1929, Eugene played for the mill team. The mill team came to Panama City to play the Panama City team and they stayed at the Pines Hotel that was once near the train depot. The Pines Hotel is gone, but the old depot still remains. This depot was very active during World War II and was used to transport military men and equipment. The ball team was carried to Shell Island in a one-cylinder boat as a special treat.

Wedding Day for Evelyn and Eugene Calloway

There were very few pleasure boats back then. Eugene thought that was the most wonderful thing that had happened to him in a long time. Eugene organized the "Calloway Brothers" softball team named after the family machine and welding business that used to be located on the water behind McKenzie Park.

Eugene learned how to weld while in high school and taught his two brothers, Arthur and Woodrow, how to weld. This became their profession. His father was well-known as a master mechanic. He helped establish many "pepper back" saw mills. He also worked for the Bay Line Railroad repairing locomotive engines. Eugene and his father worked at the sawmill in Bay Harbor. Evelyn worked in the sawmill cafeteria where Eugene and Tom would frequently eat lunch. Evelyn and Eugene first met on a blind date at the old Vickery house on Panama City Beach where the car almost got stuck in the deep sandy trenches. There were very few houses on the beach at that time and the roads were not paved. They continued to date and see each other at the cafeteria until Eugene left to find work at another mill. The sawmill business was thriving in many communities so Eugene and Tom traveled from mill to mill pursuing work.

Eugene was later hired as a welder to help with the construction of Tyndall Air Force Base, then called Tyndall Field. When the work at Tyndall was completed, he went to Jacksonville to help construct a base there for war was imminent and the nation was in the process of building many military bases. He phoned Evelyn one day and said, "Get your things ready, I'm coming to get you and we will be married." They were married in 1936 in the old First Methodist Church that used to stand on the corner of 4th St. and Magnolia.

Submitted by: Barbara Calloway Gaddie. Written by: Barbara

Calloway Gaddie, 4618 Baywood Drive, Lynn Haven, Florida 32444.

Barnes/Calloway Family Part 3

I was born the second child, my brother Gary being the first, on March 13, 1938 in Dr. Robert's clinic on Cove Blvd. The building still stands near the Women's Club, but is now a residence. The family frequently moved since dad was following construction work on the military bases. I remember the little garage apartment where we lived in Jacksonville near the base. World War II was underway. As a child about five years of age, I would stand on the sidewalk and watch the women "Waves" and "Wacs" march in the street. Much of children's clothing at that time was designed around the military styles and mom bought a Wac outfit for me. It had the little brown strap that went over the shoulder and I thought I was "really something" in that uniform. I marched on the sidewalk along with the Wacs pretending I was just as big

Noah's Ark Float. Barbara (in middle) with runner ups Carol Law and Janice Coonradt

as they were. The air raid sirens would sound off at night and we had to pull the shades down and turn off all the lights. Enemy submarines had been spotted off the coast near Jacksonville.

Dad had received the limit of three deferments because of his work to help build the military bases when the war ended and the armistice was announced. I was relieved that my dad did not have to be sent over seas to be so far away from me. Dad's brothers and mom's brothers were either drafted or enlisted in this war but they all returned home safely. Mom's brother, Earl Barnes, experienced much overseas action in the Navy on a battleship and had many war stories to tell when he returned.

Our family built a little home on North Palo Alto in the Cove where we were living when my sister Cynthia was born in 1944. A lot of special memories were made while living in this house. My brother Gary, sister Cynthia, and I went to Cove Elementary School, Jinks Junior High School, and Bay High School. I attended Jinks the first year it was built. Before this, there were no middle schools, only elementary and one high school. Bay High was the only high school for years until Rutherford was built. I graduated from Bay High in 1956. The most fun thing I did at Jinks was deciding to be a majorette and twirling a baton marching in front of the band at the football games or marching down Harrison Ave. in a parade. When I was attending Bay High, I was elected queen of the Bible Club one year. My dad made a float in the shape of Noah's Ark. He built it in the back yard of our house and stretched chicken wire around the sides. I invited many of my classmates over to help stuff the little holes of the chicken wire with facial tissues. We stuffed and stuffed and thought we would never get it finished praying that it did not rain before the homecoming parade! I was one of the finalists for homecoming queen that year and felt so proud riding on that float waving to the bystanders as we rolled down Harrison Ave.

My Dad, Eugene, became a strong Christian during my junior high days. His ministry began as a lay speaker in First Methodist Church. Later, he attended Emory University to become an ordained minister. The Methodist conference assigned him to be pastor of the Springfield Methodist Church, which he helped establish. My job was to play the piano and help with the music. He also pastored the rural churches of Williams Memorial and Red Oak near Blountstown, Florida. After he retired, he devoted full time to jail ministry concentrating on the juvenile center where

he reached many wayward youth. Again, I helped provide music for many of the jail services by playing my accordian. He had stacks of letters from young people he helped expressing their appreciation for him. After his death in 2000, the family had a special plaque with his picture placed in the Juvenile Detention Center honoring him for his service.

Submitted by Karen Wilson Bryant and David Wilson, 3210 Florida Ava., Panama City, FL 32405. Written by Barbara Calloway Gaddie.

Eudell Agnew Barrett

Eudell, better known as "Top," "Topsy," "Chief," and by his family as "Big Daddy," was born 20 Oct. 1877, in Flower Branch, Hall Co., GA. Eudell was the son of Frank Stanton and Marie Josephine (McGee) Barrett. Frank was a veteran of the Civil War as a Confederate soldier. Eudell was the grandson of John R. and Martha (Sewell) Barrett.

As a young man, Eudell worked in his father's business as a tanner, leather goods; he also sang and directed Vaudeville shows.

Eudell had a son by his first marriage; the son was Eudell Marion "Red" Barrett. Red was born 14 Jul. 1902 in Hall Co. Georgia, but grew up in Panama City, Fla; he died 30 Sept

Alice A. (Leonard) and Eudell A. Barnett 1940s

1950. Red is buried in Greenwood Cemetery, Panama City, Fla. Red was a musician and served in the army during World War II.

Eudell went to Jasper, AL about 1908. In Jasper, Eudell met and married Alice Arista Leonard in Sept. 1909. Alice is the daughter of James Lewis and Maranda Caroline (Brown) Leonard. Alice was born 08 Jul. 1881, a twin, in Jasper, Walker Co. AL. James Lewis was a Confederate veteran of the Civil War.

Eudell and Alice had four children: Carolyn Josephine, b. 1911 in Jasper, AL; Cecil Alice, b. 1913 in Jasper, AL; Stanton Agnew b. 1914 in Panama City, FL; and Margaret Elaine b. 1917 in Panama City, FL. These children grew up in Panama City, FL.

Eudell and Alice left Jasper, AL and moved to Panama City, FL in 1913. Eudell went into the pressing and tailor business on the "dock" in Panama City, FL, known as "Barrett the Tailor." Later, he moved up to Harrison Ave. and opened a men's clothing store. Alice was the seamstress.

Eudell was selected as the Master of Ceremonies of the Annual Splash Celebration on 2nd, 3rd and 4th of July in 1926.

Eudell and Alice were members of the First Baptist Church of Panama City, FL. Eudell sang in the choir for a while.

Eudell was elected/hired as the Chief of Police for Panama City, FL. Eudell served from 1926 to 1933. While serving as Police Chief, he was in at least two "shoot-outs." He shot and killed S.M. Hutto. (See News Herald, , "Panama City Pilot" 19 May 1932). He was shot in the stomach while trying to arrest R. O. Hannah. (See News Herald, "Panama City Pilot" 17 July 1930). Eudell served as City License Inspector until his death.

Eudell and Alice lived on Bruce Street in 1920 (census) later moved to 423 Massalina Dr. where they lived out their lives. This property was on Massalina Bayou.

Eudell always had a garden with turnip greens, tomatoes, peas, etc. Eudell also had scuppernon vines: bronze and purple. Eudell grew pecan, fig, and pear trees; at times they had chickens. Ashes from the fireplace went on the fig trees.

Eudell enjoyed fishing and taking Sunday afternoon car

rides out into the country. On these Sunday afternoon rides, he took his grandchildren. They went to the lakes and rivers around Bay County.

Alice belonged to the Garden Club.

Eudell died 18 April 1950 in Panama City, FL; Alice died 30 Jan 1958 in Panama City, FL. They are buried together in the Greenwood Cemetery, Panama City, Bay Co, FL.

Submitted by: Walter C. Sherman. Written by: Walter C. Sherman, P.O. Box 609, Panama City, FL 32401-0609.

Stanton Agnew Barrett

Stanton, born in 1914 was the son of Eudell Agnew Barrett (Panama City Chief of Police in 1933) and Alice Arista Leonard. Stanton had a busy lifestyle from the start. He said, "At the age of five I would paddle across Massalina Bayou in an old metal wash tub and mother never found out!" As a boy Stanton caught and sold fish from the bayou where he grew up, which was located at 423 Massalina Drive.

Stan in the year 1987

"Stanton had an outgoing personality and was well liked," said his high school classmate, Mitt (Evelyn Barnes Callaway). Throughout high school he played football and baseball and became a star on the field. Times were hard back then. Ms. Cora Stanley, the Economics teacher, kept the teams uniforms patched up.

Throughout high school, Stanton showed a real talent for singing. Mitt said, "He would always be humming a tune." Stanton was continually being called upon to sing during school assemblies. He competed in voice competitions and did well. His voice teacher, Ms. Louise Blackshear, took Stanton to Winter Haven, Florida where he sang in a statewide competition and won a scholarship to Rollins College. This trip to beautiful south Florida impressed Ms. Blackshear so much that she started *The Panama City Garden Club.* She said, "If it were not for the trip with Stanton and the beautiful azalea gardens, I might never have started the garden club."

After graduating from Bay County High School in 1933, Stanton entered Rollins College in Winter Haven on scholarship. A few years later, on February 18, 1937, on the front page of the Panama City News Herald, were the words, "BARRETT GOES TO NEW YORK TO STUDY VOICE." Stanton left for New York where he studied voice under the direction of Manly Price Boone in the *Metropolitan Opera House.* Stanton began singing with the "Student Prince Operetta" and the "Merry Widow Operetta." In 1944, during a tour, Stanton met and married Kathryn Graves. After traveling and singing for some time Stanton decided this was not what he wanted for his future family. Upon his return to Panama City, Stanton became a Baritone soloist at First Baptist Church, Panama City.

Reaping from his harvest

He started working as a Civil Service artist illustrator at Tyndall Field but soon started his own business. For twenty-eight years he built fine masonry block homes throughout Bay County. They were homes that will be standing for many more years to come. Using his artistic skills, Stanton started a decorative stone business. His concrete stonework can still be seen on many of the homes around town today.

After a hard days work, Stanton and Kathryn would enjoy a game of golf or tennis. Sometime they could be seen on the courts playing with the best-Bro. Si Mathison, and Bro. N.B. Langford. Stanton also enjoyed gardening and often helped the Rescue Mission from the abundance of his harvest. There were times he supplied the Salvation Army Church with enough speckled trout for a fish fry.

Stanton and Kathryn had four children: Janice Sharp, Frank Stanton Barrett, Diane White, and Carol Wright. They have 9 grandchildren and 13 great grandchildren as of 2003. Stanton showed his family good Christian ethics. He showed the heart behind the man and taught the meaning of good old-fashioned values. At home, Stanton enjoyed playing all the old classics on the old victrola as he sang along. The home was always filled with beautiful music.

Stanton taught compassion to his family, and to others who were struggling, both physically and spiritually. Upon his deathbed at the age of 86, Stanton's main concern was that his work was not finished...sharing Jesus became his greatest compassion. Stanton was a Panama City native son who will be remembered for his Christian values, for the many fine homes he built, and for helping to make our community what it is today.

Submitted by: Diane E. White, 700 Harvard Blvd., Lynn Haven, Florida 32444.

Clarence Henry Beach and Cali Elizabeth Quigley Beach
World's Most Beautiful Beaches

Clarence Henry Beach and wife, Cali moved to Bay County in 1934 from Defuniak Springs, Florida. They were both descendants of early Northwest Florida settlers. About 1890, the Beach family migrated from Warren, Ohio to Defuniak Springs. For a short time they also ran a sawmill in Grand Ridge, Florida. Clarence's father established a sawmill, later known as the Beach - Rogers Lumber Company in Defuniak Springs.

Cali and Clarence Beach

These Beaches, among the first to Florida, were direct descendants of John Beach. In circa 1650, brothers John, Thomas and Richard Beach settled in Stratford Colony of Connecticut. The family originated in St. Albans, Devenshire, England when John Beach was born June 3, 1623. Descendants of John Beach were to become the "World's Most Beautiful Beaches" for Panama City, Florida.

Clarence, born July 9, 1903, was the youngest son of Arthur and Jennie Downs Beach. Arthur was the first Republican mayor of Defuniak Springs, Florida.

According to a youthful Defuniak Springs friend of Clarence, a Dr. M. C. "Brother Si" Mathison, Clarence could play a trumpet very well. He attended Palmer College in Defuniak Springs, Birmingham Southern in Alabama, then studied electrical engineering at the University of Florida in the

Home at 720 Cherry Street in Cove. Built in 1935

1920's. In November, 1927, Clarence married Cali Elizabeth Quigley, born January 11, 1905, a 4th generation Floridian, the daughter of Edward John and Sarah Jane Andrews Quigley of Pensacola. In 1934 when the young couple moved to Panama City, Clarence worked for Van Kleeck Hardware, then opened his own electrical business. He became the City of Panama City's Building Inspector. Later he was associated with Dave Robertson Electric Company, which he purchased. Clarence was best known for his electronics business, which started in the Beach's garage. The business was one of the first in this area of Florida to service 2-way radio equipment for government and private business. First known as Radiotelephone Service Company, the business closed in 1992 after Clarence's death. It was last known as Southern Communications and located at 708 West Fifteenth Street in Panama City.

Clarence built the first electronic score board for the Bay High football team and assisted the late Orin Whitley; band director of the Million Dollar Band with many lighting projects. Clarence was a HAM radio operator and his call letters were "WBJF" ("Big Jumping Frog"). He built and ran the sound system for his church, served on the city's electrical board and was a leader with Civil Defense.

The Beaches had two sons: John Lyman "Skip" Beach and Richard Henry "Dick" Beach. Grandchildren were: John Larry Beach, David Mitchell Beach, Iris Beach Hendley, Richard Henry Beach, Jr., Jennifer Lynn Beach Ramsey, and Margaret Elizabeth Beach Biddle. Clarence died July 23, 1991 in Tupelo, Mississippi, and Cali died March 17, 1998 in Panama City. Both are buried at Evergreen Cemetery, Panama City. Clarence and Cali were "The World's Most Beautiful Beaches" to many friends and relatives.

Submitted by: Patricia N. Beach, 315 South Bonita Avenue, Panama City, Florida 32401.

The Bennett Family

Joseph Thomas Bennett arrived in Panama City in 1916 and opened a wholesale grocery store. He sold it some years later and became an insurance agent for Hartford Insurance. He was Mayor for two years: 1917-1919.

Six Bennett children and their parents (Walter C. and Laurie Ann Bryan Bennett) eventually came to Panama City. They had grown up on a farm in Butler County, Alabama, near Georgiana. Joseph died of a stroke on New Year's Day 1944, never knowing that his son "Jokey" was killed at sea, World War II. His ship was torpedoed in the N. Atlantic. Joseph left a widow, Clifford, known as "Tippy" and a daughter Jean.

Joseph had asked his brother Fred to come to Panama City and help him operate the Wholesale Grocery business. Fred came in 1919 and found his bride, Annie Judson, whose husband Dr. Wells had died and left her owner of a Ford dealership on Harrison Avenue at the L. Fred operated it for some years and asked his brother-in-law Will Cook, who was married to Estelle, Fred's oldest sister, to move to Panama City and help him run the Ford Motor Co. The Cooks moved to Panama City in 1920.

In 1925 Joseph built a home at 302 W. 9th St. where he lived out his life.

Fred and Annie Bennett bought a one-storied house from a Moore family at 939 Beach Dr. Mrs. Bennett added a second story and the white columns so she could bring her parents, the Judsons, to live with them. Most natives know it today as the Mayor Fannin house. The Fred Bennetts had two daughters, Catherine and Helen. Catherine said Helen was born in that house. The Fred Bennetts later moved to a farm near Chipley, and Fred was appointed a judge. Annie Bennett lived to be 98 yrs. old.

Estelle Bennett Cook and husband Will Cook moved to Wewahitchka in 1926 when Gulf County was formed and opened a Ford Dealership there. He moved back to Panama City in 1930 and bought the dealership from his brother-in-law Fred. He named it Cook Motor Co. The dealership has been at several locations thru the years, and it is still in existence today. Miss Essie's only son Bill Cook, Jr. took over the dealership after his father's death. Some years later he took Charles Whitehead as a partner, and it became Cook Whitehead Motor Co.

Miss Essie Cook, as she was called by all her family even her

son, graduated from Judson College with two degrees: Music & English. Will had left school after the third grade, but he was a very successful businessman. He served on the Board of Directors of First Federal & the Commercial Bank. He was City Commissioner for Ward 2 from 1940-1946.

Miss Essie was active in the community. She belonged to the Woman's Club, Wednesday Bridge for many years. The Cooks were active in the Baptist Church, St. Andrews Bay Yacht Club, and many community activities. Miss Essie always said that her brothers paid for her college education. She had the same maid and cook for 45 years. Louise Baker came to work for the Cooks when she was 16; her brother rowed her to work from Red Fish Point in the beginning. Miss Essie was nearly blind in her later years and could no longer drive. It really upset Louise. She said to Bill "But I tells her if a car is coming" (on Cove Blvd.)

Miss Essie's two sisters, Annie & Myrtle, moved to Panama City in the early 30's. They had a wonderful sisterly relationship. They met together every day and made unanimous decisions concerning the whole Bennett family, sometimes to the chagrin of the brothers' wives.

Relf Julian Bennett, the 5th of seven children, came to Panama City in 1920. He opened the first Chevrolet dealership.

The Bennett Family

He lost it in the Depression of 1929. Relf (later called Ralph) lived with his parents at 522 Magnolia Ave. Later they lived on Jenks Ave. near the post office.

The Cooks at one time lived next door before they built the Dutch Colonial brick house at 504 Cherry St. The second loan made by the First Federal was made to Will Cook to build the Cherry St. house. Ralph Bennett courted Elmo Bullock, the only daughter of a prominent banker, Ferdernand Bullock who with J.H. Drummond opened the Bank of St. Andrews in 1907. This was the first bank in the county.

Ralph & Elmo were married 5th December 1926. They had two sons, Julian, who was a lawyer, and Don, an electrical engineer at the Navy Base. Ralph Bennett was appointed with John Scott as policemen for the City 1 Feb 1934. Ralph built the Monterey style house on Beach Dr.

The last two children moved to Panama City in 1934. Annie Bennett Moseley was married to Frank Moseley who earned a pharmacy degree from API now Auburn University. They came to P.C. to help with Annie's elderly parents. They had two daughters, Annie Laurie and Frances, who attended local schools and graduated from Bay High. They both married young men stationed at Tyndall Air Force Base and later moved to Texas. Annie Moseley lived to be 101 years old and was loved by everyone who knew her.

Myrtle Bennett, the youngest child, attended Judson College and Julliard School of Music. She was married to a Mr. Jemison and later to Ed DeWitt, a wealthy newspaper publisher from N. Jersey who was 25 years her senior. He built the first two-storied house on DeWitt Ave., named for him, and lived to be 92. Myrtle, who was an excellent bridge player, died at 96.

The Bennetts were always a close knit family, a religious family. They came to Panama City all Baptist, but the three youngest later became members of Wallace Memorial Presbyterian Church. Their grandfather had been a Baptist Minister.

Submitted by: Ann Cook Humphreys, 240 Harmon Avenue., Apt. 108, Panama City, FL 32401.

Arthur William Betcher and Florence O'Kelley Betcher

Cpl. and Mrs. Arthur William Betcher (Florence) came to Bay County in June, 1946. Mrs. Betcher's mother Martha Lou

Suggs O'Kelley and her daughter Joyce came the next month.

Cpl. Betcher was a veteran of 34 months service during WWII. He was an aircraft mechanic stationed at various bases in the South Pacific where he had experienced enemy fire. His turn came to receive Rest & Recuperation (R & R) and he was sent stateside to Washington State. He was met there by his bride-to-be Florence Fincher and her daughter Joyce. The marriage ceremony was witnessed by his brother Rudolph and his wife Frieda, and other family and friends on Aug. 5, 1945. Cpl. Betcher was quite ill from malaria he had contacted in the Philippines. Nevertheless the new family was in Seattle for V-J day.

Since the war had ended Cpl. Betcher was transferred to Maxwell AFB, AL, and shortly thereafter to Tyndall AFB, FL. This base had just reopened and the housing area was inhabited with lots of snakes and skunks. Joyce as an elementary student was bused to Parker Elem. Crossing over the old DuPont Bridge, students were entertained by porpoises at play in the bay.

Sgt. and Mrs. Betcher bought a new home in the Old Orchard section of town. Then the Korean conflict erupted and Sgt. Betcher volunteered for duty. He was sent to Korea for 90 days and served there for 18 months. He had specialized in work on the P-51 airplane that saw heavy duty in Korea. Upon his return he was stationed at Moody AFB, GA. He retired from the military after 26 and one-half years of active duty. He was working as a civilian employee on aircraft at Tyndall when he suffered a major heart attack and passed away at the Tyndall hospital on Nov. 28, 1962. He had recently received his 30 year pin for military service. He was 51 years old.

Arthur William Betcher and wife Florence O'Kelley Betcher

T/Sgt. Betcher was a first generation American born in Snohomish, WA. He joined the military as soon as he was eligible and continued in the service of his country until his death. He and his beloved wife, Florence, are buried in Greenwood Cemetery.

Sgt. and Mrs. Betcher are survived by their daughter Joyce Betcher Yount and her husband Albert Bruce Yount (Maj. USAF ret.). Their children are Jan and Perry Ashe and children, Billy and Johanna. Joylyn Betcher Rogers and her children, Joseph and Joshua Betcher Rogers. Jonilou and Phil Wilken and her children, Brandon, Dustin, Patrick and Nathan Everett. Joseph Benjamin (Jobe) and Loree Roberts and their daughter Aimee Love.

Submitted by: Joyce Betcher Yount, 2128 Squirrel Run, Lynn Haven, FL 32444

John Newton Boggs, Sr.

"Hard Times Ahead" could have been the headlines in 1930. But there was also some great news. Florida's first paper mill was under construction and would start production in March, 1931, offering one thousand jobs, paying $20 for a 40-hour week. That was at a time when $1 to $2 was the wage for a sun-up to sun-down job. In 1926 International Paper Company, the largest pulp and paper company in the world had recruited engineers, skilled tradesmen and operators from northern mills to move south, using the vast pine tree forest for pulp and paper manufacturing.

My father, John Boggs, was one of the first of this vanguard. He was known throughout the paper industry as one of the finest experts in machinery. His wife, Nettie, two boys, Harry and John, Jr., and five girls, Bessie, Carol, Della, Alice, and Ellen, left West Virginia, moving first to Bastrop, Louisiana, then Camden, Arkansas, and finally to Panama City in 1930. We traveled in a 1928 Studebaker town car and Model A Ford with a rumble seat, loaded to the hilt. Our first

night was spent at the Tennessee House, a wooden two-story building at 4th St. and Harrison Avenue. We had breakfast at McCall's Restaurant in the next block and then walked down Harrison Avenue to behold the beautiful St. Andrews Bay.

With the influx of families to construct the new mill, housing was scarce. We rented a house on Illinois Avenue in Lynn Haven. It was like heaven to us kids with fishing and swimming. I remember vividly our first 4th of July. There was a big celebration and baseball game and a parade with Civil War Union veterans who had retired in Lynn Haven. They wore their hot blue wool army suits and had long flowing white beards.

We only lived a short time in Lynn Haven, because it was a long trip, about 15 miles on a gravel, shell, and dirt road to the paper mill in Bay Harbor. We moved to downtown Panama City to a big two-story house on Fifth Street and Harrison Avenue, where presently the Marie Hotel is located. My brother and sisters and I loved to sit on the large front porch and watch the cars driving down Harrison Avenue. At that time in Panama City you could even name the driver of every car.

We moved even closer to the mill when we bought our first house in the Old Orchard on Watson Bayou, Mama's dream house. It was a great neighborhood, especially for boys. You could hunt, swim and fish. You could slip under the fence to the

John Newton Boggs, Sr., and his wife, Nettie.

old orchard and there were cows where the Prows Dairy was, which is now the Rosenwald School. Most of the time, there were friends and relatives staying temporarily with us who had come to work at the mill. My usual place to sleep was a cot in the dining room. Two of my sisters had already married two Quickel brothers, and many of the Quickel family came. My brother, John, Jr., and I secretly wondered if Papa had made a deal with them that when they moved out they had to marry one of the girls, as eventually, four Boggs sisters married four Quickel brothers.

I grew up during "Depression" days, but I don't remember my family or anyone being mentally depressed. It was the norm for people to help others in any way they could. I have fond memories of the townspeople. There were "Mom and Pop" businesses all over, on Harrison Avenue, everywhere, from the grocery stores to the hardware stores.

My fondest business person was "Lady" Lillian West, the editor of the St. Andrews Bay Newspaper. This grand lady provided my first job. On my 12th birthday, my family had chipped in $12 to go towards the purchase of a new bicycle. I was ready to work. So I went to Lady West and asked for a paper route. She asked me if I had a bicycle which you had to have, and I said, "No, but if I get the route, I have a down payment on one. I've just spoken to people at Wilson's Furniture Store, and they have one that I want to buy." So she gave me the paper route. I paid $7 down and they came down from the price of $40 to $30. I paid fifty cents a week and I owned a new bicycle and had a paper route on the west side of Harrison Avenue. The papers cost 10 cents, five cents for me, five cents for Lady West. She only gave the delivery boys 30 customers each so more boys could have jobs. She also gave us two free tickets (one for a friend) to the Ritz theater weekly.

My route was mainly businesses with a Mom and Pop attitude. Roy VanKleeck owned a Hardware store and let me charge fishing gear and shot gun shells, paying small amounts weekly. Another friendly stop was Ralph Sorrentino's Barber Shop. Mr. Sorrentino was an Italian immigrant from Sicily, and was famous for his music ability. He led the first band in Panama City. He was such a cheerful, friendly man. He offered not only haircuts, but he had showers for the fishermen from Tarpon Dock where they could take a shower, get a haircut and a shave, because a lot of these men didn't have a home here, they lived on the boats. It was a lot of fun hearing the stories told in his shop. I gave him a daily newspaper and he gave me a free haircut. Another good customer was the Coca Cola Bottling Company. I received a free coke or two every day. Paul Conrad had a gym that was another great gathering place. He taught me and many others to box and wrestle and I don't remember ever paying a fee.

In later years I would work at International Paper Company, which included traveling extensively. In 1985, I retired in Lynn Haven. I now spend as much time as possible fishing in the beautiful waters surrounding Bay County that I learned to love as a small boy.
Submitted by: Harry Boggs, 2212 Washington Avenue, Lynn Haven, FL 32444.

Paul Brent

Paul Richard Brent is a Panama City artist whose work is known worldwide. He first came to Bay County in 1969 and his paintings have deftly portrayed the many aspects of the area capturing the innate beauty on paper and canvas.

Paul Brent was born in Oklahoma City in 1946. His father, Paul Leslie Brent, and his mother, Aledo Render Brent, were both educators. From the age of five until he was thirteen, Paul Brent lived in southwest Oklahoma in the community of Alden where his father was the superintendent of the

Paul Brent Gallery

school system and his mother taught first and second grades. Interested in art at an early age, his mother encouraged him by providing art supplies and working with him on arts and craft projects. In 1959 he moved with his parents and his older sister, Carolyn, to Long Beach, California. His father had accepted a professorship at California State University at Long Beach and his mother began teaching in an elementary school in Westminster, California. After graduating from high school, he decided to major in art at California State University at Long Beach. There he studied for two years before he decided to change his major to architecture and transfer to the University of California at Berkeley. He completed his Bachelor of Architecture degree in 1968 and following graduation he joined the Air Force where, after training, he was stationed at Tyndall Air Force Base in Panama City in 1969.

He began residing at Mexico Beach and was enthralled with the beaches and the wildlife on the shores and began collecting shells and constructing them into works of art. He also began painting watercolors of the beach and the wildlife. At Tyndall he began his Air Force career as a first lieutenant filling the position of Avionics Officer with the 4750th Test Squadron. A few months after he arrived in Bay County, he met Lana Jane Lewis and in 1971 they were married (see Lana Jane Lewis-Brent). Finishing his tour of duty in 1972 in the rank of Captain, he worked for two local architects before he returned to the University of California in 1972 to complete his Master of Architecture degree. Upon graduating in 1974, Paul and Lana Jane returned to Panama City where Lana Jane resumed her work at Sunshine-Jr. Stores Inc. and Paul worked briefly at Flagala, a construction company, as a designer and draftsman. In 1975 Paul began to design homes from his home studio on

Lana Jane Lewis-Brent, Jensen, Anders and Paul Brent

South MacArthur Ave. in the Cove and pursue his interest in art. With the encouragement of a friend who was an artist, David Bush, and Mary Ola Miller, the owner of the Gallery of Art in Panama City, Paul began to sell his work at outdoor shows and in art galleries in the Southeast. In 1978, Paul and Lana Jane moved into a new home that Paul had designed in the Cove on Dewitt St. The design of the home was totally different for Bay County and was a statement of modern design that responded to the sloping lot and the water view of Lake Van Vac. The new home also incorporated a studio and office for Paul to continue his art and residential design business. Paul also designed the graphics for the Sunshine-Jr. annual reports during the years from 1971 to 1990.

By 1986, Paul's business had grown and he began marketing prints of his watercolors. In 1987, he became a licensed interior designer and member of ASID, designing interiors for local businesses and homes. Paul initially painted wildlife and progressed to beach scenes, landscapes, underwater scenes, garden subjects and paintings from his travels, including views of the Southwest, the Caribbean, lighthouses, and historical scenes of Bay County. He was accepted as a signature member into the Florida Watercolor Society, the Southeastern Watercolor Society and the National Watercolor Society. He moved his business into an office and studio at 747 Jenks Ave. and in 1990 he built an 8000 square-foot gallery, studio and distribution center at 413 W. 5th St. on the corner of Beach Drive in downtown Panama City that he designed. In 1992, his wife, Lana Jane, joined him in his business in the position of president of the company, Paul Brent, Designer.

Every year he continued to add new subjects to his repertoire. He began licensing his work in 1988, beginning with bookmarks, bed linens and insulated barware. In 1996, he illustrated the book, *J. Rooker, Manatee*, by author Jan Haley. Following its publication he was inducted into the Society of Illustrators in New York. He later had a one-man show in their galleries. Articles on Paul Brent's artwork have appeared in *American Artist, Decor, Art World News,* and *Florida* magazines. In 2002, Paul was a winner in the Best Artist category in the Best of Florida Awards sponsored by *Florida* magazine. In the same year he was nominated by LIMA, a licensing industry organization, for Best License and Overall Best License for the year 2001. He had just completed a book entitled *Wonderful Watercolors with Paul Brent* for North Light Publishing that will be released in 2003. Paul has published over 350 images in print of his work that includes his well-known watercolors as well as his recent oil paintings. He currently licenses his images to over 50 manufacturers who produce products such as wall coverings, textiles, bedding, shower curtains, apparel, paper products, gift items, housewares, decorative home accessories and furniture. He has created posters and limited edition prints for organizations such as FSU Panama City Campus, the New Orleans Aquarium, and the Sanibel Jazz Festival. He is also known for his portrayal of local scenes on calendars for Boyd Brothers, The Red Cross, and Arizona Chemical.

Paul has been active in Arts and planning organizations both locally and in the state of Florida. He served on the board and was president for four years of Bay Arts Alliance. He was on the board of the Friends of the Bay County Libraries and the Greater Downtown Association. He served as Secretary on the Florida Arts Council and was a board member of the Florida Humanities Council. He has donated his art for many local charities including the Spring Festival of the Arts that he participated in for 25 years and he painted two life-sized dolphins for the community's "Dolphin Splash" fund raising event.

Paul and Lana Jane have two sons, Jensen, who attends Miami University in Ohio, and Anders, who attends Holy Nativity Middle School in Panama City.

Submitted by: Paul Brent, 413 W. 5th St., Panama City, FL 32401. Written by: Leona Lewis.

Maria Brooks
Our Grandmother's Immigration to Bay County in the 1890s

My 29 year old Grandmother and her four year old son came directly from Ellis Island to North Bay in early 1897. She found employment as a housekeeper for William Brooks, 76 and Eliza Brooks, 74 and their 33 year old son, James Spencer Brooks. The Brooks, who were originally from North Carolina had made their way to Florida after living the war years in Georgia where their son was born. Some years before the arrival of my grandmother the Brooks had settled at Tompkins, a now extinct settlement on North Bay. If the Tompkins settlement had survived it would be near Resota Beach and on Deer Point Lake instead of the Bay.

My grandmother was born Maria Josefina Eriksdotter on a lake called Manjarvtrasket in the mountainous region of Norrbotten, Sweden where her father Erik Helm settled after retiring from the army. Four years before Maria's birth, Erik built a large house in 1864 and named it Bergbacka as the Swedish custom was for addresses to use names instead of numbers. The lakeside farmhouse and barn comprising Bergbacka remain with Erik's decedents and can still be found on Swedish tourist maps today. The

Maria Swinson Brooks with her children and their spouses

nearest town of any size is on the Baltic Sea, about 30 miles to the east called Pitea. Maria recalled that the farm was often crossed by Laplanders, an Eskimo-like, nomadic people who customarily ignored borders and property boundaries. The lake behind Maria's house was about 800 meters across. In summers when there was 24 hours of light, Maria used to row across the lake to deliver hay to the livestock on the other side. Winters she only had four hours of light in which to deliver the hay and return. She used a sled pulled by reindeer to cross the frozen water. The customary use of the suffix "dotter" in the names of unmarried females was dropped by later generations and the suffix "son" came to be used for both sexes, like it always was for males.

When Maria was old enough she took a job as a maid at a farm near Langtrask, a small crossroads some 12 miles closer to Pitea. At the age of 19 she married the farmer, 38 year old Per Svenson in 1886. The family lived near Langtrask ten years before Per's physician advised him to relocate to a warmer climate. On August 19, 1896 the couple sold their farm and set off for Florida with two sons and three bags. The four of them arrived at Ellis Island October 26, 1896. However, within weeks Per Svenson, 48 and Sven Svenson, 7 were dead. When Maria emerged from six months in quarantine, she and her youngest son Gustof continued their trek to Florida with the Americanized surname of Swinson. The boy was now called Guster.

During the months Maria housekept for the Brooks, she must have often juxtaposed her life at Tomkins to memories of her first job in that Swedish farmhouse only a dozen years past. Within six months, just shy of a year after her arrival in this country, she and the Brooks' son were married. Maria

and James Brooks soon had a son Frans and twin daughters, Alberta and Bertella as half siblings to Guster. All these children attended school in Southport and probably grew up at Tompkins.

Maria learned to speak and read English in Florida. She was a smart,

Gradie Murfee Swinson with her daughters and grandson

kind woman, loved and respected by those who knew her. Shortly upon their arrival here, she had given much of what money she had to a fellow immigrant who wanted to return to Sweden. She was a good Christian woman of the Lutheran faith who worked hard for her husband and children. She tended a garden, kept house, milked cows, raised chickens, made soap, laundered and sewed clothes, and quilted. She also sat for the babies and children for many people. She was a midwife who delivered babies in the area and cared for sick children and adults.

Some time before 1920 James Brooks obtained a permanent job at the Pensacola Navy Yard and the family moved there. Maria continued her midwifery in Pensacola until well past middle age. Guster Swinson remained at Southport after he married the new school teacher Gradie Murfee in 1919. After three years and two children, he took his family to Chipley where he started a bakery in 1923 but closed it in 1924 and he joined his people in Pensacola where he practiced carpentry the rest of his life.

Maria Swinson Brooks died in Pensacola at the age of 93 on June 17, 1960. She was survived by her sons, Guster Swinson and Frans Brooks, her two daughters, Alberta Brooks and Bertella Courtney, and eleven grandchildren, Evelyn Elsie Swinson de la Rua; Hilda Swinson Conrad; Dorothy Swinson Gilmore; Oscar Brooks; Oleita Brooks Cook; Orin Brooks; Doris Brooks Ward; Harvey Young; Frank McMichael; Maxine Williams Adams; and Joe Courtney Jr.

Submitted by: Doris Brooks Ward, #2 North 69th Avenue, Pensacola, FL 32506.

The Fateful Voyage of Frank Brown and Arline Cushing

Bay County Florida has a sunny, hot and sultry climate during the months of July, August and September. September is officially the last month of summer, yet the heat will sometimes last well into October. Frequent thunder and lightening will bring showers that give quick relief from the oppressing heat. Local people recognize the signs of approaching storms when the salt air blows over the bay waters causing white capped waves to splash onto the shores outlining the waterfront portions of the county. Such was the weather on October 8, 1894 in a small community of Cook Bayou, Florida.

Captain Torrence Franklin Brown known as "Frank" was loading his schooner the ANNIE with provisions for a fishing trip across the bay. He was excited because this was the time of year that mullet could be seen off Sand Island by the thousands. Being in the right place at the right time was crucial to commercial fishermen who

Cynthia Harriet Cushing Brown

made their living from local waters. Choosing the most opportune time for catching large quantities took experience and wisdom to make a trip worthwhile. Two other boats accompanied Captain Brown on this fishing expedition, Captain Henry Cushing master of the LIZZIE B and Captain Tom Fowler at the helm of the sloop ARROW. So much depended on this run of fish for Frank and the other members of this party.

The three captains and their crews were confident this trip would be no different than previous trips to the same area. They listened to the community warnings of the approaching storm but assured everyone that should a storm manifest itself they would take refuge at the nearest island as they had done before when the weather had become more than they could manage. The lighthouse keeper, Mr. Edward Porter, was most fervent in his advise to them not to go. His concern for their safety was evident by his repeated pleading for them to reconsider making the trip at that time. The urgency to get to the area where the fish would be most plentiful was paramount to them because this would bring enough money to make it easier for them through the winter.

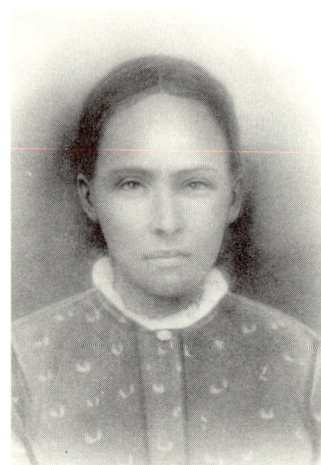
Elizabeth Cushing, Mother of the four Cushing brothers

Red sun in the morning, sailors take warning. The men knew this truism but believed they could beat the odds of a storm coming. Family and friends watched as the crews boarded their vessels that fateful morning and gazed wistfully after their loved ones as the boats glided from their sight. Voices were heard calling out well wishes for a bountiful catch and silent prayers were lifted for a safe return home. The well wishes and the silent prayers were futile because that was not to be the end results for the sixteen men of East Bay.

They sailed all day and reached their destination of Sand Island late in the afternoon of October 8, 1894. They quickly set up camp and prepared supper, all the while taking notice of the increasing wind and the waves as they became higher and much more forceful than when they left home several hours earlier. All too soon, trees were bowing groundward, loose objects were moving across the island and nothing could restrain them. The tents, cooking utensils and other objects seemed to take on a life of their own as the wind and rain gathered momentum. By this time the men could barely stand upright against such torturous hammering of the elements and they tied themselves to trees or any thing that seemed stable enough to hold against the tugging of the wind. The raging lasted for hours. The men called out encouragement to each other until no sounds could be heard over the howling, screeching devils in the storm. One by one the sixteen men of East Bay were torn from the frail security of the twisted ropes and swept to sea. The lighthouse attendant kept vigil throughout the night. He watched helplessly as the men struggled to stay above the rising waters, then, he could see nothing more than the blinding rain that blanketed the bay. Later, Mr. Porter related to

Lillie Scott daughter of Frank Brown

the families what he witnessed through his spyglass of the gallant battle their fishermen fought against the vicious elements.

The next morning Mr. Porter stared with sorrow at the floating debris and empty shores where a fishing camp had been the afternoon before. The bay was so very quiet. For days and weeks after the storm, bits and pieces of bodies were found washed upon shores in many different places, most could not be identified. Records show that only one body was recovered, that of Frank Brown and he was buried somewhere on Sand Island. The men lost their struggle against the storm, but their valiant efforts against odds too great for them will never be forgotten. They fought a battle they could not win.

Mr. P. G. Harding wrote a letter to Mr. W. H. Parker in Parker, Florida informing Mr. Parker that the community of Apalachicola, Florida had taken contributions of sixteen black dresses and a monetary gift of $100 to assist the widows with the loss of their loved ones. To the knowledge of anyone living today the dresses nor the financial gift ever reached the sixteen families. Tragically the letter was lost behind a desk in the Parker Post Office and was found by one of Frank's great nephews approximately 71 years later. Some of the descendants of the sixteen lost men still live in this area today and the author of this story is one of them.

Following are the names of the lost men of East Bay: Frank Brown, Henry Cushing, Arling Cushing, Martin Cushing, Frank Cushing, Tom Fowler, Joe Fowler, Dr. Jim Nesbitt, William Linton, Green York, Nathan Ward, George Chatterson, John Stanley, Mr. Lightfoot, Mr. Smith, and Mr. Ellerbee.

Submitted By: Marjorie Arnold, 2304 Foxworth Drive, Panama City, FL 32405-1938.

Henry Clay Brown Family

Christine Walker was born in Donalsonville GA to A. D. Walker and Johnnie Caldwell Walker. She is the oldest of two daughters. Her younger sister is Genevieve Walker Casey, married to Jack Casey and living in Thomasville, GA.

Henry Brown was born in Birmingham, AL to Charles Brown and Annie O'Neill Brown, the seventh child of eight. He had one older brother; five older sisters and one younger. Two sisters are still living - Anna Neil Brown Lane, Birmingham, AL and Carolyn Brown Bailes, Talledega, AL.

Henry Brown at Panama City Beach, 1940

Mother always claimed Thomasville, GA as her home as they moved there from Colquitt when she was 10. Her father was a druggist and had stores in Colquitt, Georgia before his drug store in Thomasville. After graduation from High School she worked as secretary for the Georgia/Florida Baseball League of which her father was the President for several years. Mother got her love of baseball from her parents at an early age and to this day is a baseball fan.

In 1940 Daddy was working in GA and AL for the Southern Liquid Gas Company located in Dothan AL. Mother and Daddy met November 11, 1940 when Daddy went to hook up a gas hot dog cooker at the Thomas County Fair. Mother had just recently had thyroid surgery and was not allowed to do much that was physically exerting. That's why she was chosen to meet the gas man. It seems that for several weeks or months Francis Tuck, a friend of Mother's kept trying to fix her up. Mother kept saying she wasn't interested and it never happened. Ironically, the man her friend wanted to fix her up with was Daddy. Apparently Daddy had been going by the drug store where he knew

Mother worked (for the Georgia/Florida Baseball League) trying to see her. Of course, Mother was not working then because she had just had the surgery. When Mother introduced herself to Daddy at the Fair Grounds, he said "I've been trying to meet you for weeks." They had a whirlwind romance and married December 14, 1940 in Thomasville, GA. Mother and Daddy were married 54 years at his death in 1994.

Christine Brown at Panama City Beach 1940

Shortly after they married Mother and Daddy moved to Statesboro, GA where David was born in October 1941. (They moved briefly back to Thomasville after David was born but relocated to Panama City in 1943 and into a home on Linda Avenue living there until 1971.) In November of 1943 Becky, their only daughter, was born. Their third child, Richard was born in Panama City in 1949. Daddy went to work for West Florida Gas after Southern Liquid Gas Co and then for Liberty National Life Insurance Co. In the early 1950's Mother worked part time at Lillian Kilpatrick's and Schneider's, local ladies apparel shops and went to work at Jinks Junior High School as bookkeeper in the late 1950s. She worked there until her retirement in June of 1983. Johnnie Walker, mother of Christine, lived with us most of the time and worked at Walgreen's Drug Store. With Mother, Daddy and Mema we three children always had a parent figure around the home.

David lives and works as a computer consultant in San Diego CA. His son, Kevin, is in Phoenix AZ. Daughter Becky Saunders and her husband Robert live in Panama City and she has worked at the Bay County Public Library for over 35 years. Her son, Steve Wallace lives in Panama City and works with the Visual Information Department at Tyndall. Richard lives in Springfield NJ and works for Monarch Housing in Montclair NJ. He and his wife Jan have two sons Jonathan and Michael.

Submitted by: Rebecca B. Saunders, 2515 Frankford Avenue, Panama City, FL 32405.

The Browns of Econfina Settlement

On the banks of Econfina Creek in Bay County, Florida, I grew up hunting, fishing, swimming and enjoying life to the fullest. There was never concern about the things to come in later years such as the Great Depression or the United States being in World War II. However now that they have come and gone, my childhood brings back many sweet memories.

James Washington Brown

I was young and my father was a farmer as most people were back then. He had cattle, hogs and even some sheep. He cultivated a hundred acres with a pair of mules. Only part of the land could be planted because it was too much work for one man. In those days if someone had these things, they had the essentials for sustaining a good living.

I have seen the clear waters of Econfina Creek turn dark in color with mullet as they came up the creek from North Bay. Today the Deer Point Dam blocks all the salt water, and collects the drinking water for Bay and other counties. Our farm had a creek that ran through it as it still does into Econfina on the east side. The Gainer Springs which today is called Emerald Springs was on the west side. The Florida Water Management headquarters is built on the place where the mules were penned and the plows were stored. I remember the big watermelons that grew nearby.

James Monroe Brown and Mattie Permelia Brown

Over the years I have seen many changes in Bay County. To me most of them have been good. Bay County has grown in population and world wide recognition. It has, without any doubt, the world's most beautiful beaches.

To continue my story, I will write a little about some of the research I have done over the years concerning my family, the Browns of Econfina Settlement. James Monroe Brown was my father. My mother was Martha, "Mattie", Russ Brown. I will write more about them later. The generations that follow is the genealogy of my family in brief from Virginia to Florida. Maybe this will help someone in their research.

Benjamin Brown was born in the year of 1710 in Albemarle County, Virginia. He married Sarah Dabney of Virginia. She could have been his second wife. I don't know for sure. Ben and Sarah are the linkage to my blood line. From Benjamin I will go to the second generation who were headed to Florida and later settled in Bay County.

Bartlett Brown was born in 1731 in Albemarle County, Virginia. He married Kathrine Holcomb. Kathrine Holcomb Brown was born in Louisa County, Virginia. Bartlett and Kathrine were married in 1754

James Brown, Sr., son of Bartlett and Kathrine Holcomb Brown, birth date is unknown. He died in Jasper County, Georgia in 1821. James married Martha. However their marriage date is also unknown. The last will and testament of James, Sr. was witnessed by his son James and a daughter named Martha who was named after her mother. I have a copy of the paper from Jasper County, Georgia.

James Brown, Jr. was my great great grandfather. He made it to Florida. He settled in Washington County a long time before Bay County became a county. James Brown was born in the year of 1800. He married Anna Gainer probably in 1828. Their oldest daughter was born in 1829 and her name was Cynthia. Sarah was the next child born. She was born in 1830. Sarah married William A. Gainer. William Gainer was of the well-known Gainer family of Econfina Creek. Grandpa came to the area with Andrew Jackson around the year 1818. He worked in the survey crew with William Gainer, Sr. James went back to Chester District, South Carolina where Cynthia and Sarah were born.

Jack Mitchell and Florida Virginia Mitchell Brown

James Brown became a prominent figure in Washington County, Florida. He served in the Florida House of

Representatives representing Washington County in 1850, 1854, and 1855. He was Justice of the Peace in 1851. While in the legislature, he served on the Committee of Schools and Colleges. He and Anna died three days apart in 1858. They are buried in the William Gainer Cemetery on Econfina Creek.

Benjamin Barlett Brown, the third child was born in Alabama. My great grandfather was born May 22, 1833, and died August 11, 1913, in Bay County, Florida. He married Louise Tabor in 1854 in Washington County. Louise was the daughter of Washington Tabor and Margaret Brown. She died in 1870 and Benjamin married Margaret Tabor, a sister of Louise in 1870. B. B. Brown joined Co. K, 6th Florida Infantry, Confederate States of America in 1861. In 1862 he became a private in the 2nd battalion Florida Partisan Rangers. This battalion became Co. E, 11th Florida Infantry and transferred to the Northern Virginia Army in Petersburg, Virginia. After the war he served on the school board of Washington County in 1873. He was trustee of Econfina School and was tax assessor from 1889 to 1891. He taught school in 1873 for $18.00 per month. On March 2, 1877, he was elected county commissioner. B. B. Brown was buried in the Millville Cemetery. He was the first Mason to be buried in Bay County. He rests with Margaret his second wife in the W. E. Spiva plot. Mollie was their daughter.

James Washington Brown (Jimmy) was born November 1, 1855. He was my grandpa. My grandma was Florida Virginia Mitchell, daughter of David Mitchell and Sarah Barfield. She was born September 11, 1859 in Washington County. They were married March 12, 1882. They are buried in the Youngstown Cemetery in Bay County. I remember them with love.

As I mentioned earlier, James Monroe Brown was my father. He married my mother in Bay County in 1915. My mother was Martha Permelia Russ. Her father was Thomas Jefferson Russ and her mother was Mary Permelia Walcomb. They were both of the Holmes Valley area of Washington County. Daddy and Mama lived all their married life in Bay County. I was the eighth of nine children.

I have the name James. I am the fifth James Brown in my family in Bay County. I married Joyce Constance Padova. We have three sons, five grandchildren and one great-grandchild. It seems that the Browns of Econfina have a home in the county of Bay in the great state of Florida.

Submitted by: James R. Brown, 7017 Highway 388 East, Youngstown, FL 32466.

The Isaac Byrd Family

The Isaac Byrd family planted its roots in Panama City in September 1930. At that time Mr. W.O. Byrd, wife Olivia Reid Byrd, and their 12 year old son Isaac Wyatt Byrd, moved from Alabama to Panama City to open a Nehi soft drink bottling plant. The Byrd and Son plant was in a 40 x 60 foot building at 328 West Beach Drive. It operated with one truck and two employees.

Isaac Wyatt Byrd, Sr. March 25, 1918—June 23, 1987

Isaac attended schools in Bay County from eighth grade until graduating from Bay High School in 1936. He graduated from South Georgia College and then attended University of Florida until at age 20 his college career was cut short when his father became too ill to manage the business.

By 1958 the business had grown until there were six buildings covering over a city block, employing 55 people and having a fleet of 28 trucks, and three transports. The company bottled Pepsi-Cola as well as Suncrest Orange, Suncrest Strawberry, 7up, and Nugrape.

By 1986 due to declining health, Isaac sold Byrd and Son Beverages Inc. to Buffalo Rock which was then located on Sherman Avenue. The business had grown to include 21 routes and multiple support vehicles, 71 employees, and an acre size building on ten acres of property.

In 1939 Isaac married Elizabeth Wing. They had five children. They are Beth Byrd McKeithen, Pam Byrd Weathersby, Olivia Byrd Cooley, Betsy Byrd Brooks, and Isaac Wyatt Byrd, Jr. All the children live in Bay County except Wyatt. There are 13 grandchildren and six great grandchildren many of whom live in Bay County.

Isaac Byrd served in the U.S. Marine Corps during World War II. In addition to his bottling business, he also served on the board of directors for the Commercial Bank of Panama City, Cpmmercial Bank of Lynn Haven, and Springfield Commercial Bank.

He was very involved in civic activities in numerous organizations. Some of those included member and president of Panama City Bay County Chamber of Commerce, chairman of Panama City Bay County Committee of 100, board member of Bay County Library Association, Salvation Army, Junior Museum, Bay Medical Center Advisory Board, and Bay County Chapter of American Red Cross. He served as chairman of the Easter Seal Campaign, Heart Fund Drive, and American Cancer Society Fund Drive. He was a member and Commodore of St. Andrews Bay Yacht Club, member of BPOE, American Legion, and Rotary Club where he received the Paul Harris Fellowship Award.

His involvement in the political activities of Bay County were many in number. He served as a Bay County Commissioner from 1962 until his death in 1987 and during that time as chairman eight different times. Some of his achievements during his time as a commissioner were the Deer Point Lake Dam, the county's purchase of U.S. 231 right-of-way, and good rates of interest on bond issues. The one he was most proud of was the purchase of land for a local Florida State University campus. His desire was "for the children of Bay County to be able to get a four-year degree without ever leaving home". As a result of his many accomplishments in 1977 he received the "Good Government" award given by the Panama City Jaycees. He was chairman of Bay County Citizens Tax Council, member of Bay County Jury Commission, Panama City Port Authority, Pilot Commissioner for the Port of Panama City, and Bay County Selective Service Board.

Isaac was a long time member of First Baptist Church of Panama City having served on its building and finance committees. He was on the President's Council of Baptist Bible Institute in Graceville, Florida.

In 1986 Isaac founded the Byrd Family Foundation which has made many contributions to various organizations in Bay County. The foundation which is managed by his daughters has continued the philanthropic spirit begun by their dad in giving back to the community.

During his many years of service in Bay County, Isaac received numerous honors and awards. He was president of Florida Pepsi-Cola Bottlers Association and a board member of Florida Bottlers Association for over 25 years. He is listed in "Who's Who in American Business" and in "Outstanding Personalities of the South". In 1962 he was awarded Boss of the Year by the Panama City Jaycees and in 1983 received the Lauren Merriam Award.

Even though Isaac was successful in business, political, and civic areas, he is best known for being an honorable man with a keen sense of humor who was always fair and cared for others. Even though he had many physical problems he rarely allowed them to stand in his way and successfully maintained an active civic and political life until his death at age 69 in 1987. When asked what he would like to be remembered for he was quoted as saying, "Bay County was a better place because Isaac Byrd had been through it." He would be pleased to know that statement remains true.

Submitted by: Byrd Family Foundation, 3310 S. Harbour Cir, Panama City, FL 32405.

Clifford Hilliard Cain
(December 31, 1919 -June 25, 1998)

I was born in a log cabin at Philips Inlet. There were no doctors. I was delivered by a colored mid-wife. My brothers and sisters went coon hunting. My father was Charles Hilliard Cain born October 31, 1877 and died October 13, 1962. My mother was Leila Charlotte Holly Cain born August 18, 1890 and died December 31, 1974. My sisters were: Vera Edna Cain born September 4, 1908 and died September 22, 1974, Amelia Ada Cain born December 9, 1909 and died December 29, 1992. One infant died at birth.

My brothers were: Guy Eugene Cain born November 3, 1912 and died November 3, 1962, Allen Percy Cain born November 24, 1914 and died April 27, 1948, William Daniel Cain born September 17, 1925 and died June 29, 1972.

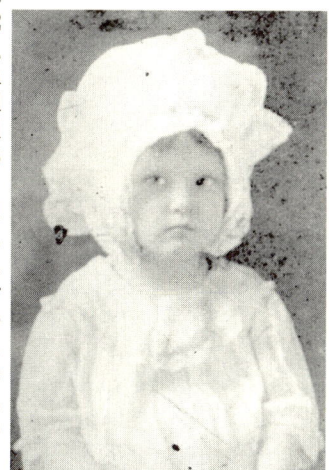

C.H. Cain approx. 2 years old 1921

We owned our home with 41 acres of land. We had cows, hogs, chickens, horses, wagons, and boats, seines and nets for fishing. We had a garden. No motor used ores and paddles. Wood stoves, stick and dirt fire place, one heater, lamps, lanterns, flamers and torches for lights.

My dad fished with a seine (commercial) and turpentined. He hunted deer, turkey, hogs, cows, squirrels, birds, ducks and geese. We had cows for milk and butter. People came down on mules and covered wagons from Alabama with syrup, meal, peanuts, from farms to trade for fish, no ice. Everything had to be salted and put in bowls or kegs or smoked.

My folks rented a house in Point Washington (the old Saltsman House from the Wesleys) so my brothers and sisters could go to grammar and high school. My father would walk and ride horses back and forth from Point Washington to Philips Inlet for one school year. I wasn't in school at that time, but we got our little school built and I went to school at Philips Inlet. Twenty-one families lived at Philips Inlet in the teens and early 1920s and we had three hotels.

My first trip to West Bay on wagon, we spent the night at Bruce Vickes house. Put the horse in the lot. The next morning got on a small boat that had a cab. We motored over to Southport, dropped the mail off and picked up mail, then motored over to St Andrews, dropped the mail off and visited my Aunt and Uncle Will Miller. Had my first ice cream. It was in a cone. We went back home the same way, by motor boat to West Bay. Then took the wagon to Philips Inlet. It was about a week's trip counting visiting.

After school was out, we raked around all the pine trees to keep fire away. We also dipped gum for the turpentine. I was too small to work at that. One morning we went out in the woods, built a big fire and they left me by the fire. While my family, all but Amelia, went to raking around them trees. I had an overcoat on and caught it a fire. I started screaming and running, but I ran towards my father. He ran out from under his hat, but he caught me, put out the fire with his hands and sand. He loaded me in that T Model Ford, carried me home, hollered to my sister Amelia to beat up some whites of eggs to put on my leg where it was burned. That did the job.

One time I got snake bit by a moccasin. I followed my brother Allen and my cousin Afred Holley down to a pond.

C.H. Cain with wife Essie and her sisters about 1945

They hid from me. I was looking for them around the pond, that snake bit me. I let out a few yells and crying. They killed the snake and carried me to the house. My leg and foot swelled up and hurt. I was real sick. My mother sit up all nite putting (poultices) and doctoring me. After about one week, I was well. We made our own medicines. No doctors in them days.

I had very few store bought clothes. One time a ship wrecked out in the gulf and washed a shore at Philips Inlet. We then had lots of cloth and all kinds of goodies. I was real lucky that my folks was rich compared to some people in them days. Very few people owned their own home in those days. When the depression came it was rough times. When I was in the second grade, the school closed down at Philips Inlet. My folks got a loan of a house in West Bay up by the Hutchinson's. We would go back to the Inlet on weekends. My Dad would come and go back and forth for four months (winter). While we went to school, he fished, hunted, trapped for four months.

We got another house in West Bay for us to live in and go to school for four months. We lived one block from the school close to the Birtchons. I was in the 3rd grade, but didn't pass. I was too short to learn much but I had lots of fun being around people to play with. My family bought a new Model T Ford car.

The Philips Inlet hotel burned in '26. My folks decided to replace it on our property. They named it Lake View Inn.

(C. H. Cain grew up at Philips Inlet. He was a fisherman and then a cook in the Army during WWII. He came back home and became a Bricklayer and built a lot of the old beach houses and motels. Later he and his wife ran a Fish Camp at Philips Inlet and Cain Road is name after him at the Inlet. He married Essie Montgomery in 1942 and had two sons, Michael and Charles, who both live in Texas now. His oldest grandson Jeffrey Cain lives in Lynn Haven with his wife Carrie and their son Kenan, who is the 6th generation of Cains in Bay County.)

Submitted by: Jo Ann Cain, 1611 Louisana Ave, Lynn Haven, FL 32444. Written by: C. H. Cain.

Malcom Carroll and Lillie Belle Eason Cain

Unfortunately, there isn't much I can tell you about my ancestry, but this much I know...My mother constantly told me, and this was confirmed by my Aunt Agnes that Grandpa Cain's ancestry was from the Isle of Man off the west coast of England. How ironic that this island features one of the greatest motorcycle races on the planet. He was born in Tarheel, N.C., migrated to Southern Florida to open a saw mill near Mulberry, Florida, in Polk County. His full name was Malcolm Carroll Cain. My mother told me that the Vikings came into the Isle of Man a thousand years ago, and that would account for my blue eyes and fair skin.

Lillie Belle Eason Cain

Apparently grandpa was quite successful, since he started to acquire land in Sarasota, eventually opening a hotel there. My mother became Miss Sarasota when she was about 18; I saw her picture in a swimsuit posing next to a single engine plane as if to start the prop. I wish I had that photo, but it got lost somewhere in the shuffle. Norma, my sister, also remembers that photo.

Somewhere along the line, Grandpa Cain moved to Panama City. This was probably after all the kids were born. He was married to Lillie Belle Eason from Surrency, Georgia, in Appling County. The only great aunt I can remember was Aunt Maggie, although I vaguely recall mention of an Aunt Sula (some names, eh!). Grandma's kids (my aunts and uncles) were, let's count "em: Ethel, Mazie, Vera, Agnes, Myrtle, Ruth, Oma and Uncle Sam (no joke).
Submitted by: Mike Hamlin, 251 SE 46th Street Cape Coral, FL 33904.

James Leamon Carter and Doris Mildred Dyson Carter

James Leamon Carter and Doris Mildred Dyson Carter were born in Holmes County, Florida. Their childhood days were spent on farms. As a young teen, James discovered he liked making things out of wood much more than he liked farming.

James and Mildred married in 1933 and moved to De Funiak Springs, Florida where James was hired by the local high school to teach shop and woodworking several nights a week. He worked at a local cabinet shop during the day, spent weekends making chests of drawers and cedar chests.

Eglin Air Force was nearby and James was hired to do cabinetwork. The Commanding Officer of Tyndall Air Force Base wrote James a letter in the early spring of 1942 requesting that he move to Panama City, as his services were needed at Tyndall AFB. In March of 1942, James and family moved to the Parker community.

During the war years (1941-1946) Mildred spent her time as a busy wife, homemaker and mother. She had one school age son and two toddlers. In 1946, money was tight and one of the officer's wives admired a dress that Mildred had sewn for herself. When asked if she would make a few dresses one of the finest self-taught seamstresses began her career. Mildred had made her first dress when she was a teenager. From 1946 through 2003, both men and women came to Mildred for sewing and repairs from all over Bay County and the surrounding areas. She had eye problems in later life, cataracts; lens implants and finally eye surgery for a tumor. Mildred quit sewing for others and *hung up her needle* after 57 years.

James worked at the military base for several years and in 1948 decided he wanted to have his own business. He had remodeled a small house he purchased when he first came to Parker. Later he bought land behind the Parker Baptist Church and built a three-bedroom home and a shop. He made custom furniture and many counter fixtures for commercial stores in Panama City. As his business flourished, James thought more and more on the idea of building pleasure boats. He hired several men from the community to work for him and soon Carter-Craft Boats was a thriving business. The Carter family and friends spent many summer afternoons on the water in the 1950's testing boats and water skiing.

In 1952 James built another home in the Callaway area that the family quickly outgrew. He built a large home on the other end of his acreage that was the third of seven homes he built in Bay County. When his mother became ill, he brought her to live with his family. In hopes of her recovering, he built a small house just below his home that would be hers.

The Carter's youngest child Wayne was still at home and in high school but the other three were grown. Their daughter Phyllis Jean had married and made them grandparents in 1958. Their oldest son, James Earl was making a career in the Navy, was married with two children. Robert Edward, their middle son, was also serving in the Navy at that time.

James purchased land between Parker and Callaway and built another home. After a year or so, he wanted a shop where he would build small fishing boats. He purchased property about a block away from his house and built a tri-level house and another shop.

After another heart attack, James sold his business and home and moved to a smaller home in the Southport area of Panama City. Before long he was feeling better, thanks to a new pace maker and he built a shop in the side yard. He was soon making cabinets and custom furniture and Grandfather clocks. Soon another business was underway and his clocks were winning prizes and selling faster than he could make them. He built another new home on the property in front of the shop. This would be the seventh house he had built in Bay County since coming to town in 1942. James had health problems again so he sold the business and home and moved across the bay to Lynn Haven in a brick home on a lake.

Mildred and James enjoyed gardening and he liked fishing in his backyard while he recovered his health. However, he soon felt the need for a "hobby shop" and he built a small shop in the backyard. He kept himself busy for several years making clocks, and a few custom pieces of furniture. He had cataracts removed and one lens implant but the glare off the lake started to bother him. Thus, he put the house up for sale and moved three blocks over near the country club in 1992.

James and Mildred Carter had four children, nine grandchildren and nine great-grandchildren as of July 2003 when their daughter Phyllis Jean Carter Sommers wrote this. James Carter was active in the community as an employer and in the church as a teacher of the adult men's class. Mildred Carter has been a professional seamstress, a Sunday school teacher of teenage girls, and was active in the Parker/Callaway communities. James Leamon Carter died on 4-5-1995 and is buried in the Parker Cemetery across from the old Carter-Craft Boat site.
Submitted by: Phyllis Sommers, 1826 Wales Dr., Tallahassee, FL 32303.

John Henry Carter

John Henry Carter is a fourth, native born, generation Floridian. His ancestors came from Colonial Virginia, Massachusetts and South Carolina. Both John Allen Syfrett who settled in Jackson County and James Hovey who received land in St. Andrews, arrived prior to 1840. Some other ancestors, Carter, Sellers, Godwin, Jones, Tiller, Edwards, Lisenby, Gilbert and Bradford arrived shortly after Florida statehood in 1845. Later, William B. (Preacher Bill) Tiller, from a staunchly Methodist family even before the American Revolution, selected

Thomas Jones married Mary (parents William and Jane Lisenby Tiller)

the wood for and became an early minister of the Moss Hill Methodist Church.

While some of these pioneers purchased government lands others were awarded land for their military service. William A. Gilbert served both in the War of 1812, in the North Carolina Militia and the Florida Indian War as a member of the 1837 West Florida Militia. James Hovey also participated in the Florida Indian War, as a member of the Alabama Militia, and was awarded land in St. Andrews.

Also answering their nation's call to the War of 1812, often referred to as the second American Revolution, was Anthony Terry Carter, Wiley Godwin and Solomon Jones. Anthony was born in Halifax County, Virginia, son of Hartwell and Sally Colquitt Carter and fought with the Virginia Militia. Anthony and Sarah Durden Carter are buried in the

Barfield Cemetery in Washington County. Wiley Godwin was a member of the Alabama Militia and Solomon Jones served with the Georgia Militia. Solomon's son, William B. Jones and Wiley's daughter, Leah, were married in Washington County. William was elected State Senator and served 1859-1863. In 1874 he became the first County Judge of Washington County. Serving in the C. S. A. Captain Jones was captured and imprisoned in Elmira, New York.

The Coroner of Washington County from 1865 to 1867 was Isaiah Bradford, a former member of the Massachusetts Militia, who married Elizabeth Wood.

Henry Sellers, from North Carolina, purchased land and was a cooper in Washington County.

John H. Carter

John Allen Syfrett, of South Carolina, traveled South with his wife Margaret C. Edwards, her parents, brothers and sisters as well as their spouses. All purchased land, beginning in 1836, in the Greenwood area of Jackson County. The home built there by John A. Syfrett is presently occupied and has a historical marker placed in the 1970s.

The first child of Neroy and Olga Syfrett Carter, John attended the St. Andrews Grammar school, Panama Grammar and Bay Hi. During these years he was active in the Boy Scouts, The Order of DeMolay and the First Methodist Church youth programs and choir.

After two years at Florida State University, although having received a deferment from the Army Reserve Officers Training Corps, John volunteered to be drafted, was sent to Fort Jackson, SC for basic training under the 101st Airborne Infantry Division and later assigned to the Occupation Forces of Germany.

In 1956 John returned to FSU and his fraternity, Phi Kappa Tau, where he was introduced to his room mate's girlfriend, Irene Rodriguez. She and John were married on June 15, 1958, following their graduations, at the Palma Ceia Methodist Church in Tampa, Florida.

John was selected by the U. S. Internal Revenue Service, before graduation and was stationed in West Palm Beach. It was here he became a father to their son, John H. Carter, II, was made a 32 Degree Scottish Rite Mason and a member of Mahi Shrine Temple, Miami.

In 1962 John was promoted to the Internal Revenue Service Center in Chamblee, Georgia as a supervisory Tax Examiner and supervised parts of the first computerization of tax returns in U. S. history.

A daughter, Melissa Ann, was born in Atlanta a few months before John was promoted to the headquarters staff of the Internal Revenue Service in Washington, D. C.

While at headquarters John was invited, by the Republic of Turkey, to assist their government as an advisor in tax administration. He was temporarily transferred to the U. S. State Department and became a member of the diplomatic corps. In addition to Turkey, where he and his family lived over two years, he was posted to Kingston, Jamaica and San Salvador, El Salvador.

Following the tour in Turkey he was invited to join the Executive Office Of The President of The United States and remained there until the U. S. Department of Energy began to form. In 1993 John retired from the U. S. Government as Director, Reference and Information Management with Distinguished Career Status.

While working in Washington John was active as an advisor to the Manassas, Virginia DeMolay Chapter, where he was awarded the Active Legion of Honor, served his church as a member of the vestry and treasurer, for many years, as

well as usher and Sunday School Teacher. During this time he was raised to the 32nd degree in York Rite Masonry and became the father of their son, Frank Thomas.

Upon retirement he, Irene and Tom returned home to Panama City. Retirement has been filled with civic activities and the birth of grand son John Lewis Charles and grand daughter Acalia Justine.

Civic activities consist of Sons of the American Revolution of which he has served as Panama City Chapter President, State of Florida President and National Society Trustee: The Society of the War of 1812 of which he is State Treasurer: Order of Founders and Patriots, the Phi Kappa Tau Fraternity and the Bay County Democratic Party, Chairman. Membership in some other Organizations are: St. Andrews Episcopal Church, Florida State University Alumni Association, Florida Pioneer Descendants, Panama City Music Association, member board of directors, The Oakland Terrace Men's Club of which he has twice been president, St. Andrews Bay Yacht Club and Visiting Resource to Wilmer Hall (Children's home) in Mobile, Alabama.

John was selected to the initial board of the Bay County School Board Sales Tax Oversight Committee and is a member of the Bay County Board of Supervisors Committee for Affordable Housing.

Submitted by: Irene R. and John H. Carter, 738 Brandeis Avenue, Panama City, Florida 32405.

Mr. and Mrs. John R. Cheshire

John and Julie Cheshire settled here in the period 1968-1970 arriving from a farm in Unionville, PA where they owned horses as an avocation. Both were avid foxhunters and John was a steeple chase rider and polo player. John is originally from Charleston, SC and Julie from Washington, DC. Her father was a WWI flyer and commanding general of the 10th Air Force in WWII.

John and Julie Cheshire

John left the Dupont Company in 1968 where he was a manager of new business development to start a shrimp farm called Marifarms, Inc. in Panama City, the first commercial shrimp farm in the world. Technicians were imported from Japan and with the help of numerous local people, permits were obtained from the State of Florida to grow shrimp around the bay. It is estimated in today's money that about $200 million was invested in the USA on shrimp farming of which Marifarms, Inc. expended $40 million. None of this money ever profited any USA investor directly. However, the industry worldwide has been an enormous success growing from Marifarm's total production of 4 million lbs. to today's 2.2 billion lbs. per year, principally in Ecuador, Thailand and other Asian countries. Adverse weather does not permit commercial shrimp farming in the USA.

John and Julie have moved to Panama City permanently and have been involved in numerous school, civic, and cultural activities. Their son, John, Jr., lives in New York City and daughter Mary (Molly) Patterson Cheshire lives in Unionville, PA. Both are involved in producing documentary films and Johnny was co-named an Emmy winner for "Mystery of the Sphinx" sponsored by NBC.

Submitted by: John Cheshire, 463 Sudduth Ave., Panama City, FL 32401.

Isaac Felix Clark
Early residents of Bay County:
{Pioneer families}

Isaac Felix Clark (1880-1965), from Abingdon, Virginia,

with his bride Cora Belle Grady (1885-1974) of Laurel, Mississippi, came to the town of Millville in the late 1800's. As a professional boiler maker, he helped to build the first boiler of the local paper mill. Felix enlarged a small three room house, on Main Street, into a very comfortable home for his family, a son and two daughters. Later, as a Building Contractor, performing electrical, plumbing and carpentry work, his company worked on many of the once "military homes" in The Cove, and all around Bay County. He constructed and owned the brick building in Millville, which housed the Millville branch of the U.S. Post office and a beauty shop. Felix and Cora's daughters were Martha Ruthmae Clark (1906-1993) and Irene Elizabeth (Bessie) Clark (1908-1999). Their son died very young. In December of 1926, Ruth married Charlie Eugene Powell (1903-1967), originally from Cottondale, whose family moved to Panama City in early 1900s. Bessie married Roy D. Laird (1906 1977), also from a pioneer family. Their daughter is Phyllis (12-15-31).

Chas. E. Powell and his brother J.W. Powell (1883-1950) were co-owners of Powell & Co. Men's Wear, located in the Sherman Arcade Building on Harrison Avenue. Roy Laird's Credit Bureau was located on the second floor of the Arcade. In the 1950's, Powell's Boys Shop, managed by Ruth Powell, was added to Powell & Company. After the deaths of his father, J.W., and his Uncle Charlie (Chas. E), Wesley Powell (10-26-28), with his mother Bettie Lee Waring Powell (1908-2003) and sisters Frances (3-10-32), and Jane (9-27-39), bought and operated Powell & Company Men's Wear Store. Later, the store was moved to a location North on Harrison Avenue. From 1939 and through the war years Charlie Powell was Bay County's U.S. Postmaster, appointed by President Franklin D. Roosevelt, and served as a Trustee with the Bay County School System.

During those World War II years, as Tyndall Field and the Navy Base grew, there was a serious housing shortage in this area. Citizens were asked to open their homes to military couples, and shipyard officials. Patriotic as they were, Ruth and Charlie shared their home with several fascinating people, who became lifelong friends. Their children Coreta (2-1-30) Margie (12-29-31) Charla (7-7-35) Martha (4-17-37) and E.I. "Butch" (3-17-44) Powell have crisp and wonderful memories of that time. They enjoyed vocal and instrumental musicians living in their home. They learned about other religious beliefs, big city life, and how to complete a jigsaw puzzle without picking up and trying out every piece numerous times.

They remember family picnics on the long stretches of clean, white beaches which, at that time, were open, and easily accessible to the public. They remember Sunday school, Training Union, and Church services at Immanuel Baptist Church, the special friendship and mentoring ministry of Rev. Adolph Bedsole and his wife "Miss Lilly". They remember attending Panama Grammar, Cove Elementary, and Bay High Schools at a time when it was safe to walk home to lunch each day. Those were the times when our doors were seldom locked and we were still enjoying peace and freedom at home, perhaps without even realizing the value of that freedom.

Submitted by: Coreta Powell Pratt, 110 Kentucky Ave., Lynn Haven, Fl. 32444; e-mail corab4@juno.com.

Ernest & Gladys Cooley Family

Ernest was born 15 July 1907, Graceville, Jackson County, Florida, the sixth of twelve children of John Wesley and Mattie Osia Bruner Cooley, Jackson County, Florida.

Gladys was born 10 March 1908, Graceville, Jackson County, Florida, the seventh of fifteen children of Franklin Levy and Julia Hays Fowler, Jackson County, Florida.

Ernest and Gladys were married 31 July 1927, Washington County, Florida. They were sharecroppers in Jackson, Holmes and Bay Counties before moving to the Tom Cane Farm, Fountain, Bay County Florida in 1934, along with their children James, John, Francis and Imogene.

130

Ernest and Gladys Cooley Family: Jean, James, Gladys, John, Ernest, Francis and Tom Cooley 1953

cousins David, Claudia and Charles walked three miles to a two-room school at Fountain, which had about twenty students in the first through eighth grades. The school was closed and moved to Youngstown about 1938.

Ernest began driving the school bus in 1935 from the Jackson County line on highway 231 to Panama City. Soon his job included supervision and maintenance of buses and later Director of County School Transportation. He retired in 1967. He was known for his strict control aboard his bus.

Ernest bought the Slick Gay place south of the Tom Cane Farm in 1937. Some land could be purchased by only paying its taxes. During 1930's and early 1940's there was no stock law, so hogs and cows roamed the woods for food.

The family grew much of what they ate, so there was always work to be done, i.e, plowing, hoeing, clearing new ground, milking cows, cutting wood, raking leaves, gathering produce, preparing vegetables and berries for canning, keeping track of hogs and cows, butchering hogs, smoking meat, growing sugar cane and making syrup, growing and harvesting rice, growing and shelling corn for cornmeal, helping wash, etc. A horse was used for plowing, hauling wood and riding while looking after our cattle and hogs.

Ernest was an avid fisherman and had fish and oysters often. John and Francis spent much of their free time roaming the woods and hunting with their hound chasing coon, fox, squirrel, possums, etc.

Thomas, the fifth child, was born at Fountain in 1941. In 1951 Ernest and Gladys moving to Panama City. Later they moved to Little Blue Pond in Bay County where they lived until her passing 27 March 1989 and his passing 13 April 1998.

All five of the children graduated from Bay County High School. James, Francis and Tom served in the Navy and John served in the National Guard.

Submitted April 2003 by: John William Cooley, 309 Dublin Circle, Madison, Alabama 35758. johnwcooley@aol.com.

Ernest worked with his brother David growing satsumas, pears, grapes, peaches, blueberries, tung oil nuts, sugar cane and other produce. Electricity was not available until 1947; so our lights were from kerosene lamps, heat from a fireplace and cooking on a wood stove.

James, John and

Glenn Cooper

Glenn Cooper was born in Caryville, Fl and moved to Sarasota as a young man. He always wanted to return to NW Florida for the hunting and the fishing. NW Florida was his paradise. In 1938, after working for the Russell News Agency in Sarasota he obtained the franchise for Panama City. With $200 borrowed dollars Glenn and his 18 year old

Fishing trip 1953

wife Mary Sue Austin Cooper came to his paradise to start their life together and their business and family careers.

Glenn Cooper loved to fish, and in the 1953 postcard (photo) is Capt. Vester Knowles, Gene Tindel, deckhand of Lynn Haven, Fl and

Glenn Cooper Sr., Glenn Cooper Jr. and Ray Austin Cooper. They are shown with Mr. And Mrs. John Franklin (wearing caps) of Atlanta, Georgia. Mr. Franklin was the inventor of the automatic phone answering machine. This led to such items as being able to call up a number and get the time and temperature. This service is still available in Panama at the same number it was when this post card was made. The boat they owned was called the Mary Dean and was moored at Tarpon Dock.

Ray Cooper while serving as deckhand on the Mary Dean enjoyed the best fried chicken and picnics that Mrs. Franklin always had aboard.

Glenn Cooper and Sue Cooper had three children, Glenn Cooper Jr., Ray Austin Cooper and June Susan Cooper Lloyd.Glenn Jr. Married Sylvia Kendrick and had two children, Paige Marie Cooper Whitaker, and Glenn Cooper III, (Bubba). Ray married Jo Bogan and had one child Kyle Austin. He later married Joyce Hoskins and had 4 children, Molly Sue who died of crib death at 2 months, then RJ Cooper, Courtney Cooper, and Matthew Cooper. June married William P. Lloyd and they had two children William P. Lloyd Jr. and Jon Robert Lloyd.

Submitted by: June Cooper Lloyd, 447 Sudduth Ave., Panama City, FL 32401.

Sue Cooper

After arriving in Panama City in 1939, Mary Sue Austin Cooper didn't share her husbands vision of paradise, but determined to make the best of things, she began her adult life dedicated to making a success of her business, her family and her community. As co-owner of Cooper's News Agency and operator of the wholesale and retail business of magazines, postcards and newspapers, Sue wanted to change Panama City for the better and provide many of the cultural and artistic opportunities available elsewhere in the world. During the war years she drove a delivery truck and ran the newsstand 15 hours a day. For 41 years she worked full time while rearing three children and was instrumental in either founding or expanding many of the organizations still playing a part in making the community better. She was listed and biographied in -Florida Women of Distinction 1952.

Sue Cooper

Sue Cooper was a founding director of the Child Guidance Clinic which became Life Management Center. President of the Panama City Garden Club, founding member of the Youth Center Board, member of the Downtown Improvement Board, founding member of the Bay Medical Center Hospital Auxiliary. The first Juvenile Detention Center was named for her. The newer facility shares her dedication with Ron Johnson. She was active in the Business and Professional Woman's Club, Chamber of Commerce, Panama City Marine Institute, American Cancer Society, Chamber of Commerce Committee of 100. She was an early director of the Panama City Music Association and was voted Panama City's Woman of the Year in 1953. She was a Jefferson Award winner the first year the contest was held in Panama City.

She was President of the Bay County Executive Committee and attended the inauguration of Jimmy Carter as President of the United States. She attended a reception at the White House the day after the inauguration.

Economic circumstances prevented higher education for Mary Sue Austin. But Sue Cooper read everything and traveled extensively after 1952 to learn and understand other people and cultures. She took her first trip to Europe in 1952 and took movies of the changing of the Guard at Buckingham Palace and came back and showed the movies to the classes at Cove Elementary School while she was president of the PTA. She toured the Holy Land and was moved greatly by the experience. She took two grandchildren to mainland China in 1982. She took another grandchild to Australia when she was 79 years old. She rode a jet ski at 72 and at 69 entered a Bill Fishing Tournament with her grandson Bill Lloyd. They placed third in the Dolphin category aboard the Christina.

She was a member of the Palo Alto Church of Christ for 62 years. As a business owner, community activist, or matriarch of her family she represented the best of the human spirit. She survived cancer at age 53, suffered several strokes in her 60's and 70's, macular degeneration in her late 70's and died October 8, 2001. You always knew where you stood with Sue Cooper and you may not always have agreed with her, but you knew she had other people's welfare at heart.

Submitted by: June Cooper Lloyd, 447 Sudduth Ave., Panama City, FL 32401.

Robert Lee Corley and Ellie Scott Corley

Robert Lee Corley and Ellie Scott were married in Quincy, Florida in 1924, and moved to Panama City, Florida in 1931. Mr. Corley's first job was in helping to build the old Hathaway Bridge. From that he began driving a city bus for Mr. Hobbs. After settling in St. Andrews the Corley relatives moved to Panama City and set up residence with Robert and Ellie. The Corleys were blessed with three children, one girl, their first born, Ethel Kathleen Corley, and two sons, Charles Lee Corley and Daniel Earnest Corley. Living in St. Andrews near the bay they had many memorable experiences. There were fishing trips and playing in the bay waters, gathering around the ice truck that brought ice to the house each day, as the driver chipped off pieces for them to eat, and although it seemed a long way, walking from St. Andrews to Panama City, to the Ritz Theatre to see the Kiddie Matinee, on Saturday was a delight. There are memories of Matties Tavern in St. Andrews

Robert Lee Corley and Ellie Scott Corley and children (L to R) Charles Lee Corley, Ethel Corley Henderson and Daniel Earnest Corley

where Mr. Corley and friends gathered for a delicious lunch each day, and an outstanding memory was the harshness of a hurricane that washed the bay right up to their doorsteps. Another landmark of St. Andrews was Mr. Brown's drugstore on main street that had an old fashioned soda fountain where he served rootbeer in frosted mugs. Next to the Corley home was the Oak Cottages. An interesting event came about when the Manager of the cottages, Mr. Harris, fell in love with, and married, Mr. Corley's sister. Another interesting thing in the family history was the marrying of Mrs. Corley's sister to Mr. Corley's brother, making it worthy to record..brothers marrying sisters. From his bus driving days Mr. Corley went to work for Standard Oil Company, and before his retirement received the honorary award for Best Driver in the company. At that time he moved his family to Panama City, which was then Palmetto Avenue, and which Mr. Corley was given the honor of renaming what is now known as State Avenue. In his bus driving days he remained at the wheel during a hurricane to insure getting the Tyndall and Paper Mill workers to their jobs. Aside from raising her family, Ellie Corley worked at Tyndall Field during World War II. During this time their daughter Ethel, who was then attending Bay High School, entered and won THE MISS PANAMA CITY title in the local pageant held at the Bay High football stadium. The Corleys were married for

74 years. Mr. Corley died in 1999 at the age of 92, his wife Ellie, died in 2001 at the age of 95. They were very much a part of Panama City's history, and very respected and active members of the Panama City Seventh-Day Adventist Church on West 11th Street.

Submitted By: Ethel Corley Henderson, 138 Sunset Oaks Drive, Cornelia, Georgia 30531. Written by: Nita Whitehurst.

Charles Cotton and Eunice Lavonia Scott

Eunice Lavonia Scott, born in 1881 in New Hope, Holmes County, Florida, to William Watson Scott and Lillie Ora Isobel Smith, was the youngest of 11 children. William, a farmer and timber man, served in the Confederate Army under General Joseph Wheeler from 1862-1864. In 1903, he served Holmes County as a representative to the Florida House of Representatives.

Charles Cotton, born in 1868 in Newton, Alabama, married Eunice Scott in 1902 in New Hope, Florida. In 1908/09, they moved to Millville, Florida. He was a partner with William Madison Brigman in the Cotton & Brigman Mercantile Company located on Third Street, between Sherman and Main Avenues. He later worked for the German-American Lumber Company and was manager of Ware Mercantile at the time of his death from influenza in 1920.

Charles and Eunice Cotton had 10 children - Fitzhugh Lee, Charles's son from a previous marriage, William James, who died at age 2, Charles, Jr., Mary Belle, Bernice Newton, Percy Scott, Eunice Elizabeth, Gladys Louise, Benjamin Francis (killed in 1943 while serving in the USAF), and Ira Melinda, born just three weeks after the death of her father. Friends often teased Charles, Sr., saying cotton wouldn't grow in Bay County. He retorted that it was evident that cotton did well here considering all the "little toe heads running around my house." Just for fun, however, he planted two rows of cotton in the backyard to prove that cotton would grow in Bay County. When Charles, Sr.'s work took him to St. Andrews, Eunice would pack some belongings and the family would move to a house near the store. They would return again to Millville when his work in St. Andrews was done. Such comings and goings were newsworthy events of the early 1910s and often were reported in the local newspaper.

Times were hard following the death of Charles Cotton, Sr. Lee and Charles, Jr., took jobs to support the family. As Bernice and Percy each reached the age of 14, they quit school to join their brothers in helping to support the family, allowing the younger siblings to complete their education. Even after they got married, the four oldest boys continued to contribute to the upkeep of the family home and their mother. Until the death of Eunice Lavonia Scott "Mama" Cotton in 1958, the Cotton Family home continued to be the

1911 Charles, Jr., Eunice Scott, Eunice Elizabeth, Percy, Charles, Sr., Mary Belle, Bernice. Standing unidentified

gathering place for the brothers and sisters and their families. Eunice is remembered as a cornerstone of Immanuel Baptist Church in Millville. Percy and Bernice were long-time employees of Nelson Buick Company, both retiring in the 1970s. Charles, Jr. (Charlie) owned Cotton's Grocery at the corner of Jenks and 11th for over 40 years. The store was a popular stop-over for school kids walking to and from Jinks Junior High School.

Submitted by: Sharon Wilkinson, 3901 Genoa Circle, Panama City, FL 32405.

Percy Scott Cotton, Sr. and Lucile Grace Pringle

Born in 1909 in Millville, Florida, to Charles Cotton, Sr., and Eunice Lavonia Scott Cotton, Percy was the fifth of nine children. He was ten years old when his father died in 1920 of influenza. Percy and his siblings - Charles, Jr., Mary Belle, Bernice Newton, Eunice Elizabeth, Gladys Louise, Benjamin Francis, and Ira Melinda - lived with their mother in their

Millville home at the corner of College Avenue and Third Street. At age 14, Percy quit school and went to work, helping his brothers support the family and allowing his younger siblings to complete their education. Percy worked several jobs, including as an auto mechanic for Chevrolet and Ford, and finally for 41 years with Nelson Buick until his retirement in 1975. He loved fishing and boats. He and his brothers built two boats

Percy Scott and Lucile Grace Pringle Cotton 1931

which they raced in the popular boat races of the 1940s and 1950s. Percy and his brothers had what may have been the first camper in Bay County. They built a shell over a 1937 Chevy pickup truck. It had a tin roof, screen sides with roll-up canvas covers, built-in bunks on both sides of the pickup bed, and custom built drawers and cabinets. Percy fished both fresh and salt water and was a regular on the Davis Queen Fleet weekend party boats.

Lucile Grace Pringle was born in 1911 in Biloxi, Mississippi, to George Christian Craig Pringle and Jessie Estelle Dolbeare Pringle. She was the fifth of eight children - Roy Fulton (d. 1902), Francis Marion, Jessie Christine (Cogburn), George Christian Craig, Jr., Vera May (d.1915), Maude Evelyn (Jenkins), and Clyde Vernon. The Pringle family moved from Biloxi, Mississippi, to Compass Lake, Florida, in 1915 and then to their newly built home at the corner of Harrison Avenue and 11th Street in Panama City, Florida, in 1920. Lucile was a member of the first graduating class to have attended Bay County High School all four years.

Percy met Lucile in 1928 when his brothers Charles and Francis, who worked at a downtown store owned by G.C. Pringle, Sr., arranged a Sunday afternoon outing with girlfriends of Lucile's. When Percy tried to sneak a kiss, Lucile "slapped the stew out of him." They were married in 1931 and in 1936 built a modest 2 bedroom house on the outskirts of town at the corner of Grace and 11th Street. There the Percy Cottons raised four children - Marjorie Grace (Peggy), Charles Christopher, Percy Scott, Jr., and Virginia Gayle. The house remained the Cotton homestead until its sale in 2003.

Submitted by: Peggy Cotton Malone, 2622 Michigan Avenue, Panama City, FL 32405.

Cotton Family of Bay County

The Cotton's came to the Bay County area in the early 1950's from Geneva, Alabama. My Dad, his sisters and brother all settled in Bay County and chose different ways to help Bay County grow. They started and successfully ran three different businesses. My parents Louie and Mary Cotton ran a successful small neighborhood grocery, gas station and game room in Springfield, which was closed when they lost my sister. My Dad retired from Tyndall Air Force Base as a Civil Service employee after 35 years of service to his country. They raised four children, Deborah Cotton Whitaker, Janet Dianne Cotton, Craig E. Cotton and Gina Michelle Cotton Deal.

My Uncle and Aunt, J. T. and Lorraine Cotton established and operated the largest produce company in Bay County for over 40 years, Cotton Produce and Egg Company, which he sold in the late 1990's. They raised two children, Larry J. Cotton and Linda Joyce Cotton Lovejoy.

My Uncle and Aunt Bill and Hazel Howell established and ran Howell Marine until their retirement, the business still operates under the same name with their son-in-law and daughter's watchful eye. They raised two children, Donna Sue Howell Gentry and Teresa R. Howell.

My Uncle Leon Harrison was manager of Glidden Paint Center for over 35 years. He and my Aunt, Rebecca "Becky" Cotton Harrison raised two wonderful children, Mark and Jeannie Harrison.

All of us have raised our children in Bay County, where they attended Bay County Public Schools, among them several successful business and professionals. One a well known local artist Donna Howell Burgess, former FSU Football All-American Jason Whitaker and Gulf Coast Community College Softball All-American Joan Whitaker.

Submitted by: Deborah Cotton Whitaker, 2002 Geralo Lane, Lynn Haven, Florida 32444.

Vici L. and John W. Crawford - Grand Lagoon

Stroked by lighter knots as fuel, a train to Panama City, Florida, carried Vici Leonard and John Winton Crawford on their honeymoon in June 1913. Vici and John enjoyed walking, swimming and sunning on the beaches along St. Andrews Bay. They visited Vici's sister, Alice Leonard and her husband, E. A. Barrett.

Returning to Panama City in 1915, they purchased a tract of land across St.

Vici Leonard and John Winton Crawford on their honeymoon

Andrews Bay on Grand Lagoon where they built a small house. Since there was no bridge across St. Andrews Bay, John traveled across the bay by small boat and motor to a lumber company in Bay Harbor where he was employed.

While living on the lagoon property, the Crawford's and other young pioneer couples living on that side of the bay fished in the bay and fresh water lakes, picnicked, climbed atop the highest sand dunes to enjoy the wonderful vista at a time when women wore high-top shoes, long dresses and wide-brimmed hats to climb atop the dunes. Many lovely

Mary Sue, John, Jr. And Alice (end of Allen Ave. in the Cove)

photos were made atop these sand dunes. On March 13, 1916, a daughter, Mary Sue, was born on the grand lagoon.

The family returned to their former home in Birmingham, Alabama and in 1922, Alice, a daughter was born, and son John Jr. was born in 1924. The family again returned in about 1926 to Panama City, moving in the Cove area. The children learned to swim in beautiful St. Andrews Bay near the Cove Hotel.

John was a self-employed Accountant and Vici owned and operated Crawford's Beauty Shop. All three children attended Bay High School. John Jr. joined the U.S. Navy in 1941, just a few weeks before the start of World War II, serving in the Aleutians then later in the Pacific Theatre of Operations. He married Mabel Meagher, and settled in Seattle, Washington. They had a daughter, Lauri, and a son, John Thomas.

During World War II Vici, John, Alice and her daughter, Vicky, along with Mr. And Mrs. Dick Bevel, their daughters, Sara and Georgia Lou, would drive to the much isolated beaches area near an artesian spring on Highway 98 and swim, walk, and gather driftwood to cook breakfast over an open fire. This was during the time of gasoline and meat rationing. On one of the breakfast cookouts, the fire was built and coffee pot ready to be put on the fire when it was discovered that we failed to pack a skillet. We cooked the bacon and eggs in a galvanized bucket and the food was great.

Vici's first hotel was the Ensley on the water on McKenzie Avenue downtown. In 1947 Vici built a small hotel, The Patio Hotel. The hotel had 21 rooms, and was the first hotel or motel on Panama City Beach that had central heat and air-conditioning. Mary Sue and her husband, Clyde Atwood operated The Patio. Mary Sue was active in the local art community as well as serving as a Vice President of the Florida Federation of Art, Inc.

Now, in the 21st Century, the property that Vici and John purchased in 1915 was developed and sold and is now called "Finis terre", lands end. This property is the beginning of North Lagoon Drive at the Grand Lagoon.

Submitted by: Ms. Alice Crawford Robinson, 105 Allen Avenue, Apt. 60, Panama City, Florida 32401-5819.

The Creamer Family
John Lafayett & Della Brookins Creamer
William Oscar & Flora Pitts Creamer

John Lafayett Creamer was born 1860 in Henry County Alabama and died at age seventy, 24 December 1930 in Bay County, Florida. He was the son of William Henry Creamer, Sr. born about 1830 in South Carolina and Jemima/Jamina Richards born about 1838 in Georgia. She was the daughter of Henry S. Richards born between 1792-1796 and Jemima/Jemina (Unknown) born between 1800-1807. Other children of William Henry, Sr. and Jemima were: William Henry, Jr., Martha J., Daniel Thomas, Jesse, Zachariah Green, George Washington, Sara Virginia, Ida Elizabeth, Rebecca, Lavonia, James Robert and Archibald Columbus. They were the grand children of Daniel Creamer born about 1798 in South Carolina and Martha born 1795 in South Carolina. John moved to Jackson County, Florida with his family about 1882-1883. John was a carpenter. He married Della Susan Brookins about 1885.

Della Susan Brookins was born 1868 in Alabama and died 1929 in Bay County, Florida. She was a daughter of Ivey Hollis Brookins born 18 September 1832 in Georgia and died 19 March 1907 in Florida, and Sarah Ann Smith born

John, Howard & Margaret Creamer - 1925

28 July 1842 in South Carolina and died 11 April 1908 in Florida. Other children of Ivey and Sarah were: Reuben, Marcus L., Lenois, Sarah, Benjamin Tapley, Cornelia, Alberta, Vesta L. and Pearl.

John and Della had the following children: Osia born 23 June 1885 and died 3 March 1950 and married John Thomas Scott; William Oscar born 31 March 1886 and died 22 April 1963 and married Flora Pearlee Pitts; Marvin born 3 March 1894 and died July 1969 and married Lucile Buffalo; Josephine "Josie" born 23 April 1898 and died 21 November 1972; Malvina born 21 May 1903 and died 17 April 1989 and married Walter Robert Potter; and Frazier born 1907 and death unknown. John, Della and five children were living at Alford, Jackson County, Florida, Round Lake Precinct, in 1910. Later they moved to St. Petersburg, Florida. In 1926 they moved to Sellers Still, Bay County Florida (now known as Hiland Park). John and Della died at Hiland Park and are buried in Oakland Cemetery, Panama City, Bay County Florida.

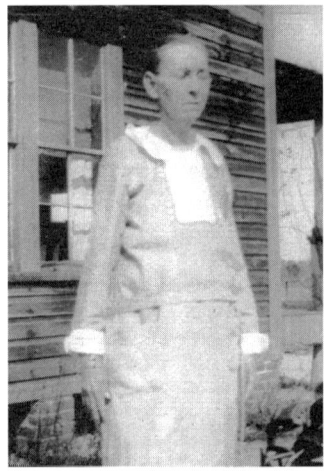

Della Susan Brookins Creamer - 1925

William Oscar Creamer, the second child of John and Della, was born 31 March 1886 in Henry County Alabama and died 22 April 1963 in Hiland Park, Bay County Florida. He is the grandson of William Henry Creamer, Sr. and Jemima Richards Creamer and great grandson of Daniel and Martha Creamer. He was living with his parents at Alford in 1910. Oscar married Flora Pearlee Pitts 26 October 1922 in Panama City, Florida and they made their home in Alford. Oscar was a carpenter and building contractor. He retired about 1955.

Flora was born 9 February 1904 near Youngstown, Bay County Florida and died 23 July 1990 in Hiland Park, Bay County Florida. Flora was the daughter of Wilburn Eli Pitts born 28 March 1868 in Holmes County Florida and died 21 July 1958 in Bay County Florida and Callie Doney Marshall born 20 May 1875 in Geneva, Alabama and died 8 June 1911 in Bay County Florida. Wilburn came to Bay County in May 1885. Flora was the grand daughter of Isaac Porter Pitts born 13 February 1841 and died 1901 and Louise Wright born 1834 and died 1900. She was the great grand daughter of Benjamin Pitts born 1815 in Georgia and died 1859 in Florida and Serena Cowart born 1817 in Georgia and died 1886 in Florida.

Oscar and Flora had two children in Alford, William Howard born 24 August 1923 and Margaret born 22 November 1924 and died 22 January 1927 in Bay County Florida. The family lived a short while in St. Petersburg, Florida before moving to Hiland Park, Bay County Florida in 1926. Their third child, Mavis Lenora Creamer, was born 17 December 1929 in Hiland Park. Oscar did oil paintings as a hobby in his latter years and won several blue ribbons. He had no formal training in art or painting. Today some of his paintings are hanging in the homes of his two children and grandchildren.

Mavis Creamer married John W. Cooley, 4 February 1950 in Hiland Park, Bay County Florida. They have three children:

William Oscar & Flora Pearlee Pitts Creamer - 1934

John Kenneth who married Barbara Ballinger and they have three children, Johnny Mac, Carrie Ann and Donald Wayne; Philip Wayne passed away three days after birth; Michael Wesley who married Sally Lee Eberhart and they have two children, Melinda and Carolyn; and Debra Sue who married Stephen Pearce and they have three children, Linda, Katie and Luke. Mavis and John have two great grand children, Nathan James Cooley son of Johnny and wife Cheryl Halley and Jacob Allen Tolar son of Carrie and husband Michael Tolar.

Howard married Flora Catherine Peterson 9 July 1960 in Wilmington, North Carolina and made their home in Hiland Park, Florida. They have one child Mary Lynn and two grand daughters Terrain and Stormy Creamer Robbins.

Submitted by: John William Cooley, 309 Dublin Circle, Madison, Alabama 35758. johnwcooley@aol.com.

Jackie Erwin and Susan Carol "Strickland" Creel

Susan Carol Strickland, born 13 April 1947 in Panama, City Florida was the daughter of Yancy Cecil and Ruby Lee "Hartzog" Strickland. Carol graduated from Rutherford High School No. 15 from the top of three or more hundred Students.

Jackie Erwin Creel, born 30 September 1945 in Cullman County, Alabama was the son of Wesley Jackson and Glader "Graves" Creel. He graduated from High School with a baseball scholarship to Gulf Coast College.

Loving baseball games, Carol met Jackie and they became engaged. Jackie was picked to play in the Minors with the Dodgers at Kenywink, Washington. After the Season was over, he and Carol were married 2 February 1968 at Hiland Park Baptist Church, Panama City, Florida. He played a second season in Bakersfield, California and was scheduled to a third season when he was drafted by the Army.

Jack and Carol Creel and family

Jack and Carol had three Children: Stillborn Son, 28 January 1969 in Panama City, Florida. Robert Christapher Creel born 9 July 1970, in Ft. Leavenworth, Kansas, where his father was stationed. Chris was married 20 January 1996 in Cullman, AL. to Tracy Carol Hartwig, daughter of Don and Edith "Haynie" Hartwig, of Cullman, AL.

Chris graduated May 2001, with a BS Degree from Athens State College. He is doing substitute teaching while working on his Masters. Chris and Tracy have a daughter, Savannah Jade born 20 December 1997 in Cullman, Alabama. They are looking to the birth of a second child in April 2003.

Craig Erin Creel born 2 November 1972 in Birmingham, Alabama, was married 28 January in Cullman, Alabama to Christi Smith. Christi was the daughter of "?" and Carolyn Smith. Craig and Christi's children are: Hunter Erin born 14 December 1997 in Cullman, Alabama. Madison Carol born 8 June 2000 in Birmingham, Alabama. The family lives in Tuscaloosa, Alabama and Craig works at Mercedes in Vance, AL. Carol received her BS degree in Athens, Alabama in 1986 and her Masters from the University of Alabama in 1997. She teaches Special Education, grades seven through twelve at Cole Springs, Alabama.

Jackie was a Deputy for Bay County Sheriff's Department in Panama City Florida. He froze his retirement after 10 years and they moved to Goodhope, Alabama (Cullman Co.) He worked for a while for the Cullman County Road Department, until he went to work for Hanna Steel in Birmingham, Alabama. The drive from Cullman to Birmingham is about 30 miles one way but this is what he grew up in, as his father did the same thing until he retired. Jack also hopes to retire when he gets old enough.

Submitted by: Craig Creel, 532 Hiland Road, Tuscaloosa, Al. 36405 Written by: Ruby L. Strickland, 2627 Game Farm Road, Panama City, Florida 32405. Source: Family Records.

Isaiah Rodolph Culbreth and Opal Emma Hendrix Culbreth - Part I

Isaiah Rodolph Culbreth, youngest of twelve children born to Eliza McMillian and Isaiah Culbreth, came to Panama City from Gordon, Alabama in 1919. After enrolling at the Normal School in Troy, he enlisted in the Army; however, World War I ended shortly thereafter and he, along with his brother Cleveland, opened gas stations in Panama City and in Millville.

It was in Millville that he first met Opal Hendrix, the youngest of nine children born to Sarah Emma Ward and Matthew Hezekiah Hendrix who followed the logging industry in the forests east of the Choctawhatchee River and west of the Apalachicola River. This had brought them to Millville and to what had been the German-American Lumber Company. Sarah Emma operated a rooming house for mill workers and Opal was a student at Millville school and later was one of the first students at Murrow's Business College.

Isaiah Rodolph Culbreth and Opal Emma Hendrix Culbreth

People were following the "Florida Boom" to Miami, and Rodolph and his brother opened a gas station there. Meanwhile, Mr. Hendrix had moved, along with many other mill workers, to the town of Sherman on Lake Okachoobee. From there, Opal went on to Miami where she and Rodolph were married in 1925; but they returned to Panama City within a few years.

Around 1930, Rodolph was hired to drive Panama City's single firetruck. The family, which included three daughters by that time, lived in an apartment on the second floor of what is now the Visual Arts Center. The firetruck was housed in a first floor garage which opened onto Luverne Avenue. One rainy night a call came in from the Cove area, and at the eastern end of the old wooden Tarpon Dock Bridge, the firetruck skidded, overturned and seriously injured Rodolph. Since that was before workman's compensation laws, a person injured on the job was out of a job-so the family moved briefly to the family farm in southeastern Houston County. After a short stay fighting malaria and depression era poverty, the family moved back to Bay County to stay with the Hendrixes who lived in Parker at the corner of what is now Tyndall Parkway and Boatrace Road. There, to provide for their families, they cultivated a garden, raised a few hogs and chickens, and fished each day in Pitts Bayou.

Submitted by: Joan Parker, 103 Harbour Pointe Dr., Lynn Haven, FL 32444.

Isaiah Rodolph Culbreth and Opal Emma Hendrix Culbreth - Part II

In 1938, the family moved to 225 Central Avenue in Springfield where they lived until 1951. People were trying to survive the Depression and life was simple-children playing "kick the can" on sand-rut roads, "oystering" at Cook Bayou, keeping a cow and chickens in the backyard. Killing the chicken for Sunday dinner was a feat that involved the whole family; first selecting and catching the chicken, wringing the neck, dousing the chicken in the boiling washpot to loosen feathers, and then plucking them. Great fun was following the ice truck to collect chips as the delivery man cut 5, 10, and 20 pound blocks for iceboxes. Fish fries on July 4 and political rallies in McKenzie Park were treats to attend.

When the country plunged into World War II in 1941, Tyndall Field came to Bay County with jobs, and the economy flourished. Rodolph found work with Civil Service and became a supervisor at the Lynn Haven Oil Terminal. This terminal received airplane fuel

Isaiah Rodolph Culbreth and Opal Emma Hendrix Culbreth

for Tyndall that was shipped through the intracoastal canal because shipping lanes in the Gulf were infested with German submarines during the war.

Opal opened the first WPA lunchroom in this area at Springfield Elementary in 1939 and the next year at Panama Grammar. As the nation entered World War II and the rationing of certain items, such as sugar, nylon, and rubber, became necessary, she was asked to serve as chief clerk of the OPA Rationing Board, which operated on the second floor of the Armory Building, now a part of the First Baptist Church campus. In the 1960's she managed the Commodity Office, distributing surplus farm food to qualified citizens.

Faith in God and regular church attendance was the family's foundation. They were members of a small group that organized and chartered Springfield Baptist Church. They also felt a responsibility for civic involvement. Both were active in PTA, and Opal served a term as president of Bay Medical Auxiliary.

From 1926 through 1938, five daughters were born into the family-Bayne Culbreth Coonce, Sara Culbreth Cooper, Helen Culbreth Schrenker, Joan Culbreth Parker, and Marynel Culbreth Adams. They all presently live in Panama City. The five daughters were educated in the local public schools-Parker, Millville, Panama City, and Bay High. Opal and Rodolph believed strongly in education and insisted the girls get a college education-and they did. In a period of ten years-from 1949 to 1959—all received degrees from FSU (four gained advanced degrees) and pursued careers as public school teachers.

The family moved to 224 Cove Boulevard in 1951 and in 1968 built a home on Massalina Bayou. Beginning in 1951, Opal and Rodolph were active members of First Baptist Church. After retirement, they spent time traveling and watching their nine grandchildren grow.

Mr. Culbreth died in 1982 and Mrs. Culbreth in 1986

Submitted by: Helen Schrenker, 2720 State Ave., Panama City, FL 32405.

Mae Johnson Culbreth

Mae Johnson Culbreth was born in October of 1878 in Henry County Alabama. Two of her brothers, Joseph and Henry Johnson settled in Bay County before the turn of the Century. Her mother Mary Jane Thompson Johnson was living with Henry and wife Julia Gardner Johnson when she died in 1911.

She told me of traveling by ox cart on her first trip to the Bay Country when only a young girl. It took a few days from Columbia, Alabama and they had to camp on the way and build fires to cook at night. After she married and had her first child, Allison, they boarded a steam boat in Columbia,

135

Gabriel Capers Johnson family: back row: Joseph Green, Mae, Barney, Eola "Opie", Blewett, Samuel; front row: Gabriel Capers Johnson, Mary Jane Thompson Johnson & Barney

Alabama and traveled down the Chattahoocha River to the Apalachicola River then stopping at Iola Landing, transferring to a train to Wetappo then again by boat across East Bay to Panama City. This was quite a trip for a young mother and baby to make but when she arrived she stayed a good month or so visiting with her family and uncle, Green B. Thompson, postmaster at St. Andrew. She also brought fabrics and notions for her sister-in-law, Jessie Palmer Johnson, Henry's first wife, from her husbands mercantile store in Columbia and were not available here. Who would think now that Columbia would have better shopping than Panama City.

When my Grandfather, Cecil B. Culbreth died in 1934, she sold her milk cow and rented a truck and driver and moved with her daughters to Panama City to be near her family.

Cecil B. Culbreth and Mae Johnson Culbreth and baby Allison

Her daughter Pattie was already a teacher at Panama Grammar having started there in 1926 and continuing until 1946, all in the fourth grade with the exception of one or two years in the third. She had been boarding with her uncle Henry and second wife Julia Gardner. He was in the dredgeing business and then became Harbor Master. Joseph had a furniture store located on west Beach Drive where the Gallery of Art is now located. Hoke, his son, had an antique store there after his dad's death. Maggie, Joseph's wife, had a news stand on Harrison. Samuel and Barney were carpenters. Barney and Carrie living in Millville and Samuel and Claudia in town. Allison Culbreth had been employed as bookkeeper with Western Auto when it was located on Harrison between 4th and 5th Street. She kept that position until shortly before her death in 1974. Mamas only son Beryl, chose the Army as his career and retired here in the Cove section shortly before his death in 1970.

Blewett operated the electric power plant in Greenwood then left and traveled north to Tennessee to work with the TVA. He married Eleanora Jansen and afterwards they also left and settled in California. Thus a large California Johnson Family was created from the decendants of Amos, Hardy and Green Berry Johnson.

Submitted by Lillian V. Stafford, 4034 Woodridge Road, Panama City, FL. 32405.

Jimmy Daffin
The Jimmy Daffin Family
and Daffin Drug Store

The Daffin family was an integral part of the development of Bay County. In circa 1901 James Horace Daffin and his family including wife, Lola (Russ) Daffin, daughter Jessie, and son, Jimmy moved by wagon to Millville from Marianna FL. Two other sons and a daughter were born in Bay County, Mitchell Jacoby, Leo and Jewel. (Leo married Mabel Green, homestead in Chattahoochee FL and owned Daffin's Ready

Top row L-R: Doc Daffin; Proctor Van Horn; Wallace Laird Sr; Les Gilbert; John Phillips; Charlie Powell; Jimmie Daffin; Roy Laird.
Bottom row L-R: Bob Ennis; Harry Phillips; Custer Russ; Doctor Lingo; Ross Phillips

To Wear there; Jewel married Vaggie Rivers from Monroe, Louisiana.) James (Mr. Jim) Horace opened a livery stable in Millville, was a deputy sheriff and ran for Sheriff in 1913 when Bay County was organized. Mr. Jim was Mayor of Millville when his wife died in 1921.

Jimmy Daffin returned to Panama City with his wife Marion Kennedy Daffin after beginning his pharmacy career in River Junction, FL. Jimmy worked for Adams Drugs until he bought J.C. Simms Drugs and opened his own store on Harrison Avenue in 1929. The Panama City Pilot recorded that on Saturday, May 25th, the opening of Daffin Drug Store was one of the greatest events in the history of Panama City. The store was decorated with flowers, Jimmy and employees were dressed in all white, boxes of Russell & McPhail's Chocolates were handed out to the women and fine cigars to the men. A local orchestra led by Jimmie Lee played throughout the entire day.

Jimmy was known for his compassion for "treating" his sick customers. Many could not afford a visit to the doctor but they knew Mr. Jimmy would listen to their symptoms and come up with a remedy. In the early years he had to mix many of the medicines and even had several "concoctions" that he patented to cure ailments from croup to "ground itch".

The Drug Store became the center of the community's political activity when Jimmy's brother M. J. "Doc" Daffin was the legendary sheriff of Bay County between 1952 and 1971. In 1960 Jimmy had the foresight to get together thirteen of his friends for a picture in front of his store. Many of these men were outstanding citizens who played important roles in the development & politics of Bay County. It was common to find various local politicians "chatting" around small tables in front of the marble top soda fountain. In fact, J. B. Lahan, dubbed the store the "Snake Pit" in reference to how the men in the community sat around the tables.

Jimmy Daffin closed the store due to failing health a few years before his death in January, 1980. He died at age 83, survived by his wife, Marion, two daughters, Marilyn Underberg and Carolyn Hoffman and one son, the Rev. Bob Daffin. Frank Pericola wrote in the News Herald that, "Jimmy Daffin was about as colorful and respected resident that this area had ever known". Pericola said, "If I wanted to know the real story behind the story, I would visit Jimmy. He would give me his honest opinion and it was invariably right".

The accompanying photograph taken in 1960 shows thirteen men who had been friends for over fifty years in front of Daffin Cut Rate Drug Company at 110 Harrison Avenue, Panama City, Florida.

Submitted by: Rev. James Robert "Bob" Daffin, 3119 Debra Blvd., Panama City, FL 32405.

The Legendary Sheriff: M.J. "Doc" Daffin

The renowned sheriff of Bay County, Mitchell Jacoby Daffin, was born in Millville, Florida on February 24, 1902 to parents James Horace Daffin and Lola Russ Daffin. "Doc Daffin" was practically born into law enforcement with his father serving both as a deputy sheriff and as mayor of Millville.

As a young man Daffin's dream was to become a medical doctor but he dropped the idea after a stint at the University of Florida. It was from this experience that he was given the nickname "Doc". After college he entered the business world as a partner in the Daffin & Cogburn Clothing Store in 1925. Later he owned Daffin's Style Shops.

Doc married Edith Stone from Blountstown in 1928 around the time when he began to take an active role in politics. He joined the Army during WW II and served in combat in Italy. Afterwards, he resumed his business and political career and was elected sheriff in 1952.

Daffin's name quickly became a household word throughout the piney woods of Northwest Florida. The people of Bay County repeatedly elected him to their highest office. Beginning in 1952, Doc was elected as Sheriff six times (five four-year terms and one two-year term).

M.J. "Doc" Daffin

Between 1959-1962 a series of articles appeared in the News Herald disclosing gambling and moonshine operations in Bay County and accusing Doc of allowing these operations in the black community. In May 1961, Gov. Bryant removed Daffin from office and appointed Charlie Abbott as sheriff. The Panama City News-Herald actually won the Pulitzer Prize for this series of articles. However, the charges were never substantiated and Doc Daffin was exonerated of all charges. Citizens of Bay County were outraged by all the "politics" surrounding the accusations. Daffin campaigned on a platform of "returning the office to the voters" and in May, 1962 "their sheriff" was reelected receiving the greatest number of votes in his political career.

Daffin prided himself on being a "round-the-clock" sheriff and on being the people's sheriff. It was along these lines that he picked up a second nickname, "Dishes". He started every public address with "Dishisyosheriff MJDocDaffin" which was shortened to "Dishes". The translation is "This is your Sheriff, M. J. Doc Daffin".

Known as "the unbeatable sheriff" Daffin reorganized the Sheriff's Department. He introduced modern crime detection methods, marked patrol cars, uniformed deputies, jail matrons, a state of art communication system and an outstanding investigation division. He solved some of the toughest cases in the annals of Bay County. Not a single major case remained on the books at the time of his death. Even though Doc had no children of his own he had a passion for their well being. He was the founder of the Junior Deputies referring to the junior lawmen as "my boys". He was one of the driving forces in the establishment of the Florida Sheriff's Boys Ranch.

Gubernatorial and congressional candidates always coveted his support. Doc brushed shoulders with powerful administrators but he enjoyed most being with the every day citizen and helping with charitable drives, listening to problems and trying to keep local teenagers out of "my dilapidated jail".

Daffin was given credit for Bay County having very few problems during the tumultuous years of desegregation due to his strong history of working with black leaders and pastors in the community. The News Herald said when integration came to the all-white schools the "Old Man," as he was fondly called, prevented what could have been a tragedy by protecting black students and saying "I will enforce the law".

On January 29, 1971, age 68, Doc died from a stroke while still in office. The News Herald eulogized him as a "living legend" in his own lifetime and undisputed king of Bay County politics. Daffin was the community's most colorful public figure who was loved by people from all segments of Bay County. Congressman Bob Sikes of Crestview said, "He was one of the greatest sheriffs I've ever known' one of the greatest men". At the time of his death, Doc had served 16 years as Sheriff (between 1953-1971). As of 2003, Doc Daffin continues to hold the record of longevity as Sheriff of Bay County.

Submitted by: The Rev. J. R. Daffin, 4006 Princess Lane, Panama City, FL 32405.

The Daffin Family

The Daffin family came to America before the American Revolution. Thomas R. Daffin left France and settled at Hillsboro, Caroline County, Maryland. He married Rebecca Dickinson whose brother was killed in a duel with Andrew Jackson in Kentucky.

All the Daffin family in the Bay County, Gulf County and also Jackson County area are descendants of Thomas Daffin and Rebecca Dickinson. Ancestors in the American Revolution for membership in the Daughters of the American Revolution are: Col. Henry Dickinson verified by Marilyn Daffin Underberg DAR# 505605, Psalmet Gregorie de Roulhac verified by Dr. Julianne Daffin DAR# 529374, John Ely verified by Florence Talley Hale DAR# 773813. Another ancestor I am sure of being a Daffin forbearer is Col. Theophilus Hunter of North Carolina.

Robert Dale Daffin, Sr., was born in Eufaula, AL on September 16, 1853. He was the father of the late Rev. Dr. Robert Dale Daffin, Jr. The Rev. Dr. Robert Dale Daffin Jr., and his wife Roberta Hall Daffin were missionaries (Presbyterian) to Brazil for 24 years. Later Dr. Daffin was minister of Springfield Presbyterian and St. Andrew Presbyterian Church where he was instrumental in getting the present structure built. Earlier they had spent time at his grandfather's home in Parker. Grandfather Robert D. Daffin, Sr., owned the two story house in Parker on Highway 98 just as the road curved away from the water.

(L to R) Rev. Robert Dale Daffin, III, Carrie Daffin Daugherty and Dr. Charles Hall Daffin

Dr. Charles Hall Daffin established a medical practice in this building in Parker on November 7, 1945. At this time he was one of ten doctors in Bay County and the entire area. There was no Bay Medical Center. Dr. Daffin and his wife, Dorothy, a registered nurse made home calls all over the county. Their office hours began at 8:00 a.m. and ended at 10:00 p.m. at night. Dr. Daffin was not discharged from the U.S. Army until March 1946. He had completed tours of duty in the Southwest Pacific for 22 months from 1942 to 1943 and Normandy from 1944 to 1945 in the 114th General Hospital. He stated that war was pure hell.

On December 5, 1948 Dr. Daffin moved his office to 536 East 4th St, Panama City, FL. His office-home saw many patients over the years. Dr. Daffin limited his practice to internal medicine. Dr. Charles Daffin and his wife Dorothy reared three children: Charles Hall Daffin II, who after graduating from Bay High went into the U.S. Navy Submarine Service, serving eight years in the Navy, then graduated from Mississippi State University, then working 25 years as a mechanical and nuclear engineer for General Electric Corp., 11 years of which were in Mexico where he met Innocencia Rivera, an Industrial Engineer. Charles and Ino married and have one child Wendy, a senior at the University of North Carolina in Charlotte, NC. Dr. Charles Daffin and Dorothy's second child is Anne Daffin Harris. She is married to Carl J. Harris who retired after 23 years in the U.S. Air Force. Anne has four children: Michael L. Gailfoil who is a Police Officer with the Panama City Beach, FL Police Office and whose wife is Deana; Christopher S. Gailfoil who sells insurance in Atlanta, GA, Shawn J. Harris of Panama City, FL who is employed at the Panama City News-Herald and Leighanne L. Newberry who graduated from the University of Florida and works for Bell Signs of Panama City, FL in Gainesville, FL. Anne Daffin Harris owns and operates Professional Office Support, Inc., a medical transcription company and MED RAD, Inc., an x-ray supply company. Dr. Charles Daffin and Dorothy's youngest child is Melinda Grace Daffin Holbert Henningfield.

Charles Daffin, II ,9th Birthday Party

Melinda has a BA degree in History Education from the University of West Florida in Pensacola, a BS degree in Nursing from the University of Tennessee, a MS Degree in Nursing from the University of Oregon and is an ARNP. She worked as a Nurse Practitioner in a Health Department in Oregon. Melinda and Dr. Thomas Holbert are the parents of Thomas Robert Holbert, Jr., and Rachel Emily Holbert.

The Daffin family has served in the armed forces with Dr. Charles Daffin serving on active duty from February 1941 through March 1946. Dr. Sidney Ely Daffin, Dr. Charles Daffin's brother served in the U.S. Army Medical Corps from 1943 to 1949. He was a Captain in the United States and Japan. Charles Hall Daffin, II, served in the Vietnam War during his eight years in the U.S. Navy in the Nuclear Submarine Fleet.

Dr. Charles Daffin was one of the few doctors who took call every fourth night in the Emergency Room at Bay Medical Center for the first four years the hospital was open. They received no pay for this all night work and most of the time the patients did not pay them either. Some of the doctors on staff declined to do call duty. The ones who did were Dr. Charles Daffin, Dr. Joe Morris, Dr. W.E. Roberts, Dr. John Benton, Dr. Sidney E. Daffin and Dr. Floyd Humphreys. Dr. Charles Daffin was the last of the original six doctors on staff at Bay Medical Center to retire on April 30, 1982.

Dorothy Ann LaRue Daffin is a life member of the Fifty Year Club of the Daughters of the American Revolution, DAR# 380614. She has verified five lines: Maj. Pleasant Henderson born in Granville Co., NC who died in Tennessee. Col. James Martin born in Hunterdon, NJ and died in Stokes Co. NC; Pvt. Thomas Lanier born in V A and who died in Stokes Co., NC; Lt. Col. Joseph Williams born and died in Halifax Court House, VA.

Dr. Charles Daffin died on December 20, 1992. Dorothy met William Stacy Randall in October 1994. Mr. Randall is a man of brilliant intellect and of the highest integrity. Dorothy Daffin and William Randall were married on June 22, 1996 at Grace Episcopal Church, Panama City Beach, FL.
Submitted by: Dorothy Daffin Randall, 5801 Thomas Drive, Unit 1224 Panama City, Beach, FL 32408.

The Martin and Lovey (Cooper) Davis Family of Parker, Bay County, Florida

Martin Davis & Lovey S. Cooper, daughter of John and Elizabeth (Harvell) Cooper, were married in Marianna, Jackson County, Florida on April 15, 1875. They moved to Donaldsonville, Georgia where their first three children were born: Emma Atwood, John Ellis & Mary Ann Elizabeth. They were living near Marianna again by October 20, 1883 when son, Lonnie Leamond was born. By September 5, 1887, when Charles William was born, they had moved to Parker, then in Washington County in the St. Andrews Bay area. Their last three sons were also born in Parker; Martin Monroe, James Otto and Delbert Franklin Davis.

Martin homesteaded 160 acres located in the area between what is now Arrow Street and Ethelyn Road, south of Business Highway 98. After 'proving up' the property for five years, Martin received his title, signed on April 1, 1892. As the children matured and began their own families, each were given a piece of the property on which to build their homes and raise their families. Seven out of the eight children all lived and raised their children in Parker, and numerous descendants still live on the land. The one son who did not stay in Parker was James Otto Davis. He married Martha Brown, who's family lived in Blountstown and they chose to live and raise their family there, where there were also numerous other Davis relatives residing.

Martin was born in Calhoun County near Blountstown in 1850, but was raised in Jackson County in the Sink Creek area south of Marianna. His parents were Ellis Fairbanks Davis and Ruth Weathington.

Ellis and Ruth had six sons and one daughter; Alford, William, Walter, John, Martin, Frank and Laura. Ruth died shortly after her 6th son, Frank, was born in 1853. Ellis married again in 1854, to Elizabeth Brickhouse, and they had one daughter, Elexena. Ellis was born in Jackson County, Mississippi in 1813 and moved to Marianna, Jackson County, Florida with his parents and siblings about 1824 when he was about 11 years old. Ellis Fairbanks Davis

Lovey (Cooper) Davis and Martin Davis
1853-1935   1850-1930

was about 50 years old on 27 September 1864, when the Battle of Marianna, Florida took place during the Civil War. He had already lost one son to the War; Walter, 18 years old, died of disease at Ft. Jackson on 28 June 1862, and another son, William E., was wounded while on the march between Petersburg and Richmond, Virginia. He was hospitalized 4 Oct. 1864 in Richmond, VA, then sent home on medical leave, where he stayed until the war was over. Ellis joined the old men and boys who volunteered to defend Marianna from the Federal Army. He was captured and taken prisoner by the Union army and was imprisoned at New Orleans on Ship Island. then sent on to Elmira Prison in New York. Thousands of Confederate soldiers died there, in the worst of all of the Union prisons, which became known as 'Hellmira', because of some of the most horrible conditions imaginable. Somehow, Ellis endured and survived seven months of it despite the cruel and sadistic treatment. He was released at the end of the war in early 1865, and made his way home to Marianna, mostly on foot, because the southern railway system was destroyed in the war.

Ellis's parents were Walter and Rebecca (Harvey) Davis, both born and raised in Effingham County, Georgia. Walter and Rebecca were married about 1800 and had at least one son, John, and 2 daughters, Elizabeth and Susanna, in Georgia. On 18 December 1809, Walter obtained a Georgia passport for his family to "travel through the Creek Nations of Indians", to move to Mississippi. They left Georgia in mid-December of 1809 and arrived in Jackson County, Mississippi by 22 January 1810, where they settled along the Pascagoula River. While living there, they had five more sons and another daughter; James H., Ellis Fairbanks, Joseph, Samuel W., Almira and George W. In 1820, Walter Davis became involved in a land claim dispute over his Land Patent. It isn't clear if the dispute was settled in his favor, but by 1824 he and his family were settled in Jackson County, Florida, where he appeared on the County Tax Return list. In 1827 he & his son, John, purchased 80 acres of land each in Marianna on what is now known as Davis Street.

Walter's parents were John and Elizabeth Davis of

Effingham County, Georgia. In 1783, John received a Headright Land Grant of 100 acres on Buckhead Creek in Burke County, and in 1790 he bought 500 acres in southern Effingham County. John died May 30, 1793, shortly after dictating his Will to his son, Joseph. His wife, Elizabeth, made her Will 3 days later on 3 June 1793 and John had already died, because she referred to him in her Will as "my late husband, John Davis". Elizabeth died a few months later and both Wills were probated in September of 1793. All of their children were named; Joseph, William, Samuel, Walter, George, James, Elizabeth and Nancy.

The history of this Davis family has not been proven beyond this point as yet, although there is very strong evidence that John's parents were John Davis, Esq. and Theodora Cook. John Davis, Esq., born about 1711, married in SC May 19, 1732, Theodora Cook, moved to Georgia from St. John's Parish, Colleton County, South Carolina about 1749, where he received grants of land in what is now Liberty and Chatham counties. A record of his Will, written 13 Dec 1773 and probated 15 June 1777 in St. Phillip's Parish, Georgia, named their children; John, William, Samuel, Sarah, Catherine, Theodora, Rebecca, and grandson, James Davis.

John, Esq.'s parents were probably Samuel and Ann Davis who resided on Toogoodoo Creek, Colleton Co., SC. Samuel's will was written 17 Feb 1730 and probated 24 Jan 1738. Named were his wife, Ann, and children John, Samuel, Jr., Martha, Ann, Sarah, Mary, Rebecca, one unnamed deceased daughter and granddaughter, Mary Cole.

Submitted by: Betty L. Robbins Day Norem, 5403 Boat Race Rd., Panama City, FL 32404.

Peggy Alice Brown Davis, mother and angel

Mother was born in the small town of Andalusia, Alabama in 1932. Her parents, Bernice and Annie Jane Brown named her Peggy Alice. She had three sisters and a brother older than her. Born to an impoverished family during the Depression, she never knew a life without poverty, but she kept an optimistic outlook.

When she was 20 years old, Peggy Alice left Alabama to move to Calhoun County, Florida where she found work on a turpentine farm. After two years of the hardest work she could imagine, she met and fell in love with Jeff Davis. They eloped to Panama City, got married and settled in. Over the next 18 years, they had four girls and three boys. Jeff worked at the Cole Shipyard and Alice cooked at the Dixie Sherman Hotel. After the seventh baby, Jeff went his own way. She had a family to raise alone. Many times there was no running water, and very little heat in the wintertime. Alice made certain that

Peggy Alice Brown Davis, an angel, with three grandchildren

her children had food, were clean and had good manners. It may not have been all good times for Mother, but seven children made playtime a lot of fun.

The children started school at Glenwood Elementary and rode the bus to the house on Massalina Bayou. Mother made sure that the homework was finished and corrected before playtime began. She raised chickens that she bought, mail order ($21 for 250 biddies), for eggs and meat. The children had fun finding the eggs of those yard birds and Mother cooked a lot of eggs. The children often did yard work to make money to help the family, too.

Mother had to be both mother and father to her children. She moved to Iowa Avenue in Lynn Haven to improve her conditions. The younger children started school at March Green Elementary, but one year later, were sent to Lynn Haven Elementary School.

Times were still tough and food was not plentiful. One day, the boys stole hot dogs from the refrigerator and went fishing. They used bits of hot dog for bait and caught 9 or 10 fish. Peggy Alice Davis didn't fuss too much about the hot dogs as she cooked fish for a great dinner.

Peggy Alice Brown Davis died in 1984. She left 25 grandchildren and her seven loving children. They all are citizens of Bay County. Health care workers, a heavy equipment operator, a police officer and a cook are her heritage in Bay County.

Submitted by: Clint C. Davis, 609 David Ave., Panama City, FL 32401.

Flossie Dawsell

My mother, Flossie Hewett Dawsell (Doswell) was born in Jackson County, Fl., in the small town of Grand Ridge, on April 23, 1917. She was one of six children born to (Ed) Edward Hewett and Lizzie Stephens Hewett. Her parents were farmers, and life was very simple and poor. She grew up and married my father, Thomas Henry Dawsell, Jr. in 1935. Daddy was a farmer, too, for a number of years. But, eventually, he decided he could make a better living doing something else. A new Paper Mill had opened in Panama City, Florida, in Bay County. So, in 1945, my mother, father and I moved to Panama City, so daddy could get a job at the mill.

I had been born Janie Ruth Dawsell in Calhoun County, Florida, in the small, rural town of Blountstown, in 1939. Our original last was Doswell. My father changed the spelling of our name somewhere along the way. I still don't know why. As a result of our move to Panama

Left Flossie Dawsell- Janie Ammons-Teresa Hires- Stormie Janie Lee Hires

City, in 1945, I completed my education in Bay County, graduating From Bay High School in 1957. I married Gene Ammons the day after my graduation.

After marrying and having three sons, I finally had a daughter, Teresa Lavern Ammons, born in 1967. She became our third generation. She was born in Shreveport, La., but finished growing up in Panama City, Fl., graduating from Rutherford High School in 1985.

Teresa married Odis Leroy Hires. It wasn't too long before our fourth generations came along, when granddaughter, Stormie Janie Lee Hires was born in 1992 at Gulf Coast Hospital in Panama City, Florida. She currently lives in Greenville, Tenn., with her parents.

Submitted by: James Ammons, Box 23, Panama City, Florida 32402. Written By: Janie Ammons Panama City, Fl. Sources: Family Records.

Janie Dawsell
Growing Up In Millville

Hair curler or bus ride, it was a big thing. As a child, growing up in the Millville area of Panama City, we would go up to Carr's Beauty Shop at the intersection of U.S. Business 98 and East Avenue to get a perm or a hair set. Afterwards, we would look like something from outer space.

There was a bus stop on Kraft Avenue and 98, where we could catch the city bus downtown, where we would go to the Christo's five and dime store. The cost of the bus ride was one token.

At home, we would play childrens's games like checkers and hopscotch. We had to use our imaginations in whatever we did. We would make a checker board out of part of a pasteboard box, and we used Coca Cola bottle caps for the checkers. When we played hopscotch, we used pieces of glass

Janie Ammons

or rock. We also would play baseball or football in the road, since there weren't many cars on the residential roads back then.

We would wash out clothes in rain water that we caught in wash tubs, which we had placed on some old wooden "saw horses" that carpenters used in their work. Our main means of transportation was walking. We would walk to the grocery store, to school, the drug store, and just about anywhere within the Millville area. I attended Millville Elementary school for six years and Everitt Jr. High School for three years.

Once in a while somebody with a car would take a group of us to the drive-in movies. There were two drive-in theaters back then, the Gulf Drive-In on west 15th street, and the Isle of View drive-in theater, closer to us on Everitt Avenue. The cost was $1.00 for a car load of people. You had to roll down the windows to set the speaker on the edge of the car door, but since cars didn't have air conditioning anyway back then, it didn't matter.

We didn't go to the doctor much. It was too expensive and only for emergencies. If you got sick, your mother would probably give you castor oil to purge your system. It would either cure you or kill you. Another activity we engaged in was climbing the chinaberry trees in our yards and throwing the chinaberries at each other. On Sundays, we could catch the church bus that ran by our house and go to church.

I had a Brownie Hawkeye camera that I took everywhere with me. Everybody would hide when they saw me coming with that camera because they knew I was going to take their pictures, time and time again. But now everybody is enjoying those pictures of the good old days.
Submitted by: Janie Ammons, Box 23, Panama City, FL 32402.

Thomas Henry Dawsell

My father, Thomas Henry Dawsell, was born 5/1/1908, in Kinard, Florida, and died 10/10/53, in Panama City, Florida. He was a farmer in Jackson County, Florida, in the Grand Ridge community. He married my mother, Flossie Hewett Dawsell, in 1935, in Calhoun County, Florida. She died 5/23/2002. I was born Janie Ruth Dawsell on 8/25/39 in Blountstown, Florida.

Thomas Henry Dawsell

We moved to Panama City, Florida, in Bay County in 1945. I was in the first grade. My father got a job at the paper mill and worked there until he died with Leukemia. We rented a house in the area around the mill known as Millville. Our rent was $15.00 a month. Daddy earned $40.00 a week. We didn't have an indoor bathroom, so we used an outhouse instead.

The house was not insulated. In the winter we would almost freeze. Our source of heat was a wood heater. There were only two rooms in the house at first, then we added a kitchen. We had a wooden refrigerator or "Ice Box". It used two blocks of ice a week, which was delivered by the ice man. A lamp was used for lighting before getting electricity on 3/8/1947, with a $5.00 deposit.

Life was simple, and seafood was plentiful in the area. We would meet the fishing boats when they came in and buy red snapper directly from the fisherman. Boy, was that good! Mom would save glass jugs for Mr. Emanuel to fill with cane juice every week. My father would buy a pint of whiskey and make a toddy by adding water and sugar. I would sneak a little when I got a chance. Neighbor women would gather for pea shelling sessions on their porches.

We would walk a few blocks to Gardner's Drug Store, an old fashioned drug store with a real soda fountain. We would buy ice cream cones and comic books. I used to work helping price groceries in a neighborhood store for Mr. Whit Curry, the owner. I made fifty cents, which was enough to walk down the railroad track to the old Bay Theater and see Roy Rogers, Dale Evans, and Gabby Hayes in a cowboy movie. The fifty cents not only paid for 9 cents admission, but I could also buy popcorn, coke and candy.

We walked everywhere back then. Like most families, we didn't have a car until later. We bought a new Blue Ford in 1955. We could catch the city bus to go down town. The fare was one token.

I went to Millville Elementary School for six years, then to Everitt Junior High for three years. There were only two high schools back then. Bay High for white students and Rosenwald High for black students. Since we lived far enough away from the school I was able to ride the school bus during my three years at Bay High. I graduated from high school on 6/3/1957. I still lived in the house and neighborhood where I grew up.
Submitted by: Janie Ammons, 2714 East 7th Court, Panama City, Florida 32401. Sources: Family Records.

Nelda Tibbits McClellan Deuerling

My name is Nelda Tibbits McClellan and I arrived in 1969 a divorced mom with Michelle, Marilyn, and Melissa McClellan my three children. I had tried living in Dothan but could not make enough money. I just meant I would not be a welfare mother. I tried many different jobs including toy

Michelle, Marilyn and Nelda holding baby Melissa

store clerk, holiday inn, and even cooking. My best money was working as a barmaid on the beach. You see I had to make enough to support us without any help. Well I found out that I was really good at remembering not only what was ordered but by whom and how much they owed. Imagine me carrying more than one tray filled with drinks and not spilling any of it. I remember many night when I would hurt so bad my feet, back and legs but it was for my children and myself. I made good tips enough to pay our bills. No, we did not have much furniture, and we rented but we were together. We did not have a decent car but I loved these kids. I missed out on a lot because of my working night and sleeping days.

We moved to Kentucky but when our chickens froze on the perches, we moved back to beautiful Bay County. You know I have never left again. I really love the beaches and warm weather. I am married to Jack Deuerling and live in Fountain.

I am a nanny to my grandchildren Christian Stinespring, Justin Stewart and Wayne Marsh. I love all my grandchildren Jade, Kyle, Aileen, Mathew and Amber McClelland, Leonia Sapp, Tabitha and Laurel Peiars. I will always be there for them.

I enjoy the outdoors especially my flowers. I can shoot a gun as good as anyone and have bagged my share of deer. I hope to live here in Fountain until I die and be buried in the Fountain Cemetery near Rev. Nellie Tibbits my mother. We attend Bayou George Calvary Temple Assembly of God church.

Submitted by: Nelda Tibbits Deuerling, 21123 Hightower Road, Fountain, Florida 32438.

Peyton Doswell

Thomas Rolfe, son of the Indian Princess, Pochohantas and the Englishman, John Rolfe, married Jane Poythress, they had a daughter, Jane Rolfe. Jane married Colonel Robert Bolling. Their son, Colonel John Bolling, married Mary Kennon. John and Mary had a son, John Bolling Jr., who married Elizabeth Bland Blaeir. Their son, Robert Bolling, married Susan Watson. Robert and Susan produced a daughter named Pochohantas Rebecca Bolling, who married Joseph Cabell. Their daughter, Mary Pochohantas Cabell, married Peyton Doswell, son of William Doswell and Elizabeth Mills. Peyton was the brother of Thomas

Standing Left to right, Leigh Anna Ammons- James Ammons- Janie Ammons- Emmett Ammons- Seated Granny Flossie Dawsell

Doswell, Sr.(my ggggrandfather), who married Elizabeth Walker of Virginia. It was Thomas and Elizabeth's son, Thomas Doswell, Jr. (my gggfather) who was married to Elizabeth Morgan of Georgia. Their son, Thomas P. Doswell, was born in Georgia in 1832, but died in Alabama. His wife was Catherine Merritt. Thomas P. and Catherine's son, Thomas Henry Doswell, Sr., was born in 1866 in Alabama and married Mineloze Collins in Calhoun County, Florida, in 1903. Thomas Henry Doswell, Jr., was born in 1908 and married Flossie Hewett in 1935 in Blountstown, Florida, and had one daughter, Janie Ruth Doswell, born in 1939, in Blountstown, Florida. I married Walter Eugene (Gene) Ammons in 1957 in Donaldsonville, Georgia. We had three sons, Emmett Eugene, 1958, James (Jimmy) Thomas (named after his granddaddy Doswell) 1959, Stephen (Stevie) Walter 1961, then we had a lovely daughter, Teresa Lavern in 1967. Teresa married Odis Leroy Hires in 1991, and my beautiful granddaughter was born Stormie Janie Lee Hires in 1992. My son Jimmy had a handsome little Blue Eyed son named Augustus McCrae Ammons. Gus, as we call him, is a typical 2 years old and full of energy. He keeps mom and dad hoping.

Submitted by: Janie Ammons, 2714 E. 7th Ct., Panama City, Florida 32401. Sources: Family Records; World Book; Pocahontas Book; Alabama and Virginia Census Records.

Frances Bunnie Douglas

My father was John William Douglas born May 14, 1917 in Southport, Florida. He was two years old when his dad died. His sister, Mable Holley, told us that their father came from Scotland. My cousin Mildred went to Scotland and there is a castle there named Douglas. We don't know which Douglas it is, but she visited a Douglas Castle. Dad and his father were named Francis Marion. I was named after my grandfather. My grandfather's brother came from Alabama.

My father was a Marine and was stationed at New Jersey. He met my mother, Emma Maude Gerlach in New Jersey and they were married November 21, 1936. While stationed at Lakehurst Naval Station, he was an eye-witness to the Hindenburg explosion May 6, 1937. My sister was born September 3, 1937 in Allentown, Pennsylvania. My father got out of the military service in 1938. After my sister, Winnie Mae Douglas, was born they moved to Panama City, Florida and lived with my dad's mother, Anna Douglas and his brother, F. M. Douglas. When my mother found out she was pregnant with me, she moved back to Allentown where

I was born. My mother was born in Allentown and she went to high school and one year of college there. She went on vacation with a girl friend to New Jersey and that's how she met my dad. Her people were from Germany. They were German-Dutch. Her great-grandparents owned the first water works in the United States and it is still there in Allentown. The steps and the wheel are now gone. We took my dad to

Frances Bunnie Douglas and family

Pennsylvania in August for a family reunion before he died in December. We looked up a lot of my mother's family and there is a library named after my great-grandparents in Allentown. His name was Kendall and that's the library's name.

When I was about four months old, we moved back to Panama City and lived on Oak Avenue. I slept in a drawer. The log house was on the 800 block of Oak Avenue and is still there to this day. My parents wanted to buy the house but was told it was eaten up with termites; but the house is still there today.

We moved to Lynn Haven and my sister started first grade in Lynn Haven School. We lived over a store and that building is still there today. I think it was at 3rd Street. My parents then bought the house at 308 Linda Avenue in the Cove area of town. It was a dirt road then and only about five houses on each side of the road. I was eleven years old when my brother George Charles Douglas was born on March 21, 1950.

I got married in 1959 at St Dominc's Catholic Church on Harrison Avenue. To an Air Force guy and we moved to East Boston, Massachusetts. I had my children and lived my adult life in East Boston. I came back for several high school class reunions. I am very proud of the quilt that I won at one reunion for coming the fartherest to the reunion.

Submitted by: Frances Bunnie Douglas Powers, 925 Oak Ave, Panama City, Florida 32401.

John William Douglas

How many people can truly say that they were there when history was made? John William Douglas, a native of Bay County who passed away on December 26, 2001 at the age of 84, is one person who can. He was in the Marines and a member of the ground crew that tried, in vain, to land the Hindenburg on May 6, 1937. The 803 foot long German airship was flying into land at Lakehurst, New Jersey on that fateful day.

It appeared that the ship was coming in too fast and people on the ground crew were relaying orders to the ship and crew through megaphones. The Hindenburg crew shut off the engine to put it in reverse, but fire burst out and ignited the ship. The hydrogen gas in the airship was highly flammable. The Hindenburg fell to the ground, killing 36 of the 97 people on board. One person on the ground as part of the landing crew was also killed.

There were radio announcers covering the Hindenburg's

Capt. John W. Douglas

landing and their on-the-air coverage of the tragic event is legend up to this day. It was radio's first recorded live news event and it lives in history.

In 1938, John Douglas and his wife returned to Panama City and raised a family. He became a member of the Panama City Police Department and worked to organize school safety patrol units in Bay County and was the first officer in charge of the patrols. He became a captain in the police department and later transferred to the Panama City Fire Department and served as Chief for several years. After he retired from public service, he became an independent insurance agent before retiring again at age 75. He was a founding member of the Bay County Sportsman's Club. He also enjoyed being a Keystone Cop with the Shriners. He drove a "paddy wagon" while the Keystone Cops performed their chase scenes in parades.

Submitted by: Bunnie Douglas Powers, 925 Oak Ave., Panama City, FL 32401.

Bobbie McClung Duncan

Our C-Mama was a very special person in the lives of her children, grandchildren, great-grandchildren and great great-grandchildren. She was born Bobbie Ophelia McClung on May 13, 1891. She married J.T. Duncan on January 1, 1915. They took the train built by Henry Flagler to Key West for their honeymoon.

C-Mama became an instant mother when she married the widowed J.T. He had three motherless children, Lester, Rignal and Louise. There was never a doubt that they were her children! The family increased over the years with the addition of Frances, Marjorie, J.T. Jr., Bob, Eularee, Joe and Jack. Sadly, Louise was fatally injured in a fire when she was six years old, and Eularee died in infancy of pneumonia. The family moved to Panama City in 1935 during the hardship Depression years.

C-Mama lost her husband in November, 1942 and valiantly continued raising her family. After he died, C-Mama was matriarch of a household consisting of Frances and her baby, Ellen, J.T. Jr., Bob, Joe and Jack. Everyone pulled together during these war years. Frances' husband, Wilkie, was stationed in Alaska. Bob joined the Navy, J.T., Jr., worked at Wainwright Shipyard, and Joe and Jack were still in school. Marjorie married H. Savely McQuagge and they also lived in Panama City.

Frances would read Ellen a poem about "going to see

Bobbie McClung Duncan our C-Mama

Grandmother" and Ellen shortened it to "see Mama" and that's how C-Mama received her name. From that time on, she was known to one and all, kin folks and friends, as C-Mama.

C-Mama was so proud of all her grandchildren and delighted in spending time with us. She taught us to love the Lord, and accept Him into all aspects of our life. She read the Bible and taught it to us. She loved Grace Livingston Hill's books and was the first person I knew who read Harlequin Romances! She loved a happy ending. She taught

C-Mama surrounded by grandchildren on her 62nd birthday in 1953

us to play Canasta and Solitaire and to love baseball. She cherished the time she spent going to baseball games to watch her grandsons play. Two grandsons played baseball at college, one at Georgia Tech and one at Georgetown.

She loved to travel whether by air, car, train or bus and made many trips to see children and grandchildren. In her later years, she enjoyed doing handiwork and made many gifts for her family.

She left us on March 2, 1988, two months before her 97th birthday but she bequeathed to us a rich heritage. She shared her love, philosophy, generosity and sweetness with her children, 25 grandchildren and 65 great-grandchildren. The number of great-great grandchildren continues to grow and currently stands at 43.

Her youngest son, Jack, a newspaper columnist, wrote about her soon after her death. Jack and his family live on the West Coast. He quoted from a letter written by his oldest daughter, Eularee, that was read at C-Mama's funeral, in which she said "You have always accepted what has come your way. I have always admired you for that quality - one I hope the years will help me to acquire... I will never stop loving you and will never forget you... You are the cornerstone of my life..."

Jack ended his column by saying that "She was once asked which of her children she loved the most. Her reply was"

The child that is sick until that child is well.

The child that is lost until that child is found.

The child that is troubled until that child's troubles end.

The child that is farthest away until that child is safely home. (He adds: "I was always the child farthest from home.")

C-Mama, we all know that you loved each of us best!

Submitted by: Ellen J. Rumph for all those who love C-Mama. 161 Marin Drive, PC FL 32405.

The J. T. Duncan, Sr. Family Arriving in Panama City

The Great Depression and the ensuing financial problems caused my father's business in Moultrie, Georgia to fail. As a boy of six, and shortly after beginning school in Moultrie, I was told we were moving to a place called Panama City, Florida, a fishing village and tourist beach town in the panhandle of Florida, on the Gulf of Mexico. I remember the long, long drive to get there. There was no such thing as asking "Are we there yet?" Or "How much longer?" In fact you had to sit as quietly as you could and didn't dare complain. My older brothers, Lester and Rignal, were adults, married and living away from home. My brother, J. T., Jr., rode in the truck bringing the furniture. The rest of the children, were crowded into my father's 1928 Buick. It was a large, black car that resembled those old gangster cars in the movies. We were so crowded that I had to sit on the floorboard of the backseat for most of the trip.

We arrived in Panama City after dark on October 10, 1935.

The house my father had rented on Harrison Avenue was dark and the electricity had not been turned on so he drove us to the Dixie Sherman Hotel in downtown Panama City where we spent the night. The hotel had opened on July 4, 1927 and was like a diamond in the center of Panama City - an awesome sight for a six year old boy that had never in his life slept in a hotel! The next morning after breakfast, my brother, Bob, took my brother, Joe and me to the roof of the 8 story building. From that rooftop, I thought that I could see forever and that I must be as high as anyone had ever been. It was a grand sight and one that is very much in my

J. T. Duncan, Sr. and wife Bobbie Duncan on Honeymoon in Key West, Florida 1915

memory even today. The smell of the salt water in the air was also different and new for me. Even today, to be in a seaport town and sniff the air brings back that memory.

The big, old darkened house I saw the night we arrived, looked different by day. The next time I saw it, our furniture had been moved in and my family, my father, J.T., Sr., mother, Bobbie, sisters Frances and Marjorie, and brothers J.T., Bob and Joe brought it to life. My sister, Frances, told me years later that mother first said she would not put her good furniture in that old house. Since we had no other place to go, she relented, but demanded that we move to a new house as soon as one could be found.

I would live in Panama City for the next ten years. It was a great place to spend a childhood. It was my hometown and if you asked me today where is my hometown, I would, without hesitation, tell you Panama City, Florida, although I lived there fewer years than I have lived elsewhere.

Submitted by : William J. (Jack) Duncan, 3663 Garden Valley Road, Roseburg, OR.

Dallas Rudolph Emanuel
Born January 29, 1919 - Died April 29, 1994

He was the second of nine children born to William Owen "Bud" Emanuel and Jessie Mae Mapes Emanuel. His nickname was "Rooster" because he had a head full of red hair. In his adult years, he was simply known as "Red." He had three red headed brothers also known as "Red." So when someone mentioned Red, we'd ask, "Which one?" He spend

Dallas Rudolph Emanuel (born January 29, 1919 died April 29, 1994) and Mavis Gibson Emanuel (born January 14, 1936 died June 19, 2000)

30 years of his life doing something he enjoyed which was the perfection of his father's vocation. His father sold dressed hogs and he grew up dressing hogs. These were the days before supermarkets so he sold to independent general merchants. At sixteen years old, he went to work in Harold Steadman's retail grocery store in Panama City. Later on he worked for the old Kelleys in St. Andrews as market manager for five years. From there he met Mr. L. D. Lewis and joined Sunshine Supermarkets where he stayed thirty years until retirement. His positions at Mr. Lewis' Sunshine Grocery Company were market manager, then supervisor of all the supermarket meat markets, supervisor over supermarket operations, manager of the Millville store, head of the produce department at Tyndall

Parkway store, and because of ill health, finished his tenure with the company as cashier at the Millville lunch counter. Red traveled with Mr. L. D. Lewis to some of the big meat packing houses in Idaho and the north. He traveled under the name of D. R. Emanuel. Mr. Lewis said they got special attention from the airlines who thought Red was a doctor.

Everyone knew Red. He was born and raised in Millville. The only time he left home was to serve in the armed forces in World War II. He was sent to the Azore Islands. His location was a secret so the family did not know where he was. The first thing he did after returning home in

Antique cars restored by Dallas Rudolph Emanuel

1946 was to buy the home and land directly across the street from the house where he was born. He lived there until his death. He married Mavis Gibson who had a son, Michael, which he adopted. They had a daughter of their own, Katrina, and a precious adopted daughter, Linda.

When Mavis' parents died, her two sisters, Laura Jean and Libby, came to live with them. Their home was a show place. There was a large catfish pond and extensive lawns and a windmill. It was a meeting place for large gatherings of family and friends where there was always warm hospitality.

Mr. Emanuel's hobby was restoring old cars to their original state. He collected parts and put together a 1915 Model T, a 1924 Model T and a 1927 Model T, and six Model A Fords. He took a trip to Disney World in 1964 in a Model T with his grandson, Rick, his daughter, Katrina, and his wife, Mavis. He said, "It took two days at 30 miles per hour." In 1968 Red drove Mr. Lewis around the county in his 1915 Model T. Mr. Lewis owned Sunshine Grocery Company and was running for State Representative. They attracted a lot of favorable attention. Red won three out of five events in the 1968 Fourth of July parade in Lynn Haven. He won best of show, slow speed contest and best driver and best costume of the era. In 1975 he took his 1915 Model T in a caravan from Sunny Hills to the fifth Annual Mackle Antique Car Tour to Marco Island in South Florida. He won another first place with his 1915 Ford touring car in the Lynn Haven parade in 1972. In 1970 he bought, restored, and drove his 1915 Model T Ford to Dothan, attracting a lot of attention on the way. His cars and family were in the local parades. His wife was a talented seamstress and designed their clothes after the era of the cars.

Mr. Emanuel was a good artist and designed effective signs to promote sales in the Sunshine Stores. His reputation as a meat cutter was well known and readily recognized for its clean, not pre-packaged, perfectly cut and displayed meat cases.

Red said, "How many people get to work all their life at a job they enjoy, with a company they love, then retire and spend the rest of their time doing something else just as enjoyable. I'm a lucky man and I know it."

Submitted by two sisters: Willowen Emanuel Harrison and Margie Emanuel Newmans, 1222 Yale Ave, Panama City, Fl 32405.

William Owen Emanuel
1878-1967

William Owen "Bud" Emanuel was born in Marianna, Jackson County, Florida. As a young man, William worked for the L & N Railroad. He also had a mercantile store in Millville. He was one of the first ice and wholesale meat dealers in Bay County. Once he went to Pensacola by train and while there he saw his first bicycle. He bought one and brought it back to Marianna. It was one with a big wheel up front and a smaller one on the rear. It had no brakes so you had to slow it down with the pedals. He gathered a crowd out on a clay hill to watch him ride it. He got it going down hill and could not stop it. It threw him and skinned him all over. He gave it to the local blacksmith and told him he never wanted to see it again. As the story goes, he was holding a bottle of whiskey in one hand as he rode down the hill. Someone asked him if he spilled any of the whiskey. He said, "Nary a drop."

William Owen Emanuel

He came to Bay County as a young man. He met and married Jessie Mae Mapes. Jessie Mae was born April 25, 1898 in St. Andrews, Bay County, Florida, and was the daughter of Lewis Nelson Mapes and Delena Swindle Mapes. Jessie Mae Mapes' grandfather, Hiram M. Mapes, helped establish Bay County's oldest church in 1886. It was St. Andrews Presbyterian. Lewis and Delena were married October 21, 1893, in Vernon, Florida, and had seven children: Jessie, Fred, Nelson (who married Alice), Raymond, Charles, Albert and Phillip. William and Jessie Mae went to their wedding in a surrey with a fringe on top pulled by a fine sorrel horse. They were married in Millville, Florida, by Judge Harrison in 1915.

William's mother was Jenny Watson and his father was Asa Emanuel. William had three sisters: Luella born 1874, Betty Elmira born 1879, Georgia Elizabeth born 1875. He had three half brothers: Kinsey, Frank and A.C., and two half sisters: Emma and Eva. William's mother died early in life. His father married again and his stepmother's name was Tabatha.

Williams' main lifetime occupation was livestock. He bought, sold and butchered in all the neighboring counties as well as Bay County. He was a professional butcher, having a big walk-in cold storage locker at the old ice plant at the end of Sherman Avenue in Millville. He could look at livestock and tell the weight on the hoof, dressed out, and profit wise, and was rarely off by much. He was widely known for treating sick animals in the days before veterinarians. He was active in politics and well known as an honorable man of his word. He was well known for his sense of humor. Many of his shenanigans are still talked about by old timers.

William had two children by his first marriage to Ida Knowles-a son, Donald, and a daughter, Willie Maude. Willie Maude was married to Al Simmons. They had no children. Donald was married to Clara Dykes. They had five sons: D.L., Odolph, Randall, William (Billy), and Nixon. With his second wife, Jessie, he had nine children: Roland Elmer born September 9, 1916; Dallas Rudolph born January 29, 1919; Marion Catherine born May 18, 1921; Christine Estelle born June 7, 1923; Margie Rhea born April 17, 1925; Willowen (named for her father) born April 13, 1927; Woodrow Caswell born May 28, 1929; Marshall Russell born August 6, 1930; and John Douglas born June 6, 1938.

William Owen Emanuel and Jessie Mae Mapes Emanuel

William raised his family on five acres of land in Millville,

Florida, which he farmed bountifully year round to feed his family and needy neighbors. He planted seven scuppernong vines, peach, plum, kumquat, mulberry and fig trees. There were chickens, horses, cows, dogs, pigs, cats and goats-you name it. There was a flock of guineas that ran loose. One day some boys asked if they could have one. William told them they could have all they could catch. Needless to say, they couldn't catch one. Always the entrepreneur, in his older age, he owned and ran a sugar cane mill at the corner of East Avenue and Business Highway 98. Also in his older age, he was endearingly known as "Uncle Bud." He grew his own sugar cane and with his faithful mule, "Peanut," and loyal bull, "Doc," hauled cane to the mill and ground juice to sell as a beverage.

Roland married Bessie Kennington and they had two sons: Roland Luther and Charles. Bessie died with complications of childbirth. Roland later married Alma Henderson of Millville who, after Roland's death, raised Roland's two sons and her three children: Thaggard, Earl and Elizabeth. Rudolph married Mavis Gibson and they had three children: Linda, Katrina and Michael. Catherine married Coy Kennington. They had two children: Ann and Alfred. Christine married Colin Shiver and they had four children: Karen, Harry, John and Jeff. Margie married Howard Newmans. They had four children: Delena, Howard, Jr., Henry and Woodrow, Willowen married Russell Harrison. They had four children: Dan, Arlene, Tom and Joanie. Woodrow never married. Marshall married Perry Jean Pettis. They had three children: Russell, Kathy and Melinda. John married Nell Gaff. They had two children: Mark and Angela.

Bud and Jessie tragically lost their firstborn, Roland, in an explosion at Arizona Chemical in Bay Harbor, Florida, on May 4, 1951. Woodrow was killed December 19, 1952, at an unmarked railroad crossing on 15th Street at 23 years of age. Rudolph died April 29, 1994, at 75 years of age. Catherine died December 12, 2001, at 80 years of age. John died August 15, 2001, at 63 years of age. William lost the love of his life, his wife Jessie, to cancer July 15, 1960, at 62 years of age. They were married 45 years. William died in 1967 of cardiac arrest at Lisenby Hospital during surgery to remove a gangrenous foot. The paper stated, "Pioneer William Owen "Bud" Emanuel passed away at the age of 89." In three months, he would have been 90 years old. Friends from near and far, of all races, attended a standing room only funeral-the largest this area had ever seen.

Bud, Jessie, Roland, Catherine, Woodrow and John are interred at Callaway Cemetery.

William's family said there are eight things to remember about their dad: He always had a full head of hair. He could read without glasses at 89 years old. He prayed on his knees before retiring at night. He was a crack shot with a rifle. He never shaved himself, always going to the barber shop or having one of his children shave him. He owned cars and trucks but never drove. He had a beautiful garden year round. He never had an enemy but a host of friends.
Submitted by: Willowen "Becky" Emanuel Harrison and Margie Rhea Emanuel Newmans, 904 Michigan Ave, Lynn Haven, FL 32444.

William Owen Emanuel
Father's Day 1990

A Tribute to my Daddy - "Uncle Bud" as he was known to many. William Owen Emanuel being his given name. As long as I can remember my Daddy was known as "Uncle Bud." As a child, I never gave it a thought why even strangers to me, called my Daddy "Uncle Bud" - now, that I am older and reminiscence - I know it was more a "Kindred Relationship" among people then - Than there is now. Too, my Daddy was a very friendly, jovial person - with a Big heart - who never met a stranger, and was never at a loss for words. I remember him as a Giving person and very patient - as well as intellectually smart - maybe not in books - But he read the daily paper - and was almost a veterinarian - Because if someone's horse was sick in those days - They came and got my Daddy to treat them. As far as I can remember, he never lost a case.

My Daddy was a Butcher by trade. He knew his profession like a doctor in our days knows diseases and antibiotics. He knew not only how to pick the cattle and hogs he butchered and cut up, but he could look at them on hoof and tell how much they would weigh out when dressed. He didn't miss them by two or three lbs. He could make homemade smoked sausage that would melt in your mouth, seasoned just right - when smoked and pork hams just as good. And how about that souse and cracklins. He didn't have to have a recipe - He went by taste-yummy! It would make Jimmy Deans' today taste pitiful! Or any of the other sausage makers on TV commercials - that are really tasty - But not like my Daddy's old timey makings.

William Owen "Uncle Bud" Emanuel

My Daddy could tell a yarn a mile long. He delighted in telling a funny - and yes, They were funny - and usually out done the one the other feller told. I still laugh over many of his 'sayings' long since he has gone to be with the Lord. He was not a bragger, and never tried to put anyone down.

My Daddy always had a garden. It was hard work, but I never heard him complain even when sweat was dripping off his face. He would pump off the water - at the old pump and drink a dipper of water and sit in an old chair under the Chinaberry tree - to rest and cool of a bit. There were no electric fans or air conditioners in those days - so he had to be made out of good stuff. He would grow the best tasting peas, Butterbeans, corn, tomatoes, hot pepper, okra, sweet potatoes, Irish potatoes, cucumbers and turnip greens. The best you ever tasted and my mother knew how to cook them. He always raised a crop of sugar cane- Because in the fall - He hooked up the wagon and loaded it with cane and headed down to Hwy 98 on the corner to grind cane juice. The only person I ever knew who would go to all that trouble to make a dollar and grind cane and make cane juice. Lots of people would stop by for "Uncle Bud's Cane Juice."

He worked hard and raised 11 children and also my Mother's Baby Brother Philip - to the age of 17 - My Mother's Mother had died at Philip's birth - so her daddy let my mother and daddy raise him as their own.

My Daddy lived to be 90 years old, so hard work didn't kill

"Uncle Bud" Emanuel cane grinding

him. He was as Honest as the days were long and I can never remember a night my Daddy didn't kneel by the old Heater or whatever using a chair for his alter and pray at least an hour. He prayed to himself, but was never in a hurry to get it over with.

Life was never easy for my Daddy or Mother when I was growing up. There were no "push buttons" to do anything. It was all "The sweat of the Brow" type - wood for the cook stove, Rub Boards to scrub clothes - no running water or electric irons, no ice or electric refrigerator. The ice man may drive by, if Daddy had a nickle, he would buy a little chunk of ice, to be wrapped in a newspaper or corn sack and put under a tub on a table under the Chinaberry tree. I thank God for all our modern day push button conveniences and wish Mother and Daddy could have known more about them and had them. Money was as scarce as chicken teeth - and there was not all the Social services which many have today - But Daddy always managed to have something Mother could fix and put on our table.

He always raised chicken, guineas, and always had a barn to keep peanuts or his mule in and he was fed and watered daily. How Daddy managed to do so much with so little to do with I still haven't figured out. I guess in those days, no one kept up with the Joneses - We were all in about the same boat!

He often went to the fish house to buy mullet fish for dinner - for the winter he would buy a box of salt fish (Mullet) that would keep because they were salted - and before cooking had to be soaked in cold water over night to remove the salt.

He would rend fat from the pigs for "Lard". The grease most people used back then to cook with - But it was delicious and "cholesterol" had never been discovered.

As I sit here, today, with all my push button conveniences - a car, microwave, television grocery store and many other helpful things, I say "How Blessed I am" and we are. And I still wonder at how my parents raised 11 wonderful children who all had professions and ability to be "stand outs" in our society.

In those days, yes, there were colds, whooping cough, measles, chicken pox - no specialists or money for Doctors. We survived. Mother sewed with a Singer pedal foot sewing machine and made clothes without patterns to look at and fit professionally - underwear, coats, shirts for the boys. Some were made from "Hand me Downs" "Has Beens" or "Hold overs" - who would ever know when mother finished with a garment.

My Daddy owned 5 acres of land where we always lived - and never moved until we were all grown and married. Its still being occupied by family members - our home place and house. I have been gone 62 years, but that 5 acres has always been a big part of my heart, and holds many, many memories. Some I will always cherish, others too painful to try to hold on to. But when it comes to my Mother and Daddy, Love abounds! It always will!

I love you both and will see you in Heaven,

Christine

Submitted by: Christine Estelle Emanuel Shiver and Becky Harrison, 904 Michigan Ave, Lynn Haven, FL 32444.

Harvey Lee Floyd Family

Harvey Lee Floyd was born 31 July 1912 to Columbus Sidney Floyd and Cora Elizabeth Pate in Holmes County, Florida. Sidney and Cora were married 9 October 1910 in Holmes County. They had six children: Johnny Leamon born 29 April 1911, Harvey Lee born 31 July 1912, Ruby D, born 26 September 1916, Albert born 16 May 1914, Robert Lee born 26 September 1921 , and Annie Lou born 23 August 1925.

Johnny Leamon left to work in Santa Rosa County, and a couple of weeks later Harvey decided to follow him. It was a little town called Jay, outside of Milton, Florida. He told me about walking down a long country road and hearing someone call Leamon's name. He had found his brother.

He met my Mother at a shindig Grandpa Stafford was having at his house on a Saturday night. He said it was love at first sight. He had thrown a string ball to another man and Mom walked in front and the ball hit her in the face. Harvey worked to save money so they could elope. They went to Bonifay in Holmes County, and Harvey Lee Floyd married Myrtle Lucille Stafford 24 September 1932. They went back to Jay, Florida where they started their family.

Houston Lebert was born 3 November 1933, Audrey Lucille was born 28 October 1935, Billie Jean was born in Holmes 11 February 1938. Dad helped move a sawmill to Lake City, Florida. Elouise was born there 24 March 1940. We moved to Bay County, Florida. Dad worked at Tyndall,

Harvey Lee Floyd and Myrtle Lucille Stafford, 1957

the paper mill, then to the Wainwright Shipyard as a fireman. Mom also worked as a spot welder. We lived in Springfield at this time. Johnnie Wayne was born 3 March 1944. Dad volunteered for the Navy 23 June 1945. They found out he had five children so they discharged him 23 November 1945.

I remember attending the Springfield Community Church when it was a sawdust floor, planks on concrete blocks, enclosed in paper from the paper mill. The pastor was Ollie Stockwell. I was about eleven when Dad decided he wanted to farm again. We moved back to Holmes County. Patricia Ann was born 1 February 1947. We were going to Live Oak School. I was top of my class; of course there were only three in my class. Mom took sick with TB and had to go to a hospital in Jackson County. It took her 2 years to get well enough to come home. Dad had moved us back to Bay County and went to work with HG Harders Cons.

In 1954 Dad bought us a home in Millville, and we have lived there since. Donald Earl was born 14 January 1955, and our baby sister was born 29 July 1961. We named her Vicki Diane.

Our brother Houston died 4 July 1997 at the GlenCove Nursing Home. Dad and Mom have 22 grandchildren, 34 great-grandchildren, and 6 great-great-grandchildren.

Dad and Mom have had a full life. They have been together 70 years. There are still seven children to take care of them.
Submitted by: Audrey Floyd Braun, 2711 E. 19th Street, Panama City, FL 32401.

Family of Leon A. Foreman and Marion Blanche Presley Foreman/Robinson

Marion Blanche Presley was born in Bradenton, Florida, in 1925, to Marion Frank Presley and Lutisha Majors Presley. Blanche's parents moved to Bay County when Blanche was just a few years old. Blanche grew up in Millville, and was graduated from Bay High School.

Leon A. Foreman, Linda Lou Foreman and Leon Franklin Foreman

Blanche married L.A. Foreman, who lived on Third Street, a few doors away. They then lived in Jacksonville, Florida, where L.A. worked with the U. S. Post Office Department. At the passing of her husband, Blanche returned to Bay County to live.

Over the years Blanche acquired a bachelor's degree, a master's degree, and a specialist's degree. She worked at different times as a guidance counselor, and as a school principal. While serving as a guidance counselor at Haney Vocational School, she established a Career Lab that was a model for the State of Florida.

Blanche was instrumental in the start of Christian radio in Bay County. She also was responsible for the bringing of Goodwill Industries to Bay County. After

Marion Blanche Presley Foreman

retiring from the field of education, Blanche worked for a time as Director of Goodwill Industries, Gulf Coast, Inc.

Blanche and L.A. had two children, Linda Lou Foreman Thomson and Leon Franklin Foreman. Linda is a high school principal in Virginia and Leon works as a corrections officer in Bristol, Florida.

In later years, Blanche married Wallace B. Robinson, a retired businessman and gospel singer. They continued to live in Bay County.
Submitted by: Judith Luann Presley Wiisanen, 1579 Misty Lake Drive, Orange Park, Florida 32073.

The Fox Family

James Knox Polk Fox and Hettina Wilhemina Kruisenga (Ettie) were married in Saugatauk, Michigan on May 28, 1871. Hettina was about seventeen years old and James ten

James Knox Polk Fox, 1844-1927

years older. They lived in Holland City, Michigan where her parents had settled in about 1848, joining a group that had migrated from Holland for religious reasons.

James evidently experienced wanderlust, for about 1875 he traveled to an area near Blair, Nebraska, along with Hettina and their two children, Evelena and Edward. James had apparently heard of homesteading in Nebraska, and the family settled on a farm there. Their stay did not last long, however. James lost an eye as a result of damage by a straw, and the winters were extremely harsh. Grasshoppers ate what few crops they were able to raise.

So, in about 1881, James returned to Holland, Michigan with his wife and four children, Kruisenga and Agnes having been born in Nebraska. Two more children were born in Holland, Josie and Jackie, who died at eleven months.

In 1886, lured by glowing reports by the St. Andrew Bay Railroad and Mining Company and the Cincinnati Land Boom claims of a Utopian place to live, James and Hettina left their home in Holland and brought their family to the St. Andrew Bay Area. The family included James' mother, Loretta Schug Fox and five children: Evelena, age 14; Edward, 12; Kruisenga (Kruse), 10; Agnes 7; and Josie, 4. They traveled by train to Pensacola, then on the sailboat *Nettie*, to St. Andrew, where they lived for a short while before moving to their tentative homestead in Callaway, Florida. James and his mother together homesteaded 320 acres. Loretta Fox died in 1894, not long after President Grover Cleveland formally granted her homestead.

Hettina Wilhemina Kruisenga 1854-1951

After arriving at their destination, four more children were born: Ida, Albertus (Bert), Frank, Elizabeth (who died at age 5), and Dell. James built a log house on what is now Cherry Street in Callaway; and later built a general store, which he ran for many years. The family fished and hunted for a living, raising their own meat and vegetables. Ettie almost died from eating poisonous mushrooms, having mistaken them for the edible type. They traveled by wagon and oxcart.

"Dad" Fox was not a doctor, but helped sick persons with his tar poultices, vinegar and brown paper, and a concoction of spices: ginger, nutmeg, cloves, and etc. mixed with a flour paste, which was used for stomach disorders. Besides having babies and tending her children, Hettina spent her time, and her strong will and energy, trying to get a School Building built in Callaway. The children had to walk to Parker to get any "book learning." She often said she believed every child should have the chance to learn to read. She persuaded Mr. Callaway, who platted the area, to give land, and through her efforts and perseverance, the school became a reality in 1911. It has been restored and still stands in John B. Gore Park, having been moved from its original location.

The small museum in Callaway, The Ettie Fox Memorial Museum, is named for her and her picture hangs there. She was a member of the Order of the Eastern Star in Parker and was a legend in her own right. When she became determined to do something, as she said, "I wait for neither God nor Man." In her later years, she became known as "Grandma Fox" to all the neighborhood children, reading and telling them stories.

The Fox family members lived long lives. James, born in Northampton, Pennsylvania in 1844, died at age 83. Hettina, born in Holland City, Michigan in 1854, died at age 97. Most of their children lived into their eighties and nineties. Edward, Kruisenga, Albertus, Elizabeth, and Evelena (Kipp) and her baby are buried in the Parker Cemetery, along with their father, mother, and grandmother. Ida Fox (Brown) is also buried there, in the Brown Plot. Agnes (Burkett), Dell (Caldwell) and Frank are buried in the Callaway Cemetery. Josie(Bush) died in Blakely, Georgia and is buried there.

James and Hettina's offspring produced at least 38 grandchildren, and their legacy lives on in the local area.
Submitted by: Bertie Burkett Shuster, daughter of Agnes, and granddaughter of James and Hettina, 5207 Teri Lane, Panama City, FL 32404.

William Augustus Gainer

William Augustus Gainer was born in Washington County January 25, 1824. The Gainers were one of the major pioneer families who settled in the Bay County area. There were seven children in the family when they followed the paths that brought them to the Econfina Creek area of Bay County. This was about 1825. Later on, a brother Walter Gainer would be born at the old homestead. They did have two or three neighboring families who also settled near Cedar Creek.

William's father must have been an educated man for this period of time when most people in the area could not read or write, because he was not only a cattleman but also a school teacher. He was hired by Mr. McRea to teach at the school his children attended.

Living near Nixon, Washington County, Florida was Col. James Brown who moved to Florida from Alabama with his family in the early 1800's. Col. Brown was well known for his deeds during the War of 1812 as an Indian fighter. William A. Gainer married Sarah A. Brown who was the daughter of Col. James Brown.

William A. Gainer was a cattleman and he also built a saw mill on Clear Creek. He shipped lumber to Apalachicola, Florida and also sold his cattle to many cities in the South. Like many other Florida Cattlemen, he also sold cattle to Cuba.

Justice of the Peace was just one of the many offices of public trust that William held during his lifetime. He was said to hold court at Old Town.

William and Sarah had ten children. One daughter,

Virginia Purcell lived in St Andrews. His son J. B. Gainer moved to Texas. Son, W. B. Gainer, was the Tax Collector and lived in Econfina. His son, S. J. Gainer, was the mayor of St Andrews at one time. A daughter, Mary Jane Thompson lived in St Andrews. Son, Robert Gainer, lived at Econfina. Daughter, Sallie Davis, moved to Chipley, Florida and daughter Katherine Gainer lived at the Gainer home place in Econfina. There were two other children who had died before 1912, John W. Gainer and Benjamin F. Gainer. William Augustus Gainer died July 27, 1912.
Submitted and written by: Ann Robbins, Heritage Book Committee member.

John Garvin Family

The first time I saw the beautiful beaches of Panama City was in 1953. We rented a cottage in St. Andrews then drove down Front Beach Road to Sunnyside going to the beach. It wasn't until we returned the next year that we learned of the Back Beach Road.

On our visit in 1955, my parents and uncle purchased lots in a newly opened subdivision, Riveria Beach. In 1956 my father, Vaughn Horton, and uncle, A. C. Killian, began construction on two houses. These were supposed to be our summer homes but after Daddy suffered a heart attack, my parents moved here permanently. I was attending college at the University of Alabama and only came on vacations. After my father's death in 1958, my mother, Fannie Horton, decided to stay here. She rented the Riveria Restaurant and managed it until September. She later worked in the furniture departments at Sears and Grants.

In 1959, after graduation from college, I was hired as a 2nd grade teacher at Cherry Street Elementary. At that time, after Labor Day, everything on the beach closed and the speed limit on Front Beach went back to 65. Webb's Grocery and Hill's were about the only businesses that stayed open. Webb's Grocery was also the post office where I would get our mail and the beach news. For our groceries, we had to go to Kwik Check located on of 15th Street and Beck Avenue. This is now St. Andrews Baptist Church.

In 1962 Mother sold our house in Riveria and we moved to Baltimore Avenue in St. Andrews. We stayed there about six months then returned to the beach where we bought a house in Open Sands. Ten days after we moved in a tornado hit and tore the top off of our house.

In 1963 I married John Garvin and we moved into a house at the north end of the Open Sands pool. Our four children were born while we lived in that house; Brian in 1964, Luke, who only lived 30 hours, in 1969, Ramona in 1970, and Anita in 1972.

In 1965, I began teaching at Beach Elementary School. In 1969, I taught at West Bay School, after the birth and death of Luke. I didn't teach in 1970 as I was awaiting the birth of Ramona. I returned to Beach School in 1971 and taught there until my retirement in 1999.

When I started teaching at Beach, there were only 250 students. These students came from Hathaway Bridge to Phillips Inlet. One bus took Bay High and Beach students to the west end of the beach.

In 1999, I decided to retire from teaching, because John had health problems and I felt I needed to be home with him. Also, my daughter, Anita, had just graduated from Florida State and was looking for a job. I retired and fortunately she got my job. I have seen many changes on Panama City Beach over the 44 years I've lived here. However, I still love it here and wouldn't want to live anywhere else!
Submitted by: Patricia Horton Garvin, 211 N. El. Centro Blvd., Panama City Beach, FL 32413.

Joan Germain

My name is Joan Germain-a name I gave myself. I was born in Coalville, Utah, in 1938 as Joan Boyden. As I turned 12 my family moved to Sacramento, California. I lived my adult life in northern California until 1995 when I moved to Bonifay, Florida, and in 2001 to Panama City. I am an assistant reference librarian at Bay County Public Library where

Joan Germain

I am responsible for and teach computer classes.

I am California educated. I attended the University of California at Berkeley, Sacramento State College in Sacramento, and a year in Salt Lake City at the University of Utah. I earned a Masters Degree in English and a high school teaching credential (five-year requirement in California). I worked as a tissue technician in a Sacramento hospital pathology laboratory to finance my education. I have been employed as a general and legal secretary and as a high school English teacher, specializing in transformational grammar and writing skills.

I have been married (11/62 & 4/72) and divorced two times (1967 & 2002). I have two children: one honored as outstanding California art scholar, the other a lifelong computer buff.

My hobbies are music (piano lessons at age 4), sewing, and metaphysical studies. I have been a member of the Rosicrucian Order since 1980. In 2003 my poem was awarded Honorable Mention in Panama City Writers Association's writing contest which covered the Southeast Region of the United States.

Submitted by: Joan Germain, POB 755, Panama City, FL 32402.

Ellen M. Gilbert

In December 1948, I was 12 years old when my father and mother moved us to northern Bay County, FL. We lived in the McQuagge homestead. Dad had retired from the army and we were headed to Sandford, FL, where he had rented a house. He decided to stop and see property he had purchased from Owen Wood, a land developer in the Fountain area.

Mother became ill and we could not travel on so we stayed and rented the McQuagge home. There were four of us children, Ellen, Dolores, Johnny and Charles. The first few days we had to carry water from Mr. Angus McQuagge's home about 1/4 mile away. I cooked our meals in the fireplace. Our beans and potatoes were a bit burned but we ate. Dad finally got the hand pump primed and we had water but no electricity, no indoor plumbing, no refrigerator. We washed our clothes in a wash tub with a rub board and hung them on a rail fence. We ironed them with flat irons that had to be heated on the wood stove or the fireplace.

The four of us children walked one mile to Highway 231 where we caught the school bus that took us to the Youngstown Elementary School. When we returned home in the evenings, after chores and supper, we laid on the floor and did our homework by the light of the fireplace. After about six months, dad got some primitive buildings built on our property and we moved into them. By this time the electric company had brought power lines down Owenwood Road. Dad was raising chickens and we cleaned and sold many of them to the Fountain House Restaurant.

On January 25, 1950, we were attending school in Youngstown and I brought to the attention of our teacher and principal Mr. O.C. Doster that there was a lot of smoke outside. He sent me to investigate and I ran back to him and informed him that the roof of the school building was on fire. He made us all evacuate the building, which was constructed of lightered pine. Within two hours the whole school was burned to the ground. They partitioned off an old church building, that was across the road from the current Waller Elementary, and we finished the school year there. I finished the eighth grade that year and would have attended Bay High the next fall had we not moved away from the area.

Even though we lived in very primitive conditions, the time that we spent in northern Bay County was a very peaceful time in my life.

Submitted by: Ellen M. Gilbert, 25 W. Government St, Panama City, FL 32401.

Arthur Lee Gill

My grandfather Elzy (A. E.) Hood was a pioneer settler of Washington County. His daughter, my mother Mamie, was

Bea and Willie's Boat at St. Andrews Beach about 1937

born there before the lines were changed and Bay County was formed. My great-grandfather James Jeremiah Tindell, was a farmer and a school teacher. He raised a large family in Geneva County, Alabama. After his first wife Eda died he married Amanda Powell. Their daughter, Lillie, my grandmother grew up in Geneva County. She was very young when she married my grandfather A. E. Hood. He was born 1861 in Dale County, Alabama, died in 1921 and is buried in Gadsden County, Florida. My mother Mamie Lee Hood was their youngest child. She was born in 1897 in Washington County, Florida. and died in 1978 in Panama City, Florida. She is buried in Evergreen Memorial Cemetery on Highway 231. Lillie died when my mother was very small, sometime before 1904. We do not know where her gravesite is. Time passes, questions are not asked, and records are lost. Mamie Lee Hood married first Arthur Mark Gill (born 1884). I was born Arthur Lee Gill. I married Verna Eve Trahan and we had fifty-three happy years together. Verna died in September 1999 and is buried in Kent Lawn Cemetery in Panama City, Florida. We have two children Gary E. Gill and Arleen Gill Curry. My four grandchildren are Matthew Gill, Steven Curry, Kevin Curry, and Lisa Curry. Steven and his wife Angela have given me two great-grandsons, Benjamin and Joshua.

Arthur and Verna Trahan Gill

I spent many hours under the big old oak tree (gone now) on the beach near where the St. Andrews Marina now stands. I built boats there to sell. I built my sisters, Bea and Willie, a boat to row around the bay. We went fishing most every day in the summer. Seafood was plentiful in the 1930's in St. Andrews Bay. As a small boy, I remember going to the Casino, which was built out over the water to see a picture show. The Casino was a popular place to go. It became the entertainment center in St. Andrews. It was located over the Bay near what is now Thirteenth Street. Then the street was not paved and the beach was wide. The waterfront was the center of activities and business. I enlisted in 1940 into the Navy and served one year aboard the USS Saratoga. I later worked at the Wainwright Shipyard as a pipe welder during World War II.

Submitted by: Arthur Gill, 2702 West 11th Street, Panama City, Florida 32401. Written by: Bea Moates, 764 Roland Road, Chipley, Florida 32428. Source: Memories, personal knowledge.

Mamie Lee Hood Gill

My grandmother, Mamie Lee Hood Gill Was born (1897-1978 in Washington Co. Fla.part of the co. was to become Bay Co. in (1913). My mother told me that she was almost born on the boat, The Tarpon; "My grandmother was traveling to Apalachicola to visit relatives in (1914)." The Tarpon made trips along the Bay during that time.

Lilly Ann Gill Ferris, daughter K. D and son John Foster Ferris

My parents are Alton and Lily Ann Gill Ferris. My mother died in (1986) She sleeps in B a r r a n c u s Cemetery in Pensacola. My father is retired from the Air Force. My brother, John Forster Ferris is married and lives in Fort Walton Beach. He has a daughter Holly Ferris. We lived in Bay Co. when John and I were small children, my mother lived in St Andrew in her childhood years .It was a peaceful little fishing community, every one knew each other. I never knew my grandfather, Arthur Mark Gill, he died before I was born. My uncle Arthur Lee Gill "Sonny", remembers the "Casino" out over the water in St Andrews. I remember my Aunt Frances Gill Kind. She sleeps in Evergreen Cem. beside grandmother Gill. I loved my aunt Willie Levonia Findley Pitts. She died (1995) She has a memorial Marker in the "Stokes" family plot in old Greenwood Cemetary. The "Stokes" are Harold Pitts' grandparents. Aunt Verna Trahan Gill died (1999). She sleeps in Kent Lawn Cemetery. I miss them all . We loved the "Bay." It is still a great place to come and watch the birds. The Bay, once so bountiful with all the seafood a family wanted to eat, is still a great Bay. I have many good memories. I am married and have a son and a daughter Michael and Priscilla. We all live in Fort Walton Beach.
Submitted by: K.D. Ferris Szosttell, 201 Spencer Drive, Fort Walton Beach Fl. Written by: Bea Moates, 764 Roland Rd, Chipley Fl. 32428. Sources: personal knowledge Census records Court House Records Cem.

Janet Lynn Gispanski

My mom Ann Ramer Gispanski is from Panama City. My father, Richard Louis Gispanski met my mom while stationed at Tyndall AFB. I was born in Hahn, Germany on January 29, 1969 while my Dad was stationed there in the Air Force. Later upon returning to Panama City when my Dad went to Thailand, I attended Panama Christian School for my Kindergarten year. Over the years we have traveled a lot and enjoyed all the places at which we were stationed. I have three brothers Johnny, Ronald and Stephen all whom were born in Panama City.

Janet Lynn Gispanski and her Dad Richard Gispanski

I married Gerald Talcott from Tucson, Arizona and we have two daughters, Desiree Ann, and Aliyah Nicole.

I have spent a lot of time in Panama City because my grandparents, Johnny and Sue Ramer have lived there most of their life. They reside at 1809 Beck Avenue in Panama City, Fl. And, ever since I can remember, Panama City has always been home to my family. I will always remember the happy times visiting relatives, my two aunts, Shirley Chismar, and Virginia McCormack and my grandparents. When visiting Grandmother and Grandfather house, there was always good times, good food on the table, and a visit to the beaches. For one particular summer, Grandmother and Grandfather operated the Goofy golf on the beach for the owners. Their presence there permitted me and my brothers to live on the beach behind the golf course. Every morning I awoke directly in the midst of all of the fun spots. Such great memories I have of the beaches, the old amusement park and Goofy golf. Panama City has really grown since I was a little girl but the people are still loving and very friendly.
Submitted by: Janet Lynn Gispanski Talcott, 431 Hatchee Drive, Crestview, Fl. 32536.

Johnny E. Gispanski

My name is Johnny E. Gispanski and I was born on November 27, 1958 at Bay Memorial Hospital in Panama City, Florida. My doctor at birth was Dr. J.J. Hollomon. He was our family doctor and a close friend of our family. My parents are Ann Ramer Gispanski and Richard Louis Gispanski. I have two younger brothers, Ronald C. and Stephen Darrell, and also a younger sister Janet Lynn. I attended Panama Christian School until I was in the 5th grade and then Drummond Park Elementary. My father was in the military stationed at Tyndall when he was transferred to Hahn, West Germany where I attended school overseas. Upon returning back to the United States after 4 years we lived in Victorville California where I attended Victor Valley High. When I was in the 11 grade my father had to go back to Thailand for a year. He moved Mom and us kids back to Panama City where I attended and graduated from Bay High School in 1975. My mom worked for Springfield Commercial Bank.

Johnny E. Gispanski

My grandparents worked for the Goofy golf out on the beach. As a benefit, we lived there temporarily on the golf course property. I and my brothers also had jobs working at the golf course where I ran the sky ride.

I remember when I was small we use to go to Econfina Creek and swim. The Place was empty back then and hardly anyone went there swimming. Someone tied a long rope to a tree limb next to the shore. From this rope we would swing out over the water. We would swing back and forth as often as we could. Each time we swung close to the tree another person would jump onto the rope. Sometimes we had 10 to 14 kids hanging onto that rope. Then we all fell into that great cold water. We also used to tube the creek. We walked the bank as far as we could upstream, then floated downstream to the tree rope. Another good memory from my days in Panama City is going hunting and fishing with my Grandfather Johnny Ramer. We visited Howard's Creek and hunted and fished all along the Wewahitchka River. Granddad was a very smart outdoorsman.

Grandmother kept a fine house on Beck Avenue. She could cook up a huge dinner to feed all of us kids in what seemed like minutes. Fried chicken, fish and fresh vegetables from Grandfather's garden were her favorite ingredients. She always had home made cakes too. Grandmother provided fond memories to me and my brothers and sisters. Those were great times back in Panama City, Florida.

Today, I am married to Leslie Webster from Melbourne, Florida. We have three sons, Daryl, Justin and Ryan aged 18 to 22. We live in Melbourne, Florida
Submitted by: John Gispanski, 128 E. Laila Dr., Melbourne, Fl. 32904.

Ronald Corbett Gispanski

My name is Ronald Gispanski. I was born at Bay Memorial Hospital on March 8, 1960. Our family doctor was Dr. J.J. Hollomon. He was also a close friend of our family. I attended Panama Christian School, Drummond Park elementary, and Jinks Jr. High. My father Richard Louis was in

Ronald C. Gispanski

the military stationed at Tyndall AFB and we were very fortunate to be able to travel and see the world. I later attended schools in Hahn Air Base West Germany, Victorville High in California and graduated from Dade High in Homestead, Florida. I have two brothers, Johnny E, and Stephen D, and a sister Janet Lynn Gispanski.

I married a wonderful young lady from Jacksonville, Florida, Susan Vestal and we have a son, Jeremy. I also have a daughter Tiffany Lynn Gispanski. I have always had the love of the ocean which I obtained from Panama City. I joined the Navy upon graduating from High School and I now own a 44 ft Sailboat that I race and travel with friends and family. Unfortunately, my boat cannot enter St. Andrews bay due to the height of the mast and the depth of the keel. So I dock it in Jacksonville, Florida.

I remember when I was small and going to the beautiful white sand beaches in Panama City. I fell in love with the blue water, white sand and huge dunes. The beaches were not crowded back then with people and condos as they are now. My Mom, Ann Ramer Gispanski is from Panama City and she always had the love for the outdoors and the beauty of the beaches. When I visit Panama City I can see big changes and growth of the beaches and the town. Even the spot we used to swing from a rope on Econfina creek is developed.

One of my fondest memories is going fishing and hunting with my Grandfather Johnny W. Ramer to Howard's Creek. He had a small piece of property there with a tiny cabin. From this cabin we would take out into the wild and unknown. He knew everything about wild animals, fishing, and alligators and especially how to catch lots of fish. He taught me how to shoot guns. I am now an avid hunter thanks to him and I pass on all I know to my son Jeremy.

Panama City was a great place to be born and raised. It used to be more peaceful and less crowded. I miss those days of my youth and time spent with my grandparents.
Submitted by: Ronald Gispanski, 2323 Eagle Nest, Jacksonville, Fl. 32246.

Stephen Darrell Gispanski

I was born in Panama City on August 18, 1961 at Bay Memorial Hospital. I was the younger of two brothers Johnny and Ronald and have a younger sister Janet Lynn.

Stephen Darrell Gispanski

Our family doctor was Dr. J.J. Holloman. My parents are Ann Ramer Gispanski and Richard Louis Gispanski. My father was in the Air force stationed at Tyndall AFB. We moved from Panama City in 1968 and traveled often and lived twice in West Germany for over 10 years. The beauty of traveling is being able to see the world and having the blessing of friends everywhere. I attended Panama Christian School, Drummond Park Elementary, Hahn Air Base School, Germany, Victorville High School, Ca, and Dade County High in Homestead, Florida. I finally graduated from an American high school in Kaiserslautern Germany.

I married Karen Wilfong from Tucson, Arizona. We have two children, Amanda, and Garrett Gispanski. We presently live in Orange Park, Florida.

When I was a young boy, my parents took me to Econfina creek and we use to swim, ride inner tubes and swing from a long rope which hung over the water. We had a lot of fun swimming in the creek and driving down the road to a farmer's garden and bringing water melons back to the creek and eating them. One time when a trip was planned to the watermelon patch, I was not allowed to go since the car was too full with others. I was angry, and climbed into our car to pout. I rolled up the windows and locked the doors. By accident I knocked the car out of gear and the car rolled into the creek. My mom jumped in the creek and pleaded with me to roll down the window. I guess I realized the emergency and lowered the window so Mom could pull me to safety as the car submerged deeper into the creek. Only the trunk lid remained above the surface. What an exciting day that was. Our family has always had the love of the ocean and water in our blood. The beaches in Panama City have always been so beautiful, the white sand and blue and green water.

My grandparents are Johnny and Sue Ramer. They live on 1809 Beck Avenue in St. Andrews. My grandmother was a great cook and my granddad worked for International Paper Company. They attended Millville Assembly of God church. They had a great love for their family and for their Lord.
Submitted by: Stephen Gispanski, 1609 Hampton Place, Orange Park, Florida 32073.

John and Margarete Gleitsmann

The Linus Gleitsmann Family immigrated to the United States from Germany in 1926, as a farming family through the sponsorship of a relative. Besides Linus and Ida his wife, there were Johannas, Willy, Elsa, Helene and Frieda. They

Margarete and John Gleitsmann on the front of their Wilmont Avenue Home

tried farming; then raising cattle; and finally raising chickens on the sand-hills farm that their uncle had bought for them in the Florida Panhandle near De Funiak Springs. Shortly after arriving, my father, Johannas (John), proposed to a young girl he had been friends with in Germany, Margarete Baeslack. Their families had been friends. They worked and saved their money for three years until she was 21 and could come over. When she arrived in New York City, the social service worker sent them straight to the Justice of the Peace to be married. After a weekend at Coney Island they traveled to Jacksonville, Florida by boat. From Jacksonville they took a bus to the farm in De Funiak.

After a few years they moved to Valpariso. While there Margarete worked as a maid for Bob Sikes and his family. There John met the Alabamians that were building vacation cottages on the Gulf beaches of the panhandle of Florida. Mr. Blue encouraged them to move to Sunnyside Beach, Florida where John was responsible for constructing about 100 houses over the next few years. In 1938 they moved into Panama City. In 1939 they bought a two-room house on Wilmont Avenue in St. Andrews. John continued in his carpentry work building over 100 houses in and around Panama City area. He eventually expanded his own house into an eight-room home with a workshop, flower-house and carport.

'Mr. John' as the GI's called him worked at Tyndall AFB in the carpentry shop for 30 years. 'Big Margarete' as she was known at the Jinks Junior High Lunchroom was their baker for 20 years. Her French bread and cinnamon rolls were known all over the county. They were faithful members of the St. Andrews Presbyterian Church for over 40 years. They grew their own flowers and Margarete put arrangements in the church almost every Sunday.

John was a 50-year Master Mason with the St. Andrews Masonic Lodge, #222. He served as Chaplain and was Past Master. He was made an honorary member of numerous lodges in the northwest Florida area.

They had one daughter, Mona Anita. She married Truett La Van Lucas and they have one daughter Ramona Gayle.
Submitted by: Mona Anita Lucas, 3235 Orlando Rd, Panama City, FL.

Jacob and Ida Godert

Sunday afternoons were always spent at our grandparents' home. Those were the days of very fond memories, exciting adventures, and life lessons worth remembering. From our youth, we would venture each Sunday after church to visit our mother's brother, sister, and parents at their home. Our grandparents, Jacob and Ida Godert, our aunt, Agnes Godert, and uncle, Jake Godert, all lived in what is known as the Schmidt homestead in the Cook's Bayou area. Our grandmother's father, Emil T. Schmidt, built the house in the late 1800's. To us as children, it was a mansion of a home, two and a half stories tall, with all sorts of rooms filled with items which were extremely old and rare. The out lying buildings and barns also held great mysteries and antiques, which each of us would come to appreciate in later years.

Grandpa and Grandmother Godert with grandchildren: Marie, Linda, William, Avis

Our grandmother, who was of German descent, was raised on the farm and loved to work in the fields and garden. She took special pride in her flower gardens. Visitors would come just to see her flowers. Grandmother even shared her faith through her garden. She planted flowers in the shape of the word JOY and was always quick to share what it stood for: Jesus first, Others second, and You last. She stressed to us if we lived by this rule we would have joy in our lives. She spent many hours in her last years just sitting out there near the garden enjoying the sunshine and flowers.

Grandpa, who was also German, was a great cook and always prepared the Sunday afternoon meal for us. Sunday dinner usually consisted of chicken and noodles or chicken and rice. He would sometimes surprise us with an unusual concoction - rice seasoned with pig's tails! Meals were always eaten around their large dining room table. The room was warmed in the winter by a wood-burning heater. On cold or rainy days, we would sit around this table and play cards with Grandpa. He loved all kinds of card games, but most of all he enjoyed winning.

Grandpa was a gentle man with a good nature and had a great love for animals. We loved the many stray and wild cats that would venture near the house. He was always faithful to feed them and give them nicknames. There were many dogs throughout the years, too. Most had been dumped nearby and wandered up to the house. Grandpa never turned one away.

Our more exciting adventures occurred when our Uncle Jake would hand crank the old 1914 Model T Ford and take us for a spin. Each of us learned to drive at a very young age in that Model T. We would hang on the side running boards as we anxiously waited our turn behind the wheel. Uncle Jake was always close at hand to prevent any accidents. We would plow along the fire lines and old dirt trails of the farm for hours. One special year, 1963, Grandpa entered the Model T in Bay County's 50th Anniversary parade downtown. We were so excited, it was our first parade. How special we felt

Uncle Jake teaching us to drive the 1914 Model T

as we rode along Harrison Avenue with our Grandpa.

Another special treat we all enjoyed was when the parlor door was unlocked and we were allowed to carefully enter and explore the many treasures kept inside. The parlor held many special antiques and memories. Pictures of our great grandparents decorated the walls. In one corner stood the old Edison phonograph. Uncle Jake would select a cylinder shaped record, hand crank the phonograph, insert the record on the cylinder, carefully place the needle on the record, and music would fill the parlor. Against another wall stood the grand old pump organ that was purchased by my great grandfather for my grandmother. She and our Aunt Agnes, both, learned to play the organ on this wonderful instrument. Its cabinet was skillfully crafted and very ornate. We would take turns perched on the swivel stool, pumping the pedals and carefully playing the keys. Although we didn't possess any musical skills, it was always a treat for our Aunt Agnes to sit and play for us. Our grandmother loved to hear one of her favorite songs, "How Great Thou Art," played and sung by Aunt Agnes.

Some afternoons at our grandparents' house were spent in the garden. Summertime brought in crops of all types of fresh fruits and vegetables, but our favorite crops were the watermelons, cantaloupes, and peanuts. We would be charged with going to the strawberry patch and picking the ripe strawberries or to the blueberry bushes and picking the blueberries. Sometimes we would sit under the shade of a tree and pick green peanuts off the bushes. It seemed there was always something that needed to be picked, shelled, husked, or cleaned. At the time it seemed like hot, tortuous work, all the while eating our fill of some of the best fruits and vegetables ever tasted. We sometimes ate more than we picked!! It seemed there was nothing our grandparents couldn't grow.

Not only did they grow wonderful fruits and vegetables, but they also raised chickens and hogs. Many times we would go to the hen house with our grandpa or our uncle and gather eggs. That was always fun, it was like an Easter egg hunt year round. Sometimes the chickens could be a little intimidating and we would go running to the nearest gate to get out of the chicken yard.

What a privilege to have been able to experience such wonderful adventures and form such precious memories in our young years and to share them not only with each other, but with our grandparents. We said goodbye to our grandmother in 1969 and our grandpa in 1972. The old homestead is now a historical site for others to come and visit, but what a special place it will always have in our hearts.
Submitted by: Marie Nelson, Linda Kelly, and Avis McGill, 606 Kristanna Drive, Panama City, Florida 32405.

Ed and "Jacque" Godfrey and the *Tip Top* Groceries

Early Panama City was a time of independent, small personal businesses. Two prominent grocers of the era were Ed Godfrey and his wife "Jacque", who owned and operated several grocery stores during the thirties, forties and fifties.

Enoch Edgar Godfrey was born November 13, 1903 in Columbia, Alabama. He came to Panama City in the mid twenties, and worked as a butcher in several meat markets. Three of which were the A and P store, located on Harrison Avenue, present entrance to McKenzie Park, Custer Russ Market, which was located on the corner of

The first Tip Top Grocery

Ed and Jacque Godfrey

Jane Godfrey Becker and Anne Godfrey Weeks

Allen Avenue and 6th Street and Stewart's Grocery, located on the corner of Harrison Avenue and 8th Street.

He met Bessie Addie "Jacque" Mayers, daughter of Melvin and Idella Mayers, owners of the Bay Hotel. They married on December 25, 1928 in Chipley, Florida. In 1930 the couple had twin daughters, Anne and Jane, born in Panama City.

In the late 30's Ed and W.C. Summers bought the A&P store, mentioned above, and renamed it *Tip Top* Grocery. After 2-3 years Ed bought out Mr. Summers and he and "Jacque" operated the thriving business. Just before the beginning of World War II the Godfreys sold the first *Tip Top* and purchased another grocery on 6th Street in the 2nd block off Harrison Avenue. Again the store was named *Tip Top* The family kept this business until around 1943-44. During WWII, many items, such as tuna, pineapple, sugar and other staples were not to be had. Again they sold the store on 6th Street and Ed decided he didn't want another grocery. "Jacque" worked during this time at the Office of Price Administration.

In 1944-45 Evon Brewton built a 2 store building in the 800 block of Harrison Avenue. Ed liked the building and purchased one half. The Shields family bought the other half and opened Superior Cleaners, which still operates in that location. The Godfreys opened the last *Tip Top* in 1945. Many grocery items were still hard to get and rationing was still in force, but the *Tip Top* had a good business. One chore that the Godfrey twins had was to take the weeks ration stamps and paste them on a master sheet which had to be turned in to the OPA. The Godfreys provided credit and delivery services. In early 1953 Ed became ill and passed away August 15, 1953. "Jacque" continued to operate the *Tip Top* until 1955-56. She sold the stock and fixtures, but leased the building.

"Jacque" later worked as Admissions Director and Director of Volunteers at Bay Memorial Hospital until she retired at the age of 70. "Jacque" passed away February 17, 1991.

The *Tip Top* building still stands, but the era of independent grocers was becoming a thing of the past.
Submitted by: Anne Godfrey Weeks, 1322 Carlotta Road West, Jacksonville, Florida 32211.

Charles G. and Alma Donnie (Oliver) Goodwin

Charlie Goodwin was born in Florida on May 22, 1873. He died in Panama City, FL, on April 6, 1965. Charlie was born in Wewahitchka. His parents were John and Quintina Smith Goodwin. John came home one day and asked Quinnie to pack him a lunch because he had to leave and he would not return. The family doesn't know the reason he disappeared. Charlie had two brothers, John Thomas born June 5, 1871,

Charlie Goodwin

and Joseph Jonas born July 6, 1875. Three days after his father left Charlie went to the logging company where his father worked and asked for a job. Charlie was twelve at the time and told them he needed the money to support his mother and brothers. They paid him the same as the others. His job was to float logs down the Chipola River.

John Thomas and his wife, Sallie, lived in Bay County forty years before his death on May 5, 1938. Joseph Jonas and his wife, Martha, lived in Bay County seventy years before his death on Sept. 28, 1964.

Alma Donnie Oliver was born on August 11, 1883, in Georgia, and died on February 17, 1954. She was the daughter of William Thomas Oliver and Rachel Morris Oliver. She married Charlie on May 10, 1894, in Calhoun County, FL. Charlie was twenty-one and Alma was eleven. Charlie was smitten with Alma and talked her father into letting her marry him. She had the first of ten children in 1895. They had five boys and five girls.

Charlie bought lots in Millville on May 14, 1907. On November 8, 1917, they bought 54 acres in Bay County. They homesteaded 164 acres in Youngstown, Florida, granted on August 9, 1919. The homestead was next door to Richmond C. McGill's farm. Their daughter, Ada, married Richmond and Katherine Whidbee McGill's son, Benjamin Elmo McGill.

Charlie owned land in Calhoun County which he leased to the Spann Brother for logging, recorded in Blountstown, FL, on May 2, 1912. Charlie sold other properties he owned in Calhoun County. Charlie didn't have a formal education, but he had a good head for business.

Their ten children are: Leola born April 7, 1895, died November 8, 1965, she married Jessie Nixon and had one son; Ada Mae born April 14, 1901, died August 3, 1980, and married Benjamin Elmo McGill and had eight children; Charlie Anderson born July 29, 1903, died December 16, 1990, married Viola Bennett and had nine children; Lovie born November 7, 1905, died November 26, 1988, married William Ira Barwick and had six children; Perry born February 2, 1908, died January 6, 1973, married Irene Batson; Omer born June 20, 1911, died August 1976, married Muriel Skipper and had six children; Iduma born October 9, 1912, died in 1990 and had one son; Adell David born January 14, 1915, died March 3, 1996, married Claire and had seven children; Richard Charles (R.C.) born September 12, 1919, married Vera Mae Broxton and had eight children.
Submitted by: Wanda Odom, 631 Tate Drive, Callaway, FL 32404.

William Edward Gore Family

William Edward Gore and his wife, Susan Elizabeth 'Bettie' Patterson Gore met and married in Shalotte,

Columbus, NC in 1891. Following the turpentine work they and their growing family moved from still to still from North Carolina, to Moultrie, Georgia, to Telogia, Florida and finally to Sandy Creek, Washington County, Florida. It was near here on the shore of the East

William Edward Gore family at a Mother's Day Reunion

Bay that they settled and homesteaded in 1906 near the community of Allanton.

Their original board and batten home there was built from the lumber of two shanties bought from the Sandy Creek Turpentine Still, floated down the creek and around the bay to the mouth of Richard Bayou. It was here that William Edward Gore set about clearing the land for farming and making a home for his family.

Their family eventually consisted of twelve children: Lenox Percy Gore who married Mary Christina Beadnell; William Henry Gore who married Allie Whitfield; Lillian Clarence Gore who married (1) J A McCumbie, (2) William Hosea Danley; Ella Gertrude Gore who married Amphion Brown; Cleveland Lee Gore who married Elsie Oliver; Gaston Sewell Gore who married Gussie Waters; Clara Estelle Gore who married Elbert 'Buck' Heldon Griffin; John B Gore who married Floyd Peacock Hammond; Elbert Ray Gore who married Helen Broxton; Gladys Viola Gore who married Herbert Coleman Moses; Alva Joshua Gore who married Lillian Marvelle Robbins; Margie Gertrude Gore who married Bernice Waters.

William Edward Gore died in 1943; Bettie died in 1962. The youngest daughter survives.

William Edward Gore with his wife Susan Elizabeth Patterson Gore

Their family was typical of the time and place. Each family member turned a hand to whatever chore was to be done. The older boys turpentined with their father or plowed the fields; some of them took to the waters to fish. They went to war when their nation called; one answered a different call later and became a minister. The girls minded the younger children, married and raised families of their own. One taught school.

They worked and lived hard. Cash money was scarce. My dad remembers working with his father and uncles in waist high swampy ponds to find fallen cypress in the swamp bottom. These were crosscut and pried out until they could be floated to shore. Then they were hauled by wagon and sold as railroad crossties for twenty-five cents each.

But they had good times too. Gladys Gore Moses recalled dancing until she wore holes in the soles of her shoes at an Independence Day celebration. There were fish fries, special family gatherings, and wonderous days of carefree hours playing with friends along the bay shore. She would say, "We were poor back then but didn't ever know it. We were too busy being happy."

They were blessed with a wonderful, loving family, and many, many wonderful, loving friends. It was a wonderful life.. . gone now... but alive and well in our memories. My parents, Bill and Jean Gore, live on part of the original homestead. And it is still home.

Submitted by: Patricia Gore Smith, 4007 Rinker Way, Bakersfield, CA 93309.

The William Edmond Hammack and Ella "Viola" (Parham) Family Story

Viola, a saint of a woman, was born on 6/21/1912 and raised in Altha, Florida, going to school and becoming a strong church woman. Because things were tough, she sought employment in Andalusia Ala. and got a job at the Halatax shirt factory facing sleeves on shirts. In Andalusia, Viola met tall, smooth talking, Ed Hammack and fell in love. Soon after, they were married on 9/26/1936. Trying to improve their circumstances, they moved back to Altha, and lived on a farm. Two daughters were born: prissy, Shirley Fay was the first, 6/23/1937. Two years later, independent Nelda Mae was born on the freezing night of 2/1/1940. Trying to eke out a living, the family moved to Mobile, Ala.

Our dad, Ed, worked on the police force in Prichard, Ala. A few years later, the family moved to Panama City, Fl. where Viola found employment at the shirt factory on 15th street, until the factory's closing around 1958. With the closing of the factory, Viola and Ed moved to Gainesville to seek employment at Sunny Land Center. About this time, their marriage faltered and they divorced in 1959. Ed stayed in Gainesville until his untimely death from liver cancer and is buried in Stark, Fl. Viola moved to Winter Haven, Fl and met Coye Hamm of Altha. They married on 1/14/1961. Both were employed at the Bordo fruit canning plant until their retirement. Our dear mother, Viola, passed away first,

Back row L to Right - Viola Parham, William Hammack; Front Row L to Right- Nelda, Shirley

due to heart complications on 4/12/1983. Coye passed away in 1987 from lung cancer. The two were laid to rest beside each other in Winter Haven, Fla.

Viola's eldest, Shirley graduated from Bay High School class of 1956 and worked in the same shirt factory as her mother. In September 1958, Shirley met and married Charles Denny Niebruegge and they moved to Vandenberg AFB, California as part of his duty for the Air Force. They reared two children. Charles "Ricky" Niebruegge was born 9/25/1959 and married Kathy Gibbs on 8/24/1994 and he has a step-son, Jimmy. Ricky is a construction superintendent for a local company and spends his free time hunting and fishing. They live in Lompoc, CA with their three hunting dogs. Terri Lynn Niebruegge was born 1/20/61 and married Richard "Dickie" Stevens in May, 1992 and have two lovely children, Richard and Nicole. They live in Goleta, CA where they own and operate a local trucking business. After Shirley's 22 year marriage to Denny ended in 1979, she went to work for the Aerospace Industry. In 1981, Shirley used her considerable southern charm and guile to enchant a wonderful man, John Aleck, of Greek and French ancestry. They were married overlooking the ocean in Pismo Beach, CA, on 7/13/1985. John's ex, does live in Texas, and he has three daughters from a previous marriage. Anne Elizabeth born 12/28/68, is married to Todd Young and they have three daughters, Devyn, Sydney and Kendyl. Christine Michele Aleck born 9/28/1970 and has one daughter, Brittany. Victoria Catherine Aleck was born 8/15/75 and has one son, Caleb. All three girls and their families live in San Antonio, TX. John and Shirley currently call Hayward, CA home.

Nelda, met Herbert Arlan ("Shorty") Shores and they were married 12/3/1961. They resided in Crestview Fl, where their son Arlan "Sherrill" Shores was born on 1/6/1962 in

Crestview. A little over 2 years later Vonda Kay Shores was born in Panama City, Fl on 9/24/1964. Arlan made a living as a master carpenter and enjoyed his free time fishing and hunting. Nelda contributed to the family income by working herself into an executive management position of housekeeping for the Gulfside Inn on Panama City Beach. Arlan passed away in April 13, 1995. Nelda retired in 1992 and lives comfortably in Panama City, where she is an ardent Bingo player and socially involved in a ladies group called the Red Hat.

Sherrill married Andy Perry of Bremerton, Washington 12/85 and became parents of a gifted daughter, Alanna Cherrill Shores. Sherrill and Andy divorced, and Alanna lives with her step dad, Todd and mother in Seattle. Sherrill continues to play a big part in Alanna's life, ensuring she keeps her southern roots. Alanna has two half-brothers, bruiser, Nash and semi-bruiser, Tucker. Sherrill lives in Portland, Oregon, where he works for a semi-conductor company and soaks up the outdoors, golfing, fishing and hunting. Vonda married James Alan Tate and they had a son, Tyler Alan Tate born 11/1/1986 and daughter, Alyssa Kay Tate born, 11/13/1989. The two bright children live with Vonda in Panama City, FL. Divorced, Vonda is a medical records and insurance administrator for a local allergy and respiratory clinic and attends Gulf Coast College.

This is a snapshot of the The Hammack side of the family. We believe Ed's life, which was very colorful and not explored in depth, could be a novel unto itself. We are certain it would make a great made-for- TV movie.

Submitted By: Nelda Shores, 913 Taylor Dr., Panama City, Fla. 32404 and Shirley Fay Aleck, 932 Fall River Drive, Hayward, Ca, 94544. Written by: Nelda Shores. Source: Family Records.

The Tom P. Haney Family

Tom P. Haney was a Tennessee farm boy, born April 28, 1913. After graduating from Minor Hill High School, he went to Nashville to live with his uncle. He attended

David Lipscomb College but took a job to pay his way. He worked for National Biscuit Company for $12.00 a week. Later he was promoted to salesman in Panama City, Florida. His territory was from Apalachicola to Florala, Alabama.

In 1937, he returned to Minor Hill and married Sarah Ingram, his high school sweetheart. They had a son, Ted, and four years later, a son, Tommy. He was in the Florida State Guard when World War II started. In 1942, he started a grocery store at 6th Street and

Sarah, Tom P., Ted and Tommy Haney

McKenzie Avenue where Grocery Outlet is located today. He was owner, stock clerk and butcher. He went into partnership with Earnest Wilder in 1947 to build a "super market", Haney and Wilder, at Highway 98 and Cove Boulevard, sharing the building with Cooper's Drugs. It was a successful business, but the long hours left little time for hunting and fishing. He was becoming more involved with First Baptist Church, which he joined a week after arriving in Panama City. He was teaching a boys class at that time, and later would serve as Deacon, Sunday School Director for 36 years, and was on numerous committees.

Tom had been an athlete in high school, so he was quick to join the amateur teams in Panama City, playing baseball and basketball, and later softball. He continued playing softball until he was 65. Besides personal play, he also coached Little League teams in the Cove for many years. He also enjoyed quail hunting and fishing.

In 1951, he was approached by a sales representative

with Praetorian Mutual Insurance Company, who thought that his sales ability and personality could earn his living in the insurance business and still leave time to follow his outside interests. He sold his share of the grocery store

The Extended Tom P. Haney family

and began his new business right away. The insurance business was a fit for him, and he soon became one of the top salesmen. Some years later, the company began an annual award in his name, honoring the sale representative who combined outstanding sales performance with service to his community. He continued in the business until his early 80's, when physical problems began to take their toll.

He was appointed to the Bay County School Board in 1952 by the governor to fill an unexpired term. He ran unopposed for three terms, and then decided not to seek the office again. Haney VoTech, the result of his vision of a school offering a quality vocational education, was completed after he left office and was named in his honor. He was very proud of that honor and actively supported the school.

His civic activities were numerous. He was an active member of the Chamber of Commerce, and held volunteer positions in the Cancer Fund, the United Way, Red Cross, Boys Club and Boy Scouts. He was a member of the Panama City Lions Club, and served as President, Zone Chairman, and District Governor. He knew one way to do things, and that was to the best of his ability. That inner drive took him to many positions of leadership in various organizations.

Sarah was also active in church and civic affairs, PTA, Girl Scouts, Cub Scouts, Volunteer with the Red Cross, Hospital Auxiliary, Woman's Club, where she served as President, Panama City Lions Auxiliary, and member of

the Garden Club. She was a long time Sunday School teacher and choir member.

In 1946, Sarah contracted Tuberculosis and had to leave home to be in the Marianna Sanitarium for treatment. For the next 15 months, Tom took over the care of their two

Haney Vocational-Technical Center

sons. He continued with his business interests and visited Sarah every week. The boys would climb up on a ladder and look in her window. Later, Sarah was able to come outside and they would picnic on the grounds.

Ted went to Georgia Tech on the co-op program with the Navy Lab, where he continued to work as an electrical engineer for 17 years after graduating. He married a local girl, Judy Gavin, and they have three children, Fara, Dina and Todd, and nine grandchildren. Ted joined his father's insurance company in 1978.

Tommy played football at Bay High and went to Florida State University on a football scholarship, but gave it up to prepare for medical school. He graduated from Emory University and married his high school sweetheart, Dianne George. They returned to Tallahassee to begin a practice in Orthopedics. They have a son, Mark, and daughter, Angela, and two grandchildren. He is proudly one of the Seminoles' doctors.

Both sons were active in high school organizations and civic affairs. Ted has been President of the Rotary Club, the Chamber of Commerce, and Gulf Coast Foundation and numerous health organizations.

In his later years, Tom enjoyed more time in fishing, hunting and golf. During hunting season his passion was quail hunting and he kept bird dogs for many years. He enjoyed bass fishing and found that to be a passion that both his sons shared. For years he spent every Wednesday afternoon golfing with a group of friends who enjoyed the fellowship as much as the golf.

Tom was diagnosed with Parkinson's disease in 1995. He died at home in July, 1999, shortly after celebrating his 62nd anniversary in the hospital with his 5 grandchildren and 10 great grandchildren visiting. He was 86 at his death.

Tom was a great tease and teller of jokes. Friends still ask Sarah to tell Tom's jokes. He was an optimist who lived his faith that the Lord would take care of his family.

Submitted by: Sarah Haney, 3304 Robinson Bayou Circle, Panama City, FL 32405.

Harmon, Murfee, Sims, Knowles... I Tie Them Together - (Part I)

I am proud to say that I am the descent of many old Bay County names, some coming to the pine woods and sandy shores of Washington/Bay County about the time of the Civil War. On my Mom's side are names like Murfee, Harmon, Sanders, Davis, Destin, Woodward, and Rubash. From my Dad's side of the family I can trace families like Knowles, Samuel W. Davis, and Sims. I am Amanda Susan Knowles Vossen. Like my parents, I grew up in the St. Andrew area of Bay County and when I graduated from Bay High in May, 2001 I was the third generation to do so.

Turner Hunt Harmon, early land holder in the Cove

My mother is Gail Murfee Knowles and she grew up in St. Andrew attending St. Andrew Elementary, followed by Jinks Junior High and finally to graduate from Bay High School in 1969. She shared with me many stories of growing up in St. Andrew. It was an old quiet area where any type of crime was practically unheard of. Doors were never locked. Many nights she would camp with her sister and friends right out in the front yard. In the summer, almost ever morning on the incoming tide she would go fish off the Villa docks and always came home with little black grouper. The Villa had in the past been a beautiful old hotel but during this time it was a run down private home. Her great aunt and uncle, Fannie and Richard Williams, lived on Cincinnati Avenue and she would always stop by there if she had caught any crabs and leave them with Uncle Richard. Richard Williams had always fished for a living originally coming to St. Andrews from Destin. Mom also shared with me stories of the frequent weekend trips up to the sand hills off Highway 77 to go camping. During the late 1950's through the mid 1970's, all of the woods up above Southport were mostly open to public use. During these years, from the Spring through the Fall, most weekends the family would pack up the camping trailer and head for the sand ponds to spend the weekend. They camped on various sand ponds but the favorites were Little Island Pond and Spring Pond. Her father had made a tear shaped board that he could pull around the edge of the water on the various ponds. The board was pulled by a rope tied to the "jeep." This was real-

ly great fun to them.

My grandparents are Patricia Ann Rubash Murfee and Rozzie Turner Murfee. They both grew up in Panama City, also. Patricia grew up in St. Andrew on Drake Avenue. For part of her early years she lived in the house adjacent to where she now resides. The home she lives in today was built during World War II by her father, John Joseph Rubash. (See article entitled John Joseph Rubash). She, her two sisters, and brother all attended St. Andrew Elementary during the weekdays and St. Andrew Baptist on Sundays. Patricia's mother was

Nancy Davis Harmon, daughter of Sanders W. Davis

Mary Jane Woodward Rubash. Great grandmother Rubash had been born at Miller's Ferry in Walton County in 1889. Mary Jane Woodward was the daughter of Jane Destin Woodward. Jane Destin was the daughter of Leonard Destin the founder of the town of Destin. Shortly after Mary Jane's youngest sister, Clara, was born both parents died and the girls, Fanny (Williams), Mary Jane (Rubash) and Clara (Mizenko) were raised by their brother Len Woodward in the area now known as Destin. At the time the area was known as East Pass.

My grandfather, is Rozzie Turner Murfee. He grew up in the Cove area. He was born directly across from the Cove Hotel in a house that still stands on Harmon Avenue and Cherry Street. He tells stories of fishing around the old Tarpon Dock area and of shark fishing just off shore on present day Beach Drive. He and his brother, Buell, along with friends would paddle out in their small skiff and drop their hook and before they could paddle back to the shore they would have caught a shark. He told me of one time when he was a young boy that a hurricane came into Panama City and he and several other boys paddled their skiffs up into the loading area and into the parking areas under the Cove Hotel. His mother was Amanda Juliette Harmon for which I am named. Her brother, Lampkin "Lamp" Harmon, was the first constable for Panama City. (See article The Harmons of St. Andrews Bay and Washington County.) Her father, Turner Hunt Harmon and one of her brothers were among the first fifteen registered voters of Harrison (present Panama City).

Ara Ethel and Amanda Juliette Harmon, daughters of Turner Hunt Harmon and Nancy Davis Harmon

Amanda's father, Turner Hunt Harmon and his wife Nancy Davis Harmon were married in Washington County in 1867. He had been in the Confederate Navy aboard both the Ironclad Savannah and the Steamship Chattahoochee. When the Savannah had blown up he had been taken prisoner. As the story has been passed down through the years, when the Civil War ended, Turner Harmon had been a prisoner of war in a hospital in Richmond, Virginia where he had smallpox. He was so angry that the South had lost the war, when he was offered a mule to ride home; he refused it, and walked back to his home. After the Civil War, Turner went to Washington County where he and Nancy Davis were married. A portion of his military naval records were lost and when after his death, Nancy Harmon applied for her husband's pension, it took her five years to receive the pension of $480 per year. A special bill was passed to grant her pension (Senate Bill No. 77) due to the fact no living veterans that served with Harmon could be found. The present "Harmon" plat in the Cove area was a small portion of the property Turner Harmon purchased from his father in law, Sanders Davis approximately 1886.

My Grandfather Murfee's other grandfather, also fought in the Civil War. He was James Glen Murfee (see the Murfees in Bay County). The little community of Murfee on Burnt Mill Creek was named for him. His wife was Susan Mitchell Murfee, for which she is one of the two great grandmothers that the Susan in my name comes.

The Bay County sand and salt runs deep in my veins and like so many of my ancestors before me, I too plan to make Bay County my home and the place I will raise my family. *Submitted by: Amanda Knowles Vossen, 1914 Frankford Av, Panama City, Fl.*

Harmon, Murfee, Sims, Knowles... I Tie Them Together - (Part II)

I am writing this article as a continuation of the above article by my daughter, Amanda Knowles Vossen. I am writing from her point of view as though she is writing it because it is through her that so many old Bay County names are connected. She wrote about my side of the family, her mother, and now I add her father's side.

My father is Frank William Knowles, Jr. All of my life he has been a harbor pilot. He has a very unique job. In 1975, he took the place of an old pilot named Ernest Spiva that retired. He has the distinction of being the last pilot to come

Amanda Juliette Harmon Murfee, wife of Rozzie Fletcher Murfee

on the "bar" under the old apprentice program. He is a state and federal licensed pilot that brings the ships in and out of the Port of Panama City. By law, a pilot must be aboard every foreign flag vessel drawing six or more feet of water when it comes into local harbors. A pilot knows the waters as a foreign captain could not. He has a small pilot boat that acts as a ferry to take him to the ship where he climbs a "Jacobs Ladder" that is let down over the side and leaves his small boat and goes aboard the ship. I have had opportunities to ride the ships with him and I enjoy meeting the captains and officers from other countries. Likewise, when a ship departs the channel, he has the pilot boat come along side the ship and he climbs down the ladder and the boat brings him back to the dock.

Frank grew up in St. Andrews next door to where he presently lives. He attended St. Andrew Elementary, Jinks Jr. High and graduated from Bay High School in 1959. He, like so many growing up in St. Andrews, fished on the boats located there during high school and later went into the Coast Guard for four years before becoming a harbor pilot. Our home is not far from Port Panama City, where during World War II the shipyard was located; and he remembers as a very small boy seeing people living in tents every where in this area. A trailer park was also located along the bay on 16th Street between Michigan and Louise Avenue for shipyard workers. In among so many houses today, it is hard to imagine at one time there were cows in the yard here and people living in tents.

Frank's parents, too, grew up in Panama City. His father, Frank William Knowles grew up in St. Andrew on the same property next door to where his son now lives. The present day Uncle Ernie's Restaurant was originally a private home

Amanda Susan Knowles Vossen, named after Amanda Juliette Harmon Murfee her great grandmother

on Louise Avenue. It was in this house at 1608 Louise Avenue that Frank, Sr. was born. Later, the house became the property of Ernest Morris. Frank, Sr. owned the first seafood trucking company out of Panama City and drove seafood to Fulton Fish Market in New York City from the area between New Orleans and Apalachicola. When Frank first married his wife Thelma Sims in 1930, he was a captain of a yacht in New York. At the beginning of World War II, Frank and Thelma returned to Panama City to live. They moved to 3700 West 16th Street on property that had been in the Knowles family since before Frank's birth. Frank Sr. died in January, 1952.

His widow Thelma remarried within a few years to Guy R. Gainer, a descendent of the Gainers from Econfina Creek area.

Frank Sr.' s father was Charlie Knowles. He was the first barber in St. Andrews and his shop was located on the pavilion. He was married to Francis "Cricket" Davis Knowles. They lived where the same property where my parents now live. My mom and dad make the third Knowles generation to live on 16th Street and Louise Avenue. Charlie Knowles originally came here with his father and brothers from Headland, Alabama. The family settled in the West Bay area and would travel to the beaches to mullet fish. They would take the mullet back to West Bay, salt them, and sell them. Eventually, the brothers came to Panama City leaving their father in West Bay. Charlie settled in St. Andrews, his brother Zack settled on Magnolia Beach, and Bob settled in the Old Orchard area.

My great Grandmother Cricket grew up in Allentown. She was the eldest of the family and upon her parents death, raised her younger brothers and sisters. After she married Charlie Knowles, she lived at 1604 Louise Avenue where my parents have their

Knowles Home circa 1925, 3700 West 16th Street, St. Andrews

home until the death of her son, Frank. After his death, her house was moved back to Allentown where she remained until her death in 1965. As a young boy, my Dad spent a great deal of time with his grandmother.

My dad's mother was Thelma Garmen Sims. Born in March, 1913, she grew up in Millville and attended Millville Elementary School. She later attended Bay High School and was in the first graduating class from Bay High School. Thelma was the second of four girls. Her parents were Lonnie and Belle Sims. Her father, Lonnie, worked at the paper mill when it first opened. He was a welder by trade. Before the mill opened he had been part owner of Panama Machinery and Supply but sold out with the opening of the mill.

My family has a very rich heritage in Bay County, Florida. They have seen Harrison (the name by which Panama City was first called), Panama City, and St. Andrew grow from small communities of dusty roads to the city which now stands in the shadows of memories of older times. I sometimes wonder what our ancestors would think if they could see how we have grown and progressed through the last century.

Submitted by: Gail Knowles, 1604 Louise Av, Panama City, Fl. 32401.

The Harmons of St Andrews Bay

The post office for the St Andrews community was located on today's East Beach Drive. Closed during the war, Thomas Gibbon reopened it in 1871 then turned it over to Mary Amanda Farley who was postmistress from August 1871 until December 1875. She was replaced by 37 year old Turner Hunt Harmon in January 1876. What follows are a few glimpses into his world and that of his wife Nancy Davis after taking that job which brought them to St Andrews Bay.

The newcomers moved their young family of four sons onto property recently bought by Nancy's father Sanders W Davis. On December 7, 1875 Nancy's father, a miller on Hard Labor Creek, had purchased 160 acres from Mrs Martha S Farley for $600. Describing the parcel using present day streets, it lay between Magnolia Avenue to the west and MacArthur Avenue to the east; between Cherry Street to the south and Third Court to the north. The

Turner Hunt Harmon and Nancy Davis ca 1868

parcel included most of Massalina Bayou and the tip of land on the northeast side now occupied by several law firms. The bayou was named after the Jose Massalina family who had lived there from the 1830s until 1856 when a hurricane wiped them out. The Harmons eventually raised ten children here and all but one played musical instruments, sometimes helping to entertain at social gatherings.

Mr Harmon served as Justice of the Peace from 1878 to 1889 and gave up the postmaster job to Lillian Ware in December 1881. He was elected county commissioner in 1889 and walked to commission meetings at Vernon from his home on the bay. He occasionally visited an Indian acquaintance who shared meals with him until one night when Mr Harmon was dishing himself another helping and the old Indian suggested that he "dig to the bottom .... that's where the grubs are".

In 1886 Nancy and her brother Dave Davis repaid their father's purchase of the Farley place. Nancy claimed the half south of Second Court. Part of this was platted and sold by her husband in 1909 and part by Nancy in 1914. Several homes were built in the cove by Mr Harmon or his sons before 1910; the last place where T H Harmon lived stands on Beach Drive, on the north side of Second Place.

The Massalinas had moved directly

Fishing Smack and Second Massalina Bayou Bridge from 1925 to 1951

across the bay to Redfish Point after the storm of 1856. However, they continued to find work around Massalina Bayou. Once, Hawk Massalina tapped Nancy Harmon's home remedy knowledge for help with stingray poisoning. The huge ray had almost drowned him while trying to break its barb free from his thigh. She treated him several times and eventually a ball of dead flesh the size of a small orange sloughed off above the knee. Hawk recovered and lived to the age of 108, dying in 1950.

About 1890 Dave Davis, his family, and Nancy's son Henry Harmon were sailing through the pass when a sudden squall capsized their boat; the craft was righted immediately but was full of water and could not support any of them. Dave and his wife Sally Gainer clung to the boat and to their infant son while Henry swam against the out-going tide to seek help from the Red Fish Point community. After four hours, the exhausted and naked young man finally reached the settlement, and Jose Massalina sent out a boat to pick up the grateful family before they were swept into the gulf.

On several occasions Nancy Harmon traveled with her children by ox cart between the bay and her parent's home south of Chipley. On one occasion in the Fall of 1887, she had stopped for the night and was preparing dinner when she noticed her ox was agitated. She turned to her baby Ara whom she had placed upon a blanket by the wagon and saw the panther. She had no weapon other than a child's small hatchet. They scared the cat off and she immediately piled the kids onto the cart and traveled all night and the next day to Davis' Mill.

Like most of their kin, Mr Harmon and Nancy alternated living between the bay and the hills southeast of Chipley. In 1892, the 54 year old T H Harmon was teacher of Rock Hill School with an enrollment of 45 and average attendance of 16. His salary was $20 a month.

In 1901 the 63 year old T H Harmon was granted a patent for a 160 acre homestead just south of Rock Hill Church. He was issued a cattle brand and raised cows.

Ivan Harmon remembered when he and his father saw a skiff adrift on the bay which they knew belonged to an old civil war veteran who lived alone near Red Fish Point. The old hermit was found dead in the boat, probably of natural causes, but they contacted the Sheriff anyway. They finally found the sheriff, who without ever seeing the body, directed them to bury it. So they rowed across the bay and buried the old veteran under a tree near his cabin.

T H Harmon had a large garden between Beach Drive and Harmon Avenue. It was occasionally inundated by storm tides which came without much warning. He sold fresh vegetables to families working in the new sawmill town of Millville. Between 1900 and 1910 he sometimes took two wagon loads a day to Millville.

In May 1910 Henry Johnson started to build a twelve foot wide vehicular bridge near the mouth of Massalina Bayou having a ten foot clearance over the water. The business owners on the bridge approaches bore the cost; it remained in service 15 years. Mr Harmon died at his homestead at age 71 a month later and never saw the completed bridge; the Panama City Pilot said that he had been closely connected with the development of Washington Co and teaching of its children.

A draw bridge replaced the old bridge in 1925 and lasted until 1951. Roz Murfee operated this bridge from about 1928 until 1942 with starting salary of $30 a month. The photo of Richard Williams' fishing smack Lucky Strike reveals this bridge with its operator's shed in the background.

Over most of the next 34 years Nancy Harmon lived with Amanda and Roz Murfee until 1944 when her daughter Amanda died. Once the tough little old lady fell and broke her arm and immediately reset it herself before going to a doctor. She liked to sit on the front porch of her house and observe traffic on the bay with her husband's old brass telescope.

Nancy Harmon filed for a war widow's pension in 1924 but it had been 60 years since that war, and she was turned down because she was unable to find the required two comrades to verify her husband's military service. After some persistence, Nancy's pension was finally approved in 1929 and her $480 annual stipend started

just in time for the depression and ran to 1947 when she died at the age of 97 at her daughter Ara Shores's home in Cottondale.
Submitted by: Jim Murfee, 15139 Highway 77, Southport, FL, 32409.

The Harries Family

The ancestry of the Harries in Bay County is a historical picture of the beginning of a new city. Many interesting events which would add to the founding picture has escaped us due to the passing of time and lack of recording. However the facts speak for the importantance of the information which has been obtained.

Harries four generations, Bowdon Foster Harries (holding daughter Mary Harries), Martha Bovis, Foster Harries and Adele Bovis Harris

Henry Bovis was born April 14th, 1843 in St. Octave County, Romiski Province of Quebec, Canada. He moved to the United States in 1876, to Pike County, Alabama. While living there he met and married Martha Frances Thomas of Thomasville, Alabama. They resided in Alabama for two years and then moved to Laure Hill, Florida. In 1900 they moved to St. Andrews Bay, and being a lumberman, he established St. Andrews Lumber Company and founded the town of Millville, Florida.

The Harries had several children, but the one who contributed the most to the historical picture was their daughter Adele Bovis, who met and married George Malcolm Harries, a tax assessor in Panama City, Florida. They had two children, a son, Bowden Foster Harries, and a daughter, Gertrude Adele Harries. The son, Bowden Harries married Mary Evelyn Welch, who was Floridas first Centennial Queen, when she was crowned in 1924, in Tallahassee, Florida at the festive Centennial Celebration. Bowden's mother, Adele Harries, became an agent for Prudential Life Insurance Company, where she remained for 32 years. After retiring she was very prominent in many organizations in Panama City. The Daughters of the Confederacy, founder of the Red Cross in Bay County, and as an artist she painted many scenes of the city, especially the bay. An avid photographer, she took memorable pictures of the area. Her home on the bay on Cincinnati Avenue, in St. Andrews is still a landmark.

Florida's first Centennial Queen 1924 Evelyn Welch

She was very active, and resided there until her passing, in February 1992 at the age of 106.

She truly contributed much to our historical city.
Submitted By: Mary Harries Pruitt, 20234 Duffy Road, Fountain, FL 32438. Written By: Nita Whitehurst.

Harry Wayne Harris - Family

Harry Wayne Harris moved to Panama City from Jackson County in 1929, soon after graduating from high school. In 1931 he married Ruth Moore of Panama City and they had five children: Kathryn, Patsy, Janet, Robert, and Kay. Harry worked as Deputy Clerk of the Circuit Court under his uncle, Harris Albert Pledger, from 1929 until he left in 1945

Harry W. Harris, Standing by the City Manager Car 1951

to assume the position of City Clerk of Panama City. He served in this position from 1945 to 1950, when he was named acting City Manager. In Nov 1951, due to failing health and at his own request, Harry returned to the office of City Clerk until his death in January 1952, at the age of 40.

Harry was a member of the Elk's Lodge where he served a term as Grand Exalted Ruler. He was also a member of the First Methodist Church of Panama City, as were all members of his family.

All of the children attended Panama Grammar School, except for Kay, who went to Cove Elementary. Janet, Robert and Kay attended Jinks Jr High School, and all five graduated from Bay High School. Janet was in the first 7th grade class to go to the newly opened Jinks Jr High in Sep 1950. Janet is the only one of the children who has lived continuously in Panama City, working for the City Clerk beginning in 1956 and later with Civil Service at Tyndall AFB until her retirement in 1994.

Ruth died in 1996, surviving her husband by 44 years.

Harry's only son, Robert, was born January 1, 1940, in the Adam's Hospital, the first baby born in Bay County that year. He was in the first class of Gulf Coast Community College when it opened in Sep 1957. He was president of the first Sophomore class and was in the first graduating class in 1959. Robert entered the USAF Aviation Cadet Pilot Training Program in 1959, graduating in Jan 1961 and served in the USAF until his retirement in 1986.

In 1987, Robert started working for the Clerk of the Circuit Court of Bay County, in the same court house that his father, Harry, had worked nearly 60 years earlier.
Submitted by: Janet Harris, 325 Bonita Ave., Panama City, Fl 32401.

Robert W. Harris

Robert was accepted to enter the Aviation Cadet Pilot Training Program in Oct 1959, receiving his pilot wings and commission as a 2nd Lt in the United States Air Force in Jan 1961.

From Aug 1966 to Aug 1967 he served in Viet Nam as a CV-2B/C-7 Caribou pilot, with the just created 536 Troop Carrier Squadron, 483rd Troop Carrier Wing. The Caribou was a two engine cargo aircraft designed for short takeoffs and landings from unprepared airstrips. For most of this time, Capt Harris flew missions in support of the Army Special Forces (Green Berets). On his initial operational mission in Viet Nam, while flying as co-pilot on the C-7, the pilot was wounded by a fragment of a shell which entered the cockpit and rendered him unable to fly the aircraft. Capt Harris took control of the Caribou and returned the wounded pilot and aircraft back to their home base. For this action, Capt. Harris was awarded his first Air Medal. Capt Harris upgraded to aircraft commander and instructor pilot in minimum time. His aircraft continued to be hit by enemy ground fire on numerous missions, so much so that he was given a nickname that probably can't be printed, except the first part which was

Capt. Robert W. Harris standing by a C-7 Caribou on the parking ramp of Can Tho Air Base, Vietnam 1967

"magnet". He was actually proud of this nickname.

On Jan 2, 1967, during an airdrop to a Special Forces camp, his Caribou received heavy automatic weapons fire inflicting fifty-three bullet holes in the aircraft and seriously wounding two crew members. Capt Harris was awarded the Distinguished Flying Cross (DFC) for meritorious achievement above the call of duty while flying under hostile conditions as the aircraft commander of a Caribou air dropping ammunition and rations to a Special Forces team engaged in combat with the Viet Cong in May 1967. By the end of this tour in Viet Nam, Capt Harris had received a total of 9 Oak Leaf Clusters to the Air Medal and had distinguished himself by being the first Air Force pilot to fly over 1000 combat hours in the Caribou.

One never knows how they will act under certain situations, such as combat, until they actually experience it.

Some of the quotes from his commanding officers, obtained from his military records, suggests that Capt Harris did OK:
"He's the coolest under fire I have ever seen." (Jan 1967); "His ability to perform under hostile fire is a well known fact which has been proven numerous times." (Apr 1967); "He has flown as many difficult missions and has been subjected to more hostile fire than any pilot in the Wing. His performance under fire has been exemplary." (Aug 1967, at the end of his year in Viet Nam)

After his year-long tour in Viet Nam ended in Aug 1967, Capt Harris was assigned to the 306th Bomb Wing, of the Strategic Air Command, at McCoy AFB, FL, as a B-52 pilot. In Sep 1968 he was flying combat missions again, this time flying bombing missions over Viet Nam in support of Operation Arc Light, operating from bases in Guam, Okinawa and Thailand. In April 1970, having flown 140 B-52 combat missions in two 6-month tours (Sep 1968 - Apr 1969 and Sep 1969 - Apr 1970), Capt Harris returned home from his last Arc Light deployment, his combat flying over, with a total of over 1800 hours combat flying hours and 16 Oak Leaf Clusters to the Air Medal.

During his Air Force career, Lt Col Harris accumulated 6000 total flying hours, of which more than 1800 hours was combat time in the C-7 Caribou and the B-52. Other aircraft included the T-34, T-37, T-33, T-29 and the T-39. He also held many administrative assignments as well, including Operations Officer of a T-39 unit, Squadron Commander of a Training Squadron, Chief of Maintenance at the Military Aircraft Storage and Disposition Center, a member of the Strategic Air Command Combat Evaluation Group (CEVG). CEVG was the standardization and evaluation organization for all flying operations of the Strategic Air Command, conducting inspections and evaluations of all SAC bases.

Robert retired from the Air Force in 1986 with the rank of Lieutenant Colonel.
Submitted by: Robert H. Harris, 435 Palo Alto, Panama City, Fl.

Bernard Hartzog Family - Part 1 of 4

Some Europeans had come to the New World and then returned to their country to give a glowing account of the Carolinas. A great German influence was in South Carolina before our Bernard Hartzog came to this land. Bernard and his young family's journey probably lasted from May to

Moses Timothy Hartzog Family Reunion Picture 1931

October, amid such hardships as no one is able to describe

adequately. The cause was that the Rhine boats from Heilbronn to Holland had to pass by 26 custom houses, at all of which the ships were examined, which was done when it suited the convenience of the custom house officials. The trip up the Rhine lasted from four to six weeks. The Hartzog family left Rotterdam, Holland, on the Cunliffe ship and headed for the New World. They made land at Charles Town, SC, during a hurricane.

The tradition of three brothers leaving Germany and coming to South Carolina has fascinated many a child as we heard Grandfather Tim Hartzog recount the story. If one examines the Giessendanner record in Salley's History of Orangeburg County, three Hartzog men appear in the record-Barnard, Tobias, and George. Also, in the land grant records, all three received grants. With this information only, one might assume that they were brothers. However, in more recent records, we have found that Tobias and George were sons of Barnard. He had two brothers, Adam and Martin. A Martin Hartzog came to Purrysville, SC, in 1734, but nothing else is known of him. As yet, we have not found Adam coming to America.

On Oct 20, 1752, Bernard Hartzog made application for land in Orangeburg District, SC. Many researchers have documented this family.

The first line of descent as we know it at this time is Henrich and Katharina Hertzog of Sandhausen, Germany. Henrich was born circa 1660 and died before 1706. This couple had at least two sons, Johannes born 1680, and Hans Henrich.

Second generation: Hans Henrich Hertzog born sometime before 1695 in Sandhausen, Germany, died Oct 4, 1744. He married Nov 16, 1706, to Katharina Kreyenbuhl who was born 1686 and died Feb 28, 1731. Their children were Johans Bernhard, Sara, Regina, Johann, Anna Margaretha, Hans Adam, Anna Katharina, and Jon Martin.

Third generation: Johans Bernhard Hertzog born Oct 23, 1707, and died after 1760. He married Jan 21, 1733, to Maria Saloma Meyer. He married the second time to widow Anne Mary Ulmer. Bernhard and Maria had the following children: Tobias, Hans Georg, Eva Barbara, Eva Elisabeth, amd Maria Eva. Bernhard and Anne Mary had John Theodore.
Submitted by: Virginia Hardy Buckalew, 4945 Guernsey Rd., Pace, FL 32571-8613.

Bernard Hartzog Family - Part 2 of 4

Fourth generation: Hans Georg Hartzog born Nov 23, 1738, and died 1782. He married 1765 to Catherine Magdalene Snell who was born Apr 14, 1747, and died 1789. This couple had John, George, Catherine, Daniel, Tobias, and Wyatt.

Fifth generation: Daniel Hartzog born 1774 and died 1826. He married in 1791 to Susannah Zorn who was born 1774 and died 1823. This couple had Tobias, William, Daniel Charles, George Henry, Susannah, Elizabeth, Sarah, and Rebecca. Daniel went farther west to Bamberg County, SC.

Hartzog Siblings-About 1957 Grady, Mamie, Cary, Lonie, Dolphie, Lessie, Perry

Sixth generation: George Henry Hartzog was born 1795 and died 1837. He first married Sarah Tyler, and they had three sons: Daniel Barney, George Wiley, and Francis. He married the second time to Celia. (We suspect her maiden name was Baxley, but have not proven it). George and Celia had James Washington, Isaac, Elizabeth, and William Henry. This family moved about 1836 to Cox Mill on present day Hwy. 53 in Barbour County. AL.

Seventh generation: James Washington Hartzog born 1830 in SC and died Dec 14, 1915, in Barbour County, AL. He first married Jul 30, 1849, to Martha A. Jane Warr, and they had William Sylvester, George W., John Aaron, Sarah Jane, James Thomas, and Moses Timothy. He married the second time to Edith Horne Beaty, and they had Nathan Alto, Maggie Bell, and Lee Cader.

Eighth generation: Moses Timothy Hartzog born Jun 28, 1875, in Barbour County, AL, and died Nov 2, 1957, in Panama City, FL. He first married Dec 27, 1891, to Margaret Arene Strickland, who was born Aug 30, 1877, in Barbour County, AL, and died Nov 16, 1916, in Coffee County, AL. She and Tim are buried at Mt. Carmel Primitive Baptist Church Cemetery, near Coffee Springs, AL. This couple had Perry James Jefferson, Dolphie Lee, Alvie Clifton, Mamie Lemarious, Cary Timothy, Grady Roan, Lonie Estelle, Leamon Fatee, Lessie Irene, Ila Mae, and twins, a boy and a girl, stillborn on Oct 6, 1916.

Submitted by: Thomas C. Hardy, 706 Radcliffe Ave., Lynn Haven, FL 32444-3039.

Bernard Hartzog Family - Part 3 of 4

Ninth generation: Lessie Irene Hartzog born Apr 6, 1911, in Coffee County, AL, and died Dec 28, 1987, in Pensacola, FL. On Nov 27, 1926, she married Thomas Hubie Hardy, who was born Feb 9, 1902, and died May 1, 1970. Hubie, as he was called, is buried at Whitmire Cemetery in Pensacola, and Lessie is buried at Bayview Memorial Cemetery in Pensacola. Hubie was a hard working man all his life. He would tell stories of working the horses and hauling cotton to the train depot. His first formal job was with Gulf Power Company. He, with other workers in 1927, put in the power poles and lines for electricity to go into the Bob Jones College, which was first located in Lynn Haven, FL. In 1933, the college was renamed Bob Jones

Thomas C. Hardy Family 2002

University, and moved to Greenville, SC. Hubie left Gulf Power after nine years, nine months, and eleven days to work for Newport Industries between 1932-1940. Then he started employment with Civil Service at Pensacola Naval Air Station from which he retired in 1965. While working with Gulf Power Company, his work took him from Graceville, FL, to Panama City, FL, where he met his bride-to-be on a double date. Hubie and Lessie married, and after their second child was born, they moved to Pensacola, FL. Lessie left school during the tenth grade to get married, but returned to school to complete a course to obtain license for Licensed Practical Nurse at which she worked for twenty years until her retirement. Lessie's gifts, talents, abilities, concerns, cares, quirks, faults, needs, and desires were many. However, the greatest thing she left her descendants was a Christian heritage.

Tenth generation: Thomas Cushi Hardy born Dec 8, 1937, in Pensacola, FL. He met Janet Marie Norris at Central Bible Institute in Springfield, MO, and they married in 1962. Janet was born Sep 24, 1930, in Flint, MI. They adopted siblings Diane Ellen Antoinette (Mull) and Erich Russell (Mull). Thomas graduated from Michigan State University in 1966 as an Electrical Engineer and served with Civil Service at the Pensacola Naval Air Station, Eglin Air Force Base, Heidelberg and Kaiserslautern, Germany, and returned to Tyndall AFB, FL, as a Research Engineer. Janet was command secretary for the 21st Support Command in Kaiserslautern and for the 23rd Air Division at Tyndall

AFB. Both retired in 1995 and reside in College Point, Lynn Haven.

Eleventh generation: Erich Russell (Mull) Hardy born Sep 6, 1962, in Melbourne, FL. In July 1995 he married Patricia Leigh Lamonica, who was born Sep 2, 1971, in Panama City, FL. Erich graduated from the University of West Florida, served as an Apache helicopter pilot in the US Army, fought in Desert Storm, and is now a pastor on staff at The Rock of Panama City. Leigh graduated from Bay High School in 1989 and was employed by Sun Bank prior to their marriage. They have two children, Ivy Grace Hardy born Aug 28, 1992, and Michael Levi Hardy born Sep 1, 1996.

Submitted by: Erich Russell Hardy, 706 Gabriel St., Panama City, FL 32405.

Bernard Hartzog Family - Part 4 of 4

Ninth generation: Dolphie Lee Hartzog born Jun 25, 1895, in Louisville, AL, and died Jul 30, 1981, in Panama City, FL. On Jun 25, 1912, he married Eura Essie Ogburn, probably in Geneva County, AL. Dolphie is buried at Greenwood Cemetery in Panama City, FL. Essie is buried at Coffee Springs, Geneva County, AL. Essie and Dolphie had six children: twins Macie Lee and Ocie Lee, Doris Marie, Abner Terrell, Alvin Huey, and Herbert Coy. On Nov 19, 1926, Dolphie moved his family to Panama City. Essie died apparently from appendicitis. Dolphie married (2) Addie Bell Cotton about 1938. Addie was a wonderful stepmother and grandmother to Dolphie's children and grandchildren. She was kind and loving to everyone she met. Addie and Dolphie lived on Highway 77 just beyond Harrison Avenue for many years. Grandmother Addie didn't like the grandchildren getting spankings at her house. If the parents got a switch out of the yard, she would sneak it away from the parents and break it up and throw it away. She made great fruit salad with nuts and cherries on top, and we children would fight over the cherries. Granddaddy Dolphie worked at the downtown post office. He had a nickname there. His co-workers called him "Cap," probably because of his thick, curly, pre-matured gray hair. He left for work at 2 a.m., and I have heard it told that he walked all the way to the post office. He said it was good exercise. Grandmother Addie died of complications from diabetes. Dolphie seemed very depressed after Addie's death. He received letters and cards from many friends, family, and loved ones. One of these letter writers was the sister of his first wife. She was living in South Florida, and she wrote such sympathetic letters. They corresponded for a while, and then he went to visit her. He came home with a new wife. When Highway 77 was being four-laned, the state bought Granddaddy's house and land. Aunt Cleetie and Granddaddy moved to Grace Avenue where both of them died. Aunt Cleetie had a little dog named "Petey." She and Granddaddy like to watch soap operas.

Tenth generation: Doris Marie Hartzog born Jan 11, 1917, in Coffee Springs, AL. Doris married Kermit Avery on Apr 15, 1938. Kermit had moved to Panama City with his parents and siblings in 1936. After serving his hitch with the U.S. Navy in WWII, Kermit became a master plumber and pipe fitter. He moved his little family all over the Southeast following job after job. When daughters Barbara Jean and Connie Lee were in middle school, Kermit and Doris decided to make Panama City their home. Kermit still followed jobs wherever they were, and on those frequent times between jobs, he would come home and work on the family business, Shady Acres Trailer Park on Highway 77, which Doris managed in his absence. Kermit's father, W.W. Avery, had bought several parcels of contiguous land for the taxes that were owed on them several years before. When his father passed away, each of the children was given several parcels. When Kermit and Doris's daughters married, each was given a parcel of this land on which to build their houses. It would be marvelous if everyone had a mother and father as wonderful as mine.

Eleventh generation: Barbara Jean Avery born May 29, 1946, in Panama City, FL. She married (1) Jerry Wayne Grantham born July 24, 1944, on Jun 1, 1963. They were divorced in 1971. They had two children: Stacey Lynn and Jerry Wayne, Jr. Barbara married (2) Bobbie Jean Tate born Jan 1, 1944. Bobbie was a Southern Bell employee for 34 years and retired in 1998 before his death in 2001. Bobbie and Barbara had one child: Jeannie Johanna. Constance Lee (Connie) Avery born Sep 13, 1949, in Panama City, FL, married Duane Randall born Jun 10, 1946, in Missouri, on Mar 2, 1968. Duane is a Southern Bell employee, and he and Connie have five children: Kimber Lee, Amy Lee, Patrick Avery, Elizabeth Lynn, and Ted Duane.

Submitted by: Barbara Tate, 821 Avery St., Panama City, FL 32405.

Cary Hartzog
Mayor Without a Town
Becomes Mail Clerk

Cary and Eva Hartzog moved to Sellars Still/Highland City/Hiland Park a suburb of Panama City, Florida in 1926. In 1947, the General Merchandise Store across the highway from their home was for sale. Cary and Eva purchased the store and operated it.

In 1952, Cary was told by the Post Office that they would take their Branch Office out of the community if they couldn't find someone to handle it. So he contracted with the

Cary T. Hartzog in Post Office with Birthday Cake

U.S. Postal Service to operate the branch office in his store. With the help of his wife and his children when they were there, the Branch Office grew as the store grew.

In 1953, some of the community wanted to incorporate into a city and some did not. A mayor and four commissioners were chosen as they voted for the city. The Mayor elected was Cary T. Hartzog and the Commissioners were: Lloyd and Barney Mashburn, Truman Hartzog and Amos Howard. The town was voted down, leaving Cary Hartzog a Mayor without a town and the commissioners out, too. Cary became known as "The Mayor without a Town" - a title he carried as long as he lived. It gave him recognition in the newspaper, television and even Time Magazine wrote an article about him.

Before the fire house was built in Hiland Park, the fire siren was put in Hartzog's store and he was responsible for ringing it and calling all of the volunteer firemen when there was a fire in the community.

In 1960, Cary was voted "The Most Outstanding Citizen" by the Civitan Club and was given a Certificate of Honor. If a record was ever made, Hartzog made it by being elected "Mayor Without a Town" in 1953 and holding that title until his death 14 March 1995 at the age of 94.

Every year he opened the store by daylight and he and Eva kept it open until 11 :00 p.m. and sometimes 12:00 if it got busy. They never closed with anyone in the store.

Cary and Eva Hartzog worked very hard all their lives and when it was time to retire, he could not retire, so he continued to work in the branch Post Office for Mr. J.K. Pettis, who contracted for it after the Hartzog store was demolished for the four-laning of the U.S. 231 Highway.

They always had a well cared for garden and grew enough for many families. It was easy to pick since all of the grass and weeds were cleaned off regularly. In the early days they had a cow to furnish milk and chickens to furnish eggs and meat.

Submitted by: Kirby Strickland, 3105 E. 8th Street, Panama City, FL

32404. Written by: Rubylee Strickland, 2627 Game Farm Road, Panama City, FL 32405. Source: Files of Sarah Rubylee Hartzog Strickland.

The Cary T Hartzog Family

Cary and Eva were blessed with the following children:

Sarah Ruby Lee Hartzog born 14 June 1923. She was married 22 June 1946 to Yancy Cecil Strickland (4 October 1921-23 August 1977) and became step-mother to his daughters, Martha Janice (6 May 1941) and Myra Jean (15 April 1943). Janice married David Spence and had Eugene, Toney, and Jana Lois. Myra married Charles Hayman and had Charles Edward Jr.

Yancy and Ruby had the following: Susan Carol (13 April 1947); She married Jackie Erwin Creel and they had Robert Christopher and Craig Erin Creel. Yancy Kirby (24 September 1949); He married first Deborah Davenport and had Rebecca Marie and Melissa Dianne. He married Tracy Reed and had Courtney Ann and Amanda Gail. His last marriage was to Darlene "Gipson" Hewett who had Joni and Jennifer Hewett. Nancy Eva (26 December 1953) was married to Lloyd Gary Norton and their children were Gary David, Desty Joanna, and Troy Joseph Norton. Joseph Phillip (7 September 1960) was married first to Angela Regina Woodrum and had Shawna Regina and Josie Necole and his third marriage was to Barbara Jo "Hearne" Chastain and they have Krista Chastain and Joshua Cary Strickland. Teddy Lee (11 March 1962) married as his second wife and her second husband Deborah Jean Steverson. She had a son Jeremy which was adopted by her mother and step-father Winston and Pat Scott. Ted and Debbie has the following: Justin Cody and Jessica Leighann Strickland.

Standing L. to R. Margaret Hartzog, Truman Hartzog, Rubylee Hartzog. Seated L to R with Jackie standing between them are Cary Timothy and Lessie Eva "Anderson" Hartzog

Cary Truman Hartzog (1 February 1927) Married Lillian Louise Bland 22 January 1947. Their children: Melanie Louise (26 March 1948) married Jack Heller (8 Sep. 1935-21 December 1983).They have Timothy Jack, Jennifer Melanie and Brian William Heller. Karen Sue Hartzog (17 May 1951) married Dewel Gail Brasher and they have David Alan Brasher. Marcie Ann Hartzog (6 March 1954) married Aaron Abreu and have Joseph Lawrence and Jason Lance Abreu. Cary Truman Hartzog Jr. (7 May 1955) married first Laura Elizabeth Landgraph and has Laura Elizabeth Hartzog. He married second and inherited two or three step-daughters.

Margaret Lavinia Hartzog (17 January 1931); married James Wesley Jordan (22 June 1929-28 April 1985) Their children were: Freida Gale Jordan, married Dwight Edward Greene and has Kevin Baxter, James Edward and Donald Eugene Green. Judith Ann Jordan is not married.

Jackie Earl Hartzog (13 January 1934-29 April 1981) was married to Carlos Ann "Maxwell" Bell. and adopted her son John Mark Bell Hartzog. Jackie and Polly has a daughter, Carlos Bridgett Hartzog.

Cary and Eva Hartzog raised their family in Hiland Park and most of them still live in or around Panama City, Florida. At their death, they had three of their children, 15 grandchildren, 35 great-grandchildren and 9 great-great-grandchildren. They lost their son, Jackie Earl with leukemia in 1981

Submitted by: Desty Jo Norton, 3922 Easy Street, Southport, Fl. 32409. Written by: Ruby Lee Strickland, 2627 Game Farm Road, Panama City

FL 32405. Source: Photo Album and Files of Sarah Rubylee "Hartzog" Strickllandd.

Cary Timothy Hartzog

Cary T. Hartzog was born 4 April 1901 in Geneva County near Malvern, Alabama and died 14 March 1995 at the age of 94, in Panama City, Florida. He is resting at Evergreen Memorial Gardens, near the Open Bible in Bay County, Florida. He was the son of Moses Timothy and Margaret Arene "Stricklan" Hartzog. His Grandparents were James Washington and Martha Ann Jane "Warr" Hartzog and Thomas Jefferson and Mary Frances "Little" Stricklan. His paternal great grandparents George and Celia "Baxley" Hartzog and John and Nancy "Bass" Warr. His Maternal Great Grand parents were John Sion and Elizabeth "Black" Stricklan and John and Martha "____" Little.

Back row: Dolphie Lee Hartzog, Parrie James Jefferson Hartzog, Front row: Cary Timothy Hartzog, Moses Timothy Hartzog holding Lonie Estelle Hartzog, Grady Roan Hartzog between mom and dad. Margaret Arene "Stricklan" Hartzog holding Lessie Irene with Mamie Lemarious Hartzog standing beside her.

The family lived in Geneva and Coffee Counties Alabama while Cary was growing up. They were members of Mt. Carmel Primitive Baptist Church in Geneva County, Alabama, near Coffee Springs. This is where his mom, Dad, Step-mom, two brothers and two Sisters are now buried. His other brother is buried possibly in Barbour County but not Sure. Cary's mother died when he was 15 years old and she was 39. She had given birth to the following children:

Parrie James Jefferson Hartzog (23 June 1893 - 19 February 1982), Dolphie Lee Hartzog (25 June 1895 - 30 July 1981), Alvie Clifton Hartzog (28 May1897 - 13 July 1898), Mamie Lemirous Hartzog (7 July 1899 -10 October 1981), Cary Timothy Hartzog (4 April 1901 -14 March 1995), Grady Roan (20 April 1903 - 3 January 1972), Lonie Estelle Hartzog (20 January 1906-16 March 2000), Leamon Fate (10 January 1908 -14 July 1909). Lessie Irene Hartzog (3 September 1911 - 28 December 1987), Ila Mae Hartzog (19 December 1914 -26 May 1915) and Twins (a boy and a girl) Stillborn (6 October 1916). Margaret died 16 Nov. 1916.

The doctor said that her stroke was caused from having too many children too close together.

In 1921 Cary's dad met Essie Lee Wilkes (16 March 1891-26 January 1973) at church. She was the daughter of John Calhoun and Cydia Antionette "Sellars" Wilkes. Moses and Essie were married 2 January 1921 and she was a wonderful mother to his children. She waited on Mr. Hartzog she called him and when they moved to Panama City she got a job and helped his children with their support. She was never able to have any children of her own but to all of us she was our real grandmother. Nobody could have been better or more loving to us than she was. When she got unable to stay home alone she stayed with Cary and Eva. I never in all of her life heard her say one cross word. I never got to know my grandmother Margaret but I was very happy with Grandmother Essie.

Submitted by: Carol Creel, 475 Higgerson Road, Cullman, Alabama. Written by: Rubylee Strickland, 2627 Game Farm Road, Panama City, Florida. Source: Family records and Memories and Bible records.

Cary Hartzog and Eva Anderson

Cary Hartzog and Eva Anderson ran away to Blakely Georgia and were married on 30 July 1922. Cary's father's asthma grew steadily worse and doctors said moving near salt water might help. Moving would be easier for Cary and Eva because his older siblings had families.

Cary and Moses made the trip in November 1922 on the train. Cary said "It like to have scared me to death when the train backed out over the water. That was the most water I had ever seen". They found a place to live and the family followed in December 1922. Cary's first job was at the German American Lumber Co. in Millville. To get there he had walk a dirt trail from near the Tarpon dock through the Cove to Millville. With

Cary Timothy Hartzog and Lessie Eva "Anderson" Hartzog

woods on both sides it was easy to be scared with animals all over. They gave him all the scraps he could carry in bags on his shoulder for the family to cook and keep warm with. One night he was walking when he discovered a pair of eyes following him. They stayed about the same distance away. He was afraid to run and the family needed the wood for tomorrow, so he kept his same pace and watched it. When he got through the woods the animal stopped following him. He never found out what kind of animal it was.

When Papa's health improved he helped Cary operate a service station at Harrison Ave. and 6th street. They also operated one at a different time near the depot.

In 1926 Cary and Moses paid $150 for two lots side by side. Cary built two small houses side by side for him and Papa. Deciding it was too far from the water Papa moved back to town and Cary's brother Dolphie moved his family into the empty house. He lost his wife with appendicitis when I was about five years old and my Mother took care of his children when he had to be at work.

Cary and brother Grady delivered bread brought in from Dothan, Alabama on a large truck. On Papa's good days, he helped Cary because he had the longest route. Cary and Grady bought a grocery store in Bay Harbor and ran it until it burned. Grady started selling insurance. Cary ran another store across from now Rutherford High School as a favor to a friend who was called to serve his country. His friend's family lived in the back of the store, while Cary ran the store.

Cary got a chance to buy the Grocery Store on 231 Highway right across from where he lived. It had been built and operated by T. C. Kinnington. Cary and Eva ran the Grocery Store with the post-office in it with the help of their son Jackie Earl and cash register clerks. In 1967, when the highway was 4-laned it cut the front off the store and Hartzog retired but went back to work in the Post-Office after it was moved.

Submitted by: Phillip Strickland, 107 E 40th Place, Lynn Haven FL 32444. Written By: Ruby Lee Strickland, 2627 Game Farm Road, Panama City FL 32405. Sources: Files of RubyLee "Hartzog" Strickland.

Hartzog Family Reunion

The Hartzog family held a reunion in 1991. Most of the Cary and Eva Hartzog family were able to attend. The following family members are shown in the photo with this story:

Back row: Tim Heller, Gary Norton, J.T. Littlepage, Polly Littlepage, Phillip Strickland. Kirby Strickland, Darlene Strickland, Theda Hartzog, Mark Hartzog, Melanie Heller, Bryan Heller, and Judy Jordan.

Third row: Desty Norton, Rebecca Stokes, Jennifer

Hartzog Family Reunion, 1991

Heller, Nancy Norton, Carol Creel, and Bridget Campbell McMillion.

Second row: Ruby Strickland, Margaret Jordan, Cary T. Hartzog, Eva Hartzog holding Jessica Strickland, Teddy Strickland, and Debbie Strickland.

First row: Cody Strickland, Vicky Campbell, Shawna Strickland, T.J. Norton, Josie Strickland, and Jonathan Hartzog

Submitted by: Rubylee Strickland, P.O. Box 23, Panama City, FL 32402. Source: Files of Rubylee "Hartzog" Strickland.

The Hartzog Family
Growing up in "Sellars Still" /Hiland Park FL.

I was born June 14, 1923 in Panama City, FL, The oldest child of Cary Timothy and Lessie Eva "Anderson" Hartzog. About two years later, my father purchased a piece of land at "Sellar's Still"(a suburb of Panama City, Florida and built a small house (about one block southeast of the railroad tracks and 231 highway). We lived at what is now 2812 Headland Avenue. To the west, across Headland Ave. was a turpentine still in operation. Except for that we were surrounded by woods.

Mr. J. D. Sellars, who owned and operated the still, lived across 231 Highway on property now owned by Highland Park Baptist church.

Playing on the Seasaw

Only there was nothing of 231, only a dirt road.. On the west, along the road, were two large houses occupied by the people who worked at the mill. Behind the last house was a commissary (Store) that furnished food, clothing etc. for the families working at the still, the bill being paid from their pay at the end of the week

Along the east side of what is now Selma Avenue was a row of small buildings called shanties, with wooden swinging shutters for windows and doors. This provided places for the workers and their families to live. On the west side of Selma Avenue, on the hill in the middle of the block was a church where all of the black people of the community attended church. This is where I, on a dare, touched my first dead person. He was an old man and his hand was so cold and stiff that I can still feel it if I dwell on it too much.

A family named Renfoe lived near Sarasota Avenue, north of Orlando Rd. but there was so many woods between us that it was like another world away.

We enjoyed "jumping board" "seesawing" and climbing through the woods on wild bullies (grape) vines swinging from tree-tops to tree-tops. It did not occur to us that the snakes we saw crawling on the ground could also be crawling up in the trees. But God took care of us cause we never did get bit by any of the animals. Sometimes at night, we could hear panthers scream in the same woods. At this time with no paved roads anywhere and woods all over, the animals could roam where-ever they wanted at night when people were sleeping.

One Christmas there was a very large Christmas tree in my uncle Frank Covington's yard, at the corner of Headland Avenue and Baldwin Rd. They called it a community tree. I never dreamed that so many people lived in houses surrounded by woods like we did, but I found out that night by the large crowd at that party. Somebody did a lot of planning cause there was a gift under the tree for every child there and we all had nuts, candy, an orange, and apple. Everyone enjoyed home made ice cream. It was one Christmas that I will always remember.

While the Still was in operation, my cousin, Terrill Hartzog worked there capping the drums of hot Rosin to sell. One day he climbed on top to use his weight to push the lid down. It slipped and his leg went in the hot liquid to his hip. Mrs. Claudie Johnson and Lem Barentine pulled him out, but the leg was badly burned. It took a long time to heal with good care.

Submitted and written by: Sarah Rubylee "Hartzog" Strickland, 2627 Game Farm Road, Panama City, FL 32405. Source: Just part of my memories of living in the same place for all my life.

Simon Bolovard Hathaway and Susan
Pearylee Pitts
The Pitts-Hathaway Family
Pioneers of Bay County

Allow me to introduce a most remarkable couple, my Papa and Granma Hathaway. First, my great-grandmother, Susan Pearylee Pitts. She was born February 8, 1881 in Bayou George, Florida to Issac Powell and Louisa Wright Pitts. They were a large family; she had six older brothers and 3 older sisters. Bayou George in 1881 was still sparsely settled, they were true pioneers. She did not have much 'schooling' but she had a keen intellect all of her life and was very wise. When Pearylee was 12 years old her mother died. Louisa had been in poor health for a while. Pearylee believed that her mother had died 'from the change of life', complications of menopause. She then lived with her siblings and also worked in boarding houses cooking and cleaning. Pearylee worked in Parker as a young woman. One of her favorite stories, and ours, was an exciting story that showed what a wilderness Northwest Florida was at that time. It was the tale of Peter Parker and the 'painter' (panther). Peter's father was away and a panther stalked the cabin because of baby Peter's crying. She could make us feel as though we were in that cabin with Peter and his mother as the panther screamed, trying to get in to the crying infant.

When she was 25, and still single, she met Simon Bolovard Hathaway. He was a handsome 30 year old man from South Alabama. Interestingly, both of their fathers had fought for the south in the Civil War. He had even saved his father's, John Marion Lafayette Hathaway, war discharge papers and the documents are still in our family. Simon spied Pearylee in Black, Alabama as she walked by and immediately told his companion she was the girl he would marry. And so, they did get married, on Christmas Eve 1905. Their first child, Archie Bell, was born September 28, 1906. Simon Perry (my grandfather) followed in 1908, Susan Ophelia in 1910, Homer Lafayette in 1912, Doll in 1914, Eva Mae, our special 'Bebe', in 1917, and Edna in 1922. Pearylee was strong and a good nurse, all seven of their children lived to have grandchildren of their own. She nursed many family members and neighbors. She was a midwife as well. She also helped prepare the bodies of neighbors for burial while the men of the families would build the coffins.

In 1914 the young family was living in Holmes County.

Simon Bolovard and Pearylee Pitts Hathaway on their wedding day, December 24, 1905

They moved to Bay County around 1915. Uncle Jasper Taylor helped load their belongings onto oxen wagons and they moved into the area that would become Bay County. Uncle 'Jasp' would later become my mothers' (Jewel) maternal grandfather. His daughter Merle married Simon Perry. They camped by night and slowly made their way to a little log cabin, a former schoolhouse on Econfina Creek.

Sometime later they moved to Majette, a small sawmill town. One of Pearylee's sisters, Liddie, lived in the hotel at Majette and several members of both families lived nearby. Simon worked for the railroad and they even briefly lived in a boxcar! They also lived in one of the small red houses by the tracks that the rail company built for their employees. Sparks from a train actually set this house on fire. The family all rushed to save their few household items from the fire. The Hathaway children attended school while living in Majette. They would take their lunch to school in old syrup buckets, whatever they had left over from supper or breakfast. Pearylee always had a garden and 'put up' vegetables and fruits to last through the winter. When fall arrived, they would butcher hogs and pack the meat in barrels filled with lard and also smoke some of the meat. They didn't have much, Doll remembers making babydolls from old towels as a child and, when older, raking wiregrass from around sapp pines for 1 cent a tree.

Around 1939 Pearylee had saved enough to buy 10 acres in Bayou George. They built their home, cutting and planing trees for the wood. The shingles were handmade from cypress bark. The house had a front room with a fireplace, a backroom for sleeping in, a kitchen off the back porch with a big black wood burning stove, and a little room off the front porch for guests to sleep in. They had a smoke house for smoking meat, and a fruit house for storing 'put up' fruits and vegetables. It always seemed dark and cool in the little houses. Men would come around on trucks in the summer selling fresh peaches by the bushel and Granma always had pear trees. Her food from those mason jars was the best. They had a barn and always had hogs for butchering and oxen to pull the plow for the large garden. Simon and Pearylee would live there the rest of their lives.

Simon and Pearylee more than 50 years after their wedding

Papa died at the age of 89 in 1964 and Granma died in 1970, also at the age of 89, in the same house they had built with their own hands. They had raised children and grandchildren, taking in my mother Jewel and her older sisters Vernell and Marie and brother John after their mother died. They even helped to raise great-grandchildren! My parents, Ronald and Jewel, and my brothers, Steve and Stan lived next door to them. They were always there if we needed anything. My great-aunt Eva, Bebe to us, lived with them and lots of other family members lived around us as well. I will never forget the love they all had for our family. Simon and Pearylee accumulated little material possessions in their lives, but a great deal of love and respect.

I feel so blessed to have known and loved such amazingly strong and wonderful people. I wish my husband, James, and our sons Simon and Tyler could have known them. They would be proud our boys are sixth generation Bay Countians who, with their cousins, will carry this family into the future.

Submitted by: Angela Dunn Miller, 1732 Courtland Place, Southport, Fl 32409.

Georgia Thomas Henry

"My mother is a woman'" I said to my mother when I was 17 years old. A revelation that she was first a person, and not just my mom. Her reply to me was, "That will be the title of my first book of poems." And it was. Her second book of poems is "Moorings."

Georgia Edith Thomas was born May 8, 1928 in Monticello, Florida to Alva and Golda Pickens Thomas, both of pioneer Bay County families. Mom was named for each of her grandmothers. She attended Panama Grammar and graduated from Bay High in 1946. Her 1946 Yearbook tells

Georgia Pearson with sons Craig, Grant and "Mike" Bradley Henry

something about her, and her school years. She won the DAR Award, was voted class secretary, Most likely to Succeed, Most Intellectual (Wallace Laird the other), co-editor (with Karl Nelson) of the school newspaper, art editor of the yearbook, secretary of the Latin Club, and majorette in the Bay High Band. She was also a majorette at FSCW/FSU, where she got degrees in 1950 and 1953. All this to say, her literary, art and musical interests in high school opened the doors to her future life.

Mom's career as an educator includes writer/director of the first Head Start program in Bay County and instructor at FSU and director of Florida's Head Start; human services consultant, curriculum coordinator, teacher and longtime employee of the Georgia Department of Human Resources. She retired in 1993 and returned to Bay County a year later.

My two brothers and I were born in Lisenby Hospital on 11th Street. Our daddy is Sid Henry and our parents met at the FSU Methodist Student House. He became a school principal and later an education consultant in Tallahassee.

My oldest brother, Craig, was born when the family lived on Highway 231, now corner of Transmitter Road on 10 acres of grandpa Thomas' land. Grant, the second child, and I were born when we lived in Woodlawn at the beach. There was no church there so the Woodlawn Methodist Church was founded in our home, with Earl and Sara Padgett, and Bill and Lou Quigley as joint organizers. Craig has 3 children (Melissa, Jessica and Phillip), Grant 1 (Mary Grace), and I have 3 (Michelle, Rachel, and Boone). My parents have 7 grandchildren and 2 greats. Craig is in the car business. He now lives in Bay County. Grant, in Atlanta has been a teacher, youth counselor, restaurant manager and collects and sells antiques. And I, with wife Susan, whom I met at the University of Georgia, moved from Atlanta to Denver where I have a media consultant firm.

But back to my mom. I asked her, from her now 75 years, what are her best memories? Her answer, "a mother and grandmother first, helping people through my work, friendship with 'the girls' since Panama Grammar days, collecting antiques and traveling, making homes out of the various houses". Then she couldn't stop - "all my friends and family, my teachers, and discovery of poetry." She has many awards for poetry and fiction and was president of the Georgia Poetry Society. Since returning home she founded the Emerald Coast Poets in Bay County. She also wrote and had published a hardback 40 year history of Woodlawn Methodist Church. But she wants her ashes scattered in her beloved North Georgia Mountains.

Mom married John Pearson, retired Navy pilot, in 1999 and now shares the volunteer job of co-producer (and writer) of the "Seniors for Seniors" television program. It won two state awards in 2001.

Mom's accomplishments are not as important as who she is. I am proud to claim this special friend, this woman, as my mother.

Submitted by: Michael Bradley Henry, 8680 Creek Trail, Morrison, Colorado 80465.

Melissa Henry-Fox

My doctor, the high risk team from Pensacola, and everyone else, said I would have to birth Brendan by caesarean section. And they had good reason.

When I was seven years old, I began living my life as a paraplegic - with my body paralyzed from my chest down. All because a 19 year old drinking driver rammed her truck into our Ford Escort. It not only changed my life, but also my family's. My Grandma Georgia described her grief in a poem: "I mourn the little things, her moments never to recapture - like the toe-feel of grass blades after a summer rain, or, the rhythmic beat of a bouncy refrain. My Melissa mourning

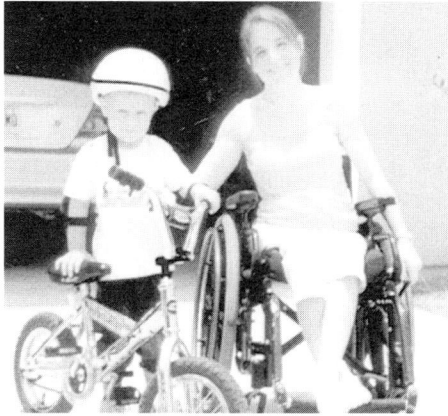
Melissa and son, Brendan Fox

mirrors me each day as I think I have accepted her way. The nightmare of the midnight phone call returns with reverberating foul weather. . . the same as any earthquake's aftershock of rumbling rocks and violent vibrations separates the field from heather." And the accident did just that. It separated my legs from my body. And some of my vital organs nonfunctional.

Just surviving was the first miracle. After being pulled out of the ditch, I was surrounded by nurses, doctors and beeping machines. After I finally became conscious, I was frightened because I never knew what was going to happen next - for a long time. After over a month in Bay Memorial Hospital, I was flown in a 4-seater plane (vomiting all the way) to Nemours Children's Hospital in Jacksonville for rehabilitation. My mom, Sue, and I entered the dark, dreary halls and the stale odor of the air. I cried, "I hate this place! I want to go home." But I had to stay. In order to be mobile, I had to master the workings of my body in a wheelchair.

Each day became one hurdle after another. I recall being at the foot of the ramp which my physical therapist, Kim, insisted I climb every day. She only said, "I don't care what methods you use to reach the top, just reach it!" And I finally did, again and again, making real the adage, "Life is an uphill battle." Then, the repetitious on and off of my clothes seemed simple, but

Melissa Marie Henry

doing it when your legs don't move is not so simple. The last major struggle was to transfer from chair to bed and back,

and using a board to help me get from chair to car and back.

After weeks at Nemours, my Grandma Georgia came for a week so my mom could go home for a few days. The occupational therapist, Jodie, told my grandma that I was not cooperating, so my grandma bribed me, saying she would take me to England to see my baby sister, Jessica, and my daddy, Craig, if I would do what the therapist said. . .And I did. (But they later moved back to Atlanta.) Also, my Uncle Brad and Susan asked me to be the flower girl in their Atlanta wedding in three months. So I had to learn to be as independent as I could.

After returning home, and to the frustration with Bay County schools which were not always ready for a wheelchair, the school years ended with almost two years at Gulf Coast College. During this period, I had experimental surgery in New York and had returned to Jacksonville for a U-shaped steel rod to be inserted from my neck to my hip for scoliosis. And I was Jerry Fox's date at the Senior Prom in my black sequined gown with rhinestone straps!

My marriage to Jerry Fox with a formal, traditional wedding at Woodlawn Methodist Church occurred on July 29, 1995. Family and friends from everywhere were there. My Grandma Georgia was my only attendant. Uncle Brad and Aunt Susan's young child, Boone, was there as ringbearer, along with a memory of my rolling down that red carpeted isle.

Looking back over the years since the accident, I see God's hand in my life. My legs may be paralyzed, but my heart and mind are not. On one of the check-ups, a new doctor asked me what bothers me the most? And I replied, "These zits on my face!" Here I have a spinal cord injury, no use of one-half of my body, and I answered like any typical teenager. Most of the time I hardly think of myself as handicapped, but as handi-capable.

On October 6, 1998, the biggest miracle of all! Brendan was born - the way I wanted. . . which no one thought was possible, even my doctor. Not by surgery, but by natural birth, to everyone's surprise. Like my grandma's poem about me: . . . "shackled in a chair of steel, but the you in you remains, your spirit undaunted, unmaimed. . . as the seagull with fractured limb refusing not to fly. . . as she soars into the limitless sky."

Submitted by: Melissa Henry Fox, 303 Brady Way, Panama City Beach, Fl. 32408.

Stormie Janie Lee Hires

My granddaughter Stormie Janie Lee Hires, from birth, was a gift to me, as was holding her in my arms and seeing a tiny smile form on her lips. As a toddler she always wanted to "Help Granny Janie." Her inner beauty blossomed as she grew into a young girl. Smiles lighted her beautiful face, her inner spirit shining through her eyes. Yet, through it all her special spirit keeps her loving heart shining bright. She had her share of scrapes and a broken arm, as she grew older.

Stormie Janie Lee Hires

Her uncle Emmett and Jimmy took her to the Movies in the Mall and also to the Under The Oaks in the Park, we would have lunch and go swimming. She remembers having dinner with her great granny Flossie on her Birthday, we had crab legs and Stormie would help her crack them. I would always take Stormie fishing with her ggranny Flossie and they would always laugh about catching all those Fish and baby Turtles. She went to Covenant Christian School for 3 years and than Lucille Moore Elementay School for 2 years, before moving to Huntsville, Al. Her mother, Teresa worked at the Marriot

Hotel and next door was the Space Center, we enjoyed visiting it.

She lives in Greenville, Tenn. now, I talk to her every week on the phone, she has new friends and they do a lot of camping in the Mountains. She says, its cooler in Tenn. than Florida. She likes the snow and school in Tenn.
Submitted by: Emmett Ammons, Panama City, Florida; Written by: Janie Ammons, 2714 E. 7th Ct., Panama City, Florida.

Dr. and Mrs. Samuel Homola

Samuel Homola and Martha Wise Surles married on October 15, 1957, establishing a permanent residence in Panama City, Florida.

Martha Wise Surles Homola was born March 10, 1928, on the Bellagio Plantation in East Carroll Parish, Lake Providence, Louisiana. She graduated from Lake Providence High School in 1946 and then attended Judson College in Marion, Alabama, for three years. When her father, Alphy Pittman Surles, died on October 28, 1948, she returned to Lake Providence to operate and manage Planter's Butane, a gas company she inherited from her father. In January of 1951, Martha and her mother, Blondell, moved to Panama City, Florida, to be near two of her mother's sisters, Maye Milner of Panama City and Lil Rimson of Dothan, Alabama. Martha worked as a clerk at the Marie Hotel for a short time and then as a typist for Howell and Conner Insurance and Real Estate. In May of 1951, she went to work at Panama Title Corporation, owned by Waldo Wallace, where she worked for 21 years.

Dr. And Mrs. Samuel Homola

In the fall of 1956, Martha herniated a lumbar disc and was treated by Samuel Homola, D.C., a Panama City chiropractor. A year later, she and Sam married. Martha retired from Panama Title Corporation in 1972. In 1988, she went to work in Sam's office as a secretary and receptionist. She and Sam both retired in 1998.

Samuel Homola was born in Dothan, Alabama, on June 10, 1929. His father, an immigrant from Revuca, Czechoslovakia, graduated from the Palmer School of Chiropractic in 1920. He practiced chiropractic in Dothan, Alabama, until his death in 1957. Sam's mother, Irene, was from Grangerburg, a small rural community near Malone, Florida.

While in high school, Sam participated in weightlifting as a sport and won an AAU gold medal in southeastern weight lifting competition in 1947. He graduated from Dothan High School in 1948 and immediately joined the U.S. Navy. He underwent boot training in San Diego, California, and then attended schools in aviation fundamentals and structural mechanics in Memphis, Tennessee. He was stationed at Miramar Air Base near San Diego until 1951 when he was transferred to the aircraft carrier U.S.S. Valley Forge for duty in the Korean War. He left the navy in 1952 with the rating of second class petty officer.

In 1952, Sam entered Lincoln Chiropractic College in Indianapolis, Indiana. He graduated in 1956 and began practicing in Panama City, Florida. His marriage to Martha Wise Surles in 1957 was the beginning of a long and productive love and partnership. While in practice, Sam wrote and published 13 books and more than 200 magazine articles, gaining recognition as one of Florida's most prolific authors (see section on Panama City authors).

Dr. and Mrs. Samuel Homola continue to reside at 1307 East Second Court in Panama City, Florida.
Submitted by: Dr. Samuel Homola, 1307 E. 2nd Ct., Panama City, FL 32401-4003.

Mamie Lee Hood 1897-1978

My mother, Mamie Lee Hood Findley, told me this story when I was a young girl. She was born 1897 in Washington County, Florida. These are her words. Papa had a wagon and he covered it like the early pioneers covered their wagons. He and Mama packed enough supplies to last us a week or more. Papa drove the two mule team wagon with Mama beside him and the children under the covered part of the wagon.

Mamie Lee Hood Findley

From Enterprise, Alabama we would travel by day and late in the afternoon Papa would pull the wagon off into the woods to camp for the night. Mama would prepare our supper over the open fire. After supper and the dishes were done we would talk, and play and then get in the wagon to sleep. Papa slept under the wagon to watch over us. In the morning after the breakfast Mama cooked over the open fire, we would be on our way. It would take a week or more of travel to arrive in St. Andrews, Florida. We camped in a big grove of trees by a natural spring. A lady came to make us welcome as we were on her land. She was riding her horse through the woods. She lived in a log cabin nearby. I know this was by the spring at the corner of Beach Drive and Frankford Avenue. The lady was Mrs. West. Just over the bay was a big fish house where mullet was salted and sold. In the early 1900's mullet was plentiful in the bay. It was salted to preserve the fish and was used during the winter months for food. Papa would buy barrels of salt fish to carry back to Enterprise, Alabama. This trip was a great adventure for Mama. This trip can be made in a few hours today, but back then life was slower and more simple, though sometimes hard.

Mama's Uncle Charlie Tindell, brother of her mother, Lillie Tindell Hood married Mary Vernon Amos, daughter of pioneer settlers of Coffee County. They had three sons. Uncle Charlie kept in touch with Mama as long as he lived. Charlie and Lillie Tindell were the grandchildren of John and Mary Powell, and children of Amanda Powell and Jeremiah Tindell. The Powells were on the 1850 Coffee County census. My mother Mamie Lee Hood(1897-1978) was the daughter of A. E. Hood (1861-1921) and Lillie Tindell (born 1877). Lillie died when Mama was a baby. Her father A. E. remarried to Isabella Cameron

Beatrice Findley Moates Birthday Dinner

Williams and she became Mama to the two little Hood girls, Mamie and Mae. Isabella was a warm and courageous lady. Elzy (A. E.) and Isabella moved to Washington County and Washington County became Bay County in 1913.

My mother, Mamie Lee Hood, married second William Nathaniel Findley (1884-1954) from Pickens County, Georgia. They had me, Beatrice Louise and my sister Willie Lavonia (1926-1995). I married Buress Moates, (1918-1984) son of Grover C. Moates (1883-1966) and Sarah Frances Wiggins (1882-1922). After Sarah died in 1922, Grover C.

remarried to Cleopatra Edmondson. She was the "Gunnie" my children knew and loved. Buress and I had a daughter and a son. I have four grandsons, a granddaughter, and six great-grandchildren.

Annette married Roy E. Sasser. They have three sons, Roy E. Jr., Kevin P., and R Keith who married Angela Green. They have a daughter Taylor Breann and son Tyler Jordan. My son Grover married Alma Ruth Hoover. They have a son Gene and a daughter Teresa A. and four grandchildren, Kimberly Dawn and Michael Devin Moates and Kera DeAnn York and Devin Stone Blackwell. I thank my Lord for these 77 years. I have had a good long and interesting life. I enjoyed growing up in old St. Andrews, attending St Andrews Grammar School, swimming in our clean wonderful bay by the old dock in St. Andrew, and diving off "Little Dock" while enjoying the long carefree summer days.

Submitted and Written by: Beatrice Moates, 764 Roland Road, Chipley, Florida 32428. Sources: Census records, Court House records, personal knowledge.

B. Hopkins

Master Pastelist, B. Hopkins, PSA-M, left her native Wisconsin in 1984 for the warmth and beauty of Panama City Beach, Florida. Her interest in two-dimensional art had taken flame in 1982 when she discovered pastels. Her fascination with their directness, versatility and luminescence has remained, for it lends itself readily to her representational style and love of pure color. "Suave", once wrote the Milwaukee Journal about her work. Another critic wrote, "In this day of painting gimmicks and sensationalism of subject, Hopkins allows the beauty of light and shadow and color to become extremely dramatic. The skill is right there. . ."

Many awards have come her way, among those most cherished have been the Philip M Lahn, the Daniel Rosenthal, the Morilla-Canson-Talens and the Ranco-Tanguay awards, all from the national competitions of the Pastel Society of America in New York City. Hopkins has won first in Still Life from the Pastel Society of the West Coast (national) and Grumbacker Silver Medallion from the Degas Society of New Orleans and the Grumbacker Gold Medallion from the Pastel Society of North Florida. Other awards are too numerous for telling, but her most recent honor was a Best of Show at the Visual Arts Centre of North Florida's Bay Annual for her pastel, "The Kid", depicting a goat eating the fringe of an Oriental carpet. Her work was included in the international show of the Societie Des Pastellists de France in Lille , 1987 and the International Pastel Exhibit in Denver, Colorado, in which she entered "Tutti Frutti" (1995).

B. Hopkins attained Master Pastelist status in the prestigious Pastel Society of America, New York, since 1988. She is also a Signature Member of the Pastel Society of North Florida and the Visual Arts Centre of North West Florida. She is listed in Who's Who in American Art and represented by the Gallery of Art, 36 West Beach Drive, Panama City, Florida, 32401

Submitted by: B. Hopkins, 121 Rose Coral Dr., Panama City Beach, FL 32408.

Roy L. Houpt, Jr.

Roy L. Houpt Jr was stationed at Tyndall AFB, when he met and married Vera Ann Pratt, daughter of Mr and Mrs Stuart A Pratt of Parker. They were married Oct 12, 1955 in the Parker Methodist Church by the Rev. W.C. Simpson.

A carpenter by trade, Roy served in the US Army Reserve, retiring from the local unit in 1986. Ann, a 1953 graduate of Bay High School, attended Florida State University. She worked for the Bay County Schools, Chamber of Commerce and News Herald before coming to the Bay County Library in 1977, where she has continued until the present. They have three children, Ronald John, Roy L. III and Melissa Ann.

Ronald has been a teacher in the Bay County Schools since 1971. He graduated from Gulf Coast Community College, attended the University of Florida, and graduated from the University of West Florida.

Roy graduated from Gulf Coast Community College where

Roy L. Houpt and Vera Ann Pratt on their wedding day

Roy L. Houpt, Jr. Family

he was sports editor of the Gull's Cry, and has been employed by the News Herald since graduation.

Melissa graduated from Rutherford High School in 1979, and attended Gulf Coast College. She was employed at the News Herald until an automobile accident resulted in her death July 19, 1981, two days after her 20th birthday.

The family has been active in the Parker Methodist Church and Parker community activities.

Submitted by: Ann Houpt, 1128 Loftin St., PC FL 32404.

James Hovey
St. Andrews Pioneer

James Hovey was born October 15, 1804 in Brookfield, Massachusetts. By 1838 he was in Jackson County, Florida where he enlisted, at Aspilago, in Captain Padgett's Company, Colonel Pittman's Battalion, Florida Mounted Militia, as a private in the Florida Indian War.

The enlistment was for one month. James was mustered in on October 1, 1838 and out on October 31, 1838. For this service he received warrant #91,749 through the Federal Act of 1850, for 50 acres of land in St. Andrews. In 1855 another act was approved by Congress and James was granted warrant #39,733 for an additional 160 acres in St. Andrews. These two acts were for "bounty land to certain officers and soldiers who have been engaged in the military service of The United States".

John and Ida Hovey Syfrett

James and his wife, Mary, had five children in Alabama. They were; James, 1838; Cullen, 1839; Eli, 1844; Frances, 1846 and Hilliard, 1849, Daughters, Caroline, 1851 and Emily, 1854 were born in St. Andrews. Sometime after the birth of Emily, Mary died at the age of 34. James and Cullen died earlier. Left with five children to raise, James soon remarried a widow, Susan Hobbs, who had two children, John 1854 and Sally 1855. On the 26th of September 1855, in St. Andrews, a son, James (Jim) was born to James and Susan Hovey.

In January of 1860, James died of pneumonia. Some months later Susan and the seven children moved to Vernon where they are listed in the Washington County Census. Family records from Alabama show that Frances, with brothers Eli and Hilliard, moved to Alabama. Frances married in 1866 and Hilliard in 1869. After his marriage, Hilliard came to Florida and took his sisters, Caroline and Emily back to his home in Barbour County, Alabama. It is not known what happened to Sally Hobbs. Her mother,

Susan Hobbs Hovey died prior to 1870. John Hobbs and Jim Hovey lived with the family of John Wesley and Roxie Ann Bradford Gilbert who welcomed the two orphans into their already large family.

James Hovey married one of the Gilbert's daughters Roxie Ann Rebecca (Becky) Gilbert and they made their home in Alford where Jim was a farmer. He and Becky raised nine children. Jim died November 19, 1937 and Becky died March 10, 1941. Becky is still remembered fondly by great grandson John Henry Carter. He can vividly recall walking with his great grandmother to a store, in Alford, for ice cream. Jim and Becky are buried at the White Pond Cemetery near Alford.

Ida, daughter of Jim and Becky, was married to John Austin Syfrett on December 25, 1910. He was the son of Thomas Abram and Sidney Lewis Syfrett who were married at the home of her parents, John William and Mary Ann Matilda Youngblood Lewis, in 1857.

John and Ida resided in the White Oak Community of  Washington County where they raised thirteen children on their farm. Ida was a remarkable woman who was 18 when her first child, Olga was born, on August 28, 1912, and 44 when the last was born. To have 13 children survive is unusual, for the time. John died June 1, 1953 and Ida on April 25, 1971. They are buried in White Oak Cemetery.

Jim and Becky Hovey

On September 5, 1931 Olga married Neroy Carter, son of Henry Hosea and Mary Alice Jones Carter of Wausau. Henry was the grandson of Anthony Terry and Sally Colquitt Carter. Anthony served in the War of 1812 and received a land grant near Wausau in 1850. They are buried near Wausau in Barfield Cemetery. Mary Alice Jones Carter was the granddaughter of the Rev. William James and Jane Lisenby Tiller who are buried in Chipley.

Neroy and Olga were active members of their church and the community. Neroy served, among other civic posts, as Master of Harry Jackson Masonic Lodge. Neroy died in 1980 and Olga in 1994. They are buried in Evergreen Cemetery in Panama City.

Olga and Neroy had two children. Lee Nell who died in infancy and John Henry. John Henry was educated in the schools of Bay County, graduating from Bay High School in 1952, after which he was accepted to Florida State University where he was a member of the Phi Kappa Tau Fraternity. In 1954 John waived his draft deferment and served with the U. S. Occupation forces of Germany.

One week after graduating from Florida State John Henry married his college sweet heart, Irene Rodriguez of Tampa on June 15, 1958 in Tampa. Their marriage resulted in the birth of John H. , II 1959, Melissa Ann, 1963 and Frank Thomas 1973. Melissa is the mother of John Lewis Charles, 1996 and Acalia Justine, 2002.

Following their wedding they settled in West Palm Beach. John became an Officer of The U.S. Internal Revenue Service in West Palm Beach while Irene taught in Lake Worth High School. While there John was made a Thirty Second degree Mason and became a Shriner. Through a series of increasingly responsible positions he was appointed to Headquarters in Washington, D. C. From here he became a part of the Corps Diplomatique and served in The Middle East, Caribbean and Central America. Following these assignments John was invited to join the Executive Office of The President of The United States. He retired as Director, Reference and Information Management, U. S. Department of Energy, Washington, D. C..

After their retirement John and Irene became actively involved in their home, Panama City. In 1994 John was awarded a Florida Pioneer Descendant Certificate by the Florida State Genealogical Society. This established descent from a documented Florida Pioneer. Among the organizations John served are The Panama City Music Association, vice president; The Oakland Terrace Men's Club, President; The Bay County Democratic Party, Chairman; General Society of The War of 1812, Florida Treasurer; The Panama City Chapter of The Sons of The American Revolution, President; The Florida Society of the Sons of The American Revolution, State of Florida President.

Submitted by: Irene R. Carter, 738 Brandeis Avenue, Panama City, FL 32405.

Henry Thomas Howard

Henry Thomas Howard came to Panama City about 1937 from Alabama. Like many he thought he was coming to the Promised Land. Instead he came to a vast wasteland (in his opinion). He had never seen a beach, was afraid of the water and had absolutely no idea of what he would do. Was not really qualified to do anything. All he had ever done was a little sharecropping. He ended up living in Hiland City (now Hiland Park). He had suffered the hardships of the Depression in Alabama and found he was really no better off in Florida.

He eventually worked a little at the turpentine still in Hiland City and as a small boat builder and various odd jobs. He was not very ambitious but had five sons and a daughter who worked hard. They were all grown when he moved to Panama City and shortly they all followed him to Bay County. The boys all came to be known as the Howard Boys. A very close knit family.

Mildred, the only girl, took in boarders who worked at the shipyard during World War II. She only had two rooms to rent but rooms were so hard to find that they actually slept, as they worked, in shifts. She washed sheets in the washpot in the yard. During this time she also worked at her brother Milburn's shoe shop and laundry as a seamstress. After the war she worked for Gilberg's fabric shop in Panama City for twenty five years, retiring at age 65. She then volunteered at Bay Memorial Hospital and sometimes "worked" there thirty hours in a week. This was the highpoint of her life. She worked there until she could no longer drive. Just a few months before her death.

The oldest son Julian worked at the shipyard until it closed and then worked at the air base as a carpenter until he retired.

The next oldest Amos worked as a mechanic at major car dealerships in town before opening his own shop and gas station. He had a wonderful business there. He and another brother Milburn also owned two hotels at Long Beach. He was very involved in the Hiland Park Baptist Church. His greatest disappointment was that he was never made a deacon there because he had been divorced. Amos was a great benefactor to that church. He also was instrumental in the development of Gulf Coast Community College. That involvement was great and fulfilled many of his dreams. He had never graduated from high school so to be able to participate and contribute to this college was a great joy to him. Amos was a large financial contributor to the college as well as serving on the board of directors.

Milburn Howard was the next son. He opened Howard's Shoe Repair in Panama City soon after arriving before World War II. This shop was extremely successful, and he eventually added a laundry and a tailor shop to accommodate the needs of the city during the war. He had a very thriving business and could repair or "fix" any pair of shoes ever made. He was also a ladies man (flirtatious), and the women thought he was sent from heaven to make their old shoes look like new. He was a partner in the hotels at the beach with his brother Amos as well as a benefactor to Gulf

Coast and to his church.

Wilburn Howard was next to youngest, and he was a whiz at mechanics. He worked for the first Hudson dealership in Panama City and worked there until Hudson stopped making cars. He then went to work for the Chrysler Plymouth dealership. I suspect many people traded in their Hudsons for Chryslers for their next cars. Wilburn retired in Hiland Park and enjoys a quiet life at age 83 with his wife Betty.

Hilburn the youngest son went away to World War II at age 17 and never came back to Panama City to live. He worked and lived in Manhattan for over forty years and now is retired with his wife Lillian in Minnesota.

The only girl Mildred was my mother. She was the third eldest. As I have mentioned the boys were known as the "Howard Boys". Mother was known as "Snow". What the boys lacked in talking, Mother made up for it. She never had a quiet moment.

Submitted by: Arlene Snow Butler, 4001 Waterbury Ct., Springfield, VA 22152.

Wilbur Brown Howell

My father, Wilbur Brown Howell, was born on a turpentine plantation out in the woods from Vernon. His father, Lewis Henry Howell, was one of 13 children of which 8 of them were twins. In 1909 my father's mother, Eula, along with her husband, Lewis and their two year old son, Brown, moved to St Andrews while they built their home at 501 East Beach Drive. When the new home was completed, the move to Beach Drive was made by horse and buggy, crossing the mouth of Massalina Bayou on a low tide where Nelson Bridge is today. Presently, the Beach Drive home is owned by Lewis Howell's grand-daughter Judy Hobbs Vandergrift and her husband Don.

Wilbur Brown Howell

In 1913, my grandfather, Lewis Henry Howell, the senator from Washington county introduced a bill in the state legislature which created Bay County from the coastal portion of Washington County. My grandfather was elected the first state representative from Bay County. He later served as mayor of Panama City.

My father's first school was in a building in downtown Panama City near Mckenzie Park south of Fourth street and west of Magnolia Avenue. Later when Panama Grammar Park School was completed he finished his schooling in that building. The building was later purchased by the Presbyterian Church.

My father often told me stories about growing up on St. Andrew Bay. One that I recall was about the building of the wooden Nelson bridge across Massalina Bayou. Before the bridge could be built a retaining wall had to be constructed. Young boys were paid a penny a stone to help shore up the sides.

Brown's father had various business interests with one being a Hudson and Essex car dealership. Brown said that he was the first young person to own a car and when he was in the twelfth grade he got a date with his teacher which he said was probably due to his having a car.

Brown started college at Washington and Lee University but later transferred to the University of Alabama which he often referred to as the country club of the South. Brown was graduated from the University of Alabama in 1930, with a degree in business administration. The great depression had started and he felt lucky to get a job with Goodyear in Akron, Ohio but was laid off within that year. He left Akron for Chicago and worked with Western Electric for two years. He missed the South and decided to move back to Panama

City. His dad helped him get a job at the paper mill paying 17 cents per hour for an 11 hour shift. After two years at the mill Brown was offered a job as manager of First Federal Savings and Loan with a salary of $22.50 per week. He became the first manager of First Federal. While working at First Federal, at age 35, Brown was elected to the Federal Home Loan Bank of Winston Salem, N.C. He served a two year term and was the youngest man to have served at that time. Eventually Brown was elected a director of First Federal, a position he held until his death in 1987. Later, First Federal was purchased by Regions Bank.

When Brown was 28 he met my mother, the lovely 24 year old Estelle Hobbs who was also raised in Bay County. Estelle was a descendant of the Porter-Mashburn clan that settled on Econfina. She was working for Cogburns Jewelry when she met Brown. He was dating another Panama City native, Louise Strickland, at the time so he began alternating his dates between the two young ladies and within a year, which was 1935, my mother and father were united in marriage.

My dad and Robert Conner decided to go into the real estate and insurance business as partners. This partnership lasted until the business was sold and Brown retired. The business was called Howell and Conner Real Estate and Insurance.

My father, like his father, believed that a person should give back to his community a portion of their time and service. He served as President of the Chamber of Commerce, President of the Rotary Club, Chairman of the Administrative Board of the First United Methodist Church during the time that the present Methodist church was built, and was secretary of the school board for many years. School board members made a salary of $8.00 a month. I vividly remember his sitting on our piano bench with a card table set up in front of him and hand signing, yes, hand signing each teacher's check in Bay County.

He and my mother built many homes in Bay County. Mama would draw out the blueprint for the houses and do the interior decorating and the landscaping My dad took great pride in overseeing the building of a quality home.

Brown, Robert Lawrence, and Robert Conner developed Santa Monica which is located between Laguna Beach and Sunnyside in Panama City Beach. That partnership was called Gulf Beach Development Company. A model home was built at Santa Monica and for several summers the Howell family lived at the beach while our mother showed the model home and lots that were for sale. Santa Monica is one of the few beaches in Bay County that has a dedicated beach on the gulf side that can never be developed. If my dad were alive today he would be amazed that a foot of gulf front is worth four to five thousand dollars.

In 1945, Brown and Estelle purchased a home on the corner of Harmon and First Court. The home had been built by the Dean family around 1917 and was only one block from the home where Brown was raised. The house sits on an old Indian shell mound and is built around a beautiful live oak tree.

Brown and Estelle had four children. I, Ruth Howell Hauser, was born in 1939, my sister, Marie Howell Goostree, was born in 1942, my brother Lewis Brown Howell was born in 1945 and my baby sister, Gwedolyn Howell O'Rear was born in 1950 All four of us attended Cove School and Bay High School. Our mother, Estelle, was in the first graduating class of Bay High in 1930. All four of the children followed in their fathers footsteps and went to the University of Alabama.

It was at the University of Alabama that I met the love of my life, Michael Rhodes Hauser. Michael was born and raised in Birmingham, Alabama. We married after he finished his bachelor of science degree in industrial engineering. We both continued school until he finished his masters degree in operations research and I finished my degree in what was then known as home economics with a specialty in interior design. After we moved back to Panama City in 1967, Michael's family purchased the old Pickens home at

703 East Beach Drive for a summer home. This home is now occupied by our youngest daughter, Elyse and her husband, John Fishel II. Our oldest daughter, Laura Hauser McCain and her husband Allen Haynes McCain live in Birmingham. Our daughters have blessed us with four grandchildren, Kaylor and Porter McCain and Brittany and Howell Fishel. Brittany will be graduated from Bay High in 2007 and will be a fourth generation Bay High graduate.

Brown and Estelle have left us a wonderful legacy. Their four children had a total of nine children and so far the Howell legacy has five great grandchildren. Estelle is 92 now and still enjoys her family.
Submitted by: Ruth Howell Hauser, 221 South Cove Terrace Drive, Panama City, FL 32401.

Robert A. "Bob" Hoxie

Bob was born May 19, 1933 in an old New England grist mill which was reconstructed into a two story home in the community of Scrabbletown, North Kingstown, Rhode Island. He was the youngest of ten children and the ninth generation since 1650. Bob cut wood and other chores on the farm. He graduated high school in 1951. He worked as a painter and carpenter for a contractor building homes. In 1951 he moved to New London, Connecticut and worked for

Robert A. Hoxie, 1990 Millville

F. W. Woolworth. In 1952 he moved to Groton and worked building submarines and served in the U.S. Navy coming to Panama City in March 1958. In 1959 he met Doris Pilcher. In March 1960 he got out of the navy and married Doris Pilcher April 1960. They moved to Connecticut to obtain a civilian job which he left. That winter it was 33 below zero and they moved back to Panama City, Florida.

Our first son was born in March 1961. Our second son was born in July 1965 and our daughter was born in November 1975. Doris and all three children graduated high school at Bay High.

Bob went to work for Sunshine Grocer Company, then Gray Lumber Company and in March 1962 he went to work for the Panama City Police Department.

Bob and family are rock hounds. Bob was instrumental in persuading the Florida Senate in naming agitized coral as our state stone. Bob and family are also collectors of palm trees and have 23 different palms planted in their front yard. They are all members of the International Palm Society, Gulf Coast Chapter. Bob is also responsible for getting the Palm Society to donate $350.00 for moving the four headed Butia Capitata (PindoPalm) from Millville to St Andrews Oaks By The Bay Park. In 1990, Bob worked with Panama City Leisure Services in caring for the palm and advised the city what was needed for it to be moved. In 1997, the palm tree was moved. In 2002, Bob donated four Coontie Palms (Cycads), also called Arrow Root and Indianbread to be placed in the four corners of the fence. Bob checks the palm and assists the city if needed. In 2002, Bob donated four large sago palms to Lynn Haven. One was placed beside their Leisure Service building. In 2003, Bob donated four large sago palms that were placed in front of the Sheriff Department building on Highway 77 and one large sago palm was placed to the left of the statute in the Lynn Haven Cemetery.

Bob belongs to several clubs, including the F.O.R., AARP and American Legion. In January 1974 Sgt. Bob Hoxie and John Hentz started the first March of Dimes "Jail For Bail" project raising $700.00.

Bob's philosophy of life that he has always lived by, was a statement he made upon retirement from the police department, "You owe the community, to make it a better place for all, from the day you are born or move into it, until the day you die or move out of it."
Submitted by: Robert A. "Bob" Hoxie, 1903 Arthur Ave, Panama City, FL 32405.

The Russell and Wilma Hudson Family

Wilma Presley Hudson was born in Bay County on East Avenue in 1924 to Marion Frank Presley and Lutisha Presley. She grew up in Bay County, and met and married

Russell and Wilma Hudson

Russell Hudson, of Fitzgerald, Georgia, in 1941. Russell worked until retirement at the paper mill. He also liked to farm on the side. Russell and Wilma lived out most of their lives in Bay County. Wilma taught Sunday school for more than fifty years.

Russell and Wilma had three sons, Larry, Jerry, and Donald Hudson. Larry passed away in 1989. Jerry and Donald are now retired and live in other states.
Submitted by: Wilma Hudson, 5613 Katherine St., Panama City, Florida 32404.

Magdalene Pollack Smith Jackson

Magdalene was born and raised in Two Egg, Florida in Jackson County. She was the only girl among six brothers who was loved by her father and mother Arlington and Luviah Pollack.

Magdalene Smith Jackson

She walked five miles one way to school each day. After completing school she moved to Lakeland, Florida with three small children.

Magdalene's first job was at a laundry working the iron pressing machine for about two years. She moved to Panama City in 1955 where she was hired as a short order cook at the Pleasant Inn Boarding House and Café. She would remain until it closed.

She then went to work at the downtown Ramada Inn for two years before moving on to work at the Sheraton Inn on the Miracle Mile Resort on Panama City Beach, Florida for 19 years aspiring to become a top award winning chef. She was a substitute for food service workers for three years with the Bay County School Board. She was married to Laulas Jackson

She was a diligent worker for her beloved Macedonia Church. She would become Director of Food Service for Funerals, a Deaconess, Chaplain and President of the Senior Mission, Vice President of the Senior Choir.
Submitted by: Bura L. Reed, 1402 Illinois Ave, Lynn Haven, FL 32444.

William H. Jennings Family
How Wilkie Met Frances

He came from Louisiana in 1939, as a crewman on a Standard Oil tanker and liked the area. He moved to Panama City and went to work at the paper mill. She came from Georgia in 1935 with her family and opened the Ritz Shop next to the Ritz Theater. They met because of The Saturday Evening Post.

On payday Friday nights, he came to the theater and as he

walked past her store, he would smile and wave at her. Then one night, he came in and asked for a Saturday Evening Post. She told him she didn't carry the Post. They still didn't know each other's name. He wanted to find someone to introduce them, so he told the cashier at the theater that he would buy her a Coca-Cola if she would come next door and introduce him to the lady there. They came in, drank a Coke, and the introduction didn't take place. She thought, well, he's interested in her, not me. But, he came right back and introduced himself. And that is how William H. Jennings met Frances Duncan. They were married on March 22, 1941 in Panama City.

William H. "Wilkie" and Frances D. Jennings

Wilkie was in the National Guard Reserves and his unit was activated in November, 1940. His unit was released in 1941 and he returned to Panama City and his job at the paper mill. After Pearl Harbor was attacked, his unit was reactivated. Wilkie and Frances were expecting their first child when he left. Frances continued to live with her family on Grace Avenue while Wilkie was away in service. His company was on the way to Alaska when their daughter, Ellen Louise, was born on September 19, 1942. It would be Christmas, 1944, before father and daughter would meet.

Following the war, Wilkie returned to Panama City and the family was reunited. They moved to 711 McKenzie Avenue and resided there until 1988, when they moved to Lynn Haven. Wilkie started working for the Post Office and for many years was the Special Delivery Carrier. Another daughter, Claire Frances, was born on January 16, 1948. The girls went to Panama Grammar, Jinks Junior High and graduated from Bay High. Claire graduated from Florida State University with a Masters Degree in Social Work. Ellen married William R. (Bill) Rumph in 1961 and they have two children, Eric Rumph and Jennifer R. Blanks, and four granddaughters. Claire is married to Christopher L. (Chris) Calohan and they have two children, Allyson and Matthew Calohan.

The family was very active at Wallace Memorial Presbyterian Church and involved in many other community activities. Frances was a Girl Scout leader for many years. She also took care of her mother, Bobbie Duncan, until her death at the age of 97 in March, 1988. After Wilkie retired, he served on the Board of Directors of the Rescue Mission, was a member of NARFE, retired Postal workers organization and the National Guard unit retirees. He passed away on April 12, 1989. Frances continues to be active at Grace Presbyterian Church, plays bridge, knits, watches the Atlanta Braves, and keeps up with her grandchildren and four great-granddaughters and is their beloved "GaGa".

Submitted by: Frances D. Jennings, 1101 Rhode Island, Lynn Haven, FL 32405.

Neta Johnson and Sam Surber

Around 1887 George Washington Surber Sr. came to St. Andrews from Washington County, Kansas. With him came his wife, Ellen Jane, and three sons: Samuel Jefferson (Age 17), George Washington Jr. (Age 15) and John William, Age 12). Two daughters of George and Ellen remained in Kansas; the couple also left behind 5 deceased children. On their arrival in St. Andrews, the Surber family set up residence where (now) 15th Street and Chestnut Avenue intersect. Their eleventh child, Henry, was born here in 1888. Shortly thereafter Ellen Jane died of stomach cancer. (Baby Henry lived only 7 months after the death of his mother. One version of the cause of his death: no canned milk could be obtained for him because the Surbers were considered "yankees" and

could not obtain credit at local stores.) Thus in 1888 George Sr. was left a widower at age 45.

Meanwhile, on a 160-acre homestead on Bear Creek, John Henry Johnson Sr. and Mary Elizabeth lived with their five children. When John Henry Sr. died in 1888 (the same year George Surber was widowed and left with teenage sons), Mary Elizabeth was left a 34-year old widow with two sons and two teenage daughters, Neta Gertrude and Mary Lola.

These sisters, Neta and Mary, would marry the Surber brothers (Samuel and George Jr., respectively)- and - their respective father and mother (Widower George Sr. and Widow Mary Elizabeth) would wed each other. They probably met on one of many camping trips made by the Surbers' to the Bear Creek area. The Surbers loved to camp in that area. They took fishing nets and seined fish from the creek - and also hunted wild pig and turkey.

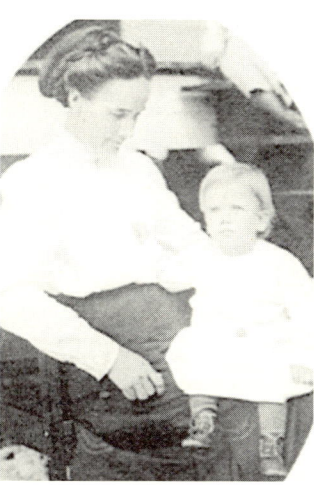

Neta Suber with baby son Charles

The three Surber families would settle on three 5-acre tracts purchased for $150 each at Pretty Bayou in St. Andrews. Pretty Bayou had deep water and high banks....and large oak hammocks shaded its shores. In later years these banks held a thriving saw mill that would supply lumber for houses and for ship building in Panama City. The banks of Pretty Bayou was also a favorite spot for covered wagon camping by Surber relatives and by other inland families.

Samuel Jefferson and Neta (she was known as "Neet") would raise a family of five sons and one daughter (and two sons who died as infants). Son Number One was Raymond Francis (nicknamed "Rinks"; he never married). The second son was Cecil Theodore (nicknamed "Cees" - married Flossie); Roy Leland was the next son (known as "Ross" - in later life married (first) Lois and after her death married Ms. Turner); Samuel Emmett was Son Number Four (he was called "Emmer" - he married Lorena); the only daughter was Elma Elizabeth (married Doc Hoskins with whom

George W. Surber, Sr's house on Pretty Bayou (6th man from left)

she had two sons (Sammy and Steve) and two daughters (Linda and Judy); the "baby" of the Sam Surber family was Charles Edward (known as "Turk" - married Vivian Montgomery; had one daughter (Gertrude Elizabeth (Bette).

The Surber cousins of Pretty Bayou would grow up together, playing in the woods, the creeks and the bay waters. The boys would bury themselves to the neck in the abundant mud bottom playing "gator" (there were live alligators around as well); they swam at "the mouth" (the Bay entrance to Pretty Bayou); they bent Pine saplings over, straddled them, and "shot" each other into the air; they dug caves in the woods; they learned the good fishing spots in the bayou and the bay and later became fishing guides to some of St. Andrews first tourists.

And...they played baseball. Raymond Surber pitched a lot of baseball in New York in a semipro league. Quoting from a newspaper article by Newton Ware, Raymond in the 1930's once saved the day in a serious St. Andrew - Millville rivalry.

"Raymond gave up only 5 hits and struck out 18 batters. He started the game by fanning the first 5 to face him." Emmett, Cecil and Charles played on the St. Andrews team as well.

The Surber brothers were popular boat builders in the area. The *Coca-Cola Kid* was constructed by them on Pretty Bayou just south of Lawrence's Cove. Most of the time, Sam Surber's back yard contained a large or small boat under construction - under a huge Oak tree still standing on their (then) lot on (now) Pretty Bayou Drive. Sam and George Surber were in-demand brickmasons as well; among others, they constructed the (then) bank in St. Andrews (now the police sub-station), the (then) bank in Panama on the corner of Beach Drive and Harrison Avenue; the print shop on Beck Avenue; and the arts building on Fourth Street at Harrison.

Needless to say, fishing was always on the mind of the Surbers. A few boats owned and captained by Roy, Emmett or *Charles The Hobo*, *The Tommy*, *The Lucky Strike*, and the *Miss Lorena*. Types of fishing included shrimping and commercial deep sea fishing. The Sam Surber family is still represented on local waters by a great-great grandson, John Petitjean. John owns and captains the charter boat *Miss Jill III*. He says he feels the eyes and smiles of his grandpa (Charles Surber) when he makes a "good catch."

Submitted by: Bette Petitjean, 3325 Robinson Bayou Circle, Panama City, FL 32405.

Robert C. Johnson and Pauline Strickland

Robert was born March 11, 1915 in Altha, Florida. The son of John Simon Johnson and Annie Eliza Blackburn, Robert had one sister Willie Marie and four brothers, Nion "N.L." Lloyd, John Russell, Edward Hopson and Jay. Robert had a nickname "Peck" but he was also known as "R. C. " by many

Pauline Strickland Johnson age 16

of his family and friends. Later, he would be called "Pa" by his family. As a boy Robert would sneak one of his mother's biscuits off his plate while eating supper. Before supper was over he would have several biscuits in his pockets to eat later. Once Russell made him mad about something and Robert chased Russell up a small oak tree. He tried to get Russell down out of the tree but Russell wouldn't come down. Robert got an axe and cut the tree down with Russell in it. He quit school in the 10th grade because his teacher wouldn't let him play ball. He joined the army and played basketball for the army. He was discharged in 1937.

Robert came back to Altha and was helping build Dr. Eldridge's house when he met Pauline at the county fair. Pauline Strickland, the daughter of Alexander Herschel Stricklen and Bessie Lee Smith, was born September 17, 1921 in Vernon, Florida. They got married and left for Texas where Robert worked on the dredge boats in Port Arthur. Later he and Pauline came home to Altha. Eventually, Robert and Pauline moved to Bay Harbor, Florida where he worked with Pauline's father doing odd jobs. He worked sometimes for 50 cents a day and was glad to get it. They moved back to Altha and stayed with Pauline's sister Pera Lee and her husband Charles Peacock on their farm. Robert worked on the farm for awhile with Charles. December 2, 1939 a daughter, Dorothy Ann Johnson was born to Robert and Pauline. The couple were now living at Robert's mother's house in Altha. It was one of the coldest winters that they had ever seen. In January and February, Massalina Bayou froze over with ice blocking small craft at their berths. There were 19 freezes that year. Robert and Charles went to Georgia to work on a pipeline and the snow and ice was very bad. He did get to go with the work crew to see

"Gone With The Wind" when it played in Atlanta, Georgia in 1939. When Dorothy Ann was five months old, April 1940, the family moved to Port St Joe, Florida. Because Robert was a good baseball player, he got a job with Kenny's Saw Mill in Port St Joe. Baseball was a very popular local sport

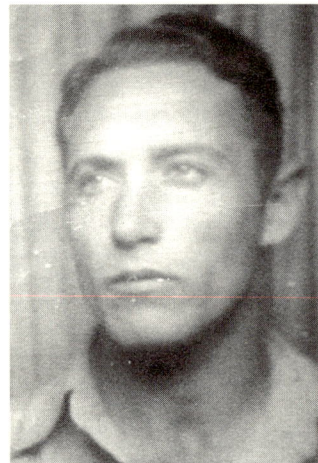

Robert C. Johnson age 24

in those days. Robert played outfield. The team was in the Gulf Coast League and they won the championship. It was after this that Robert went to work at Port St. Joe Paper Mill. They hired him to play baseball for the mill. Jobs were frozen during the War but the paper mill wasn't working Robert enough. He couldn't support his family on the hours of work they were giving him, so he left the mill and went to the Wainwright Shipyard and got a job. When the Port St Joe Paper Mill found out, they got a federal agent to go to Wainwright Shipyard to get him fired. The shipyard office called him in to explain his side of the story. They believed his story, told him to go back to work. The Federal agent left the shipyard to go investigate the St. Joe Paper Mill. Robert continued to work at the shipyard. Wainwright Shipyard employed the greatest number of workers in Panama City. It was dedicated May 22, 1942. By October 20, 1942 there were 3,900 employed, by March 1943, 13,000 and by 1944, 18,000. In the last year of the war the shipyard laid off the remaining 10,000 workers. The first Liberty ship slid into the water on December 31, 1941 and the last Liberty ship (108th) slid into the water on September 13, 1945. Robert left the shipyard and went to work for International Paper Mill. Robert worked at the paper mill until he retired in 1977.

Pauline Strickland is a descendant of Archie Smith a pioneer settler in Bay County when it was still Washington County. Archie Smith came to this area after the Civil War. He married Rebecca Hinson and they had a son Joshua Franklin Smith. Archie and Rebecca divorced and Archie remarried Queen Victoria Davis. Joshua Franklin Smith married Zena Elizabeth Johnson and they were the parents

of Bessie Lee Smith. Pauline has been a housewife all her life, devoting her life to her husband, daughter, grandchildren and great-grandchildren. A wonderful cook, great housekeeper, she always finds time to be there when anyone in her family needs her.

Robert, Pauline and Dorothy Ann were a family that

Robert Johnson, Ann Johnson Robbins, Richard Robbins and Pauline Strickland Johnson

did activities together. An avid bird hunter and fresh water fisherman, Robert was first of all a family man. In later years, Pauline not only went fishing with him (which she loved) but also would often go bird hunting with him (just to watch). Once Robert took his son-in-law Richard Robbins bird hunting. Robert had a hurt back and had to sit on a stool while waiting for the doves to fly over. Richard was amazed when Robert shot a dove flying toward him and caught the bird in his hand while still sitting on the stool. Grandfather to Cynthia Renee Robbins, (husband Brenton Eugene Peacock), Pamela Teresa Robbins and LeAnne Marie Robbins,(husband Jon Michael Lusk) and great-grandfather to Debra Ann Lusk and Lorena Colette Peacock who will remember Robert saying, "Do you think the rain will hurt the roof garden?" and his motto, "I won't go no higher than corn pullin' and no lower than tater diggin'." Robert died December 26,2000. Pauline Strickland Johnson, devoted wife and homemaker cared for Robert at home for ten years when he was disabled by a stroke. She is called "Mama" by all her family.

Submitted by Dorothy Ann Johnson Robbins, 435 South Palo Alto Ave, Panama City, Florida 32401. Sources: Washington County Tombstone Records, Sampson Johnson Family Bible, Family interviews.

Jones / Thompson Family

I generally tell people that I am a "native" of Panama City. That's not strictly true. I was actually several months old when my parents moved here. My dad, James Nelson (Jimmie) Jones, grew up in Eufaula, Alabama. My mother, Suselee Thompson Jones, grew up in Columbus, Georgia. They both came from large families. My parents were married in 1929 and attended what is now Auburn University after they were married. Before they married, there were two or three years when my dad worked in the steel mills in Birmingham, and lived with his older brother and family. My mother worked as a secretary for her brother, an attorney in Columbus, and lived with her parents. At Auburn they lived in an apartment in a large old house near the campus. My dad majored in textile engineering, as did his brothers. His father was the mill superintendent in Eufaula. [The owners of the mill in Eufaula had searched for my grandfather and brought him to Eufaula from North Carolina to run the mill; I have heard that he, my grandmother and the older children came to Alabama in a horse-drawn wagon—this is mentioned in a book called "Alabama." My mother took a 2-year degree course in teaching kindergarten, specializing in the Montessori method. My understanding from her was that this was something called a "Peabody" course. Over those years they, along with others of my mother's siblings and their spouses, periodically lived with her parents in a large house in Columbus.

James Nelson "Jimmie" Jones and wife Suselee Thompson Jones in costume at "Gay 90's" play, 1940's

After college, my dad was hired by Pepperell Mills and the two of them moved to Opelika, Alabama. At this point, my dad began to expand on his hobby of photography and amassed huge boxes of photos of Pepperell, the people there, river baptisms, President Roosevelt at Warm Springs, and more-all of which my brother and I still have.

When World War II was declared, my dad was turned down by all of the armed forces as his eyesight was very poor. Anxious to contribute, he hired on with the shipyard in Panama City and he and my mother moved here in 1942. They moved into a tiny new house in the Cove section and he walked to town and rode the bus to the shipyard and back daily.

My mother ran a nursery school first and then a kindergarten in our little house. I started kindergarten at age 3

James Nelson "Jimmie" Jones and wife Suselee Thompson Jones at a Bay High Dance in 1950's where they were taking pictures

because it was there. My bedroom was the coat room, and there were coat hooks all around the wall. The living room and dining room held the long table, the little chairs, the piano, etc. My dad, who was an excellent artist, put up wallboard around the living room walls and drew or painted scenes on the wallboard. My brother was born in 1951 and a few years later we moved deeper into the Cove into a larger house (without an internal kindergarten).

When the war ended, instead of going back to the excellent job he left at Pepperell, my dad followed his dream of photography and bought out a small photographic studio above Brake's Hardware on Harrison Avenue. He moved the studio to 412 Magnolia Avenue, next to Freeman's Seed Store (later called Covington's Seed Store). The studio was there until he retired.

My mother taught kindergarten out of our home for several years. At some point several members of the Chamber of Commerce approached her and asked that she become the Welcome Wagon Hostess for Panama City. They sent her to New York for training, and she acted as Welcome Wagon Hostess for 6-8 years. She started the Panama City Newcomers Club during that time, and she thoroughly enjoyed meeting and greeting the new people in town. After that time, she went back to her kindergarten vocation and started the First Methodist Church Kindergarten where she had been teaching the Sunday School kindergarten class for years. I'm not sure how long she stayed there but when my older son was three years old she was already teaching educable mentally retarded at the Cerebral Palsy Clinic. After my dad died, my mother went to work at Cove School and stayed there until she retired.

Submitted by: Susan Jones Moore, 310 S. Palo Alto Ave., Panama City, FL 32401.

Charles James King, Jr. Family

Charles James King, Jr. was enrolled in the University of Alabama when World War II was declared but he immediately enlisted and left college. Possession of a coveted Captain's license to operate heavy water vessels in the waters around Eglin Field, FL enabled him to perform his military duty in a most proficient manner close to home.

Charles James King, Jr. and Mary Carolyn Littlefield Walden were married on July 11, 1944 in a beautiful ceremony. She was the drum majorette of the Walton High School band and attended Shorter College where she held high scholastic honors.

Left to Right rear: "Chris", "Holly", Niles, "Chuck" Front: Charles James, Jr. and Mary Carolyn King

Charles, Jr. was active for many years in Independent Oil Company and King's Motels with his father. He owned several service stations in this area and served as Chairman of the Board of Directors of the First Federal Savings and Loan. Charles, his father and a Mississippi cousin, J. W. King, purchased the largest remaining parcel of land in the city limits of Panama City - 126 acres - which is presently being developed as an apartment complex. The Bay County Conservancy was pleased to accept a portion of the land to be preserved in honor of the King family. Charles, Jr. was an accomplished heavy equipment operator and enjoyed working with his bulldozer on his lakes on his Walton County ranch.

Charles "Chuck" James King, III and Janet McLeod married in Hawaii while he was in the Navy and became the parents of two children: Charles "Chip" James King IV and Catherine Cannaday King. "Chip" married Patricia "Trish" Marie Sharkey and they have three sons: Cameron James,

Carson John and Griffin Patrick King. Catherine married Wilbur Lee Matthews of Texas and they have a daughter, Mary Lamar McLeod Matthews.

"Chuck" owned and operated a Gulf Oil Jobbership and served on the Board of Directors of the First Federal Savings and Loan. He remarried to Judith "Judy" C. Hill of Missouri and they reside in Destin.

Niles Nelson King served in the Navy and attended the University of Florida. He and Sally Sanders married and had two children: Niles Nelson King, Jr. and Kristen King. Niles, Jr. married Carla Herring. Kristen married Jason Van Howell and have a son, Pete Van Howell. Both Carla and Kristen are teachers in Walton County Schools.

Rubye Holland "Holly" King earned degrees from Gulf Park College, Florida State University and Medical College of Georgia and is a certified Occupational Therapist with the Walton County Schools. She is married to Allan Steven Kroland, a chiropractor and published author. They were parents of one son, Glenn King Kroland, who died at birth on November 2, 1992.

Christopher "Chris" Till King earned a degree in Education from Troy State University. He and Tammy Bass married and had two children: Sarah King and Daniel Elliot King. Chris remarried to Debra Faye Tiller whose son, James Steven Hicks, is a linebacker coach at the University of West Alabama. After a long career in education, Chris is presently the owner of King Property Management.

Submitted by: Jeanette King Howell, 3106 W. 27th Street, Panama City, FL 32405-2144.

Charles James King, Sr. Family

Charles James King, Sr. was a son of Charles M. King and his wife, Lillie Jane Rivers. His wife, Frankie Till King, was a daughter of Julius Franklin Till and his wife, Pearl Hodges. Both were born and reared in Lauderdale Co., MS where their ancestors were pioneers by 1830.

Charles James King Sr.

About 1935 they moved to DeFuniak Springs with their two children, Charles James King, Jr. and Pearl Jeanette King. The family were members of the First Baptist Church. C. J. King was the owner of Independent Oil Company which he began in Birmingham, AL.

C. J. King built his first wholesale oil terminals in Freeport and Basin Bayou in South Walton Co. Later, on Beach Drive in Panama City, C. J. built a third terminal with large steel tanks to store petroleum products and canned his own brand of motor oil, SuperLube. Prior, this was the site of the old ice house which burned and the present site of the Landmark Apartments. His tugboats and barges kept the tanks filled with petroleum products which his tanker trucks hauled to his own retail service stations as well as supplied other oil companies. Another terminal was later built and operated in Lynn Haven now owned by McKenzie Tank Lines. C. J. King had a most amazing mathematical ability and could tell at a glance the capacity of any truck, tank or barge. He was a great judge of character and was very proud that his many employees were dependable and loyal friends.

In 1949, C. J. and Charles, Jr. built King's Motor Court, Restaurant and Service Station in Tallahassee, FL which his daughter managed and later owned until 1997. About 1952, they built King's Motor Court, Restaurant and Service Station on West Highway 98, presently, Howard

Frankie Till King

Johnson Motel. For many years, Grace and Earl Lee were associated with the Kings in successfully building both the oil business and the motel business.

A favorite residential project of C. J. & Charles King, Jr. was King's Point in Panama City. It was a large parcel of beautiful waterfront property with ancient oaks and native palms which reached from Pretty Bayou to North Bay to Robinson Bayou to Frankford Avenue to 27th Street.

Jeanette King married first to Curtis Wilmer Sutton and second to Maxwell Wayne Howell. Their son, Charles Wayne Howell was born on December 4, 1960 and died on June 19, 2002 at age 41. Son, Mark Wade Howell was born July 18, 1964 and died on October 30, 1995 at age 31.

Jeanette earned a Bachelor of Science degree at Huntingdon College and later was awarded the Master of Arts degree from FSU. She was a Chemist for the Florida State Food, Drug, Cosmetic and Vitamin Laboratory four years and retired from education administration and teaching in Leon and Bay Counties with 26 years service. Jeanette has held a real estate broker's license since 1955. She is a member of the United Daughters of the Confederacy, Daughters of the American Revolution, Colonial Dames of the Seventeenth Century, and Dames of the Magna Charta.

Submitted by: Jeanette King Howell, 3106 West 27th St. Panama City, FL 32405; <JKHowell@digitalexp.com>

The Alfred Walter Kirvin Family

Alfred Walter Kirvin states on his Confederate Pension Application that he came to Florida the 11th of March 1866. He settled into Calhoun County, Florida doing odd jobs of manual labor, working as bookkeeper at James Bennett Stone's saw mill, and eventually contracting to teach Union School #8, Calhoun County, Florida. He continued to teach at least through 1881.

According to census records Alfred Walter Kirvin was born ca 1839 in Alabama. Where remains a mystery, as does the names of his parents.

On 6 June 1861 AWK enlisted in Captain John Glascow's Co. G of the 13th Alabama Infantry Regiment CSA in Montgomery, Alabama. Serving until the end of the war and participating in some twelve battle engagements Alfred Walter Kirvin rose from the entering rank of Private to that of Captain. "At the Battle of Fredricksburg [Kirvin] was wounded by Rifle ball;" at "Gettysburg on the banks of [the] Potomac [he was] wizzed on the head by saber," and again, he was "wounded in the left leg by Rifle ball in May 1864 at the Battle of the Wilderness."

Mary Ann Kirvin Whitfield with her husband and two daughters

The war left AWK reflective and melancholy. In the quiet of solitary evenings he wrote personal essays questioning and reflecting on such things as the meaning of life, and the horrors and futility of war. In March of 1868 he wrote, "At home. All alone. The subject I am going to write is on the shortness of human life," and "In my writing this afternoon I will try to give the description of the battle the horrors of war..."

On December 29, 1868 Alfred Walter Kirvin wed Mary Ann Stone, the eldest daughter of James Bennett Stone and Tina Jincy Yon Stone. They would be parents to eight children: Mary Ann Kirvin (1869), J B Kirvin (1871), Jincy Kirvin (1876), Walter Jason Kirvin (1877), Josephine Lucinda Kirvin (1879), Jesse Lack Kirvin (1881), Della B Kirvin (1884), and Joseph Rodney Kirvin (1888). All but the youngest were born in Calhoun County,

Mary A. Whitfield Gore (Allie), granddaughter of Alfred Walter Kirvin

Florida; Joseph Rodney Kirvin was born after the family moved into Washington County, Florida.

In 1885 Alfred Walter Kirvin in a letter to his wife's sisters, Lucinda and Jincy Stone, wrote that "... in a short time me and my little family will be off to the Bay, where I hope we will live in peace and quietude." Leaving Calhoun County they did indeed move to Washington County and settled on what is called Kirvin Bayou on the East Bay near the community of what is today Allanton, Bay County, Florida. The move in this year is also supported by the family having been listed in both the Calhoun and Washington Counties, Florida censuses for the year of 1885.

It was in 1888 that Alfred Walter Kirvin filled out his completed but unsubmitted Civil War Pension Application. In May of that same year his name also appears in a petition to the First Assistant Post-Master General in Washington, D.C. requesting that a post office located at his homestead site with him being appointed as its Post Master. The last evidence of Alfred Walter Kirvin existence appears in 1889 when his signature is found on an uncompleted and unfiled Washington County, Florida Tax Notice.

In 1898 Mary Ann Kirvin filed for their homestead in her own name, and in the 1900 Washington County, Florida census she was listed as a widow. His grave is in the old Farmdale Cemetery, Bay County, Florida on what is now the Tyndall Air Force Reservation. Mary Ann Kirvin continued to live there on their homestead until her death in 1919. She, too, was buried at the old Farmdale Cemetery.

Alfred Walter and Mary Ann Stone Kirvin's oldest daughter, Mary Ann Kirvin, married Joseph Weldon Whitfield in 1891. They had three children: Allie, Minnie, and Joe. Mary Ann Kirvin Whitfield died from injuries received from a kick from a mule when Allie was about six years old. Mary Ann was laid to rest in what was the Burgess Creek Cemetery near Wewahitchka (a cemetery since built over). Allie and her two younger siblings were taken to Allanton to live with their maternal grandmother Mary Ann Stone Kirvin. It was here where Allie would grow up and eventually marry William Henry Gore, son of William Edward Gore and his wife Bettie, who lived down the way on a neighboring homestead.

J B Kirvin, called "Ben," died early in life in Washington County, FL.

In 1901 Walter Jason Kirvin married Suzie Selemity Raffield. They lived at Auburn, Florida until they were forced to move when the land was taken for the establishment of Tyndall Air Force Base. Born to this union were the following children: Jason W. (1904), Bertha (1906), Jesse L. (1906), Hazel A. (1909), George H. (1909), Ethel A. (1913), and Grace (1915). Walter and Suzie Kirvin are

buried at the Magnolia Cemetery, Apalachicola, Franklin County, Florida.

Jincy Kirvin married John Davis in 1893. She died soon after and is buried in the Old Shiloh Cemetery, Calhoun County, Florida near her grandparents, James Bennett Stone and Tina Jincy Yon Stone.

Josephine Lucinda Kirvin married John Beadnell. They lived on the Beadnell homestead at Allanton, Florida and raised three children: Mary Christina, Julia Dollie, and Ocey L.

Jesse Lack Kirvin married Florence Dyer in 1910. They named their son Herbert. Jesse Lack Kirvin was killed in 1929 when following a hurricane at Apalachicola, Florida he went outside to check on damage and accidentally stepped on a downed electrical wire. Jesse, wife Florence, son Herbert and his wife Doris Eddings Kirvin, and grandson Jesse Kirvin are all buried at Greenwood Cemetery, Bay County, Florida.

Della B Kirvin married Thomas T. Allan in 1907. Their children were Alfred A., Etta Mae, Myrtle M., Maude Olga, Thomas Curtis, Della Leola, Ruth J, and Evelyn J. Allan.

Joseph Rodney Kirvin married Lemma Corn. Their son was named Joseph Rodney Kirvin, Jr. They are all buried in the family plot in the Callaway Cemetery, Bay County, Florida.

Submitted by: Patricia Gore Smith, 4007 Rinker Way, Bakersfield, CA 93309.

Cindy Kleback

My parents and I moved to Bay County in 1979; it was the summer before I started second grade. My dad, James Kleback, was born and raised in Pennsylvania, and my mom, Linda Pazics Kleback, was born in Washington, D.C. and had lived in Pennsylvania since she was five. I was born in Lancaster County, Pennsylvania in 1971. Florida was a lot different than Pennsylvania - hurricanes instead of snow, beaches instead of mountains - but it was a good different once I adjusted to our new life in the Sunshine State.

Cindy Kleback

I attended Lucille Moore Elementary for the first half of second grade, but I changed schools mid-year to Oakland Terrace Elementary when we bought a house near the school. I also attended A.D. Harris when it was a sixth grade center, Mowat Junior High (we had moved to Lynn Haven when I was in sixth grade), and A Crawford Mosley High School.

I remember typical kid things: school plays, riding bikes with my friends, the first time we got a dog, and riding the school bus. While I do not remember all of the facts and dates I was taught in school, I remember fondly a couple of the teachers who influenced my life. In elementary school, I was lucky to have Mrs. Ceceila Howard as my fifth grade teacher, and she taught me that it is okay to say something is too challenging for me. When I was older, I was taught English by Mrs. Beth Deluzain in ninth grade and by her husband, Dr. Edward Deluzain, when I was a senior. This dynamic duo of teaching excellence taught me how to appreciate literature and how to nurture the creativity in me. I cannot thank them enough for the many lessons I learned and for the support they always provided me.

I graduated from Mosley in 1989 and then attended the University of West Florida in Pensacola where I earned a Bachelor of Arts in Political Science. In 1994, I enrolled at the University of Arizona where I completed a Master of Arts in Information Resources and Library Science while working as a Constituent Services Representative for U.S. Senator Jon Kyl in Tucson, Arizona. After graduation, I spent a year as a Medical Librarian at Mercer University in Macon, Georgia, 2 years as the Head Librarian at Oldfields School in Glencoe, Maryland, and am now a Branch Librarian with the Enoch Pratt Free Library in Baltimore.

When I was growing up, I was always waiting for when I could escape what I thought was too small a town. Now even though my life has led me elsewhere, Bay County will always be home because this is where I grew up and where my parents still live. Sometimes you have to leave somewhere to truly appreciate where you have been.
Submitted by: Cindy Kleback, 5 Nightingale Way, Apt. B-2, Lutherville, MD 21093.

The Kleback Family

Although my husband Jim, daughter Cindy, and I had experienced many winters in our home state of Pennsylvania, 1978 and 1979 were two of the worst. Each year had at least one snowfall of over 20 inches. In 1979 I was working nights in a factory so I could go to college during the day. While I was working, a tremendous blizzard hit. Twenty-six inches of snow obliterated everything. My coworkers and I shuffled single file to a nearly Holiday Inn and spent an uncomfortable night. That was enough for me. We had visited my parents in Okaloosa County and knew what a lovely area this was. My husband Jim and I immediately started looking for Florida jobs.

Jim, Linda, and Cindy Kleback - 1985

We were both lucky. Jim was hired as a contractor at the Navy Base. A year later he became a Civil Service employee. He is currently a Supply Systems Analyst at CSS. I joined the Reference Department at the Bay County Public Library. A year later I became Circulation Supervisor. Today I work as the Circulation Supervisor, Volunteer Coordinator, and my favorite - Genealogy Specialist.

Our first home in Bay County was at Turtle Lake Apartments. We enjoyed living there but were eager to buy a house. We found our first home on Fountain Drive across from Oakland Terrace School. It was a concrete block house on a cul-de-sac with warm and friendly neighbors. The pecan trees in the yard kept us and our northern relatives supplied with fresh nuts for baking. Since Cindy attended Oakland Terrace and went to Girls' Club after school, this was a perfect location. We also had joined St. John the Evangelist Catholic Church which was also close to our house. Jim joined the St. John's Men's Association, serving as vice president from 1987-1988, president from 1988-1990, and treasurer from 1990-1996. He was also secretary of the Parish Council while a new church was built in 1990-1994.

In 1983, we decided it was time for a bigger place - with central heat and air! We had visited friends in the Derby Woods subdivision outside Lynn Haven and really liked the neighborhood. We bought a house under construction on Belmont Blvd. For several years we had no neighbors. Two houses that had been built next to ours were vacant, and no development had started across the street from our house or behind us. Once the houses on our street were purchased, the empty lots were soon filled, and the subdivision was fully constructed. We're members of the Derby Woods Homeowners Association; Jim served as secretary from 1987-1991.

In the last few years, a long dormant interest in gardening

and wildlife has awakened in me. We've added a variety of wildlife-friendly plants and several backyard feeding stations. During daylight hours we're visited by birds and squirrels. After having a backyard light installed, we've discovered some nocturnal visitors as well. We've had up to five raccoons and three opossums at one time!

Living in Bay County has given us lots of opportunities for social activities. Jim and I have both been active members of the local chapter of the Cherished Teddies Club, the Bear Beach Club. I've participated in other organizations, including the Greater Panama City Doll Club and the Bay County Genealogical Society. In 1996 I was awarded a life membership in the genealogical society for my years of service as president, newsletter editor, and board member.

Jim and I are both glad that we picked Bay County for our home. It was a wonderful place to raise our daughter and a great place to call home.
Submitted by: Linda Pazics Kleback, 1607 Belmont Blvd., Lynn Haven, FL 32444-3343.

Foster Henry Kruse and Helen Elizabeth Kuhnhein Kruse

They had only been married a year when Granddaddy Kruse, Arnold Herbert Kruse, asked them to move to Panama City, Florida from Muncie, Indiana. The newlyweds Helen and Foster - were married June 26, 1937. Foster my Father had graduated from Indiana University with a degree in Business Administration and had planned on joining Granddaddy's bank as a Trust officer, however the depression changed all that. Instead, Foster was working with Owens Illinois Glass Company and had just received a promotion. But again, life was to change in an unforeseen way.

Foster was born May 31, 1912 to A. Herbert and Kathryn Kruse in Richmond, Indiana. Herbert was a banker and the family soon moved to Muncie. Kathryn died when Foster was only 2 years old. Herbert married Greta Coil; the youngest daughter of William D. Coil or "Pop Coil" as my Father always called him. Greta adopted Foster. Greta and Herbert had two daughters Elizabeth Ann born September 8, 1919 and Mary Virginia born June 4, 1925.

Foster Henry Kruse and Helen Elizabeth Kuhnhein Kruse

"Pop Coil" died in 1935 and Herbert Kruse was settling his estate. Granddaddy traveled to Panama City to meet a Mr. Avery. Mr. A. P. Avery had borrowed money from "Pop Coil" to start a real estate business in Panama City. While staying at The Cove Hotel, Herbert Kruse was approached by Mr. WL McAnulty, the owner and operator of Domestic Laundry. Mr. McAnulty wanted to sell the laundry to Granddaddy Kruse. Actually, Granddaddy was not interested, but Mr. McAnulty was persistent. Finally hoping to get rid of "Mac", Herbert made him an offer. Herbert would buy the plant, if McAnulty would operate it. Granddaddy Kruse's health was not good and his doctors had suggested that Florida's warmer climate would be better than the colder climate of Indiana. To Granddaddy's surprise, Mr. McAnulty accepted his offer, but before the purchase could be completed Granddaddy had another heart attack. So he asked the newlyweds Foster and Helen to move with him, Grandmother Kruse and "the girls" to Panama City and Foster to operate Domestic Laundry.

Family came first, so move, they did in 1938. Foster attended the American Institute of Laundering in Joliet, IL to learn "the business". Domestic Laundry and Dry

Cleaners grew under Foster's management and with the dedication of many fine employees to include family laundry and a commercial laundry business — operating three shifts a day during the summers to service a growing tourism industry. Domestic had routes covering all parts of town picking-up and delivering to homes and businesses, plus a fur storage vault, dry cleaning, rental uniforms and linens. During the 1960's and 70's, Domestic Laundry was one of Bay County's largest employers. In May of 1980 after 42 years, Foster and Helen sold the business and retired.

Foster helped form the Gulf Coast Community College Foundation, the Panama City Music Association and was a Deacon at Wallace Memorial Presbyterian Church. Helen (b. October 16, 1915, the daughter of Alma Adeline Cunningham and Robert Eugene Kuhnhein) helped organize the Girl Scouts, was a President of the Junior Woman's Club and an honorary member of the Jr. Service League. They had one child, Elizabeth Ann born September 3, 1950.

Submitted by: E. Ann Kruse Percival, 322 Bunkers Cove Road, Panama City, FL 32401-3912.

Landgraf

In 1886, Valentine Landgraf left his home in Minnesota to make his way south for health reasons. Born in Hesse Darmstadt , Germany on 12 December 1831, he had immigrated to the United States in 1849. After serving in the Minnesota Infantry during the Civil War, he determined to head for Florida. Leaving his wife, Elizabeth Tobin, and eight children, he traveled to St. Andrew, then in Washington County. After staying in St. Andrew for a time and being unhappy with land he found available, he homesteaded land at Cromanton, at that time in Calhoun County. He was receiving a pension from the government of $20.50 each month and expected to be

Valentine Landgraf

joined by members of his family. However, they chose to stay in the comforts of established homes in the North, rather than pioneer the unknown South. One son, Anton Valentine, came to join his father, who died on 4 November, 1912 and was buried in the Catholic Cemetery in St. Andrew. At his death, he left 120 acres of land at Cromanton. It was later taken by the U.S. Government to become part of Tyndall Air Force Base.

Anton Valentine, also known as Charlie, was born 13 October 1873 and died 30 May 1962. He is buried in the Catholic Cemetery in St. Andrew. He was married to Edna Ruth Wehnes of Elmira, New York. She was born 18 October 1893 and died 12 October 1990. They were parents of one son, Raymond, who is also deceased.

Another son of the elder Valentine, was William, born 9 February 1869, who made his home in Mishawaka, Indiana. He married Elizabeth Kline in 1894. He died 24 February 1946. Elizabeth was born 8 August 1873

A.V. Landgraf, Emma Wehnes, Edna W. Landgraf

and died 10 November 1941. They are buried in St. Joseph Cemetery in Mishawaka, Indiana. They were the parents of six children.

One of their sons, Frederick Francis, born 27 February 1899 in Mishawaka, married Marie Dorothy Phillips on 5 July 1921. She was born in Chicago, Illinois on 17 September 1899 and was the daughter of Jacob Phillips and Emma Gotto.

After visits to this area and having established a summer home at Cromanton, Fred and Marie sold their holdings in Mishawaka and moved, with their three children, into their home at Cromanton in 1934.

Fred Landgraf and wife Marie, Lester, Rita, and Fred Jr.

They lived there until the land was taken in 1941 to establish Tyndall Field.

Their children were: Frederick Francis, Jr., born 2 May 1922, Lester Phillips, born 18 September 1925 and Rita Ann, born 13 February 1928 in Mishawaka, Indiana. Marie died 12 June 1949 and was buried in the Catholic Cemetery in St. Andrew. In 1953, the elder Fred married Gladys O'Brien and they had one daughter, Leta. Gladys and Leta moved to New Orleans after Fred's death on 14 September 1961. He is buried in the Catholic Cemetery on Frankford Avenue.

Lester served in the Navy during World War II and married Jeannette Patricia Graham of Greenville, South Carolina on 8 October 1949. They settled in Silsbee, Texas and are the parents of seven children.

Rita Ann married David P. Robertson, Jr. , of Panama City on 10 June 1949 and has three children. They live in Decatur, Georgia.

Fred Jr. served in the Marine Corps during the war and married Laura Mae Smith on 26 September 1947. She was born 6 April 1928, the daughter of Charles D. Smith and Lillie Mae Hayes of Panama City. Fred and Laura parented five children. Fred Jr. died on 4 July 1999 and is buried in the Catholic Cemetery in St. Andrew. Their children are Lillian Marie born 6 August 1951 , Frederick Francis III, born 10 November 1953, Laura Elizabeth, born 21 November 1955, Linna Ann, born 18 November 1960 and Lorena Sue, born 6 April 1963.

Lillian married Michael T. Cooper of Evansville, Indiana. They reside locally and are the parents of Lisa Marie and Townsend. Lisa is the wife of John Dustin Barr. Townsend is married to Dawn Davidson and they have two daughters, Lucie and Robin.

Fred III married Jan Dillane of Indianapolis, Indiana. They have three children, Lyndsey, Lauren, and Frederick IV, known as Erick. They live in Atlanta, Georgia.

Laura married Truman Hartzog, Jr. of Panama City. They became parents to Laura Elizabeth. After a divorce, Laura married David Randall Lewis. They make their home in Panama City.

Linna married William Lee Dennis of Decatur, Alabama. They had one daughter, Marianna Francis. After that marriage ended, Linna married Michael Lee Falzone of Panama City. They reside in West Palm Beach, Florida.

Lorena married Jerry W. Kelly of Crestview, Florida. They reside in Panama City.

Submitted by: Laura S. Landgraf, 2358 Pretty Bayou Drive, Panama City, FL 32405.

Capt. Ruben Buck Lee

The Lee Family, of which Capt. Ruben Buck Lee was a descendent, first settled in north Florida in the 1850's. The Lee family lineage originated in Scotland. Capt. Buck

Capt. Ruben Buck Lee

Lee's grandfather had a homestead which encompassed much of what is now the main headquarters area of Tyndall Air Force Base, including the runway area. Capt. Lee's father, Jim Lee, and his mother, Dorothy Lee, who was a Carden, had their homestead on Pearl Bayou near San Blas. Capt. Buck Lee was born at San Blas on January 9, 1913.

The Lee homestead did what many of the others all had to do to survive and that was to work hard at a variety of endeavors, including Turpentining, Farming, Cattle, Hogs and of course Fishing. For Buck Lee the fishing was his calling. From the time of his childhood he spent many hours on the waters of St. Andrews Bay, Crooked Island Sound and St. Joe Bay. He learned to master castnetting, gill netting and did a lot of oystering. When he was old enough he began to commercial fish and fished with well known captains, such as George Curvin, and Candy Carden, engaging in gillnetting, seining and snapper fishing. He always said that the two captains he admired the most were Capt. Roy Ecker and his own father-in-law Capt. Peter Parker. He married Capt. Parker's daughter, Mary Frances Parker, in 1935.

During World War II Buck Lee volunteered for duty in the Navy. He obtained the rank of Chief Petty Officer. He was stationed on a Destroyer Escort for duty in the North Atlantic and the Mediterranean Sea escorting convoys through German U-Boat patrols and past air attacks going into the Mediterranean Sea. During this duty at sea in the North Atlantic Buck Lee became very ill with a ruptured appendix and was near death for weeks and underwent a critical recovery over months, involving several surgeries. After discharge from the Navy at the end of the war he returned to Panama City and again pursued his love of fishing.

Capt. Ruben Buck Lee

Immediately after the war Capt. Lee helped his brother-in-law, Capt. George Davis, to install the first diesel engine in a fishing boat. Buck's training in the Navy diesel schools aided him greatly here. Capt. Lee later began to develop a long association with a company that owned private boats. This company was an Alabama textile group, Avondale Mills, and they had a summer camp and several boats located in north Florida.

Capt. Roy Ecker, one of Buck's mentors, was a captain early on for Avondale Mills and also one of Roy's sons, Capt. Bobby Ecker. Bobby & Buck were good friends and as time passed the Eckers moved on and Buck continued with the company and ran their boats for over 30 years. Avondale had several boats during the 50's and 60's, including a 52' Sailboat, the "Sculpin", a 40' Sportfish, the "Skipjack", and a 80' motoryacht, the "Gomol". They fished extensively in the Panama City area and all over both coasts of south Florida and the Keys in the winter time.

Capt. Buck Lee loved fishing these boats for the company and was considered one of the best captains in this area. He also learned fishing in other areas in south Florida and excelled there. He fished with many good anglers and captains, including Ted Williams in the Keys, and Buck was considered one of the best Tarpon fishermen in Boca Grande. He also, early on, developed a relationship with Capt. Bob Lewis in the Miami area, who had helped pioneer the use of Kite Fishing in the ocean for Sailfish, etc. Capt. Lee recognized the effectiveness of this technique and utilized it. He was always keen to new innovations and incorporated them, which is key to success in fishing. Another factor in his success was that he utilized his instinctive ability to find fish and figure a way to catch them. This is something that is not learned by practice but more by innate ability. Many of the old Cracker fishermen had this ability, almost as though it was a genetic thing, or maybe from a deep awareness of things on the water from a life lived on it.

In 1965, Capt. Buck realized one of his long held dreams. He was able to have a fishing boat built of a design that he had in his mind for some time. From early childhood he had drawn pictures of boats that he liked and over the years he had begun to focus on what he wanted. He contracted with Julian and Will Gurtherie of Harkers Island North Carolina to build a 57' boat. It was built with double planked Juniper and monel fasteners and proved to be a great sea boat and a boat with finesse in handling, a feature which greatly aided in fishing.

This Carolina boat, he named the "Sunrise", was to become somewhat of a legend in the fishing world of Florida. Aided by some great captains in their own right, such as Buster Niquet and Johnny Spinks, Capt. Buck, on the Sunrise, helped to pioneer the early Marlin fishing in the Gulf during the mid 60's. The Sunrise was also involved in extensive bottom fishing, and Capt. Lee was known for having secret spots, such as the "Crack" off of Naples and the W.W.II. Freighter wreck off Boca Grande, that no one else could find.

Capt. Buck Lee led the life he wanted to, close to the sea that he loved so much as a child and he also made many great friends and enjoyed the camaraderie of the other fishermen he respected so much. He lived and worked on the sea in the old Cracker tradition of hard work, and he was fortunate to have met the two criteria in life to be happy in your work. Do what you are good at and what you love.

Submitted by: Ruben J. Lee. 5206 Teri Ln., Panama City, FL 32404.

L. D. Lewis and Leona Mae Johnson Lewis

L. D.(Luther Darius) "Sunshine" Lewis was born in Blakely, Georgia in 1907. His parents were Martin Titus Lewis and Sarah Frances Richardson Lewis. His mother had been born in Port St. Joe, Florida, where her father had been a physician and the keeper of the lighthouse at Cape San Blas. As a young boy L. D.'s family lived in various towns around south Georgia and northwest Florida where his father worked as a lumber grader in various sawmills. After the death of his father in 1924, L. D, his mother, two brothers and two sisters moved to Bagdad, Florida. L. D. was almost 17 when he became a breadwinner for the family working at the lumber mill in Bagdad. At the age of 20 he became the operator of the hotdog concession for the sawmill and began his entrepreneurial career in the food business. He greatly enjoyed fishing and played amateur baseball. In 1925 he met Leona Mae Johnson and, after a courtship of five years, they were married in 1930.

Leona Mae Johnson was born in Galt City, Florida in

Lewis Residence, 451 Sudduth Ave., circ 1946

1909. Her father was John Martin Jhonson (Jensen) and her mother was Amelia Straagaard Jhonson. John Martin Jhonson had emigrated from Denmark in 1889 and had traveled first to Illinois after arriving in the port of New York City. He Americanized his native Danish surname from Jensen to Jhonson looking forward to his new life as an American citizen (later some of his children further Americanized their last name to Johnson). In Illinois he met Amelia Straagaard whose parents had also emigrated from Denmark. Searching for a future together in Florida they traveled to northwest Florida after they were married and settled in Galt City in Santa Rosa County. The family moved to Milton around 1920 where Leona's father became the bridge tender for the draw-bridge over the Blackwater

L. D. and Leona Lewis 1946

River. Leona had four brothers and two sisters when her mother died. Along with her older sister she accepted the role of mother for her younger siblings. She completed eleven years of public school and then attended a business school. She quickly got a job taking shorthand and transcribing letters for a group of lawyers in Milton.

With little concern for the Great Depression that lay before them, Leona and L. D. were convinced that with hard work and perseverance that they could make a success of their lives together and in the process help their younger brothers and sisters for whom they had responsibility. L. D. began construction of a café and when it was finished he quit his job at the mill and Leona joined him to work together at their first business, the Overpass Café on State Road 90 near Milton. They worked long hours serving the men and women who worked at the mill and many other local residents and business travelers who regularly stopped by. Leona cooked and L. D. ran the business end of the café.

In the year 1942, they saw another opportunity and moved to Marianna, Florida, to open their first grocery store with L. D.'s two brothers. In 1944, L. D. and Leona made the decision to move to Bay County and Panama City and open the first grocery store on their own, a Jitney Jungle Food Store, on Harrison at 7th Street. Jitney Jungle was a franchised store chain that was headquartered in Jackson, Mississippi. They arrived at a time when Panama City was beginning to bustle with the ship building effort for WWII and people were flocking to the area for the jobs that were opening up. They lived first on North Cove Blvd. and later on Cherry St. in the Cove. In 1945 they purchased a home at 451 Sudduth Ave. that would be their home for almost 30 years. Their home was in the Spanish Colonial Revival style and had been built around 1925 by H.

L. D. Lewis 1980

L. Sudduth who had also constructed the Cove Hotel. The home was on the water, had a fire place with a five foot high mantel, hardwood floors with broken tile insets in the living room and pecky cypress ceilings that came from the lumber left over from the construction of the Cove Hotel. A room on the second floor was called the Mexican

Room because of its high arched windows.

Children in the neighborhood used to call the house the Alamo because of its arched parapet on the roof that was reminiscent of the shape of the Alamo in Texas. Leona continued to work in the grocery business until the arrival of their first child, Lana Jane, in 1946. Two years later their daughter, Donna Sue, was born and in another two years their son, Luther D. Jr. was born.

L. D. and Leona were both actively involved in their community being members of the First Baptist Church and many other organizations. L. D. was a member of Kiwanis and the Elks Club. He served as president of the Chamber of Commerce, as a deacon of the First Baptist Church of Panama City and was a founding member of the Econfina Club. Leona was an active member of the Women's Club, Kiwanianns, and the Garden Club. Their children attended Cove Elementary, Jinks Jr. High, and Bay High schools. From fishing trips to Central Florida, to fish fries and church parties around their swimming pool, to trips throughout the world, the Lewis family enjoyed a multitude of activities. L. D. and Leona had many friends and through their success they were able to help many family members with jobs, and in need, the comforts of their home and their open hearts. They were well known for their generous contributions to community organizations and their willingness to help those who struggled in hard times.

Leona J. Lewis 2003

More Jitney Jungle Food Stores were added in Panama City; #2 in Millville on Business 98, #3 in St Andrews on Beck Ave, #4 in the Cove on Cherry St, #5 in Lynn Haven on Highway 77, #6 in Callaway on Highway 98, and #7 in Panama City Beach on Front Beach Road by the county pier.

Seven other grocery stores were added in other towns in Northwest Florida and South Alabama. In 1961, L. D. made the decision to build the first convenience store in Bay County. Located on 11th Street across from Jinks Jr. High School, the Jr. Food Store, as it was named due to its small size of 60'x40', featured an open front with sliding glass panels that were open during operating hours and closed at night. The hours of operation were from 7 a.m. until 11 p. m. and the store sold basic groceries plus items of hardware, health and beauty aids, as well as newspapers and magazines. It was a store type that served the growing needs of Bay County and L. D. Lewis was able to repeat that successful formula many times. During this time of expansion in the early 60's L. D. decided to break with the Jitney Jungle franchise. He built a warehouse and office at June Ave. and 17th St. and renamed the grocery stores Sunshine Food Stores. He quickly acquired the nickname L. D. "Sunshine" Lewis that he enjoyed being called for the rest of his life.

In 1968, L. D. decided to try his hand at politics and made an unsuccessful run for State Representative. He moved on with his career in the grocery business and the 100th convenience store was opened in 1971. That same year L. D, as Chairman of the Board and C.E.O. of Sunshine Jr. Stores, Inc, decided to take the company public, making it the first public company to be head-quartered in Panama City.

By 1981, the chain of Jr. Food Stores had grown to 354 stores in the five states of Florida, Alabama, Georgia, Mississippi and Louisiana. The stock, SJS, was being sold on the American Stock Exchange. The generic name for a convenience store in Bay County had come to be "Jr. Food

Store", the place to meet your friends and purchase the necessities of life conveniently, and at times when other stores were closed. In August of 1981, L. D. Lewis suffered a heart attack while working in his office and passed away. Leona J. Lewis assumed the position of Chairman of the Board and along with her daughter, Lana Jane Lewis-Brent as president and CEO, continued running the company. In 1990, at the age of 81, Leona retired from her role as Chairman of the Board of Sunshine-Jr. Stores and began an active life fishing and enjoying her grandchildren and friends.

Submitted by: Paul Brent, P O Box 2209, Panama City, FL 32402. Written by: Lana Jane Lewis-Brent.

Lauvenia Johnson Holmes Lewis

Erstwhile Lauvenia Johnson Holmes Lewis was born June 1, 1900 in Jackson County, Florida to Alfred Johnson Sr. and Jane Daniels Johnson. She had

seven brothers Brock Daniels, Joe Daniels, Alfred Johnson, Jr., Henry Johnson, Cledious Johnson, Denmark Johnson and Emmit Johnson. And five sisters Ruc Daniels, Linnie Daniels, Eva Johnson, Fannie Johnson and Waver Virginia Johnson.

She grew up in the country on the family farm. She walked to her one-room school that was housed in a church until completing the sixth grade. As an adventurous young lady she ventured to Panama City in her late teens. She settled on East End Avenue, later to be renamed Harmon Avenue, to start her own business. During this time she opened her first boarding house and rented a room to Johnnie Belle Hicks Murray, developing a life long friendship.

Lauvenia Johnson Holmes Lewis

Lauvenia was married to Harrison Holmes and later she would marry Fred Lewis.

She was an active member of the Women's Civic Club during the 1960's hosting numerous fund raising projects for church and community. She, along with others, was instrumental in the re-location and building of the present day Greater Bethel A.M.E. Church, Macedonia Baptist Church and the Glenwood Recreation Center that is now the present day Martin Luther King, Jr. Center.

As a young enterprising woman she would later own and operate many businesses including the Pleasant Inn Boarding House and Cafe and the Pamela Denice Motel and Hotel in Panama City, Florida.

Lauvenia Johnson Lewis's life came to a sudden stop on April 30, 1969.

My Great Aunt Lauvenia Johnson Lewis's short life was a non-stop succession of business and civic adventures. She was one of those dauntless people who confront the world head-on with enormous clearness of vision, to make it a better place for all of us. In my heart, her gallant spirit is still with us.

Submitted by: Bura L. Reed, 1402 Illinois Ave, Lynn Haven, FL 32444.

Lana Jane Lewis-Brent

Lana Jane Lewis was born in 1946 at Lisenby Hospital in Panama City, Florida. Her parents were L.D. and Leona Johnson Lewis who owned the Jitney Jungle Food Stores at the time of her birth and later Sunshine-Jr. Stores Inc (see L.D. and Leona Mae Johnson Lewis for other information). She attended Cove Elementary School, Jinks Junior High School and Bay High School where she was active in Keyettes, Student Government and other school clubs. She went on to attend Stetson University in DeLand, Florida where she majored in English and was a member of the Alpha Xi Delta Sorority. Upon returning home in 1968 she

taught as an interim teacher at Bay High during a teacher strike but went back to work at her family's business when the strike was over. She had worked at some of her family's food stores as she was growing up and after college began her career at the corporate office. It was an exciting time of growth for the company and Lana Jane was ready to take on any challenge. One of her first jobs was to take the bookkeeping department from hand entry of figures into the new technology of data processing. She studied the process at the Bay Line Corporate offices in Dothan, Alabama and coordinated the purchase and set up of a mainframe computer, one of the first in Bay County. She also instituted a new consumer relations department. Later, she became Senior Vice President of the company following its public offering in 1971.

In personal matters Lana Jane had met her future husband, Paul Brent, in 1969, and in 1971, they were married at the Garden Club in an outdoor ceremony. She left Panama City in 1973 to live with Paul in Berkeley, California, where he was working on his Master's Degree at the University of California. She took a leave of absence from her job for a

year and a half while they were in California but continued to write the company's corporate annual report during that time. In 1974, Lana Jane and Paul returned to Panama City and she resumed her position with the company.

In June of 1981 her first son, Jensen, was born and in August of that same year her father died. By then, the company was comprised of six Sunshine Food Stores in Bay County and 354 Jr. Food Stores in five states. With the support of her mother and other board members, she became the president of the company, the first woman in Florida to be the president of a

Lana Jane Lewis-Brent

publicly held company. This was only the beginning of a series of firsts for Lana Jane. She joined the board of the Retail Grocers Association of Florida, the first woman on their board, and later became chairman of the board. She was elected to the board of directors of the National Association of Convenience Stores (NACS), again the first woman on that board. In her position as the chairman of NACSPAC (NACS Political Action Committee) she became involved in the political process nationally. Over the next several years she was appointed by Governors Graham, Martinez and Childs to the boards of the Governor's Energy Council, Public Facilities Financing Commission and Regional Interstate Banking Advisory Committee and the Florida Commission on Government Accountability to the People.

The Florida Chamber of Commerce was her focus from 1984 to 1990 when she was a board member. Prior to that, in 1981 she joined First National Bank on the board of directors until 1986. Following this, she served as Chairman of the Jacksonville Branch of the Federal Reserve Bank of Atlanta in the years 1992, 1994, and 1995, and served on the board from 1986-1993.

One of the organizations that highlights her achievements is her membership in the Committee of 200, the preeminent business women's association in the U.S. Locally, Lana Jane was a founding member of the Bay County League of Women Voters and served on that board. Other local board memberships have included the Northwest Regional Library System, the United Way of Bay County, as well as the Bay County Chamber of Commerce.

Many honors have come her way, having been listed in both the Outstanding Young Women of America publication, in addition to Who's Who of American Women. In 1989,

Working Women magazine selected her to receive the Hall of Fame Business Achievement Award. Earlier in 1986, she was listed in Savvy magazine as number 10 in the top sixty women running businesses in the United States. The year 1990 welcomed the birth of her second son, Anders.

In 1992, Lana Jane retired as President and CEO of Sunshine-Jr. Stores, Inc. and joined her husband, Paul, as president of their fine art publishing and licensing firm, Paul Brent Designer, Inc. She has served on the advisory board of Toland Enterprises, a home decor company. Other business affiliations include several key positions. She currently serves on the board of Tootsie Roll Industries, a New York Stock Exchange company. She also serves as a member of the board of directors of Vision Bank FSB.
Submitted and written by: Paul Brent, 1216 Dewitt St., Panama City, FL 32401.

The Lloyd Family

My husband, Rayford L. Lloyd, Sr., and I moved to Panama City from Eufaula, Alabama on August 15, 1936. Rayford's aunt Bertha Carter, who lived in Birmingham, had learned while here on vacation that the property where the Ramada Inn is now located was available. She suggested our buy-

ing the property and building cottages to rent to summer vacationers. At that time Panama City Beach and Long Beach were not developed. There were only five or six cottages across the road from Long Beach.

Lloyd's Bay Point Cottages, St. Andrews, 1935

Together with my husband's father, we bought the property in St. Andrews and built seven cottages-some facing the street and the others facing the bay. We named them Lloyd's Bay Point Cottages. There was a two-story frame house on the property that we lived in. A few years later Mr. Young from Columbus built another larger cottage with an eight year lease.

St. Andrews was a thriving community at that time. There were two grocery stores with a drug store in between in the next block. Farther up the street was Mattie's Tavern where we could get delicious meals. In fact, we had a full meal at noon for fifty cents.

After a few months of managing the cottages ourselves, my husband went into business with Joe Hutchison who had a Standard Oil filling station and the Pontiac franchise on the site where Merrill Lynch now stands across from the Post Office. The Dixie Sherman Hotel was across the other direction. Joe later sold his share and started the MoJo Oil Company. Rayford later acquired the Cadillac franchise. Rayford was also Chairman of the Bay County Airport Authority in 1946 when the first Bay County Airport was being built.

Our daughter Kay was born on July 4, 1937. When she was little she always thought the parades up town were for her birthday. We soon moved in to Panama City and Rayfords sister, Myrtle, and her husband Joe Rutherford, Sr. along with their two children Joe, Jr. and Jeanne moved to St. Andrews from Hurtsboro, Alabama to manage the cottages. Joe Rutherford, Sr. became an active member on the Bay County School Board, and Rutherford High School was named in his honor. Joe, Jr. was a much-loved teacher at Jinks Jr. High School for many years.

Our son Rayford, Jr. was born on August 9, 1941, and our son William "Bill" was born on April 16, 1948, making our family complete. We moved our church letters from our home churches in Alabama to the First Methodist

Church on Fourth and Magnolia. After that frame church burned a new beautiful brick church was built at 903 East 4th Street. It is now the First United Methodist Church. Each of our children joined the church at an early age. Being active in our church has been an important part of our lives.

Life in Panama City was so enjoyable. Borden's Dairy delivered milk every morning, even placing it in the refrigerator along with orange juice if needed. Rayford Jones had a fish market at Tarpon Dock. He also had a delivery service and would even peel shrimp if you asked him. Hill's Grocery was a nice family-owned and operated business on the corner of 6th Street and Cove Boulevard.

After graduating from FSU Kay worked in Atlanta before marrying and moving to Longview, Washington and from there to Portland, Oregon where her two children Elizabeth and Tom Edwards were born. Kay, her husband Tom and son Tom now live in Dundee, Oregon.

Rayford, Jr. graduated from Auburn University with a Master's degree in electrical engineering. He married Eugenia Price and they have two daughters, Lisa Hamlin and Sherrill Brown. After thirty-four years in the automobile business he decided to sell and is now retired.

Bill graduated from the University of Florida and received the Doctor of Business Administration from Indiana University in Bloomington. He taught finance at the University of Georgia six years and at Auburn University eighteen years. He married June Cooper and they have two sons, Bill, Jr. and Robert. He is retired and they live here.

Bill and Rayford, Jr. worked hard getting the old Cove School restored. We now have a beautiful building housing the upper grades of the Holy Nativity Episcopal School.
Submitted by Lillie Pitts Lloyd, 100 Cherry Street, #104, Panama City, Florida 32401.

George Logue, Sr.
The Logues of Panama City

In 1935, the Logue family was living in Dothan, Alabama. George Logue, Sr. was a traveling salesman employed by Solomon Brothers Wholesale Dry Goods Co. of Montgomery, Alabama. Part of his territory was northwest Florida, which included Panama City. The town was on the move as a paper mill had started operations three years earlier.

George and Gladys Logue November 16, 1948 - 25th Wedding Anniversary

Logue had to purchase his own gasoline for his travels and he became interested in the independent service stations as they sold gasoline two cents a gallon less than the major oil company stations. He noted that Panama City had only one small independent service station and that it was located in a rather obscure place. He found an ideal location on West Highway 98, on Watson Bayou, between Panama City and the new paper mill. The highway was an excellent place for a service station, and Watson Bayou provided the waterway to the petroleum refineries in Texas. Logue put a deposit on this piece of property. He returned to Dothan, sold his home, and moved his family into a one bedroom apartment. He resigned his job and started chasing his dream.

His first step was to visit his friend and customer, C. C. Liddon, Jr. in Graceville, and got him and his brother, Ben, to join him as partners in this venture. They saw the possibilities in this business and each invested $5,000. This, along with the $10,000 that Logue had received from the sale of his home, gave them enough capital to purchase the land, construct the service station and build two storage tanks.

As there was a housing shortage due to the new paper mill, he could not locate a suitable rental house, so he invested another $800.00 in building a small house on the oil company property. He then returned to Dothan, and moved his wife, Gladys, and their two sons, George Logue, Jr., and W. Dayton Logue, ages 10 and 6 respectively, to their new home on Watson Bayou.

The Sunny State Oil Company prospered and he later opened a store on Harrison Avenue, originally named Neal Logue Company and later renamed Logue's Inc. He and his brother, Wilbur, also purchased and operated Solomon Brothers in Montgomery, Alabama where they both began their business careers.

George Logue, Jr. and his wife, the former Alice Godwin of Selma, Alabama, and their son Bill still reside in Panama City, as well as Dayton and his son Lance.

Submitted by: George Logue, Jr., Bay Point Box 27366, Panama City Beach, FL 32411.

Clifford E. Loper
Why Berniece and I Choose to Retire in Panama City

When I retired from the Air Force at Tyndall AFB in 1980, I moved to Norman, OK where my youngest son was attending dental school. My wife, Lucretia, wanted to be near her "baby". I worked for five years during which time I inserted about 1200 full dentures before I was offered a position I could not refuse. I went to Saudi Arabia to be chief of the huge new dental clinic. After three years I couldn't stand it any more so I returned home until my old boss asked me to come to Al ain, in the United Arab Republic. I was the only dentist in a large hospital. I did surgery full time. I was offered a better paying job in a new hospital in Dhahran Saudi Arabia so I took it. That is were I met Bernice Zeidler who was the head nurse of the female ward. We had arrived in the KSA on the same airplane and were good friends for two years. When Lucretia

Clifford E. and Berniece Loper

died, I returned to the states. The following year Berniece and I were married. I wanted to move away from "Tornado Alley", so we decided to move to Florida. I wanted to be in the panhandle closer to my remaining family, it was not as expensive as living in South Florida and I preferred the four seasons. I knew many people here and I was already familiar with the area, I thoroughly enjoy eating seafood and somehow it is always better near the seashore.

A few readers may be curious why I chose Panama City instead of one of the other places I had been assigned. I have lived (while in the US Navy) in Miami, FL; Lafayette, IN; Chicago, IL and Asbury Park, NJ. The Air Force sent me to: San Antonia, TX; Biloxi, MS; Lakenheath, England; Cape Cod, MA; Concord, MA; Mountain Home, ID; Tokyo, Japan, Vietnam in 1968 and lastly, to Tyndall AFB, FL. I enjoyed living at every one of them but one, the reader will know which.

Panama City is a great place to live for Berniece and me. She is now president of the Bay County Genealogical Society and has been for about seven years. She is the past president of the Master Gardeners and still active, she takes the "Over fifty" classes at GCCC every year, swimming exercises each weekday morning at GCCC, attends her church every Sunday, helps me in the garden does 95% of the grocery shopping and meets friends everywhere, often accompanied by a big hug.

She even gets hugs from our family doctor and the pharmacist at the Air Base. I could go on, but I fear I have already written more than most readers care to read. To sum this up: Yes, Berniece and I are very happy we chose Panama City as our final place to live.

Submitted by: Clifford E. Loper, Colonel USAF Retired, 2846 Longleaf Rd., Panama City, FL 32405.

Lovett

We know little about my great, great, great, great, great grandfather, David Lovett. He had five children: James, David, Moses, Aaron and Joshua. My great, great, great,

Wiley Lovett (standing on the right) behind his brother Aaron

great grandfather, Aaron Lovett was married to Esther Rahn, having nine children. The second child born to Aaron and Esther was my great, great, great grandfather, James Grant Lovett, born 1821, was married to Sara Fain Strickland, born 1827. He was a farmer and worked in a sawmill. James Emanuel, the fifth of eleven children of James Grant and Sara Lovett, was my great, great grandfather, born 1853, was married to Susan Kelly, born 1848. My great grandfather, James Aaron Lovett, born 1882, in Cairo, Georgia. He married Edna Young, born 1893. Both my great grandparents are buried in the Southport Cemetery. James Aaron Lovett came to Bay County with his mother, Susan Kelly Lovett, in 1890. Around 1915-1916, he was an Engineer on a log train that traveled between Graceville and Southport. In later years he got a job as engineer at the Wainwright Shipyard in Panama City. It was unfortunate that he died as a result of injuries received in a train accident there during World War II.

My grandparents, E. Y. and Sadie Ruth (Odom) Lovett are retired and live near my family. E. Y. retired from Gulf Power Company and Sadie Ruth from Bay County Property Appraiser's Office. They have two sons, Aaron and Edmond. Aaron and Jacquelyn Graham Lovett have four children: James, Jennifer, Graham, and Patrice. Aaron and Jacquie own Grease Pro and most of their children help in the business with them. My father, Edmond Y. Lovett, Jr. and my mother, Debra Gilmore Lovett are employed by the Bay County School

Aaron Lovett standing on the left

Board. They have three children: Adam, Ruth and John.

We as young people should take time to sit with our elders and hear the things they have to share. Most times they will tell you something you can learn from, and you will probably always leave with a chuckle. Here are a few of the stories my grandparents have passed down to us.

My grandfather's brother, Aubrey, and other men from Southport, worked on building the Jetties at St. Andrews State Park. This was about 1936. They drove a Model "A" Ford to Panama City and then took a boat to the Jetties. They had to then jump from the boat over to the seawall being built. Once, Aubrey missed the jump and fell in the water. Nearly drowning, with shoes and coat on he treaded water and floated to near Long Beach, where Mr. Buster Vickery had somehow made it across or around and pulled him from the water.

My great grandfather, Aaron Lovett and his friend Arnie King, had several interesting experiences: One night they were driving a Model "T" Ford on a dirt road. A young calf ran into the truck, hitting the radiator. The calf jumped up, ran blindly off and still "addled", charged the truck. The second time he stayed down. In 1904 my great grandfather's brother, Wiley Lovett, was living in Texas. With work being hard to come by, he and a cousin traveled by train to Salt Lake City, Utah to find work. There they worked for the railroad company building a bridge over the Great Salt Lake for $4.50 a day in gold pieces. He worked five months and traveled to the World's Fair in St. Louis, Missouri. He returned to Salt Lake City a year later, worked all summer, seven days a week, this time for $5.00 a day in greenbacks. Wiley then traveled from Texas to Apalachicola, where he saw John Gorrie's "Ice Making Machine". He went back home to Texas and told the people at church about it. They told him not be telling things like that, that it could not be true. So he told them if they did not believe him, "to get on the riverboat, go and check it out."

Submitted by: Adam Y. Lovett, 7841 Hwy 2302, Southport, Florida 32409.

Willie Faye and Bertie V. Lucas

My parents, Willie Faye Lucas and Bertie Vonceil Kirkland were married in March of 1935. Both their families lived in Holmes County. I was born in December of that year. Shortly after that, my father's parents moved to Panama City. My parents came to live with them. My father tried his hand at farming but then decided to move to Panama City. They lived with my grandparents while they were building a house. The house was at the corner of what is now Sanders Lane and 4th Street, at the time the streets were un-named. He worked as a carpenter in town and was a carpenter at the Wainwright Shipyard. Later he worked at the Fire Department at the Shipyard. At the time that the building was built on Jenks Avenue for the Chamber of Commerce and later the Public Library, he was working on the WPA project and

Bertie and Willie Faye Lucas and son Truett, 1966

helped build that building. At the close of the shipyard, he worked as a meat cutter and grocery clerk at Clifton's store. My father worked as a clerk at the Marie Hotel/Motel downtown and met many interesting personalities in that position. He retired when he became sick with emphazema at the age of 48. He tried his hand at raising crickets. We had a shed in the back yard and large wooden packing boxes lined the walls. He did that for a few years.

My mother went to work in 1950 at Christo's 5 & 10 cent Store on lower Harrison Avenue. When it closed, she went to work with Sunshine Stores as cashier in the Cove Shopping Center. An opportunity came for her to work at the new Woolworth's 5 & 10 cent store that was built on Harrison Avenue. She worked there for a number of years till her retirement.

They moved to E. 8th Court where they lived until their death.

My parents raised 8 children of which I am the oldest. They are Howard Lucas, deceased, Patricia Ann Canning, Peggy Wingate, Gwendolyn Barrett, Diane Miller, Wanda

Pennington and Charles Lucas.
Submitted by: Truett L. Lucas, 3235 E. Orlando Rd, Panama City, FL.

Marvin and Lenda McCain

Marvin and Lenda McCain came to Bay County in 1953, Marvin to teach at Jinks Junior High School and Lenda as Librarian at Bay County High School. Marvin was born November 9, 1923, in Cay County, Alabama, the youngest son of Reuben Glover McCain and Anna Martin McCain. Lenda, the daughter of Crawford Clift Haynes and Gulema Harrod Haynes, was born October 19, 1929, in Randolph County, Alabama.

Marvin was a World War II veteran, serving in General Patton's Third Army, 90th Reinforcement Battalion, landing in Ireland, then on to England, France and Germany. At

Marvin and Lenda McCain

the end of the war, he spent time in Switzerland for R and R, and attended the Nuremberg War Trials before returning home in May 1946. He immediately entered college, graduating in 1950 from Peabody/Vanderbilt with a B.A. in Economics, and in 1953 with an M.A. in Economics and School Administration. Lenda received B.A. and M.A. degrees from Peabody/Vanderbilt in History and Library Science in 1949 and 1951 and an Ed.S. from Florida State University in 1975. Married May 19, 1949, they taught in Tennessee and Georgia before coming to Panama City.

Marvin served as a teacher and administrator in the Bay County School System for thirty years, including the assistant principalship at Jinks Junior High School, Principal at West Bay and Callaway, and Assistant Superintendent for eight years. He was the founding principal of A. Crawford Mosley High School, retiring after ten years.

Lenda was a high school and elementary school librarian for ten years and for twenty years was a county media center librarian. Supervisor of Interns at Florida State University, she concluded her work with FSU after teaching at the London campus in 1999.

After retirement from the school system, Marvin and Lenda formed Marlen Developers, and developed Mowat Highlands and Key Estates subdivisions, with Marvin as president and Lenda as secretary-treasurer. They are also involved in commercial development.

Their oldest child is Eleanor Anne, born November 14, 1955. She is a graduate of Agnes Scott College in Decatur, Georgia, and the University of Florida School of Medicine, Gainesville. She did her residency in Internal Medicine at UAB and is a practicing physician in Fort Walton Beach, Florida. Her husband is John Bert Jinks, Jr. the son of Bert and Jan Jinks and is a graduate of the University of Florida. He has an MBA from Wharton School of Business, University of Pennsylvania. Married June 24, 1979, they have two daughters, Elizabeth McCain Jinks, born March 30, 1985, and Anna Ross Jinks, born April 21, 1993.

Their son, Allen Haynes McCain, born December 28, 1961, graduated from Georgia Institute of Technology in 1984. He is President of Haymaker Corporation, an electrical engineering firm in Birmingham. He and Laura Marie Hauser, the daughter of Mike and Ruthie Hauser, and a graduate of Auburn University, were married June 28, 1984. Their two sons are Kaylor Allen McCain, born October 13, 1987, and Porter Michael McCain, born January 31, 1991. They live in Homewood, Alabama, where they are active in church, school and community activities.

Marvin is a past president of the Lynn Haven Rotary Club and a Paul Harris Fellow, past president of the Sons of the American Revolution, and a member of the Sons of Confederate Veterans. He is a past elder in the First Presbyterian Church.

Lenda is a past president of Delta Kappa Gamma, the Daughters of 1812, the United Daughters of the Confederacy, Regent of the St. Andrew Bay Chapter of the Daughters of the American Revolution, and Florida State Librarian, NSDAR.

Submitted by: Lenda Haynes McCain, 712 West Pierson Drive, College Point, Lynn Haven, Florida.

Malcolm Edwin and Mary Emma Carmichael McCorquodale

Malcolm Edwin McCorquodale, native of Havana, Florida, was living with his family in Chipley, Florida, in 1925. He heard the government was offering 160 acre homesteads to anyone filing in Gainesville. Since his job as a demonstrator of shade tobacco growing was not doing well (the climate of Washington County proved to be unsuitable), he decided to go to the Gulf beach area to assess the value of such a venture.

He returned to Chipley determined to file. He and his wife, Mary Emma Carmichael McCorquodale, native of South Carolina, moved to Bay County to a site, later named "Sunnyside," on the Gulf. With them came their children

Malcolm E. McCorquodale and Mary E. McCorquodale

Grace (13), Lawson or "Corky" (11), Ruth Ellen (5) and Mary Emma (6 mos.). Their other child, Mattie (9), died in May before they moved in August. Needless to say, there were many hardships: traveling over sand-rut roads, clearing the palmettos and scrub-oaks from the land in order to grow vegetables, etc.

They joined with the other dozen or so homesteaders to hire a teacher for the children. He taught them in a small school they built near Phillips Inlet.

Since the coastal highway was delayed in being built, the McCorquodales had to leave their homestead after two years (1927). They moved back to Chipley, then to St. Andrews, where Mrs. McCorquodale ran the Villa Hotel, a three-story building on the bay with a cottage on the grounds behind it. They only stayed there one year before moving to Panama City, where Mrs. McCorquodale ran the Park Hotel across the street from what is now called McKenzie Park.

After a year, Mr. McCorquodale heard about the profitable truck farming south of Lake Okeechobee and decided to try his hand at that; but after one year there, the lush vegetation in the area caused him to suffer allergic reactions and the family returned to Sunnyside.

This was 1933 and the construction on the remainder of Highway 98 had begun. There was now a bridge over St. Andrews Bay and a highway which turned north at the "Y," five miles east of Sunnyside. Ruth Ellen and Mary Emma had to catch the school bus at 7:00 AM and walk home in the afternoon from the Y that year. The highway was completed by the next school year.

Now began the hard but thrilling job of building and developing Sunnyside. Mr. And Mrs. McCorquodale wanted to develop a family resort area where families would have a wholesome, safe place to come for their vacation. Mr. McCorquodale had the land platted into lots with four streets and alleys behind each row of lots. He had six small cottages built to rent and began selling lots where

Malcolm, Mary Emma, Mary Charlotte Carmichael, Lawson, Mary Emma, and Ruth Ellen

individually-owned cottages were built. He laid pipe lines down the alleys and would furnish water from the well, pumped by electricity and a windmill.

They were able to get electricity brought out by Gulf Power Company by paying for the poles. They had a grocery store with a meat market, a gas station, the first telephone on the beach, and the first post office on April 5, 1940 (this entailed two or three trips to Washington with Mr. "Bab" Brown, their attorney). The McCorquodales' home was always the "gathering place" for vacationers. They even had church services in their living room and front porch with vacationing ministers, judges, or lay leaders preaching. They flew the flags denoting warnings for the Coast Guard. During World War II, they were the official gas station for all the branches of the military- Coast Guard, Navy, and Air Force. The McCorquodales rented cottages to ship yard workers from St. Andrews.

By 1945, Mr. McCorquodale's allergies were much worse, and he sold his business-store, post office, and house-and moved to Havana, Florida. He had the land south of Highway 98 dedicated to the property owners of Sunnyside, thereby preserving the sea hill and coast line-the vegetation, palmettos, scrub-oaks, and sea-oats, held the sand and prevented erosion. He had always urged others to do this, but they did not heed his advice.

Sunnyside remains a quiet resort area where most cottages are individually-owned. There is only one small cottage belonging to a McCorquodale. The youngest, Mary E. McCorquodale Munson, spends her summers here and often thinks of the " good old days."

Submitted by: Mary M. Munson, P.O. Box 242, Clinton, LA 70722.

Bose McCrary
Part I - At Work

Bose McCrary was born on October 14, 1912, to the union of Andrew and Anna McCrary near Graceville, Florida in Jackson County. Graceville was a thriving family farming community. The McCrary family grew in size to 8 boys and 1 girl. At age 9, his father, Andrew, died, and later Bose dropped out of school in the 7th grade to help work the family farm. The family owned 160 acres and 4 mules. In those days there was no mechanized farming equipment.

Bose was an energetic, self motivated

Woodyard Maintenance Crew. Kneeling (L to R) foreman Houston Gilbert, J.B. Brogdon, Jerry Barker, Donnie Boykin, Austin Taylor. Standing (L to R) Dallas Owens, Bill Platt, D.R. McBride, Mike McKenzie, F.E. McCraney, Bose McCrary and Herman Theus.

and disciplined young man even though his education was limited. At one time in the early goings, most of his older brothers were self-employed. He knew that special opportunities existed and he was willing to spend time and effort to look for them, taking him away from family and home. He took advantage of job opportunities as they came about. When a great employment opportunity occurred at the

Wainwright Ship Yard, he left a good paying job at the paper mill, and took new employment because he wanted to learn more about procedures and techniques for handling, fabricating and welding steel pieces and parts.

Bose first came to Panama City in 1927 at age 15 to visit his brother Frank. Frank was self employed and hauled logs for Millville and Springfield sawmills. The Millville Sawmill also had a tram road stretching to Indian Bayou and was used for transporting logs to the mill. In 1930, the mill was shut down; later caught fire and was destroyed. The sawmill was located near the island on Watson Bayou.

At age 18 (1930), he traveled back and forth to Bay County for 3 years which allowed him to alternate farm work with part time work with his brother Frank and also with Bob Wester hauling pine logs and paper wood at $l/day. The paper mill started up in 1931.

About 1933, he moved to Millville and then hired in with the Padgett Sawmill in Springfield on Highway 22 at $l/day doing edging and tailing work. He would feed raw lumber to the edger to trim the edges. The tailing task was the separation of the edging strips from good boards. The sawmill had about 12 employees, and a capacity of approximately 35,000 board feet per day. The mill had a planer, drying kilns, also steam boilers to power the steam engines driving the busy machinery. A steady supply of pine and cypress logs was trucked or hauled by tram from surrounding forest and swamps (as far away as Indian Bayou).

In mid 1936, Bose went to work at the paper mill for $0.32/hr as a construction laborer on an expansion project. After the project, he was hired by the paper mill for the labor gang and was later laid off. For the next year he worked odd labor jobs and was then rehired by the paper mill.

During those early days young men would gather at the mill's main gate hoping to be hired. Bose was one of about 12 men at the gate one morning when he was hired. The labor foreman came out and hand picked Bose for the job that paid $0.32/hr (no red tape and no tests-the foreman would hire at their discretion and on the spot).

After about a year in the labor gang, he became a 3rd class welder (helper); then 2nd class welder; then journeyman welder (at $0.78/hr).

He continued in this job until 1942 at which time he left the mill and hired into the Wainwright Shipyard to help build Liberty ships at $1.20/hr.

Bose worked at the shipyard for about 3 years starting as a 1st class burner, and then become a foreman of a crew of 10 burners (men and women). He witnessed the launching of the first Liberty ship in 1944. In 1945 he was rehired by the mill as 3rd class welder since they knew Bose and his excellent work history. He progressed to journeyman level again and retired as such.

During time at the mill he was a skillful worker welding boiler tubes with a mirror, burning large roller bearing from shafts, and creating gear teeth by welding and grinding. He was regarded by his peers and supervision as one of the best gas and electric welders in the mill; and, he was assigned special welding and burning jobs by supervision. One supervisor said in front of a group of men (mostly welders) at a social event that Bose was the best welder he had ever supervised.

His welding crew at the mill was composed of 11 men. Those 11 men with their children shown in parenthesis that graduated in the Bay High Class of 1957 are as follows: Bose McCrary (James), Oscar Barnes (Wanda), Levy Brock (Jerry), Ammie Lee, Jr. (Joe), Fulton Bryan, Cubie Hicks, Bertis Register, Pete Laramore, Russell Hudson, Buford Long, and Homer Mills.

Bose retired from International Paper at age 62 in 1975, and put in a welding shop at home. He took in all the welding work that he wanted for about 5 years, then really retired and went fishing. He celebrated his 91st birthday on October 14, 2003.

Submitted by: Mike McCrary, 5844 Shannon Circle, Youngstown, Florida.

Bose McCrary
Part II - Family Life

Bose was born on October 14, 1912, to the union of Andrew and Anna McCrary near Graceville, Florida in Jackson County. At age 15 (1927) Bose first came to Bay County to visit his brother Frank in Springfield. Frank was self employed, owned a log hauling truck, and later allowed Bose (at age 18) to work part time with him. Bose traveled back and forth to Bay County for about 3 years to work with his brother Frank and another log hauler Bob Wester; pine and cypress logs were hauled to the Millville and Springfield sawmills from the surrounding forests and swamps.

In 1933, he moved to Millville and went to work with Padgett sawmill in Springfield making $1/hr. Bose married Ruth Widincamp on February 17, 1934. He met Ruth in 1931 at a cottage prayer meeting at Eva and Tom Aplin's home in Millville. Bose and Ruth were God fearing people. Ruth could not afford a church wedding so they were married by a court house Judge in Panama City. In 1936, Bose and Ruth bought a small frame house on Gray Ave in Millville; lived there about 15 years; and, had their first child (Juanita born at home in 1935). An outhouse was locat-

Bose McCrary's 90th Birthday 2002. (front row L-R) James McCrary, Carolyn McCrary, Ruth McCrary. (back row L-R) Bose, Sherry Wall, Wayne McCrary and Mike McCrary.

ed on the back side of the lot. The back porch had a pitcher pump and a water bucket and ladle for drinking water. A porcelain pan was used for washing face and hands. The kitchen had a kerosene stove and a wooden ice box that required block ice on a daily basis. Block ice was delivered to the neighborhood from either the Millville or Springfield Ice Plants.

Bose made a dining room table and some baby furniture. A baby high chair was hand made by cutting an apple crate in half and attaching hand made legs (in those days apple crates were made from solid wood). Economic times were hard and Bose had to make the best of his time and money.

In 1947, Bose borrowed money and bought 5 acres of land in the north eastern end of Springfield on what is now East 14th Street. The newly acquired land was fenced and divided for raising hogs, sweet potatoes and sugar cane. The land was covered with palmettos, scrub oaks, pine trees and pine stumps and required clearing. Within the first year, a water well was driven by hand, and about one acre was cleared for planting sweet potatoes and sugar cane, also a location for a house.

During the first two years of hog raising, the hogs were fed with livestock feed, stale bakery products, home made hominy and food scraps that Bose hauled by the drum twice per week from Walgreen's Cafe on Harrison Ave. Also, the hogs were allowed to cleanup the remains of the cane and potato patches after harvest time. Supplementary pork meat and sweet potatoes were part of the McCrary family diet before they moved to Springfield. Some of the sugar cane was ground for juice.

By 1949, there were seven children in the McCrary family (4 girls and 3 boys), Juanita, Nell, James, Carolyn, Wayne, Sherry and Mike. Two girls are deceased, Juanita (1997) and Nell (1952).

Bose enjoyed fishing the Sand Hill Ponds, Dead Lakes and Brothers Rivers. He would take James, his oldest son, fishing and they would catch their limits many times. In those days, large freshwater fish were plentiful. In the early goings Bose would rent a wooden bateau and paddle it from the landing to their favorite stumps and tree tops. Eventually Bose bought his first outboard motor from Sears on Harrison Ave, a 6HP Elgin. This motor allowed him to navigate and fish the Brothers Rivers and their tributaries. Bose also enjoyed squirrel hunting in the river swamps. In 1949, Bose bought a wood frame house from his employer (International Paper Co.), and had it moved from mill property in Bay Harbor to Springfield. The house was moved by Tom Aplin and his moving crew. To accommodate the McCrary family, the house was renovated and a third bedroom added. Bose moved his family to their new home in 1950.

Bose and James, his oldest son, cleared another 2 acres of land by hand for a very large garden. It took about 2 years to remove all growth and roots to prepare the land for planting. With 7 growing children, there was a need for a large vegetable garden, milk cow, chickens and hogs, all of which took considerable work. All livestock had to be fed and watered and the cow had to be milked twice daily.

During these years Bose worked at the International Paper Mill from 1936 until 1942. In 1942, he quit the mill to work at the Wainwright Ship Yard building Liberty Ships for the war effort until 1945. After the ship yard, he was rehired by the paper mill and retired from the mill in 1975. At 90 years young, he continues to plant a garden on his original 5 acres and still goes fishing in the Brothers Rivers.

Submitted by: James L. McCrary, 12277 Brookshire Ave., Baton Rouge, LA 70816.

James L. McCrary
Part I - Millville

James was born on October 29, 1939, to the union of Bose and Ruth McCrary who lived on Gray Ave in Millville. He was born at home and the attending physician was Dr. Middlebrook. In those days doctors made house calls as a matter of routine. The house had, for a while, an outhouse at

James McCrary with Stringer 1954 age 15.

the back side of the lot; and, a hand operated pitcher pump on the back porch. Next to this pump was a water bucket with ladle for drinking water and a wash pan for hands and face. The kitchen had a kerosene stove and a wooden ice box. Block ice was delivered to the neighborhood daily, by truck, from either the Millville or Springfield ice plant. The neighborhood kids enjoyed getting ice chips as the iceman broke large blocks weighing several hundred pounds into smaller increments of 50 and 25 pounds, popular sizes for the home.

By 1949, there were seven children in the Bose McCrary family, four girls (Eunice Juanita, Linda Nell, Theadus Carolyn and Sherry Francine) and three boys (James Lawrence, David Wayne and Michael Lamar), James being the third child and the oldest boy. Two sisters are deceased, Juanita (1997) and Nell (1952).

James remembers the paper mill whistle blowing and the local sirens screaming, signaling the end of WW II in 1945, when Japan surrendered. His dad, Bose, worked three years at the Wainwright Ship Yard during the war helping build Liberty Ships. Ship building was necessary due to the large number of ships being sunk by the German Navy. During the war years, many food and automotive items were rationed to benefit the war effort.

About the early age of seven, James developed a bone disease in his left leg and hip. During this time he had to use crutches and wear a sling or brace on his left leg to keep his weight off the leg. He spent two summers in a children's hospital for treatment in Pensacola. Being away from home and

family was traumatic and upsetting for such a young child. Finally the bone healed and he was able to get back to running barefooted through the Panama City sand and doing what little boys enjoy. There were many prayers said on his behalf for a speedy healing.

He was enrolled in Millville elementary in 1945 and attended through the 5th grade. During part of this time, Millville had classes through the 9th grade. He remembers Miss Bessie Gainey (First grade teacher), Mrs. Pollock (Second grade), and Miss Ryan. Millville had a wood working class for 5th grade boys for teaching them how to use various saws for some basic wood cutting skills and creating small ornamental wood work. During one year James helped the school janitor dump waste paper containers from each class room for pennies per day as the school population generated a huge quantity of waste paper daily. When he was first enrolled, East Avenue was a dirt road from Highway 98 to the paper mill, but was paved with asphalt before his 6th grade. Liquid asphalt was trucked in and mixed with sand in the road bed with cutting disc, and then compacted with a roller. He enjoyed watching the road construction.

Circa 1947 James' parents bought five acres of land in Springfield and in 1949, bought a house from International Paper (Bose's employer). The house was moved from paper mill property in Bay Harbor to Springfield by Tom Aplin (a Millville resident) and his crew. The house was renovated and additions made to accommodate the McCrary family. In 1950 Bose and Ruth moved from Millville and James was enrolled at Springfield elementary for the 6th grade.

Submitted by: James L. McCrary, 12277 Brookshire Ave., Baton Rouge, LA 70816.

James L. McCrary
Part II - Springfield

In 1950 Bose and Ruth McCrary moved their family from Millville to a new house in Springfield, and James enrolled at Springfield elementary for the 6th grade.

After the family settled into their new home, about 2 1/2 acres of land were cleared by hand for a very large garden. The land was full of palmettos, scrub oaks, pine trees and

James McCrary and his three grandchildren Jordan McCrary, Jessica McCrary and James Esteven.

pine stumps which had to be removed. James was a key worker in the land clearing since he was the oldest boy. With seven children, there was a need for a large garden, milk cow, chickens and hogs, all of which required considerable work.

During his early childhood and teenage years, his dad took him fresh water fishing. Their favorite fishing spots were the sand hill ponds, Dead Lakes and Brothers Rivers. They caught fish in good numbers and size in those days.

At Springfield elementary there were two sixth grade classes taught in old temporary military barracks. His teacher was Miss Parkman. There were no air conditioners for summer cooling; but, there was a wood burning potbellied heater for winter. On very cold mornings, the boys would climb through a sliding glass window before the janitor arrived and fire up the old wood heater in Miss Parkman's room. The heater would get cherry red and heat the room to a cozy temperature.

James attended Everitt Jr. High; and, then Bay High and graduated from Bay High in 1957.

During junior high he had a paper route. During high school he worked in the school cafeteria, and he worked part time after school and on Saturdays at Panama Cycle Shop on East 6th Street. At Panama Cycle he repaired bicycles, reel type and power lawn mowers, small electrical appliances, safes and locks for three dollars per day. He became proficient at unlocking house and automotive locks. Also, he overhauled his first car engine at home at the age of 15.

After graduating from Bay High, he worked during the summer of 1957 and saved enough money to cover tuition for one school quarter at Georgia Tech. He worked on several fishing boats and as a stevedore loading ships at the paper mill. Most of his fishing time was spent on the "Jeanette H." owned by J. D. Holmes Fish Market. Fishing with gill nets or scalloping with drags, all fishing was done at night.

He enrolled at Georgia Tech in September 1957, as a co-operative student in mechanical engineering. His first job (for three months) was with Ball Construction Company building a housing project at Tyndall. His next work quarter (summer 1958) was at a Gulf Power Generating Plant located in Sneads, Florida working as a laboratory technician. James continued co-oping there until 1961.

In 1961 he married Hilda Sharp from Metaire, LA. They met in Chattahoochee, Florida where he lived while working with Gulf Power and she was studying psychiatry at the State Hospital. He graduated from Georgia Tech in 1963 BME (Bachelor Mechanical Engineering). Hilda graduated as a R.N. from a nursing school in New Orleans, LA.

As a mechanical engineer, his first job was with Monsanto Chemical Company in Pensacola, Florida. He then hired in with Texaco in Port Arthur, Texas; BASF near Baton Rouge, LA; Georgia Pacific Chemical Division and Georgia Gulf Chemical Company near Baton Rouge, LA. Georgia Pacific Chemical Division was bought out by Georgia Gulf in 1985.

James and Hilda have lived in Baton Rouge for 31 years (as of 2003) and have two children (a girl Pamela Louise and a boy Timothy James); and, each one has advanced degrees from LSU in Baton Rouge. They have three grandchildren (two grand daughters Jordan and Jessica McCrary and one grandson James Samuel Esteven).

James retired from Georgia Gulf in January, 2000. He has a continuing garden year round and enjoys fresh water fishing. He built a cabin on the Bayou (a 3 1/2 year project) in the swamp which he really enjoys when he goes fishing.

Submitted by: Hilda S. McCrary, 39736 Highway 75 Pigeon Bayou, Plaquemine, LA.

Richmond C. & Katherine E. (Whidbee) McGill Family

Richmond C. McGill was the son of Joseph Palmer McGill and Julia Allen. He was born in Baldwin County, AL, on July 29, 1872. He died during the flu epidemic on November 21, 1918, in Youngstown, Bay, FL. Katherine Elizabeth "Kitty" Whidbee was born on March 10, 1876, in Baldwin County, Alabama, to Thomas Whidbee and Elizabeth "Bette" Dunnings. Kitty died on December 10, 1957, in Ft. Myers, FL. Richmond and Kitty married on May 22, 1895 in Baldwin County, AL.

Richmond came to Bay County about 1908-9 to live and work with his cousin, Frank Cypret McGill. Frank worked for the German-American Lumber Co. in Millville. After about a year, Richmond bought a farm in Youngstown and sent for his wife and children to join him. Kitty brought their five children to Bay County on the steamship *Tarpon*. It cost the family five dollars each to make the trip. Kitty brought their children to Bay County: Willie Richmond b. April 17, 1899, Virginia Pearl b. April 5,

Richmond Church McGill and wife Katherine Elizabeth McGill about 1892.

1901, Royal Lawrence b. June 18, 1903, Benjamin Elmo b. February 27, 1905, and Reuben Carey b. November 20, 1907. Richmond and Kitty had four more children after moving to Youngstown, they were: Joseph Ernest b. March 3, 1910, Clifton Eugene b. August 3, 1912, Lula Mae b. March 8, 1916, and James Cypret b. June 28, 1918.

Kitty farmed with the help of her older children for several years after Richmond died. She sold the farm in 1922 and moved to Mississippi and then to Ft. Myers, FL, where she lived until her death.

Benjamin Elmo stayed in Youngstown after his mother and siblings left the area. He married Ada Mae Goodwin b. April 14, 1901, daughter of Charley and Alma (Oliver) Goodwin on May 21, 1921, in Bainbridge, GA. They had eight children: Gladys Marie b. December 12, 1923, Richmond Elmo b. December 2, 1925, Clarence James b. September 25, 1928, Charles Edward b. January 30, 1931, Claude Earnest b. December 31, 1935, Pearl Mae b. March 3, 1938, Joyce Ann b. February 25, 1941, and Ronald Paul b. February 2, 1944.

Elmo farmed and worked as a longshoreman in Panama City until his retirement. Elmo died on May 4, 1988, at the home of his daughter near Marianna, FL. Ada died August 3, 1980, in Panama City.

All eight children continue to live in either Bay or Calhoun Counties. Gladys married Benjamin Frank Odom and had five children: Jessy, Gloria, Jerry, Wayne, & Bobby. Richmond Elmo married Evelyn Beach and had two children: Ricky & Connie. Clarence J. (Johnny) married Lucille Daniels and they had four children: Larry, Ray, Donald, & Billy Joe. Charles married Jane Ann McGill and they had four children: Charles, Sharon, Tony, & Kenneth. Claude married Bertie Lou Daniels and they had four children: Lillian, Carolyn, Irish, & Claude. Pearl married Charles E. Skinner and they had two children: Paul & Dianne. Joyce married Franklin Hatcher and they had five children: Cynthia, Roger, Tammy, Ronald, & Randal. Ronald married Mary Ester Byrd and they had two children: Rhonda & Ronald.

Submitted by Gloria Bullock, 10900 McGill Road, Panama City, FL 32404-5405.

The McKenzie & Gay Families

Andrew Jackson Gay and his wife Mary moved to what is now Bay County in December, 1884, from Early County, Georgia where he owned a rather large plantation called Liberty Hill Farms.

He purchased 20,000 acres from the State of Florida for 37 cents an acre and established the town of Gay, Florida. The land was virgin forest and was located on North Bay and Beauty Bayou - where the Panama City Country Club is today. He established a sawmill on this property, which was one of the only two mills serving the St. Andrew area during the "Cincinnati Land Boom" in the 1880s.

A.J. Gay was also the first man to

The McKenzie family

manufacture and ship naval stores from St. Andrew Bay. The turpentine still, which he began to build on December 1, 1897, was located near his home at Gay, Florida. He shipped his first 9 barrels of turpentine on April 1, 1898. The barrels were carried by Captain L.M. Ware to St. Andrew and transported aboard the steamer Altha to Carrabelle, Florida. In 1898 spirits of turpentine brought 23 cents a gallon, and resin sold for $2.00 a barrel.

The Post Office at Gay Florida opened in 1895 and remained in operation until 1911 when it was moved to the newly established town of Lynn Haven. Just before it was moved, the mail was taken to Lynn Haven from Gay in a wheelbarrow. Mary E. Gay (wife of A.J. Gay) was Post Mistress of Gay, Florida.

After years of prosperous business ventures, the Gay family moved to Panama City in 1912 and leased the property in Lynn Haven to W.L. Sawyer. In 1927, Walter C. Sherman established an 18 hole golf course on the site. The International Paper Company purchased the property, which is still known as the Panama City Country Club.

A.J. invested $50,000 in a railroad venture and lost every cent - one of the few bad investments he ever made. He purchased and sold a track of land of approximately 27,000 acres known to all as the "Cove." He paid $2.25 an acre or $60,000 for the track. He was founder of the first telephone system in this part of the panhandle. The system connected Chipley, St. Andrew, Pinelog, and his home. This was the beginning of the present Bell System in Bay County.

A.J. Gay

He was also a director of the first bank to be established in the new city - the Bank of Panama City, located at First Street (Beach Drive) and Harrison Avenue. A young man was cashier of the bank and was later to marry A.J. Gay's granddaughter, Vesta Gay. The young man was Oscar McKenzie.

In addition to Oscar three other brothers of the McKenzie family moved to the panhandle from Macon county Georgia in 1902: George McKenzie went into real estate; R.L. McKenzie became partners with A.J. Gay in both his real estate and naval stores businesses; and Ed McKenzie opened a general merchandising business in the 200 block of Harrison Avenue.

Among other ventures, Oscar opened the first motion picture theater in Panama City. Unfortunately, the theater burned down on opening night. Mother never forgave Dad for that. She had taken her shoes off and had to exit the theater barefoot. She was very embarrassed.

R.L. McKenzie was Vice President of the Gulf Coast Development Company whose purpose was to buy more land and develop it into a town site and secure more waterfront property for a railroad terminal. In 1906 this purpose was realized when George West and R.L. McKenzie persuaded J.B. Steele of Atlanta to choose the Gulf Coast Development Company's land for the new railroad which would continue south from Dothan with connections to Atlanta. Steele said, "I want this to be Atlanta's outlet to the Panama Canal" which suggested the new city's name.

Both the Gay and the McKenzie families were active in politics. A.J. Gay was Tax Collector for Washington County for a number of years and was instrumental along with R.L. McKenzie in the formation of Bay County.

R.L. McKenzie was elected the first Mayor of Panama city in 1909. George McKenzie followed his brother as Mayor. A.J. Gay was the first Chairman of the City Council and Oscar McKenzie served as Secretary - Treasurer. R.L. McKenzie served two terms in the State Legislature representing Washington County (1909-1913.) L.C. Gay (son of A.J. Gay) served as a Bay County Commissioner from 1913 -1923.

The McKenzie family continued in politics. Andy McKenzie tried to follow in the footsteps of his great great grandfather and ran for Tax Collector of Bay County in 1992. Unfortunately A.J. Gay was the better politician - Andy lost.

188

Submitted by: Robert McKenzie, 105 Camelot Circle, Panama City, FL 32405.

Marjorie Gladys McLawhon

She was born February 5, 1918, the daughter of George W. McLawhon (1875-1930) and Ellen Pearl Jenkins (1892-1974). She had two brothers and two sisters: George Bernard, Frank, Edith Pearl and Dorothy Mildred. George married twice. His first wife was Dorothy Mary Etta Williams. Their children were Ralph Bernard and Dorothy Mary Etta. George married second Audra Juanita Byrd and they had four children: Edith Nanette, George Bernard, Jr., Michael Stephen, and Donald Clair. Frank McLawhon died at the age of 24 months. Dorothy Mildred married Dr. Bernard Claude Kehler and had two sons: Bernard Claude, Jr. and Keith Gordon. Edith Pearl married twice. She married Joseph Harris and had three children: Robert Joseph, Marjorie Lee and Norman Peter "Rocky" Harris. Edith married second George Milward Funk. They had no children.

Margie McLawhon Real

Marjorie's father George was killed in a saw mill accident when she was just a child. He fell from a catwalk into a vat. Later when she was eight years old, she was run over by an automobile in Arcadia, Florida. It was a miracle she survived. People from everywhere sent her cards, toys and flowers.

Marjorie lived in Apalachicola, Florida most of her young life and met and married Nonwell Robbins in Apalachicola. Nonwell was the son of Horatio Bayard Robbins (1878-1928) and Nellie Kate Fry (1883-1935). Nonwell had nine brothers and sisters: Eva Florine, Edwin Noel, Henry Bayard, Mamie Fry, William Marion, Charles Lawton, Annie Kathryn, Minnie Sue and Clifton Weems.

Marjorie and Nonwell married and had identical twin boys born November 28, 1939, Richard Nonwell Robbins and his brother who died at birth. Not long after that, Nonwell went into the service in the Navy. Our country was in World War II.

After the war, Marjorie and Nonwell divorced. Eventually, Marjorie and Richard moved to Panama City, Florida. Richard grew up and married Dorothy Ann Johnson. Marjorie met and married Charles Vincent "Vince" Real Vince worked with dog tracks in different parts of the country, but mostly in Florida. He and Marjorie traveled quite a bit until he retired. Charles Vincent Real was a true Irish gentleman. As the years went by, he lost most of his eyesight but never his memory. He loved sports and could tell you any statistics you wanted to know from memory. Charles Vincent Real died March 21, 1997 in Panama City, Florida.

Marjorie can trace her ancestors back to George McGlohon, father of Jeremiah McGlohon (1818-1894) Ayden, North Carolina. Her great-great-grandfather was Jonathan Jenkins who came from Wales to America before 1800.

Marjorie is called Margie by all her many friends.
Written by: Ann Robbins; Submitted by: Marjorie Real, 335 South Bonita Ave, Panama City, Florida 32401

Angus "Jim" Mcquagge and Gilla Ann McCormick McQuagge
The McQuagge Cigar Factory

Angus "Jim" McQuagge and his wife Gilla Ann McCormick-McQuagge were early residents of Fountain, Florida. Angus Jim was the third generation of earlier

McQuagges who had settled into Northwest Florida. His great-grandfather, Duncan McQuagge (ca. 1765- ?), had migrated from North Carolina down to the Euchee Valley of Walton County, Florida around the year 1821. Angus' grandfather, Daniel A. McQuagge, was a pioneer settler in Marianna, Florida. Angus Jim McQuagge, a true scottish-irish, had a bright red beard and was known as *Red Beard Jim.*

McQuagge Cigar Factory

Angus Jim and Gilla Ann McCormick-McQuagge were born in 1851 and 1860 respectively. They had twelve children: Thadious, James Angus, John Edward, Herbert Gerald, Cassie, Randall Amos, Annie, Beatrice, Daniel, Cora, and two sons who died in infancy. Their children's births ranged from 1878 through 1905. Angus Jim died in 1936, and Gilla Ann died in 1950. Both are buried near Econfina Creek at Brown-McQuagge Cemetery in Northern Bay County.

The McQuagge family owned and operated a store in Fountain, Florida from the late 1920's until around 1950. During the early years of its operation, and due to The Great Depression of the 1930's, business was slow. During this time, two of the children, Beatrice and Cora, went to work in the cigar industry. They had to travel to various places to find work, going as far as Abbeville and Enterprise, in the state of Alabama.

Angus and Gilla Ann McCormick McQuagge, early residents of Fountain, Florida

During this time, the tobacco industry was a booming business in the tri-state area and it didn't take Beatrice and Cora long to learn the art of making cigars by hand. However, working away from home was not agreeable with Beatrice and Cora, so they decided to return home. At home in Fountain, an additional room was added onto the house, which became the McQuagge Cigar Factory. They purchased the tobacco and made each cigar by hand. These homemade cigars were called *Florida Favorites*, and were sold at two for five cents. Beatrice and Cora continued to sell hand-made cigars from home and the family store for many years.

Writen by: Gerry Dale McQuagge; Submitted by: Emory G. McQuagge, 7103 Escambia Ave., Southport, FL 32409.
Credits: William Duncan McQuagge, Calvin Johns Sr., Kinie Johns-Reeder, and Ann Robbins.

Duncan Gillis McQuagge

My grandfather was Duncan Gillis McQuagge. He was born November 25, 1888 in Chipley, Florida in the area known as Orange Hill. He died November 1, 1952 in Panama City, Florida. Duncan married Lulia Dart Barrett on January 17, 1915 in Marianna, Florida. Lulia was the daughter of Manley Barrett and Sarah Myers Barrett. They had three children Inez, Houston Savely, and James Gillis McQuagge.

He was appointed the first Agricultural County Agent of Washington County, Florida in 1915-1916. Duncan moved to Georgia and farmed near Albany, Georgia in the early 1920's. He came back to Florida and Panama City during the Florida Land Boom in the late 1920's to sell real estate.

In 1932 Duncan ran his first campaign for Tax Assessor of Bay County, Florida. His campaign expenses consisted of the cost of twelve cards that were printed plus five dollars worth of gasoline. He would hand a voter the card to read and then ask for it back saying he was running a "depression campaign". The voters were told he would save them their tax money just as he had saved his campaign expenses. Duncan was well known for his style of telling stories. He had a special talent for story telling. He never made serious promises during his campaigns but people knew he was honest and he could tell a good story. The people of Bay County must have loved his stories and the man because he was elected for five consecutive terms.

Duncan Gillis McQuagge

One of Duncan's most famous stories was about being depressed during an election campaign while sitting out on the porch listening to the crickets saying... wayne, wayne, wayne... ... (His opponent was Wayne Lee). Then he heard a bull frog deep in the swamp bellow.... dunk, dunk, dunk. After that he said he knew everything would be alright.

His political philosophy was: "If somebody accuses you of something, admit it. If you don't, they'll prove it on you." He started every new campaign by picking a public argument with the local slum lord and the bolita kingpen so everybody would know that they were not on his side.

Duncan's nickname at the courthouse was King Dunc. Where the big hallways cross on the main floor of the Courthouse, right next to the Coca-Cola machine, that was Dunc's Court. When Dunc went into session, a crowd would gather. Wit and wisdom were dispensed by King Dunc. No matter how blue you felt, no matter how high your troubles had piled, King Dunc would lighten your load. He was the Tax Assessor of Bay County from 1932 to 1952.

Written by: William Duncan McQuagge, P.O. Box 767, Panama City, FL 32402. Sources: Family information "Steel Tanks and Tank Builders" by E. W. Brown, Sr. (husband of his niece Gertrude Blue)

McQuagge Family
Which McQuagge Are You Related To....?

McQuagge or McQuaig is not a common name, except, in Panama City, Florida! When I, Sandra, married William Duncan McQuagge in 1969, and moved back to Florida, he was the only McQuagge I had ever known. He was named for his grandfather, technically speaking. The Grandfather was, Duncan Gillis McQuagge, who had been the Bay County Tax collector in the 1930s. Duncan Gillis McQuagge II, a first cousin, is also named after his grandfather. The confusion of who was named for whom comes from the other side of the family. My mother-in-law's maiden name was Duncan. Her nickname was "Bill". We frequently received calls from people looking for Bill McQuagge. My husband went by his middle name Duncan. But that's not the worst of it.

My father-in-law was Houston Savely McQuagge, a descendent of the Gainers. But I digress. He went by Savely. "Savely" and "Sandy" look very similar when handwritten so mail would often go awry when Duncan and I were first married.

My name is Sandra Lee Ballard McQuagge. This is where the story gets stranger. (Mary) Sandra Hussey McQuaig is married to J. R. McQuagge. Sandi and I both grew up in Gulfport Mississippi, married, and moved to Panama City. We both drove Volkswagen "bugs" and belonged to the Panama City Garden Club. She and her family own "Sandi's Feed and Seed". Her husband and mine grew up within 2 blocks of each other, went to the same schools, etc.. You get the picture. Duncan and his father were in real estate. I am now a reference librarian at the Bay County Public Library.

Stranger still, after Duncan and I divorced, he married (can you guess?) Sandra Leigh McIver. Same first and second names. At one time there were (4) four, totally unrelated, Sandra McQuagges (McQuaig) in Panama City Florida. We are back down to two, as far as I know. Pleeez, don't ask me about the Susan McQuagges. At one time there were 3 of those, two of them related by marriage, one of them Duncan's sister.

I named my daughter after me. I thought I might avoid confusion by spelling her name differently. Wrong. Her name is Sondre Lyn McQuagge now Quigley. She is nicknamed 'Sunny'. We were both students at Florida State University at one time. I think they're still confused in Tallahassee.

I wish I could tell you about the other McQuagges that I am not "related to." At one time in the late 1980's there were four separate clans. I still get calls now and again from people looking for 'their' relatives.
Submitted by: Sandra B. McQuagge, 25 W. Government St., Panama City, FL 32401.

Duncan McQuaig/McQuagge (ca. 1765- ?)

A long time ago, a sea of magnificent evergreen long leaf pines covered the land of Northwest Florida. With their stalwart trunks firmly anchored into the earth, they stood like sentries, towering over the other trees of the forest. Their height seemed to reach into the sky, as they stood strong, refusing to be moved. Between these majestic forests were lush green valleys where the air and water possessed a pristine quality of pureness, for this was a time before industry and pollution. This was the world my ancestors found themselves in.

As words describing the beauty of this land reached settlements in the New World, few would have the courage to leave the safety of their village to become the first pioneers in those primitive woods, which held many dangers. Bears, wild panthers, wolves, and Indians made their homes here. During this time, only a few families dared venture into this untamed land, but later more would come. Most of these early Northwest Florida pioneers were the rugged and self-reliant Scottish-Irish.

Among these early settlers was the family of Duncan McQuaig/McQuagge. Born about 1765 in North Carolina, his family's roots can be traced back to the Isle of Islay in Scotland. One folklore tale passed down from generation to generation about the earliest McQuagges to arrive in the American colonies, tells a story about three Scottish brothers. Legend has it that these three brothers had been detained by the King's guards for killing the King's deer. Customarily, the English did not view the Scottish favorably. They considered all Scots as uncivilized renegades and outlaws, mainly because they would not bow to the King of England. Also, the Scots wanted their own country and no affiliation with the Church of England, for most Scots were of the Presbyterian faith. Considering what the English were doing to the Scots during these difficult times, the McQuaig boys likely considered themselves to only be taking from the rich and giving to the poor. However, this was not their first offense. Previously the King's guards had confiscated their weapons, but being gunsmiths by trade, the boys would return home and fashion new weapons. For their latest trespass, as fate would have it,

McQuagge Gristmill, Fountain, Florida operated from 1890 until late 1940's The McQuagge families of Fountain, Florida were descendants of Duncan McQuagge (ca. 1765-?)

the McQuagge brothers were placed on a prison ship and sent to the furthest outpost of the colonies,—this being the southern colony of North Carolina.

This rings true, for the McQuaig/McQuagge name does not appear on any ship's passenger list of the 1700's. The 1790 census of Richmond County, North Carolina shows Duncan McQuig as over sixteen years of age and with a wife. Other censuses, such as the 1820 census of Conecuh County, Alabama shows him as Duncan McQuaig; then in the 1821 census of West Florida as Duncan McQuagge; and finally in the 1830 Walton County, Florida census as Duncan McQuagg. He obtained a land grant on May 15,1829 in Walton County, as Duncan McQuaig.

Lured farther and farther south, Duncan McQuagge and his family eventually migrated from North Carolina all the way to the Euchee Valley of Northwest Florida around 1821. The Euchee Valley is located forty miles Northwest of Panama City and ten miles southeast of DeFuniak Springs, in Walton County, Florida. Descendants of Duncan McQuagge later settled into Holmes, Washington, Jackson, and Bay Counties. Three of his sons; Daniel A. McQuagge born 1794, Norman McQuagge born 1799, and Samuel McQuagge born ca 1812 had migrated with their parents to the Euchee Valley.

Like many Scottish-Irish settlers in America, the McQuagge pioneers continually placed themselves in the

Annie Finch-McQuagge with her children: (L-R), Eva, John D., Annie, Bessie, & Bertie McQuagge. ca. 1919

forefront of the new frontier. During this time, life was difficult, and people by the thousands were constantly on the move. For some, the desire to make their own way by conquering life's difficulties, along with the fear of wild beasts and Indians, offered a kind of excitement which could not be found in the tameness of life in a city. From North Carolina, they trudged southwest into South Carolina, then to central Georgia, and over into Alabama, finally reaching their destination of Northwest Florida.

Travel was slow, their wagons being pulled by a pair of mules or oxen. These were hardy animals, which were also used to clear and plow the fields. Stopping along the way to make camp for the night, the pioneers could hear the howling of wolves. Bears often attacked their livestock and there was the constant fear of being attacked by Indians. Given the many dangers and obstacles, these first settlers migrated together with other families. This group of families would form the nucleus of a new settlement. The young and ambitious were often drawn to newer settlements. Duncan's son, Daniel A. McQuagge would later become a pioneer settler in Marianna, Florida. Samuel was an early pioneer in Holmes County, but unfortunately was killed in 1858. Also one of Norman's sons, Murdock Gillis McQuagge, became a pioneer settler and sharecropper in the Orange Hill area of Washington County. Descendants of both brothers later settled in the Econfina Creek basin of Bay-Washington County. Their sons and daughters settled in Chipley, Marianna, Fountain, Lynn Haven, Southport, Panama City, Clearwater, in Florida, and in Dothan, Alabama, as well as Wiggins, Mississippi.

The McQuagge pioneers of the 1800's were primarily farmers, and by necessity they made or grew most of what they needed to survive. There was strength in numbers, and as the 1850 census of Washington, Walton, and Jackson Counties reveals these early pioneers had large families. They had to be in order to accomplish the many chores of tending to their farm animals and crops. This usually meant working from sun-up until sun-down.

Along with their fearless spirit of adventure, a strong faith in God was evident among the early pioneers. One of the first structures erected in a new settlement, was the church. Later, as more and more families came to the settlement, the church would serve dually as church and school. These early settlers to Walton County built the first church there, The Euchee Valley Presbyterian Church. Like most pioneers, their faith in God helped them survive through poverty and hardships. They remained optimistic and hopeful. Nothing could hinder their belief that life would eventually get better for all...over the next hill.

Due to the lack of roads, new settlements on the frontier were often near rivers, or other bodies of water, such as bays and bayous. The rivers were the highways of commerce where goods could be transported from one settlement to another. Also, the river's tributaries were often used to power gristmills, which were needed to grind their corn crops into meal. Corn, being the kind of crop which had a multitude of uses for people and animals, and needing little care, was widely grown by the early pioneers of Northwest Florida. One of Norman's sons, John G. McQuagge, built one of the first gristmills in this area, located northwest of Fountain, Florida on Goshen Branch, a tributary of Econfina Creek. John G. McQuagge and his son Steadman operated this gristmill from about 1890 until the late 1940's. Currently, this gristmill is on display at the Junior Museum of Bay County where it was relocated. Duncan McQuagge and his family were among the first pioneer settlers into Northwest Florida. His exact date of death is not recorded, but the 1830 census of Walton County shows him as being in his 60's. Duncan is buried in the Euchee Valley Presbyterian Church Cemetery. According to the 1920 census of Fountain, Florida, direct descendants of Duncan McQuagge comprised nearly 10% of the population of this community. Today, many of his descendants live throughout Bay and the surrounding counties.

As you travel around Northwest Florida, you are likely to meet a descendant of Duncan McQuagge, and if you will take the time to pause and be observant, in some old cemetery, you will also find earlier descendants of these early Florida pioneers.

Submitted by: Gerry Dale McQuagge 1608 Georgia Ave. Lynn Haven, FL. 32444-3753. Written by: Gerry Dale McQuagge.
Credits: Genealogy research provided by William Duncan McQuagge and his father, the late H Savely McQuagge of Panama City, Allene McQuagge Carl of Pensacola, and Patricia Ann Johnson Roberts of Marianna.

D. D. "Jack" Mashburn

My brother Jack was a member of the 1946 Bay High School football team that was undefeated and only two teams scored on them. He later played two years of semi-professional football and two years semi professional baseball. He used his "nub" as an asset when he played ball. (Jack was born with one hand with no fingers). He taught himself typing and uses both hands when he types.

In 1952 Jack was elected to the Florida House of Representatives from Bay County. During the 1953 session, and back then the legislature met only every two years, Bay County was well represented by Jack Mashburn and Ed Stokes.

D.D. "Jack" Mashburn age 24 1952

The following House Bills were some of those that Jack pursued and achieved: House Bill #1147 which authorized the Bay County Commissioners

Jack Mashburn 2003

to provide $15,000 to the Bay County Library for operation, maintenance, construction, establishment and advancement of any library facility in Bay County. This allowed the Bay County Public Library Association to drop the charge of $1.00 for membership cards. This Bill really established a free public library for the first time. House Bill # 1162 which authorized the Bay County Commissioners to provide $4,500 to pay per annum as compensation for a qualified librarian employed by the Bay County Public Library Association. House Bill #1880 which set aside $10,000 each year from gambling taxes including race track funds, for twenty years to allow the Bay County School Board to build the Bay High Stadium. House Bill #651 and 650 which authorized the State of Florida to build the four-lane Hathaway Bridge and the four-lane DuPont Bridge. House Bill # 69 was cosponsored by Jack Mashburn which created the Shands Teaching Hospital in Gainesville, Florida. House Bills # 953, 954, and 955 which created the cities of Panama City Beach, Long Beach Resort and the town of Edgewater Beach. These were the first cities created in Bay County west of the Hathaway Bridge. House Bill # 1641 which helped establish St Andrews State Park as a permanent park for Bay County.

These are some of the many things that Jack has done to help build a better Bay County. Like his father, Mansel Deshong Mashburn, before him, he has left his mark on Bay County. In 1996 he helped lead the fight to create Camp Helen State Park at Phillips Inlet Bridge in West Bay County. Now, Bay County is probably the only county in Florida that has a State Park on each end of a beach.
Submitted by: Velma P. Land, 6741 Campflowers Road, Youngstown, Florida 32466.

The Daniel Mashburn Family
Part I – "The House"

In 1896, before the advent of the airplane, automobile, or TV (at least on a commercial basis), Daniel Mashburn, who was born September 5, 1857, built his first home near his birthplace at Econfina Creek, Florida. The house was erected from the virgin longleaf pine of the Econfina woods. In the early 1900's, the German American Lumber Company cut many trees from the same area. Logs from those never-before-harvested forests found their way down the Econfina River (or Creek) to Bay Head, and ultimately on ships across the Atlantic to Germany and most likely to neighboring European countries.

The Mashburn house originally had two porches - south

The Daniel Mashburn Home c 1972

and west, the latter being the front of the house. A porch in those days was where relatives, neighbors and friends gathered to exchange news, and, no doubt, a little gossip, too. Whenever someone was sitting on a porch, it was always an open invitation for anyone passing to stop by for a friendly chat.

Not long after the house had been built, neighbors and relatives, several of whom played the fiddle or banjo, were asked to gather in the south room for a dance. The young bride, Annie Vickery Mashburn, was reported to have been "very light on her feet," as she danced the popular square dances and reels.

After five children, Daniel and Annie utilized all the rooms (except the kitchen) for sleeping purposes. Originally,

Daniel L. Mashburn

there were no closets - they weren't needed because there wasn't an excess of things or clothes. In those days, their few items of clothing were hung on nails on the walls of this modest home.

Today, one hundred seven years later, the house remains only slightly altered from its original construction – 'heart of pine" ceiling, walls, and floors. There are seven outside doors and thirteen windows. When the house was constructed, there were no interior doorways. Each room had access to one of the porches. Probably in the late 20's, three interior doors were cut.

Before electricity in the area, light in the evenings was at a premium. In the early days, candles were the principal source of light for the Mashburn family. Later, kerosene burning table lamps (with wicks) were used. Finally, Aladdin lanterns that emitted a brilliant light were hung from the 10-foot ceiling. The house moved into the 20th century when the Rural Electric Cooperative came to Bay County in 1948. Electricity allowed for running water and indoor plumbing; in addition, an electric stove replaced the old wood stove with its flue.

Submitted by: Barbara Bishop, 4443 Ashland Rd., Panama City, FL 32405.

The Daniel Mashburn Family
Part II – "Activities Around the Homeplace"

When old enough to assist with a multitude of chores, the Mashburn children (three girls and two boys) were up before daylight, feeding the horses, cows, pigs, and chickens, milking the cows and taking the milk to the cool waters of

Annie E. Vickery Mashburn and children Mamie, Eloise and Wilson c 1906

the spring several hundred feet from the house. There was no idle time; if not attending the log schoolhouse, a couple of miles north of their home, they were in the field with their father, Daniel, hoeing the corn, sweet potatoes, and other food crops for the family. In those days, rice, which is an unusual grain for this area, was grown on a section of the Mashburn property that was quite low and wet. Corn was fed to livestock, and chufas were planted exclusively for the animals.

With the arrival of summer, Annie and her daughters, Mamie, Eloise, and Clara, made many delectable cobblers and jams from the varied and abundant fruits - pears, black-berries, huckleberries, and amazingly disease-free peaches.

In the fall, the family harvested sweet ribbon sugar cane. Chewing pieces of the cane was a treat for the Mashburn children. Most of it was crushed in a cane mill or grinder and the juice boiled in a "sugar kettle" to make delicious cane syrup. The family consumed many light, fluffy buttered biscuits, using them to sop the mouth-watering syrup

Smokehouse at Daniel Mashburn home place c 1970's.

from their plates.

In the cold winter months, Daniel with sons Wilson and Clayton assisting, slaughtered both hogs and cattle. The pork hams, backbones, ribs, and bacon were smoked in the adjacent "smokehouse." Using salt as a preservative, these meats were placed in oak barrels until ready for the family's use.

On warm spring or summer days, it was always possible to get a "mess" of chinquapin bream from Econfina Creek. Fish were also very plentiful in the sand hill ponds. Wild turkey and squirrel were abundant in the woods near the house, and those meats were often found on this pioneer family's table.

Annie made everyone's clothes, stitching by hand with exquisitely tiny stitches. Her sewing scarcely would have been distinguishable from that done on a sewing machine.

Even during July and August when the temperatures often exceeded 90+ degrees, the Mashburn girls pressed the family clothes using flat irons, which had been heated in front of a roaring fire. The family wore these nicely ironed clothes when they attended the Sulphur Springs Methodist Church.

Submitted by: Gwynelle Spell, P.O. Box 18258, Panama City, FL 32417
*Granddaughter of Daniel

The Daniel Mashburn Family
Part III – "Activities Away from Home"

Daniel was often away from Econfina, peddling salt mullet. He purchased the mullet from fishermen in St. Andrew, cleaned it, salted it, packed and loaded it onto his wagon. The fish was peddled to South Georgia and South Alabama. Annie and children might not see him for weeks. The earn-

The Coca Cola Plant, Panama City, early 1900's

ings from the salt mullet "sorties" enabled their family to pay for flour, salt, and other essentials that they purchased from a "rolling store," which periodically came to Econfina.

Barely arriving at adulthood, Wilson and Clayton, the two young men of the family, often endured the rigors of extremely difficult physical labor. Their father had passed away in 1929. They took upon themselves the responsibility of supporting their mother and some of the other siblings.

This was the era of the depression, and few jobs were available. Participating in federal programs, such as CCC (Civilian Conservation Corps) or local government infra-structure projects, the Mashburn brothers were out many frigid mornings before daylight, building roads or bridges or perhaps loading tons of fat lightwood on railcars for the sum of $1.00 per day. Another of their occupations was "dipping" turpentine.

Their maternal uncle, Leland Vickery, founded the Coca Cola Companies in both Quincy and Panama City. As young men, both brothers worked for Coca Cola, Wilson continuing to work there until his death in 1957.

The "rolling store" was also the Mashburn family's source for herbs and extracts — used as medicines or for poultices made to relieve fevers, cramps, croups, and other ailments. Those herbal remedies were sufficient for most illnesses, but were not effective against the terrible flu epidemic of 1918 that took a catastrophic toll worldwide. Every member of Daniel's family came down with the flu, and everyday they heard the wagon hearses go past their home on the way to the cemetery. A young man they knew from the community took care of them all. His good-Samaritan assistance and the mercy of God enabled them to pull through the frightening epidemic.

Wilson Mashburn in Coca Cola uniform in front of homeplace

Submitted by: Sandra Mashburn Tuten, 815 Garden Club Drive, Panama City, FL 32401.

The Daniel Mashburn Family
Part IV – "Clayton at the Homeplace"

When Dan and Annie Mashburn's children were born (all at home), the house was in Washington County. In 1913, when Bay County was formed, the southern part of Washington County became the northern part of newly formed Bay County.

Ultimately, all of the children established homes in Panama City except the youngest, Clayton, who lived his entire life in the Econfina home. There he and his wife, Maxine Whitehurst Mashburn, raised two daughters, Patricia and Sandra.

During the course of Clayton's 83 years, there were many changes in his small world, and many people from the lowly to the esteemed pulled up in front of his home - from oxcart drivers to Panama City businessmen, one of the latter once stopping by with the then governor of the State of Florida, the

Clayton and wife Maxine at The Daniel Mashburn House c. 1942

Honorable Bob Graham (now U.S. Senator). Most of the residents near his home came there on a daily basis in the 1930's when the Daniel Mashburn house served as the U.S. post office for the community of Bennett, Florida. His mother was the postmistress. (Some maps still show the Econfina area as "Bennett.")

With a home that allowed cold winds and humidity to penetrate the walls, unusual weather was not easily forgotten. At one point, in the 30's, ice in a bucket outside the house did not melt for 40 days and nights. Clayton recalled that his father had witnessed a most unusual occurrence (in the 1800's) when he plowed all day in *June* wearing an overcoat.

Clayton was actually an environmentalist before the coining of such a word. He was not a sports hunter or fisherman and only participated in

Annie Mashburn and children; Mamie, Wilson, Eloise, Clara and Clayton c. 1942

those activities to furnish fresh food for his family. He was concerned about the diminishing of any given animal species. Whether because of spearfishing or other methods of fishing, sturgeon became very rare if not extinct in Econfina Creek. These gigantic fish, which were one-third to one-half the length of a truck, were commonly seen in the 1950's.

In approximately the late 1930's or early 1940's, the federal government indiscriminately sprayed the chemical DDT over local rural forest areas. This action almost decimated the buzzard or vulture population. DDT was also sprayed inside many homes. (The home in Econfina was one of them.)

Not all changes were detrimental. In the 1960's, where for 100 years or more cattle had grazed free-range, a paved road connected the Econfina area to Youngstown, the pavement beginning scarcely one-half mile from the old Econfina home. And, in May of 1962, the Mashburns at Econfina were able to connect with the outside world when telephone lines were brought to that part of Bay County. From that time on until Clayton's death 33 years later, the era of the 'pioneer" ebbed away and with it the lifestyle his father, Daniel, had known.

Submitted by: Patricia Mashburn Meredith, 13646 Mashburn Road, Youngstown, FL 32466.

James Mannon Mashburn and Clara Rebecca Sealey

James Mannon Mashburn was born January 1821 in Decatur County, Georgia. He was the son of Daniel and Elizabeth Mashburn. In 1839 in the area of Quincy, Florida James married Clara Rebecca (Annie) Sealey. Clara was born Feb 8, 1823 near Quincy, Florida. Their first child Richard Byrd Mashburn was born January 28, 1842 in Gasden County, Florida. October 20, 1843, Sara Joyce (Sally) Mashburn was born. Stephen Edward Mashburn was born May 11, 1845. January 11, 1847, Mary Ann Mashburn was born. The last child born in Gasden County was Elisabeth Jane Mashburn born April 21, 1849. James and Clara then moved with their five children to Econfina, Washington County, Florida where their daughter Missouri Mashburn was born August 6, 1851. Four more children would be born in Econfina, James Mannon Mashburn, II born May 21, 1853, Charles Monroe Mashburn born June 13, 1855, Daniel Layfayette Mashburn born September 5, 1857 and Louisana Frances Mashburn born August 28, 1859.

Richard Byrd Mashburn 1927, Confederate Soldier son of James Mashburn

James Mannon Mashburn had settled on 200 acres of rich farm land and on that land with the help of his children and slaves, he raised large crops of tobacco, corn and cotton. He transported these crops by wagon down to the Cedar Creek and Bear Creek Landings where they were shipped to ports along the Gulf Coast.

James Mannon Mashburn died March 1859 at the age of 38 years. It was said that he died from a stroke while roofing a house. He was buried on his plantation in the Mashburn Cemetery off Mashburn Road. James Mannon Mashburn is the first person to be buried in the Mashburn Cemetery which is on the Econfina Creek near Bennett, Florida.

James' death left Clara alone with nine children and she was six months pregnant with their last child Louisana Frances Mashburn.

Richard Byrd (Dick) Mashburn married Roxie Ann Nixon. He was a Confederate soldier in the Civil War. He joined the

Confederacy in Apalachicola, Florida. Richard was in the Confederate Army under General Johnson who had positioned troops near Dallas, Georgia to impede General Sherman's march to Atlanta. General Sherman's troops overran General Johnson's position and Richard was captured on May 28, 1864. He was a prisoner of war at Rock Island Prison Camp, Rock Island, Illinois. He was released May 28, 1865, one year from the day he was captured, and walked most of the way home. May 28, 1866 was the day he finally arrived home, it had taken a year. The Mashburn family celebrates his return home with an annual Mashburn Reunion. This Reunion is one of the oldest continuous reunions in the United States. May 24, 2003 marked the 138th continuous family Mashburn Reunion. Richard died March 15, 1928.

Sara Joyce (Sally) Mashburn married Henry Loftin Porter. Sara died November 18, 1910.

Stephen Edward (Ed) Mashburn married on November 26, 1863 Eliza Ellen Porter. Eliza was born 1840 and died 1918. She was the daughter of Colonel William Loftin Porter. Stephen was a Union soldier in the Civil War. Some say he was opposed to slavery and others say he was just a confused 18 year old teenager. Whatever the reason, he slipped off to Bay Head, a few miles down the creek. He borrowed a small boat and rowed around St Andrews Bay to Hurricane Island, which was the headquarters of the Yankees. He waved a white flag, then they took him to Key West where he joined and served with the 2nd Calvary of the Union Army from Florida. When he first returned home after the end of the war only his mother would speak to him. After about a year, other family members finally accepted him back into the family. Stephen died June 9, 1925.

Mary Ann Mashburn married Walter R. Gainer in 1882. Mary Ann died December 15, 1912.

Elisabeth Jane (Lizzie) Mashburn married on January 29, 1867 Joseph Martin Porter. Elisabeth died March 31, 1916.

Missouri Mashburn married Jessie Lassiter. Missouri died November 5, 1891.

James Mannon Mashburn, II married Sarah Mathilda (Tillie) Vickery. James died July 25, 1883.

Charles Monroe (Charlie) Mashburn married on May 5, 1878 to Eliza Snead Folkes. Charles died December 13, 1942.

Daniel Layfayette (Dan) Mashburn married May 1899 to Anna Eliza (Annie) Vickery. Daniel died August 3, 1929.

Louisana Frances (Lou) Mashburn married Samuel Burris Cox. Louisana died June 18, 1930.

Clara Rebecca Sealey Mashburn managed to carry on after her husband's untimely death at such a young age. Raising her large family, worrying through the war, torn with the emotions of having sons fighting on opposite sides of the war, making do with a blockade that kept supplies low and made such a hardship for the people of the South. She was truly a pioneer. She died in 1900 and is buried in the Mashburn Cemetery.

Submitted by: Jack Mashburn, 6741 Campflowers Rd., Youngstown, FL 32466.

Mansel DeShong Mashburn

At the time Mr. Mansel Deshong Mashburn married my mother, Lillie Seay Land, I was about six years old. This was in 1927 and my mother, my younger brother, Milton Gavin Land, and I moved from my Grandfather William Seay's home in Jackson County, near Alford, Florida to Mr. Mashburn's farm on Camp Flowers Road near Youngstown, Florida. My father George Land had died from pneumonia sometime earlier.

On April 21st in 1928, it was a clear beautiful Saturday morning with a gentle breeze blowing in the trees. The birds were singing and my mother was out sweeping yards. Yes, sweeping the yards. This was done with a "yard broom" made from several low bush gallberry bushes

Jack Mashburn age 74 my brother

bound tightly together with twine. The leaves were picked off by hand and this made a very effective "yard broom." The reason everyone who lived in the country kept the yards swept clean of grass was twofold, one was when the woods caught on fire as it did from time to time, if you had grass in the yard, the fire could burn up under your home and set it on fire. And two, my mother was afraid of two kinds of snakes; live ones and dead ones. So, our yard was never allowed to have one blade of grass grow in it. The yard was swept clean every day so my mother could tell if a snake had crawled across the sand. She would hunt it down and dispose of it.

It was about 8 a.m. and my mother stopped sweeping the yard, sat on the porch and called me to go fetch Mr. Mashburn from the field, that it was time for the baby to be born. I found Mr. Mashburn plowing in the field, he stopped, came to the house and talked with my mother and then put a saddle on the horse and rode as fast as the horse could run to Bayhead, Florida, about four miles from our house, to the Cummings home. They had the only telephone in all of north Bay County. He called Dr. Whitfield and asked him to come as quickly as possible. It took Dr. Whitfield about an hour to drive from Panama City to Camp Flowers Road. That may be partly because of the road conditions and partly because Dr. Whitfield was having a "toddy" along the way. He arrived about 10 a.m. and shortly thereafter the baby was born.

Mansel DeShong Mashburn 80 years old about 1950

The baby was named Dempsey D. Mashburn, much later he was given the nickname of 'Jack', which has stuck with him all his life. How he got the nickname is another story which I will get to later. After the doctor left, a Negro lady who was helping with the housework, noticed the umbilical cord was not tied tight enough, so she retied it and saved my brother's life. He would have bled to death.

When I was allowed to see the new baby, I noticed there was something unique about the right hand, there were no fingers, only part of the hand, and a wrist. Three years later another brother was born, Donald Hayward Mashburn, but he had all his fingers on both hands. Even as a child and young boy, Jack never let his shortage of fingers bother him, or stop him from doing anything he wanted to do. He never believed he was handicapped and he never has been. When he was assigned work on the farm, like picking peas or peanuts, he picked as many as anyone else. He made a point not to be outdone. Mr. Mashburn told him that his was a birth asset and that a handicap is what you put in your head, to never put that in your head.

Now about the nickname "Jack". There are two schools of thought as to how he came by the name. One, is that Mr. Mashburn admired the boxer Jack Dempsey, so the name Dempsey and later added the "Jack" to it. But, a more likely story is that at the time of his birth Mr. Mashburn had an old mule that was certified as the most stubborn mule in all of Florida and Jack was said to be even more stubborn than the mule.

Submitted by: Zane L. Gorsline, 6741–B Campflowers Rd., Youngstown, FL 32466.: Written by: Velma P. Land, 6741 Camp Flowers Road, Youngstown, Florida 32466.

Mansel Deshong Mashburn 1869-1954

My father Mansel Deshong Mashburn, "Uncle Manse" as he was known to all his friends, was born February 2, 1869 in Bay County, Florida. The place of his birth was north of "Cherokee" Landing and south of County Road 2301 near Canada Landing on Bear Creek. He was the son of Stephen Edward (Ed) Mashburn 1845-1925 and Eliza Ellen Porter 1840-1918.

Mansel was married twice. His first wife was Alice Savannah Strickland Mashburn. They had five children, Mansel Malone Mashburn born August 8, 1901, Minnie Alice Mashburn born January 9, 1904, Mary Ellen Mashburn born February 19, 1906, Ara Lee Mashburn born August 24, 1908, and Eva Rebecca Mashburn born November 11, 1912. Mansel's second wife was Lillie Seay Land Mashburn. They had two children, D. D. (Jack) Mashburn and Donald Hayward Mashburn. Lillie had two children from a previous marriage that Mansel raised, Velma Pauline Land and Milton Gavin Land.

Mansel Dahong Mashburn Age 24, 1843

I tell everyone that I picked the right father, he was 59 when I was born and 62 when my younger brother was born. My mother said, if she had not cut him off, the yard would have been full. My mother was 29 years younger than my dad. I thought the yard was full, but we had 40 acres.

My father helped build Bay County. He worked on building the first railroad to Bay County. In 1913 when Bay County was created, every able-bodied man had to work building county roads one day a month. If you had money, you could hire someone for 50 cents a day to work for you. To save 50 cents, he worked.

Prior to 1900, my father hauled oysters in the winter, salt mullet at other times, from St. Andrews to Marianna. This was in a "covered" wagon with a Bow-Frame on top. It was a two day trip. He would make it to "Sweetwater" Branch, about 28 miles north of Panama City. The common campground was just south of the railroad overpass in Fountain. Everyone going to Marianna and everyone coming from Jackson County to St. Andrews would camp there, for it was about halfway. The next morning he would leave early and get to Marianna before sundown. He would set up on the grounds at the court house so everyone would know he was in town.

On one winter trip with a load of oysters, it was really cold. He slept in a hammock that he had sewn in the top of the Bow-Frame. When he awoke the next morning, all the oysters were frozen solid. But he was warm as a bug in a rug. (His words).

My father worked at many things during his life. For a period of time he dove for sponges with the Greeks in Tarpon Springs, Florida. For several years he worked as a commercial fisherman. During most of the time he served as cook and one particular time near Carrabelle, they struck their nets around a large school of mullet. While the rest of the crew was pulling the net ashore with all the mullet it could hold, he took several mullet and was cleaning them at the edge of the water. He was almost finished when he looked out over the water and near the shore saw a dorsal fin sticking out of the water headed straight for him. He jumped to

one side just as a large shark drove itself out of the water onto the shore. The shark had followed the blood and scent of the fish to its source. The shark was completely out of the water and my father without hesitation jumped on top of the shark and

M.D. Mashburn family July 4, 1912

stabbed it to death with the butcher knife he had used cleaning the fish. When he cut open the shark it was full of mullet.

In 1896, he was appointed postmaster at Bayhead (now head of Deer Point Lake), Florida. He remained postmaster for six years. During that time he would be up before daylight and row his boat to Lynn Haven, Florida to pick up the mail. And then row his boat back and open the post office at Bayhead.

In 1902 he homesteaded the 40 acres my sister and I currently live on. He was a farmer, rancher, and fruit grower all of my life. My father's goal was to have fruit that ripened each season of the year. And we did, peaches, pears, plums, grapes, satsumas and then Japanese Persimmons in the Fall.

One of his favorite times was in the Spring when we would saddle up the horses and go to the woods to round up his wild cattle. We would bring them in, especially the cows with young calves and mark the calves in each ear. We would let the cows out in the morning and they would come back in the late afternoon because we kept the calves penned up. When we milked the cows, it would take several to get one gallon of milk, until we got them fattened up on pea-vine hay. One of my favorite memories was churning the milk to make homemade butter.

During the Second World War we grew a lot of sugarcane and made gallons of the best syrup in the world. We would cook one batch of cane juice into cane sugar and bleach it in the sun. Sugar was rationed, but we did not have to buy any. My father would only grow "Blue Ribbon" sugarcane. And to this day, nothing can match the taste of Blue Ribbon Cane Syrup.

Mansel Deshong Mashburn died in 1954. Mansel Malone Mashburn was Bay County School Superintendent 1940 and a retired principal. Minnie Alice Mashburn Cavanaugh is a housewife and mother. Mary Ellen Mashburn was a physical therapist and a retired Army Major. Ara Lee Mashburn taught school 19 years and was a registered nurse until retirement. Eva Rebecca Mashburn was a registered nurse for 43 years. Velma Pauline Land is still living in 2003 at the age of 81 years. Milton Gavin Land served in the U. S. Navy in World War II. D. D. (Jack) Mashburn was elected to the Florida Legislature in 1952 and is still living 2003. Donald Hayward Mashburn died at the age of 63, the only one who smoked.

Submitted by: Jack Mashburn, 6741 Campflowers Rd., Youngstown, FL 32466.

Annie Mae (Dykes) Masker

Annie Mae (Dykes) Masker was the youngest daughter of John Henry and Sarah Alice (Mims) Dykes, born August 25, 1900, in Millville, FL. John Henry worked at sawmills in many places. Millville, St. Andrews, Fountain, West Bay, Southport, or anywhere he could find work. I remember my mother telling me one time about her family moving back from up around Chipley, FL. They had ridden the train part of the way and the rest by wagon. They were running short of food, so Uncle Bill, the oldest boy went out hunting and killed some crows and grandma made some crow and dumpling soup.

Annie Mae went to the old school in St. Andrews located

Annie Mae (Dykes) Masker 1954

at 15th Street and Beck Avenue. She took a business course at Mrs. Monroe's Business College on Magnolia Avenue in Panama City. She went to work at Ware's Mercantile Store in St. Andrews where the St. Andrews Seafood Restaurant is located. She rented a room from Mrs. Comstock at the "Villa" (located on the hill at 14th St and Deer Ave. on the bay where Dr. Tim Smith's residence is located today).

Annie Mae met and married Tom W. Masker in 1920. They had two daughters, Sarah Mae and Lillian. Annie Mae went to work for her sister, Mattie Campbell in the early 1930s-across the street from the St. Andrews Grammar School. It was a service station, grocery store and restaurant. From there, Aunt Mattie built Mattie's Tavern in 1936 located on the corner of Beck Avenue and 12th Ct.-next door to West's Printing Press, also the Three Sons Drive Inn on the corner of 12th St. and Beck Avenue where Hunt's Oyster Bar is now. The Tavern, Carson's Tavern and Rose's Tavern were the only eating places in St. Andrews. I remember when Clark Gable was stationed at Tyndall Field, I was living at the Tavern at the time and he and some more officers came in one night to eat. He was the first movie star we all had ever seen.

Aunt Mattie sold the Tavern to Mr. Byrd and later built Daisy Lee's Restaurant in Panama City on Mulberry St. and 5th St. Annie Mae went to work there as manager until Mattie sold the restaurant. She continued to work for Mattie as bookkeeper for her dress shop and the St. Andrews Florist Shop. She also worked for Stedman Hobbs who owned the Panama Transit Company. She retired at 62 but later worked another three years as manager of the St. Andrews Bay Yacht Club and again retired. She had no greater love than that of her family to include four grandchildren and six great-grandchildren, as well as the members of her church family at St. Andrews Baptist Church. She thanked her Lord every day for the blessings he bestowed upon her. She died in 1994 at the ripe old age of 94. She is loved and missed by all.

Submitted by: Lillian M. Welch (Daughter), 3101 W. 20th Ct, Panama City, FL 32405. Written by: Lillian M. Welch.

Thomas Wesley Masker

My father, Thomas Wesley Masker was born Feb 10, 1882, in Peoria, IL. His parents

Tom Masker, 1940

Jonathan and Anna Calvert Masker owned a Soap Company in Peoria. Jonathan was killed in a Train wreck in Newcastle, Colorado, in 1897. My grandmother sold the Soap Company and divided the money among their six children and herself. My father and Uncle Ed Masker came to St. Andrews in 1910. They came by train to Mobile and then by steamboat—probably the Tarpon. They each had a boat built—Dad's was the "Lu Lu", and Uncle Ed's was the "Sharpshooter". They would take excursions out and around the bayous and bay. Uncle Ed went into photography, and Dad ran the boats. He also worked as a taxi driver and even bootlegged a little whiskey at times. He and my mother (Annie Mae Dykes) were married in Dothan, AL, in 1920. They had

196

my sister (1922) and I (1925). When I was about four, we lived at Crystal Lake, north of Southport on Hwy 77. My Dad ran the commissary-at that time there was the big Seminole Plantation. The commissary was on the left (west) side of the road and there were a number of little houses that the workers lived in on the right (east) side. There was also a school where my sister attended her first year. The railroad ran nearby to transport the fruit that was picked until the big freeze came and killed most of the fruit trees-they say there are still some blueberry bushes there. We later lived on the corner of 15th Street and Cincinnati Avenue in St. Andrews. Dad was a night watchman at Tarpon Docks before he retired. He would take my sister and I down to the Oaks Dock at the West end of 23rd St. and at the Villa Dock to swim. We learned how to swim when we were very young. My Dad died in October 1953.

Submitted by: Sarah A. (Welch) Hamm, 1903 Connecticut Ave., Lynn Haven, FL 32444; Written by: Lillian M. Welch.

The Maxwell House: Still Standing firm

Our history in Bay County is very short compared to most; however, it is no less important to me. I was born in 1960 to Samuel and Louise Maxwell. I was the 4th son and the last child. Having been born and raised in Davidson

Don Maxwell

County Tennessee my family vacationed in Panama City Beach every summer. As early as I can recall we always spent our vacations here. Panama City Beach was like a second home. Coming back each year was like viewing the growth and changes of home.

I became ill in 1988 and suffered from numerous bouts of bronchitis. Having to go on several medications to simply be able to breath. In the spring of 1989 my parents and I came down to spend a week. Upon arriving my health seemed to improve with my breathing becoming easier. It was a wonderful feeling.

Upon arriving back to Tennessee I inquired about feeling better while in Panama City Beach, FL and my doctor explained that the reason I was feeling better was that all of my treatments had been saltwater based and that living in Tennessee was the worst place for me.

Attempting to spend one more year in Tennessee only proved that I'd continue to fight with bronchitis and deal with breathing medications. Therefore in the Summer of 1990 we came down on vacation as usual; however, it wasn't the usual vacation. I decided I wanted to move and live here. With my dad having retired from work a year prior we moved on a trial basis. But, by October I had a full time teaching position and by November I had purchased a home. Things were working out better than expected and the move was becoming a permanent situation.

We've now lived here for several years and it's almost impossible to think that we've lived any where else. I worked for several years in the Bay County Schools as a teacher until I was forced into retirement after being injured in an accident. My parents and I have found a church family at the Beach Church of Christ and feel so blessed to have them as family.

Currently we are building a new home in the Colony Club area directly across from the entrance to the Holiday Golf Club. This is our dream home and for it to be located in the city in which we love it feeling more like a Paradise on Earth. This is where we want to stay for the remainder of our lives until that time that God calls us to spend our eternity in Heaven with Him.

So, with our belief in God, our church family and now

our dream home we are set! God has been so wonderful and awesome to bless us so much.

Submitted by: Don Maxwell, 137 Sandollar Dr., Panama City Beach, FL 32408.

The Maxwell House

The Maxwell House was established on April 2, 1949. That was when 18 year old Samuel Maxwell married 16 year old Louise McClard in Franklin, Kentucky despite the almost comical series of events that almost caused the marriage not to take place. It

Samuel and Louise Maxwell

wasn't a big production of a wedding. Just a simple exchanging of vows at the Justice of the Peace's office. Samuel borrowed his brothers new car to make the ride to the Court House a bit more special. With everything looking good they, Samuel, Louise, Louise's Mother and Step-father, headed out for the Court House. But, as luck would have it the car broke down on the way. Things weren't looking good. Eventually they made it as they had planned to marry at the Court House in Nashville, TN where the two of them lived with their families; however, upon arriving at the Court House they discovered they hadn't obtained license they needed for the required three day waiting period. It was then that they asked if there was anything they could do since they had obtained the blood work the necessary 3 days ahead. The judge told them the only way the could marry was if Louise was expecting. With a resounding, "NO!" to that question Louise's mother chimes in saying, "She isn't, But, I am!" The judge just laughed and said, "I'm sorry. But, that won't help." Following was the disappointing ride back home where Samuel's mother laughed and said, "I guess you won't be getting married after all today." He then looked at his mother and said, "I'll be getting married today no matter what! Even if we have to go to Kalamazoo!" Now, the question was, How do we get there? Samuel called Clyde Exum asking he and his wife to drive them to Kentucky. Clyde agreed. He and his wife Josephine were heading to Kentucky for a wedding! With all the problems behind them they were married later that afternoon. Arriving back home to a wonderful dinner that Samuel's mother had prepared.

Samuel and Louise lived in the Nashville area having 4 boys. Samuel Yancey, Jr. born 1 year and 11 days after their wedding (died when he was 6), Tommy Vance born 3/52 (died in 2/95), Robert Wayne born 7/54 and William Donald born 10/60. Samuel provided for his family by working as a local Truck Driver for 39 years. Louise worked as a homemaker ensuring that her families needs were met. Every summer the family took a vacation. And every summer this vacation brought them to Panama City Beach, Florida.

Samuel was forced to retire from work after a back injury in 1989. It was after their youngest son, Don became ill with upper respiratory problems and talked of moving to Bay County that Samuel and Louise decided that was a great idea. Why not live where we wanted to spend our summers? That's when they moved and became a real part of Bay County, FL.

Submitted by: Samuel and Louise Maxwell, 137 Sandollar Dr., Panama City, FL 32408.

The Mayers Family and the Bay Hotel

Melvin Mayers was born August 1, 1871 in South Carolina. Prior to 1894 he moved to Moultrie, Georgia. A printer by trade he was co-owner of the Moultrie Observer in 1894-95. Sarah Idella Veal was born February 25, 1875 in the Pelham, Georgia area. She was living with her parents, Louis Napoleon and Annie Jane Lewis Veal when she met and married Melvin on April 26, 1896.

Left-Right: "Bill", Idella Mayers, Lois Era, Frances and "Jacque" Eighty-ninth Birthday

While residing in Moultrie, five of their daughters were born. Era Annie Mayers Krick was born on December 4, 1897. Era died November 19, 1970 and is buried in Pensacola, Florida. Willie Ella "Bill" Mayers Smith was born August 4, 1899. Bill died November 3, 1981 and is buried in Baxley, Georgia. Mary Dell Mayers was born September 22, 1902 and died of diptheria October 3, 1905 and is buried in Moultrie. Bessie Addie "Jacque" Mayers Godfrey was born July 18, 1906 and died February 17, 1991. She is buried in Greenwood Cemetery, Panama City. Minnie Lois Mayers Mobley was born July 18, 1909 and passed away September 6, 1983 and is buried in Evergreen Cemetery, Panama City.

The family resided in Moultrie until around 1910 when they moved to Camp Walton, which is now called Fort Walton Beach, Florida. There they managed a hotel located on Santa Rosa Sound for Idella's brother.

Melvin made a trip to Panama City to investigate the possibility of purchasing the Bay Hotel. The Mayers purchased the Hotel and moved by boat, "The Swan",

Bay Hotel, 1950

in December of 1913. On June 25, 1914 the Mayers had their sixth daughter, Frances Lee Mayers Nelson. Frances passed away May 19, 1996 and is buried in Evergreen Cemetery, Panama City.

The Hotel was a boarding house where meals were served. It was a favorite place for fishermen to stay while fishing from the party boats that left from the city dock. Many single and married people, who were employed by Southern Bell, International Paper or Gulf Power boarded there.

Melvin passed away March 7, 1940 at the age of 68. Idella continued to operate the Hotel until May of 1965 at which time she leased it. She died August 28, 1965 at the age of 90. Both are buried in Evergreen Cemetery, Panama City.

There are articles about the Bay Hotel and the Mayers family in the Panama City News Herald dated March 17, 1977, October 16, 1982 and July 18, 1999. These articles give more history of the family and the Hotel.

The descendants of the Mayers family placed a marker at the corner of Park Street and West Beach Drive, the site where the Hotel was located.

Submitted by: Jane Godfrey Becker, 2314 Oakwood Street, Panama City, Florida 32408.

Dolores Gilbert Mefford

I am the fourth child of my parents Bertha & Willis Gilbert. Dad was retired military and mother a housewife. We were living near Ft. Knox, Kentucky when dad saw an advertisement for some property for sale for $10.00 down and $ 10.00 a month in northern Bay County, Fl. He decided to move the family. It was like moving back in time. We had never seen oxen pulling carts or farm animals roaming free.

Dad entered a VA program for veterans to raise chickens. We lived in the old McQuagge homestead, which we rented from Ms Cora McQuagge who was also the postmistress for the Fountain post office. This house was across the road from the property dad had purchased from Owen Wood. We lived there until he built us a house on our land.

We had almost no money and Christmas was approaching. Dad received his retirement check the first of each month and that went for food, chicken feed, and building materials. Dad and mother went to the Salvation Army to ask for gifts for us four children. My sister Ellen and I went out in the woods and cut a small pine tree and we used Christmas cards to decorate it. Mom kept telling us not to expect Santa to stop as we had no money. When we got up Christmas morning, under our crude little tree was a large array of gifts for all of us children and food for our special dinner.

I had always wanted a doll buggy and real dishes for my sister and I to put in our playhouse. We were so excited that Santa had brought us just what we ask for. My sister and I took a rake and made a floor plan out of pine straw. It was a glorious day and many happy hours were spent with our baby dolls, baby buggy, and real dishes. It was the best Christmas of my life and has always stood out in my memories.

After the Korean War broke out, Dad felt the call to serve our great county again, so we packed up and moved to Fort Smith, Arkansas. Living on Owenwood Road in northern Bay County always stood out as the best years of our lives.
Submitted By: Dolores Gilbert Mefford, P.O. Box 59625, Panama City, FL 32402..

Marilyn Virginia Siford-Broom-Middleton

Once upon a time there was a bootlegger who ran booze from one end of Florida to the Keys. He fell in love with a beautiful young woman named, Oddie, and they were married December 22, 1927. This love brought forth a little girl who became the apple of their eyes. Oddie made little dresses with lots of lace and embroidery for this little girl and crocheted her a little coat. This child was a joy to John and Oddie.

Two years later they added Jimmie to their family.

Their happiness was short lived. On March 4, 1930, the little girl was left in the care of Teddy, one of John's employees, while he and Oddie went for groceries. When they returned, the still had been raided by Federal men, and John was arrested. The little girl was taken into custody and placed in an orphanage. Oddie did not see her little girl's picture in the local newspaper with the caption, "WHO AM I?"

Virginia Broom Middleton

Oddie packed the pretty little clothes she had made except one yellow dress, and took them to a Social Worker to take to their little girl. The Social Worker assured her that their daughter would be returned.

Oddie and her mother, Lena, went about the task of collecting $200.00 owed to John to get his release from jail. Oddie and Lena then went to get this child only to be told that she had been adopted and was no longer in the orphanage.

John and Oddie, heartbroken, left Jacksonville and moved to Sarasota. John took up his old trade as carpenter but still maintained a still to provide for his increasing family. One son died at birth in 1930 and another died 18 months later. On December 13, 1932, Oddie gave birth to identical twins, Mac and Price. Twin girls, Jean and Joan, were born on July 18, 1939. But John passed away two years later.

In the meantime, there were Mayoma and Velma Broom in Chipley, Florida with their son, Fulton. Fulton got an envelope in church to be filled and sent to the orphanage. He went about the neighborhood collecting money and advising all the neighbors he was going to buy himself a "little sister:'

Mayoma and Velma, after hearing this story, adopted a little two year old girl. They loved her as their very own. She grew up, in Panama City, knowing she was adopted but her Mother assured her she was a "Special Child" because they picked her out. She always knew that because of her December birthday during the Christmas season, her birth mother was thinking of her.

In 1982, the little girl, now an aging woman, lost the Mayoma mother who loved and cared for her as only a mother could. Before she died, she suggested she might want to locate her birth Mother.

At Social Security age, this woman contacted the orphanage to secure a birth certificate. She was given the name of her parents, Oddie Johnston and John Owen Siford, with the birth date and place.

In January, 1990, she went about the job of locating her birth mother. With the help of Molly from "Orphan Voyage," she located in Jacksonville a half-brother, Leland and a half-sister, Helen, who were her father's children by a previous marriage. They said that John was dead and Oddie died in 1963 at the age of 59 in Sarasota. And that Oddie never stopped looking for her.

On September 19, 1990, she spoke with Owen, a half-brother 2 years older than she. There was an immediate love and warmth over the phone. Yes, he thought about the little girl and wondered if she had a good home. She spoke with Joan in Kissimee, Florida and Jean in Akron, Ohio. Her brother, Jimmie, had passed away 6 months before in Johnson City, Tennessee, only 100 miles from where she is living. His daughter, Debra, lives in Asheville, 20 miles away. She learned that Mac died in 1980, but she has not been able to locate the other twin, Price.

On October 19, 1990, the little girl was united with Jean and Joan in Hendersonville, North Carolina. It was as if they had never been apart. They laughed, cried and loved as little girls again. They roamed the streets and shops of this mountain town exclaiming to everyone, "We are sisters!" They played with the dolls on display, with toys at the Farmers Market and ate chocolates at the candy shop. The twins sang,"Poor Babes in the Woods" to the now silver-haired little girl. They said Oddie sang it to them when they were little girls and told me it was their sister's favorite. At the end of 4 days, the little girl knew this was only the beginning of a sister love which she had never experienced before.

In that year of 1990, God put his hand on this little girl, Marilyn Virginia Siford-Broom-Middleton and gave her the blessing of a new-found family.

Jean, Joan, and I flew to California the following January to meet Clara and Sweet Josephine, half-sisters. All of Oddie and John's children had a reunion the following July in Sarasota.

How Oddie and John would love to know their little girl's daughter, Georgia, had twins! And that their little girl's other children, Mark and Cindy, had produced offspring with their very own genes.

Yes, Mother Mayoma, you were right. I am a Special Child.
Submitted by: Mrs. Bill (Virginia) Middleton, Rt. 23, Box 1459, Lake City, FL 32025.

Buress Moates

The following story of the Associated Press, appeared in the Panama City News Herald, Friday September 1, 1944 with the following headline "General Aides St. Andrew Man in Fixing Line". A brigadier general assisted Corporal Buress Moates, St. Andrew, artillery man of the 34th "Red

Bull" division, as the latter repaired a break in communication wire recently on the Fifth Army front in Italy. The Florida soldier had proceeded along the sun-baked road for several miles, tracing the line, when a jeep stopped by him. A little man with a shiny silver star on his helmet stepped briskly out of the vehicle. "What are you doing?" the general asked. Repairing the line, Sir. "Well, lets get at it", said the general in a friendly manner, and he took the field phone from Moates and checked various lines. "Where are you from?" queried the general. And when Moates told him he was from Florida, the general asked, "How did you get in my Yankee outfit?" "It sho wasn't my fault," replied the Corporal. Moates wife, Mrs. Beatrice Moates, resides with their two years old daughter at St. Andrew. His father, Grover C. Moates, also lives in St. Andrew.

Buress Moates, Red Bull Division, 5th Army World War II Europe

Another newspaper story, by the Associated Press, appeared in the Panama City News Herald, Sunday, October 15, 1944. The headline read "Corp. Moates Takes Part in P.O. Offensive. Serves with First American Unit to Fire on Nazis". Corporal Buress Moates of St. Andrew, Wire Corporal, serving with the 175th Field Artillery Battalion, "Red Bull" division, the first American unit to fire its howitzers on the Nazis in this war, is now participating in the Fifth Army offensive driving towards the P. O.

Beatrice Moates and baby daughter Annette Moates

River in Italy. The distinguished battalion of which he is a member, has been in action on the Italian front since landing at Salerno over a year ago. Facing its third rainy winter in combat, the 175 is now engaged in the difficult drive forcing the enemy into Northern Italy.

Buress was drafted in 1941, soon after he married Beatrice Findley in St. Andrews, and shipped overseas with his unit in May 1942. His daughter Annette, was born in June 1942. Buress was promoted to T5 Sergeant and served until July 1945 when he returned home to St. Andrews, where he met his daughter for the first time. Their son Grover born 1947. Grover was named after Buress' father, Grover Cleveland Moates, and his friend, Eugene, who was killed during the war. Grover and Annette attended

Grover E. Moates, son of Buress Moates, U.S. Navy

St. Andrews Grammar School as did Buress and Beatrice earlier. Buress worked for the Coca Cola Bottling Company in Panama City for many years. He died September 4, 1984 and rests beside his father in the Greenwood Cemetery in Panama City.
Submitted by: Grover Eugene Moates, 6295 Frank Reeder Road,

Pensacola, Florida 32526; Written by: Beatrice Findley Moates, 764 Roland Road, Chipley, Florida 32428. Sources: Panama City News Herald, Personal Knowledge.

Grover Eugene Moates

Grover Eugene Moates (Gene) was born at Lisenby Hospital. Gene is the great great great grandson of A.E. Hood (Elzy) pioneer settlers to Washington Co. A.E. and Lillie Tindell Hood moved to Washington Co. in the late 1800 years. His great grandmother, Mamie Lee Hood was born in Washington Co. Fl. Gene is the grandson of Fern and Eric Lee Forbes and great grandson of Clarence Forbes. Genes' great great great granparents James M.and Ruth Ann Dew Moates lived in Washington Co.in 1800. Part of Washington Co. became Bay Co. in 1913. Gene lived in Ohio with his mother, he spent his summers in St. Andrews visiting with his Father and grandparents.

Bea Moates, grandsons Roy Sasser and Gene Moates

One day after a trip to the beach with his family, aunt Willie Pitts asked Gene if he wanted a bag of candy to take home with him, little Gene said no thanks he would take a bag of lemons. Willie and Gene went to the store for lemons and he went to grammas house with his bag of lemons.

I am Michel Walker. I grew up in Ohio. I married Gene and we have a son, Michael Devin

Kevin and Keith Sasser

and a daughter Kimberly Dawn Moates. We lived in St. Andrews for a time. We now live in Ohio.
Submitted by: Michel Walker, 252 East Main St., Piqua, Ohio 45356. Sources: Census records Marriages Cert.Court House Land records Cemetary records,..Memories.

Grover Cleveland Moates

Grover Cleveland Moates, born May 30, 1883 in Alabama, was the son of James Marion Moates, confederate war veteran who served with the First Florida Infantry Company E as a Private, and Rutha Ann Dew Moates, daughter of Baptist Minister, Thomas Spencer Dew. The family moved to Alabama from Orange Hill, Florida shortly before he was born. Grover married Sarah Frances Wiggins September 8, 1901 in Dale County and they settled on a farm in Houston County near Cottonwood.

Sarah was the daughter of James Perry Wiggins and Frances Lewvince Phillips. Her grandfathers died during the Confederate war. Daniel Stephen Wiggins, James Perry's father, died of measles soon after enlisting. Corporal Lewis Quincy Phillips, Frances' father, died at the battle of Peachtree Creek in Atlanta. He was with the 57th Alabama Co. E.

Grover and Sarah were young when they married and his father had to consent. Their firstborn was Jasper E. Marcus, (1902-1917). A handsome young man, he injured a leg while working in the fields and with few antibiotics available, he died at age 14. Their first daughter, Lula May (1904-1922) also died young, of pneumonia, at 18. Two years after Lula's birth Rita Benard (1906-1983) was born. She married Herb Capan, and lived near Dothan. Fannie Myl (born August 15, 1908)

Grover Cleveland Moates and Granddaughter Annette Moates Sasser About 1946

married Manuel Woodham and raised her family near Dothan. Another son, Grover C. Moates died at birth February 10, 1910. Ada Bell (1911-1992) married Bob Hinson and lived outside Slocomb. Flora Adel (1914-1993) married Tommy Lindsey and lived in Florida. Buress (1918-1984)was the only son to live to adulthood. The youngest, Opal, (1920 -1995) married Jake Dykes and lived in Florida.

Sarah Frances died from complications of childbirth Jan 26, 1922. Grover remarried a neighbor, Cleopatra Edmondson (1892-1967). She helped raise his children and was "Gunny" to his grandchildren, as she was affectionately called by them and neighborhood children. They sold the farm and moved to Panama City, Florida about 1930 when Buress was twelve years old. He had quit school as many young boys did during the depression to help the family. Buress met Beatrice Louise Findley (born 1924), daughter of William and Mamie Hood Findley, in St. Andrews. They were married September 19, 1941. Buress was inducted into the Army on December 2, 1941. He served for over three years in Algeria, French Morocco, Tunisia, and Italy. Buress and Beatrice had two children Annette and Grover. Grover Cleveland gave them land on which to build a house next door to him.

Grover Cleveland worked as a carpenter and for the Panama City Water Department. He owned a fish camp on Howard's creek and loved to fish. A favorite thing for Grover and Annette was to help Gunny and Grandpa "snore up" worms so they could go fishing. The house where Grover and Cleo lived no longer stands, but the memories still live. They are buried in the Greenwood Cemetery in Panama City near Buress, Opal, and Adel.

Source: Census records, personal knowledge
Written and Submitted by: Annette Sasser, 2908 Orange Hill Road, Chipley, Florida 32428.

The Moates Saga

Frances Merrion Moates and Mary Peel were married in Eucheeana, Walton County, Florida on March 31,1859. Francis Merrion joined Company F, 1st Florida Infantry, Confederate Army, at Camp Walton in March 1862. Records show that he was captured by the Union Army on November 25, 1863 and was imprisoned in Rock Island Barracks, Illinois on December 11, 1863.

On October 17, 1864, on condition of release from prison, Francis Merrion agreed to be loyal to the Union Army and was inducted into the United States Army as a private. He was then sent to fight the Indians; he was discharged from the United States Army at Levinsworth, Kansas, on July 10, 1865. It is said that he and some others walked all the way home to Florida.

After returning to Walton County, he and Mary, with two children, moved to Orange Hill in Washington County for awhile. Mary's father, Rev. James Peel, was a Baptist minister in that area. Francis Merrion and Mary moved to St. Andrews, then in Washington County, in February 1879.

He purchased a large tract of land from a Mr. Thomas Hannah and wife. It was recorded as Fractional Segments of Section 35, South Range 15 West. He platted this land into blocks and lots, and this subdivision was known as Bayside Addition to St. Andrews.

Francis Merrion built a large house on two lots just east of what is now Stephens Avenue. This house burned in about 1915. On the next two lots east, their youngest daughter and her husband erected a two-story house. This house no longer stands; The House of Chan now occupies this property. In 1910, Columbus Perry and wife Nettie built a large house on

Francis Merrion Moates, 1837-1879

the eastern two lots. This house still stands and is the home of a large house on the Eastern two lots. This house still stands and is the home of Canopy's Restaurant. These three pieces of property were known as the Moates Preserve.

In 1883, Francis Merrion and a Mr. Willet constructed and operated a small sawmill right on the bay beach just west of what is now Danford Avenue. This might have been the first mill in the area after the Civil War and was in operation until about 1893.

In 1897, tragedy struck this family. On March 29, the sloop AMELIA was lost in a storm on Pensacola bar. Drowned were daughters Mary Stephens and Carrie Constantine, along with Captain John Constantine and their three children. The only survivor was a son, Benjamin Franklin (Ben).

Then on November 16th that same year, Francis Merrion died from complications resulting from injuries received in a run-away horse and wagon accident. Mary was left alone in a big house, with three children: John Bunion (Bun), Columbus Perry (Lum), and Annie Castor. Records indicate that Mary first applied for a widow's pension about 1897, there is no record of when she received the pension or the amount. At her death in 1928 she was receiving $50 per month from the U.S. War Department.

Between 1859 and 1886 this couple had eleven children: two born in Eucheeana, Florida, six in Orange Hill, Florida, and three in St. Andrews, Florida. All of them at one time lived in St. Andrews, Bay County, Florida.

William Noah, born in Eucheeana September 14, 1861. Died in St. Andrews May 23, 1946. Buried with wife, Adele, in St. Andrews Cemetery. Seven children; none living today.

Mary Frances, born in Eucheeana October 10, 1863. Died at sea, sloop AMELIA, March 29, 1897. Married William Stephens. Two children; none living today.

Emma Ellen, born in Orange Hill October 2,1866. Died in St. Andrews December 7, 1943. Married Clem Gwaltney. Seven children; none living today. Emma and Clem rest in Greenwood Cemetery, St. Andrews, Florida.

James Augustus (Jim), born September 28, 1868. Died September 9, 1952 in Mobile, Alabama. Jim left St. Andrews in 1915 to work in shipyards in Pascagoula, Mississippi, and in Mobile, Alabama. Never returned to St. Andrews to live. Married Emma Brock of St. Andrews. They had seven children. The youngest son, Woodrow Wilson Moates is the only one living today. He and his wife, Julia, (both 90) live in Mobile, Alabama.

Nothing is known about this son. (5th child in family).

Benjamin Franklin (Ben) was born in Orange Hill, Florida, February 28, 1872. Died in St. Andrews September 1, 1953. His life from 1879 to 1953 was lived in St. Andrews. He married Nora Thompson of St. Andrews. They had one daughter who died as an infant and is buried in Greenwood Cemetery with Ben and Nora.

Carrie E. was born in Orange Hill,

Standing L-R: William Noah Moates, James Augustus Moates, Benjamin Franklin Moates. Seated L-R: John Bunyon Moates, Annie Porter, Columbus Perry Moates.

Florida, July 26, 1874. Died March 29, 1897 at sea, sloop AMELIA. She married John Constantine; they had three (3) children; Nick, Tony and a baby.

Noah Webster (a twin) was born in Orange Hill, Florida on July 26, 1874 and died as an infant.

John Bunion (Bun) was born November 16, 1880 in St. Andrews. Died in Pascagoula, Mississippi, June 1974. Married Annie Purcell of St. Andrews. This couple had six children, two girls and four boys. None are living today. Bun and Annie built a home on Moates Avenue and Cedar Point Road in Gautier, Mississippi and lived there the rest of their lives. Bun and Annie are buried in Machapelah Cemetery in Pascagoula, Mississippi.

Columbus Perry (Lum) was born April 16, 1884 in St. Andrews, Florida. He died in St. Andrews February 9, 1974. In 1908 he married Nettie Rose who was born in Pender, Nebraska on July 8, 1888. Nettie died June 15, 1968. Lum never left St. Andrews to live. During World War I, he worked in the government Shipyard in Pascagoula, Mississippi. He retired from Sherman Shipyard about 1965. This couple had seven children. Living today are second son Edward Ray Moates and first daughter Martha Frances Bukota. Lum and Nettie are resting in Greenwood Cemetery with three of their children.

Annie Castor Moates was born June 19, 1886 in St. Andrews, Florida. She died December 4, 1961 in Panama City, Florida. She married Charles T. Porter. They lived all their lives in St. Andrews and Panama City. The couple had three children. Annie and Charlie with their three children are buried in Greenwood Cemetery, St. Andrews, Florida.

Edward Ray Moates was born January 19, 1910 in St. Andrews, Florida. On March 31, 1932 he married Henrietta Louise Montgomery who was born in St. Andrews on December 13, 1913. Ray retired from International Paper Company in 1972 after 37 years of continuous service. Henrietta retired from the Bay School Support System in 1973. Both are lifelong residents of St. Andrews and make their home at 1411 Bayview Avenue. The couple has two sons: Fred Houlton Moates of Houston, Texas, and Samuel Ray Moates of Panama City, Florida.
Submitted by: Ray Moates, 1411 Bayview Avenue, Panama City, FL.

Mount Family
Part I

I was born in Panama City, Florida on October 13th 1952. I grew up in Lynn Haven and went to school there, most of my youth was spent in Bay County, Fla. My Father was a truck driver and when my Mother wasn't working at Bay Memorial Hospital, she was waiting tables at the Fisherman Wharf. I even remember that she worked at the Holiday Inn out on the beach once because she got Janet and myself jobs busing tables. I was the 2nd born child and the eldest daughter born to James Wabon (J.W.) and Betty Jean (Pitts) Mount. My older brother was Armand Kelly Mount, (whom we all called "Kelly") and my youngest brother was James Michael, whom we called, "Mikey." I still call him Mickey just to see his eyes twinkle. My only sister whom now is gone, was Janet Lynn Mount, we fought as sister do, but I sure do miss those moments now. We were all born about 11 months apart, so we were very close growing up. It was fun growing up in Lynn Haven, you could walk down to the bay to go swimming, you could walk to the ball park, Lynn Haven was a safe and fun place to grow up in. You could play outside at night without any fear. My grandparents lived nearby as to were my Aunt

Beverly Mount, age 15, 1967

and Uncle and cousins, Rocky and Eric, we all were very close. There was old man Lloyd's store to buy candy at, the was Mr. Hanson's drug store to get cherry cokes and you could roller skate down the street and on the side walks, but me I loved the little white building in the city park called the Library.

Some of the things I can remember from my childhood is going to the picture show and seeing all those Elvis Presley movies. Daddy had this car with a crazy sounding horn on it, and we loved to get out of the car and play on the play ground equipment that was located up in the front of the screen, there were seats up there also I think they were concrete, any way he would honk this horn and we would come a running back to the car. The name of this Drive-In was the Bud Davis Drive-In. It was located at 15th and Lisenby Ave, where the K-Mart Store is now. Anyway back than Lisenby Ave was a dirt road, and I remember when we would head back to Lynn Haven we would have to past this cemetery and I was scared so I would hide in the floorboard of our car until we past it.

I left home in 1969, leaving Lynn Haven was hard, but I was growing up and I was at the age that you get when no one can tell you anything. I got a job at the Margaret K. Lewis school and an apartment on corner of 11th Street and Chestnut (1107-A) in St. Andrews, (just think 30 years before me my grandparents lived right here almost on this same corner), later that year I was over in Port St. Joe visiting a girlfriend of mine and she introduces me to my future husband, not realizing that that following November I would run off to Ga. and marry him. So at the age of 18 I was married and had a new family.
Submitted by: Beverly Mount-Douds, 460 Redfish St., Port St. Joe, Fla. 32456.

Mount Family
Part II

My Daddy, J.W. was born in Opp, Alabama. That's in Covington County and my Momma, Betty Jean Pitts was born Frink, Florida, over in Calhoun County. They met when Daddy was driving a furniture truck, he was driving down a old dirt road in Calhoun County and there she was, setting on the front porch shelling butterbeans bare footed, he says it was "Love at first sight." They married in 1950 and Kelly was born there in Ma Pitts house. The rest of us kids were all born in Bay Memorial in P.C.

J.W. Mount, Betty Jean holding cousin Kim, (background) Beverly Mount in swim suit. In front of Gas Station early 1960's.

Granny and Pa only had two sons, my daddy, J.W. and Uncle Pete, they all ran a gas station in Lynn Haven called the Mo-Jo Gas Station, it was on Ohio Ave which is also Hwy 77.

We moved to Lynn Haven when Mike was a baby this was across the street from Mam Maw and Paw Paw Christian, they were my Aunt Ann's parents and every one called them that. Aunt Ann and Uncle Pete lived next door and around the corner was Granny and Pa's house. My Daddy only had one brother and his name was Albert Lewis Mount, but every one called him "Pete Mount", he was kind of famous in our town, people still remember him from long ago.

Uncle Pete was a car salesman, but that wasn't all he was a race car driver and he owned the "Purple Passion". He raced for Bill Cook at the Ford Company where he worked, later it became the Cook Whitehead Ford Company, Pete raced for until we kids were in our teens and than he got in one too many wreaks and Aunt Ann asked him to quit. So he did and than he and Woody Woodham open up the Leisure Used Car lot in Lynn Haven, this was around 1972. Pete and

Ann's boys Rocky and Eric now run the Car Business and Eric does the racing in the family.

Submitted by: Mike Mount, 2421 Minnesota Ave., Lynn Haven, FL 32444; Written by Beverly Mount Douds, 460 Red Fish Street, Port. St. Joe, FL 32444.

Mount Family
Part III

Granny (Foy Mount) and Pa (James Orell Mount) came here to Bay County back in the 1940's. They first lived over in St. Andrews. Pa worked at the Standard Ice Company for Mr. J.E. Pruett and Granny took in boarders. Their neighbors and best friends were the Gandy family. Kenyon Gandy told me that my Granny was the world's best cook. Daddy they tell me worked at the Sinclair Gas Station down on Harrison Ave in P.C......Pa had an Uncle (Martin) that come to Panama City earlier, he

owned a store called M.L. Mount Department Store, "The Popular Price Department Store" later it became the Mount-Harmon Department Store in downtown P.C. I remember it when I was growing up, Uncle Martin and Aunt Sarah moved to DeFuniak Springs and died there, they are buried in the Magnolia Cemetery there.

As a child we loved hanging around the gas station, Pa and Uncle Pete had a zoo out back behind the buildings, Pete was always hunting, he had a friend I can remember that we called

Pa and Granny Mount in front of car St. Andrews, FL early 1950's

"Snake Bill", I never really knew why but I figure it was because he hunted snakes. Pa used to pay us to catch frogs to feed these snakes, we had turtles, squirrel monkeys, gators, a deer, a tiger, and my favorite was Blackie, he was my bear, he loved for me to wash him down with the water hose and then put it in his mouth, he could eat a lot of light bread too. Than there was Jocko, he was a monkey. Daddy never liked cats and every time Janet and I would bring home a cat, it would disappear. Turns out that Jocko was a very good mother to kittens. I ready loved being at the gas station, we had this ice house, where daddy had these big blocks of ice, and Kelly and I would get in there and eat all the oysters we could hold down. They also had cold watermelons in there to, depending on the time of year it was.

Granny ran a drive-in next door to the gas station, she had the only car-hops I knew of until you went to Panama City and there was the Tally-Ho and Jimmy's Drive-In and the Chicken Box. I don't remember seeing them, I was still to small but my mother in-law tells me she was one of them. Our Drive - In was called "Mount's Drive-In", and Mrs. Skipper and my Granny was the best cooks in the world!

As time when on Granny and Pa got to old to work any longer, so they retired and Daddy went to work for Mr. Bill Pitts, driving a dump truck, and Pete went to his Cars. We lost the animals and that hurt a lot. Granny and Pa got into the bait business then, this they could do at home. I remember going to the bus company with granny to pick up crickets and with her to deliver worms, we would take them to other fish camps like Tharp's Fish camp out at Deer point, and to Red Cloud and to Bakers Ackers. I loved running all over town with my Granny, but she died in 1988 and I miss her so.

Submitted by: Betty Jean Pitts Mount, 3937 Scurlock Lane, Southport, FL 32409; Written by: Beverly Mount-Douds, 460 Red Fish St., Port St. Joe, FL 32456.

Munson Family

The Munson Family lived in the old home place at 4308

Munson Family Home, 4308 17th Street

17th Street which was one of the oldest homes in St. Andrews. Henry C. Munson, Senior purchased the land at an auction in Vernon, Florida in 1887 for $1.25 and built the house.

As a young person Henry Munson lived in the New York or New Jersey area and ran away from home as a teenager. We don't know anything about his background. After running away, it is said, he went back home one night and looked in the window and saw his mother setting in a rocking chair, but he never went in. He left and never went back. He came south and married Martha Givens and raised their family of four boys: Edward, Henry, Lambert and William (Bill) and three girls: Genivieve, Ollie and Stella.

We don't know anything about Edward. Henry was a Captain of a large ocean-going ship.

Lambert was Captain of a fire boat in Jacksonville Harbor. Bill was a second mate aboard large ships for awhile, then came ashore and worked as a surveyor.

We don't know anything about Genivieve. Stella was a local school teacher at St. Andrew Grammar School and also in Parker. Ollie was a housewife and lived in St. Andrews all her life. Henry C. Munson, Sr. was buried in Greenwood Cemetery along with his wife and his son Captain Henry C. Munson.

Submitted by: Clifford H. Munson, 1117 Fairland Avenue, Panama City, FL.

Eugene Murfee and Alice Wachob
The Bridge at Murphee

In 1902 Eugene Murfee and his wife Alice Wachob homesteaded on the east side of Burnt Mill Creek around the

site of the Highway 388 bridge. Their place was contiguous to homesteads of Lucius Johnson to the north, William Artis and Earl Wellman to the east, Rufus Ellis to the west, and Gene's brother Sylvester to the south. Alice established a post office there in 1904 and they named the community Murfee. Because of the sandy soil most of these homesteaders sold their lands to turpentiners or timber companies for cash as soon as they could. Those who intended to stay awhile leased their trees to turpentiners.

Claudius Eugene Murfee and Alice Melissa Wachob Murfee ca 1902 Murfee, Florida (now listed on map as Burnt Mill Creek)

Gene Murfee leased most of his place to turpentiners for $25 per thousand boxes plus a dollar an acre cash in 1904. The same year he sold his most northerly eight acres to the Dupree Brothers and 24 contiguous acres to Parrish and Edwards all for $5 an acre. This land had commercial value to the timber and gum naval stores industries because it was on the creek and about as far upstream as a boat could travel. Within less than a dozen years it would serve as the eastern terminus of a bridge across the creek. Parrish and Edwards bought out the Dupree Brothers and held the site only two months before selling it to another turpentiner, the Buie and Vickers Company, who built a still on the creek. That partnership went broke in only ten months and was bought out by

Vickers and Sale Turpentine Co in 1905. Six months later the Sale-Davis and Southern Timber companies bought the site and kept it until 1925 when it was transferred to the St Andrews Bay Corp. So, this property was in possession of Sale-Davis when a 300 feet long wood-

Dedication of construction of first Burnt Mill Creek Bridge Murfee, Florida ca 1917

en bridge was built over Burnt Mill Creek about 1916.

Sale-Davis most likely funded the bridge construction. They owned the site at both bridge termini in 1916, they had the funding capability, and they had the most to gain from a bridge. It was also probable that Sale-Davis funded the road from Murfee to West. Back then counties had little money and entities needing a road or bridge had to build their own. The State Road Department (SRD) was established in 1915 with an annual budget of only $10,000.

It is likely that Sale-Davis hired or contracted with Gene Murfee for the construction because family history credits him for building the roadway and the bridge across Burnt Mill Creek. In fact, Alice worried when her husband committed to build something of which he had no experience. This photo of young people at the dedication of the Burnt Mill Creek bridge at Murfee about 1917 includes Perry Kyser and Gradie Murfee on the left and the Southport twins Alberta and Bertella Brooks near the right. In 1949 the SRD built Highway 388 north of the old 1917 road from Murfee to West Bay. The old route turned north at Burnt Mill Creek, crossing the new route there, and continued on northeast to Lake Merial. Some of the old bridge's support pilings are still visible 150 feet upstream from the current bridge. The current concrete bridge is 17 feet above the creek bed and 300 feet long.

Within a year following the dedication of the old bridge things began to sour at Murfee. Despite the new access to West Bay, most of the people sold their homesteads and moved on. Alice's ninth child was born in November 1918 and lived only six days. Gene who had been house bound for some time because of Alice's travail went out to check his cows. When his horse returned without him, a search party went out and found him face down in some pooled water, apparently drowned after a fall. Alice used the new road to bury Gene at West Bay Cemetery where the two of them had placed their son less than a week earlier.

Submitted by: Dorothy Swinson Gilmore, Carpenter's Creek Assisted Living, 5918 N. Davis Highway, Pensacola, FL 32503.

The Murfees in Bay County

After four years of civil war, James Murfee returned to Montgomery with the remnant of Company A, 17th Alabama, and he married Susannah Mitchell in nearby Pike County. The couple ran a grocery and farmed near the Alabama town of Greenville until 1883 and then, near the Florida towns of Chipley and Vernon until 1902. The following stories happened after 1902 when the old couple moved south to Burnt Mill Creek where their sons Eugene, Sylvester, and Roz had homesteaded and built them a house and grocery store and Susie's yeast rolls had a market.

Mr. Murfee operated the grocery near the present Highway 388 on property belonging to Eugene on the east side of Burnt Mill Creek. The family hoped a town would grow around the grocery. A post office opened inside the store in 1904, and a large sign was raised over the wooden building to identify the community as "Murfee". Eugene's wife Alice Wachob was postmistress, and Sylvester carried the mail by sailboat to other settlements. Sails were retired when Perry Kyser brought his motor launch Cupid 1 out of Bay Head into Murfee about 1916.

James Murfee was proud of his heritage including the

spelling of his name; he would explain that it was the way Scots spelled it. One day he saw his granddaughter Ruth's homework with her name signed with "phy". He inquired as to why and she told him that a classmate's father had pointed out that the name was misspelled on the sign above the Murfee post office. The old man confronted the fellow and in the ensuing argument banished him from his store, telling him he could pick up his mail at the window but get his groceries elsewhere. The argument could also have been about whether Murfee had the right to name the community in the first place as there were other settlers there.

When Buie and Vickers opened a turpentine still at Murfee in 1904, they contracted with Eugene to supply the associated buildings. This probably included shanties, house, still, barn and lot for the work animals, commissary, and sheds for the cooper, blacksmith, and wagons. The influx of woodsmen into the already rough community resulted in a couple of unsolved murders. On the other

James Murfee and Susie Mitchell Murfee

hand, the families the turpentiners brought with them added the labor and skills a growing town needed. The Indian midwife and healer Dora Durrant was the wife of a turpentiner at Murfee. She stayed on at the creek after her husband was shot and killed. She was a petite woman who could verbalize musical instruments and dance at nearly 100 years old. She delivered most of the children at Murfee and helped nurse many through illness.

Initially, land travel to Murfee was over a sandy road from Lake Merial. In 1907 James Murfee's 64 year old sister Emily traveled to Murfee from Alabama in an automobile. The Murfee community had seen its first horseless carriage only a year earlier. Emily chastised her brother for attending a soldiers' convention in Montgomery and not stopping at Greenville to see his relatives. She urged him to return to Alabama, where he might prosper and see his grandchildren educated. James, who had not seen any of his family in 24 years, told her she was welcome and so was her driver, but he would not hear of returning to Alabama.

About 1916 a road was built from Murfee to West Bay along with wooden bridges of considerable length and height over Burnt

Vester and Seth Murfee's Children at Lake Merial in 1932

Mill and Crooked Creeks. Eugene Murfee was the builder, and the Sale-Davis Company was the owner.

Gene was drowned in November 1918 after a fall from his horse shortly after the dedication of his bridge at Murfee. Apparently the idea of a town at Murfee rested squarely on Gene's shoulders because the family gave up the vision and drifted away upon his death. Alice transferred the mail service to Southport in June 1919. With her younger children she moved just south of Rock Hill, east of Chipley but did not sell her property at Murfee. Alice's oldest daughter Gradie boarded with the Olen Hobbs family at Bay Head and taught public school at Southport a few months until she married. Gradie photographed her students with her box camera in early 1919. Aden Richardson had recently moved

203

to Southport from the mouth of Burnt Mill Creek and appears to be the young man in the hat to the right.

Sylvester Murfee's family stayed on the creek until he could sell his place; then, he relocated to Lake Merial where Vester "stumped", that is, extracted pine stumps from the ground which had over time become light wood. He raised satsumas awhile, and, like many others, he cut pulpwood. James and Susie were living at Lake Merial during the 1920 census. Later, they operated a small store along the BC & St Andrews Line tracks at Lake Merial. James was 79 years old now but also took on the job as a station master there.

The BC and St Andrews Line operated between Southport and the L & N at Chipley from 1911 until about 1940; Lake Merial was one of several stations along the route. When the railroad noticed some packages missing from the station after Mr. Murfee took over, the conductor John W (Big Six) Williams thought the old man was responsible. Now, James Murfee had always taken himself too seriously, and he was not about to let some whippersnapper thirty years his junior dismiss him as negligent, or worse, a thief He assailed his accuser, whacking Big Six with his cane one end of which was filled with lead. The time in convalescence gave Mr. Williams time to reflect on his poor judgement, and he was said to have avoided the Lake Merial depot as long as the old man remained there, which was not long. The conductor was more circumspect when he caught several youths hopping a ride north of Wausau. One of the hitch hikers, Earnest Owen described Big Six as almost compassionate.

For several years, Mr. Murfee grew a goatee big enough to hide a lip cancer; the photograph of the couple taken at Murfee about 1918 illustrates this. A few months after the altercation with the conductor, the cancer was so obvious he could no longer hide it and had to quit work. For privacy, he and Susie moved to their daughter Ella McCullough's large farm northeast of Chipley where they lived in a cabin in the yard. James was at another daughter Kate Miller's place in Bonifay when he died in 1925 at the age of 82. Susie died on Ella's farm in 1934 at age 88. Daughters were our social security in those days.

Today it appears that the Murfees' vision of development around their store on Burnt Mill Creek might be realized around an airport. Ironically the site is attractive for an airport a century later largely because it is the least developed place in the county.
Submitted by Michael Murfee, 236 Allen Avenue, Panama City 32401

Johnnie Belle Hicks Murray

Johnnie Belle Hicks Murray was born October 14, 1905 the oldest child of four sisters and one brother in Elba, Pike County, Alabama.

She arrived in Panama City, Florida in the 1920's with her young son, Willie Hicks, and took up residency on East End Avenue now known as Harmon Avenue.

She worked as a dentist helper for Dr. Fellows whose office was located in downtown Panama City, Florida on Beach Drive.

She assisted in the lunchroom under the managership of Pauline Washington at Rosenwald High School during the principalship of Calvin C. Washington.

During the 1960's, Johnnie was President of the Women's Civic Club. She was very active in fund raising events for children's charity and civic events.

Johnnie Belle Hicks Murray

Two major fund raisers were for the relocation and building of Greater Bethel A.M.E. Church and the Macedonia Baptist Church and the building of the Glenwood Recreation Center which is the present day Martin Luther King Jr. Center.

She was also an astute business person owning many rental units.

She was married to Harry Murray from 1954 until his death in 1983.

She remained active with her beloved Greater Bethel A.M.E. Church and community until 1999 when failing health caused her to relocate to Beaumont, Texas to live with her granddaughter Pamela Denice Hicks.
Submitted by: Bura L. Reed, 1402 Illinois Ave, Lynn Haven, FL 32444.

The Frank McGill Nelson Family

Frank McGill Nelson, Sr. and Helena Olivia Appelberg Nelson moved to Bay County in 1912. A large sawmill, constructed by Sale-Davis Lumber Company in Southport, lured Frank Sr. to Southport to join the mill.

Rasmus John Nelson, a Norwegian immigrant and Frank Sr.'s father, located in Bagdad, Florida in the late 1800's to work in a large sawmill there. He married Margaret Adeline Prescott of Black Water (Santa Rosa County) Florida in 1872. Frank's father became a saw-filer, one of the highly skilled trades in the sawmill industry.

Helena Olivia's father, Isaac Gideon Appelberg, had immigrated from Finland, located in Pensacola, Florida and there married Esther Annie Peake, who had been born in Plymouth, England. Olivia, a child of this union, married Frank Sr. in Pensacola on October 2, 1911.

Bubber in front of the Nelson home on Fifth Street

While residing in Southport Frank and Olivia's first two children were born. Frank McGill Nelson, Jr. was born August 5, 1912 and Marion Gustaf Nelson, born January 13, 1914.

After graduation from Bay County High School, Frank Jr. attended the University of Florida in Gainesville. However, the Great Depression canceled his plans and he did not graduate. Frank returned to Bay County and played semi-pro baseball for several Bay County teams. Frank began a gas appliance business and later joined the West Florida Gas Company as a staff member. He remained there until his retirement and subsequent death in 1980. Frank Jr. married Frances Lee Mayers, whose parents were owners and operators of the Historic Bay Hotel. Frances Carol Mills and Frank Hubbard Nelson are children of that marriage.

In 1914 Frank Sr. and Olivia moved to Panama City and occupied a home at 535 Magnolia Avenue. This avenue was lovingly called "Incubator Avenue" because so many young couples with infants and young children resided there.

Frank Sr. opened the first Buick agency in Bay County and it was originally located on First Street, now known as West Beach Drive, near the present Elks Club. The Nelson agency built a new building at 613 Harrison Avenue in 1931. Two years later the Chevrolet agency was purchased from Ralph Bennett and the business became Nelson Chevrolet and Buick Company, Inc. The Buick agency continued in business until 1990 when it closed its doors. It was the oldest family-owned agency in the Southeast and was one of the oldest in the United States.

During the period of residence on Magnolia Avenue, Helena Olivia Nelson was born, September 15, 1915. She attended Florida State College for Women and later married Elliott (Bill) Williams of Mobile, Alabama. The couple resided in Mobile until their deaths. Helen, affectionately known by the family as "Teeta" (Sister) died in 1998. Bill and Helen have two daughters. They are Joan Nelson

Kivlighan of Staunton, Virginia and Helen Delores Sporl of Birmingham, Alabama.

Frank Sr. acquired automobile agencies in Apalachicola and Marianna, which he operated for a number of years. The family moved to Marianna in 1917 and remained for one year. During that time Warren Amos Nelson was born and was the only Nelson child who was not born in Bay County. Little Warren was killed by a delivery truck in 1920 while standing on the corner of First Street, now known as West Beach Drive, and Fifth Street.

Soon after the family's return to Bay County Kathleen Inez Nelson was born at the Magnolia Avenue address on April 27, 1919. Kate was the first woman employee hired at Tyndall Field during World War II. It was there she met and later married John Blakeley of Andrews, South Carolina. The couple lived in Andrews for many years and Kate died there in 2002. One child, Julia Anne Blakeley Thornton, was born of that marriage and Julie resides at Litchfield Beach, South Carolina.

In 1920 Frank Sr. agreed to work for W.C. Sherman as Superintendent of the St. Andrews Bay Lumber Company in Millville. He divided his time between the mill and the automobile agency and the family moved to Millville that year. Two more of the Nelson children were born in the mill town; Louis Athniel Nelson (Ike) on June 24, 1921 and Hugh Appelberg Nelson on May 23, 1923. These two brothers served their country in World War II. Upon his return to Panama City after graduation from the University of Florida Hugh became the Vice-President of Commercial Bank and remained in that position until his death in 1978. Hugh married Lila Winn Merriam of

Parents and children in living room of Fifth Street home

Panama City and they are the parents of Karen Winn Ringelberg of New London, Connecticut; Susan Olivia Johnson of Milton, Florida; Barbara Cay Commander of Perry, Florida, and Helen Elizabeth Mapoles of Panama City.

Before entering World War II Ike married Mary Alyce Pettus of Dothan, Alabama. After his return from the war he became the General Manager of Nelson Chevrolet and Buick Company, Inc. In the late 1980's Ike became an owner of Nelson Buick Company and remained in the automobile business until his death in 1990. Ike and Mary Alyce are the parents of three children. They are Louis Michael Nelson, Mary Angela Lewis, both of Panama City, and Roy McGill Nelson of Tallahassee, Florida.

The Nelson family moved back into Panama City from Millville and resided on McKenzie Avenue near the Bay County courthouse. Their last move was to the Nelson home on Fifth Street and Oak Avenue.

At this last home the final two children of the "Nelson Nine" were born. Hazel Anna was born October 31,1926 and Karl Bertel on October 12, 1928. Both attended Florida State University and Hazel, who became a teacher, married John William Hawkins of Pensacola, Florida. The couple has lived in Pensacola for almost 50 years and they are the parents of John William Hawkins, Jr. and Joyce Ann Cobb, both of Pensacola. Karl married Aimee Jo Lee of Panama City and they are the parents of a son, Karl Bertel Nelson, Jr. of Wilton, Connecticut and a daughter, Aimee Olivia Smith of Phoenix, Maryland. Upon completing his education Karl Sr. was employed by International Paper Company. In early 1973 Karl, Aimee Jo and their children moved to Wilton, Connecticut and

Karl retired in 1991 as an executive of I.P.C. in the New York central office. The couple returned to Panama City after Karl's retirement. Karl is currently employed by Merrick Industries, Inc. in Panama City.

Leadership in civic and community affairs by the Nelsons has been extensive and productive down through the years. Frank Sr. was named to fill out a term as Sheriff of Bay County from 1915-1917. He was Superintendent of Bay County Schools, 1918-1921 and Chairman of the Bay County School Board, 1921-23. Frank Sr. represented Bay County in the Florida Legislature, 1917-19. Frank's brother, Oscar Nelson, served as Bay County's first judge during this same period of time. Mrs. Nelson's brother, A.G. Appelberg, was Bay County Tax Collector for many years, retiring from that position. Michael Nelson, Ike's son, served as a county commissioner (1979-1987.)

Frank Sr. and Jr. are the only father-son combination to serve as Panama City mayors. During Frank Sr.'s term, 1923-1935, greater Panama City came into existence (1926) by act of the Florida Legislature. Panama City, St. Andrews and Millville and a portion of Bay Harbor were united into one city. Frank Jr. served as mayor from 1955-1961.

M.G. (Bubber) Nelson attended Panama Grammar School, as did all the Nelson children, and then graduated from Bay High School in 1931. After graduation Bubber followed his older brother, Frank, to seek employment in Gainesville so that he could attend the University of Florida. However, during this period of time jobs were scarce and he returned home to seek employment.

Bubber's first business venture was in 1931 as manager of the newly constructed Pan-Am Service Station located at Harrison Avenue and Sixth Street. When International Paper Company opened, he was employed as a crew chief cruising timber for the mill.

Bubber entered business for himself in 1933 when he built a lean-to type building next to his father's automobile agency on Harrison Avenue. He installed Bay County's first hydraulic grease rack called "Master Service Station."

Barbara Wing and Bubber met when she came to Panama City to live with her aunt and uncle, Mr. and Mrs. Harry Fannin, while attending Bay High School. Bubber and Bobby were married on January 14, 1935, one day after Bubber's 21st birthday. The couple are parents of Gretchen Scott Vann of Panama City and Marion Gustaf Nelson, Jr. of Springfield, Illinois. Gretchen is the mother of two sons, James Carey Scott, III and Marion Nelson Scott, both Panama City businessmen. M. G. (Bubba) Nelson, Jr., who is in land development, and his wife, Donna Drendel Nelson are the parents of two children, Tricia Lee Becker and Mark Gustaf Nelson, both of Springfield, Illinois.

M. G. Sr. purchased half-interest in Nelson Chevrolet and Buick Company from his father, who died of pneumonia a few weeks later in March of 1937 at the age of 49. In addition Bubber later became President of Commercial Bank; was appointed by Governor Fuller Warren to the State Road Board (1949-53) and has been active in many other local and state organizations. These include serving as co-founder and first Chairman of the United Way; Chairman of the Bay County Defense Council during World War II; Chairman of the Bay County Water Board; Past President of the Florida Bankers Association; former Director of the Southern Company, Gulf Power Company and The Atlanta and St. Andrews Bay Railway Company.

Members of the Nelson family were pioneer members of the First Presbyterian Church, formerly Wallace Memorial Presbyterian Church, in the early 1900's when it was organized in an abandoned school building. Several family members continue to maintain active memberships there.

Helena Olivia Appelberg Nelson, affectionately known as "Mama Too", became a young widow and continued to raise her children in the Fifth Street home with the help of the older children. No one was turned away from her door and young people flocked there for wonderful food, laughter, genuine love and affection. There was not a happier or livelier place to be. Mama Too also provided a sympathetic ear, loving hugs and a generous lap which many of us grandchildren utilized until we were big enough for our feet to touch the floor!

Olivia left the Fifth Street home when the last of the children were grown and she lived her remaining years in a smaller home built for her by her son, M. G. Nelson, on DeGama Avenue. During these years she continued to enjoy her family, her friends, her church, baking amazing cakes and other sumptuous dishes and playing canasta. Helena Olivia Appelberg Nelson went to be with the Lord on October 29, 1975 after several years of declining health. Memories of Mama Too and memories of other deceased family members live on in the hearts of those who loved them all so dearly.

Submitted by Gretchen Nelson Scott Vann 1015 West Caroline Blvd., Panama City, Florida 32401.

Florence Patricia Arledge and James David Nixon, M.D.

Flo was napping on the living room couch when her "blind date" arrived to pick her up. Jim's first impression must have been favorable because they were married on August 28, 1948 in St. Ludwig's Catholic Church of Kingston, Pennsylvania.

Florence Patricia Arledge was born at home to Nell and Martin Arledge on November 10, 1924 in Forty Fort, Pennsylvania. Immediately after her birth she was placed in the kitchen oven to keep her nice and warm. She graduated from Forty Fort High School where she was a drum majorette.

Flo met Jim while she was working as assistant director of nurses at Northeastern Hospital, Philadelphia, PA. She graduated with a R.N.B.S. degree in nursing in 1946 from Temple University in Philadelphia. After her marriage she moved to Panama City in 1952.

Flo was an active member and prominent leader of many service organizations. She was chairman of the American Red Cross nursing services, vice-president and chairman of the Women's Auxiliary for Florida Medical Association, president of both the Women's Auxiliary of Bay Medical Center and the Junior Woman's Club of Panama City. She was a longtime member of the Junior Service League of Panama City.

Flo and Jim Nixon

Flo's professional career involved work as a teacher, nurse, and manager. She was a nursing instructor for five years and acting director of nursing for one year at Gulf Coast Community College, receiving the Outstanding Teacher's Award for 1968-69. She also managed Dr. Jim's office.

James David Nixon was born June 15, 1924 to Iris and James M. Nixon, M.D. in Bay Harbor. He graduated from Bay County High School in 1942, playing the trombone in the school band. He attended the University of Florida and Temple University School of Medicine, returning to Panama City to practice general medicine in 1953. He was a devoted and respected physician for 40 years (See Medical Practice - Dr. Nixon).

Jim enjoyed taking Thursday afternoons off work to play in the "dog fight" golf rounds at the Panama City Country Club with his friends. They were both active members in the St. Andrews Bay Yacht Club, Panama City Country Club, and the First United Methodist Church.

This couple loved to play bridge together. Both were life masters and accredited teachers for the American Contract Bridge League. They taught bridge lessons in the basement of their home and enjoyed playing in several bridge clubs. They were members and officers of the Panama City Duplicate Bridge Club and the Northwest Florida Bridge Board. Jim and Flo shared a passion for the game and they will always be remembered as natural yet gracious "card sharks".

Boating and beaching were also activities that they enjoyed. In later years they relaxed at "Flo's Folly", their Laguna Beach townhouse, with their children and grandchildren.

Jim and Flo had three children: Robert Craig born May 30, 1949; Beverly Jean born November 11,1950; Judy Ann born September 28, 1953. Jim died from a series of strokes on January 31, 1996 (age 71). Flo died from breast cancer on January 3, 2000 (age 75). They are buried at Evergreen Memorial Cemetery in Panama City.

Flo and Jim had three children and eight grandchildren who dearly loved and greatly admired them.

Submitted by Judy Nixon Dusseault, 1804 Rhode Island, Lynn Haven, Fl 32444.

Iris Boyer Nixon and James Montgomery Nixon, M.D.

It was bright and early at 6:00 a.m. on June 8, 1915 when Iris Genoa Boyer married Dr. James M. Nixon at the Millville Methodist Church. Dr. Nixon was a popular doctor

Iris and James M. Nixon celebrating his 70th birthday

at the lumber mill and the workers wanted to attend the wedding before their 7:00 a.m. shift. The church was filled and people spilled onto the front yard of the church. The only train going out of town each day was the 7:30 a.m. "special", which they took to Jacksonville for their honeymoon.

Iris was born at Braddyville, Iowa on January 23,1897 to Genoa and Silas Boyer. They lived in that area until her family moved to Florida when she was 14 years old (1911). James was born November 5, 1886 at Mt. Pleasant, Florida (near Quincy) to Mol and Daniel Lafayette Nixon. After completing medical school and his internships he moved to Lynn Haven in 1913 to set up his medical practice. Later that year he moved to Millville to work as a lumber mill doctor. It was there that he met and fell in love with Iris.

One favorite story about them is that after becoming engaged, Iris was spending the summer at the family homestead at Yellow Bluff (Seagrove area). To visit his fiancee, Dr. Nixon arranged to ride the mail boat to Seagrove via the Gulf of Mexico and then swam to shore. True love finds a way.

They had three children: Ray Boyer born August 15, 1916; Margaret born January 14, 1921; James David born June 15, 1924.

Dr. Nixon served in the Army medical corps during WWI, where he was on the front line in France. He returned to set up his medical practice in Bay Harbor, working for Moore Timber Company the first year and in private practice for seven years. In 1925 he moved his practice to Panama City. He was a dedicated and respected medical doctor in this area until his retirement in 1968 (See Medical Practice: Dr. J.M. Nixon).

Although always busy as a wife and mother, Iris was a natural community leader. She served in the First Methodist Church of Panama City in numerous capacities, teaching Sunday school for over 30 years. Her love of flower gardening was exemplified by her charter membership in the Panama City Garden Club which she enjoyed throughout her life. She became a State Flower Show Judge and traveled throughout the state. Painting in watercolor was another hobby.

Iris was a charter member and first president of the Women's Auxiliary of Bay Memorial Medical Society. Also, she was an active member of the Panama City Woman's Club. In 1965 she was their state candidate for "Mother of the Year", attending a formal tea at the governor's mansion (Gov. Burns) in Tallahassee as one of the 18 state finalists.

"Jimmy" always took off work on Wednesday at noon to go fishing for bream in the nearby Dead Lakes area with his lifelong friends Leland Caswell and Grady Ellis. His other relaxing hobby was "week-end" farming on five acres in Callaway. He loved to play bridge with Iris or enjoy a game of poker at the Elks Club.

Dr. Nixon died December 14, 1976 of Alzheimer's disease (age 90) and Iris died April 20, 1982 of a heart attack (age 85). Both are buried in Evergreen Memorial Cemetery in Panama City.

Iris and Jimmy had three children, eight grandchildren and 21 great-grandchildren who deeply loved and respected them

Submitted by Margaret Nixon Downer, P.O. Box 27118, Bay Point, Panama City Beach, FL 32408.

James E. and Mary McClellan Nixon

The years following the Civil War were hard in the South but the Nixon family in the area around Bear Creek, later known as "Nixon", managed to survive and even thrive off the land. James Nixon had inherited a large sheep ranch when his father, Robert, died. James and his wife Mary (McClellan) Nixon were generous with sharing their home for a meal, or a night, to those traveling from Marianna to the coast. Hospitality in those days, of necessity, extended not only to the family but also to the animals that pulled the carriages that brought them. In those days there was no bridge over Little Bear Creek. The only way to traverse the creek was by ferry. Later a toll bridge was built, and at one time was operated by James and Mary's son Dan.

(Nixon can still be found on most Florida maps just west of U.S. Hwy 231 near Bear Creek.)

In addition to overseeing the sheep ranch, James was a circuit-riding preacher, traveling from one small community to another in the area around Bear Creek. Permanent

(L to R) Lily Nixon-Nolan, Stella Nixon-Whitehurst-Waller, Mary Nixon-Nolan, Sally (Sarah) Nixon-Thompkins, Tom Nixon, Dallas Nixon and Dan Nixon

ministers in the area were scarce and James felt called by God to serve in this manner. During the times that James was traveling the circuit to preach, he entrusted the care and safe keeping of his family to an elderly black man, "Uncle Joe", a former slave.

As the Nixon children grew and started their own families, they spread throughout Florida.

Sally (Sarah), the oldest daughter of James & Mary, married a young pharmacist, Otto Thompkins, from New York state. At that time, there were no licensed medical doctors in the woods around Bay Head, the community where he and Sally settled, and he became highly valued for his medical knowledge. Otto was fondly called "Doctor" Thompkins by the people he treated.

Judson Nixon, son of James and Mary Nixon

Lily and Mary married brothers, Newell and Glen Nolan and moved (to what seemed in those days) far away from their Bear Creek home to the Suwanee River area where Glen was a "sawyer" at a sawmill and Newell was a farmer.

Dan was an educator at a time when there were few school teachers in this part of Florida. His sisters Stella and Lily could attest to his effectiveness as a teacher and as a strict disciplinarian. Eula Simmons was Dan's wife.

Stella and her husband, Mike Whitehurst, raised their children in Birmingham, AL where he was in the building business. Ten years after being widowed, Stella returned to Youngstown in Bay County where she met and married Rufus Waller. Stella's children cherish the memory that their mother was proposed to the first time in a horse and carriage on the way home from church and yet lived to see a man on the moon.

Tom and Emma (Williams) moved to Palm Beach after they were married. Tom was a "finish" carpenter and Emma was a highly sought after dressmaker.

Dallas and his wife Esther (Williams) spent many years in Vernon where Dallas served the community in several ways. At one time he followed in the steps of his Grandfather Robert Nixon and became a County Judge in Washington, Co.

The largest family of descendants of James E. and Mary Nixon in the Florida Panhandle are the family of Judson and Clara (Sewell) Nixon.

For all families growing up in those years following the War Between the States, it was a time of huge changes. They all experienced breathtaking advances in science and technology never dreamed of when they were growing up among the tall pines and scrub oaks of Northwest Florida. From a horse or a horse and buggy as the primary source of travel (which makes for a romantic setting for a marriage proposal but hard riding), many of these rugged pioneers lived to see electricity, telephones, automobiles, air planes and some even lived to see man explore space. It was an extraordinary time to be in this exciting beautiful place on the Gulf Coast of Northwest Florida.

Submitted by: Helen W. Pippen, 100 Cherry # 704, Panama City, FL 32401; Written by: Ann Gallagher, 235 S. Glades Trail, Panama City Beach, FL.32401

Medical Practices of James M. Nixon M.D. and James D. Nixon M.D.

In November of 1952, a crowd of over 1500 people attended a community birthday party in honor of Dr. James M. Nixon's 66th birthday. A huge cake, baked in the shape of Bay Memorial Hospital by Mr. Martin Jones, was enjoyed by the guests at Lions Park. Dr. Nixon had delivered more than five thousand babies by that time and about 500 of them attended. The Bay High School Band that performed that day was half "Nixon" babies. Mrs. Clyde Blackwell and Mrs. Charlie Powell served as co-chairmen for the event and received cards and letters from every state. Mr. Tom Bingham was Master of Ceremonies. The first baby boy that Dr. Nixon had delivered was present and it was Carl Gray, mayor of Panama City. The first baby girl, Mrs. U.D. Paul who ran Catherine's Fabric Shop in Millville, was also there. The community presented Dr. Nixon with a TV set (television was brand new then). Later a tree was planted in his name on the hospital grounds.

Dr. James M. Nixon, left; Dr. James D. Nixon, right (printed in the News Herald, June 20, 1971, Father's Day)

James Montgomery Nixon was born November 5, 1886 at Mt. Pleasant, Florida (near Quincy) to Mary and Daniel Lafayette Nixon. After completing school at Mt. Pleasant he walked 25 miles to Tallahassee to attend Florida State College. He did not return home for two years, but he did send his laundry back and forth to his family on the local train! He attended Chattanooga (TN) Medical College and graduated in 1910. His medical internships for two years at Erlanger Hospital in Chattanooga and one year at Bellevue Hospital in New York City prepared him for his occupation.

Dr. J.M. Nixon moved to Lynn Haven in 1913, the same year that Bay County was incorporated. He then moved his office to Millville and was associated with one of the lumber companies there. He entered the service in WWI and served in the Army Medical Corps for two years. After WWI he returned to Bay Harbor and worked with the Moore Timber Co. for one year in addition to his private practice. In 1925 Dr. Nixon moved his medical practice as well as his family to Panama City. He and Drs. D.M. Adams, Sr. and W.J. Blackshear operated the Panama City Hospital, which could accommodate six patients. It was later named Adams Hospital. Until Bay Memorial Hospital was established in 1949, he remained on staff there.

Bay Memorial Hospital was a "dream" of Dr. J. M. Nixon. To select the location for a new hospital, he served on a committee appointed by the county commissioners. He decided where it should be and pointed it out to the others. Since it was an equal distance from either side of the county, they all agreed with him. On December 10, 1949, Dr. James M. Nixon was made President Emeritus of Bay Memorial Hospital for his services as Chief of Staff for the first six months of the new hospital. He had worked long and hard to make the hospital possible.

Medical offices of Dr. J.M. Nixon and Dr. J. D. Nixon on 806 E. 6th Street, Bay Memorial Hospital in background

James David Nixon was born June 15, 1924 to Iris and James M. Nixon, M.D. in Bay Harbor. Upon graduation from Bay County High School in 1942, he attended the University of Florida for two years. He graduated from Temple University School of Medicine in Philadelphia, Pennsylvania, in 1949 and then completed his internship from 1949 to 1951 at Philadelphia General Hospital. After medical school he was a First Lieutenant in the U. S. Army and served in San Antonio, the Letterman Army Hospital in San Francisco, and the U.S. Air Force Hospital in Wiesbaden, Germany.

In 1953 Dr. James D. Nixon returned to Panama City to join his father in the general practice of medicine at 806 E. 6th St. (across from Bay Memorial Hospital). Each doctor delivered about 7000 babies during his career in general practice (family medicine).

One main change during their lifetimes, which affected the medical profession, was the mode of travel. Dr. J.M. Nixon began his practice making house calls, often by horse and buggy or by boat. He would occasionally be gone for two or three days and would return with chickens, eggs, or fresh vegetables as payment for his services, especially during the depression years. When Dr. J.D. Nixon began his practice in the early 1950s, house calls (by car) were an important part of his daily practice. At the end of office hours he received a list of his patients needing a house visit. A knock on the door or a phone call would always mean "go" for both doctors.

Both Drs. Nixon served as Chief of Staff at Bay Memorial Hospital and were members of the Bay County Medical Society, Florida Medical Association, and the American Medical Association.

After his retirement, Dr. James D. Nixon continued serving the community by volunteering hours each week at the Bay County Council on Aging. In March 1997, after his death, the Council on Aging dedicated the Respite Center in loving memory of Dr. James D. Nixon.

Between father and son, the doctors Nixon treated Bay County residents for more than 100 combined years. Dr. James M. Nixon retired Jan. 1, 1969 at age 82 after 60 years of practice. He died December 14, 1976 at age 90. Dr. James D. Nixon retired Jan.1, 1993 at age 68 after 40 years of practice. He died January 31, 1996 at age 71. They are buried next to each other in Evergreen Memorial Cemetery in Panama City.

Submitted by Beverly Nixon Dusseault, 624 Beachcomber Dr., Lynn Haven, FL 32444.

Robert W. and Mary Knight Nixon
Dirt Roads and Deep Roots

One day well before daylight in the early 1930's, my family left Miami, Florida heading for Vernon, Florida. Later in the day while traveling on a wide white sand and shell-rock road out of Blountstown, my dad pulled the car to a stop on the roadside. Dad got out and we followed. "Look, children", Dad said, "this is virgin timber", pointing to tall pine trees. My childish eyes saw just that...tall trees. My dad saw something special, something he, Thomas Nixon, had seen as a boy in Washington County. So had his father James E. Nixon and his grandfather Robert W. Nixon. All were pioneers of Calhoun, Washington and Bay County, Florida. This story is about them....

Standing L to R: Thomas Nixon, Mary Nixon, Green Davis. Seated L to R: Lester Simmons, Johnnie Simmons

Around 1841 Robert W. and Mary Knight Nixon with their children Daniel and Mary left their native Georgia. They moved to Coffee County, Alabama where children Cofield, Samuel, Roxinia, Sarah, Matthew, Lena Ann and James were born. After 1850 Nixon, 36, again moved his family to Abe's Springs near Blountstown, County Seat of Calhoun County, Florida.

The Knight family followed. Robert's sister Lena Ann had married the widowed minister Gabril McClellan in Georgia. Among McClellan's children was Van, 16. Also in the household was Martha Nixon, 72, possibly the mother of Robert and Lena Ann. The McClellans moved to Calhoun County.

An humble man of integrity and faith, honest and just, Robert was just the man to serve as Justice of the Peace of Calhoun County. Two generations later his grandson James Dallas Nixon would portray these family traits while serving as County Judge of Washington County in Vernon, Florida.

James Nixon (seated center) with sons and daughters

A son Robert was born at Abe's Springs but there Robert would bury his beloved Mary. Later, he married the widow Louisa Lewis. They had a daughter Josephine.

But the winds of war were blowing. Robert's oldest son, Daniel 23, volunteered for the Confederate Army and left for war. There would be more losses for this brave man. Before he would see his son again, both Louisa and Martha passed away. A broken-hearted but strong Irish farmer, our beloved Great Grandfather once again moved his family, this time to Econfina in Washington County.

It was a rougher country, different, with creeks and bayous, mosquitos, moccasins and rattlesnakes, cypress trees as well as pine. Family stories tell of hunting deer and wild turkey and of encounters with bears.

To help with growing sons and daughters in 1864 Robert married Elizabeth Singleton, a widow with 10 year old Elton. Thirty years later Elton still lived near both Daniel and James. Sarah married Charley Vickery; Roxy Ann married Richard Mashburn.

As they married, family members settled around Little Bear Creek. Linnie Ann and Joe Stone built a home but later moved to Stafford Creek near Blountstown. James E. and Mary E. McClellan Nixon lived there as did Matthew and Elton and their families. There was a log cabin school which their children attended. Robert W. reportedly had a 2000 acre sheep ranch at Little Bear Creek. He died sometime before 1880. Family members tell of his and other family members' burial in the Nixon cemetery somewhere in the area.

In the late 1880's as Northerners began discovering the delights of St. Andrews Bay, the area began to develop. A road was blazed out between Marianna and the Bay. A toll bridge operated by Dan Nixon was built about 300 yards west of where Bay County Highway now crosses Bear Creek. Wagons traveled the 60 miles, camping as they traveled. Often people living along the way opened their homes to them. Discriminate travelers found a warm welcome at the nearby Nixon home.

Around 1893 Mr. McNeal and Mr. Chub from the Land Office of the Interior, Gainesville, Florida were returning home from St. Andrews. While staying the night at the Nixon home, they met his lovely seventeen year old daughter Alice.

The men were impressed by the girl. She spoke of the difficulties of having correspondence with the nearest post office eighteen miles away. Mr. Mc Neal asked if she would like to have a post office. She assured him they would be happy to have one. His reply was, "I'll see that you get it". Alice soon heard from the Post Office Department. A post office was established at Nixon, Florida. Alice Nixon Murray would be the first Postmaster.

Focus now turns upon James E. and Mary McClellan

Nixon. There are other descendants of Robert Nixon living but the largest living group descends from James. The birth order of their children is (1800) Daniel W. 11/23/77, Sarah E. 2/16/79, Linny A. 8/19/80, Esther B. 12/5/81, James D. 9/7/83, Robert E.4/16/85, Thomas C. 3/28/88, Samuel J. 4/7/90, Mary E. 3/24/92, Stella E. 3/26/94, and Lilly M. 9/3/96. Linny, Robert and Esther died young.

Dan and Dallas received some higher education. Dan taught school. Dallas was County Judge of Washington County. Sarah married Otto Tompkins, a pharmacist. This large family produced educators, bankers, medical, builders, scientists, law enforcement, business men and women, many others who contributed to the growth and development of the State of Florida and elsewhere.

Dallas and Esther Williams Nixon raised their family in Vernon. Judson's family was in Chipley. Stella Nixon Waller spent many years in Bay County. The rest settled throughout the State. Three of Dallas' daughters live in the Panhandle.

As far as known, the only third generation descendants of James Nixon still residing in Bay County are two daughters of Stella Nixon Waller. Helen W. Pippin was associated with Bay Medical Center for thirty-six years as Director of Medical Records Department. She resides in the Cove section. Burton Ann Waller Gallagher and husband Ronald E., Chaplain, U.S.A.F., Ret. recently returned to the Bay area after thirty years military service.

My childish eyes saw a lot of strange things on that Vernon trip like squeeling pigs, green figs, dirt roads with deep ruts. But most of all a love was born in my heart for a family that would last a lifetime. It was love born in the hearts of the descendants of a humble pioneer who braved the trials of new territory making a path for many to follow. They gather the second Sunday in June at Parker, Florida annually for a Reunion expressing that love.

Submitted by: Jean Nixon Lucius, 255 Grand Royale Circle #104, Vero Beach, Fl. 32962. Sources: U. S. Census 1850 Coffee Co., Ala.; U. S. Census 1860 Calhoun Co, FL; U. S. Census 1870 Washington Co., Fl.; U. S. Census 1900 Washington Co., Fl.; Courthouse records Calhoun and Washington Co., Fl; Family history records; Personal history.

James E. and Mary Nixon Descendents

These are the descendents of James E. Nixon and Mary Nixon. They are the children and grandchildren of Dan Nixon, Dallas Nixon, Tom Nixon, Sally Nixon, Stella Nixon, Mary Nixon and Lily Nixon. This picture was taken at a gathering of the Nixon descendents on May 1944 in Youngstown, Florida.

In the far background (left to right) are Esther Nixon wife of Dallas Nixon, Floyd Nixon son of Dallas and Esther, and Dan Nixon. In the left middle background is Jean Nixon daughter of Tom and Emma Nixon and partially obscured by Jean Nixon is Emma Nixon.

On the back row (left to right) are Barbara Nixon granddaughter of Dallas, Betty Nixon, daughter of Tom, Bernice Whitehurst daughter of Stella and Thelma Dykes granddaughter of Sally.

On the second row (seated left to right) are Patricia Mashburn granddaughter of Stella, Juanita Pippin granddaughter of Dallas, Betty Nolan daughter of Lily, Rose Marie Pippin granddaughter of Dallas, an unknown person,

James E. and Mary Nixon Descendents

Ann Waller daughter of Stella, Sylvia Nolan (Mary's grandson) holding Eddie Glass great grandson of Sally and Philip

Wester, grandson of Stella.

The boys on the ground are Bobby Nolan son of Lily, Green Nolan son of Mary, Donny Ross, grandson of Dallas and Raymond Nixon grandson of Tom.

Submitted by: Ann Gallagher, 235 South Glades Trail, Panama City, FL 32407.

The Norris Family
Bay County Florida

The Norris family truly represents the pioneer spirit we all know so well here in Northwest Florida. The family patriarch W.O. Norris and his wife Teretha Sellers Norris and their children Janette, Oakley C., John (Walt), Wynell, and Durrell relocated from Holmes County to Bay County in the early 1930's. "Pop Norris " as he was known was a multifaceted man who knew many occupations and participated in Masonic Orders. He retired from Tyndall Air Force Base in the mid 1960's to his Bayou George farm. He instilled in his children the merits of hard work, which had been a hallmark of his life and would set the stage for his children's future successes.

The second generation of this family became successful with education at state universities after their participation in World War II and the Norris daughters married and began to rear their children and teach service to others following the example set by their father. This generation had the opportunity to see Bay County change from a small bucolic community to an area which flourished after the war coming into its own as commerce began to thrive. The rural existence of the county began to slide into obscurity. Their participation in the community not only enhanced their lives, but those of others. They were educators, small businessmen, postal service and civil servants. The profound effect of their adolescence was once again passed on to their children to face the future with resolve knowing that service to others was where their true wealth laid. The third generation of the Norris family was the most prolific and with the benefits of their parent's wisdom and education this family prospered and became more diverse. At this time the sheer size of this family was impressive and they were involved in all aspects of life here in the county. They became mill workers, foresters, educators, public servants and bankers. This generation saw and participated in the growth of the county, as we know it today. A vibrant thriving community we call home.

Once again the theme of hard work, education and the profound influence of previous generations ushered in the fourth generation of the Norris family. They too were to know the importance of family and service to others. The challenges they faced were just as substantial as those before, but the resources which previous generations had worked for were finally coming to fruition. The community was modern with services that were previously unknown.

The pioneer spirit continues to this day in the lives of the fifth generation of the Norris family and we look forward with anticipation to what their future holds. The lessons previously learned, humility, hard work, pride in self and compassion for others will keep the pioneer spirit we all know so well alive.

Submitted by: Wavine Norris, 2110 East Baldwin Road, Panama City Florida, 32405.

Gary Lloyd and
Nancy Eva "Strickland" Norton

Nancy Eva Strickland Was born 26 December in Panama City, Florida, the daughter of Yancy Cecil and Ruby Lee "Hartzog" Stricklin. At age five, Nancy was stricken with Rheumatic Fever, and was confined to her bed for one year. Luckly there were no scars left on her heart. I believe that was because she was a model patient, eager to do everything just as the doctor told her to do.

Nancy was married 22 April 1972 in Donaldsonville, Georgia, to Gary Lloyd Norton, born 27 April 1953. He was

the son of Earnest and Myrtice "Congo" Norton and the grandson of David and Myrtice B "Black" Congo, of Atlanta, Georgia. Some call it "Conger."

Gary and Nancy have three children:

Gary David Norton born 16 June 1973 in Panama City Florida. David finished high school at Cullman High in Alabama. He was married in August 1994 in Cullman, AL. Courthouse to Shannon Stricklin. She was born 12 August,

(Standing left to right) T. J. Norton, David Norton, Shannon Norton, Desty Mathis and Willie Mathis, Their son, Austin Mathis. (Seated) Gary and Nancy Norton and grandson Weston Norton

daughter of Joe and Jane Stricklin of Cullman. David and Shannon have one son, Weston Brooks Norton, born 30 November 1999. Weston is looking forward to the birth of a baby brother in March 2002. David works in Birmingham Alabama in a Cabinet Shop and Shannon works in Cullman County Hospital as a therapist.

Desty Joanna Norton was born 17 October 1975 in Panama City, Florida. She was married 2 April 1994 in a church in Lynn Haven Florida, to Willie Edward Mathis. Willie was born 29 May 1975, son of Dalton and Judy "Pettis" Mathis of Lynn Haven, Florida. Their Son, Austin Blake Mathis was born 21 September 1994 in Panama City, Florida. Desty has IGA Nethropathy and having another child would probably kill her and the baby if not killed would be deformed. This makes it impossible to have another child. Desty is working with handicapped children at M. K. Lewis School and Willie is Working for Pepsi Cola Company.

Troy Joseph "T.J." born 16 August 1984, in Panama City, Florida. He has recently finished High School at Rutherford High, in Panama City Florida.

Nancy has Fibromyalgia from a work related accident. But she works with handicapped Children at M. K. Lewis School with Limited responsibilities. Gary was injured on his job causing RSD, and now he is not able to work at all. These accidents caused them to have to sell or lose a treasured piece of property. This was the home which Nancy's Grandparents had built and lived in until their death, and her mother had lived in until her marriage.

Submitted by: David Norton, 420 County Road, #453 Cullman, AL., 35057; Written by: Ruby Lee Strickland, 2627 Game Farm Road, Panama City, FL 32405. Sources: Research Files of Family History.

Charles Joseph (Joe) and
Lennie Virginia Nowell

Joe and Lennie first arrived in Panama City, October, 1934. Due to the Great Depression, they sold their property in Dothan, Alabama and bought a run down house in West End, St. Andrew. This property had once been the home of the Manager of the German-American Lumber Company, but more recently had been occupied by squatters. In 1935 they rented rooms in the house next door while they tore the old house down. The lumber was rough virgin pine. Since money was still in short supply, he bartered with Mr. Muterspaugh who operated a small saw mill on Pretty Bayou to plane smooth the rough lumber for half of the material. Using this like new lumber he built a new home for his family.

Joe descended from Peter Gilstrap, who sailed from London, England 1726, indentured to Benjamin Aydelott, Jr., Somerset County, Maryland. In 1728 he married Rachel, Benjamin's daughter. Through Rachel his ancestors go back to Huguenot, David Aydelott, born 1610 in France. Joe's Gr/Gr/Gr Grandfather, Idolet Gilstrap was born 7/1/1737 in Maryland and married Eve about 1760. He served in the Revolutionary War, and he and Eve died in Burke County, Georgia 1803 and 1806. Their son, Henry owned slaves in Georgia. Henry's son, Charles was born 1799, and his wife Challey 1805, both in North Carolina.

Joe Gilstrap Family: Lennie, Joe, Joseph and Cordette

Joe's Grandfather, Charles Gilstrap lived in Houston and Lee Counties Georgia before homesteading in Henry County, near Ashford, Alabama after 1850 and before 1860. Joe's father, John Wesley also homesteaded there at the same time. John Wesley served in the C.S.A. and after the war, married Eliza Silcox, 3/17/1872. Joe was born in their log home, 3/22/1881, six months after his father's death.

Joe married Lennie Virginia Nowell in Headland, Henry County, Alabama 1/15/1913. Lennie, daughter of John Jefferson Nowell and Salina Josephine Locke also was born in a log home, 10/21/1885. Since Joe had loaned his horse and buggy to a friend, he walked thirty miles round trip to the County Seat after their marriage license. They were married sitting in his buggy in front of the Pastor's home. Their first son, Paul Cordette was born 08/10/1914 on a farm near Ashford. Their second son, Joseph Cortez was born 09/14/1925 after they moved to Dothan, Alabama.

In Dothan, Joe built a store building and operated a neighborhood grocery until he was forced to close due to the Great Depression. After moving to Panama City he built a grocery store/gas station/tourist court on the corner of Mound Avenue and Highway 98. These buildings were the first new construction after the Depression in the area from downtown Panama City to Panama City Beach. Since several, "Dothan families" lived nearby, the new enterprise was aptly named, "Little Dothan." He continued in the building/construction business until his early death. Charles Joseph (Joe) died 2/13/1938 and was buried in Greenwood Cemetery. Lennie lived to raise their youngest son, Joseph Cortez and to know all their grandchildren. She died 4/29/1962 and was buried along side Charles Joseph.

Submitted by: Joseph Cortez Gilstrap, 2428 Reservation Road, Gulf Breeze, Florida 32563. Sources: Census and Public records MD/NC/GA/AL/FL including Marriage/Death Records; Military Records; Family Bibles.

Sisters Mary Etta Owens and Hattie Gray Nicholson Reunited after 41 Years

Both my grandmother Mary Etta Gray Owens and her sister, my Aunt, Hattie Gray Nicholson were born in Geneva County, Al., in 1883 and 1880 respectively. Their father and grandfather had arrived in Geneva County in the 1860's. The family then moved to the Panama City area at Bayhead, Fl. From there the sisters married and drifted apart, neither knew of the others whereabouts for **41 years**.

Then in 1951, Mrs. Bessie White, a stepdaughter of Aunt Hattie, (age 73)who was then living in Pensacola, read in an obituary the name of a survivor who was a brother-in-law of Hattie. Mrs. White took Hattie to the funeral hoping to meet some of her family. None of the Panama City family attended the funeral but they learned from others that Hattie's youngest sister, my grandmother Mary Etta, (age 68) was alive and living in Panama City.

Mrs. White contacted the sheriff in Bay County, who it turned out was a good friend of Mary Etta's family. The sheriff delivered the wonderful news to my grandmother that her sister was trying to locate her. The next Monday a

letter arrived in Pensacola with the happy response.

The Panama City News paper and the Pensacola News-Journal reported the story in this way. "The women came to the News-Journal office this week arm in arm with bright , cheery smiles". "Learning where she lived," Mrs. White said, 'we took Mother to Panama City and never a happier meeting has anyone seen. They each thought the other was dead and can you imagine how they felt when they met each other. They just clung together for about 40 minutes." The article went on to say that the sisters were so happy they were staying together for about a month, recalling childhood experiences and remembering other family members and declaring precisely that another separation would never occur again.

I was about 9 years old when this reunion took place and remember it well. I also recall how much fun it was to have two loving "granny's" in the family. My grandmother, Mary Etta and aunt Hattie lived together in Panama City until their deaths. They are buried side by side, just as they wished, in the Youngstown, Fl. Cemetery.

Submitted by: Sherl Horne Morden, 4502 Brook Forest Dr., Panama City, Fl. 32404

The Joe Parrott Family

Joe Parrott, a native of upstate New York, arrived in Bay County in 1941 at the age of 26 and found lodging in the Hamilton Avenue home of C. R. (Boots) Roche. He took a job with Angus Watts, owner of Panama Billiards which was on Harrison Avenue close to the corner of Harrison and Fourth. With his quick senses of humor and easy manner, Joe quickly became acquainted with the downtown crowd of young and old working people in pre-war Panama City.

Sybil's Grill, the neighborhood diner owned and operated by Mrs. Joe Mizell, was a favorite breakfast spot of Joe's. There he met Claire Rubash, daughter of Joe and Mary Rubash of St. Andrew, who was working at Sybil's as a waitress. Claire joined the staff as a clerk at the Panama City Post Office in November of 1942, graduated from Bay High School in 1943, and married Joe the following January.

Joe Parrot

Shortly after Joe joined the U.S. Army, the Japanese attacked Pearl Harbor. He took his basic training in Hawaii and served his active duty in Saipan where the Japanese hid in caves during the day and climbed trees at night to shoot at the Americans. He served with the occupation forces after Japan surrendered and returned to the States in January of 1946.

Upon his return Joe took a job as car salesman for P. D. Heath, owner of Heath Motor Company. He later opened Good Used Cars, located on Harrison Avenue a few blocks north of Nelson Buick Company. He opened Parrott Motors on Harrison Avenue and then on Beck Avenue in St. Andrew. He was later the used car manager with Tommy Thomas Chevrolet. Because of his love for the automobile and his knowledge of used cars, Joe had his own following of loyal

Claire Rubash Parrot

customers who bought used cars from him until his death in 1976.

Joe and Claire made their home on the corner of Eighteenth Street and Drake Avenue in St. Andrew where they raised three daughters: Patricia Ann, Gwen Marie, and Susan Yvonne (Bonnie). Patty married Lamar Sikes, son of Mr. and Mrs. Hubert Shorter Sikes of Panama City. They have three children: Hugh, Julie and Joe. Gwen also married a local boy, Freddie Mack Johnson, son of the late Ted Johnson and Mrs. Mary Johnson Pogue, also of Panama City and they have three children: McKenzie Lane, Bonnie Katherine, and Carter Mack. Bonnie married David Ramirez, son of Mr. and Mrs. Joe Ramirez of Panama City.

Joe's friends best remember him for his smile and his cigar, his funny jokes and his jovial disposition. He passed away in 1976 from heart disease, which plagued him for most of his adult life. Claire remained at the Post Office for 38 years, working her way up from window clerk in the downtown office to the Superintendent of the Panama City Beach Branch and later St. Andrew Station. In 1971 she became Supervisor of Support Services (responsible for banking, budget and finance). She is retired and living in St. Andrew where she is enjoying her many friends and activities in the Agape Bible Sunday School Class of the St. Andrew Baptist Church, the St. Andrew School Reunion Committee, the Crape Myrtle Circle of the Panama City Garden Club, her Bay High luncheon group, and the Captain James Day Chapter of the Colonial Dames Seventeenth Century.
Submitted by: daughter, Patty Sikes, 6445 Dunleith Place, Pensacola, FL 32504.

Bob Pascoe
How I Wound Up in Panama City

There comes a time in every Yankee's life when he looks out the window, sees six feet of snow in the driveway, realizes he's going to spend the next two hours digging his car out, again, for the third time in two weeks, and says, "Enough."

If he's smart, and not all Yankees are, he turns to his atlas on those long, cold winter nights, and begins to look for places where a civilized man can partake of the good things in life (like fishing, sailing, tennis, dining alfresco, etc.) on a year-round basis. Inevitably he finds himself drawn, like the early Spaniards, to maps of Florida.

"Bob's Boat" at anchor, Santa Rosa Key

If he's adventurous, and few Yankees are, it occurs to him that there are other ways of getting there than driving a U-Haul crammed with things that could just as well be unloaded at a garage sale and replaced later, if need be. It might even occur to him, after he sets aside all the things he can't part ways with, like tennis rackets, fishing rods, diving gear, etc., that they would all fit in his boat, if carefully packed, and that if he got rid of the car and trailer as well, to be replaced later, if need be...

And so an idea is born. Over the cold winter months it grows into a plan, a plan that will take him from the frigid shores of Lake Michigan to the sun-drenched coast of Florida. On paper it looks good, but then so did the builders plans of the Titanic. The following fall still finds him tidying up his business affairs, the sailing date postponed three times, the weather turning cold. But Yankee ingenuity will find a way, it always does.

In this case it finds a sailing date that coincides exactly with the earliest Midwestern blizzard in recorded history.

The cold snap that follows also sets records, again and again, from the upper Mississippi to the headwaters of the Tombigbee waterway. If a Yankee was religious, and some still tend to be, he might jump to the conclusion that God was punishing him for abandoning his ancestral home. On the other hand, he can't turn back if the river keeps freezing over in his wake, so maybe God is trying to tell him something else.

But what? A line from Poe springs to mind. "Ride boldly ride, the shade replied, if you seek for Eldorado."A lone Yankee voyager chips the ice from his sheets and halyards and presses on, seeking his personal Eldorado. The log entry from February first reads, "Cleared Mobile Bay 10:30 AM. Winds southwest 15 knots and steady. Skies clear. Barometer rising. Temperature 72 degrees. The Gulf of Mexico is awesome. Awoke this morning at anchor in Dog River to find my boat surrounded by pelicans. Saw something in the water just outside the pass, a big shark maybe. Incredible. Sailing in shorts and a tee shirt in February. Called a friend back home last night. Lake Michigan is frozen solid. Think I'll steer a course eastward and try my hand at fishing. The rest will work itself out."
Submitted by: Bob Pascoe, 426 McKenzie Ave., Panama City, FL 32401.

John B. Pascoe
Why I Moved to P.C.B.

I had never planned to live at the beach but I have since learned that man plans and God laughs.

My ex-wife and I lived in the Atlanta area and bought a modest townhouse at Gulf Highlands in 1991. We bought it as a getaway and an investment. While visiting down here at the urging of a co-worker who had a townhouse on North Lagoon Dr., I discovered that my ex-wife wanted a place close to the beach and knew someone who had a unit at Gulf Highlands, so we went there to look. We made an offer but the deal "fell through". I had to get back to work so my wife came back and found the place where I live now at Gulf Highlands.

I had vacationed here several times over the years and liked the friendly people, beautiful beaches and proximity to Atlanta. I was glad when the "deal" went through.

We came here often between 1991 and 1995 when we got a divorce (after 26 years). I somehow wound up with the beach condo after replying that it didn't matter to me, she could have it if she wanted. I'm glad it worked out like it did because when I took early retirement in 1997, I decided I would move to the beach. I've never been sorry!
Submitted by: John B. Pascoe, 162 White Sandy Dr., Panama City Beach FL 32407.

Ernest Roger Patterson and
Vicki Riffe Patterson

Ernest Roger Patterson (b 2/18/1942, d 5/20/1988) was

born in Dothan, Alabama and graduated from Ashford High School. His parents, William Ernest Patterson (b 1/1907 d 1980) and Alma Martin Patterson (b 8/1911-) grew up in Dothan, Alabama. Roger joined the Air Force directly after high school graduation and made it his career.

Vicki Riffe Patterson (b 7/31/1943 -) was born in Noble, Oklahoma. Her parents Victor Hamilton Riffe (b 12/1912 d 7/1943), Carnegie, Oklahoma and Ruth Highsmith Riffe (b 7/1912 d 5/1996), Altus, Oklahoma, were married in Noble, Oklahoma, 1941. Vicki grew up in Hobart, Oklahoma; and graduated from

Roger and Vicki Patterson with children Paula and Roger Wayne 1983

Southwestern State College in Weatherford Oklahoma. Roger and Vicki were married 2/1/1964 in Hobart, Oklahoma. Roger and Vicki lived in Elk City, Oklahoma, Hobart, Oklahoma and Denver, Colorado. While in Denver, 1965-1967, Vicki worked for the Colorado Fuel and Iron Company. In 1968, Roger was transferred to Bentwaters Royal Air Force Base, England and they moved to a little village called Little Glemham in East Suffolk. Vicki worked at the Air Force Library before their daughter Paula was born (5/20/1968) at Mildenhall RAFB, and Roger worked coordinating the finances for the Service Club as a second job. They returned to the United States in 1969 to live in Sacramento, California. Their son, Roger Wayne was born in Roseville, California (7/18/1971) While in California, Roger discovered his love of fishing for salmon in the American River. Vicki worked as an administrator for the Hemophiliac Foundation.

In 1972, during the Vietnam conflict, Roger was stationed in Thailand while Vicki and the children moved back to Hobart, Oklahoma. While waiting for Roger's return, Vicki worked as secretary for the chairman of the board of Broadway Insurance Company in Hobart. Paula started school there.

In 1973 the Patterson family moved to Panama City, Florida. They almost immediately moved onto Tyndall Air Force Base and lived there for 8 years. Both children attended Tyndall Elementary School, Everett Junior High and Rutherford High School. While Roger worked in the pay and travel units of Tyndall Air Force Base, Vicki was employed at the Bay County Public Library.

When Roger retired from the Air Force in 1981, he was employed as bookkeeper for the Tropical Isle Time Share Resort and was promoted to general manager after six months. In 1986 Paula married Charles Allan Muehlebach (children - Cherles Anthony 7/1986 and Corey Scott 11/11/1992) Roger retired to due health reasons in 1985 and expired 5/20/1988 from colon cancer. Vicki and family continue to live in Panama City, 2003.
Submitted by: Vicki Patterson, 719 Clarence Lane, Panama City, FL 32404.

Brenton Eugene Peacock and Cynthia Renee Robbins Peacock

Brenton Eugene Peacock was born August 1, 1964 to Carl Eugene Peacock and Barbara Ann Nichols Peacock. Brenton was born and raised in Marianna, Florida. He came to Panama City, Florida to attend college. There he met and married Cynthia Renee Robbins. Cynthia is the daughter of Richard N. Robbins and Dorothy Ann Johnson Robbins. She was born in Panama City, Florida October 16, 1963. She attended Cherry Street School, Rosenwald Junior High and Bay High School. Cynthia and Brenton both graduated from Florida

Brenton, Lorena and Cynthia Peacock

Pauline Johnson (great-grandmother), Ann Robbins (grandmother), Lorena Peacock and Richard Robbins (grandfather)

State University.

Brenton got a job at Gulf Coast Community College with WKGC radio. He worked with the programming and taught classes. Later when the college got involved with the Work Force program, Brenton went to work with Work Force. Brenton is listed in the 2000 edition of *Who's Who Among America's Teachers*.

Cynthia works as a Kindergarten teacher at Lynn Haven Elementary School. She was Teacher of the Year at Lynn Haven Elementary School in 1999 and got her Masters Degree in 2002.

Lorena Colette Peacock age 2

Brenton and Cynthia are the proud parents of Lorena Colette Peacock. Lorena who is also called Rena, was born October 31, 1999.

Brenton can trace one of his ancestors to William Peacock born about 1642 in Raleigh, Virginia. Cynthia can trace one of her ancestors back to William Shipp born 1572 in Suffolk, England. One famous descendant of this same Shipp family is Harry S Truman, 33rd President of the United States.
Submitted by: Cynthia Peacock, 504 Lori Lane, Lynn Haven, Florida. Written by: Ann Robbins, 435 South Palo Alto Ave, Panama City, Florida 32401.

Charles Franklin Peacock and Pera Lee Strickland Peacock

Charles Franklin (1914) and Pera Lee Peacock (1923) were married in Calhoun County and brought their family to live in Panama City in 1950. They moved into a little home in Hiland Park, on Selma Avenue. They brought their children, Stony, Charlotte, Carolyn, Robert, and Pauline. Shortly after, they moved their little family to a larger frame home on Bradenton Street.

Charles worked each day at the Standard Oil Canning Plant, while Pera Lee was a fulltime wife, mother, and homemaker. With this family, both Charles and Pera Lee stretched their energies to provide for their children and each other. They taught their children old-fashioned values built around honesty, kindness, responsibility, and education. As the stair-step children became school age, they walked the dusty road leading to their school. At midday, they often walked home for lunch. When they were out of school they enjoyed lazy, long days, playing nearby, climbing trees, and walking to "Hartzog's Store" to spend pennies they earned.

In 1953, Charles and Pera Lee bought a partially constructed

Charles Franklin and Pera Lee Peacock and children

home on 12th Street in Callaway. Charles completed the interior with pine from their timberland. In May, Charles and Pera Lee moved their big family to a beautiful home sitting on five acres.

Charles used their compact acreage as if it were a tiny farm, tending cows, pigs, chickens, and a garden. Pera Lee made the girls' dresses, sewed quilts, crocheted beautiful pieces, and kept the freezer full of tasty produce from the garden. And she cultivated beautiful daylilies, making their circle driveway a springtime bouquet! Together, with God's blessing, they provided the clothes and mountains of food that their growing children needed.

And in 1957 the last baby Peacock was born to Charles and Pera Lee. She was named Roberta Lee after her big brother Robert and her mother. The family shifted to make room in their hearts and home for this sixth child.

Their children grew up seeing their parents work hard and enjoy small pleasures: fishing for great catches of bream and shellcracker, going into town for square-dances, swimming at the "Jetties', visiting family, and piling everybody into the car and taking Sunday drives! The children had their fun playing with neighbors, forming "boys clubs" and "girls clubs", "grunting" for fishbait to sell for pennies and going to summer "fun school" in Springfield.

As each child grew up and graduated from school, Charles and Pera Lee were continually loosening parental ties and putting their faith in the foundation their children had been given. One by one the children sought their fortunes and in 1979 Charles and Pera Lee retired to Dead Lakes outside Wewahitchka, where they found fishing and gardening a daily pleasure. For many years they filled their freezers with fish, vegetables, and fruits harvested at their lakeside home.

In 2002 Charles and Pera Lee returned to Panama City and Bay County, Fl., where they reside today. They are frequent visitors to their Dead Lakes home where they find peace within themselves. Their Bay County gardens keep their freezers full and they realize great pleasure in sharing their home grown produce. Pera Lee tends her beautiful flower gardens and vegetable garden while Charles F. tends his vegetable gardens and writes and sings his songs as a testimony. They are blessed and continue to be a blessing to their children!

Submitted and written by: Charlotte Peacock Davis, 9210 Lake Forest Drive, Youngstown, FL 32466.

Henry David and Rosa Belle Pitts Pennington

Henry David Pennington was born in Henry County, Alabama on November 18, 1892 (d. 22 October 1977). He was the son of Thadeus Ioleus (b. 3 May 1861, d. fall of 1914)

Rosa Pitts Pennington and Henry David Pennington

and Mary Taylor Pennington (b. 13 February 1856, d. 31 October 1943). Other children of this marriage were John William (b. April 19, 1882), Penelope Jane (b. Oct. 11, 1883, d. 30 December 1980), James Palestine (b. Oct. 4, 1885), Hardy Lamuel (b. Feb. 29, 1887, d. 18 December 1947), Velina (Dec. 2, 1891), Laura Belle (b. Apr. 3, 1894, d. 31 March 1916), Carrie (b. Oct. 8, 1897, d. infant) and Ann Mary (b. Dec. 4, 1898).

In approximately 1914, Henry David moved to Panama City, FL with his mother Mary and brothers and sisters who still lived at home. In 1922 he married Rosa Belle Pitts, (b. 4 January 1902, d. 25 September 1966) a descendent of Peter Ferdinand Parker who came over from Danzig, Germany and settled in Parker, FL. She was the daughter of Noah W. Pitts (b. 16 February 1837 d.

Henry David and Rosa Pitts Pennington and children

Mar 22, 1924) and Rebecca Parker Pitts (b. 6 March 1871, d. 14 June 1923). Rosa's siblings were Jessie, Lenora, Susan and Morris. Susan and Morris both died as infants. Children of Rosa and Henry are Argie Gunn, Henry Douglas, John Gordon, William Edward, Charles Whitfield, Rosemary Moser, Laura Ruth Grace, James Horton and Donna Ann.

Henry David was a carpenter and also served for a number of years as business agent of the local carpenter's union. He was a Boy Scoutmaster and was also involved in politics. Rosa was postmistress of Parker at one time and in later years worked for the Bay County Sheriff's office.

For many years we lived in the house that belonged to Rosa's grandmother on the big curve of U.S. highway 98 in Parker. Being on the bay, we swam, crabbed and fished a lot. Fishing was Rosa and Henry's favorite pastime. We celebrated many holidays together in this house and the memories are precious.

Submitted by: Rosemary Pennington Moser, 3515 W. 19th St, Unit #8, Panama City, FL 32405.

Pennie Pennington

Aunt Pennie Pennington was born in Henry County, AL, Oct. 11, 1893, where her father, Thadeus Pennington, was a brick mason and her family farmed. The crops were usually cotton and there were times when the children could not go

Pennie Pennington

to school because the cotton was ready for picking. After picking in her family's fields she would then work for her Uncle John Taylor. In approximately 1914 she came to Panama City with other members of her family and in 1916 she and her brother, Henry David, bought a house on Pine Street from Mrs. McKenzie, the mayor's wife. She continued to live in this house until her death at age 97, on Dec. 30, 1980. She also joined the First Baptist Church in 1916 and it became a source of much joy in her life. She never married and had children of her own but the nine children of her brother, Henry, were very dear to her and they loved her like a mother. When life became overwhelming in the large family we would pack our clothes and go to her house for a stay and we always received a big welcome. She was a very good seamstress and made all of the girl's clothes until we grew up. She also sewed for many of the women in the Cove section. Her house was divided into four little apartments, which she rented, and this was her source of income. Aunt Pennie was the happiest person I have ever known. She found joy in the small things in life. She always drew on her faith in her Lord when there were troubles. Her way of life was a lesson for us all and we cherish our memories of her.

Submitted by: Laura Grace, 3515 W. 19th St. Unit #7, Panama City, FL.

Randle A. Penton Family

The Penton family arrived in Panama City, FL. in the year 1933 to begin new life experiences. Randle Adolph "Bob" Penton and his wife Hettie Vera Warner Penton were "paper mill folks". Randle was enticed to come to Bay County to the new paper mill as many of his co-workers had moved here.

His eldest son, Hewitt H Penton moved the family as soon as school was out, to the area. He drove our old Dodge auto from Bastrop LA, with mama, Hettie in the front and sisters, Ruby Nell and Mildred in the back. The hi-way between Mobile and Pensacola was just being "paved". When they saw the tall white sand dunes, they thought it was snow!

Temporary housing was the Bay Harbor Hotel, the John Boggs family home in Old Orchard, a company house in Bay Harbor then the move to a rental house on Harrison Avenue, next door to the Presbyterian Church. The Catholic Church and rectory was on the corner of 6th & Harrison, the O. E. Addison family home, the church, our house, the Smith home and one other home, then a service station on the corner. We were a half block away from Panama Grammar school where Ruby Nell began first grade, Mildred was in the third.

Son, Hewitt H Penton went to work at the Southern Kraft Paper Mill where his dad was millwright foreman. Son Joe William joined the family to finish his senior year at Bay High. He later went to work at the mill. Hettie remained a housewife, keeping up with shift work.

Randle then moved his family to a rental at 835 Jenks Ave. (which was not paved) where the family lived until the early 40's. He rented from J. C. Stewart who had a grocery store on the corner of 8th and Harrison. He had several rentals in the area.

Randle was a handicapped person who worked with a wooden leg. He lost his leg on Christmas Eve as a result of the sawmill job related injury. He never stopped to feel sorry for himself. He climbed ladders and did all sorts of maintenance work at the paper mill. In fact, as soon as he could, he opened his own machine shop in Bogalusa, wearing a wooden peg-leg. He eventually got him an artificial limb which he wore all of his life.

While living here, Hewitt married Jo Thelma Thomas, daughter of Joseph & Adnie Ethridge Thomas on April 11, 1937. They had two daughters, Madeline & Dorothy Jean. Joe married June 12, 1941 Mildred Wert Morris daughter of William Wirt & Ella Riles Morris. They had two sons, George Oliver & Jeffrey. Mildred married February 18, 1943, Adrian D. "A.D" Richbourg, son of Chester L & Mattie Dykes Richbourg. They had two sons, Adrian Colter "Colt", and Randal Wade. Ruby Nell married April 21, 1945 John Albert Delcomyn, son of Albert & Mazie Nobles Delcomyn. They had a son, John Albert Jr, died at birth, and Laura Suzanne & Carrie Ann.

Randle was employed over 30 years with the paper industry as a master mechanic and millwright foreman, a member of The Quarter Century Society, Inc., an avid hunter and fisherman. It was not until 1946 that he pur-

chased his first home at 506 Magnolia Ave. This was before Southern Bell purchased the corner land across the street. He remodeled as he could.

Randle was a strong man, had pride in his family. Many times he would work on shut-downs for a week at a time without even coming home. He read encyclopedia and non-fiction, along with his Bible daily, which gave him a broad education. He chewed Penn's and Reynold's Natural Leaf tobacco, always wore long sleeves and a hat while in the sun as he was so fair. He kept a daily log, who came by, what bills he paid, special news happenings which his children enjoy reading. Costs of groceries, weather conditions are also recorded.

Randle Adolph Penton was born Sept 20, 1890, died May 19, 1977. Hettie his wife was active in the First Methodist Church and Sunday School. She volunteered to make items needed at the hospital. She was a member of the Women's Missionary Society of the church. Hettie Vera Warner Penton was born January 12, 1896 Tylertown, MS, died April 23, 1983. Both are buried in Greenwood Cemetery, Panama City, FL near their grandson.

Submitted by: Dorothy Jean Crawford, 801 Main St., Greensboro, AL 36744. Written by: Mildred Penton Richbourg.

J. K. Pettis Family

My name is Wanda Pettis McMullon. I was born at Bay Memorial Hospital in August of 1949. I was raised in Bay County in the area of Hiland Park. My parents were J. K. (1912-1979) and Hazel McNeal Pettis (1924-1985). They had four children James Kenneth (Kenny), Robert Charles, Wanda Kay and Sandra Faye. My

J. K. Pettis Family

parents and grandparents were raised in Washington and Jackson counties. They came to Bay County in the early 40's.

My parents were hard working self employed people. They owned and operated two businesses for over thirty years here in Bay County. One was a bar located on Highway 231, one mile north of the busy intersection of East Avenue and Highway 231. This busy intersection was known as the Hiland Park intersection. It was also the location of the other business, a grocery store, "Hiland Park Meat Market". This store, and this neighborhood holds many happy memories for me and my siblings. People would drive from miles away to get fresh meat from the market. My dad was a great butcher! This was the era before the junior stores. The local neighborhood grocery store served the communities needs.

I have many memories of my dad making sure people had food whether they had money or not. Many people received food on credit. It did not matter, when times were hard, if their credit account remained unpaid. They still got their groceries.

I remember men getting up early and drinking coffee around the kerosene heater in the grocery store. We often wondered what they were discussing, politics, or just talking about other events of the day. Politics and the love of our nation were important to my parents. The candidates visited and talked with my dad often.

Owning the local bar put extra pressure on my parents to teach us high moral standards. Good character skills were also drilled into us constantly. We did not want to disappoint our parent's, or grandparent's expectations for us. However, if we did, they taught us to accept our responsibility and to make amends for it the old fashioned way.

My memories of growing up in Hiland Park are all good!

Left-Right: Mildred Penton, Joe William Penton & wife, Mildred Morris Penton, Hewitt Hillard Penton holding first daughter, Madeline D'Ree & wife, Jo Thelma Thomas Penton, Ruby Nell Penton. Standing back center: Randle Adolph Penton and wife Hettie Vera Warner Penton (Picture made late September, 1942, next door to 835 Jenks Ave, J. B. Seaborn home)

In the Hiland Park Community, everyone knew everyone else, and might even be kin to them. Everyone helped raise everyone's children. Hiland Park people were a close knit group. They respected each other. They and their children still share this special closeness many years later. Many of the original Hiland Park people still live there or close by. The neighborhood was a safe happy place where we never locked our doors.

In those days families were also very close. Our grandparents, uncles, and aunts were part of our daily lives. Cousins were like brother and sisters, and still remain so today.

Holidays hold special memories. Christmas and Thanksgiving were the only holidays our businesses were closed! We had big dinners because all the family was there as well as the customers that didn't have family. Meals were known as breakfast, dinner and supper and we were all required to be there. It was our "family time".

I can look back on my early years with pride. I am proud of the many things my parents taught and instilled in us. I am thankful for parents who loved us and stayed together even through the rough times. I am blessed they raised me properly. I am proud they taught us manners, to respect adults, authorities and to love our country.

I'm delighted to say my daddy's word and or his handshake was as good as any legal document. I am happy to say that my parents taught us to be successful parents, because good parenting was important to them. Their love for their children came first.

These are the memories, along with love, and a strong belief in God that I want to pass on to my grandchildren. Finally, I want to pass on a heritage with deep roots and a fine lineage that will never be forgotten.

Submitted by: Wanda Pettis McMullon, 6120 John Pitts Road, Panama City, Florida 32404.

Golda Edith Pickens

Of the precious stones that Peter Zeno and Edith Coppedge Pickens had named their daughters, my mother, Golda Edith, was the gold. Her sisters were Ruby, Pearl,

Peter Zeno Pickens and Edith Coppedge Pickens

Jewel and Opal, the first born being Flossie. And then Essex and Marquis. The latter retaining the French name spelling, a reminder that the Pickens (Picons) go back to the French Huguenots - the Picons abdicating their roles in the royal court after the revocation of Nantes that revoked religious freedom. They fled to Scotland and later to Ireland. And then on to Pennsylvania where the six sons and families spread into Virginia, the Carolinas, and, our branch into Alabama.

Grandpa's daddy, James McKee Pickens, enlisted in the Confederate Army at the age of sixteen years. He and his fiddle made it through the war and returned to Greenville,

Alabama where he married the war widow, Martha Cheatham. Years later, Grandpa Peter Zeno brought his family to Millville, Florida. He operated the dredge for the land for the Dixie Sherman Hotel at 4th Street and Jenks Avenue. He was also the superintendent of the German American Lumber Company in Millville. They lived at the second house (still standing) from the corner of East Avenue and 3rd Street. There my mother was born November 2, 1908. Aunt Ruby said that their mama's daddy, John Wesley Coppedge, a preacher, had delivered the first six of her mama's children when they lived in Greenville, Alabama and Ponce de Leon, Florida. Their father's daddy, James McKee Pickens, was a Justice of the Peace in Holmes

County, Florida and signer of charter in Westville, also in Holmes County.

Alva and Golda Pickens Thomas, Millville, Florida

At age eighteen years, Golda Edith was married to Alva F. Thomas on May 9, 1926 at the St. Andrew Baptist Church. My daddy was in the turpentine business between Bainbridge, Georgia and Monticello, Florida where I was born in 1928. Five years later, in Arcadia, Florida, my sister, Joyce Elaine was born. Upon moving to Panama City, daddy owned/operated a service station (gift from his father, F. J. Thomas), later worked for Nelson Chevrolet, then was state tag inspector before being elected as Sheriff of Bay County. My parents retired to the Thomas Turkey Farm in Mill Bayou. My mother never worked outside our home.

Our cousin, Tulita Pickens, was in and out of our home on 913 Mckenzie Avenue. She was the aunt of the popular Pickens Sisters (Jane, Patti and Helen) who were on radio in the 1930's and went on the first and some succeeding USO Tours. Their daddy, Montezuma, (Monte) also a musician, is buried in Panama City. His brothers operated Pickens Dairy, first located in Callaway before moving to Highway 231. Jane (Mrs. Walter Hoving) had a child who had cerebral palsy, was one of the founders of the United Cerebral Association. She went on to launch a national volunteer organization in the 1970's. The family talked a lot about the renown ones - Revolutionary heroes General Andrew, Captains John and Joseph, and governors of South Carolina and Alabama, etc. but whispered low about the "skeletons in the Pickens closet," There were hints of American Indian heritage, also.

Double cousin (Pickens and Coppedge) Joe Atkins from Blountstown told me that the town lit up like a Christmas tree when my mother and her sisters visited them. "Those Pretty Pickens Sisters," he called them. Those sisters, too, could carry a good tune. When the Arcadia sisters came to

Golda and Alva Thomas at Dead Lakes

Panama City each summer, they would strike up a tune, each one harmonizing in key to the latest tunes (and some old Irish ones). And dance they would, with Grandpa P. Z. shuffling his buck dance. Always vying for attention, grandpa was silently pouting during one meal, but at the end

of the meal, he muttered, "The peas surely would have tasted good if anybody had just passed them to me."

One of their summer rituals was to swap clothes, the sisters returning home with new clothes. Until the next year, when they looked forward to their annual fashion show and swap meet. They liked recalling memories of their deceased mother, to whom they were very devoted. Three of her grandchildren were given the middle name of Edith.

Some of their stories remembered - when my Aunt Jewel went upstairs to put on her new organdy Millville School graduation dress that she had laid out on the bed, the dress was missing but the pet billy goat was there - still chewing! . . . I liked to hear my mother tell about her school lunches. She would take her mother's fat baking powder biscuits, punch holes in the tops and pour syrup in the holes. She would meet at the corner and exchange lunches with a friend whose mother baked cakes for her lunches. The exchange was made and they would walk on to school. . . . And Aunt Jewel kept the story alive about daddy courting her but he married my mother, six years younger than he. Aunt Jewel said that when Alva came calling, shy Golda would sit in the corner making eyes at him!

My mother, who had coarse black hair, penetrating brown eyes and olive skin, died at the age of 51 on January 21, 1959. However, her shortened life did not limit her gifts to me. Her elegance and grace, quiet love, perseverance, her devotion to home and family, and especially her encouragement and faith in me to make my own decisions are not forgotten. And all this given with a good dose of unqualified love. And there were other times, like when she would buy herself a coat, bring it to me, saying, the color was just not right for her - her knowing I needed a coat and my knowing her need to give.

Each time I open a lid of guava jelly, the lid opens up memories of our kitchen with its robin blue table and benches, with my mother cooking guava jelly while I skim the foaming bubbles off the top. As a child, the kitchen was a special room where (when daddy left early) mother let us drink coffee and choose the non-traditional breakfast of sausage or bacon sandwich, or homefries. . And we knew when she was feeling blue. Chocolate fudge would be boiling on the stove. She missed her mother, too.

I do not remember a day when she was not at home greeting and waiting for me when I arrived home from school. My parents had built a home at 913 McKenzie Avenue between Panama Grammar and Bay High School so that my sister and I could walk each way. Returning to the house several years ago, I observed a few changes but no change in the comfort I felt inside those walls. Yes, you can go home again.
Submitted by: Georgia T. Henry-Pearson, 7752 Shadow Bay Drive, Panama City, FL 32404.

Pierce Family Story

"She was the most beautiful girl that I had ever laid eyes on". That's what my father, Smith Pierce, always said about the first time that he saw my mother getting out of a taxi one hot summer day. Dad had been working in Panama City at the saw mill for a year or so. He was from Dallas County Alabama and had come south looking for work. He was a big strapping guy and very young. He was living in what was called Jenk's Quarters, a settlement for African Americans working for Jenks Lumber Company's Saw Mill. Daddy had made lots of friends in the Quarter but his best friends were Sadie Bender Brown and her husband Alex Brown. Sadie always looked out for Daddy. She made his lunch each day just as she did for her husband. Daddy ate a lot so she always sent something extra for him because he was always hungry. The Bender family in Alabama, included 15 children and it turns out they lived right across the river from where Daddy grew up in Alabama, but Daddy only knew the Bender Boys, they were notorious in that area, known to not take much from anyone. But he didn't know any of the girls.

Smith and Elizabeth Bender Pierce

Family members were expected to help other members of the family in need. This time it was Sadie's younger sister Elizabeth Bender, nicknamed Honey, who needed the help. She came to live with Sadie to finish high school. It was Elizabeth who caught Daddy's eye that hot summer day. She had shoulder length black hair and beautiful brown eyes. He decided to ask her out that very day. She accepted. Daddy's favorite pass time besides playing or watching baseball was going to the movies, so he asked her to go down town to the Ritz Theater to see a western. Now this is where the story differs, Daddy said that Mamma fell asleep in his arms at the movies. He said it was because he was "handsome and irrestible". Mama always said it was because she was "too tired from the trip". I suspect it was a little of both.

Mama attended school and played on the girls basketball team. She went on to become one of three people in the first graduating class from Rosenwald High School in 1939. After she completed school she and Daddy were married at the Bay County Courthouse in September 1940. Daddy said they walked down the railroad track to the Courthouse in the middle of town and walked back home. He went back to work and she went back to doing laundry.

My mother once told me to never say that I didn't want children. I asked her why and she said it was because she had made the same statement when she was my age and ended up having 12, three sets of twins. In birth order they are Willie Ann, Edna Earnestine, Barbara Jean, Mary Jewel, Patricia and Peggy (twins died at 3 months), Louis Allen and Luther Grant (twins), Judy Belinda, Sandra Gail, and Kathryn Ann and Kennieth Alvin (twins). Some say my father fainted at the news of the third set of twins.

Both my parents worked hard to raise their family. Elizabeth worked at a dry cleaners and Smith was a truck driver. Janie Sims, (Ma Jane) my father's mother, came to live with us to help out. She lived with us until she passed away in 1977. She made sure that we were never home alone. My father's constant prayer was that he would be able to see his babies finish school. He always stressed the importance of an education and encouraged us to seek higher education. His last child graduated from college in June 1977 and he passed away in November 1999 after 59 years of marriage. Smith and Elizabeth Pierce were truly Blessed. Elizabeth is now 84 years old and has 26 grand children and 24 great grand children. She is still beautiful with light brown eyes and long gray hair.
Submitted by: Sandra G. Pierce, 1635 Louisiana Ave., Panama City, FL 32405.

The Pierce Family Reunion

In 1985 the Pierce Family met for their very first family reunion. The reunion was held at "Mary's Place," a small restaurant in Lynn Haven, Florida. The children, grand children and great grand children of Smith and Elizabeth Pierce got together for church service at Mount Calvary Baptist Church prior to the dinner at Mary's Place. Attending the reunion from left to right First Row was: Louis Allen Pierce Jr, Breland Lewis, Deanna Bowick, Moraynikki Pierce, Jason Pierce, Laquisha Pierce,

The Pierce Family

Mia Oates, Christopher Allen. Second Row: Justin Bowick, Sonya Myrick, Sherry Pierce, Angela Samuels, Luther Pierce Jr, Elizabeth Pierce, Regina Myrick. Third Row: Smith Pierce, Edna Pierce Sullivan, Ann Pierce Lewis, Mary Pierce Bowick, Licresha Bowick, Juwan Lewis, Lutrelle Pierce, Robert Lewis. Fourth Row: Judy Pierce Allen, Kennieth Pierce Jr., Kennieth Pierce Sr., Mary

Pierce, Sandra Pierce, Barbara Pierce Myrick, Kathryn Pierce, Luther Pierce and Louis Pierce.
Submitted by Edna Pierce Sullivan, 25 West Government St., Panama City, FL 32401.

Allie Vee Pitts

Allie Vee Pitts was the daughter of William Mose and Pearl Irene Forbes Pitts. She was born in Bayou George on September 8, 1930. She attended Bayou George Elementary School and was graduated from Bay County High School in 1948.

She married Gene Carroll Frost on February 28, 1953 in Panama City, FL. Gene was born in Jamestown, NY on December 11, 1929. Their children are Robert Charles, Randy William and Jeaninne Carol.

Mose and Pearl made sure that their children accepted responsibility as they were growing up. The older children helped to care for the younger ones and did their share of chores around the house and on the farm. The girls had the task of cooking. Vee became a champion at pie making and still holds that honor. As a teenager she worked for Christo's Five and Ten Store and Jitney Jungle. After high school she attended Montreat College in Ashville, NC. She returned home and attended and worked for Morrow Business College until she went to work for Adams Hospital in Panama City.

Vee met Gene when he was in the Air Force stationed at Tyndall Air Force Base. After their marriage they lived in Panama City until he was injured in an airplane tire accident. He was sent to the hospital at Maxwell AFB in Montgomery, AL. When he was medically retired from the Air Force, they moved to Cherry Creek, NY where his parents lived. Each year, they and their children returned to Bayou George to visit Vee's parents and family. After Gene's retirement from NRC-SKF in Falconer, NY, they built a winter home at Bayou George and spend the winter months there. They can be found there from October to May searching out antiques for their collections. They collect lunch boxes and iron skillets among other things.
Submitted by: Allie Vee Pitts Frost 6439 Wendy Road Panama City, FL 32404

Ammond Pershing Pitts

The youngest son of Mose and Pearl Pitts was Ammond "Amm" Pershing Pitts. He was born February 21, 1934 and died February 9, 1994. He is buried in Evergreen Memorial Garden Cemetery. He married Eula Nell Kay daughter of Charles and Effie Nunnemaker on September 18, 1959. She was born September 18, 1941 in Port St. Joe, FL. They had two children Ammond Thelton and Cynthia Kay Pitts.

As a child, Amm worked on the farm. Like his brothers and sisters, he did not particularly enjoy planting seeds, pulling weeds, hoeing the weeds, and harvesting the crops. As a youngster, as he rested from hoeing and wiped the sweat off his brow, he said, "I know one thing that when I grow up, I'm not going to be a farmer." Needless to say, farming was in his blood, and he had a large garden that supplied the family with fresh vegetables.

In addition to going all over the neighborhood with his brother Doug and their yoke of oxen, he rode his bicycle and the pony. Later he bought a horse and he and his friends went horseback riding. He enjoyed hunting and fishing. At first they hunted small animals that were killing the chickens. As a youngster he liked to go raccoon hunting. He and Doug dressed the raccoons and preserved their hides. They either sold or gave away the meat to people that would eat it. They even went after the alligators that were eating the goats and ducks. Amm especially liked fishing at the Dam. He could throw the net like a pro. If there were fish out there, he netted them.

To earn money, Amm delivered the Panama City News Herald in Bayou George. He had help with this for his brother, Doug, and younger sisters, Margie and Rosie delivered papers too. He did some caddying at the golf course and

helped at the Turkey Shoot held each year near Evergreen Memorial Gardens.

Amm served in the United States Army. He was trained to be a radio operator and was the lead tank driver while stationed in Germany. He was a Private First Class and upon completion of his tour of duty he received the Good Conduct Medal and was honorably discharged.

Amm worked for Bond's Tile Company for several years before he and Gene Richardson decided to go into business together. They owned P & R Tile Company located in Bayou George. Amm bought out Gene's interest in the Company and continued to run a successful business until his death.

After Amm's father died, Amm checked on his mother everyday when he finished work. He would walk around the electric fence to make sure it was working and the animals could not get out. He collected produce and fed the animals. He helped to take care of his Mother when her health failed. She looked forward to his daily visits.
Submitted by : Ammond Thelton Pitts, 22445 Northwest Apache Road, Fountain, FL 32438.

Doris Frances Pitts

Doris Pitts was born September 14, 1923. She married Coot Hill on October 4, 1952. He was born on September 9,

Margie Pitts, Doris Pitts, Mom (Pearl Pitts) and Rosie Pitts

1921 in Sampson, Alabama and died in Bay County, Fl on December 6, 1999. He is buried in Evergreen Memorial Gardens. Their children are Leon Curtis, Elva Allene, and Daniel Calvin Hill. They have lived in Bayou George since their marriage.

Doris attended grammar school in a little school where the Night Owl was. The school was then moved to old cabins that once housed turpentine families. In order to get to school Doris and Pauline had to cross the Bayou George Bridge. It was made of planks and because Doris was afraid of falling off, she crawled across the bridge. When Pauline stopped school, Doris stayed out a year until her brother, Junior, started school. After graduation from Bay County High School, Doris attended a nursing school and then returned home. She and Laurice took an apartment in Panama City to be closer to their work. They worked as waitresses at the Splendid Restaurant on Harrison Avenue.

Doris returned to Bayou George and began working at Gay's Grocery and Gas Station. She lived with them until she married Coot. Her younger sisters and brothers had to catch the school bus at the store, and each morning she carefully inspected their faces and ears to make sure they were clean.

Doris and Coot moved into a house near the store until they built their present home on Highway 231. She opened up a gas station there, and Coot continued to be self-employed with Laird Timber Company cutting and hauling pulpwood.

In addition to keeping house, raising the children, helping Coot and operating a gas station, Doris still found time to take care of the garden and raise chickens, ducks, cows, and hogs. Early one morning, she called her father, Mose, and told him that there was a big bear in the hog pen trying to kill her hogs. Mose went down and killed the bear. It was lean and hungry. Doris and Coot also farmed. They had men who came and farmed the land for them.

Coot's parents were Charlie and Nettie Hill. Coot and Doris built a house on their land and his mother lived there until her death.

Submitted by: Doris Hill, 6813 N. Highway 231, Panama City, FL 32404.

Douglas Coleman Pitts

Douglas Coleman Pitts was born October 3, 1932. He married Betty Jean Martin, February 28, 1958. She was born February 21, 1938. She is the daughter of Thomas Eugene and Mozelle Martin. Their children are Beverly Gail and Rodney Coleman Pitts.

When Doug was a child, he helped out on the farm. He and his brother, Ammond, had a yoke of oxen. These were their pride and joy. They hitched them to a little cart and went all over the neighborhood. Doug was very healthy as a boy, but a ground rattler did bite him when he was crossing the railroad tracks. His father, Mose, gave him first aid and then carried him to the doctor. The younger brothers and sisters were afraid that he would die. He had another accident by standing too close to the fireplace. His pants caught on fire and he has scars from that on his legs.

After graduating from Bay High School, Doug went to work for Miller's Feed Store. He worked there until he was drafted into the army on Feb. 25, 1953. He was sent to France where drove a semi truck and trailer and worked as a Mail Clerk. He served in the Army until Jan. 27, 1955, then the reserves until Feb. 1961. When he returned home, he went back to Miller's Feed Store. When it closed, he began work in the Arizona Chemical Plant Aug. 1955 until his retirement Feb. 1994. He worked as assistant operator, operator and then supervisor until his retirement.

Doug and Betty love the outdoors and go to the river fishing every chance they get. While Betty works with her flowers, Doug works in the yard and garden.

Submitted by Beverly Segers, 5138 Star Ave., Panama City, Florida 32404.

Elva Pauline Pitts

Pauline was the oldest of Mose and Pearl Pitts' children. She first married Joseph Preston Courtney. After his death of a heart attack on July 18, 1953, she married James Richard "Smitty" Schmid on July 13, 1956. Smitty died on October 22 ,2003. He is buried in the Bayou George Cemetery in Bayou George, FL. Preston and Pauline had the following children—Lottie Irene, Joseph Marion, Lewis Harold, Margaret Eloise, Mildred Elizabeth, William Osceola, Sandra Diane and Janice Lanell. Mildred died November 8, 1944 when she was 3 years old. William Osceola, "Billy" died December 25, 1980.

Children of Elva Pauline Pitts (L to R) Irene Domico, Joseph Courtney, Jr., Harold Courtney, Eloise Hudnell, Sandra Keethler and Janice Phillips.

After Preston's death, Pauline worked for a while at Baker's Acres as a waitress, she also worked at Bay Medical Hospital. She was a person that had to keep busy. She would bring her children over and spend the day with her mother, Pearl. The children enjoyed it, for they had someone to play with since some of her children were about the same age as their aunts and uncles. The children became best friends and remain so.

Pauline was a good cook. She could cook collards and cut them so that they looked like a master chef had done it. She didn't believe in wasting food, so that when they had bread or rice left over, the children could count on bread or rice

pudding. She must have liked apple butter because she always had a supply of it. Needless to say, her children didn't always share her enthusiasm for pudding and apple butter.

Husband and family of Elva Pauline Pitts Courtney

Preston worked at the shipyard during World War II as a tacker on the ships. He later joined the Millwright and Carpenter Union and worked as a millwright and carpenter until his death. The lived out in the country and had a small garden to supply the family with vegetables. Like most families, they had a milk cow.

When Mose's eyesight got to the point that he couldn't safely drive, Pauline was the one who chauffeured him around. She took him to pick up produce for the cattle, to the animal sales in Cottondale and Chipley. She took her mother shopping and wherever else she needed to go.

Submitted by: Irene Courtney Domico, 2916 Evelyn Avenue, Panama City, FL 32405.

Margie Marie Pitts

The youngest child of Mose and Pearl Pitts is Margie Marie Pitts. She was born October 11, 1939, in Panama City, FL. She married Charles William Goodman on August 20, 1961 in the Bayou George Presbyterian Chapel. This was the former location of Bayou George School and is now a Baptist Church. Charles was born December 28, 1932 in Bay County in the area now known as Springfield. His parents were William M. (Mr. Willie) and Vera J. Goodman. Mr. Willie owned a pulpwood company and Vera was a homemaker. They were married May 4, 1930. Charles was the oldest of six children. William died in 1997 and Vera died in 1996. They are buried in the Callaway Cemetery in Callaway (Bay County, FL). Margie's parents are buried in the Evergreen Memorial Gardens Cemetery in Panama City, FL. Margie and Charles's children are Charlotte Marie Fraser, Phyllis Carol Henderson and Timothy Charles Goodman.

Margie, age 6 sitting on oldest brother's 1936 Ford.

Margie attended Bayou George School through the third grade. She was in the last class to attend that school. Students were sent to Highland Park School when she entered the fourth grade. It was a big change going from a school with only four in your class to a school with 24 students in a class. Margie was graduated from Bay County High School in 1957.

She worked at Belk's Department Store during high school and after graduation. She later went to work for Florida State Road Department, known today as Florida Department of Transportation. That is where she met Charles. After they were married they lived in Cedar Grove until he was transferred to Tallahassee. He worked for Southern Prestressed Concrete Company until 1977. Then worked for Fairchild Florida Construction Company until 1985. He then worked for The Florida Department of Transportation until his retirement in 2001. Margie worked as a kindergarten teacher's aide and was a homemaker.

Margie was the youngest child of ten. Her Father called

her "Runt" until a family friend wanted to call her "Little Mose." He nicknamed her "Mozell." She is listed in the 1940 Census as Mozell Pitts. When anyone asked her name she would say, "Mozell Margie Marie." She was asked that question often because everyone thought that she was cute. Now she is known as Margie.

It was not all work and no play in the Pitts' household. Margie rode her brothers bicycles, played kick the can, see-sawed, jumped the board, rolled barrels, played hop scotch, jump rope and played with her dolls. She took over her brothers' paper route when they gave it up.

One of her main jobs was to cook supper at night while her mother did the "night work" The night work was gathering eggs, feeding the chickens and milking the cow and putting the animals where they needed to be for the night.
Submitted by: Margie Pitts Goodman, 2528 Pecan Road, Tallahassee, FL 32303.

Michael Louie Pitts

My name is Michael Louie Pitts. I was born in Fraser Clinic on Grace Ave. in Panama City FL. I was named after my grandfather Pitts. The Pitts family lived in Millville and Mothers family lived in St. Andrews. The St. Andrews kids did not associate with Millville kids. Dad must have been brave to venture over to St Andrews. Mother said "When the Millville baseball team came over to play St Andrew Grammar our team always whipped them, every game. I attended St. Andrew grammar school, we lived a mile away. Dad and Mother both worked and sometimes my grandmother would come over to clean up the house for Mom and do other little things for us. I remember the one day I decided I would stay home from school,

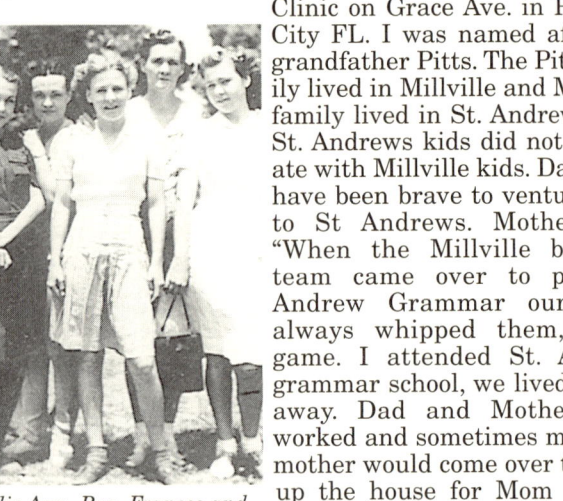
Lillie Ann, Bea, Frances and grandmother Mamie Lee Findley

since Mom was not going to be home that day. I walked as if I was going to school for a few blockes, then turned and went home. I was enjoying myself, my freedom, no school today. I could do what I wanted when low and behold I saw grandmother walk up on the porch, well needless to say I could not be caught out of school. I hurried to get under the bed. I had to listen to grandmother discuss with herself the shortcomings of Mom. Now, I knew that Grandmother talked things over with herself sometimes. She always said when she did this she was talking to a very wise person. I also knew she loved Mom, so that did not bother me. I did not want to be under that bed but I could not be caught out. My grandmother was a grand Lady and I loved her. After a few hours, and it seemed longer grandmother left to go to her home. I had to confess to Mom when she returned home that afternoon. We did not tell grandmother until years later. We all could have a good laugh about that day so long ago when I took a day off from school. I am the son of Harold E Pitts and Willie Levonia Findley. Mom died Feb. 3rd 1995. I miss her, she was my anchorage. She has a memorial Marker in old Greenwood Cemetery. My Dad died March 28th 1995. He sleeps beside my Grandmother Mamie

Mike Pitts and wife Debra Eanes Pitts

Hood Findley and my aunt Frances W Gill Kind in Evergreen Mem. Cemetery. I miss them all. I married Debra Eanes. We have a daughter De De she is married. We all live in Va. My Grandmother was born in Washington Co. My Great Granparents were pioneers, before Washington Co became Bay Co.
Sources: Memories, personal knowledge, Marriage Cert., Birth Cert.
Submitted by: Mike Pitts, 5 Rutland House, Mansfield Court, Harrogate N. Yorkshire, HGI 2QR U.K.; Written by: Bea Moates, 764 Rowland Road, Chipley, FL

Rosa Lee Pitts

Rosa Lee "Rosie" Pitts was born February 17, 1937, to Mose and Pearl Pitts of Bayou George. Rosa Lee married Alvin Morris Powell, Sr., on August 29, 1959, at the Bayou George Presbyterian Chapel. Al was born March 16, 1936,

Aric, Alvin, Rosa Lee, and Al Powell

in Norfolk VA. to Edward Lee Powell and Ada Angeline Stetson Powell Cherry. Their children are Alvin Morris Powell, Jr. and Aric Matthew Powell.

Rosa Lee attended Bayou George School through the fourth grade and then Highland Park School. She was graduated from Bay High School in 1954. With financial help of a scholarship from Wallace Memorial Presbyterian Church, workships and summer employment, she graduated from King College in Bristol, Tennessee in 1959. In 1977, she received her Masters degree from Old Dominion University in Norfolk, Virginia. She followed in Pearl's footsteps as a teacher and retired in 2001 after 42 years of teaching. Al was a Presbyterian Minister and pharmacist. He retired in 2000. They reside in Portsmouth, Virginia.

Rosa Lee earned spending money and money for education by working. She began by delivering the Grit, and News Herald. She sold seeds. When she was old enough, she baby sat, worked at Christo's and McCrory's. After high school, she worked for A. G. Appleberg, (the tax collector), Whatley Typewriter Company, Tax Assessor, and New Car Super Market in Panama City.

There are many happy memories of growing up in a household with 10 children. Fishing trips to Babe Lake, the Bayou, and the river. Her mother, Pearl, loved to fish. They would fish with neighbors and then have a fish fry. Mose would take the whole family to the river in the wagon or his model- T. They would fish and swim, and if they were lucky would have fried fish before they returned home. Just before Al and Rosa Lee got married, Pearl took them fishing. Al was not familiar with redbugs, but he got well acquainted with them as he scratched all the way back to Virginia.

Mose and Pearl believed in family and took them to visit his father, George Washington Pitts in Chipley and his mother, Drucilla Daniels Pitts Bailey in Blountstown. They would also visit his brothers and sisters while there. Pearl kept in close contact with her sister, Lillian. Rosa Lee would ride with her father to her Aunt Lillian's and visit with her each day while she waited for a ride to get to her work. Just about every Sunday, the married children would all be at their parents for Sunday dinner.

Rosa Lee was the tomboy of the family. She went 'coon hunting' with her brothers, followed them around when they hitched their oxen to the cart, went horseback riding, climbed the fruit trees, and swam at the branch where her Mother did the washing before electricity was installed in the house. She had several narrow escapes.

Al, Rosa Lee, and Alvin, and Aric visited her parents

each summer. They wanted to make sure the boys knew their roots.
Submitted by: Rosa Lee Pitts Powell, 103 Ben Hogan Drive, Portsmouth,VA 23701.

William Mose Pitts, Jr.

William Mose Pitts, Jr., known as Bill or Junior, was born March 20,1925 in Pinellas County, Florida. He moved to Bayou George in Bay County, Florida when he was one year old. As a youngster, he liked to tinker with things, especially old cars. He attended Bayou George schools and recalls helping to move desks out of the old school house into the new one. Before completing high school he was drafted into the United States Army in 1943.

Bill was given a choice of any branch of the service, but chose to follow in the footsteps of his father, Mose and joined the United States Army. He was a Staff Sergeant with Company 'E', 27th (Wolfhound) Regiment, 25th Division. He served in the Philippines and was wounded April 27, 1945 on Luzon Island. He was sent back to the United States to recuperate at Lawson General Hospital in Atlanta, Georgia. December

William Mose Pitts, Jr., and Elsie Stephens Pits

1945 he was discharged with the following declarations and citations: Purple Heart, Good Conduct Medal, Three Battle Stars and Asiatic Pacific Theater Ribbon.

While recuperating in Lawson General Hospital he met his future wife, Elsie Inez Stephens. Elsie, daughter of Cline and Lester Stephens, was born on January 1, 1929 in Buford, Georgia. They were married August 3, 1946 and settled in Youngstown, Florida where they owned and operated a gas service station and little grocery store until December 1949.

They then moved to Panama City, Florida where Bill resumed his studies and received his high school diploma from Bay High School and attended Morrow's Business College. He went to work for A.W. Loan Company for about 3 years. He built a Gulf gas service station with a small grocery store on the corner of Highway 231 and Highway 390. He and Elsie remained there until the four laning of Highway 231 acquired the business property.

They formed Pitts Sand Company in 1963 and provided services to the construction industry until their retirement in January 1989. Their two oldest sons, Donald and Mike Pitts, purchased the business from them at that time and continues the family business in the same location.

Bill and Elsie, an honest, hard-working, Christian couple, raised their five children, William Donald, Douglas Michael, Richard Dennis, Deborah Marie, and Delora Ann in a godly home. They continue to live at the junction of Highway 231 and 390 in the same home that they built in 1954.
Submitted by: Deborah Pitts Riley, P.O. Box 23, Panama City, FL 32404.

William Mose Pitts, Sr.

William Mose Pitts, Sr. was born December 3, 1893, in Frink, Florida, the son of George Washington and Drucilla Daniels Pitts.

Mose served in World War I.

On October 07,1922 in Bay County, Florida he married Pearl Irene Forbes. Pearl was born March 12, 1895 in Harrison, Michigan, daughter of Edward Clarence and Alice Mae Sherwood Forbes.

Before marrying Mose, Pearl and her sister, Lillian Mae, taught school in Frink, Florida. (Interestly Pearl's sister,

Lillian Mae, married Mose's brother Joseph Benjamin Pitts.)

After their marriage Mose worked in a logging camp in Frink before they moved to Youngstown, Florida where he and Pearl ran a store for the loggers. Later they moved to Pinellas County

William Mose Pitts Sr. and Pearl Forbes Pitts

where he drilled wells for pumps. Finally in 1926 they moved to Bayou George, Florida so that Pearl could take care of her ailing father.

Mose worked for Bay County as a prison guard in the late 1930's. He supervised the prisoners while they cleared ditches, cut brush, built bridges, and worked on the roads. He helped build the Bay County Pier and earned $1.50 a day while helping to build Highway 98 along the Gulf of Mexico. Cataracts and age forced him to retire from the County, but did not stop him from farming.

Mose and Pearl farmed about 60 acres in Bayou George, Florida. They raised most of the food that the family and livestock ate. In the summer the family had plenty of fresh vegetables and in the winter they had dried or canned vegetables from the farm. In the winter, animals were slaughtered and smoked or salted down for future use. People came to their house to buy excess vegetables and Mose had a regular route where he took vegetables to sell. They raised and sold cows, pigs, chickens, ducks, guineas and goats. Both loved their livestock but the goats were Pearl's favorite.

Pearl was a midwife and delivered many babies around Bayou George. It was not unusual for someone to come get her in the middle of the night. She also taught school at the 2 room schoolhouse in Bayou George. As a matter of fact she taught many of her own children. Her daughter Rosa Lee was in the first grade the last year Pearl taught.

Both Mose and Pearl were well known to help those in need. They taught their children to work hard and treat everyone right. They were wonderful parents to their 10 children Elva Pauline, Doris Frances, William Mose Jr., Laurice Allene, George Edward, Allie Vee, Douglas Coleman, Ammond Pershing, Rosa Lee, and Margie Marie.

Mose died May 23, 1977 and Pearl died June 16, 1990. They are buried in Evergreen Memorial Gardens in Panama City, Florida.
Submitted by: William Mose Pitts, Jr., 4811 East Highway 390, Panama City, FL 32404.

The Porter's of Econfina

I am not certain of the year that Charles L. Porter came to Econfina but he married Eliza Loftin in 1834. They had 10 children, which one was my great grandfather, Henry L. Porter who married Sara J. Mashburn. They had 6 children. They settled in Enconfina and raised their family, My grandfather Samuel S. Porter was their son. As a young man he tried to make a living by hauling salt fish to Georgia by mule and wagon. Then he met and married Lillie McCall and settled down to farming. They had 1 son and 3 girls Boyd Porter, O'Dessia Porter Shipes, Gladys Porter Pittman and Luvern Porter Green. Econfina was in Washington County at the time it was settled. It became part of Bay County when Bay County was formed. The Porter cemetery was located in the middle of the homestead. And is still used to bury any Porter descendent that wish to be buried in it. Econfina was settled by farmers, who made there living from the sandy soil. They also raised a few cattle & hogs mostly for there own use.

My ancestors settled near a spring and a small branch of water that ran through the land as they had no pumps, it was very necessary to have this water close by for drinking,

Lillie McCall Porter and children. Boyd, Gladys Lee and O'Dessia Porter

cooking and to keep milk and other perishable items cool in the running water. They also used them for bathing, washing clothes and watering their garden. All water used in the house and to water the garden had to be hauled or carried by hand in buckets.

The settlers of Enconfina was not interested in making there settlement a large city. They enjoyed the quiet farming life. Some where around 1920 my grandparents, Sam and Lillie Porter moved to Karo, Fl which was south of Youngstown, Fl.

There they continue to make their living by farming and raising cattle and hogs. In those days farming was not a easy job as everything was done by horse and wagon. There was no irrigation system to water your garden so you had to plant your seeds and water them by hand caring your water in a bucket and watering with a dipper.

As a little girl about four years old, I would carry a jar of water out to the field and spend the rest of the morning trying to follow in my granddaddy's foot steps until lunch time and then he would let me ride the horse back to the house. He would also let me go with him on the horse to round up the hogs to be branded with the Porter's branding iron. He would not let me go on the cattle drives when all the men would get together to round up the cattle to be dipped each year. I got to go to the dip and watch as the cattle was dipped.

He was very interested in politics and served quite often on the grand jury for Bay County.

I am very proud of my heritage in Bay County

Submitted by: Dorothy Pittman King, 257 Arlington Drive, Springfield, FL 32404.

Powell and Clark Family
Early residents of Bay County

Isaac Felix Clark, from Abingdon, Virginia, with his bride Cora Belle Grady of Laural, Mississippi, came to the town of Millville in the late 1800's. As a professional boiler maker, he helped to build the first boiler of the local paper mill. Felix enlarged a small three room house, on Maine Street into a very comfortable home for his family, a son and two daughters. Later, as a Building Contractor, performing electrical, plumbing and carpentry work, his company worked on many of the once "military homes" in The Cove, and all around Bay County, He constructed and owned the brick building in Millville, which housed the Millville branch of the U.S.

Charlie Powell (1903-1967) and Billy Kirkland (on right)

Postoffice and a beauty shop. Felix and Cora's daughters were Martha Ruthmae Clark and Irene Elizabeth (Bessie) Clark. Their son died very young. In December of 1926, Ruth married Charlie Eugene Powell, originally from Cottondale, whose family moved to Panama City in early 1900s. Bessie married Roy D. Laird, also from a pioneer family. Their daughter is Phyllis (12-15-31).

Chas. E. Powell and his brother J.W. Powell were co-owners of Powell & Co. Men's Wear, located in the Sherman Arcade Building on Harrison Avenue. Roy Laird's Credit Bureau was located on the second floor of the Arcade. In the 1950's, Powell's Boys Shop, managed by Ruth Powell, was added to Powell & Company, After the deaths of his father, J.W., and his Uncle Charlie (Chas. E.), Wesley, with his mother Bettie Lee Waring Powell and sisters Frances and Jane, bought and operated Powell & Company Men's Wear Store. Later, the store was moved to a location North on Harrison Avenue. From 1939 and through the war years Charlie Powell was Bay County's U.S. Postmaster, appointed by

July 4th (1943 or '44) Parade. Coreta and Wesley Powell. Ruth Powell (holding umbrella)

Franklin D. Roosevelt, and served as a Trustee with the Bay County School System.

During those World War II years, as Tyndall Field and the Navy Base grew, there was a serious housing shortage in this area. Citizens were asked to open their homes to military couples, and shipyard officials. Patriotic as they were, Ruth and Charlie shared their home with several fascinating people, who became lifelong friends, Their children Coreta (2-1-30) Margie (12-29-31) Charla (7-7-35) Martha (4-17-37) and E.I. "Butch" (3-17-44) Powell have crisp and wonderful memories of that time. They enjoyed vocal and instrumental musicians living in their home. They learned about other religious beliefs, big city life, and how to complete jigsaw puzzle without trying out every piece numerous times. They remember family picnics on the long stretches of clean, white beaches which, at that time, were open, and easily accessible to the public, They remember Sunday school, Training Union, and Church services at Immanuel Baptist Church, a special friendship and mentoring ministry of Rev. Adolph Bedsole and his wife "Miss Lilly". They remember attending Panama Grammer, Cove Elementary, and Bay High Schools at a time when it was safe to walk home to lunch each day. Those were the times when our doors were seldom locked and we were still enjoying peace and freedom at home, perhaps without even realizing the value of that freedom..

Submitted by: Coreta Pratt, 110 Kentucky Ave., Lynn Haven, FL 32444.

Arthur Llewellyn Pratt

Arthur Llewellyn Pratt, son of Lucius H. Pratt and Ellen Rogers Pratt was born July 15, 1871 at Becker, Minnesota.

Arthur L. Pratt and Gertrude Parker Pratt on the front porch of their home on the Bay in Parker with their family. Children (left to right) are Vera, Donald, Angus, Harvey and Stuart. Note the grapefruit from the family trees.

His early years were spent in and around Sherburne County where he lived on a farm and attended public school. About 1890, his father and the younger members of the family came south to Cromanton, Florida where his father and he established homesteads.

Arthur worked as a carpenter and helped build some

of the sawmills on St Andrew Bay. He bought land and an unfinished two-story house on the bay in Parker and worked in his spare time to finish it.

On October 6, 1901 he married Gertrude Parker, daughter of John W. Parker and Amanda Folkes, prominent fisherman in the area.

He joined the Lighthouse service, becoming a foreman in 1908, serving an area from the Rio Grande to South Florida up toward Lauderdale. In 1911 he resigned from the service because a shifting of districts would cause him to live in Key West.

Arthur L. Pratt and wife Gertrude Parker Pratt 1901.

The outbreak of World War I brought shipbuilding to Bay County and Arthur became a first class ships carpenter. He followed that trade for years, and worked after retiring age to accumulate some social security credits. The last place he worked was the Sherman Shipyard in Millville.

He also maintained a small farm on the property in Parker with a nice garden, fig trees and citrus trees. He had a boatways on Pratt Bayou where he did sailboat and yacht repair. In his sailboat the Silver Spray he won a free-for-all race sponsored by the St Andrew Yacht Club.

He transformed a lapstrake wooden yacht dinghy into a sailboat for the grandchildren, putting a keel on the bottom of the hull. He cut a pine tree, fashioned a mast and Gertrude sewed the canvas sail on her pedal-driven Montgomery Ward sewing machine.

He and his family were founding members of Parker Methodist Church, which they attended from their marriage in 1901 until their deaths. In his 80's, when he was deaf, someone asked why he attended, since he couldn't hear the sermon.

"Well, at least the devil knows whose side I'm on!' Arthur replied.

He drove a 1928 Ford Model-A until he suffered a stroke in his 80's. He taught himself to walk again, using a kitchen chair as his "walker" and he intended to drive his car too, but it had fortunately become disabled.

He and Gertrude had five children, Stuart Arthur, Harvey Augustus, Vera Bernice, Donald Edmund and Angus Loring.

Arthur died at home in Parker on August 17, 1959. Gertrude died at home on July 9, 1961.
Submitted by: Bernice Anderson Pratt, 1126 Loftin St., Parker, FL 32404.

Lucius H. Pratt

Lucius H. Pratt brought his family to Cromanton in 1890, homesteading on the Gulf Beach. He and his wife, Ellen Rogers Pratt, had eight children. Lucius (August 8, 1832) and Ellen (January 13, 1844) both were born in Maine, moving to Minnesota later, where they were married Nov 29, 1860. Lucius enlisted in November 1861 in the Minnesota Second Light Artillery. He served three years two months, was sunstruck marching through Mississippi, resulting in injuries for which he received a pension from the government.

The Pratts owned a prosperous farm near Anoka, Minnesota prior to moving South.

He later said he had three

Lucius H. Pratt, Minnesota Second Light Artillery

main crops at Cromanton: mosquitoes, sand spurs and rattlesnakes. Cromanton later became part of Tyndall AFB and all the family property was acquired by the government.

His eldest child, Carrie, married and remained in Minnesota. Edmund, Lucius L, Arthur, Willard, Lillian, Rosetta Belinda and Hattie came to Cromanton with their parents.

Arthur homesteaded land adjacent to his father's property. Arthur and his brother Edmund married sisters Gertrude and Wilhelmina Parker, daughters of John and Amanda Folkes Parker and granddaughters of Peter Ferdinand Parker and Anne Loftin. The Parkers were prominent fishermen on St Andrews Bay and the Gulf.

Ellen Rogers Pratt

Lucius died January 1, 1905. Ellen died Sept 17, 1912 at the home of her son Arthur. Both are buried in the Cromanton cemetery on Tyndall AFB.
Submitted by: Ann Pratt Houpt, 1128 Loftin St., Parker, FL 32404.

Stuart Arthur Pratt

Stuart Arthur Pratt, a great grandson of Peter Ferdinand Parker and Anne Loftin Parker, was born Dec 19, 1902 , to Arthur L. and Gertrude Parker Pratt at their home on the Bay in Parker. He was one of the first baptized in Parker Methodist Church. He attended Parker Grammar School, Millville High School and Panama City High School.

He worked in the shipyard in Millville to save money to go to the University of Florida, graduating in 1928 with a bachelor's degree in Business Administration. There being no jobs available, he became a cargo checker on the steamer Tarpon. While working on the Tarpon, he met and married Bernice Anderson, daughter of George and Palestine (Monk) Anderson.

He went to work at the Southern Kraft Paper Mill in

Stuart Arthur Pratt and Bernice Pratt

the labor crew (bull gang), worked his way up through paper testing in the lab to become a statistical clerk. At the time of his retirement in 1967 he was chief clerk.

Stuart and Bernice had two children, Vera Ann in 1935 and Stuart Arthur Jr., in 1939. The family attended Parker Methodist Church at which Stuart served as treasurer for 40 years. He was one of the trustees of the Parker School, an officer of the Cemetery Association, secretary of the Parker Men's Club. Bernice Pratt was active in the church and PTA and was an accomplished seamstress and cook.
Submitted by: Ann Houpt, 1128 Loftin St., Panama City, FL 32404.

Wilhelmenia Ophelia Parker Pratt – Dec. 15, 1879-Oct. 5 1943

Mama was the fifth child of John William and Nancy Amanda Folks Parker. Their homeplace was on Martin Bayou in Parker, where she said she was once confronted by a large black bear at the door of their house. One of her brothers shot it and they had a feast of bear meat. She also told about their peach tree which had an abundance of fruit she and her sisters had to can each year. I remember when I was a very young child, Mama showed me the remains of

223

Mrs. Pratt's store on what is now Pitts Avenue, Parker

the old log school house she attended in the 1880s or 90s. It was near where U.S. 98 runs through Parker.

She married Edmund S. Pratt in 1905, and they lived in Millville, where Daddy went to work at the shipyard. Their first child was a boy and stillborn. Their little girl was born while Mama had measles, The baby contracted them and lived only two weeks. Mama and Daddy, grief-stricken over their tragic losses, decided to remain childless and did so for nearly eight years until their son Harold was born in 1914. Huell came in 1917 and I was born in 1919. When I was still a baby, they sold their home in Millville and bought her family's home place on Martin Bayou. Daddy traveled to work by boat and would row across the bayou, then cross the bay to Millville, which was approximately three miles,

Daddy died when I was a year old, and Mama sold the bayou farm and bought a general merchandise store in Parker on the St. Andrews Bay. Originally the store front was at the water's edge attached to a dock. Groceries and supplies were delivered by boat and unloaded on the dock, Later, the building was moved away from the water and turned toward the road, which was only a sandy wagon rut. I was about 3 years old when the county had the road topped with shells.

Mama's hair was reddish gold in those days. And her eyes were the color of blue summer skies. She wore her hair long and usually twisted on top of her head. When bobbed hair came in style in the mid-20s she had it cut and always wore it short after that. She was an active member of Parker Methodist Church, and I remember her singing "The Old Rugged Cross" and "Saved by Grace," She always told me, "You don't have to like people, but love their souls," "Pretty is as pretty does" and "Chickens always come home to roost."

The Pratt home still stands on Maine Avenue in Millville

We lived in the rooms behind the store, and Mama worked hard to make a home for us while still doing well as a business woman. She had a long dock built on the side of the store for all the neighborhood to use when swimming. She also had springboards, high dives and a long wooden slide called a shoot-de-shoot, which reached up to a high platform with a small seat at the top. You sat in the seat and went flying into the water. The shoot-de-shoot was lots of fun and quite an attraction for all the locals as well as the summer people. It was also good for Mama's business. One afternoon Huell and I counted over 100 cars parked all around, the people taking advantage of free swimming facilities.

Mama did well in the store and we were some of the first in Parker to get electric lights. In 1926, she bought a Model T Ford sport roadster, which she never did learn to drive. She tried, but was never able to master the mechanics of the automobile. It was the only test I ever remember her failing.

She certainly succeeded as our protector and many nights walked the floor in the wee hours holding her pistol, ready to shoot when someone tried to break into the store. And as

her children grew, Mama continually struggled with our well-being. Once Harold's appendix ruptured, gangrene set in and we thought he would surely die. After two weeks, our prayers were answered and Harold recovered. When I was small, a bruise on my thigh abscessed and the doctor was afraid it would leave me crippled for life. I was in bed for six weeks before the abscess finally healed and I was back to normal. In addition, Huell suffered a head injury from a fall and the doctor said he would not live to adulthood. Huell proved the doctor wrong in that instance, but a few years later he was hit by a car and died without ever regaining consciousness.

Edmund and Wilhelmenia Pratt wedding portrait, April 2, 1905

We lived well because of Mama's business sense. But when the stock market crashed in 1929, she lost the money in her savings account. Jobs became scarce and it wasn't long before the store shelves were almost empty. Finally, she was forced to close the store for good. She continued to live in the rooms behind the old store building until she came to live with my husband Bob and me in our home next door. For two years before she died at age 63, she was bedridden from the results of a stroke.

Although her existence was one of constant struggle, I believe for the short time they had, Daddy and Mama's life together must have been a great adventure. They reached that exalted pinnacle to the stars - they experienced true love. As I look back on all life's sorrows and disappointments that Mama had to bear, I am convinced that it was her strong faith in Christ, her love for us and the sterling qualities she possessed that carried her through it all. I am forever indebted for the Christian training she gave and the example she was to us, plus the sacrifices she made for us. I loved her and missed her after she went away. She was my friend.

Submitted by: Charlotte Woodham, 1290 Menna Street, Jacksonville, FL 32205; Written by: Catherine Pratt Woodham.

The John Titus Presley and Myrtle Perkins Presley Family

John Titus Presley was born in Southport in 1916 to Marion Frank Presley and Lutisha Majors Presley. When Titus, as he was called, was very young, the family moved to Millville, and soon to the East Avenue homestead.

John Titus Presley and Myrtle Perkins Presley

Titus completed high school at Bay High School, and worked for a time at the paper mill. Then he began to work for the U. S. Post Office in Jacksonville. His career was interrupted by military service during World War II, and during that time his family returned to Bay County.

Titus and Myrtle had five children over the years, with four of them born in Bay County. Both Titus and Myrtle eventually retired from the Post Office in Jacksonville. By that time, Titus had acquired a bachelor's degree and a master's degree. Titus and Myrtle were world travelers, and were in the first tourist group to enter China after the bamboo curtain fell, and China was opened up to tourism.

Of the five children born to Titus and Myrtle, Frances Merle Presley Parker and Lawrence Preston Presley still live in Bay County. John Earl, Kathen Elaine, and Judith Luann live in the Jacksonville area.

Titus was buried in 1981 in Jacksonville, Florida, and his widow, Myrtle, still lives in Jacksonville, Florida.

Submitted by: Melanie Bell Boudreau (granddaughter), 6512 Hawkeye,, Circle Colorado Springs, CO 80919.

The Marion Frank Presley Family
Early Settlers in Bay County

Marion Frank Presley (original name Ritchey) and his brother, Thomas Warren Ritchey, were siblings from Red Level and Butler County, Alabama. They married sisters and moved to Bay County in 1912. Later, their sister, Leeoma Thomas, followed.

Marion Frank Presley and Wife Lutisha

Frank had two years of college, which was significant education for his day. He worked at different times as a millwright, a carpenter, and contractor. He built some of the older frame homes on Beach Drive in Panama City. He also worked as a machinist. In 1912, he was working at the sawmill in Millville. Many years, he helped to build and install equipment in the new paper mill.

At a dock in Millville, people often gathered to watch the boats come in to the dock. An evangelist began to visit on a boat, and got out and began preaching to the people standing around. This led to many converts, who soon began having prayer meetings at the Hammock, west of the south end of East Avenue, named because of the stands of trees. The location soon became known as Holy Hammock. It was there, on Easter Sunday night in April of 1914, that Frank and Lutisha became fervent Christians.

Their lives changed. After a long day at work, Frank and "Ludy" walked door-to door on deep sand roads carrying a lantern, and established many cottage prayer meetings in different nearby areas. Many of these groups eventually became churches.

Frank and Ludy previously had had children who did not survive beyond infancy or early childhood. Now they began having a family that survived, and they continued the door-to-door ministry. Their children accompanied them. A daughter, Wilma Hudson, remembers that a cottage group met at the Hughes home at Seller's Still, later called Dirego Park, in the woods. Some of the Hughes girls got together, cut wood, collected branches and limbs, and built a brush arbor, complete with benches and pulpit, for the children. This is a fond memory for Wilma.

John Titus Presley, Wilma Rebecca Presley, Marion Blanche Presley and Wm. Theodore Presley

Meantime, Frank bought the materials himself and with the help of others, built a church for the little group of believers. The church became known as Millville Assembly of God. Today, the church is known as First Assembly of God and stands at 1701 N. East Avenue.

Frank and Lutisha Presley had four children: John Titus Presley (my father), Wilma Lois Rebecca Hudson, Marion Blanche Foreman/Robinson, and William Theodore Presley. William Theodore ("Ted") was an Assembly of God minister for more than fifty years. Most individuals of that generation and some of their children returned to live in Bay County. The original homestead is located at 313 East Avenue.

Submitted by Frances Merle Presley Parker (Granddaughter of Frank and Lutisha Presley), 1834 N. East Avenue, Panama City, Florida 32405.

The Rev. William Theodore Presley and
Barbara Keith Presley Family

William Theodore Presley was the youngest child of Marion Frank Presley and Lutisha Majors Presley. He was born in Westville in 1929, but his parents moved to Bay County when Ted was an infant. His father died when he was approximately six years old, and he grew up under the watchful eyes of his mother, his two sisters, Blanche and Wilma, and his older brother, John Titus.

Rev. William Theodore Presley and Barbara Keith Presley

Ted, as he was called, completed Bay High School, and then was graduated from Southeastern Bible College. He became an ordained minister of the Assemblies of God. While at college, he met and married Barbara Keith. Barbara was musical and the two of them often sang together as a part of their ministry. Ted worked in the ministry in different cities and states across the nation, but returned to Bay County when his work was done. He spent more than fifty years in the ministry. Ted passed away in 2003 after an extended illness. He was widely known and much loved because of his kind and unselfish nature, and is missed by many people.

Ted and Barbara had four children, Darlene, Michael, Timothy, and Teddy. The families of both Darlene and Michael live in Bonifay, where Michael is an associate pastor. Timothy lives in Panama City, and Teddy lives in Bristol. They spent much of their lives in Bay County and call it home.

Submitted by Barbara Presley, 313 East Avenue, Panama City, FL 32405.

The Arnold Lee Price Family

Arnold Price was born January 21, 1918 in Waurika, Oklahoma, son of Henry Marvin Price and Dulcie Holman. On April 17, 1942, he married Mary Frances Givens, born December 31, 1927 in Dothan Alabama, daughter of James Leslie Givens and Mamie Lee Hollingsworth.

Arnold Lee Price Family

Arnold's first job was with the Civilian Conservation Corps (CCC) during the middle of the Great Depression era. This job took him to the state of Washington where he worked on the construction of the Grand Coulee Dam. President Franklin Delano Roosevelt had authorized $60 million to get the project started which eventually would bring electricity to eleven western states and irrigation to over 500,000 acres of farmland in the Columbia Basin.

At the beginning of World War II, Arnold joined the U.S. Coast Guard and served on the "Boutwell" stationed at Panama City, Florida, and this is where he met his bride-to-be, and where their children were born. He was later assigned duties on a naval supply ship which took him to many foreign ports around the world.

Their children were, Audrey Elaine born February 21, 1943, Lola June born August 14, 1946, James Marvin born October 27, 1951 and Joy Elizabeth born August 31, 1953.

After the war, Arnold went to work for the Panama City Fire Department and, along with his wife's uncle, Mr. J. C. Givens, opened up an upholstery business in Panama City, which later became known as "Price's Upholstery Shop". Arnold was known for his fairness and was one of the best upholsterers in Northwest Florida.

A very Christian man, Arnold taught Sunday School and was a deacon at Westview Baptist, Brannonville Baptist Church, and St. Andrews Baptist Church.

Mary Frances was a very kind person. She taught Sunday School and helped her husband in his business and tried to raise her children well.

Tragedy struck this family more than once. In 1963, their little girl, Joy, was struck by an automobile while crossing the street and was killed instantly. This family never got over the loss. But the worst was yet to come. On a Sunday morning in April 1975, Arnold and his wife were on their way to church and they stopped at a nearby convenience store to purchase Kleenex. Arnold walked into the store and found the clerk, Ann Patterson Butler, on the floor dead. Seeing no one in the store, he called the police and while talking to them he looked out the window and saw his car backing out, with the killer inside along with his wife. The killer drove his car to Greenwood Cemetery where he took the life of Mary Frances as well. This double murder was highly publicized and the killer was on death row for several years but is now serving a life long sentence for these two brutal murders.

Arnold Price was very beloved by his children and grandchildren. He went to be with the Lord on March 29, 2000 and is buried in the family plot next to his wife and little daughter at Greenwood Cemetery.
Submitted by June Price Thomason, 510 Marion Street, Attalla, Alabama 35954.

William Lawson Pridgen

William Lawson Pridgen was born on a farm in Washington County, Georgia in 1873 to Alsbury L. Pridgeon and Elizabeth Mosley Pridgeon. He married Ella Anna Louvinia Braddock, daughter of Wiley G. Braddock and Tempe Etna Cooper Braddock in 1895.

William Lawson Pridgen, 1958

He learned early that farming was not for him and, after their third child, the couple headed to Florida with their family, settling first in the Sarasota area where he opened a store and post office. He started a shell exchange with one of his steady customers being Thomas A. Edison. When South Florida became a "boom" area, he moved the family back to Georgia and then, in 1910, to Northwest Florida, where he homesteaded 100 acres of Federal land.

Lawson built a home in what became Bellisle on the peninsula that eventually became Tyndall Field. He cut down trees on his own property and dragged the logs to the site by tying a rope around his waist and around the logs. He became a professional photographer, catching the ferry to Panama City, going door to door taking pictures as permitted, bringing the film home and developing it, returning the pictures the following day, and starting the process all over again.

Lawson became the first Justice of the Peace in the area in 1929 and also established the only church in the area- holding services in his home until a school was built, which was used for both church and community center.

He had seven children — Esther, Thomas, Bertha, Ruby, Elzie, Alma, and Lucille. They maintained the garden and the grape arbor that he developed. As they married, they built homes within walking distance on land given them by Lawson. He eventually gave up photography and, with the family, built a service station and store that carried everything from cattle feed to work clothes and groceries. By then the boys were away at work, so Ella and the younger girls ran the store, did the gardening, and tended the animals. Lawson built a body onto the back of a Model A pickup truck and started a "rolling grocery," taking goods from the store into remote areas of the panhandle for sale or barter. This life continued until the late 1930s, when the Government displaced all the residents of the peninsula for the development of Tyndall Field.

The Pridgen family then lived in Millville, Lynn Haven, and, finally purchased land in Parker. Lawson continued the "rolling grocery," but now it was mostly fish and scuppernong grapes that he took inland. He continued to be the mainstay of the First Church of God and visiting ministers always stayed with the Pridgen family. When the Church was able to hire a permanent pastor, the young man, Walter Kufeldt, lived in the Pridgen home.

Lawson died on 2 May 1962 and is buried in Parker Cemetery alongside his wife, Ella, and many members of his extended family.
Submitted by: Jeanne Williams, 4506 Northpointe Place, Pensacola, Florida 32514.

George Christian Craig Pringle and Jessie Estelle Dolbeare

George C. (1868-1946) and Jessie Estelle Dolbeare Pringle (1881-1978) and their children moved from Biloxi, Mississippi, to Compass Lake, Florida in 1915 where they resided for 5 years. The family moved to Panama City in 1920 into their new 4-bedroom, 2 bath house at the corner of 11th Street and Harrison Avenue. The site for the new house was almost out of town. Electricity had not been extended beyond 7th Street at Panama City High School (which became Panama

George Christian Craig and Jessie Estelle Dolbeare Pringle, 1900

Grammar upon completion of Bay County High School in 1926). The Pringles had to pay for the installation of service poles and wiring across the four blocks to their new home.

226

City water was not available so a deep well was installed. Harrison Avenue was not a paved road and often became nearly impassable in heavy rain.

G. C. Pringle, Sr., was born in Sims Chapel, Alabama, to Francis Marion and Corinia Younge Pringle. He was a surveyor for the railroad and traveled throughout the southeast and to Central America. He also was in the turpentine business, managing stills in Compass Lake, Betts, York, Youngstown, and Sandy Creek. He held three patents: for the Pringle Turpentine Cup, the mounting nail to hold the cup, and the Pringle axe. He owned a *Clarence Saunders* grocery store and later partnered with Waldo Wallace in the Pringle & Wallace grocery store. He was instrumental in founding the St. Andrew Bay real estate company and was still active in the firm until his death in 1946.

Jessie Dolbeare Pringle was born in Jackson, Alabama, to Robert Fulton and Nancy Holder Dolbeare. She and George C., Sr., were married in 1900. The G.C.C. Pringles raised six children at their Harrison Avenue home — Francis Marion "Frank", Jessie Christine (Cogburn), George Christian Craig, Jr., "Buster", Lucile Grace (Cotton), Maude Evelyn (Jenkins), and Clyde Vernon "Sonnyman." Jessie remained at the Harrison Avenue residence until the property was sold in 1967. She then moved into a newly constructed home next door to her daughter, Lucile, living there until shortly before her death in 1978.

Submitted by: Lucile Pringle Cotton, 1033 Grace Avenue, Panama City, FL 32401.

The Robert Roy Prows Family

Robert Roy Prows married Alice Snowflake Sconiers (12-16-1891 / 12-22-1968) on December 25, 1907 in Millville. Alice was born in DeFuniak Springs, FL. Her parents, John Lockhart (8-22-1861/11-11-1942) and Monty Crosby Sconiers (5-22-1872/10-22-1963) later moved to Panama City (called Harrison then).

Robert Roy Prows

They camped along Beach Drive for a short period of time, then moved to Cedar Creek just north of Panama City. John Sconiers homesteaded in that area for the timber and fishing. Alice and her family were visiting family friends in Millville when Robert met and was smitten by her. After a decision was made by Alice's father to move the family to Oklahoma, Alice was given a choice to go with them or to stay and marry Robert. She chose the latter and as a result was the mother of eight children, being Jewel Juanita (Cannon-Harris) (8-26-1910), Vic Roy (6-22-1915), Gertrude (Anderson-Shanander) (3-2-1917), Earl Lee (1-18-1919), Monty Monette (Townsend) (2-6-1921), Rudolph Simeon (6-29-1924), Gwendolyn (Groseclose) (3-24-1927), and Florrie Ovida (Blankenship) (7-3-1930).

Robert and Alice Prows built a dairy where the present Rosenwald Middle School stands. Prows Dairy was the first dairy in Panama City. Robert delivered milk by horse and wagon to homes in the area. The housewife of the home would meet him with a pitcher/jug in hand allowing him to pour the milk from his ten-gallon can into her container. After Mr. Prows died, Mrs. Prows continued working the dairy with the help of her son, Vic Roy. Of course, the other children contributed in the milking and caring for the cows. At times, Mrs. Prows took needy young people into her home. She fed them and gave them shelter and in return they helped on the dairy farm. Madie Hamm Lindsey, Grady (Bud) Hood, Leroy (Ross) Hood, Marvin Hall, and others had great admiration for Alice for caring for them during those hard times.

During the Depression, Robert had invested money in the Bank. He was deeply saddened when the news was out that the bank owner had absconded with all of the bank's holdings and left the country going to South America. The money was never recovered.

Mr. & Mrs. Robert Prows were instrumental during the early years of present Trinity United Methodist Church in Millville, supporting it in various ways. All eight of their children attended Trinity while growing up. Mr. Prows took pride in picking up other children on the way to church, allowing them to ride standing on the running board if there was no room inside the car.

(L to R) (Front Row) Monette, Gertie, Earl Lee, Vic Roy, Rudolph Simeon (Back Row) Jewel, Robert Roy and Alice about 1927

In the 1940's, Alice gave right of way to Bay County to build a permanent road to be called Eleventh Street through her property. She donated much of the dirt to the county to build up Eleventh Street between Harrison and East Avenues. The dirt pit was on Redwood Avenue between Eleventh and Fifteenth Streets, now owned by the City of Panama City.

Alice opened Prows Convalescent Home in 1948 with the help of Sadie Holmes McKinney. This was the very first convalescent home in the area. Alice took pride in caring for the sick and the elderly. The convalescent home was sold in the early sixties to Lela Wagner.

Both Robert and Alice were dedicated to their church and family while being instrumental in the development of present Panama City. They were truly pioneers of this growing city.

Submitted by: Carolyn Prows, 4347 College Station Rd., Panama City, FL 32404.

The Simeon Carter Prows Family

Simeon Carter Prows (2-28-1837 / 6-16-1907) was born in Dearborn, Indiana, to Thomas (4-14-1792 / 7-3-1856) & Eleanor Kouns Prows (1-4-1802 / 10-3-1842). In 1842, at the age of four, he traveled with his parents and siblings into Nauvoo, Illinois. It is believed that his parents had accepted the gospel of Jesus Christ of Latter Day Saints and headed for Nauvoo in order to be near the body of the church in that city. His mother died of bilious fever shortly thereafter leaving a family of older boys and at least seven small children, the youngest being only eighteen months old. Twenty-five days later, their four-year old son, Joseph, died of whooping cough. Feeling helpless, with several small children who needed the loving stroke of a mother, Thomas asked a town widow who he had met to marry him. After a short courtship, Charity Arms and Thomas were married.

Simeon Carter & Polly Ann King Prows son of 3rd Thomas Prows

There was a period of political dissension following the martyr of Prophet Joseph Smith and it had become no longer safe to live in Nauvoo. Since Charity was determined to follow the saints as they headed west and Thomas could not bear thought of the hardships that would lie ahead, they parted ways. The story that has been passed down is that the couple "sat on the bank of the Mississippi River and divided the children". The outcome of this event was Charity took the couple's only child, Alvin, and continued west. Thomas took all of his children, got passage on a flatboat headed to Cincinnati eventually settling in Harrison County, Kentucky. There, Thomas married his third wife, Mrs. Sarah Fooks Mullen on November 5, 1851. They had two children before Thomas died on July 3, 1856.

Simeon grew up and at age twenty one he married Polly Ann King (5-18-1840 / 9-7-1933) on September 7, 1858 in Harrison County, Kentucky. God blessed this couple with thirteen children, all born in Harrison County. Simeon used the Kentucky fertile land to grow tobacco. In 1887, at age sixty, he and Polly moved to Florida seeking a milder climate. They, along with three of the children, [Maggie May (Johnson) (1876 / 8-27-1946), Eugene Sue (1-30-1878 / 5-23-1948), and Clara (Roche) (1-18-1880 / 4-21-1962)] traveled by R&N Railroad to Pensacola, Florida, and then by boat to what is now Panama City. Their furniture was brought down by rail to Pensacola and accompanied by their sons, Martin Luther (3-17-1866 / 3-8-1949) and Robert Roy (4-17-1874 / 2-20-1934) (ages 20 and 13 respectively). The family had begun to worry about the welfare of the boys since it took several months for them to arrive in Florida.

Simeon, like other Prows members of the past, had become a cooper (barrel maker) by trade. With the eighty acres he homesteaded (along present Eleventh Street between present Redwood and Bay Avenues) he planted vineyards and sold wine. He also raised sorghum cane and sold barrels of molasses. His homestead (application in 1898, #20548, certificate #13183) had been established and duly consummated in conformity to law for the eighty acres as officially surveyed and signed by U.S. President McKinley.

Simeon built a two-story frame heart pine home that was well furnished with a red carpet, lace curtains and nice furniture. The lumber was shipped from Pensacola. This home later burned on a windy March day in 1942 caused by a faulty kerosene water heater. Had it not been for the 300 feet to the windmill the home might have been saved. In 1905, prior to Simeon's death, an agreement was made between he and Robert for Robert to take care of him and Polly until their death in exchange for the title to the homestead. Robert held true to his words; however, Robert lived only five months after his mother's death in 1933. Polly Ann was 93 1/2 years old at her death. Robert was only 58 years old.

Submitted by: Rudolph S. Prows, 4340 College Station Rd., Panama City, FL 32404.

Descendents of Simeon Carter and Polly Ann King Prows

Simeon Carter and Polly Ann King Prows were married in Kentucky and moved to Panama City in 1887 seeking a milder climate. Accompanying them were five of their thir-

teen children, one of which was Robert Roy Prows. Robert was thirteen years old at the time. He later married sixteen-year-old Alice Snowflake Sconiers at the age of thirty-three years old. From this marriage eight children were born.

Robert started a

Gwendolyn Prows Groseclose, Gertrude Prows Shamander, Ovida Prows Blankenship, Vic Roy Prows, Earl Lee Prows, and Rudolph Simeon Prows 1942

dairy in around 1900. The dairy barn was in the southeast corner of present Bay Avenue and Eleventh Street. Rosenwald Middle School is now at the site of the Prows Dairy Farm. He used to deliver milk by horse and wagon. Later, the milk was delivered with a milk truck to surrounding areas. All of the

cows were milked by hand until Alice bought an automatic double milking machine.

Jewel, the eldest of the eight children, remembers milking the cows at an early age and assisting her mother with the younger children. She began college at Bob Jones College in Lynn Haven, Fl., and followed the college when it moved to Cleveland, Tennessee. She had graduated and was enjoying teaching at the college when her mother sent a telegram saying her father was very sick and she needed to come home. Being the 'apple of her father's eye', she came immediately. Her father always delighted in Jewel playing the piano for him. She remembers him asking her to play "Shanty in Old Shanty Town" many times. Jewel taught school at Millville Elementary and Everitt Junior High

Schools. She taught piano lessons to many of Panama City's children, one of which is Pat Hughes McCormick, one of her favorite students. Jewel also raised chickens and sold eggs. She still plays the piano at the age of ninety three.

Jewel Prows Harris, Vic Roy Prows, Gertrude Prows Shamander, Earl Lee Prows, Monty Monette Prows Townsend, Rudolph Simeon Prows, Gwendolyn Prows Groseclose and Florrie Ovida Blankenship 1990

Vic Roy worked on the dairy farm from an early age until he left to go to Oklahoma in 1950, except for a period of two years when he attended Bob Jones College in Cleveland. Vic Roy loved sports and was preparing to become a coach but could not complete his degree because his mother needed him to help run the dairy after Robert's death. He became the father figure for his younger siblings. Ovida, the youngest of the eight, recalls fondly him buying her clothes and other needs for the family. LeRoy (Ross) Hood has fond memories of being Vic Roy's helper at the dairy. Roy eventually settled in Ft. Lauderdale, Fl.

Rudolph was only nine years old when his father died. His father and mother trained him in early, at the age of three, by giving him a small shovel and pail and had him picking up the cow manure to be used for fertilize. He, Broward Hall, Pete and Junior Hamm, Speedball Jackson, and Bill Newberry used to ride their horses down present Fifteenth Street and also present Airport Road when they were dirt roads. Rudolph remembers when their cows would graze along present Sherman Avenue north of Fifteenth Street, they would eat the houses that were made out of brown paper mill paper. He and Jewel are the only two of Robert and Alice's children that stayed in Panama City after World War II.

Earl helped his older brother with milking the cows and also delivering the milk. Roy, Earl, and Rudolph would deliver in Panama City, Port St. Joe, Blountstown, and West Bay. They would deliver to the supply boat for the Blackwater Dredge along the Apalachicola River. Sometimes Marvin and Broward Hall, serving as helpers, would accompany the boys during their deliveries. Rudolph recalls every day Earl would follow the cow herd from the barn up to Fifteenth and Sherman and would sit down leaning against a huge oak tree in the northeast corner of that intersection and go to sleep while the cows grazed in the woods. That afternoon he would round up the cows and herd them back home to be milked. Earl went into the Navy and settled in Oxnard, California, opening up his "Blue Bird Real Estate Office".

Gertrude went to Bob Jones in Cleveland also. She became a school teacher, first at Callaway School. On Sunday afternoon Rudolph would take her to a Mrs. Brown's home where she resided until Friday afternoon when Rudolph picked her up to bring her home. She taught at Springfield Elementary for five years, then after visiting her Aunt Dessie in Washington State, she moved there. She settled in Oregon and eventually in Phoenix, AZ.

Monette served in the Army of Nurses Corps overseas. She then moved to California and worked as a school nurse. Monty, as she was called by friends and relatives, settled in Petaluma, Ca. She received her nurses degree at Charity Hospital in New Orleans, LA.

Gwendolyn always said she wanted to marry a West Point Cadet. That she did. She and her husband, Lt. Col. Robert Groseclose, traveled abroad while serving in the military and eventually settled in Altamonte Springs, Fl. They are now volunteering with the Orange County Welcome Center.

Ovida was the baby girl. She and her sister Gwen remember sneaking around and finding the 'pecan stash' that Rudolph would hide. They would turn around and hide it from Rudolph, even on the roof of the house. She remembers milking the cows although it was not a lot, and also riding the ponies around the dairy. Ovida eventually settled in Riverdale, Ga.

Submitted by: Vic Roy Prows, Box 1020, Ft. Lauderdale, FL.

Pumphrey's Pilgrimage to Panama City - Part I

The progenitor of the Pumphrey family of Gloucestershire, England appears to be John Pomphrey (1410-1472). A descendent Walter Pumphrey (1655-1721), according to the *History of the Colony of New Jersey*, immigrated to Burlington, New Jersey in 1678 to work as a carpenter and a builder. He had four children by his first wife and four by his second wife. There are more descendants of his son Lazarus Pumphrey living today from any other of Walter Pumphrey's sons. The Pumphrey family from Jackson County, Florida are descendants of Lazarus Pumphrey (1686-1766).

Thomas Sylvanus Pumphrey and Minnie Lee Davis Pumphrey

Thomas Sylvanus Pumphrey married Minnie Lee Davis June 22, 1905 in Jackson County, Florida and made their first home in Carr, Florida in Calhoun County. He owned a saw mill for several years in Carr before moving to Panama City. Their only child, John Walter Pumphrey was born in October, 1914. Six months later in early 1915 this family moved to Panama City in a Model T Ford when Tom Pumphrey began working for the Coca Cola Bottling Company for the next seventeen years. They purchased a home at 515 Oak Avenue which was the family home until 1991 when it was purchased by the Coca Cola Bottling Company as a parking lot. He then worked for Southern Kraft, (the paper mill). In 1936 Thomas Pumphrey served as Chief of Police of Panama City. A stroke left him bedridden until he passed away in January 22, 1944. Minnie Lee Pumphrey took excellent care of her husband and ran a boarding house for a number of years. Working folks report going to "Miss Minnie's" house for lunch because she served the best home cooked food. One favorite dessert was Granny's Sugar Cookies. She loved to fish and taught her son and her grandchildren how to make a cane pole with a line, cork, and hook. She would bait the hook and watch for the cork to move and say, "PULL." Her son John remembers the first fish he caught in Bayou George, a beautiful Red Breast Brim. Granny Pumphrey invited her son's family over often for delicious home cooked meals after church on Sunday. She was skilled in making quilts, tatting lace,

embroidering, and other sewing skills. She passed away in September 25, 1970 at age 97. Thomas S. Pumphrey and Minnie Lee Davis Pumphrey are buried in Oakland Cemetery on 11th Street.

Submitted by John Walter Pumphrey, 120 Linda Avenue.

Pumphrey's Pilgrimage to Panama City - Part II

John Walter Pumphrey graduated from Bay County High School in 1934 and in 1937 married a classmate Genevieve Sorensen. John Walter worked for the Standard Oil Agent as a delivery man. After five years he began employment for the United States Post Office in Panama City as a carrier and then as a clerk until 1964 when he transferred to the Navy Base as a Photographer. He retired in 1972. John served in the Navy during World War II as a photographer. John's interest include traveling to foreign countries which he captured in movies and still photography, traveling in his mini-motor home first with his wife then

John Walter Pumphrey Family

with his grandchildren. He enjoyed time on his boat, the Capt. John and scuba diving. At 67 he dove the Great Barrier Reef in Carnes, Australia then took his grandson Donald Jr. to Cozumel, Mexico diving and later accompanied his daughter Jeanette to Freeport in the Bahamas for a dive trip. John is also a gourmet cook and has enjoyed making a cake every Sunday for the library staff at his church for a number of years. John served for several years as President of the National Pumphrey Genealogy Society. He presided at the national reunions in Baltimore MD and visited many regional Pumphrey reunions. Genevieve Pumphrey worked in the United States Post Office for twenty years until retirement in 1972. She was active in the Postal Clerks Union and the Auxiliary. She worked in the five year old Sunday School Department for several years at First Baptist Church. They had three children: Jeanette Pumphrey born in July 1938 and identical twins: Charles Edwin and Donald Anson Pumphrey born in April 1942. Jeanette is a retired reading teacher from Muscogee County School District in Columbus GA and lives now in Panama City. Charles and Don Pumphrey retired from the Tallahassee Fire Department and each started a successful business. Don and Pam Pumphrey own a home on Tyndall Dr. in the Cove. Genevieve Sorensen Pumphrey passed away in September, 1975, Charles Pumphrey passed away in May 2002.

Submitted by: Donald A. Pumphrey, 1927 Tyndall Drive.

Pumphrey's Pilgrimage to Panama City - Part III

In 1942, John and Genevieve Pumphrey purchased a home on Linda Avenue in the Cove so their children, Jeanette, Charles and Don could walk to Cove Elementary School. Neighborhood children used the school's cement court for roller skating, basketball and tennis. Growing up

(L to R) Jeanette Pumphrey (Brightwell) age 11 and Janine Galbraith (Cosson) age 10, 1949

in the Cove was quiet and safe for children to play and to ride tricycles and bikes. Children could walk down South Linda Avenue, just past Cherry Street, past the Cook home and use her wooden steps to walk down the high cliff to the beach. Mrs. Cook was sweet to the children who went to her home for trick or treat by inviting them into her house and serving delicious treats. Mrs. Harris, of the Cove Hotel, was very nice to the Cove children by allowing them to use the Cove Hotel dock and beach for swimming. While swimming there Don Pumphrey saved the life of a neighborhood boy by diving in, pulling him to the beach, getting first aid help and calling the ambulance. Due to a shortage of nursery schools for children of working mothers during World War II, Genevieve opened a nursery school in her home where 25 children came during the working mother's day. Many of the students became friends to the Pumphrey children and are still friends today. One of the nursery school students was a girl named Janine Galbraith who became a friend to Jeanette. Janine's grandmother, Mrs. Lamar Dale, wanted them to continue their friendship so she purchased the home, at 116 Linda Ave. next door to the Pumphreys. Janine and Jeanette have maintained their friendship since they were four and five years old and enjoyed growing up the in the Cove together. With such wonderful memories of this beautiful Cove area, it is not surprising that children who grew up here are returning. Janine and her husband, Larry Cosson retired and moved back to her grandmother's house. Jeanette Pumphrey Brightwell retired and moved back to a South MacArthur Ave home in the Cove. Don Pumphrey and his wife Pam own a home on Watson Bayou where they dock the Capt. John. John Pumphrey continues to live in his Linda Ave. home of sixty years.

Submitted by: Jeanette Pumphrey Brightwell, 439 South MacArthur Ave.

Lucy Mell McLemore Raffield
Forbidden Fruit

Nothing taste sweeter than forbidden fruit. It seems that no matter what the age, if we aren't supposed to have it, that is what we crave, whether it be the ice cream we are not supposed to have because of Lactose, or the tomatoes because of allergies, or the coffee that keeps us up all night. There is just something so irresistible about it, Adam is a prime example, even in the Biblical days of old.

When you are a child it is even worse, no snacks before dinner, no desert before you eat your meal, no drinks after 6:00p.m., and so on and so forth.

With me the irresistible temptation was Granny's strawberries, she had bunches of them, but there were a select few that were meant for preserves and pies alone. You could eat all you wanted from one place, but it was absolutely forbidden to touch the ones from her prize strawberries.

There were so many strawberries in her garden, and there was no way that she was going to miss a few. I just had to have some of the prize strawberries, they were always so fat and sweet, not like the smaller ones that often had a bland, grainy taste.

Granny was busy with the wash, and with dinner, and I knew it would take her some time in the kitchen, so I devised a plan to sneak where she could not see me, and get me a hand full of those delicious strawberries, just a few, that would tide me over for a while.

I checked to see if she could see out the window, and sure enough she was so busy that she did not even see me go to the window and wave at her. "Perfect," I thought, now is the time. So I snuck into the strawberry patch being careful to keep a watchful eye on the window, I reached down and got me about four big ones, when all of a sudden, "Vincent Earl", I had been caught red handed.

Granny had me go get my own switch, and that hurt me as bad if not worse than the whipping I knew I was fixing to get. It had better be a good one, not a small one, and not a broken one, we had already played that game and I knew better, first of all I would have to go with her to pick another one out and she would whip me all the way back, and it

would be a lot worse than if I would just go ahead and get it over with.

The fact that she caught me was bad enough, and then the humiliation of getting my own switch, and having Granny mad at me. I took it like a trooper, and it stung with every little pop on those bare legs.

All I wanted was a few strawberries, and she had plenty, the more I thought about it, the madder I got, so I devised another plan, I would get Granny back for being so mean about those strawberries, besides if she had not seen me pick them she had so many she would never have known they were gone.

In a little while when I thought Granny had forgotten about our little incident, I told that I was going out to play. Granny told me it was okay but to stay out of those strawberries, so I promised her I would and ran outside. I played in the yard a few minutes and saw her look outside a few times to make sure I had listened to her this time.

I slipped around to the side of the house where the chicken coops were, there had been a couple of hens that had baby chicks, Granny was so proud of those chicks, she had taken me out there and showed them to me shortly after I got there. "I'll fix her." I said to myself, as I grabbed one of the chicks and put it into my shirt, then I grabbed another and another. I started around the back of the house about the time I say Granny look out the window, so I scurried to the outhouse as quickly as I could.

Granny did not have indoor plumbing, so the old outhouse was down a little path in the back yard. I took one biddy out of my shirt and dropped him into the hole, he chirped and made the most awful fuss, I pulled another one out of my shirt and was about ready to drop him when I heard "Vincent Earl"., stand right at the door was Granny, and I knew my butt was in deep trouble this time.

When Granny got through with me, I did not ever want to see another strawberry or another baby chick, then when Mom and Dad got through with me, I sure did not want to see either of them.

I honestly don't know what hurt worse, the whippings, or Granny making me feel so bad about all that I had done, and then telling Mom and Dad when they got home. It is for certain that Granny taught me some very valuable lessons.

Of course with me being a child, not knowing I was in the wrong, I never stayed mad at Granny, and as a matter of fact I loved her dearly, but I will never forget the lesson on forbidden fruit.

In Loving Memory Of: Lucy Mell McLemore, Raffield
Submitted by: Chuck Raffield, 2830 East Baldwin Road , Panama City, Florida 32405; Written by: Vince and Linda Raffield.

Captain Winton Earl Raffield – "Big Bird, Momma!"

Prior to 1941 and what is now known as Tyndall Air Force

Big Bird, Momma! Illustration by Vince Raffield

Base, our families, the Raffield's, were among some of the families who had settled in small communities like Farmdale, Auburn, Belle Isle and Cromanton where Tyndall is today.

When the family relocated it was just up the bay a little in a place many people still know as Bull Point. Dad couldn't have been much older than seven, and there was much talk about the government, the move, and the impending threat of war.

Being too young to really know or understand exactly what it all meant with the exception of their already hard times being made more difficult, Dad carried on much as usual trying to help put food on the family's table. No doubt he had to be aware of the surroundings and would have already been cautious in his daily routines of bears, panthers, snakes, gators and the dangers of the waters edge and the thick woods where they called home.

Dad had never saw a plane, at least not up close, he had heard them off in a distance, and may have even caught a brief glimpse of one way, way, off in a distant sky. He had heard the older people talk of them and he knew they were there, but had no idea how big they were, or what they looked like.

He certainly did not have any knowledge of the P.40 War Hawk, the "Flying Tigers", or that the Flying Tigers were volunteers who had sacrificed a lot to protect many lives including the Chinese children who called them "Fei Hu" for the fearsome teeth that were painted on the planes.

Little did he know that on this day in particular you might say that he was about to get an education about the air plane, and what you might say was a "Birds Eye View" so to speak, up close and personal.

Dad walked down the beach with his prize cast net in hand, feeling confident and secure in the skills he had been taught as a young fisherman, the day was beautiful and perfect for the promise of a good catch.

Lora Nell and Winton Earl Raffield, Mom and Dad

His trained eyes and ears ever cautious of his environment, as his intent was to catch supper, not be supper for a lurking panther, or a lazy gator that was an ever-present danger in the underbrush of palmetto bushes and marshy spots, which was a natural part of the landscape.

Dad had ventured a little farther from home than usual, but he had saw some boat traffic and heard the putter of their engines. He admired the boats, as his family was used to the hand made wood boat that they either poled or rowed in the little coves, lagoons, and bayous, or wherever they had to go.

Once realizing he was a little farther from home, and after the boats were out of sight his mind once again focused on the task at hand. With cast net in hand he soon spotted some bull minnows. To him and his family fishing was not just a task; it was a necessity to survive. It did seem like however that the Raffield's took much pleasure in fishing all the same, and dad was no exception.

As he walked the waters edge ever carefully, and slowly stalking his prey, his eyes trained on the bull minnows and cast net in hand ready to throw at any moment, once again his attention was taken from the pursuit to a strange noise.

It gave him a bit of a start, and he cautiously looked around to survey his surroundings. The noise seemed to be muffled at first, then it became louder and louder, nearer and nearer. His heart quickened as he realized the noise was coming from the sky. He looked up, at first he could see nothing, then he began to make out a dark silhouette of something. The silhouette grew larger and larger, and the sound louder and louder. In his little mind at least it seemed to be fixed towards him, and in that instant he feared that he had just become the prey instead of the hunter.

At that very moment the bull minnows and the prize cast net meant absolutely nothing to him, as he got out of the waters edge as quickly as he could and threw the cast net to the side, running to the hill for cover as fast as his little legs could carry him.

As he glanced back over his shoulders, he could see the big bird truly was after him, and his heart almost leaped from his chest as the thing actually came along side him well enough for him to really see it all clearly. "Oh God", how horrible, not only was the bird huge and ugly... with fierce looking teeth,

It clearly was a man eater because he could see a man on the birds back in some kind of bubble, and he was not about to be the second meal if he could help it, the sound of it alone would be enough to scare someone half to death but the size of this thing and the looks, it was the most monstrous bird he had ever seen. Just as he swallowed hard knowing with that kind of sound he was a goner for sure, it seemed like the bird flew off in a different direction, and as it did, it tipped from side to side, and it looked like the thing was coming back, sizing him up, it gave dad just enough of an opportunity to dive under the porch in a mad dash screaming to the top of his lungs, "Big Bird, Big Bird Momma." As that was all it seemed he had breath left to say.

Granny hearing the commotion of course and the child's screams came out the door. As she looked up she knew what a plane was and tried to explain to the terrified seven year old under the porch that it was okay, it was only a plane... she spent the better part of a day trying to get him out from under that porch. Dad said she would laugh a while, coax a while, but there was no convincing him that thing was not after him.

In later years before my dad died he would tell us this story time and again and we were always delighted to hear him tell it as it made him laugh. He said he knew later that the pilot was not trying to frighten him in any way but to give him a thrill of seeing an air plane up close, and he tipped his wings to say hello, but it had scared him the worst of any time he could ever recall at that age, and would be something he would never forget.

In Loving Memory of: Captain Winton Earl Raffield
Submitted by: Vince Raffield, 45 Lunsford Road, Eufaula, Alabama 36027. Written by: Vince and Linda Raffield.

Woodrow Raffield

Many years ago, I would listen intently as the stories from family members were told. My favorite was a Ghost Story believed to be true. My Great Uncle Woodrow, a serious man, did not take things lightly, or joke around.

Uncle Woodrow had lost a leg in an accident on a shrimp boat, and had a wooden leg. It was hard for him to get around. Even still he would go oystering at the head of East Bay, known by many in the area as Bull Point. He would go for two or three days at a time, so he would stay at the old homestead where my Grandpa Willis had lived.

Grandma had been dead for years, and Grandpa Willis had joined her five years later. After he died, the house was in such need of repair, and it was so far out that the only way you could get in and out was by boat.

The old house wasn't much anymore, but at least Uncle Woodrow had fresh water, a roof over his head, and a floor to lay his bedroll on.

Grandpa David Willis Raffield, Bullpoint, FL about 1945

In its prime the old home was something to behold. It was a wood framed house that sat about 1 & 1/2 to 2 feet off the ground on brick pillars. It had vertical lapboards, and a cedar shingled roof. There was a walkway down the middle of the home and rooms on each side. The kitchen and pantry/storage room were located in the back of the house. Once strong enough to weather almost any storm, the house stood weathered and beaten from all the years of neglect, and the elements.

It sat back off the beach, in a wooded area with majestic

oaks, large palms, palmetto bushes and sand spurs. The porch was as wide as the home, and remained in tact. Many evenings had been spent there talking to friends and family, and enjoying the sunsets.

There was a fresh water well, about eighteen inches in diameter, made of brick with just enough room for a bucket and rope to retrieve the cool, clean water, worthy to coin the phrase "Nectar of the Gods".

Woodrow enjoyed the solitude, and the memories of the old place were fond ones to him. As he lay on the bedroll he thought of how peaceful the sounds of the night were, the

Grandpa David Willis Raffield's Place, known as Bullpoint, across bay from Tyndall Air Force Base 1946

breeze felt cool and comfortable, it smelled salty and crisp. The sounds of the waves lapping on the beach were soothing; he could hear a bobcat, and an owl in the distance. The moon was bright and full, the shadows of the trees danced across the floor through the window in an almost mesmerizing effect, lost in thought and dead tired, he had no trouble going to sleep.

Woodrow was awakened by what he thought were voices coming from the backyard. Unafraid, he managed to pull himself up to the window to see if he could find out who was out there, he rubbed his eyes in disbelief...

There, arm in arm, in what was once Grandma's prized garden walked Grandma and Grandpa Willis.

He rubbed his eyes, but they were still there, he could even hear them talking, they were discussing what needed fixing around the house before winter set in.

He could not move, could not utter a word, not out of fear, it was pure joy to see them again, he simply stood there in utter amazement, enjoying every moment, until, a foggy mist came rolling in suddenly, and they disappeared, as did the fog.

He sat back on his bedroll and thought about it for a few minutes, and a peace that he had never felt before came over him. He had no problem going back to sleep.

The next morning the first thing that was on his mind was a pot of fresh coffee, he stirred the hot coals left from the night before, and put the coffee on.

His mind replayed the nights events as he pondered over what had happened, still in half disbelief, and amazement, the coffee soon brought him back to the present. He looked out over the bay at the fluttering sea gulls, the glistening sun on the water, pelicans fishing for breakfast, dolphins playing, and in a distance he could see a small boat. His thoughts were interrupted abruptly by someone calling his name, "Woodrow," "Woodrow."

A few minutes went by, he began to think he was just imagining things, again he heard his name, "Woodrow." This time he got a fix on where it seemed to be coming from. It sounded like it was coming from the corner of the house.

He walked to the corner; there was no one there. Again he heard his name, "Woodrow," this time it sounded like it came from the other corner.

This continued until he realized he had made almost three complete trips around the home. Just when he thought that he surely must be loosing his mind, he heard the voice again, this time it was behind him, he looked around to see an old tabby tomcat.

He laughed at himself, thinking that the cat could not speak, but that a husky plea for food must have been what he had mistaken for his name. As he looked at the cat, there was something very familiar about him. He looked like the cat that Grandma and Grandpa had. It sure did look like

232

Old Tom, even down to the tear on the left ear. As he looked close for comparisons sake, again he heard "Woodrow," only this time he was looking dead in the face of the cat, and the voice definitely came from his mouth.

Before he even thought about it, Woodrow replied, "Tom, get out-a-here you old devil," and much to Woodrow's surprise the cat vanished like a puff of smoke. Woodrow then gathered all his things and returned home, to tell the tale of "Woodrow."

Submitted by: Larry Charlton Raffield, 3607 East Game Farm Road, Panama City, Florida 32404. Written by: Vince & Linda Raffield.

Raffield Family – "No Fish Tale"

Go just about anywhere in Panama City and say the name "Raffield" and most people will associate it with fish. The Raffield story however is no fish tale. Along the mid to late 1880's the Raffield settled in communities all around the area of Bay County. They had originally come to this area looking for work, and for years they traveled back and forth between Georgia and Florida.

Most of my husbands folks settled in the Tyndall area, back then it was small communities like Farmdale, Cromanton, Auburn and Belle Isle to name a few. They scratched out a living the best way they could, some farmed,

David Willis Raffield and wife Rosa Lee Bailey Raffield, Bullpoint 1945 or 1946

others worked in logging and turpentine mills, saw mills, or what ever would bring food to the family table.

Eventually they turned their hand to fishing, and the rest is just about history. The Raffield's were known to have caught some of the biggest catches around, Clayton Raffield, according to the Panama City Pilot, March 28, 1918, caught 30,000 pounds and it went for .15 per pound. The Raffield Brothers brought in 1,800,000 Pounds of fish in 1935, fishing nine boats and employing 67 men, January 9, 1936 headlines in the Panama City Pilot.

Charles F. Raffield started the first Raffield Fish Plant, January 1, 1923 according to the Southern Fisherman Magazine, October 1946 issue, which eventually was known as Bay Fisheries.

Coy & Charlie Raffield started a subsidiary plant in Port Saint Joe in 1943. Some time later, Carl Raffield bought it, and what was once known as Gulf Fisheries is now known as Raffield Fisheries of Port St. Joe. Around this time the Charter Boat and Sports Fishing Industry was also getting started.

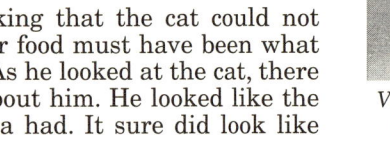
Vince and Linda Raffield with dog Popeye December 2003

The Raffield Family took to fishing like they had been born to it, and some of them have, as many of the Raffield's who were born in this area still carry on the traditions of their forefathers.

As hard hit as they were when the threat of war approached them personally in 1941 and many lost their businesses, homes, possessions and many of their dead in some of the 11 cemeteries, to Flexible Gunnery School #9, or what was later called Tyndall Field, (named after Lieutenant Frank B. Tyndall) who was not officially an ace but had received the Silver Star for his bravery behind enemy lines.

Like always the Raffield's pulled together, as family, doing what had to be done to provide for their families. Although this caused great hardship on all of the families of that area, they too played a big part in sacrificing in some cases all they had to the greater good of the area.

A house belonging to Henry Raffield, which was once located in Tyndall was brought across the bay by barge to Grace Avenue. His wife could not stand the thought of leaving their home, and so Henry had it shipped by barge across the bay just for her.

Clayton Raffield donated the land over at Auburn for the school, and the Raffield's as well as other families from the area donated materials, and labor to get the school built. The school and a bell which was called the New Auburn School, is now located in Callaway.

When asked of an older Raffield, "Why has no one ever entered the Raffield's in the Heritage Series?" The reply was "Well, I recon cause everybody knows us." Just like that, the Raffield's have always had pride in who they are, where they come from and what they stood for.

Their strong faith, determination and backbone was their driving force. It was not just the men, the women had to be strong too, they had to take care of things while the men were away, often times weeks at the time fishing, hunting or doing what was necessary to survive.

Selemanthy Raffield, The wife of John Henry Raffield was a midwife and gave medical aid during the Civil War, while her husband was off fighting in the Civil War. Nancy Raffield crocheted the first fishing net for her husband Charles Jackson, as they did not have the means to get a store bought one.

Against all odds the Raffield's survived the worst, with their faith abound. They prospered in spirit and numbers. Much like the Compass Rose they spread out all over, and there have been many who have sacrificed in every war, and every branch of the service, proudly serving for their country. Their occupations range and differ as much as the changing tides with many professions, not all being in the fishing industry. Their pride however of who they are, where they came from and of the family heritage will forever be tied to Bay County.

Whether they have a little or a lot materially, they are among the richest people I know in their love for each other, the family, and their faith in God. I am very proud to be a part of their family.

Dedicated to: My Family.

Submitted by: Benny Raffield, Post Office Box 6017, Panama City, Florida 32404. Written by: Linda Raffield.

Ann Ramer

My name is Ann Ramer Gispanski. I was born in Geneva, Alabama on December 2, 1939. My parents are Johnny and Henrietta Ramer. I am the oldest and have two sisters: Virginia and Shirley. My parents came to Panama City in the year of 1940.

When I was five years old we moved to St. Andrews on 1809 Beck Avenue. That was home for me all my life - and it is still home today. I attended St. Andrew's Elementary School, Drummond Park, Jinks Jr. High School and then graduated Bay High in 1957.

Since I never had any brothers, I always participated with Dad in the "boy" type activities of fishing and hunting. I was the boy he never had. Ha. Dad loved to fish. In fact, we ate fish sometimes every day of the week. I loved to fish, too, and Dad would take me spear fishing with him to the jetties. We would go every Saturday in the summer. I remember going to the jetties before it became a state park and before there were roads or bridges across the bay. We had a small 17 foot boat with a Mercury motor.

Normally Dad and I were the only people at the jetties. My dad had some special friends, and I was always included in their plans of adventure. Our typical way of fishing was that Dad tied a belt around his waist and I would hang onto this belt as he dove to the bottom of the jetty looking for fish. On one Saturday I was "hanging on" to my dad as he dove to the bottom of the jetty spear fishing. Suddenly, I saw a large octopus coming towards us. This really scared me and I surfaced as quickly as I could and climbed up on the rocks. I was scared to death, but Dad and his friend found much humor in my action. They laughed at me for years remembering that incident. I still laugh too remembering that special Saturday. But it was a real experience I will never forget. Ha.

Ann Ramer

I also squirrel hunted with my dad and his friend Johnny Delcomyn. On my 16th birthday I got my own 410 rifle.

My first job after school was working for J.D. Holmes Fish Market. I walked from Bay High to the market on 6th Street. I usually worked 4:00 p.m. to 8:30 p.m. every evening and all day Saturdays. After graduation I began a banking career working at Springfield Commercial Bank.

My mother, Henrietta Ramer, best known to her friends as Sue Ramer was a great cook and taught us girls how to cook, have pride in ourselves, and respect others. Mother had tremendous personal pride and was a caretaker for my father. Mother and Dad had strong religious backgrounds. They ensured we attended church often.

Growing up in Panama City was fun, exciting and special to me. I'll always have white sand in my shoes and salt water in my blood.

Submitted by: Ann Ramer, 6064 Blueberry Lane, Crestview, Florida.

Henrietta Davidson Ramer

I was born on August 17, 1920 in Samson, Alabama. I was the youngest of five children and was one of a few that graduated with a high school education in Geneva County. My father had rheumatoid arthritis which paralyzed him from the waist down. His business was a horse and wagon (rolling store) in which he traveled through Rural Alabama and Southern Florida selling to the farmers. Money was not available during the Depression and Dad always returned home with chickens, butter, milk, and garden vegetables. His business was good and we lived a life better than many.

On one occasion in 1934, I was traveling with my dad on one of his selling trips. The wagon ran off the road and I received a broken ankle. Telephones were not available nor were the roads routinely traveled where help was close by. With Dad paralyzed, I had to walk on my broken ankle a mile or so to get help. For years the ankle would not heal and I had to live with an open sore. Finally, in 1957 after many surgeries, the doctors were able to successfully close the wound.

Johnny William Ramer and Henrietta Davidson Ramer

The first time I ever met my husband, Johnny, was on a day when he and two of his friends were walking past me in Geneva, Alabama. They came upon me, a young 10 year old, playing hopscotch barefooted. I asked them where they were going. I was told to the movies. Not being shy, and liking the cute young boy named John; I asked if I could go with them. Johnny responded by saying, "If I would be wearing shoes next week I could go with them to the movie". All week long I wore shoes waiting and hoping to see Johnny again. When the next Saturday arrived, I was certain to be wearing shoes and to be playing hopscotch when Johnny walked by. To my delight Johnny kept his word and I accompanied the boys to the movie. That began a casual relationship that was not serious, because, after all, I was ten years younger than Johnny.

After some time, I became close to another boy and Johnny had become serious with another girl. Unknown to Johnny, I had a secret crush on him. On a Friday night Johnny and his girlfriend and I and my boyfriend were double-dating. During the evening we all decided to go to Panama City and get married. However, on the way down to Panama City, Johnny and I began talking seriously for the first time. We decided that we loved each other, and that we should get married. Arriving in Panama City, I married Johnny and his girlfriend married my boyfriend.

In 1940 we settled in Panama City where we raised three daughters. John worked in the shipyard and I was a homemaker and taught Sunday School at the First Assembly in Millville. We had a good life and I really enjoyed Panama City as my home.

Submitted by: Henrietta (Sue) Ramer, 1809 Beck Avenue, Panama City, Florida.

Johnny William Ramer

I am known as J.W. Ramer. I was born in Ponce de Leon, Fla. on October 15, 1910; my wife Henrietta Davidson was born in Samson AL on August 17, 1920. In 1937, we traveled to Panama City and were married in the garden of a local judge.

In 1940, I moved my wife and two daughters, Ann & Virginia, to Panama City. I enjoyed hunting and fishing. I especially enjoyed spearfishing with a special gun that I made of wood and strong rubber straps. I really speared a lot of fish. My daughter Ann usually went with me every Saturday to the jetties. We would bring home enough fish to last us until the next Saturday. I had a little boat with a Mercury motor. One day on the return trip home the propeller fell off the motor. I could see it lying on the bottom of the bay. However, I didn't

Johnny William Ramer, Henrietta Davidson Ramer, Ann, Virginia, and Shirley Jean Ramer

have a spare shear pin to reattach it. After retrieving the propeller from the water, I rowed to a dock located on the south part of the bay. Upon arriving I saw a big yacht moored at the dock. I spoke with the owner. He said he would get me a shear pin if I would dive down and disconnect some ropes that had become tangled around his propeller. With Ann helping me, we repeatedly dove under the yacht and removed the ropes. That day we returned home tired and very hungry. Ha.

In 1947 we had our third daughter, Shirley Jean Ramer. My wife Henrietta Ramer, better known as Sue, was a great cook. She taught the girls how to cook, have pride in themselves and to respect others. We attended First Assembly of God Church in Millville. I became a Deacon in the church and my wife taught a women's Sunday School class.

I worked for J.A. Jones Construction Company, Inc. at Wainwright Shipyard as an electrician. In those days you didn't need experience to obtain a trade job. On-the-job training was always provided. World War II was ongoing. You stood in line on a certain week day and applied for the job in which you wanted to be trained. I wanted to be an electrician. I was hired, trained and became a career electrician. When the

war was over, I went to work for International Paper Company and retired early in 1968. The reason for retiring early was while working an electrical circuit in the paper mill, someone removed the lock-out/tag-out device and energized the circuit. I was electrocuted and fell thirty feet. I was burned severely throughout my right side, lost use of one finger, had extensive muscle damage and received a severe concussion. I thank the Lord Almighty for sparing my life.

Panama City has always been home to me and my wife. It has really grown; it doesn't look like the sleepy, little town we moved to in 1940.

Submitted by: J.W. Ramer, c/o Bay Center, 1336 St. Andrews Blvd., Panama City, Florida 32405.

Chester Lee Richbourg

Chester Lee Richbourg was a well known barber in and around Bay County until his sudden death from a massive heart attack on 9/12/1978, age 88.

My dad began barbering while working at the saw mill at West Bay Mill located at the East end of the present Hathaway Bridge. There was no shop but he applied his skill on porches or anywhere the customer needed a barber. He

Chester Lee Richbourg (Left), Richbourg Barber Shop, 1012 Beck Ave.

continued barbering when he, his first wife Mattie Lee Dykes [whom he married 7/3/1917 Bay Co.], his children Daisy Lee & Horace Mitchell, started following the fruit picking season in South Florida. It was in Nocatee, DeSoto County, Florida that I, the third child, A. D. was born on April 21, 1923. Dad would barber "on the side", pick and pack fruit as his primary income. My parents divorced on July 20, 1929.

Chester, or Lee, as some called him eventually became a full time barber. Around 1950 he was a barber and Councilman [Commissioner] for Ocoee, Orange Co, FL. His political logo was "Working For the Future of Ocoee".

There are at least six barber shops he owned and operated in St. Andrew and Panama City, Florida and numerous shops he worked in within Bay County and Marianna, Jackson Co., FL. One of the earliest permanent structures he barbered in was located in a large wooden frame building across from what is known as the old bank building in St. Andrew, address 1001 Beck Ave. He then located across the street, 1012 Beck Ave., the north end building complex which housed The Bank, Brown's Drug Store, the Serve-U-Well Grocery, which was owned by his wife's cousin, Oscar Dykes and family. He had a bath-house with hot water for his patrons to use in this location.

Expanding, he moved across the street to his own building which was north of 1001 Beck and next door to Henry Aaron's Filling Station on the corner of Beck and 11th St. He remained in this location a number of years where he gave many a child their first haircut!

Not too many years after, he opened a shop at 119 West 6th Street on March 1, — across the street from the First Baptist Church and next door to his brother-in-law, Floyd J.

Chester Lee Richbourg Barber Shop next door to Henry Aaron's Service Station, Beck Ave.

Canterbury's Shoe Shop and Elton Warren's Radio Shop.

Later on, he had a shop in part of his home, 305 Airport Drive, where he, his second wife whom he married September 16, 1929, Dora Lee Canterbury and son Wilson lived. Dora had a Botique there, also. They sold this, and moved to 1502 W. 11th Street and he continued to barber in various shops in the community, commuting to and from work on the City Transit Bus.

My dad was a meticulous dresser, well groomed, trim and fit, of average statue, was witty, loved gardening & good food. He had the hereditary receding hair-line which is characteristic in the Richbourg line. His Grandparents were William Middleton Richbourg and Rebecca Nettles, daughter of Benjamin Nettles of Escambia Co., FL. Both granddads voted in the first statewide election of Florida in 1845. Chester's Great-g-g-g-grandparents were Rev. Claude Phillipe de Richebourg, a French Hugunot Minister, and Anne Chastaine who arrived on the "Mary and Ann" in Maninkin Town VA, in 1700.

Submitted by: Adrian D. Richbourg, son of Chester Lee Richbourg, 3909 W. 16th St., Panama City, FL, 32401-1108. Sources: Census, Marriage, Divorce, Birth & Death Records of Bay Co. FL, Escambia Co. FL, Panama City News Herald, and personal knowledge.

Mattie Lee Dykes Richbourg-Campbell
Restaurant Pioneer -
Part I

Mattie Lee Dykes Richbourg-Campbell was a pioneer in cafes, drive-ins and restaurants in St. Andrew and Panama City, Florida. There is very little written about her well known food establishments in the many histories of Bay County. Mattie was a visionaire in food establishments.

How did it all begin? After 7/20/1929, Mattie was the sole supporter of her three young children. She did have a home and a filling station next door on Beck Avenue across from the St. Andrew Grammar School. Both structures are still standing today, 2003. Her mother, Sarah Alice Mims Dykes, widow of John Henry Dykes of Jackson Co. FL, lived with her caring for the children.

Pumping gas did not provide enough income so she took in washing and ironing for private families. Somewhere along the way, she began

Filling Station with Capt. Jack, Mr. Tam, insert of Mattie Campbell.

selling groceries and making sandwiches for her filling station customers. Then came hamburgers and soup. Some of the students from the school would come over to eat as well as her own children. There was no school lunchroom at that time.

On 1/24/1930, Gulf Co. FL, Mattie married her second husband, Talmadge William "Tam" Campbell. He had been employed at the station while Mattie engaged in other endeavors to make a living. Mattie's station was the only place to eat at this time, so there was always many locals and out of towners coming by. One of their friends who worked as a cook on the dredge Binyard (opening the new "pass"), was Capt. Jack, called Uncle Jack by some, taught Mattie how to make hushpuppies. Even though hushpuppies were widely cooked she had not made them. She began serving them at the filling station cafe. She also served some of her own homemade home-brew to special customers.

Circumstances began to improve and Mattie, always the opportunist, managed to purchase land frontage between 11th Court and 12th Street, next door to the West Printers building. It was a steep sandhill. She sold her home and station, built a restaurant on the sand lot which was partially

levelled, included living quarters and opened the famous MATTIE'S TAVERN! All of her children worked in it as well as some of the nieces. By this time alcoholic beverages could be legally sold, so they had a small bar separated from the dinning area, which Tam served his many patrons.

Sources: Census, birth/death records, Dykes Bible, Bay Co. land records, personal knowledge.

Submitted (Part I): Horace Mitchell Richbourg, son of Mattie Dykes Richbourg-Campbell, 5917 Highway 90, Marianna, FL 32446.

Mattie Lee Dykes Richbourg-Campbell
Restaurant Pioneer -
Part II

MATTIE'S TAVERN opened in the 1930's. The menu included: Red Snapper, fried 50 cents, KC T-Bone including potato 90 cents, Whole fried or broiled chicken $1.50, Hamburger 10 cents, BQ Beef or Pork sandwich 15 cents, Coffee or Tea 5 cents. You could get a Martini or other popular mixed drink for 30 cents!

Mattie's Tavern

Not long after, MATTIE'S was enlarged to give more dining area and a dance floor was installed. Mattie and Tam had a son, William Kenneth "Bill" Campbell on 12/29/1936, who never worked in the restaurants. MATTIE'S TAVERN was a very popular eating establishment where families could come together in a warm, friendly and safe atmosphere. Paper mill employees, locals, tourist and high schoolers found Mattie's place an excellent and reasonable place to dine and dance.

From the beginning, Mattie had her large wood burning stove in the kitchen on which she cooked vegetables, soups and maybe even cornbread. There was more modern cooking equipment, too. Her fried chicken and hushpuppies were the rave among patrons!

Other restaurants began to open

Mattie's Tavern after addition

in the area, such as Carsons, L. T. Byrd's Cafe, and later the Shrimp Boat. All during the years Mattie was purchasing land, especially in the area of the "Tavern". She did this independently of Tam as he was not quite the visionary as Mattie. Mattie's Cottages, St. Andrew Drug Store and Post Office were built. Her children were moving out, Daisy Lee married Steadmon Hobbs, Horace moved to Marianna to run the "farm" and take care of Grandma Dykes, A. D. was off to The University of Alabama and soon to WWII and their other business interests were increasing. She built a home on Bayview Ave. (1118) which now houses an antique shop, business buildings up to where Kelly's Super Market was on Beck Avenue. The shipyard was booming and so was business. Mattie and Tam decided to sell Mattie's Tavern to J. B. Lahan in 1943.

Submitted by (Part II): Colt Richbourg, grandson of Mattie Dykes Richbourg-Campbell 5712 Bayou George Rd. Panama City, FL 32404.

Sources: Census, birth/death records/ Dykes Bible, my parent's genealogical research, Menu from Mattie's Tavern in possession of the family.

Mattie Lee Dykes Richbourg-Campbell
Restaurant Pioneer
Part III

Mattie soon began to have a calling to "cook them vittals" again. She owned some land at 508 Mulberry Avenue in

Three Sons Drive In corner of Beck Ave. & 12th Street

Panama City, and on 4/24/1947 opened DAISY LEE'S RESTAURANT, named for her daughter. The opening menu included: Cocktail, Salad, Entree, Vegetable, Dessert and Drink for $1.75!

The tables had to have white linen table clothes with a matching overlay which was always changed after each customer—white folded napkins a must! All employees wore hairnets, had health cards from the

Maude longtime cook for Daisy Lee's Restaurant

Health Department, were taught how to handle all eating utensils and none handled money. Mattie ran a very clean and healthy restaurant. Her kitchen was spotless! Customers were allowed to pick and choose their own steak or fish from the large walk-in cooler The Gulf Power Crew often came off a long hard job and were served on the large back screened porch. Black patrons were served in the same area.

Most of the employees were still there when the restaurant closed. Mattie, Mr. Tam, Miss Annie Mae, Mattie's sister, worked the kitchen as well as some of Mattie's children when they came by to work or eat. Some of the kitchen help were Maude, Wistee, Ethel, and Matthew to name a few.

All had the skills to mix up a batch of hushpuppies, grill a good steak, fry fish, shrimp or scallops, and chicken in fresh deep-fry grease and large clean grill. Miss Annie Mae always kept the salad greens washed, cut, and chilled.

Condiments were made from scratch: tartar sauce, cocktail sauce, oil & vinegar dressing, and Thousand Island

Daisy Lee's

dressing, also the shrimp batter, hushpuppies, gravy and turkey dressing. Mattie did not have her wood stove here!

Mattie was always venturing out. She had had a restaurant named for herself, one named for her daughter, Daisy Lee, and then she had a drive-in which was built on the north corner next to Mattie's Tavern which was by then owned by Lowe Smith. She named this eatery, "THE THREE SONS" for her sons, Horace, A. D. and Bill. The best hamburgers in town were made here. Horace and wife Ruth, A. D. and wife Mildred, had opportunities to operate

the drive-in at different times. A. D. & Mildred finally sold it and Mattie opened a Gift Shop there. Hunt's Oyster Bar is there now.

Age, health and competition began to take its tole. The family all ventured into their own callings, so Mattie and Tam finally retired to operate their other business interests in St. Andrew: the motel, a beauty parlor, gift shop, and even a dime store.

Mattie never lost her love for cooking and preparing good food! She always enjoyed a good pot of greens and several batches of pone cornbread.

Born in Jackson County Florida, Mattie had lineal descendants who voted in the first statewide Florida election in 1845: Benjamin Stephens (Stevens) and John Stuart (Stewart). She attended St. Andrew Grammar School for a year or two.

Mattie died the day after her 81st birthday, March 8, 1978. *Submitted by (Part III): Randy Richbourg, grandson of Mattie Dykes Richbourg-Campbell, 1106 Bayview Ave., Panama City, FL 32401. Sources: Census, birth/death records, Dykes Bible, Florida Voters In Their First Statewide Election, May 26, 1845 by Brian E. Michaels, Florida State Genealogical Society, 1987, my parent's genealogical research; Menus from Mattie's Tavern, Daisy Lee's Restaurant, Three Son's Drive-In in the possession of the family.*

Richey, Presley and Majors

Once upon a time there were two brothers and one sister. Their names were Marion Frank, Thomas Warren and Leoma. Frank & Thomas was originally from Redlevel, AL. Frank was the oldest of the three, then Thomas, then Leoma with her curley blonde hair and blue eyes. Their parents were Maddie & Warren Richey. Maddie died young so Thomas went to live with the Dunivan's, Maddie's brother,

they would not take Frank, the cause is unknown. Frank was adopted to Doctor & Ms. Presley. Leoma was born then adopted to the Thomas family in Butler County, AL. When Frank was 19, Dr. Presley passed away and Ms. Presley divided the estate with Frank. Thomas Warren Richey married Mary Elizabeth (Lizzie) Majors while his older brother Marion Frank, married Mary's older sister, Lutishia (Lu).

When the girls were still in school Leoma used to walk with them to school (about 4 miles) since they were neighbors. There was a story that a ghost haunted the woods they had to walk through. None of the girls

Thomas Warren and Mary Elizabeth Richey

had ever seen the ghost so one day as they were walking home Leoma threw her hands up in the air and shouted to the Lord, "Lord! I have never seen the ghost of these woods! If there is one, show it to me!" Leoma screaming to the Lord like this scared Lizzie and Lu to death! But what else happened, scared all three girls. When Leoma screamed out, she scared a pack of hogs in the woods and they charged throughout the woods. The girls heard them and thought the ghost was after them. They never ask after the ghost again.

Perry, the Major girl's older brother, moved with the two couples to Panama City, FL in 1912. The Majors were from Butler County, AL. Eventually both couples settled in Millville. The Presleys bought a house on East Avenue and the Richeys on North Gray Avenue where the two houses were back to back. Thomas and Lizzie had seven sons and one daughter, Quinie, Ernest (Windy), Paul, Vernon (Red), Jack, Ruby Estelle, James and Floyd. Frank and Ludie had two sons and two daughters, Titus, Blanch, Wilma and Theodore (Ted). Perry Majors married a lady named Josephine (Jo) and he had two daughters, Lennie and Lucille. Thomas worked as a carpenter and circuit preacher on the side, who traveled by horse and buggy to Wewahitchka, Blountstown and Port St. Joe. His daughter Ruby Estelle went with him a lot of the time. Frank worked as a minister on the side, a carpenter & contractor, millwright and a stevedore. It was an accident during his stevedore work that caused his death.

One time an electrician was repairing a light fixture at Frank's when he was electrocuted. Lutishia could find no pulse so they all prayed over the man till he started breathing again. I don't think the electrician charged her for his services that day.

All the women in the paper mill and Millville area agreed to pray at a certain time each day. They did this with dedication and vigor and saw the results of answered prayer which resulted in this practice going on for years and years. Thus, the name of "Holy Hammock" came about.

One of Thomas' sons, Vernon (Red), died one day of a fever. Thomas carried his son in his arms and walked to the little church his brother, Frank, had helped finance and build on East Avenue below where Millville School sits. When Thomas got there he laid Vernon on the altar. Thomas gave his son up to God and before they left Vernon was awake and hungry.

Thomas' daughter, Ruby Estelle, had skin cancer on her face while she was yet young and beautiful. She listened to R.W. Shambach, a renowned faith evangelist still alive and well on TBN today, and he called out a lady with cancer on her nose was being healed. Ruby said she felt Jesus' fingers wipe over the bridge of her nose where the cancer was physically evident. When she looked in the mirror, the cancer was gone. In 1980, on the urging of Frank Presley's daughter, Wilma, Ruby Estelle's daughter, Ruby Gail, went to the church that had grown from the little church on East Avenue. She didn't hear one word of the sermon J.B. Davis preached that Sunday morning, but the words to an old hymn, "Love Lifted Me" brought her to that same altar. She knows her family has never been perfect but one thing she will always be thankful and proud of, is a family entrenched within a Holy Ghost movement that still burns today in all our hearts.

Submitted by Ruby Gail Scruggs Sims Layton, 312 North Gray Avenue, Panama City, FL 32401.

Pamela Teresa and LeAnne Marie Robbins

Pamela Robbins was born January 6, 1965 in Panama City, Florida to Richard N. Robbins and Dorothy Ann Johnson Robbins. She has two sisters Cynthia Renee Robbins Peacock and LeAnne Marie Robbins Lusk. Pamela went to school at Cherry Street Elementary School, Rosenwald Junior High School and graduated from Bay County High School. She attended Gulf Coast Community College for awhile and volunteered at the Springfield Public Library. Later she volunteered at the Bay County Public Library where she

Ann Robbins, Pam Robbins and bullmastiff Apalachee's Gale Force Wind

was hired to work in the Circulation Department in 1983. She's now an assistant supervisor in the Circulation Department.

Pamela is a member of the Greater Panama City Dog Fancier's Association and a member of the Southeast Bullmastiff Association. She breeds and shows bullmastiffs

Debra, Jon and LeAnne Lusk

and in the past she also bred and showed basset hounds. One of her bassets, Apalachee's Pretty Persuasion, was featured with her picture in six different books on dog breeds and also in numerous calendars, bookmarks, etc. Pamela can trace one of her ancestors back to Caleb Calloway born about 1638 in Isle of Wight County, Virginia.

LeAnne Marie Robbins Lusk was born March 3, 1971 in Panama City, Florida to Richard and Ann Robbins. She attended Cove Elementary School, A. D. Harris Middle School and graduated from Mosley High School. She attended Gulf Coast Community College for awhile and then married Jon Michael Lusk of Panama City, Florida. LeAnne and Jon lived in Panama City when they married and later moved to Dothan, Alabama. LeAnne is a professional dog groomer and works for Pet Smart in Dothan. Jon worked in Panama City for Bell Signs and when he and LeAnne moved to Dothan he went to work for I. D. Associates. They are the proud parents of Debra Ann Lusk.

Jon Lusk can trace his ancestors back to William Lusk born 1720 in Chester County, Pennsylvania and LeAnne can trace one of her ancestors back to Haute Wyatt born June 4, 1594 in Allington Castle, England.

Submitted by: Debra Lusk, 202 N. Bonita Ave., Panama City, FL 32401; Written by Ann Robbins, 435 South Palo Alto Ave., Panama City, Florida.

Richard N. Robbins and Dorothy Ann Johnson

Richard N. Robbins, is the son of Nonwell Robbins and Marjorie Gladys McLawhon. Richard was born November 28, 1939 in Apalachicola, Florida. He had an identical twin brother who died at birth. World War II took Richard's father off to war. The war changed Nonwell and he was never able to cope with family life again. Marjorie and Nonwell divorced and she and Richard eventually moved to Panama City, Florida when Richard was ten years old. They lived in the Cove and Richard made friends with Robert W. Harris who would later be Best Man at Richard's

Ann and Richard Robbins 25th Wedding Anniversary

and Ann's wedding. Richard attended Cove Elementary School, was in the first 7th grade class at the new Jinks Jr. High and attended Bay County High School where he graduated in 1957.

He was in the first class at Gulf Coast Community Junior College and there he met Dorothy Ann Johnson who was also in the first class at Gulf Coast. Richard and Ann attended three years of high school together but never met in high school.

Dorothy Ann Johnson was born December 2, 1939 in Altha, Florida. The daughter of Robert C. Johnson and Pauline Strickland, she moved to Panama City, Florida when she was two years old and her father worked at the shipyard. Growing up in Millville, she attended Millville Elementary, was in the first 7th grade class in the new

Everitt Jr. High and graduated from Bay County High School in 1957. She was also in the first class at Gulf Coast Community Junior College. Richard and Ann were elected by the student body as the first Mr. and Miss Sophomore. Ann was in the first graduating class of Gulf Coast Community Junior College in 1959.

Ann Robbins and her bullmastiffs Shawney and Buck

Richard worked in construction at Tyndall Air Force Base and then got a job with Domestic Laundrey and Cleaners as a route man. One Thursday, he decided to collect for his route a day early at Panama City Beach. At a hotel near the Hangout, he was collecting from a lady when she noticed her toddler was not in her play yard. Richard and the mother began frantically searching for the child. In the distance Richard saw the little girl fall face down in the calm surf. He ran as fast as he could in the sand, which was not easy wearing work shoes. It was about a hundred yards to the surf and when he got to the child he swept her up and ran back on the beach. He thought he would have to do CPR but she began to cough up the water and was all right. The mother collapsed from the shock of seeing her child almost drown. Richard thought he was going to have to do CPR on the mother for awhile. The beach was empty of people that cold winter day and if Richard had not gone collecting one day early the story might have had a different ending. He saved that toddler's life and years later it made him feel good when he read in the newspaper that she had graduated from Bay High. Richard got an offer to work for Associates Finance Company and he worked with that company until he retired in 2000.

Ann got a job working at the Bay County Public Library in May of 1959 and she is still employed there. May of 2003 she celebrated 41 years working at the library. Starting out as a library clerk, she has worked on the bookmobile, reference and circulation department, radio program "Vietnam Voice" on WKGC, story telling and tutoring ESOL to adults from other countries. She is now Public Services Supervisor at the library and the Literacy Administrator for the Bay County

Richard Robbins and Ann Johnson at a college dance age 19

Public Library. For the past four years Ann has been listed in Who's Who In America. She and Richard were married January 16, 1960. They bought a house in St Andrews and had two daughters Cynthia Renee and Pamela Teresa. When Ann became pregnant with their third daughter, LeAnne Marie, they moved to the Cove and bought a house on South Palo Alto Ave.

The girls grew up and Cynthia became a teacher at Lynn Haven Elementary, Pamela works at the Bay County Public Library and LeAnne became a professional dog groomer. Cynthia married Brenton Eugene Peacock and they have a daughter Lorena Colette. LeAnne married Jon Michael Lusk and they have a daughter Debra Ann.

Richard, Ann and Pamela exhibit and breed bullmastiffs. They are members of the Greater Panama City Dog Fanciers Association where Ann is Secretary and Richard is a former President. They are also members of the Southeast Bullmastiff Association and Ann is President of that organization. Ann has devoted 40 years to genealogy research of both their families. Richard and Ann collect primitive antiques, Civil War antiques and Ann does talks to organizations around Northwest Florida on the pioneer life of Florida.

Richard is a descendant of Thomas C. Robbins (1621-1678) of Virginia and Ann is a descendant of James Oates (1660-1703) North Carolina. Richard's family moved from Virginia to North Carolina to Georgia and then to Florida. Ann's family moved from North Carolina to Georgia and then to Florida. The two families followed the same migration path and usually could be found in the same cities in the same years or not more than 200 miles apart most of the time. Yet the two families have never intermarried and only once did we find them actually meeting. Ann's ancestor was an attorney for one of Richard's ancestors in the late 1700's. Richard's family arrived in Florida in the late 1870's and Ann's family got to Florida in the late 1840's. Her great-great-grandfather Archie Smith, was a pioneer in Bay County when it was Washington County. Ann is also a descendant of Tolbert Parrish who was living in Holmes County before Florida was a state.
Submitted by Pamela T. Robbins, 2510 West 16th Street, Panama City, Florida 32405.

Modell Long Robinson

Modell L. Robinson was born and reared in Jackson County, Florida. Her parents were Solomon and Linnie Daniels Long. She had five sisters and three brothers.

She attended and completed Florida Normal College in St. Augustine, Florida and Tuskegee Institute in Tuskegee, Alabama majoring in Elementary Education.

She was a devoted teacher at Glenwood Elementary School for 26 years under the principalship of Mr. A.D. Harris.

Modell was a charter member of Phi Delta Kappa Sorority Inc. in Panama City, Florida.

She was a loving and devoted aunt and mentor to her niece Bura L. Reed whom she raised.

Modell Long Robinson

After retirement from teaching she owned and operated the Pamela Denice Motel and Hotel from 1969 until 1986. She owned and operated the Pamela Denice Apartments from 1987 until December of 1999 when it closed and was demolished.
Submitted by: Bura L. Reed, 1402 Illinois Avenue, Lynn Haven, FL 32444.

John Joseph Rubash

My father, John Joseph Rubash, (Joe) was born February 8, 1883 in the small town of Keystone located in Polk County, Minnesota. He was the son of Frank Rubash, Jr. who was born 1852 in Tukleky in the County of Pocov, Bohemia. Frank, Jr. having immigrated in 1876 along with his father, stepmother and siblings settled for several years in Wisconsin. There he met Barbara Chloupek, whose parents were also immigrants from Bohemia. The original family name at the time of their immigration was actually Rubes but Frank, Jr. changed his name to Rubash when he applied to homestead land in October, 1879 in Polk County, Minnesota. After applying for the land, he went back to Wisconsin where he and Barbara were married in January 1880 in Carlton, Wisconsin; and shortly, thereafter, they moved to Minnesota to improve their homestead. It was here that my father was born. They lived there until dad was about seven years of age. The family had a small store and traded with the Indians. I have heard the story from my dad that one time while he was playing with the Indian boys, Chief Setting Bull came through the village. Joe said he was the biggest, meanest looking Indian he had ever seen.

About 1889 the family moved to Chadron, Nebraska. They remained there a few years before moving to Oklahoma. Some time later they relocated to the Florida panhandle, settling for a while in the small community of Shoals on or near Choctawhatchee Bay between Destin and Sandestin. My grandparents remained there just a few years before returning to Oklahoma. My dad fished at East Pass, which is known today as Destin, Florida, where he met my mother Mary Jane Woodward. She was the daughter of Frederick H. Woodward

John Joseph Rubash and Mary Jane Woodward Rubash

and Jane Destin. Joe and Mary were married in 1919 in New Orleans, Louisiana where dad had enlisted in the merchant marines. They lived there a little over a year before moving to Bay County, Florida.

In the mid 1930s, my parents paid the back taxes on a piece of property in the St. Andrews area. After paying the taxes for the required number of years, in 1941, they went to the courthouse and upon paying $23.75, (the current year taxes) they were able to have the property recorded in their names. In 1941, that amount was the taxes on an entire block of property in present day St. Andrews. They built their home on this property and raised their family of three daughters and one son.

Written by: Patricia R. Murfee, 1714 Drake Ave, Panama City, Fl. 32405.

The Rubash Family of St. Andrew

John Joseph (Joe) and Mary Jane Woodward Rubash married on 31 JAN 1919 in New Orleans, Louisiana and moved to St. Andrew where they settled and raised four children, three of whom still live in Bay County. Joe was born into a mid-western mining family on 8 FEB 1883 in Crookston, Minnesota, to Frank and Barbara Chloupek Rubash, immigrants from the Austro-Hungarian Empire, the present-day Czech Republic. Mary Jane Woodward was a third generation native Floridian, a descendant of two early Panhandle pioneers, Leonard Destin and Frederick Harlow Harris Woodward, both nineteenth-century settlers of Washington County. Mary was born 8 MAY 1889 at Miller's Ferry where her father owned a general store. After his store

The Rubash Family

was lost in a fire, the Woodwards moved to Point Washington where her father opened a second general store on the banks of the Choctahatchee River, supplying area neighbors, fishermen and lumbermen with necessary staples. Mary's mother, Jane Destin, was the daughter of Leonard Destin, who, after fishing Connecticut waters, settled at East Pass, Florida, now known as Destin, the "World's Friendliest Fishing Village."

The oldest Rubash daughter, Grace Mae, married Grover Dempsey Kent, son of Jewel Rex and Etta Tharp Kent of Bay County. Grace and Dempsey had three daughters, Marilyn Sue, Carolyn Lee, and Shirley Anne. Marilyn married Bill Todd of Panama City, and they had three sons: Greg, Troy and Kyle. She is presently married to Tom Jones. Carolyn married Bill Pitts, also of Panama City, and they also had

three boys: Mike, Russ and Steve. She is presently married to Oscar England. Shirley married another Panama City boy, John Daffin, son of Mr. and Mrs. H. E. Daffin, and they were the parents of two daughters and one son: Leigh Anne, Kelly and Jason.

James Joseph Rubash married Joyce Newborn, daughter of Mr. and Mrs. J. A. Newborn of Liberty, Texas. They have two sons, Mark and Bradley. Mark is married to the former Ginger Killian, and they live in Friendswood, Texas. Bradley married Page Curtis. Today Jim and Joyce live in Liberty, Texas.

Claire Juliette married Orvis (Joe) Parrott, son of Fred and Cynthia Allen Parrott of Plattsburg, New York. They had three daughters: Patricia Ann (Patty), Gwen Marie, and Susan Yvonne (Bonnie). Patty married Lamar Sikes, son of Hubert and Rosalie Finlay Sikes of Panama City, and they are the parents of Hugh, Julie Ann and John Joseph (Joe). Gwen married Freddy Mack Johnson, son of Mary Lassiter Johnson Pogue and the late Ted Levoyd Johnson of Panama City. They are the parents of MacKenzie Lane, Bonnie Katherine and Frederick Carter. Bonnie Parrott married David Ramirez, son of Joe and Voncille Ramirez of Panama City. Patricia Ann Rubash married Rozzie Turner Murfee (Murf), son of Rozzie Fletcher and Amanda Juliet Harmon Murfee, pioneer residents of the Cove section of Panama City. They raised two daughters, Linda Gail and Charlotte Annette. Gail married Frank William Knowles, son of Frank and Thelma Knowles, also early settlers of St. Andrew and a maritime family. Gail and Frank have one daughter, Amanda Susan. Charlotte is married to Glen Strickland, son of Horace Lee and Dorothy Jean Nichols Strickland. They have four children: Cory, Misty, Jessica and Joshua.

Submitted by: Claire Rubash Parrott, 1415 Cincinnati Avenue, Panama City, FL 32401

John Chesley and Audrey Rumph

Among the people who moved to Bay County during the World War II years was a young family from Quincy, Florida. John Chesley Rumph came to work at the Wainwright Shipyard. He lived in a tent with several other men until his family was able to join him. He was born and raised in Georgia and met his wife, Audrey Hatcher Rumph, in the Albany, Georgia area. They married on October 17, 1937 at the Hatcher family home in Eldorendo, Georgia.

Chesley, Audrey and their two sons, William R. (Bill) and Raymond H. Rumph were among the first residents of the new homes built for the shipyard workers in Drummond Park. For awhile the parents each worked a different shift at the shipyard. Later, Audrey joined other residents who rented a bedroom in their homes to two men who worked the night shift. The boys had the room during the night, and the men slept there in the day time.

John Chesley and Audrey Hatcher Rumph Wedding Day 1937

After the war ended, they bought a house on Chandlee Avenue and Chesley began working for the Bay Line Railroad at the engine round house off of Highway 231. He worked for the Bay Line until he retired in 1975. Audrey was an accomplished seamstress and worked for several years making drapes. She also worked at Panama Grammar school and for Cooper's Drug Store on Harrison Avenue. Chesley was an avid gardener, raising wonderful vegetables, flowers and scuppernongs at their home. They both enjoyed fishing. They attended First Baptist Church, Highland Park Baptist Church and were Charter Members of Northside Baptist Church where Chesley was a Deacon and Audrey sang in the choir and taught Sunday School. Following Chesley's death on March 7, 1980, Audrey eventually moved to The Towers and then to Glen Cove. She passed away on May 3, 1999.

Bill married Ellen Jennings of Panama City on June 24, 1961 at Wallace Memorial Presbyterian Church. They have two children, Eric and Jennifer. Eric, his wife Deborah and their daughter, Abbey, live in Alexandria, Virginia. Jennifer married William Blanks and they have three daughters, Katie, Lauren and McKenna. They live in Panama City. Bill and Ellen moved back to Panama City following Bill's retirement from the Federal Bureau of Investigation.

Raymond married Barbara Bass of Dothan, Alabama, on September 17, 1966. They live in Southport, Florida. They have two children, Pamela and Michael. Pam married Ernest Schubert and they have two children, Jason and Sarah. They live in Pennsylvania. Mike lives in Southport. Raymond retired from the Panama City Police Department and Barbara works at Johnson Brothers.

Submitted by: William R. Rumph, 161 Marin Drive, Panama City, FL 32405.

Joshua Mercer Sapp

A native of Manatee County, Florida, Joshua Mercer Sapp, was born October 3, 1878. Mr. Sapp was the son of William and Harriet (Wells) Sapp. His paternal grandparents were Luke M. and Catherine O. Sapp. His maternal grandparents were Henry H. and Catherine Wells. His grandparents migrated to Washington County in North Florida in about

J. Mercer Sapp, father of Herbert and Howard Sapp

1857. After his parents married they moved to Manatee County and later to Key West. There his mother died in the yellow fever epidemic. With the five children William Sapp moved back to Washington County. Joshua was placed in the home of his grandparents, Henry H. and Catherine Wells. The country schools were poor in quality and the terms were only three months a year. He began his education under the tutorship of John R. Thompson, William Griffin, Frank Russ, Alonzo W. Weeks. In his early teens he was determined to gain an education and worked in logging camps and on farms to earn his way through school. After a time he began to teach in the country schools of West Florida, he would teach for a term and then go to school for a term. He took the full four years' course in the Florida State Normal School at DeFuniak Springs and graduated with the degree of L.I., at the head of his class in 1903. He worked in the Holmes County School system for a year and then studied law for two years at Washington & Lee University in Lexington, Virginia graduating with a Bachelor in Laws. While at the university he took a course with the literary societies and won the orator's medal.

After completing his law course he opened a practice in Vernon, Washington County. Experiencing financial difficulties he took the position of principal at a Thomasville, Georgia high school. Then he again entered the law field in Vernon. After two years of a successful practice he moved to Chipley and in two more years he moved to Panama City in 1912. In Panama City he was a prominent attorney and served as attorney for the Board of County Commissioners from 1915-1921. Mr. Sapp was prosecuting attorney for County Court of Bay County for three years. He was a fair but fearless and incorruptible prosecutor. He served on the Board of Public Instruction for Bay County in 1919 and 1920. He was city attorney for Bay County: The City of Panama City, City of St. Andrews and the Town of Millville. As a member of the Methodist Church, South, he served as

Ella Mae Sapp

superintendent of Sunday School and on the Board of Stewards. Mr. Sapp was a member of the Board of Directors of the First National Bank of Panama City, one of the largest and strongest banks of West Florida; he also served on Boards of several other corporations.

In Apalachicola, Florida, on March 4, 1909, Joshua M. Sapp married Miss Ella May Patton, daughter of George A and Hephzibah (Pearson) Patton. Ella May attended the State Normal School at DeFuniak Springs. She was quite active in social and church affairs in Panama City. They had two children: Herbert Patton and Howard William. Mr. Sapp delighted in serving as scout master and going on hikes and hunting trips in the wild and unsettled sections of West Florida with his boys. Both sons became lawyers and joined their father in practice.

Herbert Patton Sapp, born February 28, 1910, graduated from the University of Florida with the LL.B. degree in 1934. During World War II he served as a Lieutenant in the Navy in the Philippines. He married Anna Louise Watson and they have three children: Herbert Patton, Jr., James Mercer and Miriam Louise. H.P. Sapp has served as School Board Attorney and Attorney for Bay County.

William Howard Sapp, born February 25, 1912, graduated from the University of Florida Law School in 1936. During World War II he served with the United States Coast Guard. He married Gene Gordon Howell and they have five children: Elinor, Helen, William (Bill), Louise and Gene, all born in Panama City.

Submitted by: Gene Sapp, 1409 Deer Avenue, Panama City, FL 32401.
Source: History of Florida, Past and Present, Historical and Biographical, 1923.

Lewis Marion Sasser and Mary Cordelia Bess

Lewis Marion Sasser and Mary Cordelia Bess were married 1857 in Early County, Georgia. By 1869 Lewis and Mary had built a log house and established residency in Geneva County (previously Henry County) as documented on a

Christopher and Arizona Kirkland Sasser with son Howard 1917

homestead application for 160 acres. Their children were John Dallas (1857-1912), Rilla Perlina (1859), Sarah Besany (1861), Bithan Bryant (1865-1934), William Preston (1867), Mary Jane (1871), Jesse Green (1873), Lewis Chesler (1873-1945), Lydia (1876), Josiah (1878).

John Dallas, the eldest, married Sarah Eliza Hall (1859-1942), a neighbor on December 14, 1879. She was the daughter of John James Hall and Sarah Ann Elizabeth West. Her father John died during the Confederate war. Sarah and John Dallas Sasser were farmers, hard workers, and provided a good home for their twelve children on the outskirts of the small community of Malvern. Their children and the known spouses were: Sarah Elizabeth (1880-1968) married John Westly Clark, John Marion (1883-1957) married Theodosia Paulk, Josiah (1885-1948) married Etta M., Richard Franklin (1887-1964) married Teimatha Kirkland,

Sanford (1889-1934) married Nancy Ardilla Kirkland, William Henry (1892) died at birth, Cordelia (1893) married Henry Smith,

Christopher Columbus (1895-1979) married Arizona Mahala Kirkland, Christian Clifford(1899-1948) married A. L. Faulk, Eliza Jane (1901-1975) married Amie Turner. Christopher Columbus (1895-1979) married Arizona Mahala Kirkland (1898-1972) August 8, 1915 in Houston County, Alabama. Their children were, Howard Milton, Hawtense, Gustavis Vanilla, Bessie Gwendolyn, Uvell, Christopher Columbus Jr., and Lydia Ruth. They moved to Bay County during WWII and lived the rest of their life here. Christopher made a living farming in his early years and worked as a carpenter later. The oldest child, Howard Milton Sasser, was my father. (1916-1980). He married Bonnie Lucille Hall (1916-1939), a neighbor, daughter of Grover Cleveland and Mary Rachel Hinson Hall.

A favorite story told by Christopher, my grandfather, was about his mother Eliza being afraid to stay alone after dark if John was not home. As dusk came, she would take the children and go through the trail behind the house to the family cemetery which was several hundred feet into the wooded area. She would keep the children there until a light appeared in the window. This was the signal that John had returned and then she would go to the house. Many years later when Christopher was sick and nearing the end of his life, he began to reminisce in his mind and talked about wanting to go to the cemetery because no one was home. The original home place existed until recently, but time took it's toll and it no longer stands.

Submitted by: Taylor Sasser, 21616 Califa St., Woodland Hills, Ca., 91367. Written by: Roy E. Sasser, 2908 Orange Hill Road, Chipley, Florida 32428.
Sources: Census records, court house records, personal knowledge.

Emil T. and Mina Schmidt

I do not remember Grandpa as I was only two years old when he died in 1924. I do, however, remember Grandma as Mama, Daddy, my sister Minnie, my brother Jacob, and I moved back to the homestead to care for her. Once when the woods caught on fire, Grandma inhaled a lot of smoke fighting the fire and afterward suffered from asthma. In those days folks often used a pine sapling to beat out the flames.

Grandma and Grandpa Schmidt were both born in Germany. Grandpa was fourteen when he came to New Orleans, where he worked in a bakery. Later he moved to Newark, New Jersey, where he married Mina Kunz in 1882. Mina had come from Stuttgart two years before. The newly married couple had a candy shop in New York City for three years. Responding to an advertisement of the Cincinnati Land Company, they came by boat to a small tract of land that is now

Ida Schmidt Godert and Jacob Godert 1914 on their wedding day

Cedar Grove. My mother, Ida Annie, was born in Cedar Grove in 1887. The Schmidts had a daughter, Mina, and a son, Edward. Both died in childhood. Edward was buried on the present Cook Bayou homestead. The grave was marked by a little white picket fence on the side of Highway 2297 for years until it was stolen.

In 1890 Grandpa acquired a half-homestead of eighty acres, where he planned to build a model farm with money he inherited from his parents. First he cleared land and built a small one-room log house. When he arrived with his wife and child, and the last load of furniture, he found the house had been burned to the ground. The remains indicated that tools and other things had been stolen and the place

set on fire. Not giving up Grandpa built another small one room house of upright boards where the family lived while he built barns and later the big two and a half story home. This was the house where I grew up.

Rev. Johnny Vickery married my mother, Ida Schmidt, and my daddy, Jacob Godert, in 1914 in the parlor of the big house. Daddy was born in St. Goar, Germany, in 1887 to a family of thirteen children. His father was a ship pilot on the Rhine River. Daddy joined the merchant marine as a teenager and sailed for nine years on German, British, and Norwegian ships. These were sailing vessels, which is why Daddy kept a picture of Old Iron Side up over the door in the dining room. In 1912 while sailing from Brazil to Australia, Daddy's ship docked at Millville for a load of lumber from the German American Lumber Company. Some of the boat crew failed to show up, so Daddy and a buddy decided not to sail with a limited crew. They skipped ship.

Ida Schmidt Godert and her parents Emil T. and Mina Schmidt

Neither spoke English, so when someone passing in a wagon told them about the farm owned by a German named Schmidt, they walked there and got jobs on the farm. The buddy soon decided to go back to his homeland, but Daddy stayed and later married Mama.

Ida and Jacob moved to a place on Callaway Bayou, then to Millville, where Daddy worked for the St. Andrews Bay Lumber Company. There their first child, Minnie, was born. Later they moved to Panama City, where Daddy worked at night as the night watchman for the Tar Plant and for J.A. Smith at Panama Machine Shop in the day. After the Tar Plant closed, Daddy remained at Panama Machine Shop located on the south side of the Tarpon Bridge until he retired. During World War II he worked briefly at Wainwright Shipyard and International Paper Company helping the war effort.

There are many memories of living on Grandpa's farm. My sister Agnes was born at home as that was the custom. Neighbors and family helped in times of childbearing and illness. My sister Minnie died there of malaria her senior year at Bay High. She was an honor student, superior in all studies and had a record of never being tardy or absent during her whole school life until the time of her brief fatal illness.

I remember well the time our feed barn burned. Mama had gone to check on some land. Lightening struck, setting fire to the pasture and picket fence catching the barn on fire, I rang the dinner bell on the tower over the well to call for help. Men from the Norris Turpentine Camp and other neighbors came quickly. To save the nearby two story hay barn, they tore out boards upstairs in order to pour water brought by bucket brigade from the well to keep the roof and side from catching fire. Before she left Mama told me to bake some sweet potatoes in the wood stove in the house. When she came home, Mama fed those baked sweet potatoes to all that helped fight the fire.

Thanks to Daddy, I recall the good times when he would take me fishing on Cook Bayou Bridge and swimming in Oliver Creek. As a teenager it was always fun riding Grandpa's 1914 Model T Ford to Callaway on Sunday afternoon with my brother when he went to play baseball. Before and after the game all the young people loved getting a ride in the old car.

After graduating from Bay High in 1941, I entered nurses training at Pensacola Hospital (now Sacred Heart). Upon graduation, I served one year in the U.S. Army as a nurse. January 10, 1951, I married Ben Cockcroft and moved to Millville. I continued for years to go home to Grandpa's farm every Sunday with my four children, Marie, William, Linda, and Avis. Those were indeed the good old days!

Submitted by: Bertha Marie Godert Cockcroft, 309 James Avenue, Panama City, Florida 32401

Emil T. and Mina Schmidt

Although I did not know either of my grandparents, I always felt that I knew them as I heard the story of their life retold by my mother and neighbors. Grandpa died before I was born and Grandma died in the fall after I was born in April. I remember older family friends telling me how surprised they were to visit the old Schmidt house one day and learn that Mama had another baby, as Minnie was 13, Jake was 11, and Bertha was 7. During my preschool days Daddy worked in town at Panama Machine Shop six days a week, boarding in town and coming home on the weekends bringing groceries and mule, cow, hog, and chicken feed. Daddy said he would come home and find one of my three siblings

The old home place

taking turns rocking me to sleep. He would say, "That baby can't sleep all the time. Let her stay awake."

About the time I started to school the school bus service began. Before this my brother Jake drove Daddy's car taking my sister Minnie and Lovie McCall to Bay High. The school board paid for the gas. First and second grade I walked with my sister Bertha half a mile to what is now Highway 22 and caught the bus to Panama Grammar School. Third and fourth grades I went to the newly re-built Cook School. There were still a few families living at the old Norris Turpentine Camp. As they came by I would join them and walk the mile and a half through the woods to school. This was the third school building at Cook. My grandfather, who was School Supervisor, helped build the first school in 1895. This was the school my mother attended. The school opened with thirty-two children, ages six to nineteen. With no compulsory education laws, few took full advantage of getting an education. A school term was five months, but a teacher could cover the material in four months with permission. A woods fire burned this school in 1922. The next year a second school was built in the same place. Minnie and Jake graduated from the eighth grade at this school and Bertha attended first, second, and third grades there. Again, a woods fire destroyed the school in 1933. Daddy helped get the third school built in 1938. Mrs. Bertie Burkett Loftin taught grades one through eight in this one room school for two years. The county later sold the land and building. Fourth through twelfth grades I caught the bus to Panama Grammar and later Bay High. All three Cook Schools were used for community activities and regular church services. Grandpa Schmidt and later Mama, organized Sunday School and church services, teaching Sunday School and getting preachers to come from Christian Advent, Episcopal, and Baptist denominations.

Mama and Daddy were both hard workers. Daddy always worked in town, farming was not for him. Mother and we children did the farm work - planting and harvesting, and caring for the mule, cow, hogs, and chickens. We always kept a milk cow for milk and butter. We raised hogs for our own use. We butchered them the first good cold spell in the fall, so they could be gutted and hung to chill over night. There

was no refrigeration, so the meat had to be salted or cooked quickly.

We always had a lot of chickens. We raised them from chicks, eating the roosters and saving the hens to lay eggs. When my brother went off to Europe and North Africa in World War II and my sister entered nurses training and became a nurse in the army, I cared for the chickens; feeding, watering, cleaning the houses, and gathering the eggs. Daddy sold the eggs at Gray's Store in Millville and gave me the money - my work for an allowance.

We always had lots of fruit, which we ate, canned and sold. People came to the house to buy pears, grapes, sweet potatoes, or cane syrup. During the depression, when money was scarce, turpentine workers often traded octagon soap or lard for the things they needed.

Sweet potatoes draws were planted in spring to make vines. With no irrigation available, we waited until a good rain to plant the vines. It seemed that it always rained on the 4th of July, so instead of celebrating by going to town to watch the parade, we had to plant sweet potatoes and carry buckets of water to the field to water the planted vines to settle the dirt. In the fall these potatoes were dug and put in our ground cellar. This was a building with a cement floor, double brick walls, pitched roof and double ceiling. This building stayed cool in the summer and warm in the winter. Potatoes were spread on the floor until cured and ready to bake. Years ago there was a song with the words, "Take an old cold tater and wait." I remember coming home from school and enjoying a cold baked sweet potato.

Making cane syrup also involved hard work. In the fall before the first freeze the standing cane was stripped of leaves, cut and carried to the shed where it was ground, the juice boiled down in the four large copper vats until thick, then put in a huge cypress tank to cool before being put in cans. This process began before day and lasted late into the night.

Growing up I never understood what Mama meant when she told Rev. Daffin how she felt close to God in working with the soil and that as she hoed she would pray. Now I understand! My sister and I grow nearly all of our own fruits and vegetables and enjoy it! Thanks Mom! !

Whether it was returning from college, seminary, teaching Bible in West Virginia, or coming home on furlough from Japan, where I was a Presbyterian missionary, it was always good to take off my shoes and be home again on Grandpa's farm!

Submitted by: Agnes Ida Godert, 134 Highway 2297, Panama City, Florida 32404.

The Scoggins and Dial Families

My great, great grandfather, John Wesley Scoggins, was a building contractor who lived in Montgomery, Alabama. He and his wife, Lorena Vaughn Scoggins, were attracted to the newly incorporated Bay County and decided to move to Panama City in 1914.

While the Scoggins lived in Panama City, he built a number of homes in and around the downtown area. Among them was the home at 224 E. 3rd Street, known today as the Sapp house. At the outbreak of World War I, he and his wife returned to Montgomery where he participated in the construction of Maxwell Army Air Base.

Jessie Mae, his youngest daughter and my great grandmother, was employed as the bookkeeper for the Panama City Chero Cola Bottling Company located on West Beach Drive. She chose to remain in Panama City where she had established many young friends, including Pearl Strickland, Nina Starling, Flora Bell McBride, Elsie Jordan Combs, R.D. Blackshear, Frank Mosley, Albertino Minto and Mr. And Mrs. J. Ed Stokes. Also included among her friends were Dr. and Mrs. J. M. Whitfield, who asked her to move into their home when her parents left.

At that time my great grandfather, John F. Dial, was serving with the American Army in France. His brother, Earl Glover Dial, was the manager of the Chero Cola

Bottling Plant and also owned a grocery-department store in the 100 block of Harrison Avenue. Upon my great grandfather's discharge at the war's end, he was invited by his brother, Earl, to come to Panama City and work for him. He accepted his offer and later became romantically involved with Ms. Scoggins.

My great grandparents were married on October 2, 1919, at the home of the groom's brother, 115 Third Street. The Rev. W. F. Moore of the First Baptist Church performed the wedding.

Jessie Mae Scoggins (R) with friend, Albertino Minto, Panama City (1915)

Since both of my great grandparents were originally from Alabama, they had many friends and relatives who enjoyed visiting with them in their new home. Roads to and from the area at that time were not well suited for travel, so lots of visitors chose the Bay Line Railroad's weekly excursion from Dothan as the best way to come to the coast. Many of the locals referred to it as the "Gall Berry Special" because of the many miles of desolate brush that it traversed along the way.

My great grandparents later moved to Marianna, where my grandfather, Charles P. Dial, was born. He and my grandmother, Lois, were married in 1949 and moved to Bay County upon his graduation from Florida State University in 1951. My grandfather was employed by Merritt Brown, the principal at the then new Jinks Junior High School. My grandmother was later employed there as the school secretary.

My mother, Darlene Dial Salsman and her brother, Pete Dial, were both born at the old Lisenby Hospital on 11th Street, with Dr. Jack Corbitt attending.

From Jinks, my grandfather moved into school administration and retired in 1987 as the principal of Lynn Haven Elementary School. My grandmother retired the same year.

Submitted by: Stephanie Lorian Salsman, 107 Chelsea Lane, Lynn Haven, FL 32444 (6th Grade/Mowat).

Charles R. (Bob) Scott and Barbara Ann Scott

Following a dream, in May 1958 my Mom and Dad left Indiana for sunny Panama City, Florida, bringing my two brothers, ages 8 and 1, and myself, age 6, with them.

The first summer, almost every afternoon when my dad got off work we would go to the beach, stopping first at a gas station to buy old truck tire tubes. Once at the beach, my older brother Lex and I would joyously ride the waves on the inner tubes, while my younger brother

"A Work in Progress" (Mom, Zane, Denise, Lex -1962)

Zane floated in a small plastic tube, holding securely onto my mother's bathing suit strap.

When I was 6 1/2, we moved to a house 3 blocks from the bay and close to busy downtown St. Andrews. Once a week we walked to St. Andrews to spend our allowance at the drugstore on an ice cream soda or comic book, and on the marina we could watch the feeding of the dolphins and sea turtles that for some time were kept there.

When I was 8 1/2 we moved to another house about 3 blocks from St. Andrews Bay. Occasionally, my mom would come down to the bay with my brothers and I, and with our masks and flip flops on, we would dive for scallops. After collecting a tub of the delicacies, we would take them home and clean them, and my mother would fry them for supper. When Dad was off work in the summer, we often went to St. Andrews State Park and swam in the Gulf of Mexico, and then we would go to the pool made by the jetties. After swimming, my brothers and I would climb to the top of the cliffs overlooking the pass, and explore the woods behind the cliffs where we helped create the nature trails that are part of the park now.

It was about this time my dad decided to take up boat building. It was amazing to watch him create a 16 foot boat using only a set of paper plans, a pile of lumber, and about a thousand brass screws. It was difficult, because straight pieces of lumber had to be gradually bent to form the inner framework of the hull, and large pieces of plywood then also bent and screwed down to form the outside.

My family had more than 10 years of adventure and fun together exploring the bays and inlets of Bay County in our boat, the Serendipity. In 1962, soon after the boat was finished, my parents had bought a house near Hathaway Bridge so we continued to live near the water. My mother continues to live there, and my younger brother lives a block away.

My parents had many dreams when they married, and together they worked to make them come true. I will be forever grateful to them in particular for moving to Florida, and giving my brothers and I the opportunity to grow up on what I truly believe are "The World's Most Beautiful Beaches".

Submitted by: Denise A. Scott, for: The Family of Charles R. (Bob) and Barbara Ann Scott, 3916 E. 11th St., Apt. N-4, Panama City, FL 32404.

E. W. Scott's Family

My grandparents, Ellis W. Scott and Dollie S. Scott moved to Panama City around 1918. They had a son, Leon, who graduated from Panama High School in 1921. This building still stands at the corner of Harrison Avenue and 7th Street.

In 1921, my mother, Mary C. Scott Holden, was born in the Cove section of Panama City. They lived in Panama City until 1929 in which they moved out to West Bay on property that was my great grandfather's, B.C. Scott. My grandfather was elected Justice of the Peace in 1948, where he served for many years.

I married a local boy, Vernon B. Anderson, whose family also has deep roots here in Bay County. Vernon and I traveled for years, had four children and returned to where we started from, Bay County, Florida.

E. W. Scott, Sr., Dollie Scott and (middle) Eva Vick

My mother, brothers, children, husband and myself were all born in Bay County.

Submitted by: Dolly Holden Anderson, 118 Church Rd., Ebro, FL 32437.

The Family of Leeoma Thomas Scott

Leeoma Thomas Scott was the sister of Marion Frank Presley and Thomas Warren Ritchey. She followed her brothers to Bay County, and lived much of her life here. She was still raising chickens as late as the age of eighty.

Leeoma Thomas Scott

She had two children, Helen Lewis and Cleston Thomas. Her grandson was Bobby Lewis, known in Bay County for his work as a sheriff s deputy.
Submitted by: Donald Hudson, 374 Foxtrot Drive, Mansfield, Louisiana 71052; Written by: Merle Presley Parker.

Sheila Day Leto Scott and John Charles Scott Family - Part I

Edward Sherman Day, originally from Minnesota, married Maud Ellen Gainer, one of the Gainers from Econfina, and they had three daughters: Margaret Louise Day, Maud Ellen Day, and Gertrude Gloria Day. Ed Day built their home at 1001 Calhoun Avenue. This story is about Maud Ellen Day and her descendants.

Maud held two different jobs during her young years. She worked at the US Post Office and she was the Weather Observer for the area. She did not have an opportunity to go to college. A young Sicilian chemical engineer, Bruno Frank Leto, came to Panama City from Tampa to work for International Paper Company, about a year after graduating from the University of Florida.

Edward Sherman Day

They were married and lived in an apartment upstairs at the Day home. A daughter was born, Sheila Day Leto, and they later moved to a rental house near Frankford Avenue and 11th Street. When Sheila was two years old, they bought a home at 2204 West Ninth Street. That was the family home until after both Bruno and Maud's deaths.

Bruno worked at International until his retirement. He was active as a Boy Scout Leader, in the St. Andrew Men's Club (which made many improvements to Trusdale Park in

Margaret Louise Day, Maud Ellen Day and Maud Gainer Day on porch of Day House

Freida Louise Whitehead and Sheila Day Leto in front of Day home (1001 Calhoun Ave)

St. Andrew), as a member of the Red Cross, and in the Elks Club. Maud was a homemaker and was active in garden club circles, the PTA of St. Andrew's Grammar School, and she took many first aid and home health care courses with the Red Cross. She planted the azalea bushes around Jinks Junior High. She had a group of friends who called themselves "The Girls" who met monthly for many, many years. Both she and Bruno became active in St. Andrew's Episcopal Church.
Submitted by: Sheila Leto Scott, 4429 Gorman Dr., Lynchburg VA 24503.

Sheila Day Leto Scott and John Charles Scott Family - Part II

Sheila married John Charles Scott in 1959. John was the son of Earl Maxwell Scott and Mildred Hill Scott. His grandfather, John Scott, had been the sheriff of Bay County. Max, like Bruno, worked at International Paper Company.

Maud Day Leto and Bruno Frank Leto

Mildred was a homemaker. She was a very creative person and wrote some poetry and painted in her later years.

John earned a Bachelors Degree in Forestry at the University of Florida; worked in Charlottesville, Virginia for three years; and returned to Panama City to work for International Paper. He eventually earned a Master of Divinity Degree from the University of the South at Sewanee, Tennessee and served as an Episcopal minister for over thirty years.

Sheila earned a Bachelor of Music Degree from Wesleyan College, in Macon, Georgia. She earned a Masters Degree, a Specialist in Education Degree, and a Ph.D. in School Psychology from the University of Florida. She taught for about 12 years and was a school psychologist in Florida for over 15 years.

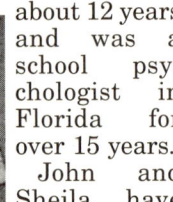

John and Sheila Scott with children, spouses and grandchildren 2003

John and Sheila have three children: Sheryl Suzanne (Born 1962), Edward Sherman (Born 1964), and Jonathan Andrew (Born 1973). Sheryl graduated from Randolph-Macon Woman's College in Lynchburg, Virginia; the University of Miami School of Medicine, and did a double residency in Internal Medicine and Pediatrics at the University of North Carolina at Chapel Hill. She married Walton Kitchin Joyner, Jr. of Raleigh, North Carolina. Walton is an ophthalmologist who attended college and medical school at UNC and also did his residency there. They live in Raleigh with their three children, Sara Elizabeth, Olivia Day, and Walton Kitchin, III ("Kitch."). Sheryl worked for eight years at Benson Area Medical Center, a rural area of North Carolina. She is currently one of two doctors at Alliance Medical Ministry in Raleigh which provides medical care to the working poor.

Edward attended Jacksonville Community College, Emerson University, and graduated from the University of

Florida in Telecommunication News. He later received a Masters Degree from Florida State University in Marketing Communication and Information Technology, and is presently working on a Ph.D. at the University of Central Florida in Texts and Technology. He married Teri-Jo Ann Baney, from State College, Pennsylvania. She graduated from The Pennsylvania State University and is a Registered Nurse. She earned a Master of Arts Degree in Adult Education after moving to Florida, and is the administrator of a home healthcare agency. They live in Clermont, Florida.

Jonathan attended Asbury College in Lexington, Kentucky where he met his wife, the former Anessa June Jeffares from Lexington, Kentucky. Jonathan and Anessa both later earned degrees from Toccoa Falls College in Georgia. Jonathan earned a Bachelor of Arts in Communication and Anessa earned a Bachelor of Science in Early Childhood Education. Jonathan works in social services and is developing a business, "Alive DJ," where they live in Lexington. Anessa is an elementary school teacher. She is working on a Masters Degree at Georgetown College in Kentucky. They have two children, Samuel Clifton and Leila Ann.

Sheila and John have lived in a number of different places over the years: Gainesville, FL; Charlottesville, VA; Panama City, FL; Sewanee, TN; Melrose, FL; Jacksonville, FL; Delray Beach, FL; North Port, FL; and Lynchburg, VA. They always think of Panama City as home and recently bought a condominium at Landmark Condominiums, less than a block from where Sheila grew up on Ninth Street. It is close to the Day home on Calhoun Avenue and St. Andrew's Episcopal Church on Beach Drive, where they were married and which was very important in their lives. They are living in Fearrington Village near Chapel Hill, North Carolina.

The Scott/Joyner family had a reunion during the summer of 2003 at Babcock State Park in West Virginia and all children, spouses, and grandchildren were present. The enclosed picture was taken at that reunion.
Submitted by: Sheila Leto Scott, 4429 Gorman Dr., Lynchburg, VA 24503.

The Charles Aubra Seal Family

Charles (Chuck) Seal and his wife, Virginia are relatively newcomers to Bay County. They met while working at Ridgecrest Baptist Assembly in N.C. and married in May of 1959 in Memphis, Tenn. -- Virginia's hometown. Chuck basically grew up in Florida (Delray Beach) and Texas (Wichita Falls) his birth state.

While at Ridgecrest the summer of '59, a mutual friend and fellow Staffer encouraged the couple to follow him to Panama City, FL—where he promised both would receive teaching positions. The friend, Jim Henry, later became the pastor of First Baptist Church in Orlando, FL.

Chuck accepted a teaching position at Panama Grammar (its last year in existence) while Virginia accepted a 7th grade position at Jinks Jr. High. Both loved their first year teaching experience and have kept fond memories of these students and others through the years.

Virginia Cobb Seal—Charles A Seal

What was to have been a one year "stay" in Panama City before moving on to Texas became 33 years for Chuck (Panama Grammar, Everitt Jr. High and Bay High School-where he served as both a football and Head Basketball coach) and 37 years for Virginia (Jinks Jr. High, Everitt Jr. High and Haney Technical Center).

In 1960 Virginia helped take the U.S. Census and was given one of the older and prettier sections of the Cove as part of her assignment. One lady, who happened to be the "sample" household and was requested to answer extensive questions—refused! She uttered some choice expletives stating that her business was none of the government's! Knowing that "a soft word turneth away wrath" Virginia drew the lady into a conversation involving one of her favorite topics—recipes. The lady was soon sharing her own copy of Hubert Humphreys" Brunswick Stew" with Virginia in her kitchen ,when she turned and said, "All right, I'll answer your questions!"

Although during this Census Virginia found many of those whom she interviewed were not native born Floridians, she and Chuck did their part. Forty-five years and four children (Merrie Dawn Seal Allen, Lisa Karen Seal Simonsen, Charles (Chip) A. Seal III, and Christopher David Seal) later, plus six grandchildren—thus far— (Amber, Andrew, Adam, Charlie, Savannah and Addie)—we're still here, and still loving Bay County.
Submitted by: Virginia C. Seal, 3412 Token Rd., Panama City, FL 32405.

The Seale Family

My family has deep roots in the sandy soil of Bay County. I don't know when my great-grandmother, Virginia Worthington, known as "Big Mama" first arrived here from Geneva County, Alabama. She raised a daughter, Jessie Mae Worthington Seale, and two sons, William and Bob Worthington, in this area. William and Bob ran charter boats from what was the dock behind the current Hawk's Nest restaurant. They also ran ferries from Panama City to Cromanton and across North Bay. William Worthington was a County Commissioner for eight years.

Jessie Seale and son Dude at the Panama City Train Depot

My grandmother, Jessie Mae, was born in 1902. She was married in 1918 to Cleveland Harrison Seale. They moved often, as my grandfather worked in the saw mills of Alabama. In the late 1930s, Jess bought a house in Lynn Haven and took in boarders to support her 5 children, Helene Seale Fisk, Glenda Seale Wadsworth, Carl Harrison Seale, Cleveland "Dude" Seale, and June Seale Poffenberger. Jess was a wonderful cook......her biscuits were my favorite!

All of Jess' children kept Bay County as their home. Glenda and Dude did welding and pipefitting at Wainwright Shipyard during WWII. Carl was a tugboat Captain, whose nickname was "Spotlight". Helene was the store manager for Mangels and the Darling Shop clothing stores on Harrison Avenue. My Mom, June, was born in Sampson, Alabama, but has spent most of her life in Lynn Haven. She went to Lynn Haven Elementary School and Bay High School. She loved spending the summers swimming in the bayous and North Bay. Her teenage hangouts were the Tally-Ho, the Beach Hangout, and the Martin and Panama theaters.

Mom met my Dad, Donald Poffenberger from Maryland, while he was stationed at the Air Force Oil Terminal in Lynn Haven. They were married October 16, 1953. She always jokes that she saved his life, since he threatened to kill himself if she didn't marry him. Dad spent 30 years in the Air Force, many of those stationed at Tyndall Air Force Base (AFB).

My sister, Ginger Poffenberger Harbison, and I were born at Tyndall AFB in the 50s. I have lots of memories of growing up around here. I was in the Tyndall AFB Elementary School cafeteria when the word came across the loudspeaker that President Kennedy had been shot. I made frequent trips to Lloyd's General Store for candy and comic books. My first horseback ride was at Pamaron Stables across from the Bay County airport. Everyone went to the Jetties at St. Andrew's State Park to swim. I remember when "going downtown" meant Harrison Avenue shopping at Sears, Murphys, and the dime stores. The train track ran next to my grandmother's house, and we'd always run out to wave as the train went by and see if we could get them to toot the whistle for us.

After moving around a lot as a teenager, and retiring from the Air Force myself, I came home to Lynn Haven. There are lots of Seale family members still in this area. It's been fun shaking the sand off these family roots.
Submitted by: Kathy Poffenberger, 429 Georgia Avenue,Lynn Haven, FL 32444.

Vera McClairen Shamplain

Vera McClairen Shamplain was born and raised in Bay County, Florida. Her parents were Sye and Florence McClairen.

She was married to the late Glasco Shamplain and is the mother of three daughters Yvonne, Toni and Yolanda with one granddaughter, Vera Chene' Shamplain Thomas.

She graduated from Rosenwald High School and attended Bethune Cookman College graduating Magna Cum Laude with a degree in Physical Education and Health. Vera did additional studies at Tennessee State A&I University, University of West Florida and Florida A&M University.

Vera Shamplain

She began her teaching career at Rosenwald High School in 1964. She transferred to Rutherford High School in 1967 and taught there until she retired in 1995. She taught Physical Ed, Health and Driver's Education. She was the Varsity girls volleyball and track coach as well as cheerleader sponsor. Under her leadership the volleyball team won one state, two regional and seven county championships. In 1982, she was honored by receiving the "Coach of the Year Award".

Vera is an active member of Allen Chapel A.M.E. Church, President of the Bay County Chapter of United Negro College Fund, Vice President of the local NAACP, President of Bay County Chapter of the National Association of Floridian Clubs, Inc. and President of Candlelite Social Club. She is a member of Delta Sigma Theta Sorority, Inc.

Shamplain was not just a teacher but mentor, friend and counselor to her many students. Her motto was "prepare the whole student to accept the challenges of the real adult world". She made history in 2001 when the sports complex at Rutherford High School, where she was an instructor for 28 years, was named the Vera McClairen Shamplain Sports Complex.
Submitted by: Bura Reed, 1420 Illinois Ave., Lynn Haven, FL 32444.

Thomas Jefferson "T .J." Sherman

T. J. was born 04 Nov 1906 in Browns Crossroads, near Headlands, Henry Co, AL. T.J was the son of Walter C. and Kate Sherman.

T.J. lived in Browns Crossroads, AL; Helton, GA; Donaldsonville, GA; Columbia, AL; Fountain, FL; and Dothan, AL. While the family was living in Columbia, AL, T. J. spent a lot of time with his father in and around Fountain, FL. The family moved to Dothan, AL in 1918; the family moved to Panama City, FL in 1926.

T.J. attended Dothan High School, Georgia Military Academy, and graduated from Marion (military) Institute.

T.J. was given a choice of going to college or a trip around the world. In Sept 1928, T.J. and his brother, John Henry,

left on their 6 mos trip.

T.J.' s first job was as a time keeper for St. Andrews Bay Lumber Company; he later went to work on the construction of the Southern Kraft Paper Mill. Later T.J. went to work at Sherman Shipyard (Sherman & Sons) in Panama City, FL.

T. J. met Carolyn Josephine Barrett in Panama City, FL; they were married 11 Jul 1932 in Dothan, AL. Carolyn was born 11 Feb 1911 in Jasper, AL. Carolyn was the daughter of Eudell and Alice Arista (Leonard) Barrett, the granddaughter of Frank Stanton and Marie Josephine (McGee) Barrett and James Lewis and Maranda Caroline (Brown) Leonard. The Barrett family moved from Jasper, AL to Panama City, FL in 1913.

In the early 1930's, T.J. was put in charge of the fish-house and ice-making operations for the Gulf and Caribbean Fisheries.

After the papermill was completed, the company received/ held the water-wood rights. The company towed on barges

the pulpwood to the mill between Pensacola and South of Tallahassee. Towed some wood for the St. Joe Papermill. T. J. ran this operation.

With the start of World War II, manpower became short, therefore, the pulpwood towing dried up. But the tugs were needed in Panama City for Wainwright Shipyard and to escort service through the bridges.

T. J. Sherman 1992

With the military services having many boats/ vessels a shipyard was needed. Sherman Shipyard went into full repair operations. T. J. worked for/ with USAF, USN, USArmy, USCG, as well as USArmy Corp of Engineers. He also worked for the State of Florida vessels. Along with the harbor tug service, T.J. operated the Sherman Shipyard. The shipyard hauled out and repaired many of the fishing boats in Panama City and surrounding towns. He also, worked on tugs and tow boats plying the intercoastal waterway.

As the steamship trade picked up in Panama City, T J. furnished the harbor tugs for docking and undocking the ships. Also, he handled the LASH barges and other barge work.

T.J. owned stock and was a director of Bay National Bank. T. J. helped start, organize, and was a VP, director, appraisal committee of the Security Federal Savings and Loan in Panama City, FL.

T. J .was a Rotarian and member of the Sons of the American Revolution.

T. J. grew up a Methodist; he helped organize and finance the Cove Baptist and Central Baptist Churches.

T. J. was an avid golfer, a member of Panama City Country Club. He played golf for 78 years.

Carolyn attended Panama Grammer School and graduated from Bay High School.

Carolyn was mostly a house wife but worked as a secretary at Wainwright Shipyard during World War II. Later she was a Gray Lady in the American Red Cross; covering Panama City down to Carrabelle (Camp Gordon Johnson).

Carolyn oversaw the construction of the Cove Baptist Church. Carolyn was a Bible teacher! She taught Sunday School, Child Evangelism, and Bible Classes. Carolyn played the piano.

T. J. and Carolyn lived from 1937 to their deaths at 110 (115) Bunkers Cove Rd.

Carolyn died 07 Aug 1989. T.J. died 27 Oct 2001. They are

buried together in Greenwood Cemetery, Panama City, Bay Co, FL.

Submitted by W. Carol Sherman; Written by Walter C. Sherman, P.O. Box 609, Panama City, FL 32402-0609.

Walter Colquitt Sherman
Part I

Walter was born 22 Feb 1880 in Stewart Co, GA, the son of Thomas Jefferson and Martha Louisana (Moore) Sherman.

Thomas was a veteran of the Civil War as a Confederate soldier; Thomas was a prisoner of war twice. Walter was the grandson of Robert Harrison and Martha Cannon (Lancaster) Sherman.

As a boy, Walter worked on his father's farm. To get off the farm, in May 1898, Walter joined Company "G" 3rd Vol Infantry of the U.S. Army. He went to Cuba during the Spanish American War. While in Cuba, Walter contacted malaria and it was with him the rest of his life.

After his discharge from the army, on May 1899 as a sergeant, Walter went West. He went to Texas hoping to help his malaria. While working in Texas, he worked for the American Express Company and then Wells Fargo Company. The road was wide open for him in the company, but he became sick and moved back to Stewart Co, GA. After getting better, he went to work for his brothers, running their saw mill business. He worked saw mills in southwest Georgia, southeast Alabama, and later, north Florida and still later in Orlando and Lake Okeechobee area.

Walter C. and Kate (Woolfolk) Sherman 1957

While working in Helton, GA, he met Anna Katherine "Kate" Woolfolk. Kate was born 17 Jul 1884 in Houston Co (now Peach) GA. "Kate" was a school teacher. Walter and Kate were married 08 Oct 1905 in Houston Co, GA. Kate was the daughter of Richard Stapler and Josephine Elizabeth (Kemp) Woolfolk. Walter and Kate had four children: Thomas Jefferson b. 1906 in Henry Co, AL; Katherine b. 1908 in Henry Co, AL; John Henry b. 1910 in Donaldsonville, GA; and Martha Louise b. 1918 in Dothan, AL.

The family moved from Browns Crossroads (Headland), Henry Co, AL to Donaldsonville, GA; then moved to Columbia, AL; to Fountain, FL; in 1918 the family moved to Dothan, AL; finally in 1926 the family moved to Panama City, FL.

Walter had a saw mill at Fountain, FL and a shingle mill at Sherman, FL (3/4 miles south of Fountain). There was also a naval stores business.

In partnership with Minor C. Keith, of United Fruit Fame, they bought the American Lumber Company, originally the German American Lumber Company, from Alien Custodian of U.S. Government in 1919.

In 1920 they owned 5 saw mills: Fountain, Sherman, American Lumber Co, Moore Timber Co, and West Bay Lumber Co. Also, there was a naval stores business, a railroad, and a shipyard.

Minor C. Keith had bought the St. Andrews Bay Line from A.B. Steele. Walter was in charge of the railroad. Walter built a repair facilities at the foot of College Ave in Panama City to keep up the railroad, timber cars, and rails. Walter increased the weight (size) of the railroad tracks of the Bay Line.

While in Dothan, besides the lumber mills, he owned a retail lumber and supply store; also, had carpenter crews which built houses. With all this wood, Walter owned a box plant. This box plant, of course, built boxes, but also built coffins! Many of the carpenters came to Panama City with him. In Panama City again, Walter had a lumber and supply business behind the Company Store. Again, he built houses; some of the houses on Bonita Ave, and the house at 110 Bunkers Cove were built as well as others.

Along with the saw mills and rail system was the well-known and regularly used Company Store. The original Company Store was located on the southwest corner of Third St. and Sherman Ave (Tarpon St); in the early 1930's. The Company Store was moved to the northwest corner of Hwy 98 and Sherman Ave.

Around 1928 the timber was "cut out"!! Walter moved men and equipment to South Florida and opened up saw mills. He had mills at Sherman on Lake Okeechobee, Lake Wales. Nictaw, and Hicore. The lumber from these mills went to Cuba; England, for rail service; and to South Africa, for the diamond mines. When the rail system ran out, Walter started a new phase of using trucks to move the timber.

In 1927 Walter started construction on the Dixie-Sherman Hotel. The hotel was financed by bonds; local men were to participate. The local men didn't follow through and the hotel was a burden on Walter. Walter sold it right before WWII.

Walter built the first bridge (wood) between Lynn Haven and Southport.

In 1931, Walter was the main instrument in getting Southern Kraft (International Paper Co) to build a paper mill in Panama City, FL.

Walter was a golfing enthusiast. He built the original golf courses in Dothan, AL and Panama City, FL. He held memberships in clubs all over the state of Florida. Walter started and put up the trophy for the "Sherman Amateur Golf Tournament" at the Panama City Country Club.

In 1935, Walter built the Sherman Arcade on the southwest corner of Harrison Ave. and 3rd Court. This was an office type building.

Walter helped organize and was Commodore of the St. Andrews Bay Yacht Club. He helped to provide the fish class sailboats.

Walter served as President of the Florida State Chamber of Commerce for many years.

During World War II, Walter was appointed by the Governor of Florida to be the Pricing (Rationing) Administrator. He served throughout WW II. Originally located in Jacksonville and later moved to Tallahassee.

Walter served as a city commissioner, finishing out the term of Tom Milam.

Walter owned the First National Bank of Panama City, and later was a stockholder, VP, and Director of Bay National Bank of Panama City.

Walter and Kate were Methodist; being members of the First Methodist Church of Dothan, AL, then Panama City, FL

Walter was known for playing dominoes at the Elks Club.

Kate belonged to the Garden Club, Woman's Club, St. Andrews Bay Yacht Club, and the Daughters of the American Revolution.

Kate died 21 Feb 1960 and Walter died 27 July 1967. Both are buried together in Greenwood Cemetery, Panama City, Bay Co, Florida.

Submitted by: Walter D. Sherman; Written by: Walter C. Sherman, P.O. Box 609, Panama City, FL 32402-0609.

Walter Colquitt Sherman (II)
Part II

Walter was born 01 Jun 1933 in Dothan, AL, the son of T.J. and Carolyn J. (Barrett) Sherman; the grandson of Walter C. and Kate (Woolfolk) Sherman and Eudell A. and Alice A. (Leonard) Barrett.

Walter attended Cove Grammar School and graduated from Bay High School in Panama City, FL. While at Bay High he served on the Student Council all four years. Walter played football, basketball, and baseball for Bay High. In 1952 Walter completed the American Red Cross Swimming

Wanda J. (Norris) and Walter C. Sherman 2000

and Life-Saving Instructions Course. Walter taught swimming and worked as a life guard.

Walter attended Bob Jones University for two years and graduated from the University of Florida with a BS in Psychology. Had one year of graduate school at the University of Miami. Walter, also, attended Gulf Coast Community College in the business area/field.

In Sept 1957 Walter joined the Florida Army National Guard. Trained for 6 months at Fort Jackson, SC. Walter served in all enlisted men ranks from Private to Command Sergeants Major, then served as a Chief Warrant Officer 2. Walter left the Reserves in Nov 1986 with 29+ years.

After college and military service, Walter went to work for Sherman Shipyard (Sherman & Sons, Inc). He worked as manager of the boat repairs and harbor tug services. Also did the scuba diving necessities.

Walter met in Panama City, FL Wanda Jean Norris and married her 28 Mar 1970 in Carrabelle, FL. Wanda was born 11 Aug 1941 in Carrabelle, FL to Manuel Ethaniel and Wilma Irene (Sanders) Norris. Walter and Wanda have four children: Wanda Carol b. 1970, Jean Elizabeth b. 1972, Rachel Anne b. 1974 and Walter David b. 1978. All children were born and raised in Panama City, FL.

Wanda graduated from Mars Hill J.C. in North Carolina with an A.A. and from Florida State University with a B.S. in education. Wanda is a school teacher and teaches piano. Wanda taught at Parker, Cove, Tallahassee Christian, Oakland Terrace, Panama Christian, and the Fine Arts Academy at Tommy Smith.

Other business experiences: WSCM radio, Harby Marina, and Sherman's Music Center.

Walter and Wanda are members of Central Baptist Church. Walter and Wanda have taught Sunday School and sung in the choir. Walter is a Deacon. Wanda plays the organ and piano for the church.

Walter is member, Director, and Treasurer of the Bay County Genealogical Society.

Walter has served as member, Secretary, Treasurer, Registrar and President of the Panama City chapter of the Florida Society of the Sons of the American Revolution.

Wanda and Walter have lived their lives at 216 S. Claire Drive.

Submitted by: Wanda N. Sherman; Written by Walter C. Sherman, P.O. Box 609, Panama City, FL 32402-0609.

O'Dessia Porter Shipes

April 5, 1905 would be a day that some people will never forget. A calm and peaceful day that was suddenly shattered by a disaster as East Kashmir in India was shook by a 8.1 earthquake killing hundreds.

Halfway across the world in the United States in Washington County in the state of Florida, it was not death that would be remembered but life, for on that wonderful day of April 5, 1905, Lillie McCall Porter and Samuel Shivers Porter, the grandson of Charles L. Porter one of the first settlers of Econfina, gave birth to a girl child O'Dessia Porter, she would be the oldest of four children of Samuel and Lillie Porter.

They was not a rich family as they made their living off of the land on Econfina by farming and raising cattle and hogs. They would be quick to tell anyone they was not poor for they had a roof over their heads, and food on their table.

O'Dessia was to grow up in the house that she was born

in with her two sisters and one brother on Econfina. She was not your average woman for that day and age. She stood six feet tall and she loved to hunt and fish. She could shoot a rifle better than most men. She was a straight forward person that told you exactly how she saw it and straight from the hip. She was a independent woman, way before they had a name for such a thing. Her favorite saying was don't worry about my end if you can handle your end I can handle mine. Maybe because of those abilities she had or her way of saying things to people that by the age of twenty, she was not married.

O'Dessia Porter Shipes and her daughter Gloria Lee Shipes

In the year of 1925, Ebenezer Shipes, or William P. Shipes (because of his intense dislike for his birth name) was on the bank of the Chipola River with some friends, when he happened to glance across the river and spied a vision in a yellow dress with long braided blond hair. He decided that he had to have a date with that woman and not one to allow a river to stand in his way, and to the amusement of his friends, he jumped in the river and swam across to the other side to ask her for a date.

O'Dessia Porter watched with some amusement as the man crawled out of the river and thinking, what a idiot and was surprised and astonished when the man walked right up to her and asked her for a date. Believing if nothing else she would not be bored, she agreed to go out with him. This date would lead to a Courtship that would end in marriage in 1926 in Vernon, Fl. They bore three children by this marriage, and continued to live together until separated by the death of William P. Shipes, after 38 years of marriage.

Things were extremely hard during the depression years for everyone. In later years for money they went out in the woods to cut and haul wood to sell to the paper mill to provide for their family.

Sadly I did not know my Grandparents as they died before I was born. All the memory I have of them is from the stories passed down in my family. They live on in this Family because of those stories. My Grandmother was a hard working pioneer woman that did what she had to do to help provide for her family.

Submitted by Tammy L. Hughey, 1200 Transmitter Road, Springfield, Fl 32401.

The Sikes Family of Panama City

Pre-War Panama City was bustling in the early 1940's as citizens began preparing for what they knew was ahead. The Sherman Shipyard had begun its extensive shipbuilding with combat and defensive action in mind. During this time Hubert and Rosalie Sikes moved to Panama City where Mr. Sikes found a job at the shipyard pouring concrete ballast for the liberty ships.

Hubert Shorter Sikes was a native of Luverne, Crenshaw County, Alabama, the son of Short and Zilla McMillan Sikes. He married Rosalie Finlay, daughter of Thomas Watson and Millie Folmar Finlay of Goshen, Alabama. They brought with them to Panama City one daughter, Jacqueline, who was nine years old, and one son, Hubert Lamar, who was three. They made their home in Drummond Park.

Following the War, Mr. Sikes found employment with Mr. Evon Brewton, at Brewton Engineering, as a concrete contractor. In 1947 he bought a small concrete mixer and went into business for himself pouring concrete curbs, sidewalks and driveways. Mrs. Sikes worked in his office with him, keeping the company books and taking the customer orders. For several years his small company was situated on the west side of St. Andrew, but as it grew, the need for more space for additional trucks and equipment became apparent. In 1950 Mr. Sikes secured seven acres from the City and began building a larger, more versatile facility. Sikes Concrete Pipe Company not only supplied ready-mix for many local contractors and homeowners, but also manufactured concrete pipe for area road builders.

Jacqueline married John Franklin Bynum, son of John Carl and Mary Rose Carlos Bynum, of Panama City. Jackie and John Franklin had five children, all of whom were raised in Panama City. They were: John Hubert, Rosalyn, Amy Louise, James Carl, and Thomas Watson. John Hubert lives with his wife, Martha Smith Bynum, in Cashiers, North Carolina. He has a son, John Gray, living in Virginia. Rosalyn married James Lowery of Callaway and they had two children, Jim Wells and Ashley. Amy married Howard Emery of Panama City and they have a son, Benjamin. Jim married JoAnn Stafford and they had one daughter, Nicole. He is now married to Valerie Colmery of Panama City. Thomas and Rosalyn are deceased.

Lamar married Patricia Ann Parrott, daughter of Joe and Claire Rubash Parrott of St. Andrew, in 1964. Upon the death of his father in 1978, Lamar became President of Sikes Concrete and is still working in that capacity today although he and Patty are now residents of Pensacola. They have three children: Hugh, Julie and Joe. Hugh is married to Lee Ann Nelson Trevathan and they have one son, Carson Hugh. Hugh has a daughter, Ashton Nicole, from a previous marriage; Lee Ann has two children from a first previous marriage, Erica and Brent Trevathan, all of Panama City. Julie is married to John Anthony Albert of Atmore, Alabama, and they live with their son, John Christian (Jack), in Gulf Breeze, Florida. Joe is a student at Florida Coastal School of Law in Jacksonville, Florida.

Submitted by Joe Sikes, 6445 Dunlieth Place, Pensacola, FL 32504.

C. D. and Lillie Mae Smith

In late 1925, Charles Darwin Smith and his wife, born Lillie Mae Hayes, left Birmingham, Alabama and moved to Seville, Volusia County, Florida. He had left the L & N Railway to work with the Florida East Coast Railroad. Making the move with them were their infant daughter, Mabel Irene, born 17 August, 1925 and Jimmie Louise Nelson, born 10 November, 1915 to Lillie Mae and her first husband, Lawrence Nelson. They had been married in Wilsonville, Shelby County, Alabama on 20 December, 1914. He had succumbed to pneumonia on 21 December, 1915. She married C.D. Smith in Birmingham on 6 May, 1923. He was born 8 May, 1878 and she was born 31 January, c1896.

After the hurricane of 1926 and an infestation of fruit flies in their orange grove, they came to Panama City and settled. Their daughter, Laura Mae, was born 6 April, 1928. C.D. died 4 February, 1960 and is buried in Pelham Cemetery, Shelby County, Alabama. Lillie Mae died 16 September, 1984 and is buried at Forest Lawn Cemetery in Panama City.

C.D. Smith and wife, Lillie Mae

Louise Nelson married Carl W. Murray and parented two daughters with him. They later divorced and Louise married Dr.Andrew Munsell. He died 28 June, 1978. She died 10 December, 1988. They are interred at Forest Lawn Cemetery in Panama City.

The first daughter of Louise and Carl, Shirley Ann Murray was born 4 February, 1936 and married Lution Hill. They had two children, Lu and Cheryl. Shirley died 8 December, 1973 and is buried at Forest Lawn Cemetery in Panama City.

The second daughter, Judith Carleen, born 25 August, 1938, married Dr. J.C. Toole. They live in Marietta, Georgia, and have three children, Jeff, Lori and Janet. Jeff has one daughter, Lori has one son, and Janet has two sons.

Mabel Smith married Joseph M. Lyer. They have two daughters, Patricia and Pamela. Pat has one daughter and Pam has two daughters. All live in Memphis, Tennessee.

Laura Smith married Fred Landgraf, Jr. on 26 September,1947. (See Landgraf)

Submitted by: Lorena Landgraf Kelly, 4333 North Shore Road, Lynn Haven, FL 32444.

George Smith, Sr.

Down in the delta, Shelby, Mississippi, was the birth place of Leola and George Smith. George and Leola were married and they both taught school in Shelby. Life was tough, the cotton fields stayed busy, the pay was pitiful. Besides teaching school, George was an excellent carpenter.

In March 1936, 2138 acres of land was bought for $17,500 to start an experiment called, "Cooperative Farming Communities." The purpose was to improve a better quality of life. Sharecroppers, white and black, who had been evicted were now facing starvation and desperation. Mrs. Roosevelt appealed for funding to aid these desperate refugees through her column "My Day," which appeared in 500 newspapers. George Smith was the building planner for the co-op farm. Imagine a place, infested by racism, where now a diverse group of people were living, praying and attending school together. Two of George Smith's children were born on the farm, George Smith, II and Mackintosh Smith. A group of Christian men headed by Sherwood Eddy were responsible for this wonderful experiment. White and black people living in harmony in a civilized manner. There are several books written about this experience.

George Smith, Sr.

One day, George Smith, Jr. was playing outside his house and a white man approached him and asked George where his father was. "My daddy isn't here," reply George. The man was offended by the abruptness of the reply. He threatened the little boy. George knew, there and then, it was time to take his family and leave Mississippi.

George and Leola took their family and headed to New York, where the cultural and educational experience would be an advantage.

Leola Smith pursued a nursing career. The Smith children, both the young men, joined the military. The daughter, Mary Alice, attended Howard University and met her future husband there. Her sister, Annetta, worked in the medical field and the baby girl, Atheleen worked for the telephone company. Annetta and Atheleen contribute to the community, volunteering their time for the less fortunate.

George and his wife Leola, in their declining years, lived in Panama City, Florida. When Leola was in her nineties, she was the exercise instructor for the Council On Aging. They loved her dearly. George and Leola lived in Panama City for over twenty years. They both died in Panama City and were buried in New York. George was a Mason and Leola was an Eastern Star.

George Smith, II was the first black Real Estate Agent in Panama City, Florida. His wife, Maureen, became the first black Real Estate Appraiser in Panama City. Their son, Andre Smith, is the first black Real Estate General Appraiser in Panama City. The oldest son, George Smith, III, is a pilot for Delta Air Lines. Roy Smith is a Lieutenant Colonel in the military and his sister Nadine is a newspaper journalist. She led a march on Washington in 1993 and received a Silver Medal for her humanitarian contributions from the National Conference of Christians and Jews which is now called the National Conference of Community Injustice.

Maureen still operates The Just Your Style Beauty Salon business. George Smith, II is still in the real estate business. He also serves as City Commissioner of Callaway.

George Smith was wise to leave Mississippi after his son was threatened. If that man who made the threat had carried it out, a great injustice would have been bestowed on this very productive and loving family

Submitted by: Maureen Smith, 1226 East 15th St., Panama City, FL 32405.

John A. Sorenson, Part I

Johannas August Sorensen (John A.) born August 31,1889, whose parents arrived in this United States from Denmark in 1888 and Ruth Leonora Tyler born July 24, 1890 whose ancestors arrived in this country in the 1600's were married June 24, 1913 in Clinton, Big Stone County Minnesota where they were born and raised on neighboring farms. John attended the Dairy Department of Minnesota Agricultural College, paying his expenses by milking cows, testing dairy products in the laboratory and teaching butter making. He became one of the leading authorities on dairying and farm management in the northwest. Ruth attended St. Cloud Normal School and taught school. After their marriage they settled in Minot, North Dakota. John became superintendent of a large stock farm showing cattle in county and state fairs. John later managed Ward County

John A. Sorenson and Ruth Lenora Tyler Sorenson

Demonstration Farm and the Old People's Home. Here he developed a herd of outstanding pure Guernsey cows. Ruth was matron of the home. They soon rented a farm near Logan ,North Dakota and he continued to raise Guernsey Cows as well as Duroc Jersey hogs, and Wyandotte chickens. Their children John, Jr, Genevieve, Henry Tyler, Jacqueline, and Ruth Tyler were born in Minot, Ward County, North Dakota.

In 1929, due to ill health, John moved his family to Bay Head, (Now Indian Bluff Road) Bay County, Florida, to manage a new dairy farm. Moving the household items, live stock and farm implements was a great undertaking. Emigrant and automobile boxcars were rented for the move. Shelves with pens were built over the hogs and sheep to house the chickens. Bunks were made for John and John Jr. for sleeping so that they could care for the live stock. On such a long trip, food for the live stock and clean straw to keep the boxcars clean was purchased along the way. Fresh water was stored in large barrels for the stock. Cows were milked twice a day and the eggs were collected each day which were all given to railroad hands or people traveling by boxcars. Arriving at Bayou George, the boxcars were put on

250

a siding to be unloaded. The larger live stock were herded down a two rut sandy road to Bay Head Farms and the smaller stock and household items were trucked to the farm. After remodeling the farm house and household items unpacked, John wrote Ruth to come with the four other children, who arrived before Christmas. Their car was driven from Minot to Bay Head by a friend who wanted to take his wife to warmer climate. The Sorensen family was the only family to move live stock, farm implements, and house hold items to Bay County by box cars.

Submitted by Henry Tyler Sorensen, 135 Belmont Road, Tallahassee, FL 32301.

John A. Sorenson, Part II

After learning agriculture in the Midwest, John Sorensen spent many hours reading and studying the agricultural methods of Florida and the diseases of plants and animals in the area to learn how to plant, what to use and what type crops to plant to get the best feed for the animals and his family. The sandy soil had to be studied and new methods used since he was used to the rich soil of the Midwest. At the

Bay Head Dairy he raised most of the feed for his live stock and in 1930 built the first silo in Bay County (2003 stands at the site of the Bay Head Farm on Indian Bluff Road) to store fodder. A water tower was built to store water from a flowing well which provided running water to home and

Silo and Barn built in 1930 Bay Head Dairy Farm

dairy. A cream separator was installed in the milk house in order to sell cream, butter and milk to customers in Panama City. Some customers drove to the dairy to purchase these items. The Guernsey dairy herd, the Duroc Jersey Hogs, and the flocks of chickens, Wyandotte and Rhode Island Red were the first in Bay County. The Wyandotte and Rhode Island Red chickens were kept in a separate barn and the eggs were used by the family. The Quail were so tame, some laid eggs with these chickens. Two large two story chicken houses were built to house White Leghorn chickens purchased in lots of 1,000 to produce eggs and fryers. When these baby chicks were big enough, the hens were separated from the cockerels These chickens never touched the ground. The nests were built in such a way that when the eggs were laid, the egg rolled into a trough for easy gathering and record keeping. The eggs and fryers were sold to customers in Panama City and the customers at the farm. The Duroc Jersey Hogs when full grown weighed 400-600 pounds were raised and sold for meat. Meat from the hogs was salted down in large crocks for family use. The sheep did not do well in the warm climate and soon died.

While living at the Bay Head Farm, John Sorensen and daughter Jacqueline contracted malaria and were deathly ill. A son was born who lived a very short time and is buried in the Bay Head Cemetery.

Submitted by Jacqueline (Jackie) Sorensen Hogan, 6151 Hogan Road, Panama City, FL 32404.

John A. Sorenson, Part III

After three years at the Bay Head Farm, John Sorensen felt he needed to move his family nearer to Panama City. In 1933, John Sorensen purchased the 40 acre Heron Fruit Farm from E.N. Pagleson located in Callaway on the north side of Cherry Street between North Gay Avenue and North Kimbrel Avenue and became a truck farmer selling vegetables and fruit In the mid 1930's the Work Progress Administration hired Ruth Lenora Sorensen to teach the ladies of Bay County to can with a presser cooker, cook, sew, and the importance of good health and nutrition. She received a teaching certificate, taught school at Millville School, and become the first librarian. She held this position until her death, April 2, 1947. John, Jr. joined the Civilian Conservation Corps (CCC) later joining the Florida National Guard Co. D 106 Engineers and worked for the State Forestry Department. After graduating from Bay County High School, Genevieve received a teaching certificate and taught her first two years in the Callaway one room school. She was one of the first to teach at the Springfield School and also taught at the Millville School. After Henry graduated from Bay County High School, he taught school and worked at odd jobs, before joining the Florida National Guard Co. D 106 Engineers. John and Henry were in Co D when the company was inducted into Federal Service on November 25, 1940, and served during World War II. Jacqueline and Ruth attended the Old Callaway One Room School, when their sister, Genevieve was the teacher. Jacqueline and Ruth were members of a Girl Scout Troop in Millville, where they attended grammar school after the Callaway one room school closed. They were also members of the Alpha 4-H Club in Callaway and members of the first Girl Scout Sea Scout troop in Bay County. The Girl Scout Sea Scouts met at the Callaway Methodist Church. "Jackie" and Ruth both graduated from Bay County High School. All the children married and at sometime made Bay County their home. Descendants of John and Ruth L. Sorensen are six children, eighteen grandchildren, twenty nine great grandchildren and six great, great grandchildren(2003).

Sorenson Siblings 1946 Genevieve, Henry, Ruth, John and Jacqueline (Jackie)

Submitted by Ruth T. Sorensen Butler, 4625 20th Ave., St. Petersburg, FL 33713.

John Sorenson, Part IV

Even though I did not know Papa (Grandfather, John A. Sorensen) I have learned a lot about him and I wished that I could have had the privilege of knowing him. He was born and raised in Minnesota, the eldest of 12 children of Danish parentage. He had to learn English before attending a one room school, Number 12. At an early age he learned to hunt and he worked on neighboring farms. By working and saving his money, he was able to travel to Minneapolis to enter the Minnesota Agricultural College. After college he was superintendent of the dairy department of the Minnesota State Fair, stock judge at county fairs in Minnesota, and a buyer of large dairy herds for many farmers and investors. He was hired to travel through the Midwest and to California showing cattle and horses at State Fairs winning prizes for his employer. He frequently wrote articles for the agricultural press and dairy journals about thoroughbred stock and farm products. When he was superintendent or a manager of a farm, he kept a registry of all registered Guernsey, Duroc Jersey Hogs, and

The First 4-H oyster Club in the Nation 1954: Donnie Wildman, Marshall Gore, Fred Waters, Albert Hogan, Bobby Seaborn, John A. Sorenson and George H. Toepfer

Wyandotte chickens. Papa and Grandmother Ruth Leonora Sorensen were charter members of the Springfield Presbyterian Church now Parkway Presbyterian Church. He was one of the first three Elders and was the first clerk of the session. He and my grandmother taught Sunday school and were very active in the church. When the young men were called to serve in World War II, the Bay County Agriculture Agent was called to service. Papa filled that position during the war years and later filled the position permanently until his death July 18, 1954. He made regular visits to the farms, of Bay County, which were many at that time, helping the farmers solve their agriculture problems, vaccinating the hogs, and other farm animals if needed. Papa was a supporter of the Bay County Fair years before he became county agent and encouraged everyone to support the fair. While he was county agent, Papa had a radio program each week on station WDLP giving the latest news and farm reports. "Old McDonald Had a Farm" was the theme song for this radio program. Many 4-H clubs, were formed, however since Bay County did not have a Home Demonstration Agent, girls were required to have boy's projects. Papa formed the first all girl 4-H cattle judging team in the State of Florida. These girls competed against 96 boys and two were in the first ten. With the help of a local fisherman and the Florida Conservation Saltwater Division, he organized the first 4-H oyster club in the nation with five charter members. For many years, Papa was scout master for a boy scout troop, who usually camped on his farm. Years after Papa's death, two of his grandsons and one great grandson became Eagle Scouts. Papa was a member of the Kiwanis Club of Panama City, Acme Masonic Lodge, Knight Templar, 32 degree Scottish Rite Mason and the Morocco Shrine Temple. Papa was religious man who was honest, fair, impartial and conscientious in his dealings with all people with whom he came in contact.

Submitted by: Glenn Calvin Hogan, 6835 Smith Road, Panama City, FL 32404.

Ralph William Sorrentino

Ralph William Sorrentino, born 1888 was a native of Catania, Sicily. No one could have guessed that this boy from a country far from the United States would enrich immeasurably the cultural opportunities in the Florida Panhandle.

It was all due to his extraordinary musical talent. In the small Italian village Ralph was considered a prodigy because of his unusual musical ability and a patron of the village paid for Ralph to pursue the study of music. Ralph's father, a

Ralph William Sorrentio and wife Lillie Smith Sorrentino

Custom's Officer in Sicily, died young and left a large family. Ralph at fourteen, over the strong objections of his Mother, got a job playing in an orchestra on an Italian cruise ship.

When the ship reached New York, Ralph visited his cousins. While staying with them he saw a line of people who were trying out for a theater orchestra. Ralph ran back to his room, got his instrument, and auditioned for a job. He was hired on the spot. Later, he joined the Ringling Brothers Circus Band and traveled all over the United States. He went to see his sister and brother in-law Agnes and Dick Taranto who lived in Apalachicola, Florida. He learned that the Chattahoochee Mental Hospital was planning to organize a band composed of employees of the hospital. Ralph traveled to Chattahoochee, Florida and was hired to organize the band.

In 1915 Ralph met a young nurse, Lillie Smith, who along

with other employees had great fun dancing on Saturday nights to the music of Ralph Sorrentino's hospital band. They were married on October 21, 1916 . Later, Ralph and Lillie moved with their two children, Ralph and Virginia to Panama City, Florida.

The family was becoming too large for the house, now three children, so Ralph bought a wooden sawmill office which he floated across the bay and placed on the lot facing Magnolia Avenue. Mr. Dick Whittington also bought one of the offices which was placed on the lot next door. Friends could not understand why he wanted to live so far in the country. Panama Grammar School was diagonal across the street. Three more girls were born in this house, Gloria, Catherine and Marie. The house is still standing today.

Ralph loved azaleas, camellias and Easter lilies. He never pruned his beloved azaleas. Grapevines, vegetable garden, Satsuma, plum, pear, kumquat, fig and pecan trees provided food for Lillie's family and whoever stopped in at mealtime.

The four surviving children of Ralph and Lillie: Virginia Granberry, Anita Pospisil, Catherine Wilson and Marie Lee have contributed to the community through their careers in Civil Service and as a College Administrative Secretary. They credit their success to good Christian parents who provided an environment of discipline, love, and learning.

Ralph became almost blind in old age but he never complained because he substituted good radio music for eyes. He died of a stroke at age eighty-two. Lillie died of a heart attack at seventy-nine. Both are buried in Evergreen Memorial Gardens.

Fond memories of these remarkable and unforgettable people make old timers stand taller to cheer the marching band because an Italian immigrant boy enriched the lives of Panhandle people.

Submitted by: Marie Sorrentino Waller Lee, 1002 Iowa Ave., Lynn Haven, FL 32444.

Spicer Family

Henry Marvin Spicer of Ludington, Michigan, married Harriet Bessie of Amber, Michigan on September 18 1879. They moved soon afterwards to Cromanton, Florida. Henry worked and traveled with a circus. They had one son, Audley Marvin. As a young man, Audley traveled to Ludington MI and Chicago IL with the circus.

In July, 1901, Audley was back home in Cromanton and married to Mattie Parker. Audley and Mattie built a lovely home on the bay in Cromanton. Audley worked in the shipyard during World War I until his health failed. He and Mattie had six children. Three lived to adulthood. Audley died in 1920. Mattie lived in their home in Cromanton until the Government took their land for what is now Tyndall Air Force Base.

Audley Marvin Spicer, son of Henry Marvin and Harriet Bessie Spicer

Their daughter Frederica was a teacher in Parker and San Blas for two years. She married Ralph Palmer in November 1929. They had five children, Ralph, Don, Ray, Gayle and Clark. All of their children married and left the area-except Clark., who married Sylvia Ecker, daughter of Bobby Ecker, in September 1963. They have a lovely home on the bay in Parker. Clark and Sylvia are teachers in area schools.

Audley and Mattie's son, William (Bill) started fishing as a young man with his uncle, Peter Parker. William married Haley McWilliams in May 1935 and they built a home on the Gulf at Pratt's Cove. They lived there until the government took the property for Tyndall. William was a fisherman and

later became a marine mechanic. William and Haley had one daughter, Carol.

Carol married Vernon Lee, son of Rudolph and Bessie Lee of Parker, in November 1958. Carol and Vernon have two sons, John and David. John married Phyllis Keefe and they have two sons, Matthew and Adam. David married Tina Lyle and they have three sons, Joshua, Jacob and Timothy.

William, a widower, still lives in the home he built in Parker after leaving Cromanton. He will be 89 years old in March 2002.

Audley and Mattie's daughter Claudia died in 1974, and Frederica died at the age of 84.

Mattie Parker Spicer, daughter of John and Amanda Parker, granddaughter of Peter Ferdinand Parker and Anne Loftin Parker

Submitted by: Carol Spicer Lee, Route 1, Box 337, Concord, GA 30206.

Spiva-Brown-Harrison-Alexander Families

Stephen Augustus Spiva came to then Washington County from Kentucky in 1880. He bought timberland and settled here. His wife, Harriet Naylor Spiva, was also a native of Kentucky. She was a direct descendant of John Alden and Priscilla Mullins of the Plymouth Colony in Massachusetts, who came over on the Mayflower. One of Stephen and Harriet's sons, William Eldridge Spiva, was one of this county's first harbor pilots. Before that, he was master of a sailing schooner that was shipwrecked off Vera Cruz. He served as a local harbor pilot until his death in 1933. His son, Ernest Raymond Spiva, Sr., was also a harbor pilot on St. Andrew Bay for more than 40 years. He was born in High Point (at Deer Point Lake) and died in Panama City in 1979. Pilot Boats have been named after both Spivas, as well as for other pilots who served.

William E. Spiva Family L to R: Mollie B. Spiva, William E. Spiva, Willie Spiva, Ernest R. Spiva

William Spiva first piloted sailing ships into St. Andrew Bay, before the advent of steamships. The pilots lived and worked at the "Pilot Station" on Hurricane Island until the station washed away in a hurricane many years ago. This was during a time before radio and telegraph communications. Pilots had to watch for approaching ships in the Gulf and go out to meet them, climb aboard, and then navigate the ship into the harbor and to the dock or anchor.

Harbor pilots lead very interesting lives. They pilot ships from all over the world. They can taste many exotic foods and learn of customs from many foreign countries. And they get to spend most of their time on the waters of beautiful St. Andrew Bay and the Gulf of Mexico. Working as a pilot in wartime was exciting as well as hazardous. During World War II, the pilot boat was painted black (to make it invisible at night) and carried no running lights. German submarines were operating in the Gulf and every night the harbor was filled with many types of ships, large and small, taking refuge in a safe harbor for the night.

William Spiva's wife was Mary Olivia (Mollie) Brown, whose ancestor first came to the Econfina Creek area with Andrew Jackson in 1820. Her father was Benjamin B. Brown, who built a school in this area and was a teacher and served in numerous local government positions, including Superintendent of Schools and Tax Assessor. He was in Co. K., 6th Florida Infantry, CSA, during the Civil War. His funeral in 1912 was the first Masonic funeral to be held in Bay (then Washington) County. His second wife, Margaret Tabour, was the mother of Mary Olivia. Her father was John Tabour, a state representative.

William and Mary Olivia Spiva's first child was a daughter, Willie. She was born and died in Bay County. She married William M. Pope. They had three children: Merritt Pope, Mary Nelle Pope Shumaker, and Nan Pope Mathis.

Ernest R. Spiva, Sr., son of William and Mary Olivia, married Florine Harrison of Lynn Haven. They had two children, Betty Sue Spiva Kimmel and Ernest R. Spiva, Jr. Florine's father, William J. Harrison, was a sawmill owner until his untimely death in 1925. He was the son of Zachary Taylor Harrison and Sarah Ann Willis of Henry County, Alabama. Zachary Taylor Harrison was the son of William Harrison and Elizabeth Sherman of Stewart County, Georgia. William J. Harrison's wife was Purlieu Alexander Harrison, who was born in Henry County, Alabama, the daughter of James and Marilda Alexander. Marilda was born Marilda Wiggins, the daughter of Martha Dortch and Joshua Wiggins, early settlers of Henry County, Alabama. James Alexander and his father, James Alexander, Sr., both served in the CSA army during the Civil War. William and Purlieu Harrison came to this area from Henry County. Their other children were: Lillie Maude Harrison, Floyd Harrison Campbell, Wallace J. Harrison, and Elaine Harrison Wiselogel. After William's death, Mrs. Harrison and her son, Wallace, were the first bridge tenders at Porter Bridge in Lynn Haven (near the present Bailey Bridge).

Numerous Spiva, Brown, Alexander, and Harrison descendants still reside in and around Bay County.
Submitted by: Betty Sue Spiva Kimmel, 115 Springhill Circle, Panama City, FL 32405.

Willard Winston Starling
Panama High School Days 1916-1919

My father, Willard Winston Starling, moved into the area called Crooked Creek near the present Highway 388 with his father, Marshall Owen (Marsh) Starling; mother, Mattie Fielding Starling; brother, Henry Guy; and sister, Nina Jane, before 1915. Turpentining had brought Granddaddy from Fayetteville, North Carolina, into Georgia and then to Mississippi and Florida. The Naval Stores industry provided their livelihood. They moved fairly often. Daddy told Mama that "when his father hitched up the wagons, the chickens jumped into their coops!"

Daddy completed eighth grade in a country school and that was as high as the grades went. When the next school term started, he figured he'd finished his schooling, until they moved where there was a secondary school. His father told him he'd better get dressed for school or "he could hit the road." Daddy went through the eighth grade again!

Willard Starling standing in front of his first car, 1924

In the young town of Panama City, students were needed in order to have enough enrollment to provide high school classes. During the ninth grade, Daddy stayed with the Judge J. R. Wells family whose home was on the east side of Massalina Bayou. By rowing a boat across the bayou and leaving it at the landing at the Sapp's place, they would walk about four blocks to the school located on Harrison

Avenue and Seventh Street. Daddy's family moved to Panama City during 1916.

Old newspapers gave me glimpses into this time period as I found Daddy's name mentioned in the school news section of these papers. One honor roll in March, 1916, named J. R. Wells, Willard Starling, Mattie Studebaker, and Ophelia Bledsoe.

In that year, the school boys organized a baseball team. In January, 1917, a basketball team was formed. Daddy and Tom Sharpless played the positions of "guards." Later, Uncle Tump, Daddy's brother (Henry Guy), was a "cracker jack" baseball pitcher and a good basketball player. A cheer to the team was "Panama! Panama! What's your cry? V-I-C-T-O-R-Y!!!"

A "Surprise Party" for Miss Flora Belle McBride included Daddy and eighteen other guests. Flora Belle was Aunt Nina's sister-in-law. She helped develop and operate Long Beach Resort with her husband, J. E. Churchwell.

The "Womanless Wedding" in 1917 caught me by surprise as I could not picture Daddy as a bridesmaid! Names I recognized included Waldo Wallace, who was also a bridesmaid!

In 1919, the second graduating class of Panama High School consisted of Daddy and Joel Reeves Wells. Mrs. G. M. B. Harries saved Daddy's graduation announcement and mailed it to him in 1978! Imagine receiving it after 59 years!

Daddy attended the University of Florida for a year. In high school. Uncle Tump was voted "best looking" boy and tied Ben Ellis for "best male athlete." Uncle Tump married Louise Gainer of Southport. Aunt Nina married T. J. (Jeff) McBride. Daddy married Estelle Cawthon from DeFuniak Springs. Daddy lived in Panama City from 1916 until his death in 1989.
Submitted by: Ruth Starling Glenn, 925 North Bay Drive, Lynn Haven, FL 32444.

The Legacy of my Parents, Marvin and Victoria Stephens

The legacy of my parents would be a blueprint for success in any generation. My father Marvin Hercules Stephens was born July 2, 1882 in Bay County (then part of Washington County). He was the son of John D. Stephens and Florida Ann Riley Stephens. He probably completed his formal education at sixth grade, but his life was a study in determination and self-reliance.

As a young man, he owned his own fishing boat and seine net and earned his living from St. Andrew Bay and the Gulf of Mexico. He married Victoria Smith, daughter of Confederate veteran Archie Lee Smith and wife Queen Victoria Davis Patterson Smith. Together they raised four daughters (Pauline, Grace, Kathleen Gwendolyn and one son Alfred) as well as building a home in the West End of St. Andrews. The home grew as the family grew and is owned by one of the grandsons today.

When we were young, we sat around the kitchen table at

Marvin and Victoria and their five children

253

night and daddy read to us by lamplight. My favorite book was The Little Shepherd of Kingdom Come.

During World War I, Marvin worked at a shipyard in Pascagoula, Mississippi. When he returned home he continued to work in shipbuilding and construction. In the depression my father often used his castnet to provide fish to supplement our family meals. My mother canned vegetables from our garden and kept chickens for meat and eggs. We fared better than most because of our parent's resourcefulness.

Marvin was not sure about an indoor bathroom so he closed in part of the back porch for this addition.

Mother and daughters studied catalog fashions. Mother would make her patterns and sew on a pedal-driven Singer sewing machine. Scraps of material were used in quilts some are treasured heirlooms in our family today. Mother often played hymns on her upright piano. She was active in PTA at our school and served as a leader in the Dorcas Society of our church for many years.

Daddy bought a new black four-door car, a STAR with curtains that snapped at the sides to keep out the cold-wind and rain. That car was his pride and joy and he drove it proudly on the mostly sand roads of our time.

On one occasion, three friends visited and tried to persuade him to enter the race for City Commissioner. They said our town needed him and they would work hard to get him elected. He said he would think about it. But his final answer was "NO".

Mother and daddy encouraged us to do our best in school and often rewarded an excellent report card.

My God-fearing, loving parents who lived by the Golden Rule forever shaped my life.

Submitted by: Grace Stephens Helms, 820 Moore Court, Panama City, FL 32401.

Dr. Robert Washington Stephens

Dr. Robert Washington Stephens and his wife, Nancy (Beaver), moved to Panama City, Florida, in 1912 from Hewins, Kansas near the border of Kansas and Oklahoma (Indian Territory). Just before the turn of the century, he had moved his family by horse and buggy from their former home in Arkansas. Dr. Stephens was a practicing medical doctor in Hewins and also owned an apothecary shop (drug store). It was the practice in those days for doctors to dispense their own prescriptions.

August 12th, 1923. Mother Stephens and family with Tom and Rosie Dickens on visit to Florida. Leo and Dorothy are standing in front of the car.

Dr. and Mrs. Stephens brought their two sons to Florida. Son Gus was suffering from asthma so Doc Stephens responded to an ad for a doctor in Panama City. The elder son was Claude V. Stephens, who was born Sept. 12, 1896, in Sharpe County, Arkansas. Augustus (Gus) C. Stephens was born April 15, 1908, in Hewins, Kansas. An older daughter, Rosa, had married and remained behind in Independence, Kansas.

Dr. Stephens built one of the best known landmarks in Panama City, the Tennessee House, at Harrison Avenue and Fourth Street. It had living quarters upstairs and two commercial businesses downstairs, one of which was his apothecary shop. The Panama City Pilot was also located there. He had dreams of a successful medical practice in Panama City. He made house calls with his horse and buggy, but his dreams were shattered in the deadly influenza epidemic following World War I. While treating victims, he was struck down with the disease and it took his life. His final resting place is Oakland Cemetery at Balboa and 11th Street. His widow operated a rooming house and lived in the Tennessee House until her death in 1941. She too is buried in Oakland Cemetery.

Son Claude married Edith Jarvis, daughter of Francis and Selina (Boyea) Jarvis. Her father was one of the Union Army veterans who settled Lynn Haven, coming from Malone, New York. He was instrumental in the erection of the statue in Lynn Haven dedicated to the Union soldiers. Edith was one of their three children who moved with them. The other two were Dave Jarvis and Alice Snell. Dave's four children — Alice, Clariece, Irene and David (Buzzy) were all born and raised in Lynn Haven. Dave was responsible for water, road maintenance, constable, and other duties for Lynn Haven. Claude and Edith had 13 children — Leo (Ruth Roush), Flora Ella (died in infancy), Dorothy Davis Pinkerton, Betty Turner Knowles, Helen (Steve) Cullen, Robert (Dorothy Furman), Howard (Sue Ann), Edith Mae (John) Pascual), Donald (Dolores Land), Nancy Roman Wellborn, Arthur (Carol Espy), Mary (Charles) Walsh, and Norma (Dick) Baymiller.

Son Gus married Ruth Sowell, whose parents lived at the present site of the Navy Base. She attended Mrs. Fleta Murrow's Business College. Her father took her in a boat across the bay. Gus and Ruth had two daughters, Martha (Jack) Todd, and Carolyn (James) Bradley. They divorced and Gus married Nellie Mae Taylor from Compass Lake. They had one daughter, Gwen (Don) Tillotson.

Many descendants of Robert and Nancy Stephens still live in Bay County.

Submitted by Edith Stephens Pascual, 124 Eagle Street, Eureka, UT 84628.

Frank Lee Strickland, Jr.

Frank Lee Strickland, Jr. is the son of Frank Lee and Marjorie (Hatcher) Strickland and was born in Panama City at Fraser Clinic in 1945. He has an older sister, Marjorie Dianne, born in Panama City at Lisenby Hospital in 1941. His mother died when he was young, and, later, his father, Frank, married Allie (Harper) Law who had been Dianne's teacher in the seventh grade. Frank, Jr. married Janice Genelle Wynn while they were in college, and both were graduated from Auburn. Frank and Janice had one child, a daughter, Jana Lee who married Eric Stephen Wibberley. Frank later married Roxanne (Tillman) Hallford who had a son, Ryan Doyle whom Frank adopted. Then, Frank and Roxanne had Frank Lee Strickland, III (Trey). (It is a family tradition to include the name Lee for at least one child since that is an early family last name and the family members are descendents of General Robert E. Lee.)

Frank, age six, with his first fish, a choffer, caught with a cane pole with a hook and line and a cork, Watson Bayou, Glen Bridge 1951.

Frank grew up in the Cove on N. Palo Alto Avenue which was a dirt road for years until it was paved with asphalt. The neighborhood children sometimes used the dirt road as a baseball diamond since there was very little traffic before the street was paved. (There wasn't much more traffic after it was paved.) Other families living in the immediate area on Palo Alto were the Haneys, the Smiths, more Smiths, the Warrens, the Hickeys, and, later, the Barbays. Nearby were the families of Prows, Parker, Hobbs, Johnson, Van Horn, Platt, and Hindsman.

Submitted by: Marjorie Dianne Strickland Hodges (Mrs. Donald Richard Hodges) sister. 406 Harvard Blvd., Lynn Haven, FL 32444.

Howard Delmas and Safronie Elizabeth "Strickland" Hall

Howard Delmas Hall was born 26 February 1906 and died 2 December 1995. He was the son of Jessie (1872) and Marietta (1875) "McLendon" Hall. His grandfather was John Jr. Hall (1850)

Delmas spent 3 years in the Army. He was in the 21st Regiment 1930 and his ID No. Was 6375508. Most of his time was spent in Hawaii because the war had already ended.

After being discharged Delmas returned home. On 10 December 1933, at Rehobeth Baptist Church in Houston County, Alabama, Delmas was married to Elizabeth Safronie Hall, born July 29, 1913. She was the daughter of Parley P (January 12, 1886) and Nancie "Hall" (January 12, 1888) Strickland. Her grandparents were Richard Franklin and Ella Jane "Buchanan" Hall and George Rufus and Safronia Elizabeth "Holland" Strickland. John Jr., above and Richard Franklin Hall, above were sons of John Sr. (April,1830) and Sarah Elizabeth "West" Hall (December 11, 1833).

Children of Delmas and Fronie Hall: Joel, Jane, and Annette.

Delmas and Fronie had three children: 1.) Elizabeth Annette Hall (March 31, 1935), married Robert Ray Mount, son of Willie S and Maggie "?" Mount. Their children were 1) Julie Mount born June 25, 1954. She married James Ray Harris and they have Heather Elizabeth and James Mathew Harris. 2) Robert Ray Jr. Mount born (November 24, 1956). He married Debra Anita Gore and had Stephanie Rae, born January 2, 1979 and Mechelle born October 18, 1980. Ray and Anita were divorced in November 1982. 3). Janet Lenni Mount born October 18, 1958 and died October 19, 1958.

2), Joel Lance Hall born February 5, 1939 was married to Jo Ann Moore daughter of Robert L. Moore. Their children were: Allen Hall born December 1, 1958 and Robbie Hall born October 25, 1963. Allen married Jamie Churchwell and has Taylor Allen and Brittney by first marriage and Carlie by second marriage. Robbie married Joyce April and has Andrew Lane Hall born April 14, 1940 and Garrett Landon Hall born November 26, 1994.

3). Melba Jane Hall born July 10, 1940 was married to Roy Lee Thornton October 18, 1936. They have Belinda Gale born October 7, 1980, married first Timothy Yates and had Jennifer Lee Yates (October 9,1980) and Timothy Lynn Yates Jr. (February 26 1985). She married second Kenneth R. Parson and Aubrey Jane Parson was born August 28,1996. Carla Elizabeth Thornton born November 3, 1960 married Joseph Bryon Ivey, born in Jasper, Alabama. They have Joseph Bryon Jr. Ivey born September 9,1984 in New Orleans, La. Daniel and Alexander Ivey born October 30, 1987 in Hattiesburg, Mississippi.

When Delmas Hall died at age 89, his son-in-law, Bryon preached his Funeral and he was buried in Evergreen Memorial Garden in Bay County Florida. His wife is living at the time of this writing. The family lived in Geneva County Alabama and Annette, Joel and Jane were born there before coming to Panama City, Florida. They have raised their family here and all three children and families still live in Panama City, Florida.

Submitted by: Fronie E. Hall 2815 Bartow Ave., Panama City, FL 32405; Written by: Rubylee Strickland Ave., 2627 Game Farm Road, Panama City, FL 32405. Source: Family Records.

Joseph Phillip and Barbara Jo Hearne Strickland

Joseph Phillip Strickland was born 7 September 1960, in Panama City Florida. When he was a young boy, he would clean out places in the yard and build a small fire with sticks and put it out with his toy fire-truck. As he grew old enough, he became a volunteer at the Hiland Park Fire Department. He worked a short time at a grocery store and learned to drive 18 wheel trucks and drove for a while. Phillip also worked at the Panama Fire Department.

Phillip was married 20 October 1979 in Fountain, Florida, to Angela Regina Woodrum Born 2 February 1961, in the Bermuda Islands (where her father was stationed). Their home was in West Virginia. Angie was the daughter of Leonard Ivan and Hilda Ruth "Marshal" Woodrum.

Phillip and Angie had two daughters, born in Panama City, Florida. Shawna Regina Strickland born 15 January 1981. Josie Necole Strickland born 9 May 1983. Their marriage ended 18 July 1984. About this time Phillip became a Deputy for the Bay County Sheriff's department for about 2 years.

Phillip Strickland, Shawna Regina Strickland, Josie Necole Strickland, Barbara Jo Strickland, Joshua Cary Strickland, and Krista Chastain

While in this work Phillip was married to Karen Leigh Price. There were no children and this marriage only lasted about a year. Phillip became a fireman for the Lynn Haven Fire Department. He went to College to get a Fire-Science degree and became a Paramedic on the Ambulance on his days off from the Fire Department.

April 8, 2000 Phillip was married to Barbara Jo "Hearne" Chastain. Barbara's daughter Krista Chastain was eight years old 9 October 2000. Their son, Joshua Cary was born 10 October 2000. Barbara finished her nursing degree and became a nurse at Bay Medical Center until about 2 years ago when she became a traveling nurse and worked in places like John Hopkins in MD. and in Bakersfield, California and Jacksonville, Florida. She is now working at Gulf Coast Hospital in Panama City, Florida.

Phillip is a Lieutenant at the Lynn Haven Fire Department and a Paramedic. He is also teaching courses on his days off at Gulf Coast Community College.

Phillip and Barbara are helping Shawna and Josie while they are both going to College. Shawna and Josie both are taking nursing courses. They plan to work in the medical field.

Submitted by: Shawna Strickland, 2538 Volusia Ave., Panama City Florida 32405; Written by: Ruby Strickland, 2527 Game Farm Road, Panama City, Florida 32405. Source: Family Research Files.

Yancy Cecil and Sarah Rubylee "Hartzog" Strickland

Yancy Strickland (1921-1977) was married 22 June 1946 in Houston County, Alabama to second wife, Sarah Rubylee Hartzog, born 14 June 1923 in Panama City, Florida. She was the daughter of Cary Timothy and Lessie Eva "Anderson" Hartzog. Her mother was born in Tinnelle, Alabama (1904). Her father was born in Geneva County Alabama (1901). Her grandparents were Moses Timothy and Margaret Arene "Stricklan" Hartzog and John Zollicoffer and Desty Lavinia "Chapman" Anderson.

Great grandparents were: James Washington and Martha A.J. "Warr" Hartzog; Thomas Jefferson and Mary Frances "Little" Stricklan;, John Wesley and Martha "Oliver" Anderson; Richard Asbury and Martha Zipparuhana "Baker" Chapman.

Great great grandparents were: George Henry and Celia "Baxley?" Hartzog; John and Nancy "Bass" Warr; John Sion

(1790) and Elizabeth "Black" Stricklan; John and Martha "___" Little; Henry and Rebecca "___" Anderson; Richard and Nancy "Goodson" Oliver; Thomas Richard and Elizabeth White Parkinson "Grimmer" Chapman; Richard and Amma "Annie" "Shouter" Baker.

Third great grandparents were: Daniel and Suzannah "Zorn" Hartzog; Thomas and Martha "Wood" Warr; Joseph and Martha "Jones" Bass; Sion and "___" Stricklan born 18  March 1776 (Bible Record). His second wife, Sallie Wilson was born 29 June 1788 and they married 16 November 1800 and gave birth to Wilson 5 September 1803 (Bible Records) John Black and Elizabeth "Irving" Black; William Washington and Elizabeth "Hester" Chapman; William

Teddy and Debbie Strickland and Cody and Jessica Leigh-Ann

C. and Flora "Montgomery" Grimmer.

Fourth Great Grandparents were: George and Catherine Magdaline "Snell" Hartzog; Henry and Elizabeth "-" Zorn; William and Patience "Wood" Warr; Joseph and Hope "-" Wood; Joseph and Jane "___" Bass; Samuel and "___" Jones; Aaron And Christina "Hill" Stricklan; Jonathon and Judith "Harlow" Black; Robert and Harriet "Smith" Hester; William and Mary "Cook?" Grimmer; David and Elizabeth "Hawthorn" Montgomery

Yancy and Ruby were blessed with five children, all born in Panama City Florida. Susan Carol Strickland born 13 April 1947 married Jackie Erwin Creel.

Yancy Kirby Strickland born September 24, 1949 married first Deborah Susan Davenport, second Tracy Ann Reed, third Genaveve Louise "Sterratt" Baker and fourth Bessie Darlene "Gipson" Hewett.

Nancy Eva Strickland born 26 December 1953 married Gary Lloyd Norton.

Joseph Phillip Strickland born 7 September 1960 married first Angela Regina Woodrum, second Karen Lee Price and third Barbara Jo "Hearn" Chastain.

Teddy Lee Strickland born 11 March 1962. His first marriage to Susan Darline Drennan lasted from 3 January 1984 to 1985. Teddy married second, Deborah Jean "Steverson" Calvert. Her first child, Jeremy was adopted by her mother and stepfather, Pat and Winston Scott. Deborah was born 7 June 1966 in Wewahitchka, Florida. She is the daughter of Gene and Patricia "Greyson" Steverson. She was 15 when her father died. Ted and Debbie have two children, both born in Panama City, Florida. Justin Cody born 6 March 1988 and Jessica Leigh-Ann born 5 July 1991. Ted is an Electricion for Stone Container and Debbie Works at Bay Walk-in Clinic.

Submitted by: Teddy Strickland, 11122 Lawrence Road, Fountain, FL 32438; Written by: Ruby L. Strickland, 2627 Game Farm Road, Panama City FL 32405. Sources: Family Research Files.

Yancy Kirby and Bessie Darlene "Gipson" Strickland

Yancy Kirby Strickland was born 24 September 1949, in Panama City, Florida, the son of Yancy Cecil and Sarah Rubylee "Hartzog" Strickland. His father and all grandparents were born in Alabama.

When Kirby was five years old, he was hit by a car on US Highway 231 at Hiland Park Florida, near his grandfather's Supermarket. He was unconscious for forty one hours and semiconscious for a week. He was in the hospital for six weeks and spent time later in a Pensacola Children's Hospital and had surgery on his leg several times.

Kirby was married first to Deborah Susan Davenport.

Children of Kirby and Debbie were: Rebecca Marie Strickland Stokes born 20 December 1968 in Panama City, Florida. Children of Becky are: Tyler Kirby "Figlliozzi" Stokes born 25 February 1996 and Kevin Lee "Pearson" Stokes born 22 July, 1999 in Panama City Florida. Melissa Dianne Strickland Stokes born 5 June 1952. Missy's son, Corey Nethaniel "Collins" Stokes was born 15 August 1992 in Dothan Alabama His father was Christopher Collins. Both girls now live in Panama City, Florida. Kirby and Debbie's second divorce was final 7 July, 1974.

January 25, 1975, Kirby was married to Tracy Ann Reed, born 3 August 1955. She was the daughter of Neal and Peggy Joyce "Andrew" Reed. Their children were Courtney Ann Strickland born 15 October 1978 in Longview, Texas.  She and husband John Montgomery have Nathaniel Reid Montgomery born 4 April 1997 and Jacob Daniel Montgomery born 5 March 1999. Amanda Gail Strickland born 7 March 1980 in Longview Texas. Amanda was married January 3, 1998 to Benjamin

The family of Kirby and Darlene Strickland

Causey, of Wewahitchka, Florida. Their children are Anna Cathryn Causey born 18 February 1999 in Panama City, Florida and Grace Andrew born 28 December 2000 in Panama City Florida. This marriage ended in divorce And Amanda lives in Panama City, Florida. Courtney and John also live in Panama City, Florida. Kirby and Tracy's divorce became final 15 May 1981.

September 18, 1981, Kirby was married to Genaveve Louise "Sterratt" Baker, who had a son, Clint Baker born 10 December 1971 and a daughter Salina Baker born 9 April 1973. Jenny was born 16 December 1950. They were divorced.

Kirby was married on November 12, 1990 in Sweetwater Texas to Bessie Darlene "Gipson" Hewett. She was born 15 May 1961 in Brownsville, Kentucky, the daughter of Lester and Dorothy "Vencent" Gipson. Darlene has two daughters. Joni Rose, who's father was David Langford. She was born 12 May, 1981 and adopted by present father James Craig Hewett on 7 August 1984. Joni has one daughter, Aja Necole Hewett born 20 September, 2002. Jennifer Ann Hewett born 6 August 1985. Darlene and John Hewett were divorced.

With no education in art, Kirby has been a gifted person in drawing and painting since he was small. I think he inherited this from his fathers family as there were several artists in the family. He loves sign painting and became a sign painter and this led to painting houses. Kirby and Darlene live in Panama City, Florida.

Submitted by Kirby Strickland, 3105 East 8th Street, Panama City, FL 32404; Written By Ruby L. Strickland, 2627 Game Farm Road, Panama City Florida Source: Family History.

Yancy Cecil and Martha Mae "Mathews" Strickland

Yancy was born 4 October 1921 in Geneva County Alabama and died 23 August 1977 in Panama City, Florida. He was laid to rest in Evergreen Memorial Gardens near the Garden of Memories. He was the son of Parley P and Nancy Hall Strickland; the grand son of George Rufus and Safronia Elizabeth "Holland" Strickland and Richard Frankland and Ella Jane "Buchanan" Hall. His Paternal great grandparents were David and Pearla Green "Wood" Strickland and Jesse and Harriet "Brumbelow" Holland. His maternal Great grandparents were John Sr. and Elizabeth "West" Hall and

Elbert and Sarah Ann "Underwood" Buchanan. Known Great Great Grandparents were Luke and Orpa "Riley" Hall and George Washington and Jane "Miller" Underwood.

Martha Janice Strickland and Myra Jean Strickland

At age 14, Yancy left home and hired out as a farm hand for a while. Deciding this was not for him, Yancy left Alabama and came to Panama City, Florida. When 18, he was married 19 June 1940 in Chipley, Florida to Martha Mae Mathews. She was born 21 June 1925 and died 20 December 1984.

Children of Yancy and Martha were both born in Panama City: Martha Janice born 6 May 1941. She was married to David Albert Spence, born 7 April 1942 in Panama City, the son of James C. and Nezzie "Pittman" Spence. Their children are Douglas Eugene born 13 December 1960, David Anthony born 10 September 1962 and Rhonda Janalois born 6 May 1964.

Myra Jean was born 15 April 1943. She was married 30 November 1968 to Charles Edward Hayman, He was born 18 November 1930 and had two Daughters by a previous marriage. Charley and Myra Jean only had one son; Charles Edward "Chip" Hayman II.

At the beginning of World War II, Yancy joined the U.S. Coast Guards. During his first month in service, it was discovered that he was totally deaf in one ear and partially deaf in the other ear. They said that could cause lots of people's death and hospitalized him until they could process him out. His medical discharge became final 12 January 1942 with only 2 months of service. He then went to work at Wainwright Shipyard in Panama City, Florida. He worked 16 hours a day for the duration of the war. Yancy's marriage to Martha ended in a divorce, which became final 9 January 1946.

Being very young, Martha wanted Yancy's sister, Safronia Elizabeth to raise these two girls. That suited him cause he would be living with his sister and her family. When Yancy was married again Fronie let the girls spend part of their time in his home.

Sources: Family knowledge.
Submitted by: Myra Jean Hayman, 377 Anclote RD #300, Tarpon Springs, FL 34689; Written by: Rubylee Strickland, 2627 Game Farm Road, Panama City, FL 32405.

Strickland/Peacock/Johnson Family

Looking back, over sixty-five years ago, a new chapter opened in the life of two lovely young ladies. It was on January 26, 1939, that sisters Pauline (9-17-1921) and Pera Lee Strickland (1-6-1923) said "I do" in pursuit of new hopes and dreams. This story began in Blountstown, Florida, and continues through today in Panama City.

Pauline, the eldest of the two, being sixteen years of age at the time, had met and fallen in love with Robert Carrell (Peck) Johnson (3-11-1915/12-24-2000) of Altha, Florida. Like Pauline, Pera Lee, age fifteen, had fallen in love with Charles Franklin Peacock (12-8-1914), also of Altha. After a courtship of approximately four months, the couples made the decision to get married. Charles and Peck made the traditional visit to ask the girls' father, Alexander Hershel Strickland (4-20-1897 /10-7-1961) for permission to marry his daughters.

That evening, at approximately 9:00pm, the girls' father went to the local judge's home. His knock on the door awakened the judge. Mr. Strickland asked Judge Leath if he would marry the two couples. Arrangements were made to meet Judge Leath later that evening at 11:00pm at the Calhoun County Courthouse. Everyone arrived on time, including the girls' mother, Bessie Lee (8-28-1899/9-24-1942), and their three brothers, Albert Franklin (8-13-24/ Dec. 1996), James Oliver (11-25-1925), and Alexander Hershel, Jr. (12-17-1928/ July 2001) and their eldest and devoted sister, Willie Mae (12-9-1919/12-06-1992).

Pera Lee and Charles Peacock

Not knowing the exact ages of Pauline and Pera Lee, the judge first asked the age of Pauline. "Sixteen" was Pauline's reply since she had just turned sixteen in September just prior to that date. By that time the judge was probably wondering if he was going to legally be able to join the second couple in matrimony. The dubious judge turned to Pera Lee and asked the same question, "How old are you?" "Fifteen", responded Pera Lee. Judge Leath then stated, "I cannot marry you, Pera Lee. You have to be sixteen years old". Willie Mae, trying to look out for her youngest sister as she always did, spoke up and answered, "She will be sixteen tomorrow." Little did the judge know that Pera Lee had just turned fifteen on January 6th, only twenty days before.

Judge Leath thought for a few moments, probably remembering his oath of office and at the same time trying to fulfill the couples' desire to be married. "Pauline and Peck, I will marry you right now; however, Charles and Pera Lee, you will have to return after midnight tonight and I will marry you." The first couple was married at 11:15pm that evening. Everyone left and returned after midnight. The wedding continued after the brief intermission. At 12:10am, on January 27th, Judge Leath joined Charles and Pera Lee in marriage.

Pauline and Peck Johnson

They headed West on January 27th in a 1931 Model A Sport Sedan with roll up windows and roll back top! They had $200 to support them until the job could be found and a payday was earned. Charles had already made arrangements for a job for both of the men with Standard Dredging. They were to meet the dredge in Lake Ponchartrain but the dredge company had already moved west. As soon as they located the dredge company, they were hired immediately and went to work.

The sisters were content having each other and felt safe in the care of their husbands. Wanting to impress their new husbands, the girls decided to cook a fine meal of beef soup. Not realizing how much macaroni swells when cooked, they used a whole box in their soup. They laugh today, describing how they had to walk down the road and dump the dry pot of soup in the ditch. They also enjoy laughing about the time they decided to surprise the men with a delicious southern meal. Not knowing the difference between a hen and fryer, the excited ladies selected a hen to fry. Biscuits were homemade by their loving hands. Needless to say, the fried hen was too tough to eat. To make matters worse, even the biscuits were a total flop, so

Pauline Johnson, Willie Mae Newton and Pera Lee Peacock at St. Andrew Trusdell Park, Christmas 1949

hard that they could not eat them.

The couples returned to Florida after working on the dredge and have since then raised their own families, enjoyed many fresh water fishing trips near Wewahitchka, and shared many enjoyable times together. Both couples have lived in Panama City most of their married life. Though they have always celebrated their wedding anniversary one day apart, they still maintain that they were married in a "double wedding".

Submitted by Carolyn Peacock Prows, 4340 College Station Road, Panama City, Florida 32404.

Alexander Hershel Stricklen and Bessie Lee Smith

Alexander Hershel Stricklen was a descendant of Matthew M. Strickland, II, 1663-1730 of Isle of Wight,

Archie Smith

Virginia and Ann Braswell 1674-1744. He was born April 20, 1897 Wicksburg, Dale County, Alabama, son of John Albert Strickland and Martha Emma Bryan. The Strickland/Stricklen name has been a bone of contention in the Strickland family. None of Hershel's brothers, sisters or children spelled their surname the same. They all believed their spelling was the correct spelling. When he was 18 years old Hershel fell in love with Bessie Lee Smith. Hershel's family worked for Bessie's father Joshua Franklin Smith at Hinson's Crossroads, Washington County. Joshua

caught Hershel "making eyes" at Bessie and fired him. Bessie knew her father would not approve of Hershel as a husband for her so she stole out of the house one night by climbing out a window. Hershel and his mother were waiting for her and they had to buy her a pair of shoes before they could get married because she was in such a hurry to get away that she forgot her shoes. They went to live with Hershel's parents. Hershel enlisted in the army August 26, 1918, a Private in the Utilities CO. QMC. He was sent overseas but the war ended when his ship got to France. Hershel was accidentally gassed aboard the ship and was discharged from the army March 1, 1919. He was a disabled veteran for the rest of his life. This was a big help financially when the Depression came along. He was getting $80 a month when most men were working for 15 cents a day. Hershel was classified as a laborer but his health wouldn't let him do any hard labor. Several times during his life the Veterans organization would come to his house and take him to a doctor because his breathing was worse.

Hershel was a beekeeper. Anytime anyone had a swarm of bees that was causing trouble, they would call him to come and get the bees. He didn't have any fancy stuff to protect him from the bees. He just knew how to handle them. He was a very good hunter and fisherman. He ran a fishing camp near Blountstown and men from Alabama and Georgia stayed at his camp so he would be their guide

Bessie Lee Smith Stricklen

on hunting and fishing trips. These men would take barrels of fish back home from their fishing trips.

Hershel and Bessie had six children. Willie Mae Strickland born December 9, 1919, Pauline Strickland born September 17, 1921, Pera Lee Strickland born January 6, 1923, Albert Franklin Stricklen born August 13, 1924, James Oliver Stricklen born November 25, 1925 and Alexander Hershel "Junior" Stricklen, Jr. born December 17, 1928. Willie Mae married Alto Conner Newton and had two children, Bessie Maxine and Monroe Durwood.

Pauline Strickland married Robert Carrell Johnson and had one daughter Dorothy Ann. Pera Lee Strickland married Charles Franklin Peacock and had seven children, Baby Peacock who died at birth, Charles Stonewall, Charlotte Marie, Georgia Carolyn, Robert Belser, Mary Pauline and Roberta Lee. Albert Franklin Stricklen was married and divorced four times. He married Doris Elaine Traylor and had Susan Jane who died at birth and Doris Ann. He married Vera Jo Porter and had Albert Franklin, Jr. He married Mary Lois Toole and had Bessie Lynn. He married Barbara Gayle Brown and they had no children. James Oliver Stricklen married Oween Chesser and had Jerry Thomas. James divorced Oween and married Shirley Lee Mullikin and had Sherri Lee and James Oliver "Jimmy" Jr. Alexander Hershel "Junior" Stricklen, Jr. married Julie Ann Foster and had four children Robert Lee, Joyce Ann, Julius Albert and Rhonda Lynette.

Bessie Lee was a very religious woman. She loved to go to church. It didn't matter what denomination she would go if they were having anything at the church. At home she always had a special place outside where she would go at night to pray. Bessie Lee was a descendant of Thomas Smith born 1767 North Carolina and his wife Jiminia. Thomas and Jiminia moved to Georgia where they had a son James who married Eleanor and moved to Pike County, Alabama. They had nine children: William born 1841, Archie born May 26, 1842, Mary born 1843, Neill born 1845, James H. born 1845, Piety E. born 1851, Americus born 1853, Sarah born 1855 and Jahaza S. born 1859. Archie married Annie Wilson May 1, 1866 in Pike County, Alabama. Later he married Rebecca Hinson and they had a son Joshua Franklin. Archie and Rebecca divorced and

Alexander Hershel Stricklen

Archie married Queen Victora Davis. He had five children with her: Archie, Jr., Alto, Mattie E. N.born 1888, Cora Lee born 1890 and Queen Victoria born 1892. Archie enlisted in March 22, 1862 at Troy, Alabama for the Confederacy. He was in Company E 37th Alabama Regiment. He was captured at Vicksburg, Mississippi July 4, 1863 and was a prisoner of war. His first battle was May 26, 1864 at New Hope Church, Georgia. He was wounded in the battle and as a result lost his right hand and two fingers and his thumb on his left hand. He was discharged July of 1865 and had to walk home from the war. It took him almost a year. Archie was a farmer and a Baptist preacher. He wore a special glove on his left hand so he could farm. Archie died June 28, 1919 and he and Victoria are buried at Cedar Creek Cemetery in Bay County. Joshua Franklin Smith married Zena Elizabeth Johnson 1877-1905 daughter of Sampson Johnson 1830-1923 and Margratte Ann Parrish 1849-1938. Joshua and Zena had six children: Charlie Franklin, Maude Evelyn, Minnie Eron, Bessie Lee, Albert Sampson and Donna Elizabeth. Zena died giving birth to Donna Elizabeth. Joshua next married Flora Nell Worthington and had seven children: Ethel J., Josie Marie, Rebecca Ouida, Sanford Malone, Godfrey F., Joshua Flornoy and David Greenwood. Hershel Stricklen died in a car wreck October 7, 1961 and Bessie Lee Smith died September 24, 1942.

Sources: Washington County Tombstone Record, Family Interviews, Sampson Johnson Family Bible.
Submitted by: Pauline Strickland Johnson, 204 Kraft Ave., Panama City, Florida 32401.

Alexander Hershel Stricklen Descendants

Alexander Hershel (1897-1961) and Bessie Lee Smith Stricklen (1899 - 1942) were the parents of three daughters and three sons.

The oldest child was Willie Mae. She was born December 9, 1919. Willie Mae worked as a waitress at the Cafe in Bay Harbor and met her future husband there, Alto Newton. She worked at Captain Jack's (behind Walgren's Drug Store), City Drug Store, Winns Drive-In, Domestic Laundry, International Paper Mill(in the Pulp Mill section) and at Tyndall Air Force Base Commissary. Alto worked at International Paper Mill until he retired. As a young man, Alto was one of the divers that worked at the St Andrew's Jetty as it was being constructed. The enormous rocks, hanging by chains, were placed by heavy equipment into the water to make the channel. The divers had to dive down, holding their breath, with no equipment and unfasten the

Frank, Alexander Hershel, Junior, James, Pauline, Willie Mae and Pera Lee

chains. Willie Mae and Alto had two children, Bessie Maxine and Monroe Durwood. Willie Mae was a wonderful cook and loved to garden, canning and freezing what her vegetable garden produced. She was always sharing her home-grown vegetables with friends and family. Willie Mae died December 6, 1992.

The second daughter, Pauline, was born September 17, 1921. She remembers that their daddy didn't like for them to play with dolls as children. He didn't think pretending was good for them. So the girls would make their play-house in the woods and hide their dolls in the woods near the house. Pauline's family (parents, siblings, aunts, uncles, nieces, nephews, children, grandchildren) have been and always will be next to her heart. Everyone knows she will be there if they need her. Pauline married Robert Johnson and they had a daughter, Dorothy Ann. Robert Johnson died December 23, 2000.

Daughter number three was Pera Lee born January 6, 1923. She and Pauline being close in age did everything together. Pera Lee married Charles Franklin Peacock and they had seven children; baby Peacock (who died at birth), Charles Stonewall, Charlotte Marie, Georgie Carolyn, Robert Belser, Mary Pauline and Roberta Lee. The Peacocks lived on the family farm many years before moving to Panama City. Charles worked for Standard Oil Company until his retirement. Pera Lee loves to fish, collect sea shells and grow flowers most of all.

Albert Franklin "Frank" the first son, was born August 13, 1924. Frank's birth was very hard on his mother. He

weighed more than 14 pounds at birth. In those days women had their babies at home with a midwife to help with the birth if no doctor could come. Frank was in World War II serving in the 28th Infantry Division in Germany. He worked in Panama City at the Standard Oil Company until his retirement. He loved to fish and in his young days pick a guitar and sang sad country songs. He was married four times. He married Doris Elaine Traylor and had a

James, Pera Lee, Junior, Willie Mae, Frank and Pauline

daughter Doris Ann. He married Vera Jo Porter and had a son Albert Franklin "Frankie", Jr. He married Mary Lois Toole and had a daughter Bessie Lynn. He married Barbara Gayle Brown and had no children. Frank died December 1986.

The second son, born November 25, 1925, was James Oliver. His father was very ill in the other bed. Alexander had been gassed in World War I and suffered with lung trouble the rest of his life. The Veterans Organization came and took Alexander away to a hospital while Bessie was in the house laboring in childbirth. She had a midwife and her mother helping her. A neighbor took the other children home with her while Bessie struggled to bring forth her next child. When James was about 13 years old, the Stricklens lived in Bay Harbor. In those days it was called "Rat Row." Bessie Lee was not well and Alexander took her to every doctor he heard about. It was while they were gone on a trip to see a new doctor that James got into trouble. He did odd jobs to earn money (sold papers, shined shoes, etc.). With the money he earned he bought comic books, took Frank and Junior to the movies and sometimes bought food for his mother's special diet. One day he was sitting on the front porch whittling on a stick. Frank came home with a neighbor boy and went into the house. The boy came out with a bunch of comic books. James and the boy got into an argument over ownership of the comics. The boy was older and bigger and pushed James off the porch. James came back swinging his knife and cut the boy under the arm bad enough to send him to the doctor. The sheriff came to see Alex and James. Alex told the sheriff that James was smaller than the other boy and he didn't believe he should be punished. The sheriff said Alex would have to pay the doctor bill but James said his father never did pay the bill.

James was too young to get into the service when World War II began but he lied about his age and joined the Navy. He served with the Navy 3rd Fleet Pacific Theater Operations for three years. He left the Navy and joined the Air Force as a Private First Class in March 28, 1947. Staff Sergeant James O. Stricklen made the Air Force his career. James married twice. He married Oween Chesser and had a son Jerry Thomas. He married Shirley Lee Mullikin and had two children, Sherri Lee and James Oliver "Jimmy" Jr. James died Oct 31, 2003.

The third son born December 17, 1928 was Alexander Hershel Stricklen, Jr. and he was always called Junior. As a boy Junior hated to go to school. Pauline would take him to his class and while she went to her class, he would climb out the window and run back home. Junior worked on tug boats for many years. He was an outstanding carpenter. He loved fishing and hunting. Laughing and cracking jokes, he made friends everywhere he went. If anyone ever needed him, he was always there. He married Julie Ann Foster who loved her family and was known to never say an unkind word about anyone. She could always find something good in everyone she met. They had four children; Robert Lee, Joyce Ann, Juluis Albert and Rhonda Lynette. Julie died May 8, 2000 and Junior died July 21, 2001.

All the girls in the family spelled their name Strickland and all the boys spelled their name Stricklen. Their mother, Bessie, was the granddaughter of Bay County pioneer Archie Smith.

Submitted by James O. Stricklen, 502 Seneca Ave., Panama City, FL 32404.

Reverend William Sutton

Rev. William Sutton was born September 23, 1886 in Muller County, Georgia. He was the son of George and Peggy Sutton. William Sutton received his diploma from St. Augustine Seminary. Pastoring at an early age, he began his pasturing at New Judson Church during the early 1900's, over at Red Fish Point across the bay which is now Tyndall Air Force Base. He later moved to Shine Town which is now Glenwood in early 1920's. He bought property and built a brick house at 724 Hamilton Ave. The house is still there. He had a grocery store next to his house. He loved and helped everyone. He was loved by every one. He was one of the Black stock holders of West Florida Gas Company. He own Glenwood Community Swimming Pool, Bay Medical properties and also sold the property which was Motel Neota, which is now ASAP property.

Reverend William Sutton
1882-1980

On March 27, 1947, he married Arletha Bracy. William and Arletha raised five children. They had three daughters, Sally Ann Sutton Waters, Venetricia Masha Sutton and Arletha L. Sutton. They had two sons, Wendell Lafayette Sutton and Tofoya Lorenza Sutton, Sr. William and Arletha had eighteen grandchildren and three great-grandchildren, Marissa Micole Waters, Chagrin Chante and Elise Alexandria Tinsley.

William worked at West Florida Gas Company. He left West Florida Gas Company to get a job at Panama City Hall in 1951 and worked there until retirement caused by failure of his health. He pastured New Bethel Baptist Church from 1945 to 1951. Rev. William Sutton was a member of the original Adversary Committee Founders of Rosenwald Junior College along with Henry C. Bailey, Immaniel Pope, Pasco Gainer, Sr., and Edward Lee, Sr.

Rev. Sutton was an outstanding, lovable man. He and Arletha loved everyone that they touched. He was a Mason and Arletha was an Eastern Star. Arletha worked at Tyndall Air Force Base. She was a great housekeeper in and out of the home.

Arletha B. Sutton

Maggie Walls was a great lady too. She helped raise the neighborhood children. She was the second Mama to William and Arletha's children.

August 1952 a club was organized from a vision of Rev. William Sutton. Five members took part in this club: Arletha B. Sutton, Curtis Lee, Nellie Marron, Eddie Davis and Beulah Lee. Also Flora Spearman who was a member

at St John Missionary Baptist Church, along with her daughter Annie W. Lee, shared her time to help. William was involved in the organization of the Greater Friendship Baptist Church. After Rev. Sutton's retirement he was still active. William and Arletha were well thought of and loved by everyone. Rev. William past this life September 9, 1980, Leroy Sutton July 8, 1965 and Matthew Sutton 1951.

Submitted by: Sally Ann Waters, 707 East 13th Court, Panama City, Florida 32401.

The Hollie B. Tate and Joanie Frances (Bailey) Family

Our grandparents met while Hollie was stationed at Tyndall Military Base in the US Army in Panama City, Florida. According to Frances, it was love at first sight, she often spoke of how handsome he was in his military uniform. Shortly after their meeting, they married in 1944. Two sons were born into this marriage. The firstborn was Ronald Wayne Tate on 4/19/1945. It wasn't until years later that the second son, James Alan Tate was born on 4/13/1958. Hollie was from Big Stone Gap, VA and Frances was from Grand Ridge, FL. Hollie was a pilot during his stay in the US Army, and Frances was employed at a drycleaners while stationed at Andrews AFB, Washington D.C. Ronald Wayne grew up to marry Virginia Lee Stanworth, formerly of Hampton VA. There were also two sons born into this marriage, Ronald Wayne Tate, Jr. on 5/1/1969 and Jason Scott Tate on 2/29/1976. To date Ronald Wayne, Jr. is still a bachelor and Jason Scott married April Tate and they have a daughter, Anna Grace Tate, born 3/1/2002 and April has a son named Andrew.

Joanie Frances Tate and Hollie B. Tate

This brings us to our parents, son of Hollie and Frances, James Alan Tate and Vonda K Tate (Shores). Two children were born into this marriage, Tyler Alan Tate on 11/1/1986 and Alyssa Kay Tate on 11/13/1989. James has spent most of his career as an avid fan of automobiles (buying and selling) while our wonderful mother has specialized in insurance sales and administration. We were never fortunate enough to meet our grandfather, with his untimely death in 1968. This is a photo of our grandparents, shortly after they married.

Submitted by: Tate Family, 913 Taylor Dr., Panama City, FL 32404; Written by Tyler, Alyssa and Vonda Tate. Source: Ronald Tate/Family Records.

Alva Franklin Thomas – The High Sheriff

"I loved your grandaddy. Like a father to me. A fair man, a good man. Taught me all the common sense I ever had. The only good man that's ever been sheriff of this county. Let's have coffee one day so we can talk about Alvie." These were the words of one of my grandpa's deputies. I also learned that my sheriff grandpa usually did not carry a gun. His billet or blackjack was his preferred weapon. Neither did he wear a uniform or drive a marked car.

Before holding that public office from 1949 to 1953, grandpa was a state tag inspector under Governor Holland and Governor Caldwell. Prior to that, he worked at Nelson Chevrolet for many years. Before the Great Depression, he owned and managed a Texaco Station at the Y of 4th Street and Beach Drive. His daddy, Franklin Joseph Thomas (F.J.), landowner and naval stores owner, had another service station on 4th and Massalina Drive. The only place I remember was the Thomas Turkey Farm in Bayou George after he retired from public service. My grandparents moved there from 913 McKenzie Avenue where they had lived since my mother, Georgia, was in the 4th grade.

Alva, husband of Golda Pickens, father of Joyce and Georgia

Grandpa married Golda Edith Pickens, the daughter of Peter Zeno and Edith Coppedge Pickens. She often uttered about my grandpa, "The cobbler's children have no shoes," referring to his generosity of spirit to friends, or strangers! Like, my mom tells about his piling her sister, Joyce, their mother, and her in the car to take food and clothing to a family of a friend in jail. The man, as it later turned out, was the father of a prominent attorney and politician. Other times, grandpa would come home with empty pockets because he said that someone else needed the money more than he.

Then, there are other sayings that came out on a regular basis: "Where there's a will, there's a way.' "The chickens done come home to roost." Plus, with a handshake, "A man's word is his bond.' And his cussing was as close to him as his pocket knife. When asked if he had a knife on him, he came back with, "I have my pants on, don't I?"

Another fixture on my grandpa's body was his hat. A felt in winter, a straw in summer. Never did he leave the house without the hat, which he constantly tipped on seeing anyone, known or unknown. In his car, his hand moved up and down from his hat, never letting a car pass without a tip of the hat.

One thing about grandpa I remember most of all. He could throw his voice" - in other words, a ventriloquist! When somebody new came into the house, the voice would call his or her name and say something to the person who would rush from one end of the house to another. - yet, there

Georgia Thomas, Golda Pickens Thomas, Alva Thomas and Joyce Thomas

would be no one else around and my grandpa's lips were closed. But before long, laughter was heard throughout the house. As it was when another incident was recalled. My grandpa was fearless, afraid of no one, no thing - not snakes or any animal. Except mice. One day he fell and broke his leg when a mouse ran across the floor - and he couldn't get out of the way fast enough. The sight of this fearless one in a leg cast (and the reason, there of) has been added to the list of family jokes and joys.

An enigma. . . a saint with a demon's temper. . . a thoughtful, unselfish one. . . a feared one, a loving one - my grandpa.

Submitted by: Craig Henry, 8837 Lagoon Drive, Panama City Beach, FL 32408.

Franklin Joseph Thomas

We do not smell the fragrance of turpentine as we drive by the pine trees. As we walk in the woods, there are no cups on the pine trees to gather turpentine.

In the early1900's, my Daddy had two turpentine stills in Bay County. One was on what is now 15th Street which was only pines and woods. In Callaway he had another still. The workers stripped bark from the pine trees, and the wounds would bleed sap into waiting cups. These trees

F. J. Thomas on right with son, Alva, in center

were left looking like cat-faces, so we had forests of cat-faces staring at us. Barges would launch in the bayou and pick the barrels of turpentine to take to market. Turpentine had many commercial uses. But we used it as a home remedy for cuts and for the times we stepped on nails since we liked to go bare-footed.

My Daddy, Franklin Joseph Thomas, and Mother, Adnie Ethridge, were pioneers in Bay County. Our home was on the hillside on Massalina Drive off 4th Street. We had a filling station there on the corner. Part of the concrete is still there today, 2002. Daddy also built a station for his son, Alva. The home my Daddy built burned so he built another one which is the first white house facing Massalina Bayou. He also owned land up and down what is now Harrison Avenue, and all over the county. We had a yacht parked on Massalina Bayou; he would take his friends to Shell Island for a day. I also remember the planning of fishfries in the park.

Daddy was a businessman, saying a handshake was the bond between two men. This trust filtered down to him from his father, Jefferson Franklin, and his father, Hezekiah. You could believe his word. He taught his children about character. His children are Ingram, Carl, Alva (Bay County Sheriff in the 1940's), Rufus, Fleida Hall, Jo Thelma Penton, Jean Smith and myself, Nona Carr.

How things have changed! When we were growing up, we would walk to school. When mother said dinner was ready, we waited for Daddy at the table. He asked the blessing, and we always ate together. At a gathering, children went to the table after the men served their plates. Today, children go first. When will the men take their "rightful" places? Mother taught us to honor our Daddy.

We went through the Depression in the 1930's. Daddy was devastated as he gradually lost his business. His bookkeeper helped the situation by stealing from him. One day, daddy decided to shoot him. They walked across the Massalina Bridge and Daddy took his gun out, but then decided not to use it. Today you sue. It's amazing how God takes care of us - I believe this. After all this, Daddy became foreman of another turpentine still. While he was riding in the woods one day, the horse came home without him. Some men took a wagon and rode into the woods to find him. He had a stroke. It was a light stroke so he could continue on in life, but not in the turpentine business.

Daddy applied with the State and was hired as bridge tender for the East Bay Bridge. Our family lived in San Blas at what is now called Wherry housing at Tyndall Air Force Base. We had a home overlooking the bay. Tyndall Field came with the war in 1941. They bought our home and land and so we moved to Parker on the other side of the bridge. Daddy continued with the State until the day he was walking out to turn the draw-bridge for a boat. He turned it by hand with a metal crank. A State truck was crossing the bridge and hit Daddy. He fell and had a stroke so the ambulance came and took him to Lisenby Hospital. He was in a wheelchair until he died in December, 1943. I really came to know my Daddy. He would ask my sister, Jean, and I to sing, which was a joy for us to do for him.

When we lived on the bay, our friends and nieces would spend time with us, swimming, crabbing, walking on the beach. Now the bay is not used for swimming much. There was no television at that time, only radio. We played cards and games like hop-scotch and statue.

When we were growing up, Mother tried to tell us about

our heritage, but we were not interested. Today, I wish I had listened; I would like to say to the children today, gather all the information you can from Mom, Dad and Grandparents.

In 1942 I married a soldier, Buck Walker, from Tyndall Field. Our children are Helen Ann, Jimmy, Rebecca and Frank.

But that is another story.

Submitted by: Nona Thomas Carr, 4039 Pipeline Rd., Panama City, Fl 32404.

Grace Thomason Sunday Morning

Taken on a Sunday morning, on her way to church. Grace was a charter member of Calvary Baptist church, and was very faithful in attendance. Most Sundays in the early years of the church the altar flowers were provided by Mama from her own flower garden.

Submitted by: James E. Thomason, 1057 Oak Avenue, Panama City, FL 32401.

Grace Thomason ready for Church

Jo and Edna Thomason

Edna was always her sister's shadow...following her

wherever she went...the youngest of the Thomason children, her brothers and sister always said she was "spoiled rotten"; but really she was a very good little girl...

Submitted by: Ronald W. Thomason, 1057 Oak Avenue, Panama City, FL 32401.

Joe and little sister, Edna, taken about 1954

Weston and Grace Thomason - Part 1

Weston Thomason, son of James Jackson and Lucy Caswell Thomason, born February 2nd, 1910, in Portland, FL, married Minnie Grace King, born April 2nd, 1915, in Noma, FL, daughter of Burrell Albert and Jessie Ruth Wallace King, on December 28, 1931, in Freeport, FL.

He moved his bride to Pensacola, where he was employed with the Army Engineers, and their first son was born. In late 1934, they moved to Panama City where he was part of the government crew that constructed the jetties. They lived in an apartment near Tarpon

Weston and Grace Thomason about 1977

Dock, and stayed briefly in a boarding house at the site which is now Bay Bank. In 1935, they lived on Magnolia behind the "Redmond" store, where their second son was born. Briefly they lived in the 700 block of Oak Avenue, where their third son was born, and for a short while on

9th Street in St. Andrews. They also lived in the old McNally house near Lake Ware. On October 6th, 1938, they moved to 1537 Mulberry Avenue where the house built for them by E. T. Hudson still stands. In those days the closest church, First Baptist, was a mile away, the closest grocery store was J.C. Stewart's near Panama Grammar (this was before Johnny Turner and Mr. Campbell opened up their neighborhood grocery stores), both the Airport Road and 15th Street were dirt roads, and the Panama City Airport had recently moved from its original location between Mulberry and Highway 231 to its present site.

In the early years, there was no electricity or running water in this area...1ife was sweet and simple... No television, you didn't lock your doors, children played outside. High adventure for children included walks along "Big Ditch", climbing trees, sandlot baseball, football, Saturday matinees at the old Panama and Ritz Theaters, eating watermelon under the huge willow trees in our backyard where all the children liked to play, chasing the ice truck on a summer day hoping to get a chunk of ice, trading comic books with Sonny King, Nancy Sampley, the Newberry kids, Bill Campbell and Billy Rumph, walking along the railroad tracks with Billy Glaze, Billy Brown and other friends, and going into the hammocks to chop down the family Christmas tree, cutting down a few extras to sell to neighbors for ten cents each. Another favorite pastime was searching for Indian artifacts (arrowheads and broken pottery) which could be found on the open field at the corner of Mulberry and Airport Road, the location of Lindsey's trailer park today. Some of the children would earn money by "picking cotton" in Mr. Hogan's cotton field located at Florida Avenue and 17th Street. Wages were one dollar per day.

The Thomason children attended Panama Grammar and were graduates of Bay County High School. Their children Ronald Weston Thomason, born May 5th, 1934, married Barbara Padgett. Darrell Wallace Thomason, born September 7th, 1935, married Selmajane Ruden, then Lola June Price. James Earl Thomason, born November 14th, 1937, married Margie Campbell, then Fay Faulk Thomas. Grace Josephine Thomason, born February 1st 1943, married William Harold Manis. Edna Ruth Thomason, born October 6th, 1951, married John Moore.

Submitted by Darrell W. Thomason, 510 Marion Street, Attalla, AL.

Weston and Grace Thomason - Part 2

In the early 1940's, Weston took a leave from the Corps of Engineers and worked in the construction of Tyndall Field to make more money for his growing family. He

returned to his government job where he worked until retirement. During his 37 year career, he was cook, deckhand, and became Captain of *The Blakely* in 1947, following the retirement of Captain Pryor. He was appointed Captain of the survey boat, *Wimico*, in the late 1950's. Captain "Wes" served as pilot of the snagboat *Montgomery* (1962-1964) when he became pilot of the dredge boat *Guthrie* where he worked until his retirement in 1967.

Captain Thomason, an expert navigator of the Intracoastal Waterways from St. Marks, Florida, to Pearl River, Louisiana, was a hard worker and well respected by all. During the early 1940's, he piloted the first boat to go through the West Bay Canal, *The Blakely*, along with Captain Pryor. Accompanying

Thomason Children (front) Jimmy and Jo (back) Ronnie and Darrell

them were Congressman Bob Sikes, General George Patton and other dignitaries.

In January 1946, Weston was serving on *The Blakely* with Captain Pryor when they spotted two men in Lake Wimico who had been missing for a couple of days. Air Force and Coast Guard search parties were patrolling the waters to locate them. The men were found half frozen to death. Weston jumped into the waters and pulled them to safety, giving them warm food and returning them safely home. These two men were Spencer Fields, a local dentist, and Bobby Carswell, owner of Carswell's Barber Shop. To hear more of this story, you only have to ask Mr. Bobby... he said the time spent in those cold waters prior to rescue was when he made his peace with the Lord.

In 1961, the Thomason's moved to Walton County, back to their roots. In 1963 they returned to Panama City, building a home at 702 West 19th Street, where they lived for the remainder of their lives.

Grace, a homemaker and mother, was a charter member of Calvary Baptist Church. She loved the outdoors, had a "green thumb," which she inherited from her father, and took pride in her flower and vegetable gardens. She was a great seamstress and raised her children with a strong hand, taking them to Sunday School, striving to teach them well and to believe in the Lord. Her children knew the meaning of "Walking the Line" way before Johnny Cash's famous hit!

Weston died April 1, 1980, and Grace died November 8th, 1982, both were buried at Hatcher Cemetery in Portland, Florida.

We are honored for our parents to be part of our county's heritage. To their descendants who may read this in the future who never knew them, in the words of Grace herself, she would say..."be proud, you come from good stock!"

To read more of this family and it's history... you are invited to visit the Thomason website at http://thomason6.tripod.com/ThomFam.html
Submitted by: Jo Thomason Manis, 1057 Oak Avenue, Panama City, FL 32401.

Weston Thomason

Weston Thomason and his first-born son, Ronald Weston, May 1934, taken at Pensacola, FL. The lady on the left was their neighbor who was from England...She was scheduled to have come to America on the Titanic, but missed the boat.
Submitted by Edna Capri, 1057 Oak Avenue, Panama City, FL 32401.

Weston and Ronald Weston Thomason

John Sellers Thompson 1908-1987 & Louise Spencer Thompson 1909-2002

His parents wanted him to sell shoes but John Sellars Thompson had other plans. The new fangled invention called the radio held a fascination for him and after building his own crystal set as a teenager, he knew others would be buying and using radios in their homes.

Growing up in Hartford, Alabama, he spent time as a young man just south of Troy where he met and married Louise Spencer in 1931. They decided to move to Panama City where the population was growing and there would be a market for radios. He worked selling and delivering furniture for Clark Chavers, but was given a small room in the Harrison Avenue store where he could repair radios.

Soon he ventured into his own shop in the Tennessee House next to the Ritz Theatre and during W.W.II, John would rise at 3-4 AM to work on repairs and then spend normal store hours waiting on customers.

In the mid forties, John and Louise bought the buildings at 6-10 East 4th Street and opened Thompson Appliance, one of the few places residents could buy radios, refrigerators, stoves, small appliances and records. Many long time residents remember the small booths with glass doors where they could listen to 78's and in later years, 45 RPM records. Thompson Tune Time, a popular radio show broadcasted the latest records with the added bonus of a Mystery Tune with a prize jackpot of silver dollars that increased a dollar a day. Some of the jackpots ran well over $100.

Recording artists Eddie Arnold and Andy Griffith, who had a comedy hit, made personal appearances at Thompson's.

When WDSU- TV New Orleans began broadcasting in the early 1950's, John put an antenna on top of the Dixie Sherman Hotel and placed a television set in a room on the top floor. Several locals had their first glimpse of television in the roof garden room.
Submitted by: Anita Thompson Segler, 2508 Pretty Bayou Island Drive, Panama City, FL 32405.

The Tibbits Family

I arrived in Bay County in the mid 1960's with my wife Nellie Albritton Tibbits and children William Terence, Valarie, Polly and Lottie. The other three were married. We were almost broke, leaving Bonifay Florida where I couldn't make a living. I am an electrician but learned to do plumbing so I could work.

It is amazing how this county has grown. Use to be a lot of open spaces.

We bought houses in Southport, Lynn Haven, and finally in Fountain where I am still living. While at Bear Creek we would go boating. My beautiful little white fluffy dog was

Nellie Mae Albritton Tibbits, Lottie, Polly, Valarie, William Terrence

swimming along side when he just disappeared. I really loved my little dog. An alligator had eaten my little dog. One minute he was there and the next he was gone. People would come by on their boats never suspecting that alligators were under that surface just waiting for their turn to get food. I would watch those gators and remember my dogs.

Nellie died of Leukemia in May of 1999 and I thought my life would end. How could I go on? We were married for 58 years and I was so lonely and life was meaningless. I still had me some horses, dog and a cat but I needed more. I have a wonderful new wife who lost her husband to cancer named Betty Dowell Lynch. We got married right here in Bay County at the courthouse. We are living in Fountain were the air is clean. Our children visiting when they can and enjoying life again. You see life still goes on and when I die I will be buried next to Nellie here in Fountain but for now I am an 82 year old man loving life.

I owned my own plumbing business until I retired and now my son Tim has taken over. I am a WWII Veteran serving overseas and just love Bay County Florida.
Submitted by: William Elphanso (Tim) Tibbits, 10936 Nonawood Road, Fountain, Florida 32438.

Lotti Tibbits Calhoun

I am Lottie Tibbits Calhoun. I came to Bay County when I was only in the fifth grade. How I hated school. Why would anyone want to learn all that mess? I finally just quit. Little did I know that I would regret that decision the

Lottie and William Calhoun"Billy," her son

rest of my life. I have tried many jobs including bartending, construction and plumbing. I had a wonderful foolproof way to get rich. With my Uncle Robert Tibbits money, I opened The Education Plus Video rentals. With all the home schooled children I just knew it would be a go. I had hundreds of educational tapes waiting to be rented. With the proper education and marketing skills, I believe I could have made a lot of money instead of going under. So all you young people please stay in school and get a good education, you will need it in the real world to make a living. Without the financial help from my parents I could never have raised my son Billy as we called him by myself.

I met and married my husband William Calhoun here on the beach. He was an Air Force man stationed at Tyndall. Our son William was born there on the base. We are divorced now. Billy turned out just fine. He finished college with a degree in engineering and business, and married his high school sweetheart Daye Allen from Bay Pointe. They have two wonderful children Caden and Cassis. I love my family.

I had the pleasure of having an ordained preacher for a mother, Reverend Nellie Tibbits. I got to visit many churches and met many people in my lifetime. I wish I had listened more to her preaching. She preached fire and brim stone. She played the accordion and piano by ear. She never took a lesson. She had her own church in Bayou George.

I feel blessed to have been able to live in Bay County and hope to live out my life here and be buried next to my mother in Fountain.

Submitted by: Lottie Tibbits, 21234 Hightower Road, Fountain, Florida 32438.

Tim Tibbits

I Tim Tibbits moved here to Bay County in 1961. I was working for a tree surgeon, I married Vivian Williams and had Timothy and Melanie both born here. I have worked with the cable company. Now I own a plumbing business. I have put the plumbing in a lot of the homes and businesses here.

I enjoy scuba diving. You would be amazed at all the beautiful fish under the sea. I have spent many hours exploring the sea. I also love to fish. I owned my own boat for a time and you would find me on the water most weekends. Now I just enjoy my grandchildren Brittany and Michael Austin. I try to take them to see their grandpa Tibbits on Sunday morning. I wish you could see

Tim Tibbits, Vivian Williams Tibbits, Melanie Tibbits, Timothy Tibbits

the two of them running along side the fence and dads little horse running on the other. He seems to enjoy running with them. He has a bad habit of biting, so you don't want to place your hands inside the fence. Brittany fell down but just got right back up and started running again. They are being home schooled by their mother. They have a play station and school video's that help them to learn. Everything is so complicated now, not just adding and subtracting but computers.

264

I guess they will have to use that thing by themselves. I just do not want to tackle it the computer I mean.

Now I am still working, but one day when I retire, maybe you will see me back in the gulf scuba diving

Vivian and I are divorced but are still friends. We have our children and grandchildren to share. We lived on 7th treet behind the Bay Medical Center and Vivian still lives there.
Submitted by Tim Elphanso Tibbits, 5802 Bayfront Drive, Panama City, Florida 32404.

The Tibbits – Grant Family

It was June of 1989 when I woke up coughing and having a hard time breathing. After months of treatment the doctors gave up and said I would have to learn to live like this and to move to the beach. So we sold our eighty acre layer house farm in Holmes County and moved to 17627 Front

Beach Road buying a gulf front townhouse. It was so beautiful and peaceful. I had always wanted to live on the beach. We would watch the dolphins playing and jumping as high as they could, playing like little children. It seems unreal that we were living on this beautiful white sands. At first I was able to go outside and even take long walks while watching the wonderful sunsets. Many little birds which came out of sand dollars. where found on the beach.

Reverend Nellie Tibbits, my mother, would try to come on Sundays and visit as often as she could. My sisters Nelda Deuerling and Valarie Zion came when they could and dad,

Sharon Tibbits Grant and William Elphanso Tibbits

Tim Tibbits. My children Marianne, Nathan and Gary came as often as they could. Marianne would leave Nicole Johnson my granddaughter to visit. Nikki would spend a lot of time just splashing in the gulf. One day she came crying that a jelly fish had stung her and boy did it hurt, yes they do hurt. Several times we would see people falling off jet skis. You have to be careful on those things. Most of the time it was just beautiful seeing all those people having fun.

My husband Leaon was driving to work nights at Fort Rucker Alabama. He was so tired. You see when you really love some one you can and will do anything it takes to be with your spouse. We met some wonderful people Melba Mackin, Dana Hicks and Betty Kniezal to name a few. But after a short time I could no longer go outside and it was just to depressing to live there. You see I have environmental illness, allergic to the world including the outside air and any odors. I will never forget the wonderful time spent on the beautiful beach here in Panama City Beach. We lived there from March 1990 until December 1991.
Written by: Sharon Tibbits Grant, 4119 Charles Circle, Pace, Florida 32571.

The Tiller and Ware Family
Growing Up on St. Andrews Bay

When you have grown up on St. Andrews Bay it is very hard to move away. I do not live in St. Andrews anymore, but I have to see the bay almost every day. I drive by the place where I grew up and to the St. Andrews Marina to look at the bay. My name is Jo Dell Tiller Breland and I am now taking my 4 grandchildren (Garrett Breland 6, Sarah Breland 6, Peyton Breland 3, and Abbigayle Breland 2) with me and sharing my childhood memories with them.

My Uncle Curtis and Aunt Pearl Ware's home was on St. Andrews Bay at 803 Drake Avenue in St. Andrews. Their son Newton and his wife, Mildred, along with Aunt Pearl's sister, Kina Newman also lived in their home. It was a big two-story house with lots of rooms, big kitchen with lots of good cooking always going on, porches with swings where we all sat and listened to lots of stories about their younger years. It was a place where a child would listen to these stories and never forget them. Aunt Pearl and Aunt Kina were sisters of my Grandfather, Rev. Hansel L. Ellis, of Southport, Florida. He was my Mother's father. They visited there often while my mother was growing up.

My Mother (Elzie Ellis Tiller) and Father (Elwood Tiller) were both born in Southport. After they were married they rented a house from Uncle Curtis located on the property where he and Aunt Pearl lived. This is where I was born (1939). So I began my growing up years in the midst of all my wonderful relatives and St. Andrews Bay.

Curtis and Pearl Ware

Uncle Curtis was the owner and Capt. of a charter boat. In my Baby Book my Mother recorded that she took me on my first deep-sea fishing trip with Uncle Curtis when I was one month old. The book says I slept the whole day!! Uncle Curtis was always bringing home some of the "catch of the day" and would throw them up on the fish-cleaning table in the back yard. They were available for family members; of course my Mother always got there first. We had the very best of seafood, which consisted of fish, scallops, crabs and oysters. We all cooked and ate together quite often. When it was mealtime I went to their house to see what they were cooking and most of the time I would eat with them. My Aunts were such wonderful cooks. They had a pantry that always had molasses cookies in a big cookie jar. Of course I was always helping myself to these delicious cookies.

The year after I was born, a new cousin came along for me to play with and boss around. He was named Sandy Ware. He was born to Newton and Mildred Ware. We became best friends. When we were small, I pushed him around in my doll buggy, I don't think he was having fun because he looks very unhappy in the photos. We did quite a few things together which got us in trouble, things that he instigated, of course. He talked me into helping him fill up his Daddy's car with gas, but instead of gas, it was sand! I held the bucket, but Sandy "pumped the gas". We got in big trouble for this. We spent most every day playing on the

Sandy and Jo Dell going fishing and crabbing

beach, swimming in the bay and catching crabs. We had a tire swing in the big oak tree down by the bay that we stayed in a lot. I loved all my family that lived there; they were a big part of my growing up. We were like one big family!

In 1945, I started first grade at St. Andrews School. Miss Bessie Bowen was my teacher; I liked her very much. During this year my Mother and Daddy gave me a little sister. Her name is Cornelia Tiller Scruggs, but called "Trig", a nickname I gave her when she was born. I thought she was as pretty as Roy Roger's horse! She has never forgiven me for this. Sandy got a little brother in 1947. His name was Mike Ware.

My Daddy decided it was time to buy a house. He wanted to "get out of town" so he bought a house in Lynn Haven on Kentucky Avenue and we moved there the year I started second grade. It was a beautiful home and there were very few houses on Kentucky Avenue at that time. This became home

to me and I continued growing up in another wonderful place. I lived in Lynn Haven for thirty-one years and am proud to have been called a "Lynn Haven girl". Sonny Breland and I were married in 1959 and had two sons, Bill and Steve, while living there. St. Andrews was still a big part of my life and we continued to visit my family there at least once a week.

I would like to tell you a story about my Mother who was born in 1908. When she was fifteen years old she was very sick with a ruptured appendix. Her Mother, Dell Ellis, was also very sick at this time and near death from complications of childbirth. The doctors did not think either one of them were going to live. Dr. D.M. Adams came to their house and told my Grandfather they might be able to save my Mother's life if she could be taken to the Ware home in St. Andrews where he would operate on her. He said she could not be carried by car because of the rough roads. He suggested that they move her by boat. So my family prepared Mother for this trip, hoping she would be alive when they got there. She was carried from their house on a homemade stretcher to the bay near my Grandfather's house. She was put on a boat and rowed very carefully to Uncle Curtis and Aunt Pearl's home. The big kitchen table was prepared for the operating table. Everything in the kitchen was sterilized as clean as possible. She was operated on and her life saved.

She was very sick for a long time and had to stay there. When she was well enough she began to ask about her Mother and why she hadn't come to see her. She did not realize her Mother was near death when she left home. Dr. Adams had advised the family that my Mother

JoDell and Sandy going for a ride

could not be told about her death because he felt it would hinder her recovery. When she was well enough my Grandfather came to tell her. It took the Doctor and three relatives to hold Mother on the bed when she was told her mother had died the same day she had been brought by boat to St. Andrews. She cried for weeks and my Grandfather felt she was not able to go home. He left her at Uncle Curtis and Aunt Pearl's for a lengthy time to recover. My Mother told me this story so many times and each time my heart ached for her. After this, my Mother visited quite often with Aunt Pearl and Aunt Kina. They became like a Mother to her. This is another reason their home and St. Andrews Bay has been so special to our family.

This property was sold in 1991 when Newton and Mildred Ware were no longer able to keep it up, but I still rode down that way every chance I had. I felt like the place was still mine even though it belonged to someone else. All of these relatives I have told you about have passed away except Newton Ware (age 93) and Sandy Ware, who still lives in St. Andrews.

In May of this year (2003), I decided to make a trip to St. Andrews to look at the bay and ride by my childhood home. When I drove up to the property all the houses were gone except the one I had lived in and it was in the process of being torn down. I was in a state of shock. I drove on the property and asked a man nearby what was happening there. He told me the property had been sold again and a new home was going to be built. I sat there and cried, my heart was broken. I finally decided I might as well realize that this property was no longer mine. I went home and got my husband and we went back for me to walk through our house one more time before it was demolished, each room bringing back such wonderful memories. We walked the property and followed the sidewalk that took us to the spot where the big house stood in which my Ware relatives lived and I shed more tears. We walked down toward the beach and my husband made my picture by the big oak tree, which the swing was in that Sandy and I enjoyed so much as children. My mind was flooded with memories of our families sitting in lawn chairs and looking out over beautiful St. Andrews Bay. I'm thankful for all the photos that my Mother made while we lived there. I look at the photos often and relive my childhood at this wonderful place.

I inquired around and found that the Scott Clemons family are the new owners of this property and are building a beautiful home there. I ride by often to see how their new home is coming along. I wish their family happiness and wonderful times living on this beautiful piece of property and enjoying lazy afternoons looking out over the bay. Maybe one day their children will write an article about their memories of this special place and their good times on St. Andrews Bay. Even though it now belongs to a new family, this beautiful place will be a part of me until the day I die. I will continue to ride by and reminisce because "my car automatically goes that way"!!
Submitted by: Jo Dell Tiller Breland, 902 Huntingdon Road, Panama City, FL 32405.

Lillie Tindell and Arthur Elzy Hood

My name is Arleen Gill. My great-grandparents lived in Washington County, in the part that became Bay County in 1913, during the late 1800's. They were some of the first settlers in Bay County. My great-grandmother Lillie Tindell was born 1877 in Geneva County, Alabama. She was the daughter of James Jeremiah Tindell and Amanda (A. E.) Powell. Jeremiah was a school teacher and a farmer. He taught school at Mt. Gilead Church. The church was also the school at that time. The Tindells owned farm land and a home site near the Church. Amanda was the daughter of John and Mary Powell. Lillie married Arthur Elzy Hood, the son of Daniel Stone Hood and Eliza Jane Jernigan. Daniel was a school teacher, a surveyor, and a farmer. He owned many acres of land in Dale County Alabama. Daniel and Eliza had thirteen children. My great-grandfather Elzy Hood (1861-1921) was the

Grandmother Mamie Lee Gill, Harrison Avenue 1942 – USO Building

last child to be born. My grandmother Mamie Lee Hood was born 1897 in Washington County, Florida. She died in 1978 and sleeps in Evergreen Memorial Cemetery beside her daughter Francis Gill Kind (1921-2000) and my uncle Harold E. Pitts (1924-1995). I never knew my grandfather Arthur Mack Gill (born 1884). He died before I was born. I am the daughter of Arthur Lee Gill and Verna E. Trahan (1928-1999). My father grew up in Old St. Andrews. He has many good memories of the beautiful old Bay. My mother was the daughter of Acar and Neola Trahan of Caplan, Louisiana. Both are deceased. I lived in old St Andrews for a while. I married Regan Curry. We have two sons Steven W. and Kevin W., and a daughter Lisa

Mamie Lee Gill and first granddaughter Annette Moates

Rene'. Steven is married to Angie and has two sons, Ben and Joshua. My brother Gary is married and has two sons, Matthew and Jackson Gill. I have many good memories of my loved ones.
Submitted by: Arleen Curry, 2420 Riverfront Drive, Little Rock, Arkansas

72202. Written by: Bea Moates, 764 Roland Road, Chipley, Florida 32428. Sources: Census, cemetery, courthouse, personal knowledge.

Winton Frederick Turner

My name is Winton Frederick Turner, born April 17, 1922, in Millville, Florida, the last and ninth child of Wilburn Frances Turner and Saphronia Elizabeth Thomley Turner. My brothers and sisters were:

Ola Mae Turner, b. June 6, 1898 d. November 10, 1910, James Henry Turner, b. October 1898 d. February, 1975, Verlie Irene Turner, b. November 14, 1902 d. November 8, 1964, Connie Ethelyne Turner, b. July 22, 1905 d. 1989, Howard Shelton Turner, b. October 5, 1904 d. May 1985, Lois Lucille Turner, b. September 21,1910 d. Oct. 7, 1997, Alma Luverne Turner, b. January 24, 1914 d. February 1999, Wallace Nelson Turner, b.

Fred Turner

June 10, 1917 d. May 25, 1992. My Grandparents were: James Marion Turner and wife, Sarah Elizabeth Collins Turner. My Great Grandparents were Beloved and Mary Turner. All my Great Grand/Grand parents are buried in Alabama. My parents were born in Wicksberg, Alabama in 1877 and came from farming families. My father attended Alabama Normal School in Troy, Alabama about 1894 for 2 years and attained a teaching certificate and returned to Wicksberg and taught in a one-room schoolhouse where he met and fell in love with one of his students, my mother. They were married at the home of the bride. Aunt Lovie (my father's sister) "made Fronie's dress and stood with them" during the ceremony. My mother had a 5th grade education but I never heard her complain about "under-educated". She once said to me: "I almost refused to marry Will Turner because he couldn't dance a step!!" She loved country music (from WSM in particular) and she would dance to the radio music in our home. She personified a home life filled with music, gaiety and dancing.

After finishing High School (Bay Hi) in 1940. I enlisted in U. S. Army Air Force October 4, 1940 and afterward attended Officer Candidate School in Miami, Florida graduating August 5, 1942 with the rank of Second Lieutenant. On September 24, 1942, I joined 308th Bomb Group (H) In March, 1943, I escorted the group equipment to Calcutta, India, and then on "over the Hump" to China. I was assign Asst. S-4 in the Group and was the youngest Staff Officer in the Air Force. We were the most accurate Bomb group in the Air Force in World War II and suf-

Lucille Newberry, Fred Turner and Alma Harmon

fered the highest casualties. We also had the only Medal of Honor winner, Major Horace "Stump" Carswell, 374th . Bomb Squadron. Carswell Air Force Base, Texas named in his honor. I served in China in 1943, 44 and 1945.

Chabua, Assam, India was our jumping-off point from India to China and we established a rear base there. We changed engines in our combat planes every 100 hours there and I threw a party for our enlisted men. The Army had a field hospital there but the nurses (officers) were not to fraternize with the enlisted personnel so I made a special request that the nurses attend and Asst Chief Nurse Spangenberger granted permission. I was on the microphone to announce an early departure to China and one nurse, Helen Wood, asked her dancing partner, "Who is that conceited Lieutenant at the mike?" After we both came stateside in 1945, I married Helen Wood on December 24, 1945, at Lincolnton, North Carolina, in the same church that her Grandmother was married in. We have three children: Drucie, who just completed her Master Degree at FSU in Tallahassee; Martha, who married Dr. Dewey Barton, a Radiologist, graduated from Duke University and Fred Turner, Jr., who is a pilot for and part of management of Flex-Jet, Dallas, Texas. Martha has two sons: John a freshman at Duke (PBK) and Andrew, not yet out of High School and Freddie's Ryan, a high school junior at Concord, NC.

Submitted by: Fred Turner, 2694 Island View Dr., Panama City, FL 32405.

Wilburn Francis Turner and Saphronia Elizabeth Turner

This short narrative is about the Wilburn Francis (Will) and Saphronia Elizabeth (Aunt Frony) Turner family who were among the early settlers of Millville. My grandfather, in search of a better life for his family, moved them from Alabama in 1917.

There were four brothers and four sisters, as well as an older sister who had died at the age of twelve. All of the children except the youngest (Circuit Judge W. Fred Turner) were born in Alabama. The four girls all married local boys. The boys looked elsewhere and found wives who added to the diversity and closeness of the Turner family.

My grandfather took advantage of the growing community and used his skills as a carpenter and a painter to provide for his family. He was also an avid gardener and there was always an abundance of food on the table. Next to his family and church (where he served as moderator and deacon), he took a special interest in politics—local, national, and international. In addition to a subscription to the local newspaper, he also received regular editions of the *Congressional Record.* He never missed an opportunity such as holidays and elections days to fly the flag and was elected Mayor of Millville.

My grandmother, an excellent cook, was a very bright woman who had a common sense approach to every problem. She used her talent as a quilt maker to provide coverlets for each of her children and grandchildren. On several occasions she was the blue ribbon champion quilter at the county fair. She always counted her blessings. She would say, "I have 31 grandchildren," (or more as time went on). She made sure that each and every child and grandchild felt special. She was never too busy to bake her special

Wilburn Francis and Saphronia Elizabeth Turner (A trip to the beach, circa 1935)

"tea cakes" for the family. She especially enjoyed talking to the many passers-by who lingered at the corner of Center Avenue and Second Plaza.

My mother was Lucille Turner. She was six years old when the family moved here in 1917. She married my father, her high school sweetheart and outstandng Bay High School athlete, Ralph "Huck" Newberry, in 1930. Their union produced four daughters and one son, of which I am the oldest.

My fondest memories are of the halcyon days spent playing in the neighborhood with other children, which are best described by the words in the old song, "Those Were The Days, My Friend."

Submitted by: Judy (Newberry) Nobles Cleghorn, 6008 Boat Race Road, Panama City, Florida 32404.

Will Turner and Saphronia Thomley Turner
Part I - First Things First

My grandparents, Will and Saphronia Turner came to Millville from Alabama in 1917. Will Turner was one of the

FIRST mayors of Millville, and according to my uncle, Circuit Judge W. Fred Turner, they had the *FIRST* telephone in Millville.

Bay County was formed the *FIRST* of July, 1913, from Calhoun and Washington Counties, and on July 24, 1913, my Dad, Harold (Dusty) Harmon, Sr. was the *FIRST* child born in Bay County, in a small house on Sherman Ave. just S. of 3rd Street in Millville. He married his Bay High School sweetheart, Alma Turner Harmon in 1934. They had 4 children, Virginia, who died at age 5 months in 1936, Emily H. Busby, (1937-1998), Shirley H. Brookins, (1940) and Harold Harmon, Jr. (1948).

We lived in Millville until 1950, when we moved to the Cove. We all attended local schools, and graduated from Bay High School. Mother was one of the *FIRST* to receive a teaching certificate from Bob Jones College, located in Panama City in the 1930's which is now College Point, and taught elementary school for several years. My dad was an electrician at the Paper Mill until his retirement in 1975. We were members of Immanuel Baptist Church in Millville.

I married my Bay High School sweetheart, Harold Brookins, who was the *FIRST* person to receive the Sam B. Hearn Academic Scholarship to Gulf Coast College, in 1957, due to being in the top fifteen when graduating from Bay High. He also was the *FIRST* person to graduate from

Harold and Shirley Brookins

Gulf Coast College in 1959, and was elected the *FIRST* head of Student Government. He was the *FIRST* president of the Student Christian Union and Vice President of the *FIRST* Phi Theta Kappa Honor Society. Our daughter was later President of this Society while attending Gulf Coast College in 1987.

Harold worked at Arizona Chemical until his retirement in 2002, having worked 43 years without missing a scheduled day of work. We were married in 1960 and have three children, Holly B. Dorr (1968) and twin sons, Jason and Jon (1970). Holly was the *FIRST* person from Bay County to give birth to quadruplets! Our quadruplet grandchildren are the *FIRST* quads in Bay County – two boys and two girls, perfect and healthy, born July 12, 2002. We now have a total of eight grandchildren, and we are now active members of *FIRST* Baptist Church, downtown Panama City.

What a wonderful life.

Submitted by: Shirley Harmon Brookins, 136 Cottonwood Circle, Lynn Haven, FL 32444.

Will Turner and Saphronia Thomley Turner
Part II - Bay County's FIRST Quadruplets

Four tiny babies, two girls and two boys, were born to Holly and Russ Dorr of Lynn Haven, on July 12, 2002 at Sacred Heart Hospital in Pensacola FL. The babies were perfect and in good health, despite low birth weights, ranging from 2 pounds 5 ounces to 3 pounds 7 ounces. The babies had reached normal weights and development by their 1st birthday

The Dorr Quads – 1 yr. old (July 12, 2003), Children of Holly and Russ Dorr, L to R – Brooke, Jacob, William & Sarah Faith

Submitted by: Holly (Brookins) Dorr, 321

Joseph Manning Vickers, Sr. and Ila Mae Scott Vickers Family
Part I – The Early Years

Our Mother's maiden name was Ila Mae Scott. Our Father was Joseph Manning Vickers. Our Mother's family came from north Georgia by way of Georgiana, Alabama, to the Geneva County, Alabama, area about the time of the Civil War. Our Father's family came from north Georgia by way of

Ila Mae Scott Vickers 1949

Henry County, Alabama, to Geneva County, Alabama about the same time. They met and married in December 1908 in New Hope, FL. About 1913 they moved to the newly formed Bay County, Florida, and settled in West Bay. They had two small children at that time, Vera and Fred. About the time of World War I the family moved to Lynn Haven. By then there were two more children, Mary Lou and Beatrice. While in Lynn Haven three more children were born, Joseph, Jr.; Edith; and Jo Ellen.

Prior to the family's move from New Hope to the West Bay area, our Mother's Father owned a large timber, lumber, and logging operation in New Hope. It was very hard work with a lot of responsibility and his health was bad. He decided to sell his business and move to Bay County. Our family decided to move also, as our Father was a partner and employee in that business. Grandfather Scott's health continued to fail and he felt he needed to move nearer to where there were doctors. He sold some timber and the small mill operation in West Bay and moved to Lynn Haven, where our family moved also.

Our Father and Grandfather went in together in the operation of the ferry from Lynn Haven to Grassy Point in Southport. We lived on Ohio Avenue which was near the ferry. There was a signal flag used to indicate that cars were waiting on the Southport side of the bay. There was no bridge from Lynn Haven to Southport, so the only way to travel north of Lynn Haven was by the ferry. The operation of the ferry was by demand so they had to watch for the signal. There was no scheduled time for ferry operation.

The children would ask their Father or Grandfather if they could ride the ferry with them. If there were four cars to be transported, there was no room, but if only one or two cars were to make the trip, they could go. They were instructed as to where they could sit and that they were not to go near the edge. Sometimes they could fish during the trip. These were happy times for the Vickers children.
Submitted and written by: Jo Ellen Vickers Mitchell, 1515 Country Club Drive, Lynn Haven, FL

Joseph Manning Vickeers, Sr. and Ila Mae Scott Vickers Family
Part II – The Homestead At The Beach

In 1925 our Father was a deputy sheriff and through contacts at the court house got the information that citizens could apply to stake a claim for a homestead. He put our name in the box for the drawing to select those who could stake a claim and we were fortunate to have our name drawn. The property was located about 1 1/2 miles east of the intersection of Highway 79 and what is now Front Beach Road. When school was out in May 1925 the family moved to the site. Our Father had already gone out with a crew of helpers to start the house. It was not completed, but enough was finished so we could move into it.

We had to immediately begin fulfilling the requirements,

meaning that 15 acres must be fenced during the first quarter; cultivation had to begin on a prescribed number of acres.

Joseph Manning Vickers, Sr. 1949

An inspector came each month to see if crops planted met the standard. The first year was very difficult, but once we got everything fenced and crops began to bear, things became a little easier. We rotated crops, as we always had to have something growing for food. This requirement was necessary so people would not just go to the homestead site and wait out their time of occupancy, not actually making it a homestead. A homestead was just that—a place that could support you and your family. We planted corn, beans, peas, okra, and tomatoes. Mother experimented to find those crops most suitable for the soil and conditions.

We had about three acres in watermelons. Every morning about 10 o'clock Mother hit the dishpan with a spoon signaling "watermelon time." The melons were kept in water overnight, keeping them cool because there was no electricity or ice. We also had to have livestock. Mother was determined that we were going to have milk, so we always had a cow for milking and also a couple of heifers. In addition we had hogs, chickens, dogs, and a horse that our Father rode.

Our Father took a job inspecting turpentine trees to see that they were not over-cut. There was a regulation to prevent over-cutting. Next, he got a job surveying all the cattle in the area, as the entire state of Florida had a problem with ticks on cattle. He had to see that all cattle were brought in for dipping in vats to eradicate the ticks. This called for three dips and after one summer the problem was solved, so that job ended. As there were not enough jobs in the homestead area to allow him to make enough money to support his family, he moved back into town to work again as deputy sheriff. He traveled back and brought provisions for his family as often as possible, but sometimes it was a month between trips. The family looked forward to those days when he drove up with the car loaded with provisions.
Submitted by Mildred Vickers Nauman, 2439 Flower Avenue, Panama City, FL; Written by Jo Ellen Vickers Mitchell.

Joseph Manning Vickers, Sr. and Ila Mae Scott Vickers Family
Part III – Life At The Homestead

While establishing the homestead, daughter Mildred was born. The schoolage children, Fred, Mary Lou, Beatrice, and Joseph, Jr. were attending school in West Bay and it was

Fred's job to drive them to school. In those days there was no age restriction and you didn't even have to take a driving test. If you had a vehicle, gas to put in it, and someone who could handle it, that was their job. There were no roads, just trails through the woods. In sandy areas he'd

1988 Vickers Family Reunion

get stuck in the sand and all would get out and get limbs and palmetto fronds to get unstuck. While going through cypress thickets the car would get mired in mud. Even though the distance from homestead to school was only about five miles, we had to leave very early because sometimes it took over an hour to get there. The second year Fred had finished the 8th grade which was the highest grade offered at the West Bay School. He would then take the rest of us to school, drive to West Bay and work at Uncle John Rodgers general merchandise store, pick us up after school and drive home.

Mary Lou tells the story that one day an alligator jumped out of the lake on the homestead property and grabbed our favorite dog. We had dogs for watch dogs and for hunting. The dog he grabbed was our favorite because he was so obedient and intelligent. He may have been wading in the lake when the gator jumped him and started ripping him to pieces. We heard him barking, knew he was in distress, and ran to check on him. We threw rocks, sticks, and anything else we could find to get the gator to turn him loose. He finally let him go. We took him to the house. Mother made him a pallet in the kitchen and we nursed him back to health.

In nice weather in the afternoon after finishing our chores, Mother would let us walk over the dunes to the Gulf and wade. Since Fred was the only child who could swim, Mother told the rest of us we could only get knee deep until we learned to swim. We'd ask how we could learn to swim in knee deep water. Anyhow, she let us wade and we had a lot of fun.

Submitted by Margaret Vickers Jencks, 3110 Country Club Drive, Lynn Haven, FL; Written by: Margaret Vickers Jencks.

The Joseph Manning Vickers, Sr. Descendents
Part I – More About Life At The Homestead

Beatrice related the incident when one day we took a picnic over to the Gulf so we could build a fire on the beach and cook, if you can imagine that. It got dark while we were there so we built our fire. Mary Lou saw what she thought was a log, so she walked over and sat on it. Well, it was that gator!! He had gotten out of the lake and followed us over to the beach. We didn't know what his intentions were—whether to get some of our food or get one of us. When she sat on him he raised up and ran back to the lake.

Other times when we were doing our chores, we'd take a break at a place set aside under the trees. This was our place to play, yell, or get involved in noisy games where we couldn't disturb anybody. We would play baseball, hopscotch, hide and go seek, and other games that were our favorites. Then, we'd read or tell stories, staying a little quieter so Mother could rest and nap if she wished.

Our Mother was a nature lover. She'd point out birds or animals she saw and we'd get the bird book or encyclopedia and identify them. All of us developed an insatiable desire to learn more about nature and the world around us, as well as other subjects.

Another thing we enjoyed after our evening meal was to sit on the porch facing the Gulf and watch the gorgeous sunsets.

After completing the homestead requirements and qualifying for the deed to the property, the family moved back to Panama City so the older children could attend high school. Vera, the oldest daughter lived in Panama City instead of on the homestead because she was attending Bay High School. She graduated in Bay High School's first graduation class. As the Vickers children grew up, all eleven of them graduated from Bay High School.

Submitted by: John Ellis Vickers, 3020 Country Club Drive, Lynn Haven, FL; Written by: John Ellis Vickers.

The Joseph Manning Vickers, Sr. Descendents
Part II – Back In Panama City

Our Father hired a tutor to bring Fred, Mary Lou, and Beatrice up to the level of Panama City schools. Her name was Mrs. Bray. She lived about a block west of the Bay County Court House. She tutored Mary Lou and Beatrice in the morning and Fred in the afternoon. She must have done a good job because we had no problem keeping up our grades or taking any courses we wanted. There were no scholastic restrictions on us and Mrs. Bray probably saved our education. Some children we knew got behind in learning and were never able to catch up on their own. Our parents always emphasized education, and hiring a tutor was a very wise move.

Our Father was in law enforcement and we lived on West 11th Street near groves of persimmons, oranges, and other fruits. These orchards were started by people who moved from the north who eventually lost all their crops to the cold weather.

From there we moved to a house on West 13th Street, across from Bay High School. After Vera graduated from Bay High she went to work for Southern Bell Telephone Company. Following this move back from the homestead to Panama City, daughter Margaret, son John, and daughter Shirley were born.

In 1929 the United States entered the depression, which affected everyone in the country. Fred got a job at International Paper Company which was under construction. The job was to remove the old, rotted pilings from beneath the former German-American Company docks so new docks for the paper mill could be built on the same site. Fred worked as a "hard hat" diver. He was to dive and tie cable to the rotted pilings about 30 feet down so they could be brought up with a crane. For that he received 25 cents per piling.

Later he worked on construction of both the DuPont and the Hathaway Bridges. As he helped paint the underside of the DuPont Bridge, he would tie a baited line onto his toe and drop the line into the water so he could fish while he was painting. That way, along with the little he was paid, he could get some food for the family. Fred told of the time he was fishing this way. He had his line over and caught about a six foot shark. Before he could let go of his paint brush and paint bucket to get a hand on his line, the shark had almost pulled his toe off!

Very few people had a job during the depression and it was a struggle to keep food on the table and clothes to wear, especially in such a large family. Everyone learned to conserve resources and do without anything except the bare necessities.

Submitted by: Shirley Vickers Snead, 735 E. Tugalo Street, Toccoa, GA; Written by: Margaret Vickers Jencks

The Joseph Manning Vickers, Sr. Descendents
Part III – The World War II Era

The depression years led into the WW II era, which brought tremendous growth to the Panama City area. During this time many changes took place in the Vickers family. Jo Ellen, while a senior in Bay High School, took a test, passed it, and was hired as a secretary at Tyndall Field, going to work upon graduation. Our Father went to work at Wainwright Shipyard, Edith started working at Tyndall Field, and Mildred worked at the shipyard between her junior and senior years at Bay High.

During the war four of the Vickers daughters met and married men who were stationed at Tyndall Field. Beatrice married Anthony Picciano; Edith married Donald MacLaren who was killed during the war (she later married Bert Rhyne); Jo Ellen married Robert Mitchell; and Mildred married William Nauman. Fred served in the National Guard and Joseph, Jr. was career Air Force.

Many people came from Alabama, Georgia, and other parts of the United States to work in defense related jobs. Significant numbers of them lived in housing built for them while working at Tyndall Field and the shipyard. One site is now Gulf Coast Community College and the Florida State University/PC campus.

In the early 1940's Gen. Patton's division came from Ft. Benning, GA, to Panama City for their summer bivouac. Soldiers (25,000 to 30,000) set up tents in the vicinity of

Oakland Terrace. At that time that area was entirely vacant, but later during the war numerous small brick houses were built that still stand today.

There were not many cars then and gas was rationed, so buses were utilized for transportation. Panama City was very busy, congested, and in many ways made an important contribution to the war effort. Following the war the economy improved significantly and continued to grow.

The three children born after the family moved from the homestead to Panama City were Margaret, John, and Shirley. John entered FSU in 1948 where Margaret was already a student. This was right after the college converted from a women's college to co-ed to accommodate the thousands of men who had been in the service and wanted to take advantage of the GI Bill. John was the first in the family to graduate from college. However, several furthered their education by taking college level courses. Margaret was at FSU about two years, but met Guy Jencks and they married before she graduated. The youngest, Shirley, met Robert Snead, Music Minister at St. Andrew Baptist Church, and soon after she graduated from Bay High School in 1953, they were married.

In spite of the challenges of raising eleven children during difficult times, Joseph Manning Vickers, Sr. and Ila Mae Scott Vickers taught their children dedication to a work ethic and strong family values that have remained with them. The have always been a loving, close-knit family.
Submitted by: Mrs. Joseph Manning Vickers, Jr. (Ginger), 1406 West 13th Street, Panama City, FL; Written by John Ellis Vickers.

George and Carol Vickery

The most frequently asked question I hear when introduced to a person in Bay County is: "Are you related to Henry Vickery. "No," I say, "not that I know of." I was born in New Orleans in 1942. My father, Dr. George W. Vickery, was born in Hartwell, Georgia in 1911. He was a Urologist who served in WWII and practiced in New Orleans and Gulfport, Mississippi. We trace our forebears to one Joseph Vickery, and as a result of that connection I am a member of the Sons of the Revolution (SAR).

I came to Bay County in 1985 to serve as the Director of the Bay County Public Library and of the Northwest Regional Library System. I like to think that my interest in libraries was preordained. I say that because I know that people have an extraordinary influence on others. Psychologists explain it as the *Self-Fulling Prophecy* or the *Pygmalion Effect*: People oftentimes become what others expect them to become. Thanks to my Grandmother, we called her 'Deah,' my childhood was packed with the sights and sounds of a bustling, exciting city - New Orleans. For years she would take me on her excursions through the shops, art galleries, antique stores, and museums of the city; it was a delightful exploration of the world of art, culture, business, and human nature. And it was 'Deah' who introduced me to the wonder of the spoken and written word. She read to me and took me to storytimes at the New Orleans Public Library. Her great expectation was for me to be well-read, well-spoken, and well-informed. No doubt her influence directed me toward teaching, toward librarianship, and eventually to Bay County.

The foundation for good public library service had been established long before I arrived in Bay County. That is a

(L to R) Drew Pridgen, Carol Vickery, George Vickery, Ashley Vickery, G Vickery and Rebekkah Pridgen

testament to the many dedicated librarians who have made this library system their career. My hope is that I have continued to build on their accomplishments. My desire is that the program of public library service will continue to expand and develop in Bay, Gulf, and Liberty Counties.

In 1988 I married Carol Lee Pridgen. Carol was a State Farm Insurance Claims adjuster who lived at Grayton Beach and worked in Fort Walton Beach. She was born in St. Louis, Missouri, the 'Show Me" State, and she is an excellent example of that state's motto. We were married in the Bay County Public Library on December 29, 1988, a first for the library. Our children, Ashley and G Vickery and Drew and Rebekkah Pridgen attended Bay High School and are now into their careers or finishing their higher education. Carol Vickery has been active in various social and civic organizations and has served as President of Anchorage Children's Home and the Junior Service League. One of her most rewarding projects was helping to restore the historic McKenzie house. This year marks her 25th year of working at State Farm.
Submitted by: George Vickery, 614 E. 1st Ct., Panama City, FL 32401.

Emmett and Lina Walden
Hindsight is 20/20

But for the biting nature of the sand fly, irritability of the no-see-um, the tenaciousness of the mosquito, and the quivering rattle of our eastern diamondbacks, I would now be a millionaire many times over.. .ah, but by the notions of a rather tightfisted man and notably somewhat narrow minded, alas, I am not.

There was a time in the late forty's and early fifties that a man could homestead parts of the beach. My grandmother's room mate at the Florida State College for Women (now FSU) kept in regular touch and told her and my grandfather (Emmett and Lina Walden) of a golden opportunity to do exactly that in what is now known as Carillon Beach and Pinnacle Port.

For five dollars a year per acre in taxes, a man could homestead up to forty acres. It did manage to pique my grandfather's interest. Not much, but enough to spend a day driving on washboard clay roads to get to Lake Powell, then rowing around the point that led to the Gulf of Mexico to see the property from all sides. My grandmother remarked some years later that Gramps enjoyed the ride in the boat though gave occasion to remark on how much hotter it was at that end of the beach. She knew he was beginning to conjure up excuses why this was not a good idea...other than paying five dollars a year in taxes. Gramps was not real fond of taxes.

The trip made, the land scrutinized from every possible angle, he concluded that anyone stupid enough to pay taxes on beachfront property was in need of professional care. Crunching on some sand that happened into the picnic lunch, he suggested Chattahoochee to my grandmother as a place for her former roomie. I am sure that was not taken well, but though she grimaced in the retelling, she never really commented. Needless to say, between the critters, the thick scrub oak, vines and various and sundry flying insects, he chose instead to purchase and build in what was then called Bahama Beach. The year was 1950.

As I retell the original telling of this story, a memory now over 30 years old, I marvel at what has become of Panama City Beach. Even as a kid in the late 50's, my memories of the beach are of a lot of sand, a few motels and restaurants, and not much else.

One acre of beachfront in Carillon Beach today would be worth more than a few million dollars.. .sighhhhh...
Submitted by: Chris Calohan, 1101 Rhode Island Ave, Lynn Haven, FL 32444.

The Waldrop Family

In the year 1918, during World War I, in Europe, a young man from the Panhandle found himself along side other soldiers marching in the "ARGONNE DRIVE", in France, where the weapon of Mustard Gas was used by the enemy. During his time of service he became a professional wrestler and exhibited this talent in Europe, but suffered as many did from the Mustard Gas. He came down with asthma, and even though he was a robust man, he had this problem throughout the remainder of his life.

William Waldrop and wife Era and baby son Malcolm

William David Waldrop returned from the war and settled in Millville, Florida. Another citizen, Lee McLeod had come to Millville in 1910 and worked in a saw mill as a sawer of logs. William Waldrop met Mr. McLeod's daughter, Era McLeod, and after a courtship they fell in love. At that time her father seeking better employment, decided to move to South Florida. Knowing Era could not stay behind, and alone, he agreed to allow her to marry William, but insisted it be done immediately, as he was ready to leave. So they hurried to Judge Harrison's house, and gently woke him and were married at midnight February 1, 1924.

The newlyweds began their marriage by homesteading in the area of Millville known as "HOLY HAMMOCK", later moving to 3rd and East Avenue. By this time they had three additions to the family. Malcolm, a son, their first born, and two girls, Helen and Viva.

Mr. Waldrop had continued his wrestling career after returning from the war and wrestled in the old Millville Theatre, which was across from the Millville Post Office on 3rd Street. The theatre eventually burned down. Mr. Waldrop decided to give up his wrestling career after he married due to the danger involved for there were no rules or regulations, but he did become a referee. In order to support his wife he had an ice, coal, and wood business, and also worked on the docks as a stevedore. One thing he did do was continue to drive his Red Roadster Automobile, which he had when they married, even though there were only dirt roads to drive it on.

After the children came along he opened a grocery store called "THE PENNY PROFIT GROCERY" which he later sold and moved to 2nd and East Avenue and built their home next to the new store, still using The Penny Profit Grocery name. He also built several rental houses using lumber from SAVELL'S LUMBER YARD, and bartered groceries for the labor. Mrs. Waldrop ran the store with the help of the children for many years.

During World War II, when rationing started he closed the store and moved the family out on the bay at the foot of, and the East end of, the Hathaway Bridge. At this writing the house and property was where what is known today as the..... "No Name Lounge". At the time Mr. Waldrop purchased the place it was know as the COCA COLA HOUSE that had been moved by barge from Allanton, which is located on East bay across the bay from Tyndall Field. After he settled the family in their new home he built cottages beside the old house as rentals....

At retirement the property was sold and he moved the family to North Michigan Avenue, just off 23rd Street, where he and Era enjoyed many years before Mr Waldrop's death on March 8, 1977. Mrs. Waldrop lived until December 2, 1990. Malcom Waldrop, their son, died May 1984. As of 2003 the two girls, Helen Waldrop Mills, and Viva Waldrop Barber, still reside in Panama City.

Mr. Waldrop's fame as a professional wrestler diminished, but his fame was regained in the area of successful business man. His ventures into many Profitable and Memorable businesses made him truly a part of Bay County Heritage.

Submitted by: Helen W. Mills, 111 W. Baldwin Rd., Panama City, FL 32405; Written by: Nita Whitehurst.

Louie F. Walker

I was born Louie F. Walker on January 18, 1923 in Donaldsonville, Georgia. The son of Harvey K. and Mary Lizzie Walker. I have two brothers, George M. Walker and Harvey G. Walker. I had two sisters, Annie Ruth Walker who is now deceased and Willie Mae Walker still living.

I served my tour of duty overseas, in the United States Army from January 6, 1943 to January 6, 1946. I served in both England and France. I married Willie Rae Gandy on January 15, 1946 and we are still married today.

Louie F. Walker

I was a contractor and a carpenter by trade. I took up photography and electronics as a hobby. Both turned into full time jobs. When I quit construction, I owned my own Radio and T.V. Repair Shop for a few years. Then my photography hobby turned into a full time news photographer job for WJHG TV Channel 7. I built a film processing machine out of fishing line spools and plastic tanks which I also built. It was a 16MM black and white processor. I had purchased a 16 MM Bolex Camera with a zoom lens, which allowed me to get close ups of people and things without getting in people's way and to keep further away from dangerous situations, such as falling power lines in bad weather and house fires and other structures.

I worked with Earl Hadaway, Earl Hutto, Joe Moore and others from mid 1961 until January 1973. I quit and went back to construction work and then to Civil Service at Tyndall AFB in 1973. I was a photographer and then an engineer for five years, after having had a heart attack on the first day of career employment, September 17, 1973.

During my twelve years with WJHG TV Channel 7, I photographed many, many bad wrecks also house and business fires. I was there on moonshine raids with the Sheriff's Department and Beverage Department. There were many plane crashes to photograph. A lot of VIPs such as John F. Kennedy, Lyndon Johnson, Farris Bryant, Claude Kirk, Reuben Askew and more were photographed by me. There were presidential candidates and congressional candidates, beauty contestants and beauty queens from Panama City, Florida to Sarasota, Florida to Atlantic City, New Jersey all being photographed.

After leaving WJHG TV and before going back into construction work, I went to work with Charlie Abbott and the law enforcement. They made a documentary training film for the Panama City Police Department. That was the last official film that I made. Bill Hudson is presently running a lot of the films on WJHG TV.

Submitted by Louie F. Walker, 803 Transmitter Road, Panama City, FL 32401.

Beatrice Alaine Walters

Welcome. I am glad to meet you. Let me introduce myself. My name is Beatrice, Beatrice Alaine Walters, that is. I am an inventor, a photographer, a writer and a maker of doll clothes. My maiden name is Sanks. Duncan and Roberts used to part of my name and Brown used to also be a part of my name. Brown was my married name when I was first married for a while. I was proud to carry this name but now I wish I never did. I have three children that are now grown that still carry this name. There is nothing wrong with the name itself. It is just the heartache that came with it. My grown children are Jose Brown, Angela Brown and Amanda Brown.

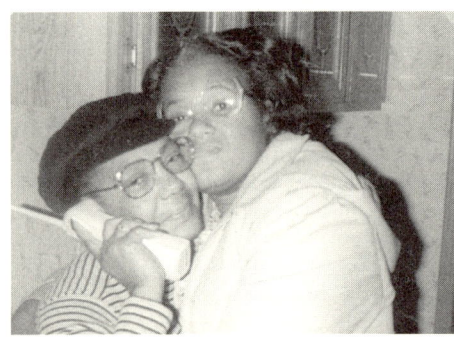

My Loving Mother Mrs. Rosemary Sanks and daughter Beatrice A. Walters.

My husband Glenn Walters and I also have a teenage son, Terrance Jacob Walters. He is 16 years old. In a few months he will be 17. This is hard for me. My baby grew so fast. They all did. We also have two granddaughters, Angela Monique Davis and Cassandra Denise Davis. They are something to treasure. You thought I was going to say they are something else, didn't you? Well, you are right, they are. They are two beautiful little girls.

Yes, I was born here in Panama City, Florida, 48 years ago. I have done some traveling but ended up back here. Mama (Rosemary Sanks) said when I was born the doctor called me snowflakes because I had some gray hair. Through the years I have been asked why don't I dye my hair. My answer is always, "No way." I have thought about it. I thought I would love to look younger.

All my family that I wanted to put into this story but couldn't, is in a way, represented here through my Mama. My link with all those relatives is through my Mama.

I am taking care of the girls today. Aunt Masie Simmons and Grandmama, Arlena Bledsoe took care of them yesterday. I have not seen my cousin, Zic, lately. She is a very nice and smart person. She has a son by the name of Larry and he is a sweet young man. Our grandmother is very frail but also nice. I have to go. The girls are getting upset with one another.
Submitted by: Beatrice Alaine Sanks Walters, 1321 Kensinger Place, Panama City, Florida 32401.

Edward Ellis Walton and Marjorie Grace "Peggy" Cotton

Born in Berlin, Alabama in 1919, to Thomas Anthony Walton and Jessie Zerette Ellis, Edward Ellis Walton came to Panama City during the summers of 1947 and 1948. He worked at the Bay Line Railroad Express Office on Beach Drive and part-time as the operator of the skating rink at Long Beach Resort. In 1948 he made Panama City his permanent home.

Marjorie Grace Cotton was born in Millville, Florida, in 1932 to Percy Scott and Lucile Grace Pringle Cotton. Born in the family home and in the same room where her father was born in 1909, Peggy, is a second-generation Bay County native. Her father called her Peggy saying she was

Peggy and Ellis at the Long Beach Skating Rink 1949

too small for such a big name. Barely weighing in at 4 pounds fully dressed in winter wear, she wore her father's handkerchiefs for diapers. Peggy, an avid skater, spent many hours on the neighborhood sidewalks, and, when she could coax her parents into taking her and 11 of her closest friends, at the skating rink located next to the Hangout at Long Beach Resort.

It was at the rink in 1947 that Peggy met Ellis. A long-time skating friend thought they would look good skating together and introduced them. In 1949, they were married and together managed the skating rink during the summer seasons until 1953. During the winter months, Ellis worked in town at Sears-Roebuck. Their first child, Deanne, was born in 1952. When she began to walk, Ellis attached wheels to the bottoms of a pair of her baby shoes. And, another generation of skaters took to the wood floors. In 1955, Ellis began working at the Navy Base, where he remained until his retirement in 1980. In 1966, the skating Walton family was recognized with the cover photo of a national skating magazine.

The Waltons raised five children - Jessica Lucille Deanne (Coffield), Marjorie Sharon (Wilkinson), Gregory Ellis, Randy Scott, and Christina Gayle (Jacquay). Ellis Walton died in 1983.
Submitted by: Deanne Walton Coffield, 408 Palmetto Court, Lynn Haven, FL 32444.

Adam and Delilah Welch

The family of Adam and Delilah Welch who were married in 1888, have been in the town of St. Andrews, Florida for seven generations. I, Elzona Welch Muenzel, born October 1913 in St. Andrews, Florida, am 89 years old and their oldest living descendant. The land my grandfather bought and built his home on is still in the family. He and grandmother had five sons and one daughter. They lived to be very old. He died September 1916 and grandmother died October 1908. They are buried in Greenwood Cemetery. My grandfather farmed and raised his family to work and he was honest and

Welch and Montgomery Clan at Wilmont Avenue home; Bessie (Welch) Montgomery is seated with first child, Henrietta, in chair. Her husband, John, stands behind her. Others in the picture are extended family members of Bessie.

a hard worker. We have a family reunion each year to honor our ancestors. All we have is a photograph of them and lots of descendents to enjoy at each reunion. My grandfather fished and farmed and taught his sons to fish. The bay was then so clean and farming and fishing was about all there was at that time. As the younger ones grew older, some drifted away to other places but they all came back home eventually to live close to each other.

It was a joy to be on the bay so many years ago. I am now 89 years old and I remember how the beach and bay was so clean and the fishing boats tied up to Ware's Dock at the foot of 10th Street. My grandfather helped build the bank building on the corner of Beck and 12th Street which is now used as a police station. It's the only original building still left except the printing building on Beck Avenue between 12th and 11th Streets.

I attended St. Andrews Grammar School when it was a wooden building and we had no lunchroom so we walked home at noon. So many things were not invented then. The car's as they are today, T.V., radios, everything electric.

Us, the older descendants, meet each month at each others homes for lunch and fellowship. We have a grand time and some of us are great grandparents so we have lots to talk about and hope they, the younger ones, will carry on our tradition.

I married a naval officer and lived in many different places but after his death I moved back to what we all call home to live out the rest of my life. I often think of what it used to be like when I was a little girl. The beaches around St. Andrews bay were clean and white, the bay water was so clear and we went swimming in it all summer. We caught big blue crabs and scallops. There was a big oak tree on the beach between Ware's Dock and 11th Street and we enjoyed the beach there in the shade. My father fished and we would watch there to see the boat come in and tie up at the dock. I am now back home for good. I have lots of Welch cousins. We often talk about when all the roads were either sand or clay roads. No electric lights, just kerosene lamps and no refrigeration, washing machine, drier or television.

The Casino, a building built out over the bay, would have Saturday night movies and after that skating. The movies were silent movies with words that came up on the screen. A lady played the piano and when there was a very scary scene that came on, she would bang real hard on the piano as the cowboys rode away. After the movie chairs were folded and moved away for dancing, a lady played the piano and the dance lasted about an hour and then we had a nice walk home. Alls well that ends well and hopefully we have a few years more labeled "the older ones."

Submitted by: Elzona Welch Muenzel, 1236 Beck Ave., Panama City, FL 32401.

Bessie Welch and John Montgomery

In the late 1800s Adam Levi Welch married Deliah Glisson. Their home was on Wilmont Avenue in St. Andrews, near the waterfront. Adam and Deliah had five boys and one daughter (Clarence James, Silas Marion, Emanuel Benjamin, Thomas Levi, Christopher Columbus, and Ester Elizabeth, known as "Bessie). When Bessie was 13 years old, her mother died. At this young age Bessie became the female head of household at the Welch home; she cooked, kept house, washed clothes, helped raise her two younger brothers - and attended school.

The St. Andrews waterfront was a center for activity, and the Welch family members were all influenced in one way or another by its presence. The little fishing community on the bay also attracted others from nearby. In 1909 John Samuel Montgomery moved to St. Andrews from Apalachicola. At first John and his brother continued the business of his family in Apalach - cattle buying and running butcher shops. But the water "called" John, and soon he owned and captained two fishing smacks (The REBA and The TWO FRIENDS) and later a seine boat (The BESSIE M.)

John Montgomery with his mandolin

These boats and Captain John carried many St. Andrews men out into the Gulf to make their living off the then abundant fishing stock. To quote the local paper, The Panama City Pilot, January 11, 1917: "The "Reba" - Capt. John Montgomery, came in Monday night with a full fare - 5,500 pounds of red snapper as a result of two days fishing. Captain Montgomery and his crew seem to have permanent "dates" with the snapper. They always find them at home."

Another interesting article appeared in the Panama City Pilot on May 24, 1917: "The crew of The REBA reports an unusual occurance off the Cape on Friday last. While fishing, a large steamer came up from the southard and headed straight for The REBA. When the steamer had approached quite near, she veered off, circled Captain Montgomery's craft and steamed away off shore again. The steamer had one stack and was apparently a merchant vessel of several thousand tons. She flew no flag nor carried any identification marks. The men on The REBA were unable to tell whether or not she was armed. The occurance was reported to Port Officer Tyre as soon as the Reba docked. "

The waterfront - Ware's dock and the markets and shops on Beck Avenue - is the probable meeting place for Bessie Welch and John Montgomery. They married in 1911, raising a family of their own (4 daughters and 1 son). Now in their golden years, these "Montgomery children" frequently reminise about childhood antics, about playing on the sandhill, and about school days at the original, wooden schoolhouse in St. Andrews.

Through the years John and Bessie stayed in close touch with their respective families. John eventually purchased the Welch homeplace on Wilmont Avenue (it was up for taxes), but its doors remained open for extended family members as they left and then returned to the St. Andrews area. When elderly, both John and Bessie's fathers were blind. They became very close as they lived out their lives together at John and Bessie's home. Their final desire was to be buried side by side; their graves rest side by side at Greenwood Cemetery in the Welch family lot.

The first daughter of John and Bessie was Henrietta Louise who married Ray Moates. They have two sons: Fred and Sam. Daughter Number 2 was Viola Deliah who married Claude Arthur Pichard Jr. of Tallahassee. Their children are David, Kay and Claude. Vivian Ardel, next daughter, married Charles "Turk" Surber and has one daughter, Bette. Daughter No, 4 was Frances Ester who married William Banks. Their two daughters are Shirley and Pat. (After the death of William, Frances married Foster Tally.) John Samuel was the only son of Bessie and John, and their last child, married Mary Jane. John's children are Sandra, John III and Linda. To date, the great grandchildren of Bessie and John Montgomery number twenty, plus fourteen great, great grand children.

The children of John and Bessie are still close knit; they and their spouses gather every weekend to relive crabbing and swimming days in the bay. They and their families have a special love of St. Andrews and St. Andrews Bay.

Submitted by: Vivian Surber, 2353 Pretty Bayou Drive, Panama City, FL 32405.

Thomas (Tommy) Alfred Welch

Thomas (Tommy) Alfred Welch was born October 22, 1922, in St. Andrews, Florida, to Thomas Lambert and Ettie Louise Brackin Welch. He was the second oldest of six children. His grandparents were Delilah and Adam Levi Welch. Adam was one of the men who helped to build the old St. Andrews Bank located at the corner of Beck Ave. and 10th St.

Tommy attended St. Andrews Grammar School located at Beck Ave. and 15th St. His family lived in a number of places - one house was located at Bayview and 12th Ct. (which was then an alley) across from the old train depot in St. Andrews-another home was located up on the hill at Wilmont and 11th St. They called it the "Goat House"

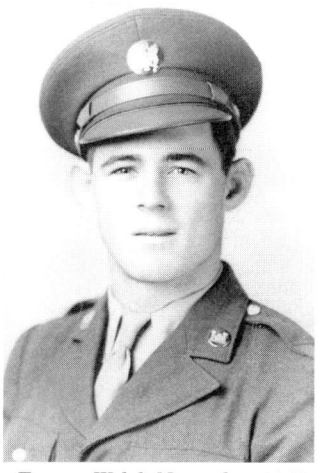

Tommy Welch November 1943

because they had a pet goat. When he and I (Lillian Masker) met, he was living at 1105 Drake Ave.

Tommy would come to Mattie's Tavern to see his buddy (my cousin), A.D. Richbourg. I lived at Mattie's Tavern (located at 12th and Beck Ave, next door to West's Printing

Press) with my family. The tavern belonged to my Aunt Mattie Campbell, A.D.'s mother. Tommy and A.D. would go crabbing and floundering at night after the tavern closed. Back in the 40's you could walk around the Buena Vista Point (where the Ramada Inn and the St. Andrews Marina are located now). The old Tillers Dock was at the foot of 11th St and Lloyd's Cottages were on the point. You could catch a tub full of crabs or a bucket of scallops in no time. They were plentiful in the bay. Tommy worked for Mr. Spencer on the Budweiser Beer Truck when he and I started going together. He fished on the "7 Brothers' Seine Boat" and also the fishing smacks "Lucky Strike", "The Tommy", and a number of other boats. I remember they would be gone out fishing for 28 days at the time and come back just loaded down with snapper, grouper, and scamp. It was a rough life in the winter time.

Tommy joined the service in 1943. He came home on leave in July and we were married in Lynn Haven, FL, by Judge Russ' secretary, Annie Mae Porter. He was discharged after the war, but enlisted in the Air Force. We had four children, 2 boys and 2 girls. During his 21 years of active military life, he was stationed in Florida, Bermuda, Nebraska, California, and Thailand. After his retirement in 1965, we moved back to St. Andrews where Tommy worked as a carpenter and plumber. In 1985 he was injured in an industrial accident-he died 19 days later on October 4th. He is missed by all.
Submitted by: Anna L. Welch, 15 Hampton Circle, Niceville, FL 32578; Written by: Lillian M. Welch.

A.D. Weller

Alfred Daniel Weller was born in Jacksonville, Florida on February 13, 1872 to the Rev. Reginald Heber Weller and his wife Amanda Look Weller; he was the last of their twelve children. Amanda died when he was five months old, but his father remarried Caroline Cordelia Veale of Jacksonville and they had one daughter who lived just three years. Alfred Weller came to St. Andrews in the early 1900s to manage the first ice plant which was located where Landmark Condominiums are now. He was the second mayor of St. Andrews. He started Bay Fisheries as a small business, but it became a major Bay County industry as its growth made it one of the largest fisheries in the Gulf Coast area. Weller made contacts through the Georgia cities of Atlanta and Birmingham and on up through Tennessee and united these contacts into a large network of customers for seafood brought into St. Andrews by the fishermen.

A. D. Weller (on the mule) the day he was elected Mayor of St. Andrews (10th Street and Beck Ave.)

Weller knew that hard work made successful business and he put in long hours to make certain that the seafood he sent out was cleaned, fresh, and properly iced before it was shipped to the surrounding states.

In 1913 he built a house for his family on Beach Drive not far from his business. There in the living room the people who would become members of what would eventually be St. Andrews Episcopal Church first met to hold services. His children Alfred, Evalyn, Ruth, and Carroll attended schools in the area; the smallest, Marguerite, was not born until 1917. On January 17, 1918 tragedy struck the family. The schooner *Annie and Jennie* sailed out through the old pass, was soon mauled by high seas and frigid winds, and was driven onto a sandbar outside the pass. Young Alfred Weller, aboard to learn the family business before attending the Citadel, drowned along with three other men. This blow to the family was devastating and they left Bay County to

move to Georgia. They returned to the Pensacola area of the panhandle in 1927, then came back to Bay County and St. Andrews. By the fall of 1928, A.D. Weller was again a force in the wholesale fish trade along the Gulf Coast. In 1936, a goodly portion of the business was washed out to sea when an unexpectedly strong hurricane struck; it recovered.

Thomas Carroll Weller was born in Pensacola on June 11, 1911 and was brought with his mother on the *Tarpon* when he was five days old; he helped with the operation of the Bay Fisheries Company, but began his own business later; he served in the Merchant Marines as an officer during WWII. He changed vocations and bought a partnership in Kelley Press in St. Andrews which he later sold. Then he worked at the college until he retired.

Thomas Carroll Weller, Jr. attended local schools with his siblings, left after his years at UF, but has recently retired as an Episcopal priest and is living in the home Alfred Weller built in 1913.
Submitted by: Gina Weller Webb, 1025 W. 19th St., 2D, Panama City, FL 32405.

Ethel J. Wheeler May 13, 1915-May 22, 1989

Mrs. Ethel J. Wheeler, born as Ethel Lucille Jenkins on May 13, 1915, was the second child of Asa and Fannie Jenkins. Her earthly life ended May 22, 1989 at her home in Panama City, Florida.

She spent her early childhood and early youth in Vernon, FL where she attended the public schools. She completed her formal education at Florida A & M University with a M. Ed. degree.

She married Mr. Alexander Wheeler on Sept. 7, 1940 and moved to Panama City in 1945.

From the beginning of her residence in Bay County until her death she was affiliated with Greater Bethel A.M.E. Church. She generously contributed her time, talents and resources to the Choir #1, Trustee Board and Missionary Society.

Ethel Wheeler

She began her career as an educator in 1937 in Washington County. The majority of her teaching career was spent as a third grade teacher at Glenwood Elem. School where she influenced the lives of many Bay County youth. She retired June 1977.

She was very active in Bay County's civic and political affairs. She was the first black citizen to serve on the Democratic Executive Committee in Bay County on which she held several offices. She was appointed to various city boards, one of which was the Panama City Zoning Board of Adjustments. She also worked tirelessly with the American Cancer Society coordinating activities for the nine-county area.
Submitted by; Bura Reed, 1402 Illinois Ave., Lynn Haven, FL.

James Oscar Whitehurst and Bera Mae Carlile Whitehurst

In this year of 2003, with it's modern marvels, man's going to the moon, and life's existence controlled by a computer world, it is fascinating to step back in time to a world of mud covered roads, horse and wagons, and ferries instead of bridges. New honeymooners, James Oscar Whitehurst, and his 17 year old bride, Bera Mae Carlile Whitehurst, arrived in Panama City, Florida just a little past the turn of the century in 1918. They had left Dothan, Alabama due to his transfer with the Bay Line Railroad, and the train stopped in front of their new home along the track, which was one of the section houses provided by the company, and was located between which is now known as West 11th Street and West 8th. They found the main street, Harrison Avenue, was dirt, as all streets were, but had wooden plank sidewalks.

Transportation was by walking, wagon or train. Recreation consisted of frequent visits to St. Andrews by train, spending the day, and returning by train, or a trip to the beach by ferry. Exciting entertainment was to view a silent movie shown in the 500 block of Harrison Avenue below the Brake Funeral Home. A walk along West Beach Drive was enhanced by the beauty of masses of wild flowers, beautiful oak and pine trees. It was said that the bay water was so clear and pure it made the fish, oysters, crabs and shrimp excellent for consumption.

Oscar and Bera Mae Whitehurst

Living facilities were far from convenient. They grew their own vegetables, cooked on a wood stove, washed and boiled clothes in a wood fired black pot outdoors, and had a hand pump on the backporch for water. The only lighting facilities were kerosene lamps. Storm warnings were unheard of and they had to endure the element of surprise. Oscar and Bera Mae were the first Whitehurst to set up residence, but their immediate families followed from Alabama. Oscar and Bera added to the population in the birth of their six children; John Darrell, Iris Yuvonne, Vivian Anita, Aubrey Donald, Nathalon Janice, and Larry Edris. All reside in Panama City but Iris Yvonne, who lives in Ohio. In future years as our town progressed, these pioneers witnessed the coming of the automobile, which could only travel ten miles an hour due to the sandy roads, the electric light, the telephone, indoor plumbing, paved streets, real movie theatres, bridges across the bay, radio and television. It is worthy to note that the first telephone installed in their home, is not only still being used, but maintains the original number that was issued to them. Oscar made a contribution to a part of the city's growth by opening the first Restaurant-Night Club, which was located on West Sixth Street.

Oscar and Bera Mae Whitehurst were true pioneers, they experienced the old and the new of our city, and from their honeymoon to the end of their lives, they called Panama City...... home.

Submitted by: Nita Whitehurst, 2710 Frankford Avenue, Panama City, Florida, 32405.

Nadine and Louis Wilkerson

My family moved from Tallahassee to Panama City in January 1955 when I was twenty months old. My brother, Barney Joe, was five days old and Mother had just been released from the hospital. She packed everything she could and moved to Springfield, where she rented a house. My father was working on the tugboat "Viking Prince," which was docked at Sherman Shipyard for repairs. Mother went to see him and asked if he was coming home for a little while. Not knowing that we had moved to Panama City that very day, my father said, "Honey, you know I don't have time to go home. I'm only here a few hours." Mom said, "Well, let's go get a Coca-Cola." So she rode to the house she had rented and my father saw all of us kids outside playing, and mother said, "Welcome home," She said my father's face lit up when he

Louis and Nadine Wilkerson

saw all of us, but my father wanted to know where the baby was. A neighbor, Mrs, Hill, kept him that night because we had no furniture. Everyone slept on the floor that night. And that's how my father found out about us moving from Tallahassee to Panama City. We lived in Springfield until September 1956 when Hurricane Flossie struck Northwest Florida. It blew the roof off our home. Mother was expecting another baby and my oldest brother, Ray, was sick in bed at the time. We moved to Millville into an apartment we rented from Mrs. Fanny Hutchinson.

My father had never driven before my mother went into labor. Since there was no one to drive her, my father drove to the hospital. Mother said he drove 5 mph and hit every bump in the road. He was driving so slow that a policeman stopped them to ask if everything was OK and got in front of them with his lights on until they got to the hospital. And that's where my brother Roy was born.

We rented a few more times, until we bought two acres of land from J.K. Golden. My brother Ray bought the other two acres off of Kimbrel Avenue in Callaway. It had an old flamed log cabin on it. The cabin had no walls and no roof. My father was

(L to R) Nadine Wilkerson with baby, Rose, Ray, Mae, and Nancy, Louis, Erma and Mary

working at Sherman Shipyard. The church we attended gave us tin for the roof. A gentleman from the church, who worked for Gulf Power wired the house so we could have electricity. We got kraft paper from the Papermill for the walls. Mr. Sherman loaned my father the money to get black tar paper for the outside of the two-room house. There was nine children- Nancy, Mae, Ray, Mary, Louis, Erma, Rose, Barney, and Roy; we slept on the floor. My parents slept on the only bed. We stayed there until we built a new home on the land.

The house had three bedrooms and a room that was supposed to be the bathroom, but was never finished So we made it into a bedroom for my older brothers. There was no inside plumbing, so we had to carry buckets of water to wash dishes. Water was heated on an old wood stove. In the summer, we would put on our swim suits and bathe outside in an old bath tub that we would fill with water before leaving for school so it would be warm when we came home. In the winter, we would use a #2 washtub. We finally did get running water in the kitchen. My father fixed us a shower outside; he built it with heavy curtains and a hose tied to the top of the pipes he used to put up the curtain. We still kept our swim suits on.

Dad and Mom had 12 Children but there were 15 in all. After my father's sister died, they took in her two kids Nancy and Mae; as their own, Jerry is Nancy and Mae's brother. He came to live with us later. He was around 13 years old. My brothers were born after we moved into our new home. John, and Charles, Terry Joe and Kerry Joe, (twins) and Donald was the baby.

I was 12 years old when we moved in our first home with inside plumbing. It was yellow with white trim and was located in Bay Harbor on Everitt Avenue across from the poolroom that Clarence Gideon was convicted of breaking into. I loved that house; it was my most favorite home that we had ever lived in. We ended up going back to Callaway, and that's another story.

I am Rose, the baby girl, as my parents use to call me. I was number 7 child and I am writing this story as a part of my history. I had to grow up too soon too fast. I had to miss a lot of school to take care of my little brothers. My sister and I were taken before a Judge when I was in the 6th grade because of missing so much school to take care of my brothers. So my mother stopped keeping us out as much after that. I was only in the 7th grade when I had to drop out of school to help out at home.

I now have four children of my own: Tracy Wayne, Theresa, David, and Kelley. Tracy Wayne married Deanne. They have three children: Ricky, Jakye, Hailey. Theresa married Dwayne they have two children: Miranda, and Michael. David married Shelby. They have three children: Jeffery, David, and Amber. Kelley married Gary. They have three children: Kimberly, Victoria, and Johnny. We all live in Bay County.

Submitted by: Rose Wilson, 5662 Glensway Rd, Panama City, FL 32404.

Winge Family
Barwing

Dogs have always been important in the lives of the Winge

Sam Walker, Sr., and dog

family. It is a trait that has been passed down through the generations. Favorite dogs or horses were often mentioned in wills and left to a son.

Samuel West Walker, Sr., a Spanish American War Veteran was Barbara Walker Winge's grandfather. He was famous in the State of Georgia for his hunting ability and his bird dogs. One in particular, Jack, could walk up to a row of bills on the ground and pick out whatever denomination he was told to select. From a pile containing a billfold, keys, and flashlight he would pick up the articles as named. At fruit stands he would select a juicy apple or orange at his police officer master's request. Several Georgia newspapers named him the "Smartest Dog in Georgia."

Winge's father, Samuel West Walker, Jr., a veteran of World War II, had a reputation for training gun dogs for the

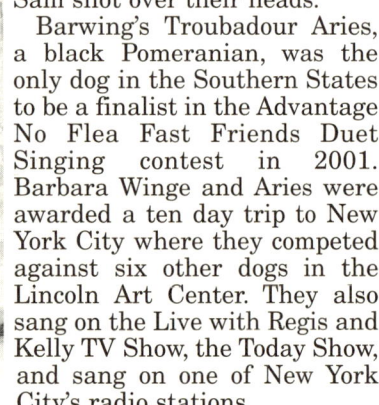
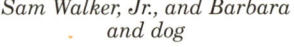
Sam Walker, Jr., and Barbara and dog

field. His Pointers and Setters were renowned for the time they could hold a point while Sam shot over their heads.

Barwing's Troubadour Aries, a black Pomeranian, was the only dog in the Southern States to be a finalist in the Advantage No Flea Fast Friends Duet Singing contest in 2001. Barbara Winge and Aries were awarded a ten day trip to New York City where they competed against six other dogs in the Lincoln Art Center. They also sang on the Live with Regis and Kelly TV Show, the Today Show, and sang on one of New York City's radio stations.

Winge has owned Pomeranian Dogs for over forty years, showing them in both the AKC Confirmation and Obedience rings. Barwing's Demure Hera has earned an AKC Canine Good Citizen award and is certified with Therapy Dog International. Barwing's Mischievous Zeus also has the AKC Canine Good Citizen. These Poms along with Poms Bel-Mei's Itzi Bitzi Mitzi and Aries visit area nursing homes, schools and other local facilities as members of Covenant Hospice and Pets Are Working Saints.

Bobby T. Winge, Jr., Winge's son, was a member of Southport Coon Hunters Association for many years. He was often one of the top four winners with his Treeing Walker Hounds.

Terre Winge Hall, Winge's daughter, fosters dogs for The

American Belgian Malinois Club and Southern States Rottweiler Rescue, as well as the Mid-Fla Australian Cattle Dogs Rescue. She has earned a reputation for rehabilitating problem dogs. Hall trains these dogs then donates them to Law Enforcement Agencies to be used as K9s or finds them a "forever home."

Submitted by Barbara Walker Winge, 103 South Gay Avenue, Panama City, FL 32404.

Loy and Marlene Womack

April 30, 1973 marked an important date for the Womack family. That's when Loy and Marlene Womack and children Jesse, age 8 and Mike, age 5 arrived in Bay County after being transferred from McGuire AFB, New Jersey to Tyndall AFB. Fred would be born at Bay Memorial eight months later.

Loy Womack's roots dated back to Dallas County, Arkansas and Marlene Minch's roots were Linden and Elizabeth, New Jersey.

When the Womacks came, the area was experiencing a housing shortage so the family took temporary lodging in Mexico Beach. A small town east of Tyndall AFB, where mail was delivered and picked up from the post office inside one of the grocery stores. Mexico Beach did not have a school so children were bussed to Highland View just west of Port St. Joe in Gulf County.

While the family was looking for a house to buy, realtors spoke of area expansion to Bayou George and a projected bypass north of Panama City. This bypass would route traffic above East Bay then cross near Allanton to connect with U.S. 98 at the eastern end of Tyndall.

On June 20, the Womacks moved into their permanent home in the Northside School district. Around Panama City, children could ride their bikes to school, stores or church without parents worrying about their safety on the sidewalks and streets.

Walt Hall ran the popular Boys Club on 19th Street. Michael sang with the Boys Club Choir at the opening of the salt works' replica on Lake Caroline during the Bicentennial of 1976.

Numerous little league, soccer and youth football teams existed around town and in Callaway, Lynn Haven, Southport and at Panama City Beach. The opening of Harder's Park near Bayou George added numerous new fields needed for these sports.

Deer Point Lake, which opened in the early 1960's, was relatively new in 1973 and attracted fishermen, both summer and winter. Property owners near what had been North Bay often commented on the way the dam changed the water level on their land and around the lake.

Lynn Haven remained as it had for decades with numerous old homes erected by retired Union veterans from the Civil War. These men and their families moved south after the town's founding in 1911. Many lots stood vacant and could be purchased at reasonable prices. Then subdivisions sprang up west of Maine Avenue and around the Panama Country Club. But few anticipated the huge growth Lynn Haven would experience in the 1990's.

More new subdivisions such as Derby Woods, Mowat Highlands and Mill Bayou popped up around greater Lynn Haven on land that had once been woods, Bob Jones College property and Mowat Dairy.

Over on the east side of Panama City, workmen finished four-laning 15th Street east of Transmitter Road to Business 98 in Parker. But in 1975 cow pastures and large wooded sections still remained along the road that would become know as Tyndall Parkway. But even with all these changes, we're still glad to call Panama City home and fortunate to live in a place with the Gulf and bay not far from our front door.

Submitted by: Marlene Womack, 2101 Norwood Place, Panama City, FL 32405.

David Wright and Agnes Lowther

The Wright family came from northern England

(Northumberland). It was during the mid 1690's. Our branch of the family crossed over into Scotland and settled in Dumfriershire the parish of Lochmaben and made the village of Hightae home.

The first branch of our family left Dumfries and came to America in 1844. John Wright born in 1805 was married to Helen Wilson on June 24, 1831 in Lochmabey. The first Wrights who came to America were John and Helen and their five children: Elizabeth, Joseph, James, John L. and Thomas Wright.

The family left Scotland and traveled to Liverpool, England where they was to take a steamship for New Orleans, Louisiana. Landing in New Orleans they boarded a paddlewheel and traveled up the Mississippi River to the Illinois River which took them to Beardstown. Then they took a horse and wagon to Springfield, Illinois and they purchased a large farm in Riverton in 1850 which the family still farms today. They had seven more children after they moved to the farm in Riverton.

The next set of Wrights to come to America were my paternal great grandparents David Wright (1846-1909) and Agnes Lowther (1846-1927). They also left the area of Dumfries and landed in New York City in 1872.

My grandfather was married in 1895 to Margaret Clark (1874-1959). They produced eight children which my father was the first set of twins.

Our father was Everett C. Wright born September 4, 1906. He married my mother, Mary Veronica Russell on October 27, 1934. She was the daughter of Joseph Russell (1868-1937) and Mary Fitzmaurice (1882-1915).

Dad lived in New York until 1963 when we moved to Florida.

We settled in Deerfield Beach, Florida and I left home to find my own place and lived in a number of areas in Florida like Ocala, Bartow and Bonifay. Then in 1962, I moved to Bay County, Florida and I have been here ever since.
Submitted: Wayne Wright, PO Box 783, Panama City, Florida 32402.

Cecil O. Young, Jr.

The spring of 1961, my father, C.O. Young, Jr. discovered Panama City, Florida and that discovery changed the course of direction for our family's life. After convincing the senior class of the rural high school in TN, which he was the principal, to alter the traditional senior trip to include Panama City, he became captivated by the white sand and sparkling surf. While the kids romped on the beach he interviewed with Earl Cochran the superintendent of Bay County Schools and was given the position of Physics instructor at Bay County High School for the next term. He remained in that position until the doors of A. Crawford Mosley High School opened and he tranferred there to the science department in 1971. In 1985 he walked out the side door to the faculty parking lot of Mosley to begin retirement.

C.O. Young, Jr., Bay County Educator 1961-1985

Retirement; What a joke! At the age of 75 years he is still going full speed ahead with his excavator, bulldozer and land development business.

While teaching was his full time career he also served as a bi-vocational pastor of several Southern Baptist Churches in the Bay County area. He pastored the mission church, Green Hills - Fountain from 1966 - 1973 and later this church became the First Baptist Church of Fountain. Onward to the mission church that was soon constituted into East Bay Baptist Church in 1973-1981. The last pastorate he had was to constitute the Kingswood Baptist Church in 1984-1992.

Through the ministry of church pastor and classroom teacher, C.O. Young, Jr. has touched many lives in Bay County, FL.

C.O. Young, Jr. married Georgia Fay Lockhart in 1946 and they have parented four daughters: Sharlet, Janet, Patricia, and Donna. Those four girls all graduated Bay County High School, Gulf Coast Community College and received degrees from various universities. Janet was crowned Miss Panama City in 1967 and became the first Miss Gulf Coast in 1967. From this legacy have been raised teachers, social workers, medical doctors, forensic scientist and a missionary in a frontier field. What a legacy! My Dad is a tall man.
Submitted by: Sharlet Young Ludlum, 226 Pine Ridge Dr., Panama City, FL 32405.

Lionel and Sara Nelle Covington Young
The Youngs Come to Bay County

When Lionel and Sara Nelle Covington Young decided to move to Panama City Beach in 1947, people said they were crazy. Friends even placed bets on how many months would pass before the couple returned to Newton, Alabama.

The couple, who had often taken trips to the beach while they were courting, continued visits after their elopement June 2, 1940, when they were married in Chipley by Probate Judge Evelyn Carmichael, one of the first female judges in Florida. During the war years Lionel worked with the Civil Service at Fort Rucker, Alabama .

In 1947, Lionel's father, William Rhett Young, decided to move to Florida. His wife, Johnie Ella Mathews Young, refused to go unless one of her children moved with them. Lionel and Sara Nelle volunteered to go. After locating suitable property, Lionel and a friend lived in a tent, cleared property and built a road, the present Young Street.

In October 1947, Rhett, Johnie, Lionel, Sara Nelle, six year old Junior and one year old Nancy moved to the beach. Friends told Lionel he was insane to leave a good government job to open a business on the beach. Not only did he not have a building to open a business in, but there were few people to sell anything to.

Rhett was to open a motel on the gulf side of Highway 98 and Lionel to open a garage across the street. Waterfront property was selling for $50 a foot.

The two families lived in rental housing while they put up the buildings. Young's Motel and Young's Garage opened for business in March of 1948, just in time for the AEA holiday. Young's Motel was located on the site of the present Trip's Motel and Young's Garage was at the site of the present California Cycles.

The garage was the only one on the beach. Lionel's "Big Boy" wrecker pulled many tourists from the sandy road-sides. In addition to repairing cars, Lionel sold Sinclair gasoline as well as some food and beach items. Sara Nelle ran the cash register and helped pump gas. Inflated car tubes for the beach rented for 25 cents an hour. The family soon included daughters Sara and Mary Frances.

In the early years, enough money had to be made in the short summer season to support the family for the entire year. There were no doctors, no schools, no supermarkets, and no fire department on the beach. When Mary Frances was bitten by a rattlesnake, Lionel outran the Highway Patrol in his fifteen mile race across the Hathaway Bridge to the hospital.

When the Beach Business Men's Club formed about 1949, Lionel was a charter member. The Club started a program to fight dog flies, later formed a volunteer fire department, and built the first wing of an elementary school. Lionel did all the welding for the new school.

Young's Garage expanded in the sixties to include boats and motors. Lionel retired in 1971, turning the business over to his son.
Submitted by: Nancy Young Sheffield, 207 Harrison Place, Panama City, Florida 32405.

Albert Bruce Yount

1st Lt. Albert Bruce Yount first came to Bay County in

Albert Bruce Yount

June 1958. He was on a three day vacation to Panama City Beach. He had recently returned from Japan where he had flown as a navigator on weather recon aircraft. His primary job was to locate and track typhoons. He made several trips into the eye of typhoons over the Pacific Ocean.

Yount attended Arkansas A & M in Monticello AK., before being accepted for Air Force Cadet Training at Harlingen AFB, TX. Upon completion he was commissioned a 2nd Lt. and awarded the silver wings of an Air Force Navigator.

While stationed at Graham Air Base in Marianna, he met and married Jeannette Melvin in December 1958. He was then stationed at Hunter AFB, GA., K.I. Sawyer AFB, MI. Castle AFB, CA., F. E. Warren AFB, WY and then to service in Viet Nam. While a navigator on the C-130 aircraft he was awarded the "Distinguished Flying Cross" for the battle of Kae San. Upon his return to the states he was stationed at McCoy AFB, and while in a KC-135 was involved in refueling operations for the SR71 Blackbird recon aircraft.

While stationed in Wyoming Major Yount graduated from the University of Wyoming with a BS in general engineering. He also holds an AS degree from GCCC in Real Estate.

Major Yount and his former wife Jeannette have two children, Kathryn Leigh McCurdy and Lisa Ann Daughtery. They also have three grandchildren Ryan Willoughby, Alex Nichols and Alisha Daughtery.

Major Yount retired in February 1974, at McCoy AFB and returned to Lynn Haven. In civilian life he managed two service stations, co-owned and operated Etheridge Marina. Owned and operated his own real estate office. He was employed as a bookkeeper at Ball Petroleum when he retired.

In 1991 Major Yount married Joyce Betcher Roberts and they make their home in Lynn Haven. Mrs. Yount is retired from West Florida Natural Gas Co. and they enjoy spending time with their children and grandchildren. They are active members of 1st Presbyterian Church of Lynn Haven where both are elders.
Submitted by: Jan Ashe, 2504 Rollins, Panama City, FL 32405; Written by: Joyce B. Yount.

LATE SUBMITTALS

Archibald Edwin Bruner and C.S. Anderson

My grandmother, Amanda Jane Granger Bruner, told me this story many times when I visited her in Cottonwood, AL. The story goes she would get up every morning about four o'clock and make breakfast. This morning there came a knock at the back door, when she answered Grandfather's buddy Capt. C.S. Anderson was there. She asked him to come in and finished breakfast for him and my grandfather, Archibald Edwin Bruner. Grandfather was the mail carrier.

During breakfast that morning, Capt. Anderson told my grandfather he needed to borrow some money to start a fishing business and asked where could they get it. Grandfather told him they could probably get the money at the Dothan bank. After breakfast they hitched up the horse and buggy and made a nine mile dash to Dothan to talk with the banker. He borrowed the money, $500, with my grandfather signing the note with Capt. Anderson. They drove the buggy home and Capt. Anderson went back to Panama City. He rode the train. It came from Dothan to Cottonwood and down through the woods to Cottondale and Panama City.

About a year later, my grandmother was cooking breakfast at four a.m. and another knock came at the back door. She answered and Capt. Anderson was there. She asked him to come in. He said it had been a year and it was about time he paid that note off. After breakfast, my grandfather and Capt. Anderson got the horse and buggy ready and went to Dothan and paid the note off.

As I was telling the story, my Uncle Grady asked if I wanted to know the rest of the story. He said, every time your granddaddy would come down to Panama City to see Capt. Anderson your grandmother would get so mad she'd have a hissy, because they were known to have a snort or two when they got together. Grandmother lived to be 96 years old.
Submitted by: R. Granger Bruner, P.O. Box 31, 224 Stinson Drive, DeFuniak Springs, FL.

MEMORIALS, TRIBUTES AND BUSINESSES

IN LOVING MEMORY
Mrs. Flossie Hewett Dawsell
April 23, 1917-May 23, 2002

*Two years ago today,
the Angels came &
beckoned you on to
the heavenly way.*

*Leaving behind
all the things of
this earth.*

*For your heavenly
eternal
re-birth.*

We love & miss you
Jamie, Emmett, Jimmy, Teresa, Odis,
Stormie and Gus.

Don't weep for me
Fishing in the
afterlife is where I'll Be.

THE GILLIANDS

Shelton Gilliland was born in Panama City on August 10, 1971. Ramona Gayle Lucas was born in Washington D.C. on April 19, 1971. Her family moved back here in 1974 when her father retired from the Army. They both attended Mosley High School and graduated in 1990. They started dating in October of that year and were married on October 5, 1991. They have lived and worked here in Bay County since their marriage. Their daughter Makenzie Paige was born on April 20, 2002. They all live in Ramona's grandparents' home in St. Andrews.

RAMONA, SHELTON AND MAKENZIE CHRISTMAS 2004

The Gleitsmanns settled in Panama City in 1939 when they immigrated from Germany. Ramona works at Bay Medical Center in Medical Records and Shelton serves full time in the

Florida Army National Guard and is a veteran of the Iraqi War. Makenzie goes to school and keeps the day-care busy all day. After school and weekends, she anxiously participates in activities with her Mom and Dad and Opa and Oma (Truett and Anita Lucas).

The Legacy of Tradition Continues

Time and service have honored the name of Battle Funeral Home since 1933. In Phenix City, Alabama in February of 1933 W.C. Battle, Sr. embarked upon the funeral service industry. To this day Battle Funeral Home continues to service the families of Russell County and surrounding areas of Alabama and Georgia.

Mr. W.C. Battle, Jr.
1934-1990

To this end W.C. Battle, Jr. founded Battle Memorial Funeral Home in June of 1963. His vision of establishing a professional funeral service for the African American Community in the Bay County area was an essential part of the legacy he wanted to foster. Located in the beginning at 605 East 10th Street, the Lord Blessed this family to build a new facility at 1123 N. Cove Boulevard which has since changed to Martin Luther King, Jr. Boulevard. This facility which was completed in 1972 offers a complete funeral service, including burial, cremation, shipping throughout the U.S. as well as international shipping arrangements.

Battle Memorial Funeral Home under the direction of his son, Victor B. Battle, LFD has remained a family owned and independent funeral home. He believes this makes a tremendous difference in the personalized care and service a family receives in their time of need. In addition it gives us the ability to offer very competitive prices. Our family vows to continue its strong commitment to the community and funeral service profession in the millennium and looks forward to continuing this fine tradition of Quality and Sympathetic Service.

Gladys Chapman
Her passion for people fueled her capacity to lead

Gladys Alford Chapman was born in rural Escambia County, Alabama, with three qualities that would emerge as themes throughout her lifetime.

She had a genuine fondness for people, a passion for learning and the capacity to lead.

Born May 1, 1913, Mrs. Chapman would excel as a student and would not be content with merely a grammar school education. As a girl, she moved, with her family's blessings and support, to a private residence in Brewton, Ala., 18 miles from her parents' home. There she attended the Downing Schefner School for Women, an accredited high school, and worked at McCrory's Five and Dime.

Her experience at the Downing Schefner School only served to fuel Mrs. Chapman's desire for further education. She enrolled at Troy State Teachers College in Troy, Ala., received her Alabama teaching certificate in 1935 and began her career as an educator during the Great Depression.

Her first assignment was teaching grades 1-8 in a one-room schoolhouse in Castleberry, Ala. Her wages were meager and she received additional

Gladys Chapman was the first woman ever to serve as a Bay County elected official.

in-kind compensation in the form of food and other necessities. Too, she continued to work at McCrory's.

In fact, on a Saturday in 1937, she worked at the dime store until 5 p.m. and married Joseph Fleming Chapman Jr. an hour and a half later.

The couple moved to Bay County that year and Mrs. Chapman brought with her a strong work ethic and dedication to teaching. In the 1940s, she joined with four other women in establishing the Bay County Classroom Teachers Association.

Formed at a time when the school district's instructional staff was made up almost exclusively of women, while all administrators and School Board members were men, the association aimed to give classroom teachers a collective voice in the education issues of the day.

The male education establishment distrusted the new association, however. Both Bay County Superintendent of Schools Tommy Smith and the Florida State Superintendent of

Gladys Chapman appears in the upper left-hand corner of this composite photo of one her third-grade classes at the Cove School.

Schools office in Tallahassee viewed it as a potentially disruptive departure from established norms and immediately characterized it as a "union" and a "radical association."

Mr. Smith summoned Mrs. Chapman to his office and asked her to sign a prepared statement whereby she would resign as Teachers Association president and renounce the organization as unnecessary.

Mrs. Chapman refused to sign the paper and an emergency meeting of the Bay County School Board was convened. There, Mrs. Chapman and other teachers, at the risk of their jobs, staunchly defended the association and its role. They prevailed and the association remained intact with Mrs. Chapman as its head.

Mrs. Chapman taught in Bay County through 1955, splitting her teaching career between the Millville School and the Cove School and earning a reputation as a fine educator and courageous spokeswoman in support of both teachers and the interests of students.

In 1960, she worked in behalf of Ferris Bryant's successful campaign for governor and, in 1961, Gov. Bryant appointed Mrs. Chapman to the job of Bay County supervisor of elections, making her the first woman ever to serve as a Bay County elected official. In eight successive elections, she retained the post, and retired in 1997 following 36 years in office. Under her watch, Bay County voter rolls grew from 15,000 people to 76,000.

Throughout her life, Mrs. Chapman was closely attuned to needs and issues affecting

women, minorities, educators and senior citizens. She was instrumental in the formation of the Bay County League of Women Voters, an organization that for starters was met with the same distrust and suspicion that had greeted the Teachers Association years earlier.

Mrs. Chapman lent her time, talents and energy to various community organizations including the American Cancer Society and the American Heart Association. She helped organize and was a charter member of the Bay Medical Center Foundation, the Junior Museum of Bay County and Friends of the Bay County Library. In her latter years, she focused especially on the Bay County Council on Aging and served on its board of directors.

Mrs. Chapman was a loyal and active member of the Democratic Party, with which she had great affinity. She inspired her son, Joseph F. Chapman III, to become active in the party and to succeed in diverse areas of endeavor ranging from public service to politics and banking to development. Mr. Chapman founded Peoples First Community Bank in 1983 and his mother chaired for many years the bank's "Prime 55 Advisory Board," whose members represent Peoples First's senior citizen customers.

Mrs. Chapman died on Nov. 7, 1999, but her life is often recalled and celebrated by people who knew and appreciated her myriad efforts toward making Bay County a better place to live for all.

History of Davis Exterminators, Inc.
2153 Frankford Avenue, Panama City, Florida
Phone: 850-763-4142 Fax 850-769-2785

Bob Davis obtained a business license along with his wife (Mary) to open a new business April 1, 1965. The name of the business was Davis Exterminators, Inc., specializing in Commercial, Residential and Termite Control Service. After receiving his Florida Certification Status in 1959 it was always in the back of his mind to fulfill the American Dream, going into business for himself.

Their desire was to live by the Golden Rule and since the nature of the profession is solely based on performance and service their aim was to perform honest, dependable and customer satisfactory work.

The employee's were to wear uniforms and drive vehicles bearing the company logo. The colors of the vehicles, white with black letters and red with black letters. The vehicles were easily noticed because the name Davis was in bold black English print.

Two of their three sons joined the company as regular employees. John came in his late teens and Steve came after a tour in the Air Force. Each have obtained their Certification Status in 1993 and 1994. The two Sons and their Dad served the industry as Regional Directors of FPMA.

Mary and Bob retired in 2000 and also a 28-year employee, Galen Mielke. They turned the business over to the two Sons, thus making it a family business and they in turn were labeled second generation.

Bob wished to conclude this article with a special thanks in three different areas. First: To his family and especially his wife Mary, who believed and stood behind him in making a dream come true. She was a tremendous asset throughout these years. Second: To achieve any measure of success in business one must surround himself with employees who share the same concept. We have employees who have been continuously employed ranging from 1 to 29 years of service. Third: Thanks to our two sons, John and Steve, second generation Exterminators and to the other 14 employees who make up Davis Exterminators, Inc. While tools, methods, and even product materials have changed, each of you are still promoting the same warm and friendly orientated concepts the company was founded upon.

REMEMBER OUR MOTTO, "DON'T TOLERATE-LET US EXTERMINATE."

Davis Exterminators Employees 2004

Davis Exterminators' Van

Springfield Community Church

Early Church, 1952

Church in 2004

Springfield Community Church was established in March of 1951 in a paper tabernacle on the corner of 7th Street and Transmitter Road by a man with a vision, Rev. J.W. Hunt and his wife. The church grew from the paper tabernacle to using tents to a basement which became known as the "Hunt Hole." In 1952, the congregation moved into a new sanctuary until it became too small. The first service in the brand new sanctuary was held on Sunday Morning October 4, 1975. The sanctuary is still being used for church services today. Rev. J.W. Hunt was the founder and pastor of the church until he passed away in May of 2001.

Rev. J. W. Hunt

Mr. Joseph Williamson Horn, Jr.
Family of Bay County

Joseph Williamson Horn, Jr. (Joe) is the son of Joseph Williamson Horn and Marie Dowling Horn of Ozark, Alabama. In 1957, after graduating from Carroll High School, he attended Auburn University. He graduated from Auburn with a B.S. degree in Electrical Engineering and began his career in Panama City, Florida at a U.S. Navy and Research Development Laboratory. He designed equipment and systems while working as an electrical engineer. Later, he was a Senior Systems Engineer and designed underwater acoustics, sonar, navigation, and diving equipments. He was a member of IEEE as long as he worked. In 1998, he retired with 36 years of service. At present, he works as a consultant in the same engineering field. Additionally, Joe is on the Regency Towers Condominium Board and also manages other properties he owns in Panama City Beach. He is a member of the First United Methodist Church Choir, St. Andrews Bay Yacht Club and a past president of the Bay Area Auburn Club. He is a past member of the Panama City Jaycees and past president of the Gulf Coast Football Officials Association. His work and play time in, on and around the water in Panama City with his family are greatly enjoyed blessings.

Martha Ann Andrews Horn is the daughter of Olin Noveller Andrews and Mignon Mallette Andrews of Auburn, Alabama. In 1957, she graduated from Lee County High School and attended Auburn University. After graduating in Vocational Home Economics Education, she taught for a year at Atwater Jr. High in Thomaston, Georgia. Then, she was an Assistant Home Demonstration Agent in the Alabama Cooperative Extension Service in Ozark, Alabama before moving to Panama City, Florida in 1963. Resuming her teaching career, she taught at Mowatt Jr. High School, Rosenwald Jr. High School and retired a math teacher from Jinks Middle School with 30 years teaching in the Bay County School System in 1998. She is a member of the United Methodist Women, Women's Bible Study, Junior Service League, Alpha Delta Kappa and Delta Kappa Gamma Professional Honorary Educator's Sororities, past member of Jr. Woman's Club and Jaycettes, Gulf Coast Woman's Club and the St. Andrew Bay Yacht Club Ladies' Auxiliary.

Joseph Williamson Horn, Jr. Family
Left to right: Sitting:
Martha Ann and Joe Horn
Standing: Joanna H. Blackburn, Lucy H.
Robertson, Marie H. Harvey

Joe 1938 and Martha Ann 1939 began dating in Ozark, Alabama in 1962 and became engaged about a year later. They married and became Mr. and Mrs. Joseph Williamson Horn, Jr. on November 10, 1963 at the First Baptist Church of Auburn, Alabama. Their wedding reception was held in the Auburn Faculty Club. After a honeymoon in New Orleans, they began their married life in Panama City, Florida. The gulf and beach was their favorite vacation spot as children. Their first home in 1963 was a one bedroom at The Morgan's duplex at 212 W. 12th. Street. In 1965, they purchased a 75-foot canal-front lot from W.E. Lloyd who developed the Pretty Bayou area. In 1966, they moved to a two bedroom at Miss Boe's duplex at 202 Hamilton Avenue to have more space for their baby. Joe began building the family home at 2441 Pretty Bayou Blvd. in November of 1966. In February of 1967, they moved into their home with their seven month old daughter Lucy Ann. They are members of the First United Methodist Church. They are the proud parents of three daughters and sons-in-law: Lucy Ann 1966 (Noel Lee Robertson 1965), Marie Mignon 1968 (Gordon Earl Harvey 1967) and Joanna 1970 (Corey Glen Blackburn 1970). Granddaughters are Twila Grace Robertson 1993 and Katherine Marie (Kate) 2002. Grandsons are Noel Joseph Robertson 1995, Jonathan Glen Blackburn 1998, Preston Stewart Harvey 1999, Hudson Andrews Harvey 2001 and Ian Williamson Blackburn 2003. Their daughters and sons-in-law are Auburn graduates. To say they are Auburn fans is an understatement! The couple enjoys family activities, traveling, boating, water sports, bridge, Auburn football games and their wonderful friends! The Horns love working and playing in this beautiful area. They recently celebrated their 40th Wedding Anniversary on an Alaskan Cruise and tour.

Lucy, Marie and Joanna attended Lucille Moore Elementary School, A.D. Harris Sixth Grade Center, Jinks Middle School and Bay High School. All were in National Honor Society, Anchor Club, Performing Arts Singers, Homecoming Queen, Azalea Trail and Junior Miss Contestants and a Panama City Tour Guide Model. After graduating from Bay High School, they went to Auburn in 1984, 1986 and 1988. They were very active and leaders in Baptist Campus Ministries where they met their spouses. They are all very involved in their churches. Lucy and Marie graduated in Elementary Education and Joanna has a Pharmacy degree. Soon after graduating, they each married their spouses at the First United Methodist Church of Panama City with reception at the Woman's Club of Panama City. They all enjoy visiting and vacationing with the family in Panama City.

Lucy and Lee Robertson live in Alhambra, California. Lucy taught in public school. She home schools their children, Twila and Noel. The children attend Friday School where Lucy teaches science and geography. She also is a water aerobics instructor in addition to being a homemaker. Lee is a High School Spanish teacher and also has a Master degree in Marriage and Family Therapy from Theological Seminary. The family enjoys camping, swimming, biking, sunning and church activities. Twila takes piano, is on the drill team and loves art. Noel plays all the sports, likes legos and the computer.

Marie and Gordon Harvey live in Monroe, Louisiana. Marie taught in Alabama for nine years and was "Teacher of the Year" at Carrie Woods Elementary School for two consecutive years for Auburn City Schools. Gordon is a history professor at ULM. He has a Masters in History from UAB and a Doctorate in history from Auburn. He wrote, "A Question of Justice" and is working on his second book about the political views of Reubin Askew, Florida Governor 1968-1972. Preston is a soccer player. Hudson also loves ball and running. They enjoy church activities, working out, swimming and attending ball games!

Joanna and Corey live in Heath, Texas, near Dallas. Joanna has worked as a clinical pharmacist at Baylor University Medical Center and Baylor Senior Health Center. She is now working part time at Walgreen's and is a full-time mom. Corey has Building Science degree. He received his Masters of Theology degree from Dallas Theological Seminary. He is a Project Engineer with Charter Builders. He also finished his first project for Blackburn Custom Homes which he designed and contracted in 2002. Jonathan enjoys T-Ball and trains. Kate is a happy people lover. Ian is a cuddly bundle of joy. The family enjoys outings to the Caldwell Zoo, church activities, AU Club and the State Fair of Texas.

Joe and Martha Ann Horn's Children and Grandchildren
July/August 2004. Back row, L-R: Marie Harvey (36), Hudson Harvey (3), Twila Robertson (11), Joanna Blackburn (34), Jonathan Blackburn (5), Noel Robertson (9), Lucy Robertson (38).
Front Row, L-R: Preston Harvey (5), Kate Blackburn (2), Ian Blackburn (8 months).

In Honor of W.R. Sowell and Nadine Sowell
Founders of Sowell Aviation Company, Inc.
Panama City, Florida

W.R. Sowell,
Founder, 1988

Nadine Sowell,
Founder, 2004

Wanting to fly was a feeling that first came over W.R. "Bill" Sowell as a young boy, when he would hang around the Tampa Airport after school just to be close to the airplanes. Bill was born in Chipley and spent part of his youth in the Tampa area before moving to Panama City where he attended Bay High School.

He bought his first plane in partnership with two buddies when he was only 17. He sold his interest to his partners three years later, in 1940, when he joined the Army Air Corps. He spent most of his military time as an instructor in multi-engine aircraft, primarily flying B-24's, B-25's, C-46's and C-47's.

Bill was stationed at Barksdale Field, Shreveport, Louisiana when he met his future wife, Nadine. Bill did not have an automobile, but he had his little J-3 Cub. They did their courting in the little airplane. He and Nadine were married in Nashville, Tennessee in 1942.

Nadine Sowell with
Flight Student, 1990

Nadine did not drive a car nor could she fly. Bill knew that to keep peace in the relationship, he would need to acquaint Nadine with flying. Bill, being a civilian and military flight instructor, taught her to fly. She obtained her pilot's license before she had an automobile license.

When his military enlistment ended in 1945, Bill and Nadine lost little time going into business, opening Sowell Aviation in December of that year at an air strip on Highway 77. Sowell Aviation Company, Inc., moved to its current location at Fannin Field in 1955 and embarked on a new instructional course.

The new concept was based on our area's appeal as a vacation destination. One of the reasons pilot training takes as long as it does is that most student pilots are available for lessons only during non-working hours, or on weekends. Sowell Aviation began promoting the idea, through extensive advertising, that one could bring the family here for a week's vacation and they could all enjoy the world's most beautiful beaches - while the student pilot engaged in a highly intensive week-long instructional program.

This accelerated training concept worked in a big way, bringing growth not only to the firm, but stimulating growth of tourism as well. Sowell Aviation has graduated as many as 3,600 pilots in one year's time from its FAA approved Flight School. Other vital parts of the business include fuel sales, charter, aircraft service, storage, sales and maintenance. The company currently employs between 25 and 30 people.

W.R. Sowell and
J. Don Sowell, 1991

Bill was active in community and business related activities. He was a Master Mason, a Shriner, a Elk, and a Rotarian. He was a member of the Chamber of Commerce, the Committee of 100, Resort Council and Military Affairs Committee. He was a founding member and three-time president of the Florida Aviation Trades Association and was also a founding member of the National Aviation Transportation Association. With the Governor Reuben Askew, he established the Florida Aviation Advisory Council - then served on it for 16 years, under four governors, twice serving as chairman.

Bill and Nadine had four children, and two of them are pilots. They divorced after 28 years of marriage, but remained business partners and friends. Bill passed away in 1995, and their son, Don, became President of Sowell Aviation. Nadine remains active in the business and serves as the Executive Vice President. Two of their daughters, Dianne and Debbie, are actively involved in the business. Their youngest daughter, Denise, works for a local Hospice organization.

Sowell Aviation Company is proud of its 60 years of service to Bay County and surrounding communities. It is our desire to continue to serve our community as well as providing personalized service to our customers.

Sowell Aviation Company, 1965

Sowell Aviation Company, 2005

SAINT ANDREWS PRESBYTERIAN CHURCH

Bay County's oldest church, the Saint Andrews Presbyterian Church was organized September 13, 1886. From the close of the Civil War in 1865, and for about 20 years afterward, several families of the Presbyterian faith moved into this area from Northern states.

After meeting in several different homes, a small group of Presbyterian met in the home of Hiram M. Mapes where the First Presbyterian Church of St. Andrews was organized. Records show it was authorized by the Presbytery of East Florida in connection with the Presbyterian Church of the U.S. of America with 16 charter members and Ruling Elders Hiram Mapes and Michael Chadwick.

Church in 1917

The first pastor was the Rev. E.H. Post, grandfather of Richard Post a long-time teacher at Jinks Junior High School. The group continued to meet in homes and raised money to construct a church building with members helping with the construction which was ready on July 22, 1888. The Rev. Luther H. Wilson was the pastor called upon Rev. Post's death in 1890.

On June 30, 1897 the church was transferred to Presbytery of Florida, "Southern Assembly U.S." The Rev. R.J. McIlwaine pastored from July 10, 1898 until 1901. The Rev. J.B. Rosebough served until 1902. Ormand C. Dolphy supplied the pulpit in 1906. The church was without a regular pastor from 1906 to December 1907. The Rev. J.D. Roundtree accepted the call and served until 1909. The Rev. W.D. Lee served til November 1912.

On November 22, 1913 the Rev. J. Marion Stafford came and pastored until 1914. From 1914-1916 the Rev. W.S. Milne served. In 1916 the Rev. James Lapsley came and pastored until 1919. The Rev. J.P. Word served the Panama City and St. Andrews churches. In 1920 he resigned to give the Panama City Church his full-time.

On June 8, 1917 the church was moved from the corner of Drake Street (Avenue) and Lorraine Avenue (14th. Street) to the Bayview Avenue and 14th. Street site. In 1920, the

Rev. Fred Schell preached monthly. Later in 1920 the Rev. Ira Miller of Lynn Haven, Florida served for a short time, being followed by a Rev Delaney of Chipley. The Rev. J.P. Word served the church again for a short time.

The Rev. E.C. Haymaker served until 1927. The Rev. J.C. Leckemby filled the pulpit on Sunday afternoons. The Rev. Hall from the U.S.A. Church in Lynn Haven preached on Sunday afternoons when possible. From 1927 until 1931, there is no record of church activities except the Sunday School.

Church in 1936

Following the reorganization in 1931, several students from Bob Jones College supplied the pulpit. They included Clifford Lewis, Ivay Palmer, Marion Bradwell and Ralph Gamewell. Fulton Lytle was the first regular pastor coming in May of 1933. He was ordained here and served for one year.

Mr. Howard Gould came in June, 1934, serving this church and Wallace Memorial. He was ordained at Wallace Memorial and after one year went to Central America as a missionary.

The Rev. Mr. H.F. Beaty of Port St. Joe, Florida came in May 1935. He served several churches as well as St. Andrews. It was in the winter of 1935 and 1936 that the Sunday School addition to the old sanctuary was built. Mr. Beaty served until the summer of 1938 and Mr. A.L. McNair, a student from Columbia Seminary, served us in the summer of 1938. The Rev. George H. Hurst, a missionary from Brazil, on extended leave served us from September 1938 to July 1939. Mr. Hurst was a dedicated and tireless servant. From 1933 to 1939 there is no accurate record of the many that served. The Rev. Thomas Watson served from 1939 until his death in 1941.

The Rev. Dr. Robert Dale Daffin, Jr. came to us in the fall of 1941 and served until November 5, 1951. During these ten years under the same Pastor the church was very fruitful. The Boy Scout Building was completed in February 1945. The two lots on Beck Avenue, where the present sanctuary is situated was purchased in 1946 and the Ship-ahoy Cottage was purchased for a manse the same year. The present sanctuary was completed in 1949 and the last notes were burned in 1951 leaving the church debt free.

The Rev. L. Samuel Magbee came to us August 17, 1952 and served until September 1955. It was during his pastorate that the church went on self-support probably for the first time in its 60 years of existence.

The Rev. Gordon E. Jowers came to us in January 1956 and served until June 1963. During this time, there has been a steady growth. The Ship-ahoy cottage was traded for the manse on the corner of Bayview Avenue and 14th Street (1317 Bayview Avenue) and in 1957 the Educational Building was completed. The Rev. Edsel Huffstetler was pastor until November 15, 1969. The Rev. Frank Havlicek served from November 30, 1969 to January 31, 1977. During this time a new manse was purchased at 1009 Balboa Avenue. Pastor Victor C. Scott came October 23, 1977. The Rev. L. Gilbert McLaurin served from July 10, 1980 until June 4, 1988. Rev. Joseph C. Eckstine supplied the pulpit during this year. The manse was sold.

The Rev. Tom Douglas pastored from 1989-1999. During the year 1999 the church steeple was replaced and stained-glass windows were installed in the side windows of the church. The Rev. Bob Lucas served from 2000 until 2002. In 2002 a new church sign was designed and installed.

The Rev. Joe Vaughn came in 2002 and is the present pastor.

Church in 2004

Pioneer History of Van Horn Transfer & Storage
850-763-3965

Van Horn Transfer & Storage is by far the oldest moving business in Panama City today, and has been serving Bay Countians for the past 97 years. It was started in 1906 by Cornelius and Jack Van Horn, the sons of Robert J. Van Horn who had moved to this area from Kansas in 1887. He homesteaded on the location of the previous "Cove Gardens".

The two sons started a drayage and ice service in Millville and Harrison (early name of Panama City) when they began to meet small boats with their horse dray (a stoutly built cart with removable sides). For several years before the R.R. came to Panama City, boats transported merchandise between the communities of Millville, St. Andrews, Harrison, Bay Harbour, Lynn Haven and Southport. They carried freight and passengers, and eventually the brothers bought the popular boat, the "Jolly Rover", and established themselves as the first major freight hauling and transfer business in this area.

Around 1912, the Bay Line R.R. extended it's tracks into Bay County and all the trains were met on schedule by the brothers. A contract was then signed with the Bay Harbour sawmill for all their freight to be hauled by the brothers. When the roads became better, and trucks began to be used, the delivery service was much more dependable.

The popular boat "Tarpon", which was used both as a passenger and freight boat between Carrabelle and Mobile, hauled more freight into this section than any other. A contract to handle this freight was also obtained by the Van Horns.

When Cornelius retired in 1927, he left the business to his two sons Earl and Proctor, who then moved the company from Millville to Panama City. They had purchased an old railway express building and had it moved to the north end of Grace Avenue where the "storage service" was initiated. It was at this time that Earl married Madge Riddick, and they eventually became the sole operators of the business. During the war years, a two-story brick building was purchased at 28 W. Beach Drive and remained the base of operations until the present complex was purchased in the 1400 block of Harrison and Grace Avenue. The facility structures presently contain 5 buildings with 15 vehicles for transfer of furniture or other needs.

Early moving was done by the local iceman, the wood and coal dealer, or the draymen at the depot. But as America became a moving nation, moving became a total business in its own right. In 1940, Van Horn Transfer & Storage became affiliated with Aero Mayflower Transfer Co., the pioneer in the modern moving industry. Through them, coast to coast services to residences became available.

Van Horn now has the capacity to offer moving service to practically all parts of the free world. Contracts with Tyndall AFB and the Naval Surface Warfare Center to ship personal effects to wherever our forces are stationed around the world, brought the moving operation increasing business.

In early years, Earl and Madge ran the business on their own, but had many employees who were with the company since its early years; some over 35 years.

Hercules Pettis Sr. joined the firm in 1946. His most important move in life was in 1943, when he touched down as an Air Force pilot in Panama City. He moved his Greek wife Clio Calogeropoulou from N.Y. to this area while he completed his tour of duty. At the end of the war, they decided to stay in Panama City and make it their home. He became the general manager in the late 50's and upon retirement of Earl Van Horn, moved up to president and owner of the organization. He was the driving force behind the growth and modern technology now employed by the company.

Hercules and wife Clio were active members in Panama City's many civic functions. Clio was a retired opera singer and quickly became the city's #1 voice and piano teacher & choral director for many years. Their close and personal association with music made them a favorite with the music association in Panama City. Supporting the local Kiwanis Club, Hercules was involved in their many projects and was known particularly as the "composer in residence" of the promotional theme songs for their annual "Pancake Days" fund-raiser. This is a tradition that has been continued by son Hercules Jr., with help from daughter Stephanie Pettis.

Hercules Jr., known as H.L., along with his sister Stephanie Pettis worked summers and weekends with Pettis Sr. They obtained good basic knowledge of the operations of the moving business. Stephanie moved on to bigger cities to pursue her professional music career, while H.L. returned to Panama City in 1984. He gradually assumed the duties of Hercules Sr., who had started slowly phasing out and "kind of" retired in 19??. During his retirement, Hercules took the opportunity to travel the world many times with wife Clio, but because of his love of the business, one would see him more times then not, back with all the action at Van Horn's. Meanwhile, H.L. totally threw himself into running the business and helping with it's continual growth, while managing to win many achievement awards as did his dad. At present, in addition to his main job of raising his four daughters, H.L. capably runs the business.

When Hercules Sr. died in 1997, daughter Stephanie moved back to Panama City with her husband Rusty Smith and son Oliver Pettis to help with the family business and continue her concert career on the Gulf Coast. She continues in her father's footsteps with her involvement in the Music Association, striving to bring culture to Panama City, as did her parents.

The families of this "Family run business", are continuing to efficiently operate a near "century old" business, and are still growing with newer techniques for a fast, low cost and safe move and storage. No job is too large or too small for Van Horn Mayflower. As Hercules Sr. always said, "we move everything but the bowels".

A family tradition that lasts forever -- Van Horn Mayflower is still here.

THANK YOU PANAMA CITY FOR A SUCCESSFUL 97 YEARS.

L-R: Hercules Pettis, Jr., Stephanie Pettis and Hercules Pettis, Sr.

Things have changed in last 97 years.

Back in the early 1930's, the Van Horns Transfer & Storage Co. consisted of one truck and moved furniture and freight in town. Bottom Picture: Today, the 97-year old business has 15 vans and moves freight to any country in the free world. Hercules Pettis displays a modern van.

Hercules Pettis, Sr.

L-R: Earl Van Horn, Madge Van Horn, John B. Smith, President of Mayflower. Geraldine Agerton and Hercules Pettis.

285

LUCAS SOO-HYUK PEACOCK

Lucas Soo-Hyuk Peacock, newest member of our family tree, was born April 15, 2004 and is the son of Brenton Eugene Peacock and Cynthia Renee Robbins Peacock of Panama City, Florida. He is the grandson of Richard N. Robbins and Dorothy Ann Johnson Robbins and Carl Eugene Peacock and Barbara Ann Nichols Peacock. Lucas is the great-grandson of Pauline Strickland Johnson and Lillie Virginia Fowler Nichols. Lucas is the first boy on his mother's side of the family for three generations. He has a five year old sister Lorena Colette Peacock who loves him very much.

Lorena and Lucas Peacock

A MOTHER WITH A VISION

Seventy years ago, Rena Diamond Windham was given a wedding present of $75.00, which she saved for several years. Then one day, she was told about some property for sale in St. Andrews for just the same amount - $75.00. She purchased the lot, now known as 1110 Beck Avenue. The young woman had a vision, and that vision has grown. As the years went by, her husband, Tony Windham, and his father, A.T. "Pap" Windham, built on the lot and opened a seafood and oyster bar called Windham and Sons.

Rena Windham and Family

Following the death of "Pap", Rena opened a fabric and notions shop. She provided sewing and alteration services for many years. When the adjoining lot came up for sale, she purchased it and rented it to the City of Panama City as a parking lot for $325.00 per year, for ten years. Church has been and important part of Rena's life being a member of the St. Andrews Baptist Church longer than any other member.

In this same building, recently, the now 88-year old Rena, along with her grandson, Mitch Holman and his wife Carolyn, have opened a new seafood restaurant - The Captain's Table.

Rena has one daughter, Lenora Holman, a retired school teacher and another grandson Mark Holman who serves as a Merchant Marine.

Ad from Windham & Son from 1938

Business card from
Captain's Table

We're in the business **of pleasure.**

Whether you choose to hold your event in our expansive convention center, along the deck of our famous lagoon pool or on our half-mile private beach, our Executive Chef, Shawn Koon, and our professional catering staff will ensure everyone in your group is well fed and satisfied. After all, it's more than our job. It's our pleasure. For more information, call our catering sales manager at 235-4948 and be sure to ask about our off-site catering as well.

PANAMA CITY BEACH, FLORIDA

www.edgewaterbeachresort.com

Lighted Signs by Freeman Electric Co., Inc.

Freeman Electric Neon Sign Early 1940's
at 534 Oak Avenue

Freeman Electric Company, Incorporated was founded in 1936 by H. Otis Freeman, Jr., and his brother, Cook Freeman. In 1948, J.T. Duncan, Jr., a licensed master electrician, was hired to run the electrical department and Otis ran the sign department. Since then, Freeman Electric has installed much of the wiring, heating and air conditioning in Bay County's homes and beach cottages, from Phillips Inlet to Mexico Beach and partnered with Sears Roebuck's Home Heating and Air Conditioning Department for many years. But their main focus has been building lighted signs.

Over the years, Freeman Electric has manufactured and installed many landmark signs, including the Sputnik sign for the Jitney Jungle Store, the Martin Theatre Marquee, the Gulf Drive-In and the Old South Pacific Motel sign, to name just a few. Freeman Electric created and donated to the city the neon Santa and Reindeer that soared over Harrison Avenue each Christmas for many years. It has been the primary sign contractor for firms such as Sunshine Junior, Peoples First, Po' Folks, Sonny's Bar-B-Q, Express Lane, Tom Thumb, Bay Bank and many others.

Neon Santa and Reindeer displayed across Harrison Avenue at Christmas time, 1950's.

This small family business, run by Otis and J.T. and their wives, Marguerite and Margaret, made a big impact on the county in other ways. J.T. became a partner in the business in 1953. J.T. was chairman of the Panama City Electrical Examining Board from the early 1960's until the mid 1980's, when the City turned its Building Department over to Bay County. J.T. was a member of the Bay County Construction Industry Advisory Board from its inception until his death in 1996. Both Otis and J.T. were primary contributors to the creation of the City and County electrical code laws. The signs they created have stood the test of time and hurricanes. Much of the neon still functioning from the 1960's was made by Marvin Helms, a true artist and craftsman, who worked with Freeman Electric for over thirty years.

Otis Freeman died in 1980. J.T. and Margaret continued to run the business. J.T. Duncan, Jr. died in 1996. The business continues to prosper, guided by the vision and integrity of these special people. Freeman Electric Company is still owned and operated by the Duncan Family.

Ritz Theatre Sign, early 1940's.

Neon Ford roof sign at Harrison Avenue location early 1940's.

LIGHTED SIGNS BY
FREEMAN ELECTRIC CO., INC.

Chavers Fowhand Neon Sign on Harrison Avenue, early 1950's.

H. O. FREEMAN, JR. — ONE OF GARLAND'S 50 REPEAT CUSTOMERS

Otis Freeman, Jr. and J.T. Duncan, Jr. and employees with new crane truck, 1952.

Gulf Drive-In Theatre 15th. Street, 1955.

Jitney Jungle Sputnik sign at Harrison Avenue and Highway 231, 1958.

Wayside Shopping Center, Panama City Beach, early 1950's. Wayside Drive-In in background.

J.P. Stephenson Court, Panama City Beach, 1957.

Sputnik sign being assembled on set by Marvin Helms, Abel and Fuller, 1958. Jitney Jungle Grocery Store at Harrison Avenue and Highway 231.

Martin Theatre Marquee sign, 1959.

Gulfwind Motel, Front Beach Road, Panama City Beach, early 1960.

South Pacific Motel, Front Beach Road, 1962. Sign survived Hurricanes Eloise, Opal, Ivan and others.

100 foot tall McDonald's sign early 1984. Mike Duncan in bucket.

Cook Motor Company sign, 15th Street, 1963.

Junior Food Store sign, early 1980's.

Harvey's Showcase sign corner of Harrison Avenue and 15th. Street.

Wilson Funeral Home

Bay County's Oldest Family Owned Business.

214 Airport Rd.

(850) 785 - 5272

292

Index

209, 221
Mashurn 39
Masker 92, 195, 196, 273
Mason 41, 75
Massalina 6, 101, 157
Mathis 37, 64, 68, 69, 210, 253
Mathison 49, 119
Mattair 61, 62
Matthews 72, 174, 256, 257, 277
Mauldin 15
Maxon 100
Maxwell 93, 161, 196, 197
Mayer 109
Mayers 152, 197, 204
McAllister 8
McAnulty 176
McBride 37, 184, 242, 253
McCabe 39
McCain 67, 69, 75, 170, 183, 184
McCalister 53
McCall 63, 113, 221, 222, 242
McCalls 9
McCarthy 43
McClairen 246
McClard 197
McClellan 140, 207, 208
McClellans 209
McClinton 54
McCliren 28
McClung 142
McClure 27
McConnel 39
McCormack 149
McCormick 188, 189, 228
McCorqadale 11
McCorquodale 5, 184
McCraney 184
McCrary 28, 61, 79, 184, 185, 186, 187
McCulloch 89
McCullough 204
McCumbie 153
McCurdy 278
McDaniel 91
McDermott 27
McElvey 71
McFatter 60
McGee 118, 246
McGill 37, 151, 152, 187
McGills 12
McGilvra 49
McGlohon 188
McIlwaine 45, 284
McIntyre 30, 85
McIver 190

McKeand 54
McKeithen 126
McKenzie 5, 49, 73, 184, 187, 188, 214
McKinney 74, 115, 227
McKinnon 55
McKnight 37
McLain 44
McLaughlin 25
McLaurin 284
McLawhon 188, 237
McLemore 9, 230
McLendon 255
McLeod 15, 20, 173, 271
McMichael 123
McMillan 3, 43, 248
McMillian 135
McMillion 163
McMullon 215, 216
McNair 284
McNally 262
McNeal 209, 215
McNeil 44, 50, 65, 68
McNulty 29
McQuagge 2, 7, 84, 113, 142, 148, 188, 189, 191, 198
McQuagges 190
McQuaig 189, 190
McRea 147
McWilliams 252
Meagher 133
Mefford 197, 198
Melvin 278
Mercer 113
Meredith 193
Merriam 64, 68, 205
Merrill 25
Merritt 141
Messer 2
Meyer 56, 159
Middlebrook 186
Mielke 281
Milam 247
Miley 89
Miller 16, 25, 29, 30, 32, 37, 42, 43, 44, 57, 64, 68, 122, 127, 164, 183, 204, 257, 284
Mills 68, 141, 185, 204, 271
Milne 284
Milner 166
Mims 92, 195, 235
Minch 276
Miner 62
Minto 242, 243
Miracle Strip Amusement Park 1
Mitchell 39, 125, 126, 203, 268, 269

Mixer 51
Mixon 63
Mizell 37, 211
Mizenko 155
Moates 44, 53, 94, 148, 149, 166, 167, 198, 199, 200, 201, 220, 266, 273
Mobley 197
Modawell 44
Monk 112, 223
Montgomery 127, 171, 201, 256, 272, 273
Moody 49, 55, 68, 82
Moore 11, 38, 39, 44, 93, 158, 173, 243, 247, 255, 262, 271
Morden 55, 211
Morgan 50, 141
Morley 111
Morris 18, 25, 26, 36, 37, 106, 138, 152, 156, 215, 292
Morrison 10, 43
Morton 44
Moseley 65, 120
Moser 67, 214
Moses 153
Mosley 226, 242
Moss 67
Mount 201, 202, 255
Mount-Douds 201
Mowbray 37
Mozley 37, 68
Muehlebach 213
Muenzel 272, 273
Mull 160
Mullen 228
Mulligan 58, 59, 64, 65, 68
Mullikin 258, 259
Mullins 48, 252
Munsell 249
Munser 11
Munson 184, 202
Murfee 3, 6, 8, 45, 123, 155, 156, 157, 158, 202, 203, 204, 239
Murphy 38, 63, 69
Murray 2, 37, 42, 180, 204, 249
Murrow 254
Musgrove 80, 116
Muterspaugh 210
Myers 39, 189
Myrick 217, 218

N
NaJu Boarding & Grooming, Inc. 291
Nale 63

Nauman 268, 269
Neal 20, 36, 42
Neeley 31, 32
Neill 63
Nelson 15, 37, 39, 45, 66, 67, 92, 151, 164, 197, 204, 205, 206, 249
Nesbitt 124
Nettles 235
Newbern 39, 63
Newberry 42, 44, 62, 73, 138, 228, 262, 266, 267
Newborn 239
Newman 30, 264
Newmans 143, 144
Newsome 50
Newton 258, 259
Nichols 213, 239, 278, 286
Nicholson 211
Niebruegge 153
Niquet 178
Nix 55
Nixon 8, 21, 152, 193, 206, 207, 208, 209, 210
Noble 16
Nobles 215, 267
Nolan 207, 209, 210
Norem 139
Norris 38, 160, 248
Norton 74, 113, 161, 162, 163, 210, 256
Nowell 15, 70, 210, 211
Nugent 66
Nunnemaker 218

O
O'Brien 177
O'Kelley 120, 121
O'Neal 116
O'Neill 81, 124
O'Rear 169
Oates 69, 217, 238
Oberst 78
Odom 152, 182, 187
Ogburn 37, 160
Oliver 20, 38, 152, 153, 187, 255
Olivers 8
Olliver 113
Olson 65
Oneal 80
Orr 31
Outlaw 55
Owen 204
Owens 3, 184, 211

P
Padgett 57, 66, 108, 113, 114, 164, 262
Padova 126
Page 46, 48
Pagleson 250

Palmer 25, 37, 136, 252, 284
Panama City News Herald 58, 75
Parham 153
Parish 15
Parker 19, 29, 38, 42, 53, 56, 68, 69, 71, 116, 124, 135, 178, 214, 222, 223, 225, 244, 252, 254
Parkinson 256
Parnell 70
Parrish 202, 238, 259
Parrott 211, 239, 249
Parson 255
Pascoe 212
Pascual 254
Pate 37, 43, 80, 145
Patrick 30
Patterson 1, 15, 152, 212, 213, 226, 253
Patton 74, 76, 84, 86, 91, 102, 103, 240
Paul 91, 208
Paulk 240
Payne 7, 23, 37, 48, 64, 67
Pazics iii, 58, 175, 176
Peace 68
Peach 20
Peacock 12, 14, 55, 172, 173, 213, 214, 237, 238, 258, 259, 286
Peacock/Johnson 257
Peake 204
Pearce 134
Pearson iii, 22, 77, 164, 165, 240
Peel 200
Pegler 85
Peiars 140
Pemberton 18
Pender 50
Pennington 38, 183, 214
Penny 42
Penton iii, 16, 17, 18, 19, 37, 38, 39, 214, 215, 261
Percival 46, 48, 69, 177
Pericola 136
Perkins 37, 116, 224
Perry 17, 154, 164
Peters 29, 37, 51, 103
Peterson 33, 37, 134

FAMILY RECORD

NAME	BIRTH		DEATH	
	Date	Place	Date	Place